Welcome to

Reading Statistics and Research, Fourth Edition

with Research Navigator™

This text contains some special features designed to aid you in the research process and writing research papers. As you read this textbook, you will see special Research Navigator (RN) icons cueing you to visit the Research Navigator website to research important concepts of the text.

To gain access to Research Navigator, go to **www.researchnavigator.com** and login using the passcode you'll find on the inside front cover of your text.

Research Navigator™ includes three databases of dependable source material to get your research process started:

EBSCO's *ContentSelect Academic Journal Database*. EBSCO's ContentSelect Academic Journal Database contains scholarly, peer-reviewed journals. These published articles provide you with a specialized knowledge and information about your research topic. Academic journal articles adhere to strict scientific guidelines for methodology and theoretical grounding. The information obtained in these individual articles is more scientific than information you would find in a popular magazine, newspaper article, or on a Web page.

The New York Times *Search by Subject Archive*. Newspapers are considered periodicals because they are issued in regular installments (e.g., daily, weekly, or monthly), and provide contemporary information. Information in periodicals—journals, magazines, and newspapers—may be useful, or even critical, for finding up-to-date material or information to support specific aspects of your topic. Research Navigator™ gives you access to a one-year, "search by subject" archive of articles from one of the world's leading newspapers—*The New York Times.*

"*Best of the Web*" Link Library. Link Library, the third database included on Research Navigator™, is a collection of Web links, organized by academic subject and key terms. Searching on your key terms will provide you a list of five to seven editorially reviewed Web sites that offer educationally relevant and reliable content. The web links in Link Library are monitored and updated each week, reducing your incidence of finding "dead" links.

In addition, Research Navigator™ includes extensive online content detailing the steps in the research process including:

- Starting the Research Process
- Finding and Evaluating Sources
- Citing Sources
- Internet Research
- Using Your Library
- Starting to Write

For more information on how to use Research Navigator go to
http://www.ablongman.com/aboutrn.com

Reading Statistics and Research

FOURTH EDITION

Schuyler W. Huck

University of Tennessee

PEARSON

Boston • New York • San Francisco
Mexico City • Montreal Toronto • London • Madrid • Munich • Paris
Hong Kong • Singapore • Tokyo • Cape Town • Sydney

Senior Editor: *Arnis E. Burvikovs*
Editorial Assistant: *Christine Lyons*
Marketing Manager: *Tara Whorf*
Editorial-Production Service: *Omegatype Typography, Inc.*
Manufacturing Buyer: *Andrew Turso*
Cover Administrator: *Kristina Mose-Libon*
Electronic Composition: *Omegatype Typography, Inc.*

To obtain permission(s) to use material from this work, please submit a written request to Allyn
and Bacon, Permissions Department, 75 Arlington Street, Boston, MA 02116 or fax your
request to 617-848-7320.

Between the time Website information is gathered and then published, it is not unusual for
some sites to have closed. Also, the transcription of URLs can result in typographical
errors. The publisher would appreciate notification where these errors occur so that they
may be corrected in subsequent editions.

Library of Congress Cataloging-in-Publication Data

Huck, Schuyler W.,
    Reading statistics and research / Schuyler W. Huck.—4th ed.
      p.   cm.
    Includes bibliographical references and index.
    ISBN 0-205-38081-6
    1. Statistics. 2. Research. 3. Experimental design. I. Title.

  QA267.H788 2004
  001.4'22—dc10

                           2003041906

Printed in the United States of America

10 9 8 7 6 5 4 3 2 1   08 07 06 05 04 03

This book is dedicated to two groups: those consumers of research reports who work at developing the skills needed to critically evaluate (and sometimes reject!) the claims made by researchers, and those researchers whose claims ought to be believed (and acted upon!) because they take the time to carefully analyze the data gleaned from thoughtfully designed studies that address worthy questions.

Brief Contents

Contents

14 *Analysis of Variance with Repeated Measures*   **357**

15 *The Analysis of Covariance*   **390**

18   *Statistical Tests on Ranks (Nonparametric Tests)*   **486**

Preface

This preface is devoted to three topics of potential interest to anyone who may be considering reading or adopting this book. These topics concern my assessment of people's need to critically evaluate research claims, the book's main objectives, and differences between the third and fourth editions. In a very real sense, the material contained in the following paragraphs contains the answers to three legitimate questions that might be directed my way: (1) For whom is this book intended? (2) In what ways will this book benefit its readers? (3) Is this simply a cosmetic revision of the third edition, and, if not, how does this fourth edition differ in significant ways from its predecessor?

People's Need to Critically Evaluate Research Claims

In earlier editions of this book, it was said that humanity could be divided into three groups: (1) those who conduct their own research studies, (2) those who do not formally engage in the research process but nonetheless encounter the results of others' investigations, and (3) those who are neither "makers" nor "consumers" of research claims. Now, nearly 30 years since that statement was initially made, I *still* believe that every person on the face of the earth can be classified into one of those three groups. However, it is clear to me that the relative sizes and the needs of the three groups are different now than they were in 1974 (when the first edition of this book was published) or even 2000 (when the third edition appeared).

Regarding the size of the three groups, the first group (the "doers" of research) has grown slightly larger, while the second group (the "consumers" of research) has expanded geometrically over the past few years. The odds are extremely high that any randomly selected person belongs to one of these two groups. The first would be populated with lots of professors, all graduate students preparing to write a master's thesis or doctoral dissertation, most employees of the many research units located in both public and private organizations, and a handful of independent researchers. Whoever isn't a member of the first group most likely is a member of the second group. That's because it is virtually impossible to avoid coming into contact with research findings.

In one way or another, almost everyone bumps up against the findings of empirical investigations. First of all, formal and full-length research reports are presented each year in thousands of professional journals and at countless international, national, regional, and local conventions. Summaries of such studies appear in newspaper and magazine stories, are presented on television and radio news programs, and crop up during informal conversations. Computer availability and the staggering increase in Internet websites make it possible for growing numbers of people to have access to the research "evidence" that stands behind online advice from "experts" regarding everything from acupuncture to Zen Buddhism. And then there are the innumerable advertisements and commercials that bombard us on a daily basis and contain the results of so-called scientific studies that supposedly demonstrate the worth of the products or services being hawked.

Everyone in the huge second group needs to become a more discerning consumer of research findings and research claims. Such individuals, located on the receiving end of research summaries, cannot be *competent* consumers of what they read or hear unless they can both understand and evaluate the investigations being discussed. Such skills are needed because (1) trustworthy research conclusions come only from those studies characterized by a sound design and a careful analysis of the collected data, and (2) the screening process—*if* there is one in place—that supposedly prevents poor studies from being disseminated is only partially successful in achieving its objective. For these reasons, consumers must acquire the skills needed to protect themselves from overzealous or improperly trained researchers whose work leads to exaggeration, false "discoveries," and unjustified claims of "significance."

Individuals in the other group—the doers of research—also should be able to evaluate others' research reports critically. This is the case because almost every research project is supposed to be built on a foundation of knowledge gleaned from previous studies. Clearly, if a current researcher cannot differentiate legitimate from unjustified research conclusions, his or her own investigation may well be doomed from the outset because it is pointed in the wrong direction or grounded in a research base made of sand. If applied researchers could more adequately critique the studies cited within their own literature reviews, they also would be able to apply such knowledge to their own investigations. The result would be better designed studies containing more appropriate statistical analyses leading to more justifiable conclusions and claims.

And so, this fourth edition of *Reading Statistics and Research* is targeted at two groups: those who conduct their own research investigations and those who are the recipients of research-based claims. I have tried to keep both groups in mind as this revision project was initiated and as it unfolded. Hopefully, members of *both* groups will benefit from this edition's textual discussion of statistics and research design, the many excerpts taken from published research reports, and the end-of-chapter review questions.

This Book's Objectives

The seven specific objectives of the fourth edition are basically the same as those of the previous editions. These goals include providing the reader with (1) an understanding of statistical terms, (2) the ability to make sense out of (or to set up) statistical tables and figures, (3) a knowledge of what specific research questions can be answered by each of a variety of statistical procedures, (4) an awareness of what can and cannot be accomplished when someone sets up and tests one or more null hypotheses, (5) the skills needed to notice the misuse of statistics, (6) a facility for distinguishing between good and poor research designs, and (7) a feeling of confidence when working with research reports.

The seven objectives just listed can be synthesized nicely into two words: **decipher** and **critique**. This book is designed to help people *decipher* what researchers are trying to communicate in the written or oral summaries of their investigations. Here, the goal is simply to distill meaning from the words, symbols, tables, and figures included in the research report. (To be competent in this arena, one must be able not only to decipher what's presented but also to "fill in the holes"; this is the case because researchers typically assume that those receiving the research report are familiar with unmentioned details of the research process and statistical treatment of data.) Beyond being able to decipher what is presented, readers of this book will improve their ability to *critique* such research reports. This is important because research claims are sometimes completely unjustified due to problems associated with the way studies are planned or implemented, or because of problems in the way data are collected, analyzed, summarized, or interpreted.

Differences between the Third and Fourth Editions

In an effort to assist readers to become better able to decipher and critique research reports, I have done my best to update, expand, and in other ways improve this edition and make it superior to the third edition. Several of these changes are quite minor and need not be discussed. There are, however, four important ways in which this edition is different from the one published in 2000. These changes *are* worth discussing.

Excerpts.   It is not an exaggeration to say that the boxed excerpts constitute the "lifeblood" of this book. I have included these tables, figures, and passages of text from published research reports to illustrate both good and not-so-good practices, to instruct via the words of others, and to demonstrate that contemporary researchers do, in fact, use the statistical procedures discussed in this text.

A total of 513 excerpts appear in this edition. The vast majority of these excerpts are new, with only 20 carried forward from the third edition. These numbers can be used to back up the claim that this book contains an *extensive* array of material that illustrates what *contemporary* researchers put into their research reports.

It should be noted that the 513 excerpts included here were not chosen indiscriminately. On the contrary, each was carefully hand selected because of its ability to help others understand a concept or practice. Moreover, a concerted effort was made to select excerpts from a variety of disciplines. This was done to increase the reader's ability to cross disciplinary lines when reviewing research reports.

In contrast to those books that focus on a single discipline (with titles such as *Statistics for Education* or *Research in Nursing*), the manifest purpose here is to help readers feel more at ease when confronted by research claims that emanate from disciplines *other than* their own. Unless people have the ability to decipher and critique research in a multidisciplinary fashion, they become easy targets for those who inadvertently or purposefully present research "evidence" that comes from studies characterized by ill-conceived questions, poor methodology, and sloppy statistical analysis. Unfortunately, some researchers begin their studies with a strong bias as to what they would like the results to show, and the results of such biased investigations are summarized on a near daily basis in the popular press. Clearly, a person is more likely to detect such bias if he or she can decipher and critique research *across disciplines,* recognizing, for example, that the purpose of and issues related to a one-way ANOVA are the same regardless of whether the data come from psychology or ecology or epidemiology.

Website.   A companion website (www.ablongman.com/huck4e) has been created to extend and embellish the material contained between the covers of this book. This website is easy to navigate, it contains different kinds of information for users with different kinds of needs, and it has been field-tested and modified on the basis of student feedback. The website and the book function to complement each other, with neither one able to successfully do alone what both can do together.

The largest and most important part of the website involves information, exercises, and links carefully organized in a chapter-by-chapter format. To be more specific, the following items are available for each chapter:

Chapter Outline	*e-Articles*
The Chapter's Best Passages	*Links to Other Sites*
Chapter Quizzes	*Recent Email Messages from the*
(interactive or printable)	*Author to His Students*
Misconceptions about the	*Poetry about Statistical Topics*
Chapter's Content	*Biography of a Famous Person*
Funny Stuff (two jokes)	*Themes of the Times*
	Link to Research Navigator

It should be noted that certain features of this book's companion website provide a form of instruction that is literally impossible to duplicate either by an instructor or a book. For example, the links to other sites bring the learner into contact with interactive exercises that actually *show* statistical concepts in operation, thereby permitting a kind of presentation that no instructor or book could ever accomplish.

Content.   Several changes were made as the third edition was transformed into this fourth edition. Three of these qualify as being major changes. First, the companion website described in the previous section has been created. Second, three topics (three-way ANOVAs, three-way fully repeated measures ANOVAs, and three-way mixed ANOVAs) have been moved to the website and exist there as supplements. Third, two new topics have been added to the website: meta-analysis and multivariate analysis of variance.

I have made a slew of other small and large changes for the purposes of increasing clarity, updating material, explaining new excerpts, emphasizing critical concepts, and improving review questions. The meaning of the word *slew* can be quantified by considering the number of typed pages of inserts that were submitted to the publisher as a part of this revision project. Disregarding the pages containing excerpts and end-of-chapter review questions, 371 pages of inserts were prepared so as to improve the quality of this book.

Research Navigator™.   In revising *Reading Statistics and Research,* I capitalized on the information and technology available in Research Navigator by connecting the fourth edition to full-text e-articles published since 2000. As a result, the book's statistical/research terms and tools "come alive" for the reader within settings where they are actually used. The book and Research Navigator™ are integrated via two features that facilitate student learning and increase motivation to learn:

- Fun end-of-chapter exercises that entice readers to examine carefully selected e-articles.
- Icons in the margin next to important terms used in the e-articles of several disciplines.

Although both features encourage use of the ContentSelect portion of Research Navigator™, it is the end-of-chapter exercises that will capture the interest of both students and instructor. Each such exercise contains (1) a brief summary of an *interesting* research investigation; (2) a question from me that asks the reader to make a "guess" about the study; and (3) directions as to which database of ContentSelect to enter, what article to examine, and where to look in the article to find out whether one's guess is correct. To illustrate, one exercise involves a study focused on college students' reported cheating behavior on tests and papers. After summarizing this investigation, the reader is asked to guess whether this study's results showed statistically significant differences between the reported cheating of male versus female and of older versus younger college students. I then indicate precisely where to look in the article to see the evidence (from a two-way ANOVA) that answers his "gender" and "age" questions.

Emphasis.   As in earlier editions, I have made a concerted effort to point out what kinds of questions can legitimately be answered by the statistical analyses considered in this book. In this edition, however, I try even harder to show that there is often a difference—and sometimes a giant difference—between what researchers are entitled to say following their data analyses and what they actually do say. My concern about this shows up throughout the many chapters concerned with inferential techniques.

Of this book's 18 chapters, 12 deal with statistical procedures that bring forth claims of "significance" or "significant differences." Such procedures inherently involve sample-to-population inference, null hypotheses, underlying assumptions, the possibility of inferential error, and "significance" that may exist in a statistical sense but not in any practical manner. I have purposefully emphasized these facets of statistical analysis more here than in the previous edition, for it is my growing observation that applied researchers often forget about inference and instead reify their sample statistics into population parameters.

I have also tried my best to assert at every opportunity that complex statistics do not have the magical power to create a silk purse out of a sow's ear. Unless the research questions being addressed are worthy, a study is doomed from the start. Accordingly, there is more emphasis here than before on critically evaluating research questions and null hypotheses as the first step in assessing the potential value of any investigation.

Finally, I have been very, very careful in selecting the 513 excerpts that appear in this edition. Many of these excerpts came from studies that dealt with important questions, that were designed thoughtfully, and that produced findings that may impact the way you think or act. Many other excerpts came from studies focused on topics that were undoubtedly fun for the researchers to research. By considering the research questions and methodology associated with these studies, perhaps more than a few readers will adopt the view that research can be both fun and relevant to our daily lives.

Using Research Navigator

This edition of *Reading Statistics and Research, Fourth Edition with Research Navigator*™ is designed to integrate the content of the book with the following resources of Research Navigator™, a collection of research databases, and instructional and contemporary publications available to you online at www.researchnavigator.com.

- **EBSCO's ContentSelect Academic Journal Database** organized by subject, with each subject containing leading academic journals for each discipline.
- *The New York Times,* one of the most highly regarded publications of today's news. View the full text of articles from the previous year.
- **Link Library** connects users to thousands of websites for discipline-specific key terms.
- **Research Review and Preparation.** A special section called "Understanding the Research Process" helps you work your way through the research process.

Connecting the Book with RN

As you read the book, you'll see special Research Navigator™ (RN) icons cueing you to visit the Research Navigator™ website to expand upon the concepts of the text and to further explore the work being done in the field of Statistics and Research. RN learning aids include:

Research
Navigator.c⊛m
Mixed methods

1. **Marginal keyword search terms.** Appearing in the margins of the text, these already tested terms will guide your search on topics relevant to the course content, and will yield an abundance of sources from a variety of perspectives that will broaden your exposure to key topics.
2. **Applied research activities and projects.** These suggestions provide more practice using the databases in Research Navigator™, and move students beyond the book to library and field research.

YOUR "Key" to Research Navigator™

It's now time to enter Research Navigator™. Purchase of this book provides you free access to this exclusive pool of information and data. You can find your personal access code to Research Navigator™ just inside the front cover of this book. The following walk-through provides a series of screen captures that illustrate, step-by-step, the various ways this valuable resource can make your research process more interesting and successful. Enjoy your entry into Research Navigator™!

Registration

In order to begin using Research Navigator™, you must first register using the personal access code found on the inside of the front cover of your book. Follow these easy steps:

1. Click "Register" under new users on the left side of the home page screen.

2. Enter the access code exactly as it appears on the inside front cover of your book or on your access card. (Note: Access codes can only be used once to complete one registration. If you purchased a used text, the access code may not work.)

1 ▶ Your Access Code   **?** Need Help? ▶

Please enter your six-word code without dashes. You can type the letters in lowercase or uppercase.

Example

SMPLE - FRILL - TONLE - WEIRS - CHOIR - FLEES

3. Follow the instructions on screen to complete your registration—you may click the Help button at any time if you are unsure how to respond.
4. Once you have successfully completed registration, write down the Login Name and Password you just created and keep it in a safe place. You will need to enter it each time you want to revisit Research Navigator™.
5. Once you register, you have access to all the resources in Research Navigator™ for six months. Each time you enter Research Navigator™, log in by simply going to the "Returning Users" section on the left side of the homepage and type in your Login Name and Password.

Returning Users

Login Name

Password

Forgot your login?

Log In

Getting Started

You're now official! The options available to you on Research Navigator™ are plenty. From Research Navigator's™ Homepage, you have easy access to all of the site's main features including a quick route to the three exclusive databases of source content. If you are new to the research process, you may want to start by browsing *Understanding the Research Process.*

This section of the site can be helpful even for those with some research experience but who might be interested in some helpful tips. Here you will find extensive help on all aspects of the research process including:

- Introduction to the Research Paper
- Gathering Data
- Searching the Internet
- Evaluating Sources
- Organizing Ideas
- Writing Notes
- Drafting the Paper
- Academic Citation Styles (MLA, APA, CME, and more)
- Blending Reference Material into Your Writing
- Practicing Academic Integrity
- Revising
- Proofreading
- Editing the Final Draft

Completing Research

The first step in completing a research assignment or research paper is to select a topic. (In some cases, your instructor may assign you a topic, or you may find suggested topics in the margins or at the end of chapters throughout this book.) Once you have selected and narrowed your research topic, you are now ready to *gather data.* Research Navigator™ simplifies your research efforts by giving you a convenient launching pad for gathering data. The site has aggregated three distinct types of source material commonly used in research assignments: Academic Journals (ContentSelect); Newspaper Articles (*The New York Times*) and World Wide Web Sites (Link Library).

1) EBSCO's ContentSelect

The first database you'll find on Research Navigator™ is the EBSCO Academic Journal and Abstract Database containing scholarly, peer-reviewed journals (such as *Journal of Education Policy* and *Assessment & Evaluation in Higher Education*).

The information obtained in these individual articles is more scientific than information you would find in a popular magazine, in a newspaper article, or on a web page. Searching for articles in ContentSelect is easy!

Within the ContentSelect Research Database section, you will see a list of disciplines and a space to type keywords. You can search within a single discipline or multiple disciplines. Choose one or more subject databases, and then enter a keyword you wish to search. Click on "Go".

The next thing you'll see is a list of articles that match your search. From this page you can examine either the full text or the abstract of each of the articles and determine which will best help with your research. Print out the articles or save them in your "Folder" for later reference. From this page you can also complete more focused searches by using the Basic Search or Advanced Search options in the navigator bar.

2) *The New York Times*

Searching *The New York Times* gives you access to articles from one of the world's leading newspapers. The first step in using the search-by-subject archive is to indicate the subject area you wish to search. You have the option of searching one specific subject at a time by highlighting the subject area or searching all subjects by highlighting "All." Click on "Go" now for a complete listing of articles in your chosen subject area that have appeared in the *New York Times* over the last year, sorted by most recent article first. For a more focused search, type a word, or multiple words separated by commas, into the search box and click "Go" for a list of articles. Articles can be printed or saved for later use in your research assignment.

The New York Times
ON THE WEB   Search by Subject Archive

Archive of New York Times articles from January 1, 2002.

Search by Subject

| Education Research | ▼ | Go | ⚠ Log in to search. |

Search by Keyword

| Mixed Methods | Go | ⚠ Log in to search. |

---

3) *"Best of the Web" Link Library*

The third database of content included on Research Navigator™ is a collection of web links, organized by academic subject and key terms. To use this database, simply select a subject from the dropdown list, and find the key term for the topic you are searching. Click on the key term and see a list of editorially reviewed web sites that offer educationally relevant and credible content. The web links in Link Library are monitored and updated each week, reducing your incidence of finding "dead links."

LINK
L I B R A R Y

Link Library provides access to thousands of web links for discipline-specific key terms. Click below to search by term, or keyword and have instant access to editorially reviewed and credible web sites for research.

Search by Subject

| Education—Educational Psychology | ▼ | Go | ⚠ Log in to search. |

Using Your Library

While Research Navigator™ does contain a vast amount of information to assist you with your research, it does not try to replace the library. After you have selected your topic and gathered source material from the three databases of content, you may need going to go to your school library to complete your research. Finding information at the library, however, can seem overwhelming. Research Navigator™ provides some assistance in this area as well, serving as a bridge to the library by helping you understand how to use library resources effectively and efficiently.

In addition, when you are ready to use the library to complete a research assignment or research paper, Research Navigator™ includes 31 discipline-specific "library guides" for you to use as a roadmap. Each guide includes an overview of the discipline's major subject databases, online journals, and key associations and newsgroups. Feel free to print them out and take them with you to the library!

CAUTION! Please note that the Research Navigator™ site undergoes frequent changes as new and exciting options are added to assist with research endeavors. For the latest information on the options available to you on Research Navigator™, visit www.ablongman.com/researchnavigator.

Acknowledgments

As with most large projects, the revision of this book was made possible because of the hard work on the part of many talented people. I wish now to express my sincere appreciation to these individuals. They are not responsible, of course, for any mistakes that may have inadvertently crept into this work. They *are* responsible, however, for initiating this project, for moving it along, and for making the finished product far superior to what it would have been had they not been involved.

First and foremost, I want to thank two individuals at Allyn & Bacon who have supported and protected this project from beginning to end. Arnis Burvikovs and Christine Lyons have been enormously helpful to me over the past two years, and I truly feel as if each one functioned, at different times, as my handler, my mentor, and my guide. Though the three of us were separated by hundreds of miles, we kept in constant communication via telephone, email, fax, and "snail mail." Without exception, the many questions I posed were answered promptly and clearly by Arnie and Christine. They also raised important questions I never would have considered, passed along a variety of relevant questions from others, and (most importantly) they offered wise counsel and moral support.

During the past four years, several students identified passages in the third edition that were ambiguous, contradictory, or unnecessarily repetitious. Many professors at other universities and a handful of independent researchers also contacted me with questions, comments, and suggestions. None of these individuals probably realizes how much I value their important roles in this revision project. Nevertheless, I am indebted to each of them for their contributions. In addition, I would like to thank the following reviewers of this manuscript: Chester H. McCall, Pepperdine University, GSEP; Takako Chris Oshima, Georgia State University; and Bethany Shifflett, San Jose State University.

Several graduate students were involved in this revision project, and I want to thank them for their assistance. Extensive library and Internet research was conducted by Kathryn Flowers, Andrew D. Sipel, Emily Musick, Allison Keeneland, and Gary Webmann. The many pages of new text were typed by David Goodfiend and Nancy Reeder. Page proofs were carefully read by Alex Traveler, Patricia Gardener, Jason Banks, Deborah Brussels, Jennifer Vail, and Joe Driver. The permission file was overseen by Candace Glide, Todd Appletown, and Keith Chessman.

Shannon Foreman and the team at Omegatype Typography, Inc., took charge of the revision project as it moved through its production phase. I am extremely grateful to Shannon and the Omegatype team for their work on this project.

My heartfelt appreciation is extended to Ammar Safar who created the companion website for this book. This website (www.ReadingStats.com) contains extensive information and interactive exercises not contained here, and it is far more than simply a book supplement. In several respects, this companion website is equivalent in importance to the book. Having such a website would not have been possible had it not been for Ammar's generous contribution of his time and talent. I want to thank him for those contributions. Moreover, I want to thank him for the friendship that developed as we worked for over two years on the creation of the companion website.

Finally, I want to thank my family for being supportive of my efforts to complete this revision project. At every step along the way, members of my nuclear and extended family encouraged me to consider this project to be the second highest priority (behind my students) among my many professional obligations. Had they not encouraged me to hole up in my little home office and to keep my nose to the grindstone, this revision project would have been delayed for months, if not years!

Schuyler W. Huck
Knoxville, 2003

1

The Typical Format of a Journal Article

Almost all journal articles dealing with research studies are divided into different sections by means of headings and subheadings. Although there is variation among journals with respect to the terms used as the headings and the order in which different sections are arranged, there does appear to be a relatively standard format for published articles. Readers of the professional literature will find that they can get the most mileage out of the time they invest if they are familiar with the typical format of journal articles and the kind of information normally included in each section of the article.

We are now going to look at a particular journal article that does an excellent job of illustrating the basic format that many authors use as a guide when they are writing their articles. The different sections of our model article could be arranged in outline form as follows:

1. Abstract
2. Introduction
   a. Background
   b. Statement of purpose
   c. Hypotheses
3. Method
   a. Participants
   b. Materials
   c. Procedure
4. Results
5. Discussion
6. References

Let us now examine each of these items.

Abstract

An **abstract,** or *précis,* summarizes the entire research study and appears at the beginning of the article. Although it normally contains fewer than 150 words, the abstract usually provides the following information: (1) a statement of the purpose or
objective of the investigation, (2) a description of the individuals who served as participants, (3) a brief explanation of what the participants did during the study, and
(4) a summary of the important findings.

Excerpt 1.1 is the abstract from our model journal article. As in most articles,
it was positioned immediately after the title and authors' names. This abstract was
easy to distinguish from the rest of the article because it was indented and printed
in a small font size. In some journals, the abstract will be italicized to make it stand
out from the beginning paragraphs of the article.

EXCERPT 1.1 • *Abstract*

This study examined the anxiolytic (anxiety reducing) effects of exercise for elderly
women engaging in a single bout of aqua aerobics. Volunteers ($N = 29$) completed
questionnaires immediately before and after participating in an aqua aerobics class.
The average age of participants was 66.4 yr. A brief form of Spielberger's State Anxiety Inventory and a question on demographic items were administered prior to engagement in exercise, and the brief form of the State Anxiety Inventory was
administered again immediately after the exercise session. There was a significant
difference on a *t* test between participants' ratings of anxiety before exercise ($M =$
16.8) compared to after exercise ($M = 13.9$); participants' ratings of state anxiety
were somewhat lower after exercising. Weaknesses of the present study and suggestions for research are presented.

Source: S. R. Wininger. (2002). The anxiolytic effect of aqua aerobics in elderly women. *Perceptual and Motor Skills, 94*(1), p. 338.

The sole purpose of the abstract is to provide readers with an overview of the
material they will encounter in the remaining portions of the article. Even though
the abstract from our model journal article contains two technical terms (*significant
difference* and *t test*) and two abbreviations (*N* and *M*), you most likely can get a
good sense for what issues were being studied, who supplied the data, and how the
investigation turned out. On the basis of abstracts like the one shown in Excerpt 1.1,

you can decide that the article in front of you is a veritable gold mine, that it *may* be what you have been looking for, or that it is not at all related to your interests. Regardless of how you react to this brief synopsis of the full article, the abstract serves a useful purpose.

Introduction

The **introduction** of an article usually contains two items: a description of the study's **background** and a **statement of purpose.** Sometimes, as in our model journal article, a third portion of the introduction will contain a presentation of the researcher's **hypotheses.** These components of a journal article are critically important. Take the time to read them slowly and carefully.

Background

Most authors begin their articles by explaining what caused them to conduct their empirical investigations. Perhaps the author developed a researchable idea from discussions with colleagues or students. Maybe a previous study yielded unexpected results, thus prompting the current researcher to conduct a new study to see if those earlier results could be replicated. Or, maybe the author wanted to see which of two competing theories would be supported more by having the collected data conform to its hypotheses. By reading the introductory paragraph(s) of the article, you will learn why the author conducted the study.

In describing the background of their studies, authors typically highlight the connection between their studies and others' previously published work. Whether this review of literature is short or long, its purpose is to show that the current author's work has been informed by, or can be thought of as an extension of, previous knowledge. Such discussions are a hallmark of scholarly work. Occasionally, a researcher will conduct a study that is based on an idea that is not connected to anything anyone has investigated or written about; such studies, however, are rare.

Excerpt 1.2 comes from our model article. Though only a single paragraph in length, this portion of the introduction sets the stage for a discussion of the authors' investigation.

Statement of Purpose

After discussing the study's background, an author usually states the specific purpose or goal of the investigation. This statement of purpose is one of the most important parts of a journal article since, in a sense, it explains what the author's "destination" was. It would be impossible for us to evaluate whether the trip was

EXCERPT 1.2 • *Background*

Many elderly (55 years of age and older) persons report anxiety. Based on survey research the prevalence has been estimated to be as high as 24% (Forsell & Winblad, 1988; Himmelfarb & Murrell, 1984). Previous studies have also indicated that ratings of state and trait anxiety are more prevalent among elderly women than men (Forsell & Winblad, 1988; Himmelfarb & Murrell, 1984; Schuab & Linden, 2000). One means of reducing state anxiety and improving one's mood is to engage in physical activity. Research with younger subjects has shown single bouts of exercise improve mood (Petruzzello, Landers, Hatfield, Kubits, & Salazar, 1991), yet little research has examined the effects of such exercise on mood among elderly people.

One drawback of exercise for elderly people is the potential for injury. However, the increasingly popular use of exercising in the water reduces the risk of weight-bearing injuries. Two studies with younger subjects have specifically examined the effects of acute bouts of water exercise and swimming on mood. Both reports indicated subjects had improved mood states after exercising (Berger & Owen, 1983; Crissman, 1999). Even though water-based exercise is a popular form of exercise for elderly persons and is often recommended by physicians, the author was unable to locate any studies investigating the effects of a single bout of water-based exercise on mood with elderly participants.

Source: S. R. Wininger. (2002). The anxiolytic effect of aqua aerobics in elderly women. *Perceptual and Motor Skills, 94*(1), p. 338.

successful—in terms of research findings and conclusions—unless we know where the author was headed.

The statement of purpose can be as short as a single sentence or as long as a full paragraph. It is often positioned just before the first main heading of the article, but it can appear anywhere in the introduction. Regardless of its length or where it is located, you will have no trouble finding the statement of purpose if the researcher begins a sentence with the words, "The purpose of this study was to . . ." or "This investigation was conducted in order to compare. . . ." In Excerpt 1.3, we see the statement of purpose from our model journal article.

Hypotheses

After articulating the study's intended purpose, some authors disclose the hypotheses they had at the beginning of the investigation. Other authors do not do this, either because they didn't have any firm expectations or because they consider it

EXCERPT 1.3 • *Statement of Purpose*

The purpose of this study was to examine the anxiolytic effects of exercise for elderly women engaging in a single bout of aqua aerobics.

Source: S. R. Wininger. (2002). The anxiolytic effect of aqua aerobics in elderly women. *Perceptual and Motor Skills, 94*(1), p. 338.

unscientific for the researcher to hold hunches that might bias the collection or interpretation of the data. Although there are cases (as you will see in Chapter 7) where a researcher can conduct a good study without having any hypotheses as to how things will turn out, and although it is important for researchers to be unbiased, there is a clear benefit in knowing what the researcher's hypotheses were. Simply stated, outcomes compared against hypotheses usually are more informative than are results that stand in a vacuum. Accordingly, I applaud those researchers who disclose in the introduction any *a priori* hypotheses they had.

Excerpt 1.4 comes from our model journal article, and it contains the single hypothesis that the researcher had in the study concerned with anxiety and exercise among elderly women. In light of the research findings cited in the article's first two paragraphs, it is not surprising that the hypothesis in this study was that anxiety scores would decrease following a session of aqua aerobics.

In most articles, the background, the statement of purpose, and hypotheses are not identified by separate headings, nor are they found under a common heading. If a common heading were to be used, though, the word *introduction* would probably be most appropriate because these three items set the stage for the substance of the article—an explanation of what was done and what the results were.

EXCERPT 1.4 • *Hypotheses*

The central hypothesis was that the average scores for state anxiety of the elderly women engaging in water aerobics would significantly decrease after a single exercise session.

Source: S. R. Wininger. (2002). The anxiolytic effect of aqua aerobics in elderly women. *Perceptual and Motor Skills, 94*(1), p. 339.

Method

In the **method** section of a journal article, an author will explain in detail how the study was conducted. Ideally, such an explanation should contain enough information to enable a reader to replicate (i.e., duplicate) the study. To accomplish this goal, the author will address three questions: (1) Who participated in the study? (2) What kinds of measuring instruments were used to collect the data? and (3) What were the participants required to do? The answer to each of these questions is generally found under an appropriately titled subheading of the method section.

Participants

Each of the individuals (or animals) who supplies data in a research study is considered to be a **participant** or a **subject.** (In some journals, the abbreviations *S* and *S*s are used, respectively, to designate one subject or a group of subjects.) Within this section of a journal article, an author usually indicates how many participants or subjects were used, who the participants were, and how they were selected.

A full description of the participants is needed because the results of a study will often vary according to the nature of the participants who are used. This means that the conclusions of a study, in most cases, are valid only for individuals (or animals) who are similar to the ones used by the researcher. For example, if two different types of counseling techniques are compared and found to differ in terms of how effective they are in helping clients clarify their goals, it is imperative that the investigator indicate whether the participants were high school students, adults, patients in a mental hospital, or whatever. What works for a counselor in a mental hospital may not work at all for a counselor in a high school (and vice versa).

It is also important for the author to indicate how the participants were obtained. Were they volunteers? Were they randomly selected from a larger pool of potential participants? Were any particular standards of selection used? Did the researcher simply use all members of a certain high school or college class? As you shall see in Chapter 5, certain procedures for selecting samples allow results to be generalized far beyond the specific individuals (or animals) included in the study, while other procedures for selecting samples limit the valid range of generalization.

Excerpt 1.5 comes from our model journal article. Labeled participants, it was the first portion of the article's method section.

Materials

This section of a journal article is normally labeled in one of four ways: **materials, equipment, apparatus,** or **instruments.** Regardless of its label, this part of the article contains a description of the things (other than the participants) used in the study. The goal here, as in other sections that fall under the method heading, is to

EXCERPT 1.5 • *Participants*

Twenty-nine elderly females voluntarily completed questionnaires immediately before and after participating in aqua aerobics classes. Their average age was 66.4 yr. (*SD* = 9.2). Participants were surveyed in aqua aerobics classes at two separate facilities, a university pool and a private club pool.

Source: S. R. Wininger. (2002). The anxiolytic effect of aqua aerobics in elderly women. *Perceptual and Motor Skills, 94*(1), p. 339.

describe what was done with sufficient clarity that others could replicate the investigation to see if the results remain the same.

Suppose, for example, that a researcher conducts a study to see if males differ from females in the way they evaluate various styles of clothing. To make it possible for others to replicate this study, the researcher would need to indicate whether the subjects saw actual articles of clothing or pictures of clothing (and if pictures, whether they were prints or slides, what size they were, and whether they were in color), whether the clothing articles were being worn when observed by participants (and if so, who modeled the clothes), what specific clothing styles were involved, how many articles of clothing were evaluated, who manufactured the clothes, and all other relevant details. If the researcher does not provide this information, it would be impossible for anyone to replicate the study.

Often, the only material involved is the measuring device used to collect data. Such measuring devices—whether of a mechanical variety (e.g., a stopwatch) or of a paper-and-pencil variety (e.g., a questionnaire)—ought to be described very carefully. If the measuring device is a new instrument designed specifically for the study described in the article, the researcher will typically report evidence concerning the instrument's technical psychometric properties. Generally, the author accomplishes this task by discussing the reliability and validity of the scores generated by using the new instrument.[1] Even if an existing and reputable measuring instrument has been used, the researcher ought to tell us specifically what instrument was used (by indicating form, model number, publication date, etc.). One would need to know such information, of course, before a full replication of the study could be attempted. In addition, the researcher ought to pass along reliability and validity evidence cited by those who developed the instrument. Ideally, the authors ought to provide their *own* evidence as to the reliability and validity of scores used in their study, even if an existing instrument is used.

---

[1]Later, in Chapter 4, we will talk more about the kinds of evidence researchers normally offer to document their instruments' technical merit.

Excerpt 1.6 contains the materials section from our model article. By reading this excerpt, we learn that the elderly women who participated in this study completed a demographic form and the brief form of Spielberger's State Anxiety Inventory. If more space had been allocated to this article in the journal, the author undoubtedly would have described more fully these two measuring instruments. In that more extended description, the author would have (1) pointed out what information (in addition to age) was gathered on the demographic form, (2) presented a sample item from the State Anxiety Inventory, and (3) indicated that Spielberger's anxiety instruments are considered to be extremely good for measuring people's anxiety levels.

EXCERPT 1.6 • *Materials*

The questionnaires assessed state anxiety and demographic characteristics. State anxiety was measured using a 10-item brief form of the State Anxiety Inventory (Spielberger, 1979). Scores on this version range from 10 to 40, with higher scores indicating greater state anxiety. Evidence of the validity and reliability are discussed by Spielberger (1979). Estimates of internal consistency for this inventory in this study before and after exercise were acceptable as coefficients alpha were .80 and .71.

Source: S. R. Wininger. (2002). The anxiolytic effect of aqua aerobics in elderly women. *Perceptual and Motor Skills, 94*(1), p. 339.

In most empirical studies, the **dependent variable** is closely connected to the measuring instrument used to collect data. In fact, many researchers operationally define the dependent variable as being equivalent to the scores earned by people when they are measured with the study's instrument. Though this practice is widespread (especially among statistical consultants), it is *not* wise to think that dependent variables and data are one and the same.

Although there are different ways to conceptualize what a dependent variable is, a simple definition is useful in most situations. According to this definition, a dependent variable is simply a characteristic of the participants that (1) is of interest to the researcher; (2) is not possessed to an equal degree, or in the same way, by all participants; and (3) serves as the target of the researcher's data-collection efforts. Thus, in a study conducted to compare the intelligence of males and females, the dependent variable would be intelligence.

In the study associated with our model article, there was one dependent variable: state anxiety. (As opposed to *trait anxiety* which remains high, medium, or low over time, *state anxiety* fluctuates depending on the circumstances of the moment.) That was the target of the primary measuring instrument used in this study. By citing Spielberger's validity and reliability findings and by presenting his own evidence on internal consistency (by citing two alpha coefficients), the author's final two sentences in Excerpt 1.6 represent his claim that the collected scores did, in fact, reveal the participants' levels of state anxiety.

Procedure

How the study was conducted is explained in the **procedure** section of the journal article. Here, the researcher explains what the participants did—or what was done to them—during the investigation. Sometimes an author will even include a verbatim account of instructions given to the participants.

Remember that the method section is included so as to permit a reader to replicate a study. To accomplish this desirable goal, the author must outline clearly the procedures that were followed, providing answers to questions such as these: Where was the study conducted? Who conducted the study? In what sequence did events take place? Did any of the subjects drop out prior to the study's completion? (In Chapter 5, we will see that subject dropout can cause the results to be distorted.)

Excerpt 1.7 is the procedure section from our model article. Even though this section is extremely brief, it provides information regarding who collected the data, when this took place, and where this was done. In addition, the researcher points out that permission was granted to collect the data.

EXCERPT 1.7 • *Procedure*

Permission to administer the surveys was granted by the supervisors and instructors at both facilities. One instructor who taught the aqua aerobics classes at both facilities introduced the researcher who briefly described the survey and asked for volunteers. Prior to exercising the participants completed a questionnaire on demographic characteristics and the State Anxiety Inventory. Immediately following the approximately 60-min. session of water aerobic exercise, participants took the State Anxiety Inventory again. There was no control group.

Source: S. R. Wininger. (2002). The anxiolytic effect of aqua aerobics in elderly women. *Perceptual and Motor Skills, 94*(1), p. 339.

Results

There are three ways in which the results of an empirical investigation will be reported. First, the results can be presented within the text of the article—that is, with only words. Second, they can be summarized in one or more tables. Third, the findings can be displayed by means of a graph (which is technically called a **figure**). Not infrequently, a combination of these mechanisms for reporting results is used to help readers gain a more complete understanding of how the study turned out. In Excerpt 1.8, we see that the author of our model article presented his results by means of a single paragraph of text.

EXCERPT 1.8 • *Results*

There was a significant difference between participants' state anxiety before ($M = 16.8$, $SD = 5.9$) and after exercise ($M = 13.9$, $SD = 4.1$, $t_{28} = 3.76$, $p = .001$). On the average, the effect size for the decrease in participants' scores on state anxiety was .71 standard deviation units (pooled $SD = 4.27$, M difference = 3.0). It is also interesting to note that the distribution of the anxiety scores changed before and after exercise. Scores before exercise had a skewness value of .37, while scores after exercise were more skewed at 1.07, that is, the majority of the subjects rated their anxiety low after exercising.

Source: S. R. Wininger. (2002). The anxiolytic effect of aqua aerobics in elderly women. *Perceptual and Motor Skills, 94*(1), p. 339.

Although the **results** section of a journal article contains some of the most crucial information about the study (if not *the* most crucial information), readers of the professional literature often disregard it. They do this because the typical results section is loaded with statistical terms and notation not used in everyday communication. Accordingly, many readers of technical research reports simply skip the results section because it seems as if it came from another planet.

If you are to function as a discerning "consumer" of journal articles, you must develop the ability to read, understand, and evaluate the results provided by authors. Those who choose not to do this are forced into the unfortunate position of uncritical acceptance of the printed word. Researchers are human, however, and they make mistakes. Unfortunately, the reviewers who serve on editorial boards do not catch all of these errors. As a consequence, there sometimes will be an inconsistency between the results discussed in the text of the article and the results presented in the tables. At times, a researcher will use an inappropriate statistical test. More often than you would suspect, the conclusions drawn from the statistical results will extend far beyond the realistic limits of the actual data that were collected.

You do not have to be a sophisticated mathematician in order to understand and evaluate the results sections of most journal articles. However, you must become familiar with the terminology, symbols, and logic used by researchers. This text was written to help you do just that.

Look at Excerpt 1.8 once again. The text material included in this excerpt is literally packed with information intended to help you. Unfortunately, many readers miss out on the opportunity to receive this information because they lack the skills needed to decode what is being communicated or are intimidated by statistical presentations. One of my goals in this book is to help readers acquire (or refine) their decoding skills. In doing this, I hope to show that there is no reason for anyone to be intimidated by what is included in technical research reports.

After reading subsequent chapters in this book, you will be able to decipher easily all of the information presented in Excerpt 1.8. Once you get these chapters under your belt, you also will be in a position to critically evaluate this investigation and judge for yourself whether the researcher's claims ought to be believed. More important, you will be able to decipher and critique the majority of the research reports you encounter in printed and electronic journals.

Discussion

The results section of a journal article contains a technical report of how the statistical analyses turned out, while the **discussion** section is usually devoted to a nontechnical interpretation of the results. In other words, the author will normally use the discussion section to explain what the results mean in regard to the central purpose of the study. The statement of purpose, which appears near the beginning of the article, usually contains an underlying or obvious research question; the discussion section ought to provide a direct answer to that question.

In addition to telling us what the results mean, many authors use this section of the article to explain *why* they think the results turned out the way they did. Although such a discussion will occasionally be found in articles where the data support the researchers' hunches, authors are much more inclined to point out possible reasons for the obtained results when those results are inconsistent with their expectations. If one or more of the scores turn out to be highly different from the rest, the researcher may talk about such serendipitous findings in the discussion section.

Sometimes an author will use the discussion section to suggest ideas for further research studies. Even if the results do not turn out the way the researcher had hoped they would, the study may be quite worthwhile in that it might stimulate the researcher (and others) to identify new types of studies that need to be conducted. Although this form of discussion is more typically associated with unpublished master's theses and doctoral dissertations, you will occasionally encounter it in a journal article.

It should be noted that some authors use the term **conclusion** rather than discussion to label this part of the journal article. These two terms are used interchangeably. It is unusual, therefore, to find an article that contains both a discussion section and a conclusion section.

Excerpt 1.9 contains the discussion section that appeared in our model journal article. Notice how the author used the first paragraph to argue that (1) his hypothesis was supported by the empirical evidence of the study and (2) there was a meaningful *effect size* (i.e., impact) associated with the exercise session. In the second paragraph, the author addresses an apparent weakness in the study's design—the lack of a control group—by presenting evidence suggesting that the study's main finding is still valid even though no control group was used. In the final paragraph, an alternative explanation for the obtained results is discussed, with suggestions offered for further research. This researcher deserves high praise for discussing these concepts of effect size, control groups, and alternative explanations.

EXCERPT 1.9 • *Discussion*

The hypothesis was supported as participants' scores on state anxiety were significantly lower after exercising than before exercising. The effect size for the lower scores was .71 standard deviation units and indicates the magnitude of the decrease is large compared to the average effect size of .23 reported in previous studies on the anxiolytic effect of exercise when the State Anxiety Inventory was given to young and middle-age adults (Petruzzello, *et al.*, 1991). An effect size of this magnitude indicates a medium to large difference (Cohen, 1988). One may infer that a single bout of water aerobic exercise reduced scores on anxiety more for these elderly women than occurred for younger adults.

The main weakness of this study was the absence of a control group. The major drawback of a one-group pre-posttest design is that it does not control for regression to the mean, which might account for the present result. However, the large effect size found suggests the validity of the current finding. It is important to note that some of the studies reviewed in the same meta-analysis by Petruzzello, *et al.* compared anxiety scores before and after exercise while other studies included control groups and exercise groups. Comparisons of the effect sizes for these two types of studies indicates that the pre-posttest studies had an average effect size of .47 while the treatment and control group designs had an average effect size of .22 to .26. The authors of the meta-analysis suggest that the decrease may be related to controlling for the threats to internal validity. However, they point out the exercise groups did report lower scores on anxiety than the control groups.

Another potential explanation for the observed result could be that the reduction in anxiety was associated with social interaction rather than exercising. Researchers could improve designs by creating several different control groups to control for social interaction. For example, one could design a study with a group of elderly people in a social setting who are not engaging in physical activity, elderly people exercising alone, and elderly people who are not exercising or engaging in social interactions with others. Researchers should also include elderly men and ascertain the effects on the anxiolytic effect of exercise of potential covariates such as personality types.

Source: S. R. Wininger. (2002). The anxiolytic effect of aqua aerobics in elderly women. *Perceptual and Motor Skills, 94*(1), p. 339–340.

References

A journal article normally concludes with a list of the books, journal articles, and other source material referred to by the author. Most of these items were probably mentioned by the author in the review of the literature positioned near the beginning of the article. Excerpt 1.10 is the **references** section of our model article.

EXCERPT 1.10 • *References*

Berger, B. G., & Owen, D. R. (1983). Mood alteration with swimming—swimmers really do "feel better." *Psychosomatic Medicine, 45,* 425–433.

Cohen, J. (1988). *Statistical Power Analysis for the Behavioral Sciences.* Hillsdale, NJ: Erlbaum.

Crissman, D. E. (1999). Collegiate females' state anxiety levels following water exercise intervals. *Dissertation Abstracts International, 59*(10-A), 3873.

Forsell, Y., & Winblad, B. (1998). Feelings of anxiety and associated variables in a very elderly population. *International Journal of Geriatric Psychiatry, 13,* 454–458.

Himmelfarb, S., & Murrell, S. A. (1984). The prevalence and correlates of anxiety symptoms in older adults. *Journal of Psychology, 116,* 159–167.

Petruzzello, S. J., Landers, D. M., Hatfield, B. D., Kubitz, K. A., & Salazar, W. (1991). A meta-analysis on the anxiety-reducing effects of acute and chronic exercise: outcomes and mechanisms. *Sports Medicine, 11,* 143–182.

Schuab, R. T., & Linden, M. (2000). Anxiety and anxiety disorders in the old and very old—results from the Berlin Aging Study (BASE). *Comprehensive Psychiatry, 41,* 48–54.

Spielberger, C. D. (1979). Preliminary manual for the State-Trait Personality Inventory (STPI). (Unpublished manuscript, Univer. of South Florida, Tampa).

Source: S. R. Wininger. (2002). The anxiolytic effect of aqua aerobics in elderly women. *Perceptual and Motor Skills, 94*(1), p. 339–340.

The references can be very helpful to you if you want to know more about the particular study you are reading. Journal articles and convention presentations are usually designed to cover one particular study or a narrowly defined area of a subject. Unlike more extended writings (e.g., monographs and books), they include only a portion of the background information and only partial descriptions of related studies that would aid the reader's comprehension of the study. Reading books and articles listed in the references section will provide you with some of this information and probably give you a clearer understanding as to why and how the author conducted the particular study you have just read. Before hunting down any particular reference item, it is a good idea to look back into the article to reread the sentence or paragraph containing the original citation. This will give you an idea of what is in each reference item.

Notes

Near the beginning or end of their research reports, authors sometimes present one or more notes. In general, such notes are used by authors for three reasons: (1) to thank others who helped them with their study or with the preparation of the technical report, (2) to clarify something that was discussed earlier in the journal article, and (3) to indicate how an interested reader can contact them to discuss this particular study or other research that might be conducted in the future. In our model journal article, there were three notes. The researcher used these notes to thank two people who helped with the study, to indicate that Charles Spielberger had given permission to use the State Anxiety Inventory, and to provide his postal address for anyone who wished to contact him.

Two Final Comments

As we come to the end of this chapter, I would like to make two final points. One concerns the interconnectedness among the different components of the research summary. The other concerns the very first of those components: the abstract.

In this chapter, we have dissected a journal article that summarizes a research study that focused on exercise and anxiety among elderly women. In looking at this particular article section by section, you may have gotten the impression that each of the various parts of a research article can be interpreted and evaluated separately from the other sections that go together to form the full article. You should not leave this chapter with that thought, because the various parts of a well-prepared research report are tied together so as to create an integrated whole.

In our model journal article, the researcher had one principal hypothesis. That hypothesis appears in Excerpt 1.4. That same hypothesis is the focus of the first two sentences of the results section of the journal article (see Excerpt 1.8), the first paragraph of the discussion section (see Excerpt 1.9), and the fifth sentence of the abstract (see Excerpt 1.1). The author who prepared this journal article deserves high marks for keeping focused on the study's central hypothesis and for showing a clear connection between that hypothesis and his findings. Unfortunately, many journal articles display very loose (and sometimes undetectable) connections between the component parts of their articles.

My final comment takes the form of a warning. Simply stated, do not read an abstract and then think that you understand the study well enough to forgo reading the entire article. As was stated earlier, an abstract gives you a thumbnail sketch of a study, thus allowing you to decide whether the article fits into your area of interest. If it does not, then you rightfully can move on. On the other hand, if an abstract makes it appear that the study is, in fact, consistent with your interests, you need to then read the entire article for two reasons. First, the results summarized in the abstract may not coincide with the information that appears in the results section of the full article. Second, you cannot properly evaluate the quality of the results—even if they are consistently presented in the abstract, results, and discussion sections of the article—without coming to understand who or what was measured, how measurements were taken, and what kinds of statistical procedures were applied.

If you read an abstract (but nothing else in the article) and then utilize the abstract's information to bolster your existing knowledge or guide your own research projects, you potentially harm rather than help yourself. That is the case because the findings reported in many abstracts are simply not true. To be able to tell whether or not an abstract can be trusted, you will need to read the full article. The rest of this book has been written to help make that important task easier for you.

Review Terms

Abstract	Notes
Dependent variable	Participants
Discussion	Procedure
Figure	References
Hypotheses	Results
Materials	Subject
Method	

The Best Items in the Companion Website

1. An important email message sent by the author at the beginning of the semester to students enrolled in his statistics and research course.
2. An interactive online quiz (with immediate feedback provided) covering Chapter 1.
3. Gary Gildner's wonderful poem entitled "Statistics."
4. Five misconceptions about the content of Chapter 1.

Fun Exercises inside Research Navigator

1. **What kind of "no-suicide" contract do college students prefer?**

   In this study, each of 112 college students evaluated three different "no-suicide" contracts on how well each one might help prevent suicides on college campuses. The three contracts differed in length and complexity. One contained a single sentence; one was made up of two sentences; one had nine sentences covering six points. Each research participant rated each contract on several criteria (e.g., effectiveness in stopping suicidal thoughts, potential for lessening depression). Which of the three contracts do you think was evaluated as being the best? Do you think the subgroups of participants who had or had not contemplated suicide felt the same way about which contract was best? To find out the research-based answers to these questions, locate the PDF version of the research report in the Helping Professions database of ContentSelect and read (on page 588) the first paragraph of the section entitled "Discussion." In addition, take a look at *all* of the article's sections and headings. This will give you a feel for the way most research articles are organized.

G. Buelow & L. M. Range. No-suicide contracts among college students. *Death Studies*. Located in the HELPING PROFESSIONS database of ContentSelect.

2. **Do college students get anxious about aging when taking a course on aging?**

In this investigation, 256 college students were measured as to their knowledge about aging, their attitudes toward elderly people, and their anxiety about becoming old. Half were seniors who had just completed a course on aging; the other half were freshmen who had never taken such a course. The researchers compared the seniors with the freshmen on each of the study's three dependent variables: knowledge, attitude, and anxiety. As expected, the seniors did better on the knowledge-of-aging measure. But what about the other two measures? Do you think the seniors differed from the freshmen on either the attitude measure or the anxiety measure? To find out, locate the PDF version of the research report in the Nursing, Health, and Medicine database of ContentSelect and read (on page 664) the first two paragraphs of the "Discussion." Also, skim through the entire article, noting the different sections and headings. Most articles are set up like this one.

L. A. Harris & S. Dollinger. Participation in a course on aging: Knowledge, attitudes, and anxiety about aging in oneself and others. *Educational Gerontology*. Located in the NURSING, HEALTH, AND MEDICINE database of ContentSelect.

Review Questions and Answers begin on page 516.

2

Descriptive Statistics

The Univariate Case

In this chapter we will consider descriptive techniques designed to summarize data on a single dependent variable. These techniques are often said to be **univariate** in nature because only one variable is involved. (In Chapter 3, we will look at several techniques designed for the **bivariate** case—that is, for situations where data have been collected on two dependent variables.)

We begin this chapter by looking at several ways data can be summarized using pictures. These so-called picture techniques include frequency distributions, stem-and-leaf displays, histograms, frequency polygons, and pie graphs. Next, the topic of distributional shape is considered; here, you will learn what it means when a data set is said to be normal, skewed, bimodal, or rectangular. After that, we examine the concept of central tendency and various methods used to represent a data set's average score. We then turn our attention to how researchers usually summarize the variability, or spread, within their data sets; these techniques include four different kinds of range, the standard deviation, and the variance. Finally, we consider two kinds of standard scores: z and T.

Picture Techniques

In this section, we consider some techniques for summarizing data that produce a picture of the data. I use the term *picture* somewhat loosely, since the first technique really leads to a table of numbers. In any event, our discussion of descriptive statistics begins with a consideration of three kinds of frequency distributions.

Frequency Distributions

A **frequency distribution** shows how many people (or animals or objects) were similar in the sense that, measured on the dependent variable, they ended up in the same category or had the same score. Three kinds of frequency distributions are often seen in published journal articles: simple (or ungrouped) frequency distributions, grouped frequency distributions, and cumulative frequency distributions.

In Excerpt 2.1, we see an example of a simple frequency distribution. Actually, there are two simple frequency distributions presented in this excerpt—one for males and one for females—each showing the ages of the people included in the researchers' sample. The numbers in the right-hand column of each distribution indicate how many people were as old as the ages specified in the left-hand column. Thus, 5 males were 12 years old, 10 males were 13 years old, and so on.

EXCERPT 2.1 • *Simple Frequency Distribution*

TABLE 1   *Age Distribution within the Sample*

Age	Males (n = 72, 53%)		Females (n = 65, 47%)	
	Percentage	*n*	*Percentage*	*n*
12	6.9	5	6.2	4
13	13.9	10	13.8	9
14	23.6	17	35.4	23
15	18.1	13	26.2	17
16	25.0	18	12.3	8
17	12.5	9	6.2	4

Source: R. A. Ellis, M. O'Hara, and K. M. Sowers. (2000). Profile-based intervention: Developing gender-sensitive treatment for adolescent substance abusers. *Research on Social Work Practice, 10*(3), p. 332.

Two features of Excerpt 2.1 are worth noting. First, the authors used the letter *n* to label each distribution's right-hand column of numbers. Sometimes you will see the word *frequency* or the abbreviation *f* used instead. Second, if you add together the numbers in either of these columns, you'll get the total number of men and the total number of women. These totals appear inside parentheses above each column.

Excerpt 2.2 shows how a frequency distribution can help us understand the characteristics of a group relative to some categorical (rather than numerical) variable of interest. In the study from which this excerpt was taken, the chief academic officers at 368 community colleges were surveyed regarding their career paths. In response to one of the survey questions, each CAO was asked to indicate the title that he or she had when first hired in a community college. Those initial positions were called *entry ports.*

EXCERPT 2.2 • *Simple Frequency Distribution for a Qualitative Variable*

TABLE 3   *Entry Ports for CAOs*

Entry Position	*Frequency*	*Percentage*
Faculty	188	51.1
Primary Academic Officer	64	17.4
Chair or Head	42	11.4
Other Administrative Position	33	9.0
Chief Academic Officer	28	7.6
Chief Student Affairs Officer	13	3.5
Total	368	100.0

Source: B. D. Cejda, C. B. McKenney, and H. Burley. (2001). The career lines of chief academic officers in public community colleges. *Community College Review, 28*(4), p. 39.

In Excerpt 2.3, we see an example of a grouped frequency distribution. In this study, data were collected from four different groups of athletic trainers (those associated with professional teams, with college teams, with high school teams, and with clinics). The variable of interest in Excerpt 2.3 is the number of concussions typically evaluated yearly by each trainer. This is a *grouped* frequency distribution because the far left-hand column has, on each row, a group of possible scores (rather than a single score). This grouping of possible scores—into what are technically called *class intervals*—allows the data to be summarized in a more compact fashion. If the data in Excerpt 2.3 had been presented in an ungrouped frequency distribution, there would have been at least 11 rows (for the scores 0 through 10), and possibly many more if one of the trainers evaluated far more than 10 concussions per year.

EXCERPT 2.3 • *Grouped Frequency Distribution*

TABLE 2   *Number of Concussion Evaluations per Year by Setting*

No. Evaluated	Professional (n = 18)	College (n = 126)	High School (n = 105)	Clinic (n = 78)	Total No. (%)
0–3	6	28	21	21	76 (23.2)
3–5	4	33	27	25	89 (27.2)
5–10	7	42	34	23	106 (32.4)
≥10	1	23	23	9	56 (17.1)

Source: M. S. Ferrara, M. McCrea, C. L. Peterson, and K. M. Guskiewicz. (2001). A survey of practice patterns in concussion assessment and management. *Journal of Athletic Training,* *36*(2), p. 146.

In addition to simple and grouped frequency distributions, **cumulative frequency distributions** sometimes appear in journal articles. With this kind of summarizing technique, a researcher tells us, through an additional column of numbers labeled *cumulative frequency* or *cumulative percentage,* how many measured objects ended up with any given score and all other lower scores (or how many scores ended up in a given score interval and all other lower intervals). This kind of frequency distribution is shown in Excerpt 2.4. Notice how the cumulative percentage of 93.00 can be obtained by (1) adding together 1,430, 569, and 206, (2) dividing the sum by 2,371, and (3) multiplying by 100. Or, you can obtain the same cumulative percentage by adding together the top three numbers in the third column from the left.

Stem-and-Leaf Displays

Although a grouped frequency distribution provides information about the scores in a data set, it carries with it the limitation of "loss of information." The frequencies tell us how many data points fell into each interval of the score continuum but they do not indicate, within any interval, how large or small the scores were. Hence, when researchers summarize their data by moving from a set of raw scores to a grouped frequency distribution, the precision of the original scores is lost.

A **stem-and-leaf display** is like a grouped frequency distribution that contains no loss of information. To achieve this objective, the researcher first sets up score intervals on the left side of a vertical line. These intervals, collectively called

EXCERPT 2.4 • *Cumulative Frequency Distribution*

Table IV summarizes author publication frequencies on the basis of pages published. More than 60 percent of the authors who published on business ethics published less than 10 equivalent pages. Many of these authors were listed as coauthors on one paper that had two or more authors.

TABLE IV *Summary by Quantity of Articles Published*

Pages Published	Number of Authors	Percentage of Total Authors	Cumulative Percentage
Less than 10	1430	60.31	60.31
10–19	569	24.00	84.31
20–29	206	8.69	93.00
30–39	70	2.96	95.97
40–49	43	1.81	97.99
50–59	13	0.55	98.32
60–69	11	0.46	98.78
70–79	9	0.38	99.16
80–89	7	0.30	99.46
90–99	4	0.17	99.63
More than 99	9	0.37	100.00
Total	2371	100.00	

Source: Adapted from M. Sabrin. (2002). A ranking of the most productive business ethics scholars: A five-year study. *Journal of Business Ethics, 36,* p. 364.

the *stem,* are presented in a coded fashion by showing all but the last digit of the scores falling into each interval. Then, to the right of the vertical line, the final digit is given for each observed score that fell into the interval being focused on. An example of a stem-and-leaf display is presented in Excerpt 2.5.

In the top row of this stem-and-leaf display, there is a 10 on the left (stem) side and a 0 on the right (leaf) side. This indicates that there was one score, a 100, within the interval represented by this row of the display. The bottom row has three digits on the leaf side, and this indicates that three scores fell into this row's interval. Using both stem and leaf from this bottom row, we see that those three scores were 27, 27, and 29. All other rows of this stem-and-leaf display are interpreted in the same way.

Notice that the 43 actual attitude scores in Excerpt 2.5 show up in the stem-and-leaf display. There is, therefore, no loss of information. Take another look at

EXCERPT 2.5 • *A Stem-and-Leaf Display*

The 1990 McCall, Belli, and Madjidi Statistics Attitude Scale was administered to 43 postgraduate education students in Transkei at the end of a course on research methodology. . . . The distribution of attitude scores is shown by the stem-and-leaf plot in Table 4.

TABLE 4 *Frequency Distribution of Attitude Scores*

10	0								
9	2	3	6						
8	0	1	2	3	6	9			
7	0	0	1	3	3	5	8	8	9	9
6	0	2	2						
5	0	2	4	5	7	9	9		
4	0	1	2	3	9				
3	0	3	4	6	8				
2	7	7	9						

Source: G. Glencross and V. I. Cherian. (1992). Attitudes toward applied statistics of postgraduate education students in Transkei. *Psychological Reports, 70,* p. 72. © *Psychological Reports.*

Excerpt 2.3 or Excerpt 2.4, where grouped frequency distributions were presented. Because of the loss of information associated with grouped frequency distributions, you cannot tell what the highest and lowest earned scores were, what specific scores fell into any interval, or whether gaps exist inside any intervals (as was the case in Excerpt 2.5 because no student ended up with any score from 63 to 69).

Histograms and Bar Graphs

In a **histogram,** vertical columns (or thin lines) are used to indicate how many times any given score appears in the data set. With this picture technique, the baseline (that is, the horizontal axis) is labeled to correspond with observed scores on the dependent variable while the vertical axis is labeled with frequencies.[1] Then, columns (or lines) are positioned above each baseline value to indicate how often each of these scores was observed. Whereas a tall bar indicates a high frequency of occurrence, a short bar indicates that the baseline score turned up infrequently.

---

[1]Technically speaking, the horizontal and vertical axes of any graph are called the **abscissa** and **ordinate,** respectively.

A **bar graph** is almost identical to a histogram in both form and purpose. The only difference between these two techniques for summarizing data concerns the nature of the dependent variable that defines the baseline. In a histogram, the horizontal axis is labeled with numerical values that represent a quantitative variable. In contrast, the horizontal axis of a bar graph represents different categories of a qualitative variable. In a bar graph, the ordering of the columns is quite arbitrary, whereas the ordering of the columns in a histogram must be numerically logical.

In Excerpt 2.6, we see an example of a histogram. Notice how this graph allows us to quickly discern the IQ scores for the individuals included in the researchers' sample. Also notice that the columns had to be arranged as they were because the variable on the baseline was clearly quantitative in nature.

An example of a bar graph is presented in Excerpt 2.7. Here, the order of the bars is completely arbitrary. The short bars could have been positioned on the left with the taller bars positioned on the right. Or, the bars could have been arranged alphabetically based on the labels beneath the bars.

EXCERPT 2.6 • *Histogram*

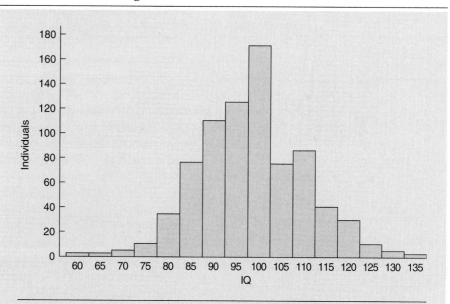

FIGURE 1   *Distribution of IQ scores for all individuals in the analysis sample.*

Source: S. J. Wadsworth, R. K. Olson, B. F. Pennington, and J. C. DeFries. (2000). Differential genetic etiology of reading disability as a function of IQ. *Journal of Learning Disabilities, 33*(2), p. 195.

EXCERPT 2.7 • *Bar Graph*

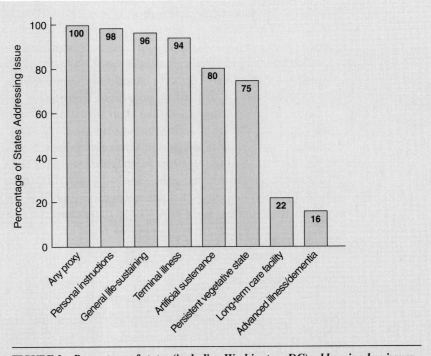

FIGURE 2   *Percentage of states (including Washington, DC) addressing key issues.*

Source: G. Gunter-Hunt, J. E. Mahoney, and C. E. Sieger. (2002). A comparison of state advance directive documents. *Gerontologist, 42*(1), p. 53.

Frequency Polygons

A **frequency polygon** is the technical name for what many people refer to as a line graph. As in a histogram, this picture technique for summarizing data has a horizontal axis that is labeled with individual scores or score intervals, along with a vertical axis that is labeled with frequencies (or sometimes percents). With a frequency polygon, however, each bar is replaced with a single dot positioned where the top of the bar would have been located. Then, adjacent dots are connected with straight lines to form the final graph.

In Figure 2.1, I have built a frequency polygon to show the ages of the 65 females shown in Excerpt 2.1. Notice how this picture allows you to discern quickly that most of these females were either 14 or 15 years old. Also notice that (1) the left and right ends of the line graph have been "tied down" to the baseline (at age 11, immediately to the left of the youngest person in the sample, and at age 18, immediately to the right of the oldest person in the sample), and (2) the horizontal axis

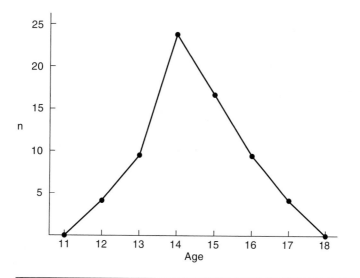

FIGURE 2.1   *Frequency Polygon for the Female Data in Excerpt 2.1*

is scaled so as to permit the frequency polygon to fill the two-dimensional space created by the two axes.

Pie Graphs

A **pie graph**[2] represents an easy-to-understand way of showing how a full group is made up of subgroups—and also of showing the relative size of the subgroups. An example of a pie graph is included in Excerpt 2.8. Here, as in all pie graphs, the size of each slice of the pie indicates the relative size of the particular subgroup represented by that portion of the circle. Because of this feature of pie graphs, one can look at Excerpt 2.8 and quickly determine that a little over half of the respondents were in the furniture, cabinetry, or lumber distribution lines of business; that only a small proportion of respondents were in the lumber retailing line of business; and that about 1 in 11 respondents had a line of business other than the eight that showed up most frequently.

Distributional Shape

If researchers always summarized their quantitative data using one of the picture techniques just covered, then you could *see* whether the observed scores tended to

---

[2]Some authors refer to this particular picture technique as a *pie chart* or as a *circle graph*.

EXCERPT 2.8 • *Pie Graph*

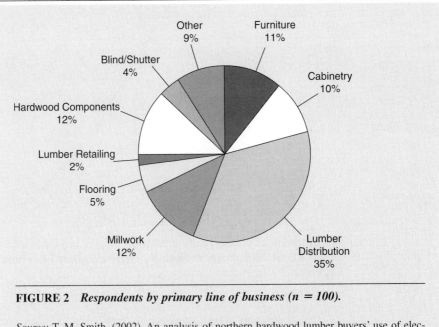

FIGURE 2 *Respondents by primary line of business (n = 100).*

Source: T. M. Smith. (2002). An analysis of northern hardwood lumber buyers' use of electronic commerce. *Forest Products Journal, 52*(2), p. 64.

congregate at one (or more) point along the score continuum. Moreover, a frequency distribution, a stem-and-leaf display, a histogram, or a frequency polygon would allow you to tell whether a researcher's data were symmetrical. To illustrate this nice feature of the picture techniques we have discussed, take another look at Excerpt 2.1. The frequency distribution for the 65 females shows nicely that (1) most of the females were 14 or 15 years old, and (2) the distribution of ages was fairly symmetrical, with ages not strung out either toward the young or the old end of the continuum.

Unfortunately, pictures of data sets do not appear in journal articles very often because they are costly to prepare and because they take up lots of space. By using some verbal descriptors, however, researchers can tell their readers what their data sets look like. To decipher such messages, you must understand the meaning of a few terms that researchers use to describe the **distributional shape** of their data.

If the scores in a data set approximate the shape of a **normal distribution,** most of the scores will be clustered near the middle of the continuum of observed scores, and there will be a gradual and symmetrical decrease in frequency in both directions away from the middle area of scores. Data sets that are normally distributed are said to resemble a bell-shaped curve, since a side drawing of a bell will start out low on either side and then bulge upward in the center. In Excerpt 2.6, we saw a histogram that closely resembles a normal distribution.

In **skewed distributions,** most of the scores end up being high (or low), with a small percentage of scores strung out in one direction away from the majority. Skewed distributions, consequently, are not symmetrical. If the tail of the distribution (formed by the small percentage of scores that is strung out in one direction) points toward the upper end of the score continuum, the distribution is said to be **positively skewed;** if the tail points toward the lower end of the score continuum, the term **negatively skewed** applies. The frequency distribution that we looked at in Excerpt 2.4 provides a good example of a positively skewed distribution, as does the histogram shown in Excerpt 2.9.

EXCERPT 2.9 • *A Positively Skewed Distribution*

A total of 253 incidents [wheelchair injuries] were reported by 109 participants while using 120 different wheelchairs, 53 (44 percent) manual and 67 (56 percent) powered. Sixty-four participants (59 percent) had experienced more than one incident during the 5-year period (Figure 1).

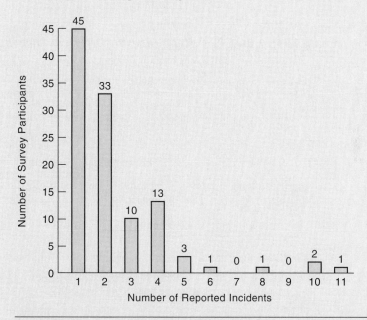

FIGURE 1 *Number of incidents reported by individual survey participants (total 253 incidents among 109 participants).*

Source: R. P. Gaal, N. Rebholtz, R. D. Hotchkiss, and P. F. Pfaelzer. (1997). Wheelchair rider injuries: Causes and consequences for wheelchair design and selection. *Journal of Rehabilitation Research and Development, 34*(1), p. 60.

If the scores tend to congregate around more than one point along the score continuum, the distribution is said to be **multimodal** in nature. If there are two such places where scores are grouped together, we could be more specific and say that the data are distributed in a **bimodal** fashion. If scores are congregated at three distinct points, the term **trimodal** would come into play.[3]

If scores are fairly evenly distributed along the score continuum without any clustering at all, the data set is said to be **rectangular.** Such a distributional shape would probably show up if someone (1) asked each person in a large group to indicate his or her birth month, and (2) created a histogram with 12 bars, beginning with January, arranged on the baseline. The bars making up this histogram would probably be approximately the same height. Looked at collectively, the bars making up this histogram would resemble a rectangle.

In Excerpts 2.10 through 2.12, we see a few examples of how researchers will sometimes go out of their way to describe the distributional shape of their data sets. Such researchers should be commended for indicating what their data sets looked like because these descriptions help others to understand the nature of the data that have been collected.

EXCERPTS 2.10–2.12 • *References to Different Distributional Shapes*

The scores were normally distributed.

Source: T. V. Crowe. (2002). Translation of the Rosenberg self-esteem scale into American sign language: A principal components analysis. *Social Work Research, 26*(1), p. 59.

- -

[The] pharmacy fills were highly skewed with 2.7% receiving >20 fills.

Source: J. Guevara, P. Lozano, T. Wickizer, L. Mell, and H. Gephart. (2002). Psychotropic medication use in a population of children who have attention-deficit/hyperactivity disorder. *Pediatrics, 109*(5), p. 735.

- -

Both distributions are bimodal (although this is less prominent in the UK), and indicate some (naturally acquired) immune recognition of the mycobacterial antigen.

Source: G. F. Black, R. E. Weir, S. Floyd, and L. Bliss. (2002). BCG-induced increase in interferon-gamma response to mycobacterial antigens and efficacy of BCG vaccination of Malawi and the UK: Two randomised controlled studies. *The Lancet, 359*(9315), p. 1395.

[3]Distributions having just one "hump" are said to be **unimodal** in nature.

As we have seen, two features of distributional shape are modality and skewness. A third feature is related to the concept of **kurtosis.** This third way of looking at distributional shape deals with the possibility that a set of scores can be nonnormal even though there is only one mode and even though there is no skewness in the data. This is possible because there may be an unusually large number of scores at the center of the distribution, thus causing the distribution to be overly peaked. Or, the hump in the middle of the distribution may be smaller than is the case in normal distributions, with both tails being thicker than in the famous bell-shaped curve.

When the concept of kurtosis is discussed in research reports, you may encounter the terms **leptokurtic** and **platykurtic.** These terms denote distributional shapes that are more peaked and less peaked (as compared with the normal distribution), respectively. The term **mesokurtic** signifies a distributional shape that is neither overly peaked nor overly flat.

As illustrated in Excerpts 2.9 through 2.12, researchers can communicate information about distributional shape via a picture or a label. They can also compute numerical indices that assess the degree of skewness and kurtosis present in their data. In Excerpt 2.13, we see a case in which a group of researchers presented such indices in an effort to help their readers understand what kind of distributional shape was created by each set of scores that had been gathered.

To properly interpret coefficients of skewness and kurtosis, keep in mind three things. First, both indices will turn out equal to zero for a normal distribution. Second, skewness is not considered to be too extreme if the coefficient of skewness

EXCERPT 2.13 • *Quantifying Skewness and Kurtosis*

The shapes of the distributions can be described by their coefficients of skewness and kurtosis. Skewness was −0.807 and 0.597, and kurtosis was 2.267 and 0.161 for the Binary and Octave procedures, respectively. Thus, the distribution of the differences with the Binary procedure was negatively skewed, indicating that the negative differences (reflecting pitch matches becoming higher in frequency during Session 2) were greater than the positive differences (pitch matches becoming lower in frequency). In contrast, the distribution for the Octave procedure was positively skewed. The kurtosis values are scaled so that a value of zero indicates a normal distribution. The distribution for the Binary differences was more positively peaked than normal (indicating more data in the central part of the distribution), while the Octave differences were more normally distributed.

Source: J. A. Henry, C. L. Flick, A. Gilbert, R. M. Ellingson, and S. A. Fausti. (2001). Comparison of two computer-automated procedures for tinnitus pitch matching. *Journal of Rehabilitation Research and Development, 38*(5), p. 561.

assumes a value anywhere between -1.0 and $+1.0$. Third, platykurtic distributions are indicated by coefficients of kurtosis smaller than -1.0 whereas leptokurtic distributions are indicated by coefficients of kurtosis larger than 2.0.[4]

Depending on the objectives of the data analysis, a researcher should examine coefficients of skewness and kurtosis before deciding how to further analyze the data. If a data set is found to be grossly nonnormal, the researcher may opt to do further analysis of the data using statistical procedures created for the nonnormal case. Or, the data can be "normalized" by means of a formula that revises the value of each score such that the revised data set represents a closer approximation to the normal.

Measures of Central Tendency

To help readers get a feel for the data that have been collected, researchers almost always say something about the typical or representative score in the group. They do this by computing and reporting one or more **measures of central tendency.** There are three such measures that are frequently seen in the published literature, each of which provides a numerical index of the **average** score in the distribution.

The Mode, Median, and Mean

The **mode** is simply the most frequently occurring score. For example, given the nine scores 6, 2, 5, 1, 2, 9, 3, 6, and 2, the mode is equal to 2. The **median** is the number that lies at the midpoint of the distribution of earned scores; it divides the distribution into two equally large parts. For the set of nine scores just presented, the median is equal to 3. Four of the nine scores are smaller than 3; four are larger.[5] The **mean** is the point that minimizes the collective distances of scores from that point. It is found by dividing the sum of the scores by the number of scores in the data set. Thus for the group of nine scores presented here, the mean is equal to 4.

In journal articles, authors sometimes use abbreviations or symbols when referring to their measure(s) of central tendency. The abbreviations *Mo* and *Mdn,* of course, correspond to the mode and median, respectively. The letter *M* always stands for the mean, even though all three measures of central tendency begin with this letter. The mean is also symbolized by $\overline{X}$ and μ.

---

[4]The coefficient of skewness for the positively skewed distribution shown in Excerpt 2.9 is equal to $+2.51$; the coefficient of kurtosis is equal to 7.55. (These coefficients were computed via formulas that involve z-scores. The notion of a z-score is discussed later in this chapter.)

[5]When there is an even number of scores, the median is a number halfway between the two middle scores (once the scores are ordered from low to high). For example, if 9 is omitted from our sample set of scores, the median for the remaining eight scores would be 2.5—that is, the number halfway between 2 and 3.

In many research reports, the numerical value of only one measure of central tendency is provided. (That was the case with the model journal article presented in Chapter 1; take a look at Excerpt 1.8 to see which one was used.) Because it is not unusual for a real data set to be like our sample set of nine scores in that the mode, median, and mean assume different numerical values, researchers sometimes compute and report two measures of central tendency, or all three, so as to help readers better understand the data being summarized.

In Excerpt 2.14, we see a case where two measures of central tendency were reported for the same data set. Excerpt 2.15 contains an example where all three averages—the mode, the median, and the mean—were provided.

EXCERPTS 2.14–2.15 • *Reporting Multiple Measures of Central Tendency*

Interviews to obtain the 24-hour recalls ranged in length from 5 to 29 minutes (mean = 15; median = 14).

Source: S. D. Baxter, W. O. Thompson, M. S. Litaker, F. H. A. Frye, and C. H. Guinn. (2002). Low accuracy and low consistency of fourth-graders' school breakfast and school lunch recalls. *Journal of the American Dietetic Association, 102*(3), p. 391.

- -

On the recent-use scale, scores were skewed toward zero, and sexually active males had a mean score of 1.7, a median of 1.2 and a mode of zero; among sexually active females, the corresponding values were 1.5, 1.1 and zero, respectively.

Source: J. S. Santelli, L. Robin, N. D. Brener, and R. Lowry. (2001). Timing of alcohol and other drug use and sexual risk behaviors among unmarried adolescents and young adults. *Family Planning Perspectives, 33*(5), p. 202.

The Relative Position of the Mode, Median, and Mean

In a true normal distribution (or in any unimodal distribution that is perfectly symmetrical), the values of the mode, median, and mean will be identical. Such distributions are rarely seen, however. In the data sets typically found in applied research studies, these three measures of central tendency assume different values. As a reader of research reports, you should know not only that this happens but also how the distributional shape of the data affects the relative position of the mode, median, and mean.

In a positively skewed distribution, a few scores are strung out toward the high end of the score continuum, thus forming a tail that points to the right. In this kind of distribution, the modal score ends up being the lowest (that is, positioned farthest to the left along the horizontal axis) while the mean ends up assuming the highest value (that is, positioned farthest to the right). In negatively skewed distributions, just the opposite happens; the mode ends up being located farthest to the right along the baseline while the mean assumes the lowest value. In Figure 2.2, we see a picture showing where these three measures of central tendency are positioned in skewed distributions.

After you examine Figure 2.2, return to Excerpt 2.1 or Figure 2.1 and look at the summary of the ages of the 65 females. By looking at the frequency distribution or frequency polygon, you will notice that the ages are strung out slightly toward the high end of the continuum. Because the data set has a slight positive skew, the mode, median, and mean assume values that are only slightly different: 14, 14.35, and 14.43, respectively.

To see a case where the computed measures of central tendency turned out to be highly dissimilar, thus implying dramatic skewness in the data, consider Excerpt 2.16. This passage deals with the number of sessions a group of marriage and family therapists had with their clients. The researchers who conducted this study deserve to be complimented for (1) including the mean and the median in their report and (2) indicating that their data set was skewed. In such situations, the median (and *not* the mean) does the best job of indicating the "center" of the distribution.

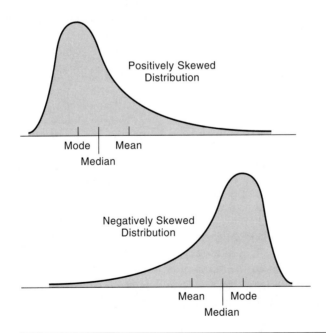

**FIGURE 2.2 *Location of the Mean, Median, and Mode in
Skewed Distributions***

EXCERPT 2.16 • *The Mean and Median in a Skewed Distribution*

The median number of sessions for the cases was 12; the mean was 25. The higher mean reflects the skewed distribution, with a large number of brief cases and a smaller number of very long cases. Of the cases reported, 41.8% lasted 10 or fewer sessions, 65.6% were completed within 209 sessions, and 87.9% were completed within 50 sessions.

Source: W. J. Doherty and D. Simmons. (1996). Clinical practice patterns of marriage and family therapies: A national survey of therapists and their clients. *Journal of Marital and Family Therapy, 22*(1), p. 19.

In a bimodal distribution, there will be two points along the score continuum where scores tend to "pile up." If the distribution is symmetrical, the mean and median will be located halfway between the two modes. In a symmetrical trimodal distribution, the median and mean will assume a value equal to the middle of the three modes. Real data sets, however, rarely produce symmetrical bimodal or trimodal distributions. Any asymmetry (that is, skewness) will cause the median to be pulled off center toward the side of the distribution that has the longer tail—and the mean will be pulled even farther in that direction.

With full-fledged rectangular distributions, the mean and median will assume a value halfway between the high and low data points. In such distributions, there is no mode because all earned scores occur with equal frequency. If the distribution turns out to be only roughly rectangular, the median and mean will be located close together (and close to the halfway point between the high and low scores), but the mode could end up anywhere.

Other Measures of Central Tendency

Although the mode, median, and mean are the most popular measures of central tendency, there are other techniques for summarizing the average score in a data set. (Examples include the geometric mean and the harmonic mean.) Because these indices are rarely seen in research reports, they will not be discussed here. If you take an advanced course in statistics, however, you will encounter these alternative methods for computing an average score.

Measures of Variability

Descriptions of a data set's distributional shape and reports as to the central tendency value(s) help us to better understand the nature of data collected by a researcher. Although terms (e.g., *roughly normal*) and numbers (e.g., $M = 67.1$) help, they are not sufficient. To get a true feel for the data that have been collected, we also need to be told something about the variability among the scores. Let us consider now the standard ways that researchers summarize this aspect of their data sets.

The Meaning of Variability

Most groups of scores possess some degree of variability. That is, at least some of the scores differ (vary) from one another. A **measure of variability** simply indicates the degree of this **dispersion** among the scores. If the scores are very similar, there is little dispersion and little variability. If the scores are very dissimilar, there is a high degree of dispersion (variability). In short, a measure of variability does nothing more than indicate how spread out the scores are.

The term *variability* can also be used to pinpoint where a group of scores might fall on an imaginary homogeneous–heterogeneous continuum. If the scores are similar, they are **homogeneous** (and have low variability). If the scores are dissimilar, they are **heterogeneous** (and have high variability).

Even though a measure of central tendency provides a numerical index of the average score in a group, we need to know the variability of the scores to better understand the entire group of scores. For example, consider the following two groups of IQ scores:

Group I	Group II
102	128
99	78
103	93
96	101

In both groups the mean IQ is equal to 100. Although the two groups have the same mean score, their variability is obviously different. While the scores in the first group are very homogeneous (low variability), the scores in the second group are far more heterogeneous (high variability).

The specific measures of variability that we will now consider are similar in that the numerical index will be zero if all of the scores in the data set are identical, a small positive number if the scores vary to a small degree, or a large positive number if there is a great deal of dispersion among the scores. (No measure of variability, no matter how computed, can ever turn out equal to a negative value.)

The Range, Interquartile Range, Semi-Interquartile Range, and Box Plot

The **range** is the simplest measure of variability. It is the difference between the lowest and highest scores. For example, in Group I of the example just considered, the range is equal to 103 – 96, or 7. The range is usually reported by citing the extreme scores, but sometimes it is reported as the difference between the high and low scores. When providing information about the range to their readers, authors normally will write out the word *range*. Occasionally, however, this first measure of variability is abbreviated as *R*.

To see how the range can be helpful when we try to understand a researcher's data, consider Excerpts 2.17 and 2.18. Notice in Excerpt 2.17 how information concerning the range allows us to sense that the researchers' sample was quite heterogeneous in terms of age. In contrast, the presentation of just the mean in Excerpt 2.18 puts us in the position of not knowing anything about how much variability existed among the responding pharmacists' ages. Perhaps it was a very homogeneous group, with everyone in their early 40s. Or maybe the group was bimodal, with half the pharmacists in their early 30s and half in their early 50s. Unless the range (or some other measure of variability) is provided, we are completely in the dark as to how similar or different the group members were in terms of their age.

EXCERPTS 2.17–2.18 • *Summarizing Data with and without the Range*

The mean age of the 24 participants was 48.30 (SD = 7.11; range = 34–59).

Source: S. W. Bowling, L. K. Kearney, C. A. Lumadue, and N. R. St. Germain. (2002). Considering justice: An exploratory study of family therapy with adolescents. *Journal of Marital and Family Therapy, 28*(2), p. 216.

- -

The majority of respondents were male (74.4%) and the mean age of all respondents was 42.2 years. The respondents have been registered pharmacists for an average of 17.4 years.

Source: D. Suh, M. R. Greenberg, D. Schneider, and J. L. Colaizzi. (2002). Pharmacists' perceptions of healthy people goals in economically stressed cities. *Journal of Community Health, 27*(2), p. 137.

Research Navigator.c⊕m

Interquartile range

Whereas the range provides an index of dispersion among the full group of scores, the **interquartile range** indicates how much spread exists among the middle 50 percent of the scores. Like the range, the interquartile range is defined as the distance between a low score and a high score; these two indices of dispersion differ, however, in that the former is based on the high and low scores within the full group of data points whereas the latter is based on only *half* of the data—the middle half.

In any group of scores, the numerical value that separates the top 25 percent scores from the bottom 75 percent scores is the **upper quartile** (symbolized by Q_3). Conversely, the numerical value that separates the bottom 25 percent scores from the top 75 percent scores is the **lower quartile** (Q_1).[6] The interquartile range is simply the distance between Q_3 and Q_1. Stated differently, the interquartile range is the distance between the 75th and 25th percentile points.

In Excerpts 2.19 and 2.20, we see two cases in which the upper and lower quartiles were presented. In both of these excerpts, the values of Q_1 and Q_3 give us information as to the dispersion among the middle 50 percent of the scores. In Excerpt 2.19, for example, the length of the follow-up period for the middle half of the individuals extended from 96 to 120 months, with one-fourth of the study's participants having a shorter (or longer) follow-up period. In Excerpt 2.20, the information regarding the interquartile range indicates that the placebo group was far more homogeneous—in terms of time to first recurrence—than the fluticasone group.

EXCERPTS 2.19–2.20 • *Quartiles and the Interquartile Range*

The median follow-up period was 108 months (minimum = 3, maximum = 144; first quartile = 96, third quartile = 120).

Source: P. K. Keel, D. J. Dorer, K. T. Eddy, and S. S. Delinsky. (2002). Predictors of treatment utilization among women with anorexia and bulimia nervosa. *American Journal of Psychiatry, 159*(1), p. 141.

- -

The median time to first recurrence was 3 days sooner in the placebo group, 22 days (interquartile range, 21–24) vs. 25 days (interquartile range, 13–43) in the fluticasone group.

Source: R. J. Dolor, D. L. Witsell, A. S. Hellkamp, and J. W. Williams. (2001). Comparison of cefuroxime with or without intranasal fluticasone for the treatment of rhinosinusitis: The CAFFS Trial: A randomized controlled trial. *Journal of the American Medical Association, 286*(24), p. 3102.

Sometimes, a researcher will compute the **semi-interquartile range** to index the amount of dispersion among a group of scores. As you would guess on the basis of its name, this measure of variability is simply equal to one-half the size of the interquartile range. In other words, the semi-interquartile range is nothing more than $(Q_3 - Q_1)/2$.

With a **box-and-whisker plot,** the degree of variability within a data set is summarized with a picture. To accomplish this objective, a rectangle (box) is drawn to the right of a vertical line labeled so as to correspond with scores on the depen-

Research
Navigator.c⊕m

Box plot

---

[6]The middle quartile, Q_2, divides any group of scores into upper and lower halves. Accordingly, Q_2 is always equal to the median.

dent variable. The positions of the top and bottom sides of the rectangle are determined by Q_3 and Q_1, the upper and lower quartile points. On the outside of the rectangle, two vertical lines—called the *whiskers*—are drawn. These whiskers extend up to the highest observed score and down to the lowest observed score. However, there's a rule that says that neither whisker should be longer than 1.5 times the height of the rectangle. If any scores are further out than this, they are considered to be outliers, and their positions are indicated by small circles or asterisks.

In Excerpt 2.21, we see a case in which box-and-whisker plots were used to show how 100 employees rated, on a 6-point scale, seven characteristics of their employer's organization. From this picture, we can tell that the employees' ratings of group focus were much more homogeneous than their ratings of the pay-performance link.

EXCERPT 2.21 • *Box-and-Whisker Plot*

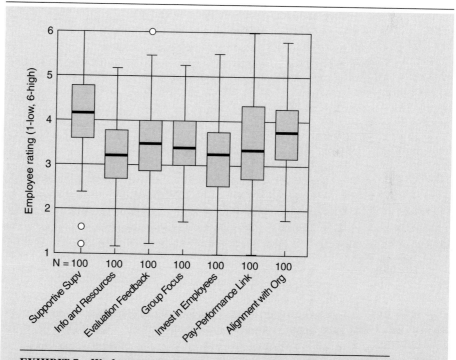

EXHIBIT 7   ***Work system assessment results for all work teams: Organizational characteristics***

Source: E. M. Van Aken, R. L. Groesbeck, and G. D. Coleman. (2001). Integrated organizational assessment process and tools: Application in an engineer-to-order company. *Engineering Management Journal, 13*(4), p. 24.

Although box-and-whisker plots are designed to communicate information about variability, they also reveal things about central tendency and distributional shape. Within the rectangle, a vertical line is positioned so as to correspond to Q_2, the median. If this median line appears in the center of the box and if the whiskers are of equal lengths, then we can infer that the distribution of scores is probably symmetrical. On the other hand, the median will end up off-center and the whiskers will be of unequal lengths in skewed distributions. (If the median is on the lower side of the box while the top whisker is longer, the distribution is positively skewed; conversely, negatively skewed distributions cause the median line to be on the upper side of the box and the bottom whisker to be longer.)

Standard Deviation and Variance

Two additional indices of dispersion, the **standard deviation** and the **variance,** are usually better indices of dispersion than are the first three measures of variability that we have considered. This is due to the fact that the standard deviation and variance are each based on all of the scores in a group (and not just the high and low scores or the upper and lower quartile points). The standard deviation is determined by (1) figuring how much each score deviates from the mean and (2) putting these deviation scores into a computational formula. The variance is found by squaring the value of the standard deviation.

In reporting their standard deviations, authors may employ the abbreviation *SD,* utilize the symbol *s* or σ, or simply write out the word **sigma.** Occasionally, authors will report the standard deviation using a plus-and-minus format—for example, 14.83 $\pm$ 2.51, where the first number (14.83) stands for the mean and the second number (2.51) stands for the standard deviation. The variance, being the square of the standard deviation, is symbolized as s^2 or σ^2.

Excerpts 2.22 through 2.25 illustrate four of the ways researchers indicate the numerical value of the standard deviation. The first two of these—in which the abbreviation SD and the plus-and-minus reporting strategy are used—are frequently seen in published journal articles; the other two—in which the abbreviation s.d. or the single letter s is used—are seen far less frequently.

Excerpt 2.26 shows how information on the standard deviation can be included in a table. In this excerpt, each row of numbers corresponds to a different group of older adults. By looking at the standard deviations presented in the far right-hand column, we can tell that the 18 individuals in the youngest subgroup were the most heterogeneous in terms of their years of education, while the 15 individuals in the oldest subgroup were the most homogeneous.

Although the standard deviation appears in research reports far more often than does any other measure of variability, some researchers choose to describe the dispersion in their data sets by reporting the variance. In Excerpt 2.27, the numerical values of the variance reveal that the ages of the 117 students were more variable than were the ages of the 110 youths housed at the runaway shelter.

EXCERPTS 2.22–2.25 • *Reporting on the Standard Deviation*

Both groups of women were relatively young (HIV—seropositive: mean age = 37.0 years, *SD* = 9.0; HIV—seronegative: mean age = 33.4 years, *SD* = 11.1).

Source: M. F. Morrison, J. M. Petitto, T. T. Have, and D. R. Gettes. (2002). Depressive and anxiety disorders in women with HIV infection. *American Journal of Psychiatry, 159*(5), p. 791.

- -

No significant difference was observed between the mean nutrition knowledge scores of men (5.9 ± 1.8) and women (5.7 ± 1.9).

Source: C. A. Rosenbloom, S. S. Jonnalagadda, and R. Skinner. (2002). Nutrition knowledge of collegiate athletes in a division I national collegiate athletic association institution. *Journal of the American Dietetic Association, 102*(3), p. 420.

- -

Faculty from research universities are in substantial agreement (mean = 3.46, *sd* = 0.76) that research is rewarded more than teaching, whereas community college faculty (mean = 1.40, *sd* = 0.72) disagree that research is rewarded more than teaching.

Source: D. W. Leslie. (2002). Resolving the dispute: Teaching is academe's core value. *Journal of Higher Education, 73*(1), p. 57.

- -

We used a *t* test for Course Score to compare the students who answered the questionnaire (mean = 78.8, *s* = 13.1, *n* = 91) with those who had not (mean = 76.1, *s* = 13.6, *n* = 43).

Source: S. A. Dellana, W. H. Collins, and D. West. (2000). On-line education in a management science course—effectiveness and performance factors. *Journal of Education for Business, 76*(1), p. 45.

Before concluding our discussion of the standard deviation and variance, I would like to offer a helpful hint concerning how to make sense out of these two indices of variability. Simply stated, I suggest using an article's reported standard deviation (or variance) to estimate what the range of scores probably was. Because the range is such a simple concept, the standard deviation or variance can be demystified by converting it into an estimated range.

To make a standard deviation interpretable, just multiply the reported value of this measure of variability by about 4 to obtain your guess as to what the range of the scores most likely was. Using 4 as the multiplier, this rule of thumb would tell you to guess that the range is equal to 20 for a set of scores in which the standard deviation is equal to 5. (If the research report were to indicate that the variance is

EXCERPT 2.26 • *Reporting the Standard Deviation in a Table*

TABLE 1   *Means and Standard Deviations of Age and Education for 92 Older Individuals*

Age Range	n	Age		Education	
		M	*SD*	*M*	*SD*
60–65	18	62.44	1.69	15.00	2.99
66–70	19	68.57	1.39	13.58	2.17
71–75	20	72.85	1.57	13.25	2.15
76–80	20	78.30	1.38	13.50	2.48
81–85	15	82.80	1.52	12.87	1.88

Source: C. C. Persad, N. Abeles, R. T. Zacks, and N. L. Denburg. (2002). Inhibitory changes after age 60 and their relationship to measures of attention and memory. *The Journals of Gerontology, 57B*(3), p. P226.

EXCERPT 2.27 • *Using the Variance to Measure Dispersion*

The total sample ($N = 227$) was composed from two groups: a clinical sample ($n = 110$) and a nonclinical sample ($n = 117$). The clinical sample consisted of youths housed at a runaway shelter in Tallahassee, Fla., as well as youths detained at three juvenile assessment centers in three Florida cities. The nonclinical sample was made up of students in grades 6 through 12 at a high school in Tallahassee. . . . The participants' mean ages were nearly identical when comparing the nonclinical ($M = 14.8$, variance = 3.83) and clinical ($M = 15.0$, variance = 2.17) groups.

Source: D. W. Springer. (1998). Validation of the Adolescent Concerns Evaluation (ACE): Detecting indicators of runaway behavior. *Social Work Research, 22*(4), p. 244.

equal to 9, you would first take the square root of 9 to get the standard deviation, and then you would multiply by 4 to arrive at a guess that the range was equal to 12.)

When giving you this rule of thumb, I have said that you should multiply the standard deviation by "about 4." To guess more accurately what the range most likely was in a researcher's data set, your multiplier will sometimes need to be a bit smaller or larger than 4. That's because the multiplier number needs to be adjusted on the basis of the number of scores on which the standard deviation is based. If there are 25 or so scores, use 4. If *N* is near 100, multiply the standard deviation by 5. And if

N is gigantic, multiply by 6. With small *N*s, use a multiplier that is smaller than 4. With 10–20 scores in the group, multiplying by 3 works fairly well; when *N* is smaller than 10, setting the multiplier equal to 2 usually produces a good guess as to range.

It may strike you as somewhat silly to be guessing the range based on the standard deviation. If researchers regularly included the values of the standard deviation and the range when summarizing their data (as was done in Excerpt 2.17), there would be no need to make a guess as to the size of *R*. Unfortunately, most researchers present only the standard deviation—and by itself, a standard deviation provides little insight into the degree of variability within a set of scores.

One final comment is in order regarding this technique of using *SD* to guess *R*. What you will get is nothing more than a rough approximation, and you should not expect your guess of *R* to "hit the nail on the head." Using the standard deviation and range presented in Excerpt 2.17 (and using a multiplier of 4), we see that our guess of *R* is a bit too big. But that guess is close, and it would help us understand how much spread was in the data if only the standard deviation had been presented.

Other Measures of Variability

Of the five measures of variability discussed so far, you will encounter the range and the standard deviation most often when reading researcher-based journal articles. Occasionally, you will come across examples of the interquartile range, the semi-interquartile range, and the variance. And once in a great while, you will encounter some other measure of variability.

In Excerpt 2.28, we see a case where the *coefficient of variation* was used. As indicated within this excerpt, this measure of dispersion is nothing more than the standard deviation divided by the mean.

The coefficient of variation is useful when comparing the variability in two groups of scores where the means are known to be different. For example, suppose we wanted to determine which of two workers has the most consistent commuting

EXCERPT 2.28 • *Coefficient of Variation*

The variation of the ABL parameters, which exhibited an almost perfect lognormal distribution, were expressed as relative standard deviation, also called coefficient of variation (CV, defined as standard deviation divided by the population mean). . . . The benefit of using CVs over standard deviation is its usefulness in representing population having lognormal distribution in which the mean of the population is proportional to its standard deviation.

Source: U. Dayan, B. Lifshits-Goldreich, and K. Pick. (2002). Spatial and structural variation of the atmospheric boundary layer during summer in Israel—profiler and rawinsonde measurements. *Journal of Applied Meteorology, 41*(4), p. 451.

time driving to work in the morning. If one of these workers lives five miles from work whereas the second lives 25 miles from work, a direct comparison of their standard deviations (each based on 100 days of commuting to work) would not yield a fair comparison because the worker with the longer commute would be expected to have more variability. What *would* be fair would be to divide each commuter's standard deviation by his or her mean. Such a measure of variability is called the coefficient of variation.

Standard Scores

All of the techniques covered thus far in this chapter describe features of the entire data set. In other words, the focus of attention is on all N scores whenever a researcher summarizes a group of numbers by using one of the available picture techniques, a word or number that reveals the distributional shape, a numerical index of central tendency, or a quantification of the amount of dispersion that exists among the scores. Sometimes, however, researchers want to focus their attention on a single score within the group rather than on the full data set. When they do this, they usually convert the raw score being examined into a **standard score.**

Research Navigator.com

z-scores

T-scores

Although many different kinds of standard scores have been developed over the years, the ones used most frequently in research studies are called *z*-**scores** and *T*-**scores.** These two standard scores are identical in that each one indicates how many standard deviations a particular raw score lies above or below the group mean. In other words, the numerical value of the standard deviation is first looked upon as defining the length of an imaginary yardstick, with that yardstick then used to measure the distance between the group mean and the individual score being considered. For example, if you and several other people took a test that produced scores having a mean of 40 and a standard deviation of 8, and if your score on this test happened to be 52, you would be one and one-half yardsticks above the mean.

The two standard scores used most by researchers—*z*-scores and *T*-scores—perform exactly the same function. The only difference between them concerns the arbitrary values given to the new mean score and the length of the yardstick within the revised data set following conversion of one or more raw scores into standard scores. With *z*-scores, the mean is fixed at zero and the yardstick's length is set equal to 1. As a consequence, a *z*-score directly provides an answer to the question, "How many *SD*s is a given score above or below the mean?" Thus a *z*-score of +2.0 indicates that the person being focused on was 2 standard deviations above the group mean. Likewise, a *z*-score of −1.2 for someone else indicates that this person scored 1.2 standard deviations below the mean. A *z*-score close to 0, of course, would indicate that the original raw score was near the group mean.

With *T*-scores, the original raw score mean and standard deviation are converted to 50 and 10, respectively. Thus a person whose raw score positioned him or her two standard deviations above the mean would receive a *T*-score of 70. Someone else positioned 1.2 standard deviations below the mean would end up with a

T-score of 38. And someone whose raw score was near the group mean would have a *T*-score near 50.

Although researchers typically apply their statistical procedures to the raw scores that have been collected, they occasionally will convert the original scores into *z*-scores or *T*-scores. Excerpts 2.29 and 2.30 provide evidence that these two standard scores are sometimes referred to in research summaries.

EXCERPTS 2.29–2.30 • *Standard Scores*

To facilitate comparison across age ranges and testing instruments, we converted all speech and language and motor test measurements to *z* scores, with a mean of 0 and standard deviation (*SD*) of 1.

Source: W. G. Mitchell, Y. Davalos-Gonzalez, V. L. Brumm, S. K. Aller, E. Burger, S. B. Turkel, M. S. Borchert, S. Hollar, and S. Padilla. (2002). Opsoclonus-ataxia caused by childhood neuroblastoma: Developmental and neurologic sequelae. *Pediatrics, 109*(1), pp. 89–90.

- -

A *T* score of 55 was chosen as the cutoff for the nonaggressive group because being within 0.5 standard deviation from a nationally standardized mean score of 50 is generally considered within the normative range.

Source: B. Aguilar, K. M. O'Brien, G. J. August, S. L. Aoun, and J. M. Hektner. (2001). Relationship quality of aggressive children and their siblings: A multiinformant, multimeasure investigation. *Journal of Abnormal Child Psychology, 29*(6), p. 481.

A Few Cautions

Before concluding this chapter, I want to alert you to the fact that two of the terms discussed earlier are occasionally used by researchers who define them differently than I have. These two terms are *skewed* and *quartile.* I want to prepare you for the alternative meanings associated with these two concepts.

Regarding the term *skewed,* a few researchers use this word to describe a complete data set that is out of the ordinary. Used in this way, the term has nothing to do with the notion of distributional shape but instead is synonymous to the term *anomaly.* In Excerpt 2.31, we see an example of how the word *skewed* was used in this fashion.

The formal, statistical definition of *quartile* is "one of three points that divide a group of scores into four subgroups, each of which contains 25 percent of the full group." Certain researchers use the term *quartile* to designate the subgroups themselves. In this usage there are four quartiles (not three), with scores falling in the quartiles. Excerpt 2.32 provides an example of *quartile* being used in this fashion.

EXCERPT 2.31 • *Use of the Term* Skewed *to Designate an Anomaly*

While many business ethics articles were published in these journals during the period under study, many other business ethics articles were published in other journals. Omitting these other articles would have skewed the results in favor of authors who published primarily in these top thirteen business ethics journals.

Source: M. Sabrin. (2002). A ranking of the most productive business ethics scholars: A five-year study. *Journal of Business Ethics, 36*(4), p. 357.

**EXCERPT 2.32 • *Use of the Term* Quartile *to Designate the*
*Four Subgroups***

The first quartile is comprised of women who had no additional sexual partners; the second quartile is for those women who report one to three partners; the third quartile is comprised of women with up to eight partners; and the last category is for those reporting more than eight partners.

Source: M. Gaughan. (2002). The substitution hypothesis: The impact of premarital liaisons and human capital on marital timing. *Journal of Marriage and Family, 64*(2), p. 412.

My second warning concerns the use of the term *average.* In elementary school, students are taught that (1) the average score is the mean score and (2) the median and the mode are *not* conceptually the same as the average. Unfortunately, you will have to undo your earlier learning if you're still under the impression that the words average and mean are synonymous.

In statistics, the term average is synonymous with the phrase "measure of central tendency," and either is nothing more than a generic label for *any* of several techniques that attempt to describe the typical or center score in a data set. Hence, if a researcher gives us information as to the "average score," we cannot be absolutely sure which average is being presented. It might be the mode, it might be the median, or it might be any of the many other kinds of average that can be computed. Nevertheless, you won't be wrong very often when you see the word "average" if you guess that reference is being made to the arithmetic mean. In Excerpt 2.33, for example, the three average scores are most likely means.

My final comment of the chapter concerns scores in a data set that lie far away from the rest of the scores. Such scores are called **outliers,** and they can come about because someone doesn't try when taking a test, doesn't understand the instructions, or consciously attempts to sabotage the researcher's investigation. Accordingly, researchers should (1) inspect their data sets to see if any outliers are present

Research
Navigator.c⊕m

Outliers

EXCERPT 2.33 • *Use of the Term* Average

The average age at death among our diabetic cohort was oldest for whites (72.0 years), youngest for Latinos (68.8 years), and intermediate for blacks (69.9 years) and Asians (69.3 years).

Source: A. J. Karter, A. Ferrara, J. Y. Liu, H. H. Moffet, L. M. Acherson, and J. V. Selby. (2002). Ethnic disparities in diabetic complications in an insured population. *Journal of the American Medical Association, 287*(19), p. 2525.

and (2) either discard such data points before performing any statistical analyses or perform analyses in two ways: with the outlier(s) included and with the outlier(s) excluded. In Excerpts 2.34 through 2.35, we see two cases in which data were examined for possible outliers. Notice how the researchers associated with these excerpts explained the rules they used to determine how deviant a score needed to be before it was tagged as an outlier. Also notice how these rules differed!

EXCERPTS 2.34–2.35 • *Dealing with Outliers*

In addition, to reduce the possibility that the evidence for a major gene could be due to the presence of the extreme outliers, all isolated and outlying residual values greater than 4 standard deviations from the mean were excluded from analysis. Five individuals were excluded from the analyses.

Source: S. K. Nath, A. Chakravarti, C. Chen, R. Cooper, A. Weder, and N. J. Schork. (2002). Segregation analysis of blood pressure and body mass index in a rural US community. *Human Biology, 74*(1), p. 14.

- -

We first examined the distributions of raw latency scores for outliers. Extremely fast or slow responses might reflect various types of errors (accidental key press, interruption of the task). To address these potential concerns, outlier scores were trimmed as follows. A lower bound for legitimate responses was set for each task on the basis of minimal response times suggested by prior research, and scores below this limit were dropped. The limits were SRT, 150 ms; CRT, 150 ms; lexical, 400 ms; and semantic, 1,000 ms. The upper bound was established by computing the mean and standard deviation separately for each of the age groups and dropping any trials exceeding the mean by three or more standard deviations.

Source: D. F. Hultsch, S. W. S. MacDonald, and R. A. Dixon. (2002). Variability in reaction time performance of younger and older adults. *The Journal of Gerontology, 57B*(2), p. P105.

If allowed to remain in a data set, outliers can create skewness and in other ways create problems for the researcher. Accordingly, the researchers who conducted the studies that appear in Excerpts 2.34 through 2.35 deserve credit for taking extra time to look for outliers before conducting any additional data analyses.

I should point out, however, that outliers potentially can be of legitimate interest in and of themselves. Instead of quickly tossing aside any outliers, researchers would be well advised to investigate any "weird cases" within their data sets. Even if the identified outliers have come about because of poorly understood directions, erratic measuring devices, low motivation, or effort to disrupt the study, researchers in these situations might ask the simple question, "Why did this occur?" More importantly, outliers that exist for other reasons have the potential, if considered thoughtfully, to provide insights into the genetic, psychological, and/or environmental factors that stand behind extremely high or low scores.

Review Terms

Average	Negatively skewed
Bar graph	Normal distribution
Bimodal	Outlier
Bivariate	Pie graph
Box-and-whisker plot	Platykurtic
Cumulative frequency distribution	Positively skewed
Dispersion	Quartile
Distributional shape	Range
Frequency polygon	Rectangular
Grouped frequency distribution	Semi-interquartile range
Heterogeneous	Sigma
Histogram	Simple frequency distribution
Homogeneous	Skewed distribution
Interquartile range	Standard deviation
Kurtosis	Standard score
Leptokurtic	Stem-and-leaf display
Mean	*T*-score
Measure of central tendency	Trimodal
Measure of variability	Ungrouped frequency distribution
Median	Univariate
Mesokurtic	Variance
Mode	*z*-score
Multimodal	

The Best Items in the Companion Website

1. An email message from the author to his students explaining what a standard deviation really is (and what it is not).
2. An interactive online quiz (with immediate feedback provided) covering Chapter 2.

3. A challenging puzzle question created by the author for use with an interactive online resource called "Fun with Histograms."

4. Twelve misconceptions about the content of Chapter 2.

5. What the author considers to be the best passage from Chapter 2.

Fun Exercises inside Research Navigator

1. Do college men and women perceive "male sexual self-control" the same way?

In this study, 523 college students (193 male, 330 female) read 15 different vignettes describing a dating situation. In each vignette, things evolve to the point where a man attempts to have intercourse with his date, she resists, and then he considers various strategies to reduce her resistance. After reading each short vignette, the research participants were asked to rate the man's ability to stop himself. The rating scale extended from 0 to 100. After being averaged over the 15 vignettes, the participants' mean ratings were summarized (separately for each gender group) via (1) a grouped frequency distribution and (2) the three most popular measures of central tendency (the mean, median, and mode). How do you think the ratings provided by the 193 males compared to the ratings provided by the 330 females? To find out, locate the PDF version of the research report in the Helping Professions database of ContentSelect. Once you have this article in front of you, examine Table 1 on page 306.

M. Shively. Male self-control and sexual aggression. *Deviant Behavior*. Located in the HELPING PROFESSIONS database of ContentSelect.

2. What do police officers say when asked why they drink?

In this study, 749 state police officers from Australia responded to a survey that asked, among other things, what the officers considered to be the major reasons for drinking in the workplace. This was not an open-ended question; instead, 10 reasons for drinking (gleaned from the literature and focus groups) were listed. Four of these 10 reasons were: "To cope with stress," "To be a part of the team," "To wind down after shift," and "To celebrate special occasion." The survey respondents rated each of the 10 reasons on a 10-point scale. One of the four sample items presented above received the highest mean rating, the highest median rating, and the largest percentage of high ratings. None of the other three reasons for drinking came close to being the top choice. Which one do you think came in first place? To find out, locate the PDF version of the research report in the Helping Professions database of ContentSelect. Once you have this article in front of you, examine Table 2 on page 146.

J. D. Davey, P. L. Obst, & M. C. Sheehan. It goes with the job: Officers' insights into the impact of stress and culture on alcohol consumption within the police occupation. *Drugs: Education, Prevention and Policy*. Located in the HELPING PROFESSIONS database of ContentSelect.

Review Questions and Answers begin on page 516.

3

Bivariate Correlation

In Chapter 2, we looked at the various statistical procedures that researchers use when they want to describe single-variable data sets. We saw examples where data on two or more variables were summarized, but in each of those cases the data were summarized one variable at a time. Although there are occasions when these univariate techniques permit researchers to describe their data sets, most empirical investigations involve questions that call for descriptive techniques that simultaneously summarize data on more than one variable.

In this chapter, we will consider situations where data on two variables have been collected and summarized, with interest residing in the relationship between the two variables. Not surprisingly, the statistical procedures that we will examine here are considered to be **bivariate** in nature. In a later chapter, we will consider techniques designed for situations wherein the researcher wishes to simultaneously summarize the relationships among three or more variables.

Three preliminary points are worth mentioning as I begin my effort to help you refine your skills at deciphering statistical summaries of bivariate data sets. First, the focus in this chapter will be on techniques that simply summarize the data. In other words, we are still dealing with statistical techniques that are fully descriptive in nature. Second, this chapter is similar to Chapter 2 in that we consider ways to summarize data that involve both picture and numerical indices. Finally, the material covered in the next chapter, Reliability and Validity, draws *heavily* on the information presented here. With these introductory points now behind us, let us turn to the central concept of this chapter, correlation.

The Key Concept behind Correlation: Relationship

Imagine that a researcher measures each of nine families with respect to two variables: average daily phone use in the home (measured in minutes) and the number of teenagers within each family. The data for this imaginary group of families might turn out as follows:

Family	Average Daily Phone Use (Minutes)	Number of Teenagers
Abbott	75	2
Donatelli	100	3
Edwards	60	1
Franks	20	0
Kawasaki	70	2
Jones	120	4
Lopez	40	1
Meng	65	2
Smith	80	3

While it would be possible to look at each variable separately and say something about the central tendency, variability, and distributional shape of the nine scores (first for phone use, then for number of teenagers), the key concept of correlation requires that we look at the data on our two variables *simultaneously.* In doing this, we are trying to see (1) whether there is a **relationship** between the two sets of scores and (2) how strong or weak that relationship is, presuming that a relationship does in fact exist.

On a simple level, the basic question being dealt with by **correlation** can be answered in one of three possible ways. Within any bivariate data set, it *may* be the case that the high scores on the first variable tend to be paired with the high scores on the second variable (implying, of course, that low scores on the first variable tend to be paired with low scores on the second variable). I refer to this first possibility as the *high-high, low-low* case. The second possible answer to the basic correlational question represents the inverse of our first case. In other words, it *may* be the case that high scores on the first variable tend to be paired with low scores on the second variable (implying, of course, that low scores on the first variable tend to be paired with high scores on the second variable). My shorthand summary phrase for this second possibility is *high-low, low-high.* Finally, it is possible that little systematic tendency exists in the data at all. In other words, it *may* be the case that some of the high and low scores on the first variable are paired with high scores on the second variable while other high and low scores on the first variable are paired with low scores on the second variable. I refer to this third possibility simply by the three-word phrase *little systematic tendency.*

As a check on whether I have been clear in the previous paragraph, take another look at the hypothetical data presented earlier on the number of teenagers and amount of phone use within each of nine families. More specifically, indicate how that bivariate relationship should be labeled. Does it deserve the label *high-high, low-low*? Or the label *high-low, low-high*? Or the label *little systematic tendency*? If you haven't done so already, look again at the data presented and formulate your answer to this question.

To discern the nature of the relationship between phone use and number of teenagers, one must first identify each variable's high and low scores. The top three values for the phone use variable are 120, 100, and 80, while the lowest three values in this same column are 60, 40, and 20. Within the second column, the top three values are 4, 3, and 3; the three lowest values are 1, 1, and 0. After identifying each variable's high and low scores, the next (and final) step is to look at both columns of data simultaneously and see which of the three answers to the basic correlational question fits the data. For our hypothetical data set, we clearly have a *high-high, low-low* situation, with the three largest phone-use values being paired with the three largest number-of-teenagers values and the three lowest values in either column being paired with the low values in the other column.

The method I have used to find out what kind of relationship describes our hypothetical data set is instructive, I hope, for anyone not familiar with the core concept of correlation. That strategy, however, is not very sophisticated. Moreover, you won't have a chance to use it very often because researchers will almost always summarize their bivariate data sets by means of pictures, a single numerical index, a descriptive phrase, or some combination of these three reporting techniques. Let us now turn our attention to these three methods for summarizing the nature and strength of bivariate relationships.

Scatter Diagrams

Like histograms, bar graphs, and frequency polygons, a **scatter diagram** has a horizontal axis and a vertical axis. These axes are labeled to correspond to the two variables involved in the correlational analysis. The **abscissa** is marked off numerically so as to accommodate the obtained scores collected by the researcher on the variable represented by the horizontal axis; in a similar fashion, the **ordinate** is labeled so as to accommodate the obtained scores on the other variable. (With correlation, the decision as to which variable is put on which axis is fully arbitrary; the nature of the relationship between the two variables will be revealed regardless of how the two axes are labeled.) After the axes are set up, the next step involves placing a dot into the scatter diagram for each object that was measured, with the horizontal and vertical positioning of each dot dictated by the scores earned by that object on the two variables involved in the study.

In Excerpt 3.1, we see the raw data and a scatter diagram associated with a recent election in North Carolina. For each of the 28 counties in the First Congressional District, the researchers found out two things: (1) the percentage of black voters who were registered and (2) the percentage of votes cast for black candidates. Those data are presented as numbers in Table 1 and then as dots within Figure 1. The dot in the scatter diagram that is furthest to the right came from Edgecombe County where the two percentages were 72.4 and 79.0. Due to the way the axes were set up, that county's dot was positioned so as to correspond with 72.4 on the abscissa and 79.0 on the ordinate. All other dots in this scatter diagram were positioned in a similar fashion.

EXCERPT 3.1 • *Raw Data and a Scatter Diagram*

TABLE 3 *North Carolina First Congressional District Democratic Primary*

County	% of Black Voters Registered	% of Votes Cast for Black Candidates	County	% of Black Voters Registered	% of Votes Cast for Black Candidates
Wayne	8.4	11.7	Nash	49.7	60.9
Beaufort	22.6	34.2	Northampton	53.4	49.7
Columbus	29.4	71.3	Warren	55.1	70.0
Chowan	31.0	36.4	Vance	55.3	66.2
Perquimans	33.4	37.8	Pender	55.4	68.3
Bladen	35.8	58.7	Hertford	55.4	49.6
Greene	36.0	21.8	Pasquotank	55.7	63.8
Martin	39.5	31.1	Bertie	55.7	56.2
Pitt	42.1	33.5	Halifax	61.0	65.8
Washington	42.2	41.7	Lenoir	61.1	51.7
Duplin	43.3	51.5	Wilson	61.3	72.5
Craven	45.2	46.7	New Hanover	61.8	88.8
Gates	45.2	37.2	Cumberland	67.4	80.6
Jones	48.5	56.2	Edgecombe	72.4	79.0

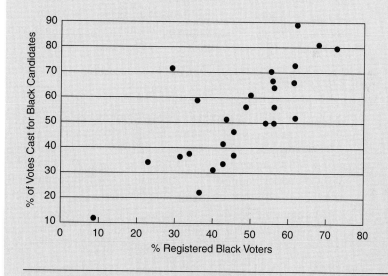

FIGURE 1 *Black Voting in North Carolina First Congressional District*

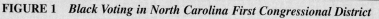

Source: D. M. Clayton and A. M. Stallings. (2000). Black women in Congress: Striking the balance. *Journal of Black Studies, 30*(4), pp. 593–594.

A scatter diagram reveals the relationship between two variables through the pattern that is formed by the full set of dots. To discern what pattern exists, I use a simple (though not completely foolproof) two-step method. First, I draw an imaginary perimeter line, or "fence" around the full set of data points—and in so doing, I try to achieve a tight fit. Second, I look at the shape produced by this perimeter line and examine its tilt and its thickness. Depending on these two characteristics of the data set's scatter, I arrive at an answer to the basic correlational question concerning the nature and strength of the relationship between the two variables.

Consider once again the scatter diagram shown in Excerpt 3.1. Our perimeter line produces a rough oval that is tilted from lower-left to upper-right. Tilts going in this direction imply a *high-high, low-low* relationship, whereas tilts going in the opposite direction, from upper-left to lower-right, imply a *high-low, low-high* relationship. (In cases where there is no discernible tilt to the shape produced by the perimeter line, there is little systematic tendency one way or the other.)

After establishing the tilt of the oval produced by our perimeter line, I then turn to the issue of the oval's thickness. If the oval is elongated and thin, then I conclude that there is a *strong* relationship between the two variables. On the other hand, if the oval is not too much longer than it is wide, then I conclude that a *weak* relationship exists. Considering one last time the scatter diagram in Excerpt 3.1, I conclude that the thickness of the oval produced by the perimeter line around the 34 dots falls between these two extremes; accordingly, I feel that the term *moderate* best describes the strength of the relationship that is visually displayed. Combining the notions of tilt and thickness, I feel that the scatter diagram in Excerpt 3.1 reveals a moderate *high-high, low-low* relationship between the two measured variables.

The Correlation Coefficient

Although a scatter diagram has the clear advantage of showing the scores for each measured object on the two variables of interest, many journals are reluctant to publish such pictures because they take up large amounts of space. For that reason, and also because the interpretation of a scatter diagram involves an element of subjectivity, numerical summaries of bivariate relationships appear in research reports far more frequently than do pictorial summaries. The numerical summary is called a **correlation coefficient.**

Symbolized as r, a correlation coefficient is normally reported as a decimal number somewhere between -1.00 and $+1.00$. In Excerpts 3.2 and 3.3, we see examples of correlation coefficients.

To help you learn how to interpret correlation coefficients, I have drawn a straight horizontal line to represent the continuum of possible values that will result from researchers putting data into a correlational formula:

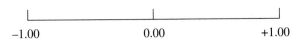

| -1.00 | 0.00 | $+1.00$ |

EXCERPTS 3.2–3.3 • *Correlation Coefficients*

The largest correlation ($r = .34$) was between HSC and loneliness, affirming that they are assessing adaptation in the same life domain.

Source: D. Birman, E. J. Trickett, and A. Vinokurov. (2002). Acculturation and adaptation of Soviet Jewish refugee adolescents: Predictors of adjustment across life domains. *American Journal of Community Psychology, 30*(5), p. 595.

- -

The two indicators of psychological health (depressive affect and self-esteem) were negatively related in both samples (unemployed $r = -.46$; employed $r = -.36$).

Source: L. E. Waters and K. A. Moore. (2002). Reducing latent deprivation during unemployment: The role of meaningful leisure activity. *Journal of Occupational and Organizational Psychology, 75*(1), p. 22.

This correlational continuum will help you pin down the meaning of several adjectives that researchers use when talking about correlation coefficients and/or relationships: direct, high, indirect, inverse, low, moderate, negative, perfect, positive, strong, and weak.

First, consider the two halves of the correlational continuum. Any r that falls on the right side represents a **positive correlation;** this indicates a **direct relationship** between the two measured variables. (Earlier, I referred to such cases by the term *high-high, low-low.*) On the other hand, any result that ends up on the left side is a **negative correlation,** and this indicates an **indirect,** or **inverse, relationship** (i.e., *high-low, low-high*). If r were to land on either end of our correlation continuum, the term **perfect** could be used to describe the obtained correlation. The term **high** comes into play when r assumes a value close to either end (thus implying a **strong** relationship); conversely, the term **low** is used when r lands close to the middle of the continuum (thus implying a **weak** relationship). Not surprisingly, any r that ends up in the middle area of the left or right sides of our continuum will be called **moderate.**

In Excerpts 3.4 through 3.6, we see cases where researchers used adjectives to label their rs. In the first two of these excerpts, we see the concepts of strong and weak being used to describe correlation coefficients. In the third excerpt, notice that the adjective *modest* is being used as a synonym for *weak.*

Before concluding our discussion of how to interpret correlation coefficients, I feel obligated to reiterate the point that when the issue of relationship is addressed, the central question being answered by r is: "To what extent are the high scores of one variable paired with the high scores of the other variable?" The term *high* in this question is considered separately for each variable. Hence, a strong positive correlation can exist even though the mean of the scores of one variable is substantially

EXCERPTS 3.4–3.6 • *Use of Modifying Adjectives*
with the Term Correlation

Teacher confidence in their ability to teach math relative to the goals of their NCTM Standards was strongly correlated with familiarity of the goals ($r = .74$).

Source: P. Maccini and J. C. Gagnon. (2002). Perceptions and application of NCTM standards by special and general education teachers. *Exceptional Children, 68*(3), p. 335.

- -

A weak correlation of $r = .15$ was found between the Attitudes of Others and Acceptance of Loss scales for women, suggesting that for them, acceptance of hearing loss may be less affected by the attitudes of family and friends.

Source: D. C. Garstecki and S. F. Erler. (1999). Reducing latent deprivation during unemployment: The role of meaningful leisure activity. *Journal of Speech, Language, and Hearing Research, 42*(4), p. 792.

- -

The correlations among our measures of health behaviors (eating breakfast, sleeping, and exercising) are modest, with Pearson's *r*s approximately .2 or .3 for all grade levels.

Source: D. J. Safron, J. Schulenberg, and J. G. Bachman. (2001). Part-time and hurried adolescence: The links among work intensity, social activities, health behaviors, and substance use. *Journal of Health and Social Behavior, 42*(4), p. 438.

different from the mean of the scores on the other variable. As proof of this claim, consider again the data presented earlier on nine families who had varying numbers of teenagers and also varying amounts of phone use; the correlation between the two sets of scores turns out equal to $+.96$ despite the fact that the two means are quite different (2 versus 70). This example makes clear, I hope, the fact that a correlation does *not* deal with the question of whether two means are similar or different.[1]

The Correlation Matrix

When interest resides in the bivariate relationship between just two variables or among a small number of variables, researchers will typically present their *r*s within

---

[1]In many research studies, the focus is on the difference between means. Later, our discussion of *t*-test and *F*-tests will show how researchers compare means.

Research
Navigator.c⊕m
Correlation matrix

the text of their article. (This reporting strategy was used in Excerpts 3.2 through 3.6.) When interest centers on the bivariate relationships among many variables, however, the resulting *r*s will often be summarized within a special table called a **correlation matrix.**

It should be noted that *several* bivariate correlations can be computed among a set of variables, even for relatively *small* sets of variables. With six variables, for example, 15 separate bivariate *r*s can be computed. With 10 variables, there will be 45 *r*s. In general, the number of bivariate correlations is equal to $k(k - 1)/2$, where k indicates the number of variables.

In Excerpt 3.7, we see a correlation matrix that summarizes the measured bivariate relationships among five variables. In the study from which this excerpt was taken, each of 60 supposedly funny TV ads was evaluated in terms of five characteristics: surprise, playfulness, ease of resolution, warmth, and humor. As you can see, this correlation matrix contains *r*s arranged in a triangle. Each *r* indicates the correlation between variables that label that *r*'s row and column. For example, the value of 0.54 is the correlation between warmth and humor.

EXCERPT 3.7 • *A Standard Correlation Matrix*

TABLE 3 *Intercorrelation Matrix: Stage 2*

	Surprise	*Playfulness*	*Ease of Resolution*	*Warmth*	*Humor*
Surprise	1.00	0.12	−0.17	−0.03	−0.72
Playfulness		1.00	0.06	0.16	0.25
Ease of Resolution			1.00	−0.11	0.48
Warmth				1.00	0.54
Humor					1.00

Source: D. L. Alden, A. Mukherjee, and W. D. Hoyer. (2000). The effects of incongruity, surprise and positive moderators on perceived humor in television advertising. *Journal of Advertising, 29*(2), p. 8.

Two things are noteworthy about the correlation matrix shown in Excerpt 3.7. First, when a row and column have the same name (as is the case with the top row and the left column, the second row and the second column, etc.), the correlation coefficient positioned at the intersection of that row and column is always 1.00. This simply indicates that the relationship between any variable and itself is guaranteed to be perfect positive. Second, no correlation coefficients appear below the diagonal formed by the 1.00 values. If correlation coefficients did appear there, they would be a mirror image of the *r*s positioned above the diagonal; 0.12 would appear on the second row in the first column, 0.06 would appear on the third row in the second column, and so on. Such *r*s, if they were put in, would be fully redundant with the *r*s that already are present; accordingly, they would add nothing. In this or any other correlation matrix, *r*s need to appear on only one side of the diagonal.

In Excerpt 3.7, the correlation matrix was set up with the 10 bivariate correlation coefficients positioned above the diagonal of the 1.00 values. At times, you will come across a correlation matrix in which (1) the values of the correlations are positioned below the diagonal or (2) the diagonal either contains dashes or is left empty. Such alternative presentations should not cause you any difficulty, for they still will contain all possible bivariate correlations which are interpreted in the same way that we interpreted the *r*s in Excerpt 3.7.

Now consider the correlation matrix in Excerpt 3.8. On first glance, this one seems just like the one in Excerpt 3.7, except that (1) there are four rows and columns rather than five and (2) the *r*s form a triangle that is positioned in the lower left rather than in the upper right. However, if you look closely you will notice two things. First, the variable names used to label the rows are not exactly the same as those used to label the columns. The variable called physical health, which labels the left column, does not appear as a label for any of the rows. Similarly, the variable called impact of UI, which labels the bottom row, does not appear as a label for any of the columns. Second, the diagonal here is filled with correlation coefficients.

EXCERPT 3.8 • *A Correlation Matrix with One Row and One Column Deleted*

TABLE 3   *Correlations between Health-Related Quality-of-Life Measures at Baseline*

	Physical Health	Mental Health	Vitality	Health Perceptions
Mental Health	.22			
Vitality	.50	.41		
Health Perceptions	.42	.35	.69	
Impact of UI	−.17[a]	−.27	−.25	−.21

a. Not statistically significant.

Source: S. L. McFall, A. M. Yerkes, and L. D. Cowan. (2000). Outcomes of a small group educational intervention for urinary incontinence: Health-related quality of life. *Journal of Aging and Health, 12*(3), p. 311.

If the correlation matrix in Excerpt 3.8 had been set up with a top row called Physical Health and a final column called Impact of UI, it would have resembled the first correlation matrix we considered, except this one would have nothing at all in the diagonal. However, nothing would be gained by the addition of those new rows and columns. That's because neither the new top row nor the new final column would have any entries. (If you look again at Excerpt 3.7, you will discover that one row and one column did not contain any correlation coefficients of interest.)

Occasionally, researchers will set up their correlation matrices like the one in Excerpt 3.8. By deleting one empty row and one column, a little space is saved. Knowing that this is sometimes done, you must be careful when trying to figure out how many variables were involved; simply counting the number of rows (or columns) may cause you to end up one variable short!

Excerpt 3.9 illustrates how two correlation matrices can be combined into one table. As indicated in the table's title, the six *r*s located above the diagonal are based on data from children, whereas the six *r*s located below the diagonal are based on data from parents. By comparing common elements in the upper and lower triangles, you can see whether or not the relationship between any pair of variables is similar or different for children versus parents. For example, the correlation between ethnicity and knowledge was very similar for the two groups: −0.32 for children and −0.28 for parents.

EXCERPT 3.9 • *Two Correlation Matrices Combined into One Table*

TABLE 2   *Bivariate Correlations (n = 1737) as a Factor of Age Group between Mediators, Ethnicity and Aggregate AIDS Knowledge (children's correlations are in the upper triangular matrix, parents' in the lower matrix)*

Variables	1	2	3	4
1. Ethnicity	—	−0.32	0.31	−0.17
2. Knowledge	−0.28	—	−0.25	.16
3. Fatalism	0.31	−0.30	—	−.09
4. Family community health	−0.31	0.27	−0.20	—

Source: J. R. Ramirez, W. D. Crano, R. Quist, and M. Burgoon. (2002). Effects of fatalism and family communication on HIV/AIDS awareness variations in Native American and Anglo parents and children. *AIDS Education and Prevention, 14*(1), p. 36.

Now consider Excerpt 3.10. This correlation matrix is different in two ways from the others we have examined. First, the mean and standard deviation are presented for each of the five variables (which are called *dimensions*). Second, there are five rows but only four columns in the correlation matrix part of the table. All bivariate *r*s are presented, however. The researchers did not deprive us of anything by failing to include a fifth column (labeled 5) in the correlation matrix. Had they included it, it would not have had anything in it.

EXCERPT 3.10 • *A Correlation Matrix with Means and Standard Deviations*

TABLE 6   *Correlation Matrix of Ratings for All Groups*

			Correlation			
Dimension	**M**	**SD**	*1*	*2*	*3*	*4*
1. Weighted total	61.40	10.650				
2. Content/organization	2.76	0.677	.940			
3. Style	3.12	0.490	.861	.739		
4. Conventions	3.34	0.529	.890	.761	.789	
5. Sentence formation	3.38	0.538	.869	.732	.732	.797

Note: Reported means are for the entire sample.

Source: N. Gregg, C. Coleman, R. B. Stennett, and M. Davis. (2002). Discourse complexity of college writers with and without disabilities: A multidimensional analysis. *Journal of Learning Disabilities, 35*(1), p. 31.

Different Kinds of Correlational Procedures

In this section, we take a brief look at several different correlational procedures that have been developed. As you will see, all of these techniques are similar in that they are designed for the case in which data have been collected on two variables.[2] These bivariate correlational techniques differ, however, in the nature of the two variables. In light of this important difference, you need to learn a few things about how variables differ.

The first important distinction that needs to be made in our discussion of variables is between quantitative and qualitative characteristics. With a **quantitative variable,** the targets of the measuring process vary as to how much of the charac-

---

[2]Some authors use the term **zero-order correlation** when referring to bivariate correlations. They do this to distinguish this simplest kind of correlation—that involves data on just two variables—from other kinds of correlations that involve data on three or more variables (such as partial correlations, multiple correlations, and canonical correlations).

teristic is possessed. In contrast, a **qualitative variable** comes into play when the things being measured vary from one another in terms of the categorical group to which they belong relative to the characteristic of interest. Thus if we focus our attention on people's heights, we have a quantitative variable (because some people possess more "tallness" than others). If, on the other hand, we focus our attention on people's favorite national park, we would be dealing with a qualitative variable (because people simply fall into categories based on which park they like best).

From the standpoint of correlation, quantitative variables can manifest themselves in one of two ways in the data a researcher collects. Possibly, the only thing the researcher will want to do is order individuals (or animals, or objects, or whatever) from the one possessing the greatest amount of the relevant characteristic to the one possessing the least. The numbers used to indicate ordered position normally are assigned such that 1 goes to the person with the greatest amount of the characteristic, 2 goes to the person with the second greatest amount, and so on. Such numbers are called **ranks** and are said to represent an **ordinal** scale of measurement. A researcher's data would also be ordinal in nature if each person or thing being measured is put into one of several ordered categories, with everyone who falls into the same category given the same score. (For example, the numbers 1, 2, 3, and 4 could be used to represent freshmen, sophomores, juniors, and seniors.)

With a second kind of quantitative variable, measurements are more precise. Here, the score associated with each person supposedly reveals how much of the characteristic of interest is possessed by that individual—and it does this without regard for the standing of any other measured person. Whereas ranks constitute data that provide relative comparisons, this second (and more precise) way of dealing with quantitative variables provide absolute comparisons. In this book, we will use the term **raw score** to refer to any piece of data that provides an absolute (rather than relative) assessment of one's standing on a quantitative variable.[3]

Qualitative variables come in two main varieties. If the subgroups into which people are classified truly have no quantitative connection with each other, then the variable corresponding to those subgroups is said to be **nominal** in nature. Your favorite academic subject, the brand of jelly you most recently used, and your state of residence exemplify this kind of variable. If there are only two categories associated with the qualitative variable, then the variable of interest is said to be **dichotomous** in nature. A dichotomous variable actually can be viewed as a special case of the nominal situation, with examples being "course outcome" in courses where the only grades are pass and fail (or credit and no credit), gender, party affiliation during primary elections, and graduation status following four years of college.

---

[3]Whereas most statisticians draw a distinction between interval and ratio measurement scales and between discrete and continuous variables, readers of journal articles do not need to understand the technical differences between these terms in order to decipher research reports.

In Excerpts 3.11 through 3.14, we see examples of different kinds of variables. The first two of these excerpts illustrate the two kinds of quantitative variables we have discussed: ranks and raw scores. The last two of these excerpts exemplify qualitative variables (the first being a 13-category nominal variable, the second being a dichotomous variable).

EXCERPTS 3.11–3.14 • *Different Kinds of Data*

Respondents were asked to rank eleven goals or aspects of their work life in order of their importance: opportunity to learn, interpersonal relations, promotion, work hours, variety, interesting work, job security, match between job and abilities, pay, working conditions, and autonomy.

Source: R. Snir and I. Harpaz. (2002). Work-leisure relations: Leisure orientation and the meaning of work. *Journal of Leisure Research, 34*(2), p. 190.

We collected the infielder and outfielder data over 219 half-innings. We recorded number of throws, distance of throws, and intensity of throws for each position.

Source: M. J. Axe, T. C. Windley, and L. Snyder-Mackler. (2002). Data-based interval throwing programs for collegiate softball players. *Journal of Athletic Training, 37*(2), p. 195.

The occupational and or domestic roles of characters [in TV commercials] shown using technology, where discernable, were coded into categories. The roles included: executive/business professional, computer expert, clerical, doctor/scientist/researcher, nurse/medical technician, blue-collar worker other than secretary, teacher, student, child, athlete/celebrity, husband or male relative, wife or female relative, or undeterminable.

Source: C. White and K. N. Kinnick. (2000). One click forward and two clicks back: Portrayal of women using computers in television commercials. *Women's Studies in Communication, 23*(2), p. 399.

Race was coded as a dichotomous variable (0 = non-White, 1 = White; 45.6% were White), as was gender (1 = male, 31.7%).

Source: S. M. Lynch and L. K. George. (2002). Interlocking trajectories of loss-related events and depressive symptoms among elders. *The Journals of Gerontology, 57B*(2), p. S120.

Researchers frequently will derive a raw score for each individual being studied by combining that individual's responses to the separate questions in a test or survey. As Excerpts 3.15 and 3.16 show, the separate items can each be ordinal or even dichotomous in nature, and yet the sum of those item scores is looked upon as being what I have called a raw score. Although theoretical statistical authorities argue back and forth as to whether it is prudent to generate raw scores by combining ordinal or dichotomous data, doing so is an extremely common practice among applied researchers.

EXCERPTS 3.15–3.16 • *Combining Ordinal or Dichotomous Data to Get Raw Scores*

A measure of externalizing behavior was constructed using 13 items appropriate for the adolescent age group. Items in this scale include a variety of behaviors such as being unruly, painting graffiti, damaging property, stealing, fighting, and using or threatening to use a weapon. Response categories ranged from 0 (*never*) to 3 (*five or more times*); these items were summed to create a single measure (observed range: 0–39).

Source: T. M. Videon. (2002). The effects of parent-adolescent relationships and parental separation on adolescent well-being. *Journal of Marriage and Family, 64*(2), p. 493.

Of interest in this study are two items [from the *Family Information* Form] inquiring about any alcohol or drug problems, coded dichotomously (0 = no, 1 = yes). The two items were combined to form an overall measure of any *parental substance abuse*.

Source: J. B. Kaplow, P. J. Curran, and K. A. Dodge. (2002). Child, parent and peer predictors of early-onset substance use: A multisite longitudinal study. *Journal of Abnormal Child Psychology, 30*(3), p. 204.

One final kind of variable needs to be briefly mentioned. Sometimes a researcher will begin with a quantitative variable but then classify individuals into two categories on the basis of how much of the characteristic of interest is possessed. For example, a researcher conceivably could measure people in terms of the quantitative variable of height, place each individual into a tall or short category, and then disregard the initial measurements of height (that took the form of ranks or raw scores). Whenever this is done, the researcher transforms quantitative data into a two-category qualitative state. The term **artificial dichotomy** is used to describe the final data set. An example of this kind of data conversion appears in Excerpt 3.17.[4]

---

[4]The term *tertile* appears in this excerpt. A tertile is one of two points that divides a distribution into three parts, each of which contains one-third of the scores.

EXCERPT 3.17 • *Creating an Artificial Dichotomy*

Depression was measured by an 11-item subscale of the 50-item version of the Hopkins Symptom Check List. Participants were assigned a score ranging from 11 to 44. A dichotomous variable was created based on the highest tertile (≥15) to indicate higher levels of depression ("1" = high levels of depression vs "0" = moderate/low levels).

Source: M. Tabbarah, E. M. Crimmins, and T. E. Seeman. (2002). The relationship between cognitive and physical performance: MacArthur studies of successful aging. *The Journals of Gerontology, 57A*(4), p. M230.

Research
Navigator.c✱m

Pearson's
product-moment
correlation

Pearson's Product-Moment Correlation

The most frequently used bivariate correlational procedure is called **Pearson's product-moment correlation.** It is designed for the situation where (1) each of the two variables is quantitative in nature and (2) each variable is measured so as to produce raw scores. The scatter diagram presented earlier in Excerpt 3.1 provides a good example of the kind of bivariate situation that is dealt with by means of Pearson's technique.

Excerpts 3.18, 3.19, and 3.20 illustrate the use of this extremely popular bivariate correlational technique. Note, in the second of these excerpts, that the label "Pearson" is used by itself without the follow-up phrase "product-moment." In the third excerpt, note that only the symbol r is presented, and there is no adjective such as Pearson's, Pearson's product-moment, or product-moment. (In cases like this, where the symbol r stands by itself without a clarifying label, it's a good bet you're looking at a Pearson product-moment correlation coefficient.)

Spearman's Rho and Kendall's Tau

Research
Navigator.c✱m

Rank-order
correlation

The second most popular bivariate correlational technique is called **Spearman's rho.** This kind of correlation is similar to the one we just discussed (Pearson's) in that it is appropriate for the situation in which both variables are quantitative in nature. With Spearman's technique, however, each of the two variables is measured in such a way as to produce ranks. This correlational technique often goes by the name **rank-order correlation** (instead of Spearman's rho). The resulting correlation coefficient, if symbolized, is usually referred to as r_s or ρ.

In Excerpt 3.21, we see a set of two ranks. This table comes from an article in which the researcher was concerned about the scholarly productivity of faculty members at highly reputable business programs. The data here simply indicate the rankings of schools by two business-oriented magazines. If we correlate these two sets of ranks, using Spearman's rho, it turns out that $r_s = 0.76$. (If you scan the two sets of ranks, you should be able to see a *high-high, low-low* relationship.)

EXCERPTS 3.18–3.20 • *Pearson's Product-Moment Correlation*

A Pearson product-moment correlation coefficient also was calculated to determine the relationship between the POPRAS and BOTMP battery composite scores.

Source: J. Flegel and T. H. Kolobe. (2002). Predictive validity of the test of infant motor performance as measured by the Bruininks-Oseretsky Test of Motor Proficiency at school age. *Physical Therapy, 82*(8), p. 766.

The Pearson correlation coefficient for the association of baseline depression score with follow-up score on basic activities of daily living was $r = 0.38$.

Source: J. C. Hays, D. C. Steffens, E. P. Flint, H. B. Bosworth, and L. K. George. (2001). Does social support buffer functional decline in elderly patients with unipolar depression? *American Journal of Psychiatry, 158*(11), p. 1853.

The correlation between packer grades and 24-h visual loin color was $r = 0.41$.

Source: H. L. Lagoda, L. L. Wilson, W. R. Henning, S. L. Flowers, and E. W. Mills. (2002). Subjective and objective evaluation of veal lean color. *Journal of Animal Science, 80*(7), p. 1911.

EXCERPT 3.21 • *Two Sets of Ranks*

TABLE VII   *Comparison of MBA program rankings*

Institution	U.S. News 2001 Ranking	Business Week 2000 Ranking	Institution	U.S. News 2001 Ranking	Business Week 2000 Ranking
Harvard U.	1.5	3	Dartmouth College	12	16
Stanford U.	1.5	11	UCLA	12	12
U. of Penn.	3	1	U. of Virginia	12	9
MIT	4	4	New York U.	14	13
Northwestern U.	5	2	Cornell U.	15	8
Columbia U.	6.5	7	U. of Texas	16.5	17
U. of Chicago	6.5	10	Yale U.	16.5	19
Duke U.	8	5	U. North Carolina	18	15
U. of Michigan	9	6	Carnegie Mellon	19	14
UC-Berkeley	10	18	Indiana U.	20	20

Source: M. Sabrin. (2000). A ranking of the most productive business ethics scholars: A five-year study. *Journal of Business Ethics, 36*(4), p. 373. [Adapted slightly for presentation here.]

Only rarely will a researcher display the actual ranks utilized to compute Spearman's rho. Most of the time, the only information you will be given will be (1) the specification of the two variables being correlated and (2) the resulting correlation coefficient. Excerpts 3.22 and 3.23, therefore, are more typical of what you will see in published journal articles than is the material in Excerpt 3.21.

EXCERPTS 3.22–3.23 • *Spearman's Rank-Order Correlation*

The Spearman rho correlation coefficient was .65.

Source: G. M. Kirchofer, J. H. Price, and S. K. Telljohann. (2002). Primary grade teachers' knowledge and perceptions of head lice. *Journal of School Health, 71*(9), p. 449.

- -

We used a Spearman rank correlation (r_s) to assess the level of consistency between the two surveys.

Source: D. Lepage and C. M. Francis. (2001). Do feeder counts reliably indicate bird population changes? 21 years of winter bird counts in Ontario, Canada. *The Condor, 104*(2), p. 260.

Research Navigator.c⊕m

Kendall's tau

Kendall's tau is very similar to Spearman's rho in that both of these bivariate correlational techniques are designed for the case where each of two quantitative variables is measured in such a way as to produce data in the form of ranks. The difference between rho and tau is related to the issue of ties. To illustrate what we mean, suppose six students took a short exam and earned these scores: 10, 9, 7, 7, 5, and 3. These raw scores, when converted to ranks, become 1, 2, 3.5, 3.5, 5, and 6, where the top score of 10 receives a rank of 1, the next-best score (9) receives a rank of 2, and so on. The third- and fourth-best scores tied with a score of 7, and the rank given to each of these individuals is equal to the mean of the separate ranks that they would have received if they had not tied. (If the two 7s had been 8 and 6, the separate ranks would have been 3 and 4, respectively; the mean of 3 and 4 is 3.5, and this rank is given to each of the persons who actually earned a 7.)

Kendall's tau is simply a bivariate correlational technique that does a better job of dealing with tied ranks than does Spearman's rho. For the two sets of ranks presented in Excerpt 3.21, Kendall's tau turns out equal to 0.58, which is smaller than the Spearman rho value of 0.76. Because of the tied ranks, many statisticians would consider tau to be the more accurate of these two correlation coefficients. In Excerpt 3.24, we see a case when Kendall's tau was used.

EXCERPT 3.24 • *Kendall Tau Correlation*

Kendall's tau correlation coefficient between age and PSE score is $r = -0.058$ indicating that age has a weak negative correlation with PSE score.

Source: R. Abratt and N. Penman. (2002). Understanding factors affecting salespeople's perceptions of ethical behavior in South Africa. *Journal of Business Ethics, 35*(4), p. 273.

Point Biserial and Biserial Correlations

Sometimes a researcher will correlate two variables that are measured so as to produce a set of raw scores for one variable and a set of 0s and 1s for the other (dichotomous) variable. For example, a researcher might want to see if a relationship exists between the height of basketball players and whether they score any points in a game. For this kind of bivariate situation, a correlational technique called **point biserial** has been designed. The resulting correlation coefficient is usually symbolized as r_{pb}.

If a researcher has data on two variables where one variable's data are in the form of raw scores while the other variable's data represent an artificial dichotomy, then the relationship between the two variables will be assessed by means of a technique called **biserial correlation.** Returning to our basketball example, suppose a researcher wanted to correlate height with scoring productivity, with the second of these variables dealt with by checking to see whether each player's average is less than 10 points or some value in the double digits. Here, scoring productivity is measured by imposing an artificial dichotomy on a set of raw scores. Accordingly, the biserial techniques would be used to assess the nature and strength of the relationship between the two variables. This kind of bivariate correlation is usually symbolized by r_{bis}.

In Excerpt 3.25, we see a case where the point biserial correlation was used in a published research article. In this study, whether or not an individual was a day

Research Navigator.com
Point biserial

EXCERPT 3.25 • *Point Biserial Correlation*

We applied point biserial correlation to the responses obtained from the questionnaires. We found a significant correlation between time of birth and whether one was identified as a day person or as a night person, $r_{pb} = .33$.

Source: B. Wallace and L. E. Fisher. (2002). Day persons, night persons, and time of birth: Preliminary findings. *The Journal of Social Psychology, 141*(1), p. 113.

person or a night person was correlated with time of birth. Since the day person versus night person variable represented a true dichotomy whereas time of birth was a raw score variable, the point biserial correlation was utilized to assess each of these relationships.

Phi and Tetrachoric Correlations

If both of a researcher's variables are dichotomous in nature, then the relationship between the two variables will be assessed by means of a correlational technique called **phi** (if each variable represents a true dichotomy) or a technique called **tetrachoric correlation** (if both variables represent artificial dichotomies). An example calling for the first of these situations would involve, among high school students, the variables of gender and car ownership; since each variable represents a true dichotomy, the correlation between gender (male/female) and car ownership (yes/no) would be accomplished using phi. For an example of a place where tetrachoric correlation would be appropriate, imagine that we measure each of several persons in terms of height (with people classified as tall or short depending on whether or not they measure over 5′8″) and weight (with people classified as "OK" or "not OK" depending on whether or not they are within 10 pounds of their ideal weight). Here, both height and weight are forced into being dichotomies.

Excerpt 3.26 illustrates the use of phi. Note that both of the variables in this excerpt—race and school type—were true dichotomies.

EXCERPT 3.26 • *Phi*

The correlation between race [white and black] and school type [urban or suburban] was high (phi coefficient = .79).

Source: A. E. Bonny, M. T. Britto, B. K. Klostermann, R. W. Hornung, and G. B. Slap. (2000). School disconnectedness: Identifying adolescents at risk. *Pediatrics, 106*(5), p. 1018.

Cramer's V

If a researcher has collected bivariate data on two variables where each variable is nominal in nature, the relationship between the two variables can be measured by means of a correlational technique called **Cramer's V.** In Excerpt 3.27, we see an instance where Cramer's *V* was used. Each of the two variables that were correlated—TV network and story type—was nominal in nature with more than two categories. In those cases where each of the nominal variables has just two categories, Cramer's *V* and the phi coefficient turn out identical to each other.

EXCERPT 3.27 • *Cramer's V*

CNN covered proportionally more health/welfare and science/technology/computer stories than FNC and MSNBC. FNC presented more diplomacy/foreign relations and social conflict stories and less health/welfare stories than CNN and MSNBC. MSNBC provided more business/economics stories than CNN and FNC. . . . The association between networks and story topics was weak at Cramer's *V* of .12, however.

Source: H. Bae. (2000). Product differentiation in national TV newscasts: A comparison of the cable all-news networks and the broadcast networks. *Journal of Broadcasting & Electronic Media, 44*(1), p. 68.

Warnings about Correlation

At this point, you may be tempted to consider yourself a semiexpert when it comes to deciphering discussions about correlation. You now know what a scatter diagram is, you have looked at the correlational continuum (and know that correlation coefficients extend from -1.00 to $+1.00$), you understand what a correlation matrix is, and you have considered several different kinds of bivariate correlation. Before you assume that you know everything there is to know about measuring the relationship between two variables, I'd like to provide you with six warnings. These warnings deal with the issue of cause, the coefficient of determination, the possibility of outliers, the assumption of normality, the notion of independence, and criteria for claims of high and low correlations.

Correlation and Cause

It is important for you to know that a correlation coefficient does not speak to the issue of **cause and effect.** In other words, whether a particular variable has a causal impact on a different variable cannot be determined by measuring the two variables simultaneously and then correlating the two sets of data. Many recipients of research reports (and even a few researchers) make the mistake of thinking that a high correlation implies that one variable has a causal influence on the other variable. To prevent yourself from making this mistake, we suggest that you memorize this simple statement: correlation $\neq$ cause.

Consider Excerpt 3.28. In this excerpt, the researchers point out that their correlational findings should *not* be interpreted to mean that clear-cut cause-and-effect connections have been identified. Whereas these researchers set a good example of how researchers should talk about their correlational results, it is unfortunately the

EXCERPT 3.28 • *Correlation and Cause*

We calculated simple correlation coefficients for the correlation between the number of bonus points awarded to a particular student and the scores he or she made on quizzes or exams. . . . In all cases, the correlation coefficients were positive, indicating that those students with the most bonus points also did the best on quizzes and exams. . . . Of course, correlation does not imply causality. It could be the case that the brightest students are the ones most comfortable with this new technology.

Source: S. E. Hein and K. A. Stalcup. (2001). Using World Wide Web utilities to engage students in money, banking, and credit. *Journal of Education for Business, 76*(3), p. 170.

case that not all researchers follow their lead. Stated more forcefully, you need to be on guard for the many instances where researchers wrongfully impute "cause" into their correlational findings.

Later in this book, you will learn how researchers often collect data in such a way as to address the issue of cause. In such situations, however, researchers typically use data-gathering strategies that help them assess the possibility that one variable actually has a determining influence on a second variable. Those strategies require a consideration of issues that cannot be discussed here; in time, however, I am confident that you will come to understand the extra demands that are placed on researchers who want to investigate causal connections between variables. For now, all I can do is ask that you believe me when I say that correlational data alone cannot be used to establish a cause-and-effect situation.

Coefficient of Determination

Research Navigator.c⊕m
Coefficient of determination

To get a better feel for the strength of the relationship between two variables, many researchers will square the value of the correlation coefficient. For example, if r turns out equal to .80, the researcher will square .80 and obtain .64. When r is squared like this, the resulting value is called the **coefficient of determination.** In Excerpt 3.29 we see a case in which a researcher presented the coefficient of determination even though it is not labeled as such.

The coefficient of determination indicates the proportion of variability in one variable that is associated with (or explained by) variability in the other variable. The value of r^2 will lie somewhere between 0 and +1.00, and researchers usually multiply by 100 so they can talk about the *percentage* of explained variability. In Excerpts 3.30 and 3.31, we see two examples where r^2 was converted into a percentage. As these excerpts indicate, researchers sometimes refer to this percentage as the amount of variance in one variable that's "accounted for" by the other variable, or they sometimes say that this percentage indicates the amount of "shared variance."

EXCERPT 3.29 • *The Coefficient of Determination*

Respondents' television viewing was measured by asking respondents to specify how many hours they spent each week viewing specific categories of Chinese and imported television programs. . . . Total viewing of Chinese and imported television was highly correlated ($r = .73$, $r^2 = .53$).

Source: Y. B. Zhang. (2002). Television viewing and perceptions of traditional Chinese values among Chinese college students. *Journal of Broadcasting and Electronic Media, 46*(2), p. 252.

EXCERPTS 3.30–3.31 • *r^2 and Explained Variation*

Relative distance traveled in primary submovement accounted for 23% ($r = -.48$) of variance in movement time for older adults, but only 2% ($r = -.13$) for young adults.

Source: C. J. Ketcham, R. D. Seidler, A. W. A. Van Gemmert, and G. E. Stelmach. (2002). Age-related kinematic differences as influenced by task difficulty, target size, and movement amplitude. *The Journals of Gerontology, 57B*(1), p. P61–62.

- -

For the association noted above for Clinton, for example, at time-one, issue and persona perceptions have 88% shared variance ($r^2 = .88$). For the associations noted for Dole at time-one, we see that issue and persona perceptions have 64% shared variance, ($r^2 = .64$).

Source: K. L. Hacker, W. R. Zakahi, and M. J. Giles. (2000). Components of candidate images: Statistical analysis of the issue-persona dichotomy in the presidential campaign of 1996. *Communication Monographs, 67*(3), pp. 233–234.

As suggested by the material in Excerpts 3.30 and 3.31, the value of r^2 indicates how much (proportionately speaking) variability in either variable is explained by the other variable. The implication of this is that the raw correlation coefficient (that is, the value of r when not squared) exaggerates how strong the relationship really is between two variables. Note that r must be stronger than .70 in order for there to be at least 50 percent explained variability. Or, consider the case where $r = .50$; here, only one-fourth of the variability is explained.

Outliers

Our third warning concerns the effect of one or more data points that are located away from the bulk of the scores. Such data points are called **outliers,** and they can cause the size of a correlation coefficient to understate or exaggerate the strength of the relationship between two variables. Excerpt 3.32 very nicely illustrates this point.

EXCERPT 3.32 • *Outliers*

The Pearson correlation between behavioral improvement and increased activation of the left inferior frontal cortex was 0.66. The scatterplot revealed a highly consistent association between performance improvement and activation increase in all but one patient. . . . When this patient was removed from the analysis, the correlation increased to 0.90.

Source: B. E. Wexler, M. Anderson, R. K. Fulbright, and J. C. Gore. (2000). Preliminary evidence of improved verbal working memory performance and normalization of task-related frontal lobe activation in schizophrenia following cognitive exercises. *American Journal of Psychiatry, 157*(10), p. 1696.

In contrast to the good example provided in Excerpt 3.32, most researchers fail to check to see if one or more outliers serve to distort the statistical summary of the bivariate relationships they study. You won't see many scatter diagrams in journal articles, and thus you will not be able to examine the data yourself to see if outliers were present. Almost always, you will be given just the correlation coefficient. Give the researcher some extra credit, however, whenever you see a statement to the effect that the correlation coefficient was computed after an examination of a scatter diagram revealed no outliers (or revealed an outlier that was removed prior to computing the correlation coefficient).

Linearity

The most popular technique for assessing the strength of a bivariate relationship is Pearson's product-moment correlation. This correlational procedure works nicely if the two variables have a linear relationship. Pearson's technique does not work well, however, if a curvilinear relationship exists between the two variables.

A **linear** relationship does *not* require that all data points (in a scatter diagram) lie on a straight line. Instead, what *is* required is that the *path* of the data points be straight. The path itself can be very narrow, with most data points falling near an imaginary straight line, or, the path can be very wide—so long as the path is straight. (Regardless of how narrow or wide the path is, the path to which we refer can be tilted at any angle.)

If a **curvilinear** relationship exists between two variables, Pearson's correlation will underestimate the strength of the relationship that is present in the data. Accordingly, you can place more confidence in any correlation coefficient you see when

strong. Although they turned out to be higher than some other *r*s and thus "consistent with the present study's a priori prediction," they suggest that academic self-efficacy accounts for only about 10 percent of the variability in written test performance and that Internet self-efficacy accounts for only about 13 percent of the variability in search-test performance.

Review Terms

Abscissa
Biserial correlation
Bivariate
Cause and effect
Coefficient of determination
Correlation coefficient
Correlation matrix
Cramer's V
Curvilinear
Dichotomous variable
Direct relationship
High
Indirect relationship
Independent
Inverse relationship
Kendall's tau
Linear
Low
Moderate
Negative correlation
Nominal
Ordinal
Ordinate
Outlier

Pearson's product-moment correlation
Perfect
Phi
Point biserial correlation
Positive correlation
Qualitative variable
Quantitative variable
Ranks
Rank-order correlation
Raw score
Relationship
Scatter diagram
Spearman's rho
Strong
Tetrachoric correlation
Weak
r
r_s
r^2
r_{pb}
r_{bis}
V
ρ

The Best Items in the Companion Website

1. An interactive online quiz (with immediate feedback provided) covering Chapter 3.
2. Ten misconceptions about the content of Chapter 3.
3. The author's poem "True Experimental Design."
4. An email message from the author to his students in which he asks an honest question about Pearson's *r* and Spearman's rho.
5. Two jokes about statistics, the first of which concerns a student in a statistics course.

Fun Exercises inside Research Navigator

1. Is IQ correlated with reaction time?

The 81 adult participants in this study were measured on two kinds of reaction time: how fast they could respond to auditory stimuli and how fast they could respond to visual stimuli. They were also measured on several other variables, one of which was IQ. The correlation between the two kinds of reaction time turned out as most people would expect—it was moderate and positive, with Pearson's $r = .69$. But what about the correlation between IQ and each of the two kinds of reaction time? These two rs were about the same size and they had the same sign. But what was that sign? In other words, do you think this study revealed a direct relationship or an indirect relationship between IQ and reaction time? After you make your guess, refer to the PDF version of the research report in the Communication database of ContentSelect and look at the correlation matrix at the bottom of page 46.

R. Stringer & K. E. Stanovich. The connection between reaction time and variation in reading ability: Unraveling covariance relationships with cognitive ability and phonological sensitivity. *Scientific Studies of Reading*. Located in the COMMUNICATION database of ContentSelect.

2. How does emotional intelligence correlate with general intelligence?

In this study, 107 undergraduate students, graduate students, and college graduates were measured in terms of their general intelligence. In addition, the research participants completed the *Multifactorial Emotional Intelligence Scale*. This instrument provided four scores per participant, three based on its subscales (Emotional Knowledge, Emotional Perception, and Emotional Regulation) and one composite score. The correlation matrix included in the research report contained 21 bivariate correlation coefficients, four of which showed the relationship between the study's measures of general intelligence and the four scores on emotional intelligence. These four rs turned out equal to .40, .23, .04, and –.03. Which emotional intelligence score do you think correlated most highly with general intelligence? After making a guess, locate the PDF version of the research report in the Psychology database of ContentSelect and look at Table 1 at the bottom of page 188.

J. Pellitteri. The relationship between emotional intelligence and ego defense mechanisms. *Journal of Psychology*. Located in the PSYCHOLOGY database of ContentSelect.

Review Questions and Answers begin on page 516.

4

Reliability and Validity

Empirical research articles focus on data that have been collected, summarized, and analyzed. The conclusions drawn and the recommendations made in such studies can be no better than the data on which they are based. As a consequence, most researchers describe the quality of the instruments used to collect their data. These descriptions of instrument quality normally appear in the method section of the article, either in the portion that focuses on materials or in the description of the dependent variables.

Regardless of where it appears, the description of instrument quality typically deals with two measurement-related concepts—reliability and validity. In this chapter, I will discuss the meaning of these two concepts, various techniques employed by researchers to assess the reliability and validity of their measuring instruments, and numerical indices of instrument quality that are reported. My overall objective here is to help you refine your skills at deciphering and evaluating reports of reliability and validity.

As a simple check to see whether you can profit by studying the material in this chapter, take a look at Excerpt 4.1. If you understand and can critique reports such as this (and if you are familiar with this chapter's review terms and can answer the end-of-chapter questions), skip this chapter and go to Chapter 5. If you are unfamiliar with the terms and cannot answer the questions, carefully read and examine the content of this chapter.

Reliability

This discussion of reliability is divided into three sections. We begin by looking at the core meaning of the term *reliability*. Next, we examine a variety of techniques that researchers use to quantify the degree to which their data are reliable. Finally, I will provide five cautionary comments concerning reports of reliability that will help you as you read technical research reports.

EXCERPT 4.1 • *Typical Description of Reliability and Validity*

Psychometric properties of the WGCTA have been reported previously. The split-half reliability for 10 norm groups ranged from .69 to .85, test-retest reliability for 96 students' responses was .73, and alternate-form reliability for 228 students' responses to Forms A and B of the WGCTA was .75. In a recent study (Gadzella, Baloglu, & Stephens, 2001), analyses on the WGCTA showed that the internal consistency was .86 for 135 students (majoring in Education), .91 for 30 men, and .83 for 105 women. The split-half reliability for the same group was .65 for the total group, .87 for men, and .55 for women. The concurrent validity for the 135 students' course grades and the total WGCTA scores was $r = .42$. Using a confirmatory factor analysis, construct validity of the WGCTA (based on the theoretical model consisting of the five subscales) was supported.

Source: B. M. Gadzella, M. Baloglu, and R. Stephens. (2002). Prediction of GPA with educational psychology grades and critical thinking scores. *Education, 122*(3), p. 620.

The Meaning of Reliability and the Reliability Coefficient

The basic idea of **reliability** is summed up by the word *consistency*. Researchers can and do evaluate the reliability of their instruments from different perspectives, but the basic question that cuts across these various perspectives (and techniques) is always the same: "To what extent can we say that the data are consistent?"

As you will see, the way in which reliability is conceptualized by researchers can take one of three basic forms. In some studies, researchers ask, "To what degree does a person's measured performance remain consistent across repeated testings?" In other studies, the question of interest takes a slightly different form: "To what extent do the individual items that go together to make up a test or inventory consistently measure the same underlying characteristic?" In still other studies, the concern over reliability is expressed in the question "How much consistency exists among the ratings provided by a group of raters?" Despite the differences among these three questions, the notion of consistency is at the heart of the matter in each case.

Different statistical procedures have been developed to assess the degree to which a researcher's data are reliable, and we will consider some of the more frequently used procedures in a moment. Before doing that, however, I want to point out how the different procedures are similar. Besides dealing, in one way or another, with the concept of consistency, each of the reliability techniques leads to a single numerical index. Called a **reliability coefficient,** this descriptive summary of the data's consistency normally assumes a value somewhere between 0.00 and +1.00, with these two "end points" representing situations where consistency is either totally absent or totally present.

Different Approaches to Reliability

Test-Retest Reliability.   In many studies, a researcher will measure a single group of subjects twice with the same measuring instrument, with the two testings separated by a period of time. The interval of time may be as short as one day or it can be as long as a year or more. Regardless of the length of time between the two testings, the researcher will simply correlate the two sets of scores to find out how much consistency is in the data. The resulting correlation coefficient is simply renamed the **test-retest reliability coefficient.**[1]

With a test-retest approach to reliability, the resulting coefficient addresses the issue of consistency, or stability, over time. For this reason, the test-retest reliability coefficient is frequently referred to as the **coefficient of stability.** As with other forms of reliability, coefficients of stability reflect high reliability to the extent that they are close to 1.00.

In Excerpt 4.2 a single test-retest reliability coefficient is presented. In Excerpt 4.3, three are presented (one for the full instrument and two for its subscales). In Excerpt 4.3, note how the reliability coefficients are referred to as *stability coefficients.*

With most characteristics, the degree of stability that exists decreases as the interval between test and retest increases. For this reason, high coefficients of stability

Research Navigator.com

Test-retest reliability coefficient

EXCERPTS 4.2–4.3 • *Test-Retest Reliability*

Test-retest reliability over a one-month period for the current sample was .79.

Source: T. Field, M. Diego, and C. Sanders. (2002). Adolescents' parent and peer relationships. *Adolescence, 37*(145), p. 123.

- -

Test-retest reliability over a 2 month time period was obtained for a subsample of 55 randomly selected participants, yielding a stability coefficient of .78 for the total POB scale scores and stability coefficients of .72 and .68 for the Career-Related and Educational subscales, respectively.

Source: D. A. Luzzo and E. H. McWhirter. (2001). Sex and ethnic differences in the perception of educational and career-related barriers and levels of coping efficacy. *Journal of Counseling and Development, 79*(1), p. 63.

---

[1]As you recall from Chapter 3, correlation coefficients can assume values anywhere between −1.00 and +1.00. Reliability, however, cannot logically turn out to be negative. Therefore, if the test-retest correlation coefficient turns out to be negative, it will be changed to 0.00 when relabeled as a *reliability coefficient.*

are more impressive when the time interval is longer. If a researcher does not indicate the length of time between the two testings, then the claims made about stability must be taken with a grain of salt. Stability is not very convincing if a trait remains stable for only an hour!

Research
Navigator.c✷m
Parallel forms

Parallel-Forms Reliability.[2]   Instead of assessing stability over time, researchers sometimes measure people with two forms of the same instrument. The two forms are similar in that they supposedly focus on the same characteristic (e.g., intelligence) of the people being measured, but they differ with respect to the precise questions included within each form. If the two forms do in fact measure the same thing (and if they are used in close temporal proximity), we would expect a high degree of consistency between the scores obtained for any examinee across the two testings. With **parallel-forms reliability,** a researcher is simply determining the degree to which this is the case.

To quantify the degree of parallel-forms reliability that exists, the researcher will administer two forms of the same instrument to a single group of individuals with a short time interval between the two testings.[3] After a score becomes available for each person on each form, the two sets of data are correlated. The resulting correlation coefficient is interpreted directly as the parallel-forms reliability coefficient.[4] Many researchers refer to this two-digit value as the **coefficient of equivalence.**

To see an example where this form of reliability was used, consider Excerpt 4.4. Notice how these researchers refer to their correlation coefficient (which turned out to be .87) as the *coefficient of equivalence* and the *alternate forms reliability*. These two terms are used interchangeably by most researchers, and both mean the same thing as parallel-form reliability coefficient.

Internal Consistency Reliability.   Instead of focusing on stability across time or on equivalence across forms, researchers sometimes assess the degree to which their measuring instruments possess internal consistency. When this perspective is taken, reliability is defined as consistency across the parts of a measuring instrument, with the "parts" being individual questions or subsets of questions. To the extent that these parts "hang together" and measure the same thing, the full instrument is said to possess high **internal consistency reliability.**

To assess internal consistency, a researcher need only administer a test (or questionnaire) a single time to a single group of individuals. After all responses have

---

[2]The terms *equivalent-forms reliability* and *alternate-forms reliability* are synonymous (as used by most applied researchers) with the term *parallel-forms reliability*.

[3]The two forms will probably be administered in a *counterbalanced* order, meaning that each instrument is administered first to one-half of the subjects.

[4]As is the case with test-retest reliability, any negative correlation would be changed to 0. Reliability by definition has a lower limit of 0.

EXCERPT 4.4 • *Alternate Forms Reliability*

The *SRES* currently exists in four versions: two alternate 95 item full forms (B, K) and two alternate 25 item abbreviated or short forms (BB, KK). The psychometric properties of the two short forms (BB, KK) of the *SRES* were examined using data from 608 undergraduate students. . . . The coefficient of equivalence or alternate forms reliability was .87.

Source: M. R. McGhee, N. Johnson, and J. Liverpool. (2001). Assessing psychometric properties of the sex-role egalitarianism scale (SRES) with African Americans. *Sex Roles, 45*(11/12), p. 862.

been scored, one of several statistical procedures is then applied to the data, with the result being a number between 0.00 and +1.00. As with test-retest and parallel-forms procedures, the instrument is considered to be better to the extent that the resulting coefficient is close to the upper limit of this continuum of possible results.

One of the procedures that can be used to obtain the internal consistency reliability coefficient involves splitting each examinee's performance into two halves, usually by determining how the examinee did on the odd-numbered items grouped together (i.e., one half of the test) and the even-numbered items grouped together (i.e., the other half). After each person's total score on each half of the instrument is computed, these two sets of scores are correlated. Once obtained, the *r* is inserted into a special formula (called **Spearman-Brown**) that makes a "correction" based upon the length of the full instrument. The final numerical result is called the **split-half reliability coefficient.**

Use of this first procedure for assessing internal consistency can be seen in Excerpts 4.5 and 4.6. In the first of these excerpts, notice that the term *odd-even split* is used to convey the manner in which the Body Esteem scale was divided into two halves. In the second excerpt, notice that "corrected by Spearman-Brown" appears. Because researchers so often do these two things when performing a split-half reliability, it's a safe bet to presume that (1) their instruments were divided into odd and even halves and (2) they used the Spearman-Brown correction, even when these two things are not stated.

A second approach to assessing internal consistency is called **Kuder-Richardson #20,** or simply **K-R 20.** This procedure, like the split-half procedure, uses data from a single test that has been given once to a single group of respondents. After the full test is scored, the researcher simply puts the obtained data into a formula that provides the K-R 20 reliability coefficient. The end result is somewhat like a split-half reliability, but better. That's because the split-half approach to assessing internal consistency yields a result that can vary depending upon which items are put in

EXCERPTS 4.5–4.6 • *Split-Half Reliability*

In a sample of 7- to 12-year-old children, Mendelson and White reported that the Body Esteem scale had a split-half reliability of $r = .85$ (odd-even split). . . .

Source: K. K. Davison and L. L. Birch. (2001). Weight status, parent reaction, and self-concept in five-year-old girls. *Pediatrics, 107*(1), p. 48.

- -

Reported estimates of internal consistency ranged from .68 to .71 via split-half method corrected by Spearman-Brown.

Source: L. O. Gonzalez and E. W. Sellers. (2002). The effects of a stress-management program on self-concept, locus of control, and the acquisition of coping skills in school-age children diagnosed with Attention Deficit Hyperactivity Disorder. *Journal of Child and Adolescent Psychiatric Nursing, 15*(1), p. 10.

---

the odd-numbered slots and which ones are placed in the even-numbered slots. In other words, if the items that go together to make up a full test are "scrambled" in terms of the way they are ordered, this will likely affect the value of the split-half reliability coefficient. Thus, whenever the split-half procedure is used to assess the reliability of a measuring instrument, we don't know whether the resulting reliability coefficient is favorable (i.e., high) or unfavorable (i.e., low) as compared with what would have been the case if the items had been ordered differently.

With K-R 20, the end result is guaranteed to be neither favorable nor unfavorable. That's the case because the formula for K-R 20 was designed to produce a result that's equivalent to what you would get if you (1) scramble the order of the test items over and over again until you had all possible orders, (2) compute a split-half reliability coefficient for each of these forms of the test, and (3) take the mean value of those various coefficients. Of course, the researcher who wants to obtain the K-R 20 coefficient does not have to go to the trouble to do these three things. A simple little formula is available that brings about the desired end result almost instantaneously.

In Excerpt 4.7, we see an example of how K-R 20 results are often reported in published research reports.

A third method for assessing internal consistency is referred to as **coefficient alpha,** as **Cronbach's alpha,** or simply as **alpha.** This technique is identical to K-R 20 whenever the instrument's items are scored in a dichotomous fashion (e.g., "1" for correct, "0" for incorrect). However, alpha is more versatile because it can be used with instruments made up of items that can be scored with three or more possible values. Examples of such a situation include (1) a four-question essay test,

Coefficient alpha

EXCERPT 4.7 • *Kuder-Richardson 20 Reliability*

An estimate of internal consistency for the *MCSDS* was high in the participant sample (Kuder-Richardson 20 = .83).

Source: S. E. Davis, I. S. Williams, and L. W. Hays. (2002). Psychiatric inpatients' perceptions of written no-suicide agreements: An exploratory study. *Suicide and Life-Threatening Behavior, 31*(1), p. 56.

where each examinee's response to each question is evaluated on a 0–10 scale or (2) a Likert-type questionnaire where the five response options for each statement extend from "strongly agree" to "strongly disagree" and are scored with the integers 5 through 1. Excerpts 4.8 and 4.9 show two instances in which Cronbach's alpha was used to evaluate internal consistency. These excerpts demonstrate the versatility of Cronbach's technique for assessing internal consistence, for the two instruments had very different scoring systems. Whereas the instrument in Excerpt 4.8 had "1" or "0" scores (to indicate correct or incorrect responses to test questions), the instrument in Excerpt 4.9 utilized a 5-point Likert-type response format aimed at assessing the respondents' attitudes.

EXCERPTS 4.8–4.9 • *Coefficient Alpha Reliability*

We used the coefficient alpha for the 20 multiple-choice questions to assess the internal consistency reliability of the indirect component of the writing assessment instrument. The coefficient alpha of 0.565 suggests that the questions comprising the indirect test are internally consistent.

Source: H. Ashbaugh, K. M. Johnstone, and T. D. Warfield. (2002). Outcome assessment of a writing-skill improvement initiative: Results and methodological implications. *Issues in Accounting Education, 17*(2), p. 130.

SoC [Sense of Community] was assessed using 6 items, each with a 5-point scale (1 = strongly disagree to 5 = strongly agree). Cronbach's alpha for the *SoC* composite index was 0.77.

Source: S. Zeldin. (2002). Sense of community and positive adult beliefs toward adolescents and youth policy in urban neighborhoods and small cities. *Journal of Youth and Adolescence, 31*(5), p. 336.

Interrater Reliability

Researchers sometimes collect data by having raters evaluate a set of objects, pictures, applicants, or whatever. To quantify the degree of consistency among the raters, the researcher will compute an index of interrater reliability. Four popular procedures for doing this are Kendall's coefficient of concordance, Cohen's kappa, the intraclass correlation, and Pearson's product-moment correlation.

Kendall's procedure is appropriate for situations where each rater is asked to rank the things being evaluated. If these ranks turn out to be in complete agreement across the various evaluators, then the **coefficient of concordance** will turn out equal to +1.00. To the extent that the evaluators disagree with one another, Kendall's procedure will yield a smaller value.

In Excerpt 4.10, we see a case in which Kendall's coefficient of concordance was used six times. In the study associated with this excerpt, three separate groups of people first talked about 11 factors, such as "team size," that can derail a software development project. Then, each group (called a panel) ranked these 11 factors. Thus, Kendall's *W* here provides an index of intergroup consistency in evaluating the risk factors.

Kendall's coefficient of concordance establishes how much interrater reliability exists among ranked data. **Cohen's kappa** accomplishes the same purpose when the data are nominal (i.e., categorical) in nature. In other words, kappa is designed for situations where raters classify the items being rated into discrete categories. If all raters agree that a particular item belongs in a given category, and if there is a total agreement for all items being evaluated (even though different items end up in different categories), then kappa assumes the value of +1.00. To the extent that raters disagree, kappa assumes a smaller value.

To see a case in which kappa was used to assess interrater reliability, consider Excerpt 4.11. In this study, undergraduates supplied the researchers with written summaries of two conversations, one that was elegant and characterized by aes-

EXCERPT 4.10 • *Kendall's Coefficient of Concordance*

In this study we measured the degree of consensus among the panelists using Kendall's coefficient of concordance (*W*). . . . This analysis focused on the set of 11 risk factors that were ranked by all three panels. Their level of agreement on the relative ranking of these 11 items was moderately strong (*W* = 0.689) though the absolute ranking of these factors (in terms of rank number given in each panel) differed markedly.

Source: R. Schmidt, K. Lyytinen, M. Keil, and P. Cule. (2001). Identifying software project risks: An international Delphi study. *Journal of Management Information Systems, 17*(4), pp. 14, 22.

thetic grace, and the other considered to be graceless and an eyesore. Statements from the summaries of the beautiful conversations were classified into seven categories (such as conversational flow); seven different categories (such as banal conversation) were used with the summaries of nonbeautiful conversations. As indicated in Excerpt 4.11, there was a high degree of consistency in how the two coders classified statements from each kind of conversation.

EXCERPT 4.11 • *Cohen's Kappa*

One coder, trained to the coding manual, then coded all of the data. For purposes of reliability checking, a second coder independently coded a randomly selected sample of 25% of the questionnaires (*n* = 60). The percentage of coding agreement for beautiful conversations was 90% (kappa = .88), and the percentage of coding agreement for non-beautiful conversations was 91.7% (kappa = .89).

Source: L. A. Baxter and D. H. DeGooyer. (2001). Perceived aesthetic characteristics of interpersonal conversations. *Southern Communication Journal, 67*(1), p. 6.

Research
Navigator.c⊛m

Intraclass
correlation

The third procedure for assessing interrater reliability to be considered here is called **intraclass correlation.** Abbreviated as ICC, the intraclass correlation is typically used to estimate the reliability of ratings. For example, each of 20 job applicants might be rated by each of five members of a hiring team. After analyzing the set of ratings, ICC could be used to estimate the expected reliability of either the individual ratings provided by a single rater or the mean rating provided by a group of raters.

Although originally developed for use with ratings, ICC is currently used in a wide variety of research studies wherein each subject is measured two or more times on the same characteristic. Such situations might be described using the terms *test-retest, test-retest-retest,* and so on, depending on the number of multiple measurements taken. The simplest of these, of course, is the same as that considered earlier when we began our discussion of reliability procedures.

Intraclass correlation is similar to the other reliability procedures we have considered in terms of the core concept being dealt with (consistency), the theoretical limits of the data-based coefficient (0 to 1.00), and the desire on the part of the researcher to end up with a value as close to 1.00 as possible. It differs from the other reliability procedures in that several ICC procedures exist. The six most popular of these procedures are distinguished by two numbers put inside parentheses following the letters ICC. For example, ICC (3,1) designates one of the six most frequently used versions of intraclass correlation. The first of the two numbers indicates which of three possible statistical models has been assumed by the researchers to underlie their data. The second number indicates whether the researchers are interested in the reliability of a single rater (or, one-time use of a measuring instrument) or in the re-liability of the mean score provided by a group of raters (or, the mean value produced by using a measuring instrument more than once). The second number within the parentheses will be a 1 for the first of these two cases; if interest lies in the reliabil-ity of means, the second number will be a value greater than 1 that designates how many scores are averaged together to generate each mean.

I will not attempt to differentiate any further among the six main cases of ICC. Instead, I simply want to point out that researchers should explain in their research reports (1) which of the six ICC procedures was used and (2) the reason(s) behind the choice made. You have a right to expect clarity regarding these two issues be-cause the ICC-estimated reliability coefficient can vary widely depending on which of the six available formulas is used to compute it.

In Excerpt 4.12, we see an example of how discussions of ICC ought to be presented. Note that the researchers specified the version of ICC used—(2,1)—but they did not provide the rationale behind their choice.

EXCERPT 4.12 • *Intraclass Correlation*

Interrater reliability during the Bayley-II Motor Scale testing was established be-tween the first 2 authors on 7 children prior to the start of the study. The ICC (2,1) for the total raw score was .97.

Source: M. E. O'Neil, R. J. Palisano, and S. L. Westcott. (2001). Relationship of therapists' attitudes, children's motor ability, and parenting stress to mothers' perceptions of therapists' behaviors during early intervention. *Physical Therapy, 81*(8), p. 1419.

The last of the four main approaches utilized by researchers to assess inter-rater reliability is Pearson's product-moment correlation. When used in this man-ner, Pearson's r has the same basic objective as Kendall's coefficient of concordance, Cohen's kappa, and intraclass correlation. With all four procedures, the goal is to evaluate the extent to which different judges or raters are consistent in the way they evaluate the people or things being evaluated. It should be noted, however, that Pearson's technique is most similar to the intraclass correlation due to the fact that only these two techniques of data analysis are appropriate for situa-tions where ratings are raw scores (rather than ranks or categorical classifications).

In Excerpt 4.13, we see an interesting case where Pearson's correlation was used to assess interrater reliability. In this study, 185 undergraduates wrote a de-tailed description of two peers, someone they liked and someone they did not like. Then, each of these written statements was evaluated in terms of its cognitive complexity. This evaluation was made by simply summing the number of psychological constructs mentioned by the writer. As a check on interrater reliability, 39 of these written descriptions were evaluated independently by two judges, with Pearson's *r* used to assess the degree of consistency across the two judges.

EXCERPT 4.13 • *Using Pearson's r to Assess Interrater Reliability*

Coding reliability was assessed by having two independent judges each score approximately 20% of the protocols (*n* = 39). Interrater reliability, as assessed by Pearson correlation, was .99.

Source: W. Samter. (2002). How gender and cognitive complexity influence the provision of emotional support: A study of indirect effects. *Communication Reports, 15*(1), p. 9.

The Standard Error of Measurement

Some researchers, when discussing reliability, will present a numerical value for the **standard error of measurement.** Often abbreviated as **SEM,** the standard error of measurement can be used to estimate the range within which a score would likely fall if a given measured object were to be remeasured. To illustrate, suppose an intelligence test is administered to a group of children, and also suppose that Tommy ends up with an IQ score of 112. If the SEM associated with the IQ scores in this group were equal to 4, then we would build an interval for Tommy (by adding 4 to 112 and subtracting 4 from 112) that would extend from 108–116. This interval, or **confidence band,** would help us interpret Tommy's IQ because we could now say that Tommy would likely score somewhere between 108 and 116 if the same intelligence test were to be readministered and if Tommy didn't change between the two testings.[5]

In a very real sense, the standard error of measurement can be thought of as an index of consistency that is inversely related to reliability. To the extent that reliability is high, the SEM will be small (and vice versa). There is one other main difference between these two ways of assessing consistency. Reliability coefficients are tied to a scale that extends from 0 to 1.00, and in this sense they are completely "metric free." In contrast, an SEM is always tied to the nature of the scores generated by a test, and in this sense it is not "metric free." Simply stated, the continuum

---

[5]By creating an interval via the formula "score±SEM," we end up with a 68 percent confidence band. If we doubled or tripled the SEM within this little formula, we would end up with a 95 percent or a 99 percent confidence band, respectively.

for reliability coefficients has no units of measurement, whereas the SEM is always "in" the same measurement units as are the scores around which confidence bands are built.

In Excerpt 4.14, we see a case in which the standard error of measurement was computed and reported.

EXCERPT 4.14 • *Standard Error of Measurement*

The Willingness to Care Scale (WTC), introduced here, was designed to reflect the domains of instrumental, nursing, and emotional care. . . . Coefficient alpha computed as .923 for the global WTC score [and] standard error of measurement coefficients (*SEM*s) were computed as indicators of measurement error for the current sample. *SEM*s for subscales were: instrumental = .251, emotional = .187, and nursing = .211. For the global WTC score, *SEM* = .151.

Source: N. Abell. (2001). Assessing willingness to care for persons with AIDS: Validation of a new measure. *Research on Social Work Practice, 11*(1), pp. 124–125.

Warning about Reliability

Before we turn to the topic of validity, there are five important warnings about reliability to which you should become sensitive. It would be nice if all researchers were also aware of these five concerns; unfortunately, that is not the case.

First of all, keep in mind that different methods for assessing reliability consider the issue of consistency from different perspectives. Thus a high coefficient of stability does not necessarily mean that internal consistency is high (and vice versa). Even within the internal consistency category, a high value for split-half reliability does not necessarily mean that Kuder-Richardson #20 would be equally high for the same data. The various methods for assessing reliability accomplish different purposes, and the results do not necessarily generalize across methods. Because of this, I like to see various approaches to reliability used within the same study. (To see a case where several reliability methods were used to assess the quality of the same measuring instrument, take another look at Excerpt 4.1.)

My second warning concerns the fact that reliability coefficients really apply to data and not to measuring instruments. To understand the full truth of this claim, imagine that a test designed for a college-level class in physics is administered twice to a group of college students, producing a test-retest reliability coefficient of .90. Now, if that same test is administered on two occasions to a group of first grade students (with the same time interval between test and retest), the coefficient of stability would not be anywhere near .90. (The first graders would probably guess at all questions, and the test-retest reliability for this younger group most likely would end up close to 0.00.) Try to remember, therefore, that reliability is conceptually and computationally connected to the data produced by the *use* of a measuring instrument, not to the measuring instrument as it sits on the shelf.

Excerpts 4.15 and 4.16 illustrate the fact that reliability is a characteristic of data, not the instrument that produces the data. Reliability can vary across groups that vary in gender, age, health status, profession, or any number of other characteristics.

EXCERPTS 4.15–4.16 • *Different Reliabilities from Different Samples*

The reliability for the four broad recommendation categories was a highly acceptable Kappa of .97 for 50 male respondents, and an acceptable Kappa of .70 for 50 female respondents.

Source: E. W. Gondolf and R. J. White. (2000). "Consumer" recommendations for batterers programs. *Violence against Women, 6*(2), p. 205

Internal consistency reliability analyses in the present study produced alphas of .84 for the total sample and .74 and .86 for women and men, respectively.

Source: P. J. Hartung and J. R. Rogers. (2000). Work-family commitment and attitudes toward feminism in medical students. *Career Development Quarterly, 48*(3), pp. 268–269.

Some researchers realize that reliability is a property of scores produced by the administration of a measuring instrument (rather than a property of the printed instrument itself). With this in mind, they not only cite reliability coefficients obtained by previous researchers who used the same instrument, but also gather reliability evidence *within* their own investigation. This practice is not widely practiced, unfortunately. Most of the time, researchers simply reiterate the reliability evidence gathered earlier by previous researchers who developed or used the same instrument.[6] Those researchers who take the extra time to assess the reliability of the data gathered in their own investigation deserve credit for knowing that reliability ought to be reestablished in any current study. In Excerpt 4.17, we see an example of this good practice.

My next warning calls on you to recognize that any reliability coefficient is simply an estimate of consistency. If a different batch of examinees or raters are used,

----

[6]Go back and look at the first paragraph of Excerpt 4.1 to see an example of this common practice.

EXCERPT 4.17 • *Assessing Reliability within the Researcher's Study*

The Perceived Stress Scale (*PSS;* Cohen, Kamarck, & Mermelstein, 1983) is a general measure of stress perception. . . . In a sample of African American adults with disabilities, Belgrave and Walker (1991) obtained a Cronbach reliability coefficient of .85. . . . The internal consistency reliability for the present study was .66.

Source: S. L. Jarama and F. Z. Belgrave. (2002). A model of mental health adjustment among African Americans with disabilities. *Journal of Social and Clinical Psychology, 21*(3), p. 330.

you should expect the reliability coefficient to be at least slightly different—even if the new batch of examinees or raters contains people who are highly similar to the original ones. If the groups are small, there would probably be more fluctuation in the reliability coefficient than if the groups are large. Accordingly, place more faith in the results associated with large groups. Regardless of how large the group of examinees or raters is, however, give credit to researchers who use the word *estimated* in conjunction with the word *reliability.*

My next-to-last warning concerns estimates of internal consistency. If a test is administered under great time pressure, the various estimates of internal consistency—split-half, K-R 20, and coefficient alpha—will be spuriously high (i.e., too big). Accordingly, do not be overly impressed with high internal consistency reliability coefficients if data have been collected under a strict time limit or if there is no mention as to conditions under which the data were collected.

Finally, keep in mind that reliability is not the only criterion that should be used to assess the quality of data. A second important feature of the data produced by measuring instruments (or raters) has to do with the concept of validity. The remaining portion of this chapter is devoted to a consideration of what validity means and how it is reported.

Validity

Whereas the best one-word synonym for reliability is consistency, the core essence of **validity** is captured nicely by the word *accuracy.* From this general perspective, a researcher's data are valid to the extent that the results of the measurement process are accurate. Stated differently, a measuring instrument is valid to the extent that it measures what it purports to measure.

In this portion of the chapter, we first will consider the relationship between reliability and validity. Next, we will examine several of the frequently used procedures for assessing validity. Finally, I will offer a few warnings concerning published claims that you may see about this aspect of data quality.

The Relationship between Reliability and Validity

It is possible for a researcher's data to be highly reliable even though the measuring instrument does not measure what it claims to measure. However, an instrument's data must be reliable if they are valid. Thus high reliability is a necessary but not sufficient condition for high validity. A simple example may help to make this connection clear.

Suppose a test is constructed to measure the ability of fifth grade children to solve arithmetic word problems. Also suppose that the test scores produced by an administration of this test are highly reliable. In fact, let's imagine that the coefficient of stability turns out equal to the maximum possible value, +1.00. Even though the data from our hypothetical test demonstrate maximum consistency over time, the issue of accuracy remains unclear. The test may be measuring what it claims to measure—math ability applied to word problems. On the other hand, it may be that this test really measures reading ability.

Now, reverse our imaginary situation. Assume for the moment that all you know is that the test is valid. In other words, assume that this newly designed measuring instrument does, in fact, produce scores that accurately reflect the ability of fifth graders to solve arithmetic word problems. If our instrument produces scores that are valid, then those scores, of necessity, must also be reliable. Stated differently, accuracy requires consistency.

Different Kinds of Validity

In published articles, researchers often present evidence concerning a specific kind of validity. Validity takes various forms because there are different ways in which scores can be accurate. To be a discriminating reader of the research literature, you need to be familiar with the purposes and statistical techniques associated with the popular validity procedures. The three most frequently used procedures are content validity, criterion-related validity, and construct validity.

Research
Navigator.c⊕m
Content validity

Content Validity. With certain tests, questionnaires, or inventories, an important question concerns the degree to which the various items collectively cover the material that the instrument is supposed to cover. This question can be translated into a concern over the instrument's **content validity.** Normally, an instrument's standing with respect to content validity is determined simply by having experts carefully compare the content of the test against a syllabus or outline that specifies the instrument's claimed domain. Subjective opinion from such experts establishes—or doesn't establish—the content validity of the instrument.

In Excerpt 4.18, we see a case in which content validity is discussed by a team of researchers. As you will see, these researchers were extremely thorough in their effort to assess—and improve—the content validity of the new measuring instrument they had developed.

EXCERPT 4.18 • *Content Validity*

The first step in the development of the *PMIEB* was to create an initial item pool. . . . The next step in the development of the pilot version of the *PMIEB* was to determine whether the *PMIEB* items provided content validity; that is, whether they provided accurate and sufficient coverage of our six target psychopathology domains. Toward this end, the *PMIEB* items were reviewed by a panel of child clinicians and experts in child psychopathology. Potential participants included seven child psychopathology experts who were editors or former editors of journals focusing on child psychopathology, as well as 22 practicing child clinicians; these individuals were located in four countries.

These individuals were sent the 19-item pool, and asked to (a) sort the *PMIEB* items into the six domains; (b) delete items that did not fit into any of the domains or were redundant with other items; (c) suggest wording changes for items that were not clear; and (d) suggest additional items if the coverage of a domain was not adequate. Twenty-seven of these 29 individuals returned the forms and provided information for this part of the study. Changes were made if more than 4 or more of the 27 members of the pool recommended a similar change. This resulted in two items being added, no items being dropped, one item being split into two separate items, and one item having minor wording changes.

Source: B. Weiss, V. I. Harris, and T. Catron. (2002). Development and initial validation of the peer-report measure of internalizing and externalizing behavior. *Journal of Abnormal Child Psychology, 30*(3), pp. 286–287.

Criterion-Related Validity.   Researchers sometimes assess the degree to which their new instruments provide accurate measurements by comparing scores from the new instrument with scores on a relevant criterion variable. The new instrument under investigation might be a short, easy-to-give intelligence test, and in this case the criterion would probably be an existing reputable intelligence test (possibly the *Stanford-Binet*). Or, maybe the new test is an innovative college entrance examination; hence, the criterion variable would be a measure of academic success in college (possibly GPA). The validity of either of those new tests would be determined by (1) finding out how various people perform on the new test and on the criterion variable, and (2) correlating these two sets of scores. The resulting *r* is called the **validity coefficient,** with high values of *r* indicating high validity.

There are two kinds of criterion-related validity. If the new test is administered at about the same time that data are collected on the criterion variable, then the term **concurrent validity** is used to designate the kind of validity being investigated. Continuing the first example provided in the preceding paragraph, if people were given the new and existing intelligence tests with only a short time interval

Research
Navigator.c⊕m

Concurrent
validity

between their administrations, the correlation between the two data sets would speak to the issue of concurrent validity. If, however, people were given the new test years before they took the criterion test, then *r* would be a measure of **predictive validity.**

In Excerpts 4.19 and 4.20, we see cases in which the expressed concern of the researchers was with concurrent and predictive validity. In the first of these studies, over 300 individuals filled out two personality inventories. One was a shortened version of the other. In finding out that the correlation between scores from the two scales was so high, the researchers established the concurrent validity of the short version of the scale. In the second study, the researchers used several techniques to validate the MSSC, an instrument designed to measure the motivations behind sport spectator consumption. These included correlating scores on this instrument with data collected, at the end of the sporting season, on relevant criteria (e.g., fan loyalty).

EXCERPTS 4.19–4.20 • *Concurrent and Predictive Validity*

To demonstrate that we were measuring proactive personality, we also examined the correlation between our short form and the original scale on a separate sample of 322 employees from a variety of organizational settings. The correlation between the two forms was .90, thereby providing support that the five items are indeed measuring the proactive personality construct.

Source: J. Kickul and L. K. Gundry. (2002). Prospecting for strategic advantage: The proactive entrepreneurial personality and small firm innovation. *Journal of Small Business Management, 40*(2), p. 89.

- -

Predictive validity was assessed by comparing the factors of the MSSC to four criteria from data that were collected at the end of the season (approximately two months later).

Source: P. G. T. Trail and J. D. James. (2001). The motivation scale for sport consumption: Assessment of the scale's psychometric properties. *Journal of Sport Behavior, 24*(1), p. 119.

In Excerpt 4.21, we see a case where the generic term *criterion-related validity* was used. When you encounter a case like this, you may have to make a guess as to whether reference is being made to concurrent or predictive validity. Sometimes, as with Excerpt 4.21, there are not many clues to use when trying to decide which type of criterion-related validity is being discussed. Here, I would guess that it is concurrent validity, for I suspect the SSRS and the criterion (the Child Behavior Checklist) were administered in close temporal proximity.

EXCERPT 4.21 • *Criterion-Related Validity*

The Social Skills Rating System (*SSRS*) is highly reliable in terms of internal consistency and test-retest reliability, and it demonstrates high criterion-related validity. The problem behaviors score from the *SSRS* and the total behavior problems score from the Child Behavior Checklist are highly correlated ($r = .81$).

Source: K. R. Minter, J. E. Roberts, S. R. Hooper, M. R. Burchinal, and S. A. Zeisel. (2001). Early childhood otitis media in relation to children's attention-related behavior in the first six years of life. *Pediatrics, 107*(5), p. 1038.

Construct Validity.   Many measuring instruments are developed to reveal how much of a personality or psychological construct is possessed by the examinees to whom the instrument is administered. To establish the degree of **construct validity** associated with such instruments, the test developer will typically do one or a combination of three things: (1) provide correlational evidence showing that the construct has a strong relationship with certain measured variables *and* a weak relationship with other variables, with the strong and weak relationships conceptually tied to the new instrument's construct in a logical manner; (2) show that certain groups obtain higher mean scores on the new instrument than other groups, with the high- and low-scoring groups being determined on logical grounds *prior to* the administration of the new instrument; or (3) conduct a factor analysis on scores from the new instrument.

Excerpt 4.22 provides an example of the first of these approaches to construct validity. This excerpt deserves your close attention because it contains a clear explanation of how correlational evidence is examined for the purpose of establishing **convergent validity** and **discriminant validity.**

It is not always easy to demonstrate that a measuring instrument is involved in a network of relationships where certain of those relationships are strong while others are weak. However, claims of construct validity are more impressive when evidence regarding both convergent *and* discriminant validity is provided. Of course, not all measuring instruments are created to deal with personality or psychological constructs, and even those that have been can be validated with noncorrelational evidence. When you *do* encounter validation evidence like that illustrated in Excerpt 4.22, give some "bonus points" (in your evaluation) to those researchers who have utilized the two-pronged approach.

In Excerpt 4.23, we see an example of the group comparison approach to construct validity. Here, evidence for construct validity comes from showing that certain groups score higher on the measuring instrument than do other groups, with these high- and low-scoring groups logically connected to the stated claims of the new measuring instrument.

Research Navigator.c⊕m

Convergent validity
Discriminant validity

EXCERPT 4.22 • *Construct Validity Using Correlations*

As can be seen in the correlation matrix [not shown here], CYN is significantly and positively correlated with both RC ($r = 0.272$) and JIT ($r = 0.306$). The relationship follows from the cynics' predisposition to impugn the motive of others. . . . To the extent each of these scales is measuring a common underlying construct, these positive correlations indicate convergent validity. In addition, the negative relationship with trust ($r = -0.272$), as with organizational commitment ($r = -0.308$) and OCB ($r = -0.233$) also support convergent validity. The relationships found between cynicism, trust, and role conflict establish construct validity. Cynicism must be negatively correlated with trust. In addition, it should be apparent that a cynical attitude would act to reduce both organizational commitment and organizational citizenship behaviors.

In addition, validity requires that the measure also discriminate among dissimilar constructs. Discriminant validity is provided by the lack of a significant relationship with constructs that should not, nomologically, be related. According to our premise that cynicism and altruism are independent moral dimensions, they should be uncorrelated. The lack of a significant correlation between them ($r = -0.094$) is evidence of discriminant validity. Further evidence of discriminant validity is provided by the lack of a significant correlation between cynicism and gender ($r = 0.061$), company tenure ($r = 0.012$), and self-report performance ($r = -0.060$). None of these should these should, by theory, be related to cynicism, and they are not.

Source: J. H. Turner and S. R. Valentine. (2001). Cynicism as a fundamental dimension of moral decision-making: A scale development. *Journal of Business Ethics, 34*(2), p. 133.

EXCERPT 4.23 • *Construct Validity Using Comparison Groups*

As shown in Table 3 [not shown here], discriminant validity was established and is illustrated by significant differences in the *FAST* total scores when administered to the different groups. Athletes with eating disorders scored significantly higher on the *FAST* as compared with athletes without eating pathology and nonathletes with eating disorders. Items that specifically pertained to training and sport were deleted from the reference group scores (nonathletes without eating disorders) to demonstrate the ability of the *FAST* to discriminate between athletes with and without eating disorders. Further, this shows that the *FAST* is specifically designed to detect eating disorders in the athlete because this measure distinguished between athletes with eating disorders vs. nonathletes with eating disorders.

Source: K. Y. McNulty, C. H. Adams, J. M. Anderson, and S. G. Affenito. (2001). Development and validation of a screening tool to identify eating disorders in female athletes. *Journal of the American Dietetic Association, 101*(8), p. 890.

The third procedure frequently used to assess construct validity involves a sophisticated statistical technique called **factor analysis.** Although I will not discuss the details of factor analysis here, I want you to see an illustration of how the results of such an investigation are typically summarized. I don't expect you to understand everything in Excerpt 4.24; my only purpose in presenting it is to alert you to the fact that construct validity is often assessed statistically using factor analysis.

EXCERPT 4.24 • *Construct Validity Using Factor Analysis*

To further examine the [construct validity] of the *PTM,* a varimax rotated principal components exploratory factor analysis was conducted. An exploratory, rather than confirmatory, factor analysis was conducted because this was the first study using the *PTM.* As shown in Table III [not shown here], 6 distinct factors emerged accounting for 63.38% of the systematic variance in responding. For interpretation purposes, items with a factor loading of at least 0.40 were considered to load on that factor (with the exception of 1 item from the altruism subscale that had a loading of 0.39). In general, the factors that emerged corresponded conceptually to the subscales of the *PTM.*

All 5 of the items making up the anonymous prosocial behaviors subscale loaded positively on Factor 1. All 4 of the public prosocial behaviors items loaded positively on Factor 2 (2 altruism items loaded negatively on this factor). The 5 items from the altruistic prosocial behaviors subscale loaded positively on Factor 3 (1 item from the public subscale loaded negatively on Factor 3). The 4 items from the emotional prosocial behaviors subscale loaded positively on Factor 4. The 2 items from the compliant prosocial behaviors subscale loaded positively on Factor 5 (although 1 item from the dire subscale also loaded positively on Factor 5). The 3 items from the dire prosocial behaviors subscale loaded on Factor 6.

Eigenvalues for each factor were > 1.0. Factor 1 accounted for 14.45% of the variance, Factor 2 accounted for 12.45% of the variance, Factor 3 accounted for 10.49% of the variance, Factor 4 accounted for 10.20% of the variance, Factor 5 accounted for 8.06% of the variance, and Factor 6 accounted for 7.73% of the variance.

Source: G. Carlo and B. A. Randall. (2002). The development of a measure of prosocial behaviors for late adolescents. *Journal of Youth and Adolescence, 31*(1), pp. 36–37.

Warnings about Validity Claims

Before concluding our discussion of validity, I want to sensitize you to a few concerns regarding validity claims. Because researchers typically have a vested interest in their studies, they are eager to have others believe that their data are accurate. Readers of research literature must be on guard for unjustified claims of validity and for cases where the issue of validity is not addressed at all.

First, remember that reliability is a necessary but not sufficient condition for validity. Accordingly, do not be lulled into an unjustified sense of security concerning the accuracy of research data by a technical and persuasive discussion of consistency. Reliability and validity deal with different concepts, and a presentation of reliability coefficients—no matter how high—should not cause one's concern for validity to evaporate.

Next, keep in mind that validity (like reliability) is really a characteristic of the data produced by a measuring instrument and not a characteristic of the measuring instrument itself.[7] If a so-called valid instrument is used to collect data from people who are too young or who cannot read or who lack any motivation to do well, then the scores produced by that instrument will be of questionable validity. The important point here is simply this: The people used by a researcher and the conditions under which measurements are collected must be similar to the people and conditions involved in validation studies before you should accept the researcher's claim that the research data are valid because those data came from an instrument having "proven validity."

My third warning concerns content validity. Earlier, I indicated that this form of validity usually involves a subjective evaluation of the measuring instrument's content. Clearly, this evaluation ought to be conducted by individuals who possess (1) the technical expertise to make good judgments as to content relevance and (2) a willingness to provide, if necessary, negative feedback to the test developer. When reporting on efforts made to assess content validity, researchers should describe in detail who examined the content, what they were asked to do, and how their evaluative comments turned out.

With respect to criterion-related and construct validity, a similar warning seems important enough to mention. With these approaches to assessing validity, scores from the instrument being validated are correlated with the scores associated with one or more "other" variables. If the other variables are illogical or if the validity of the scores associated with such variables is low, then the computed validity coefficients conceivably could make a truly good instrument look as if it is defective. Thus, regarding the predictive, concurrent, or construct validity of a new measuring instrument, the researcher should first discuss the quality of the data that are paired with the new instrument's data.

My next-to-last warning concerns the fact that the validity coefficients associated with criterion-related or construct probes are simply estimates, not definitive statements. Just as with reliability, the correlation coefficients reported to back up claims of validity would likely fluctuate if the study were to be replicated with a new batch of subjects. This is true even if the test-takers in the original and replicated studies are similar. Such fluctuations can be expected to be larger if the validity coefficients are based on small groups of people; accordingly, give researchers more credit when their validity investigations are based on large groups.

---

[7]This is true for all varieties of validity except content validity.

Finally, keep in mind that efforts to assess predictive and concurrent validity utilize correlation coefficients to estimate the extent to which a measuring instrument can be said to yield accurate scores. When construct validity is dealt with by assessing an instrument's convergent/discriminant capabilities or by conducting a factor analysis, correlation again is the vehicle through which validity is revealed. Because correlation plays such a central role in the validity of these kinds of investigations, it is important for you to remember the warnings about correlation that were presented near the end of Chapter 3. In particular, do not forget that r^2 provides a better index of a relationship's strength than does r.

Three Final Comments

Within this discussion of reliability and validity, I have not addressed a question that most likely passed through your mind at least once as we considered different procedures for assessing consistency and accuracy. That question is simply, "How high do the reliability and validity coefficients need to be before we can trust the results and conclusions of the study?" Before leaving this chapter, I want to answer this fully legitimate question.

For both reliability and validity, it would be neat and tidy if there were some absolute dividing point (say, .50) that separates large from small coefficients. Unfortunately, no such dividing point exists. In evaluating the reliability and validity of data, the issue of large enough has to be answered in a *relative* manner. The question that the researcher (and you) should ask is, "How do the reliability and validity associated with the measuring instrument(s) used in a given study compare with the reliability and validity associated with other available instruments?" If the answer to this query about relative quality turns out to be "pretty good," then you should evaluate the researcher's data in a positive manner—even if the absolute size of reported coefficients leaves lots of room for improvement.

The second of my three final comments concerns the possible use of multiple methods to assess instrument quality. Since there is no rule or law that prohibits researchers from using two or more approaches when estimating reliability or validity, it is surprising that so many research reports contain discussions of only *one* kind of reliability and (if validity is discussed at all) only *one* kind of validity. That kind of research report is common because researchers typically overlook the critical importance of having good data to work with and instead seem intent on quickly analyzing whatever data have been collected. Give credit to those few researchers who present multiple kinds of evidence when discussing reliability and validity. To see an example of this good practice, take another look at the first excerpt included in this chapter.

My last general comment about reliability and validity is related to the fact that data quality, by itself, does not determine the degree to which a study's results can be trusted. It's possible for a study's conclusions to be totally worthless even though the data analyzed possess high degrees of reliability and validity. A study can go down the tubes despite the existence of good data if the wrong statistical procedure is used to analyze data, if the conclusions extend beyond what the data legitimately allow, or if the design of the study is deficient. Reliability and validity are important concepts to keep in mind as you read technical reports of research investigations, but other important concerns must be attended to as well.

Review Terms

Accuracy	Equivalent-forms reliability
Alpha	Factor analysis
Alternate-forms reliability	Internal consistency reliability
Coefficient alpha	Interrater reliability
Coefficient of concordance	Intraclasss correlation
Coefficient of equivalence	Kuder-Richardson #20 (K-R 20)
Coefficient of stability	Parallel-forms reliability
Cohen's kappa	Predictive validity
Concurrent validity	Reliability
Consistency	Reliability coefficient
Construct validity	Spearman-Brown
Content validity	Split-half reliability coefficient
Convergent validity	Test-retest reliability coefficient
Criterion-related validity	Validity
Cronbach's alpha	Validity coefficient
Discriminant validity	

The Best Items in the Companion Website

1. An interactive online quiz (with immediate feedback provided) covering Chapter 4.
2. Ten misconceptions about the content of Chapter 4.
3. An online resource entitled "Multitrait-Multimethod."
4. An email message about convergent and discriminant validity sent from the author to his students to help them understand these two measurement concepts.
5. Chapter 4's best paragraph.

Fun Exercises inside Research Navigator

1. **How reliable is measured empathy in medical residents over a one-year time period?**

   In this study, nearly 100 medical internists completed the *Jefferson Scale of Physician Empathy* during their residence. Of these interns, 41 had their empathy measured on two occasions: at the beginning of their first year and then again a year later. Pearson's product-moment correlation was used to assess the reliability of these 41 pairs of scores. After presenting the value of *r*, the researchers asserted "this magnitude of test-retest reliability over [a] one-year interval supports the conclusion that the empathy scores remained stable during this time period." How large do you think that test-retest reliability was? After making a guess, locate the PDF version of the research report in the Nursing, Health, and Medicine database of ContentSelect and read (on page 71) the last paragraph of the "Results" section.

S. Mangione, G. C. Kane, J. W. Caruso, J. S. Gonnella, T. J. Nasca, & M. Hojat. Assessment of empathy in different years of internal medicine training. *Medical teacher*. Located in the NURSING, HEALTH, AND MEDICINE database of ContentSelect.

2. **How valid is a 10-item instrument for measuring alcohol withdrawal symptoms?**

The data in this study came from 60 patients receiving alcohol withdrawal treatment in a London psychiatric hospital. These individuals were evaluated with the SAWS, a 10-item self-report instrument designed to measure alcohol withdrawal symptoms. (This assessment instrument is quite simple; the patient simply indicates, using a scale of 0 to 3, how severe each of 10 conditions—such as sweating or tremors—has been within the past 24 hours.) To assess concurrent validity, 46 of the patients were also measured with the CIWA-Ar, another more complicated procedure for assessing alcohol withdrawal symptoms. After reporting the correlation between the SAWS and the CIWA-Ar, the researchers said, "since the SAWS and the CIWA-Ar have both been designed to measure the same phenomena, a substantial degree of correlation between the two scores is to be expected." You might be surprised to see the actual size of the validity coefficient! To see what it was, locate the PDF version of the research report in the Biology database of ContentSelect and then read the last full paragraph on page 42.

M. Gossop, F. Keaney, D. Stewart, E. J. Marshall, & J. Strang. A Short Alcohol Withdrawal Scale (SAWS): Development and psychometric properties. *Addiction Biology*. Located in the BIOLOGY database of ContentSelect.

Review Questions and Answers begin on page 516.

5

Foundations of Inferential Statistics

In Chapters 2 through 4, we considered various statistical procedures that are used to organize and summarize data. At times, the researcher's sole objective is to describe the people (or things) in terms of the characteristic(s) associated with the data. When that is the case, the statistical task is finished as soon as the data are displayed in an organized picture, are reduced to compact indices (e.g., the mean and standard deviation), are described in terms of distributional shape, are evaluated relative to the concerns of reliability and validity, and, in the case of a bivariate concern, are examined to discern the strength and direction of a relationship.

In many instances, however, the researcher's primary objective is to draw conclusions that extend beyond the specific data that are collected. In this kind of study, the data are considered to represent a sample—and the goal of the investigation is to make one or more statements about the larger group of which the sample is only a part. Such statements, when based upon sample data but designed to extend beyond the sample in terms of relevance, are called *statistical inferences.* Not surprisingly, the term **inferential statistics** is used to label the portion of statistics dealing with the principles and techniques that allow researchers to generalize their findings beyond the actual data sets obtained.

In this chapter, we will consider the basic principles of inferential statistics. We begin by considering the simple notions of sample, population, and scientific guess. Next, we take a look at eight of the main types of samples used by applied researchers. Then we consider certain problems that crop up to block a researcher's effort to generalize findings to the desired population. Finally, a few tips are offered concerning specific things to look for as you read professional research reports.

Statistical Inference

Whenever a statistical inference is made, a **sample** is first extracted (or is considered to have come from) a larger group called the **population.** Measurements are then taken on the people or objects that compose the sample. Once these measurements are summarized—for example, by computing a correlation coefficient—an educated guess is made as to the numerical value of the same statistical concept (which, in our example, would be the correlation coefficient) in the population. This educated guess as to the population's numerical characteristic is the **statistical inference.**

If measurements could be obtained on all people (or objects) contained in the population, statistical inference would be unnecessary. For instance, suppose the coach of the girls' basketball team at a local high school wants to know the median height of 12 varsity team members. It would be silly for the coach to use inferential statistics to answer this question. Instead of the coach making an educated guess as to the team's median height (after seeing how tall a few of the girls are), it would be easy to measure the height of each member of the varsity team and then obtain the precise answer to the question.

In many situations, researchers cannot answer their questions about their populations as easily as could the coach in the basketball example. Two reasons seem to account for the wide use of inferential statistics. One of these explanations concerns the measurement process while the other concerns the nature of the population. Because inferential statistics are used so often by applied researchers, it is worthwhile to pause for a moment and consider these two explanations as to why only portions of populations are measured, with educated guesses being made on the basis of the sample data.

First of all, it is sometimes too costly (in dollars and/or time) to measure every member of the population. For example, the intelligence of all students in a high school cannot be measured with an individual intelligence test because (1) teachers would be upset by having each student removed from classes for two consecutive periods to take the test and (2) the school's budget would not contain the funds needed to pay a psychologist to do this testing. In this situation, it would be better for the principal to make an educated guess about the average intelligence of the high school students than to have no data-based idea whatsoever as to the students' intellectual capabilities. The principal's guess about the average intelligence is based on a sample of students taken from the population made up of all students in the high school. In this example, the principal is sampling from a **tangible population** because each member of the student body could end up in the sample and be tested.

The second reason for using inferential statistics is even more compelling than the issue of limited funds and time. Often, the population of interest extends into the future. For example, the high school principal in the previous example probably would like to have information about the intellectual capabilities of the school's student body so improvements in the curriculum could be made. Such changes are made on the assumption that next year's students will not be dissimilar from this year's students. Even if the funds and time could be found to administer an individual intelligence test to every student in the school, the obtained data would be viewed as coming from a *portion* of the population of interest. That population is made up of students who attend the school now *plus* students who will follow in their footsteps. Clearly, measurements cannot be obtained from all members of such a population because a portion of the population has not yet "arrived on the scene." In this case, the principal creates an **abstract population** to fit an existing sample.

Several years ago, I participated as a subject in a study to see if various levels of consumed oxygen have an effect, during strenuous exercise, on blood composition. The researcher who conducted this study was interested in what took place physiologically during exercise on a stationary bicycle among nonsedentary young men between the ages of 25 and 35. That researcher's population was not just active males who were 25–35 years old at the time of the investigation. The population was defined to include active males who *would be* in this age range at the time the research summary got published—approximately 18 months following the data collection. Inferential statistics were used because the subjects of the investigation were considered to be a representative sample of a population of similar individuals that extended into the future.

To clarify the way statistical inference works, consider the two pictures in Figure 5.1. These pictures are identical in that (1) measurements are taken only on the people (or objects) that compose the sample; (2) the educated guess, or inference, extends *from* the sample *to* the population; and (3) the value of the population characteristic is not known (nor ever can be known as a result of the inferential process). Although these illustrations show that the inference concerns the mean, the pictures could have been set up to show that the educated guess deals with the median, the variance, the product-moment correlation, or any other statistical concept.

As you can see, the only differences between the two pictures involve the solid versus dotted nature of the larger circle and the black arrows. In the top picture, the population is tangible in nature, with each member within the larger circle available for inclusion in the sample. When this is the case, the researcher actually begins with the population and then ends up with the sample. In Figure 5.1, the lower picture is meant to represent the inferential setup in which the sequence of events is reversed. Here, the researcher begins with the sample and then creates an abstract population that is considered to include people (or objects) like those included in the sample.

Excerpts 5.1 and 5.2 illustrate the distinction between tangible and abstract populations. In the first of these excerpts, the population was the full set of newspaper articles containing the word "cancer." This was a tangible population, for any of those 1,027 articles could have ended up in the sample. In Excerpt 5.2, the 67 undergraduates who composed the sample were not pulled from a larger group; instead, they got into the sample because they voluntarily responded to newspaper advertisements. Because the researchers used inferential statistics with the data collected from those undergraduates, it's clear that they wanted to generalize the

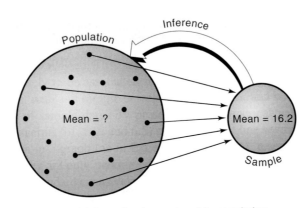

(a) Sampling from a tangible population

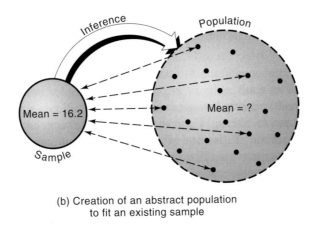

(b) Creation of an abstract population
to fit an existing sample

FIGURE 5.1   *Two Kinds of Sample/Population Situations*

study's findings beyond those 67 students. The relevant population was abstract be-cause it existed only hypothetically as a larger mirror image of the sample.

The Concepts of Statistic and Parameter

When researchers engage in inferential statistics, they must deal with four questions *before* they can make their educated guess, or inference, that extends from the sam-ple to the population:

1. What is/are the relevant population(s)?
2. How will a sample be extracted from each population of interest, presuming the population(s) is/are tangible in nature?

EXCERPTS 5.1–5.2 • *Tangible and Abstract Populations*

Newspapers were searched for articles that included "cancer" in the headline. Medical advice columns, obituaries, letters to the editor, and recipes were excluded. From 1,027 articles collected, a random sample of articles, with a sampling fraction of 30%, was drawn for an in-depth content analysis.

Source: M. M. MacDonald and L. Hoffman-Goetz. (2002). A retrospective study of the accuracy of cancer information in Ontario Daily Newspapers. *Canadian Journal of Public Health, 93*(2), p. 143.

- -

Participants were 67 undergraduate students at the University of Utah (32 men, 35 women). All participants were solicited through campus advertisements and were paid $5 per hour for their participation.

Source: M. K. Gardener, D. J. Wortz, and B. G. Bell. (2002). Representation of memory for order of mental operations in cognitive tasks. *American Journal of Psychology, 115*(2), p. 260.

3. What characteristic of the sample people, animals, or objects will serve as the target of the measurement process?
4. What will be the study's statistical focus?

The first of these four questions is completely up to the researcher and will be dictated by the study's topical focus. The second question will be considered in detail in the next section. The third question, of course, is answered when the researcher decides what to study.[1] The notion of a measurement process is also involved in this question, thus making the issues of reliability and validity (covered in Chapter 4) important to consider when judging whether the researcher did an adequate job in measuring the subjects. This brings us to the fourth question, a concern for the statistical focus of the inference.

After the researcher has measured the sample on the variable(s) of interest, there are many alternative ways in which the data can be summarized. The researcher could compute, for example, a measure of central tendency, a measure of variability, a measure of skewness, or a measure of relationship. But even within each of these broad categories, the researcher has alternatives as to how the data will be summarized. With central tendency, for example, the researcher might decide to focus on

---

[1] You may, at times, disagree with the researcher as to whether the characteristic of the people, animals, or objects in the population is important. Nevertheless, I doubt that you will ever experience difficulty determining what variables were examined. A clear answer to this question is usually contained in the article's title, the statement of purpose, and/or the discussion of dependent variables.

the median rather than on the mean or the mode. If relationship is the issue of interest, a decision might be made to compute Pearson's product-moment correlation coefficient rather than other available correlational indices. The term **statistical focus** is used simply to indicate the way in which the data are summarized.

Regardless of how a researcher decides to analyze the sample data, there will always be two numerical values that correspond to the study's statistical focus. One of these is "in" the sample—and it can be computed as soon as the sample is measured. This numerical value is called the **statistic.** The second value that corresponds to the study's statistical focus is "in" the population, and it is called the **parameter.** The parameter, of course, can never be computed because measurements exist for only a portion of the people, animals, or objects that compose the population.

Because researchers often use symbols to represent the numerical values of their statistics (and sometimes use different symbols to represent the unknown values of the corresponding parameters), it is essential that you become familiar with the symbols associated with inferential statistics. To assist you in doing this, I have developed a chart (Table 5.1) that shows the most frequently used symbols for the statistic and parameter that correspond to the same statistical focus. As you can easily see, Roman letters are used to represent statistics whereas Greek letters stand for parameters.

Now that I have clarified the notions of statistic and parameter, I can be a bit more parsimonious in my definition of inferential statistics. When engaged in inferential statistics, a researcher uses information concerning the known value of the sample statistic to make an educated guess as to the unknown value of the popula-

TABLE 5.1   *Symbols Used for Corresponding Statistics and Parameters*

Statistical focus	*Statistic* *(in the sample)*	*Parameter* *(in the population)*
Mean	$\bar{X}$ or M	μ
Variance	s^2	σ^2
Standard deviation	s	σ
Proportion	p	P
Product-moment correlation*	r	ρ
Rank-order correlation	r_s	ρ_s
Size of group[†]	n	N

*Unfortunately, the symbol ρ is used to designate the value of the product-moment correlation in the relevant population. This is the letter rho from the Greek alphabet. In Chapter 3, we saw that Spearman's rank-order correlation is also referred to as rho.

[†]In many articles, the symbol N is used to indicate the size of the *sample.* It would be better if the symbol n could be used instead of N when researchers give us information about their sample sizes.

tion parameter. If, for example, the statistical focus is centered on the mean, then information concerning the known value of $\overline{X}$ is used to make a scientific guess as to the value of μ.

Types of Samples

The nature of the sample used by a researcher as a basis for making an educated guess as to the parameter's value obviously has an influence on the inferential process. To be more specific, the nature of the sample will influence either (1) the accuracy of the inferential guess or (2) the definition of the population toward which the inferential guess is directed. To help you understand the way in which the sample can affect the inferential process in these two ways, I need to distinguish among eight kinds of samples that fall into two main categories: probability samples and nonprobability samples.

Probability Samples

If all members of the population can be specified prior to drawing the sample, if each member of the population has at least some chance of being included in the sample, and if the probability of any member of the population being drawn is known, then the resulting sample is referred to as a **probability sample.** The four types of probability samples that we will consider are called *simple random samples, stratified random samples, systematic samples,* and *cluster samples.* As you read about each of these samples, keep in mind the illustration presented in Figure 5.1a.

Simple Random Samples. With a simple random sample, the researcher, either literally or figuratively, puts the names of all members of the population into a hat, shuffles the hat's contents, and then blindly selects out a portion of the names to determine which members of the total group will or won't be included in the sample. The key feature of this kind of sample is an equal opportunity for each member of the population to be included in the sample. It is conceivable, of course, that such a sample could turn out to be grossly unrepresentative of the population (because the sample turns out to contain the population members that are, for example, strongest or most intelligent or tallest). It is far more likely, however, that a simple random sample will lead to a measurement-based statistic that approximates the value of the parameter. This is especially true when the sample is large rather than small.

In Excerpts 5.3 and 5.4, we see examples of simple random samples being used in applied research studies. In the first of these excerpts, notice the word *simple;* in other cases where only the phrase *random sample* is used, you should assume that the samples being described are simple random samples. In Excerpt 5.4, notice the term **sampling frame.** Generally speaking, a sampling frame is a list that enumerates the things—people, animals, objects, or whatever—in the population.

EXCERPTS 5.3–5.4 • *Simple Random Samples*

The sample consisted of 4,892 individuals randomly selected from the population of individuals (rather than households). In this simple random sample, 3,014 participated in paid work.

Source: C. Cheung. (2002). Gender differences in participation and earnings in Hong Kong. *Journal of Contemporary Asia, 32*(1), p. 75.

- -

The sample was purchased from a supplier of the American Medical Association (AMA) Masterfile. The vendor constructed a sampling frame consisting of all physicians in the AMA Masterfile who (a) indicated that they spend the majority of their professional time on direct patient care and (b) listed primary specialties of obstetrics/gynecology, family or general practice, emergency medicine, pediatrics, or general internal medicine. The sampling frame was restricted to these five specialties because they account for 85% of all STDs diagnosed. . . . A simple random sample of 300 physicians was selected from this sampling frame.

Source: D. Kasprzyk, D. E. Montano, J. S. St. Lawrence, and W. R. Phillips. (2001). The effects of variations in mode of delivery and monetary incentive on physicians' responses to a mailed survey assessing STD practice patterns. *Evaluation and the Health Professions, 24*(1), pp. 8–9.

Research
Navigator.c⊕m
Stratified random
sample

Stratified Random Samples.   To reduce the possibility that the sample might turn out to be unrepresentative of the population, researchers will sometimes select a stratified random sample. To do this, the population must first be subdivided into two or more parts based upon the knowledge of how each member of the population stands relative to one or more stratifying variables. Then, a sample is drawn so as to mirror the population percentages associated with each segment (or stratum) of the population. Thus if a researcher knew that the population contained 60 percent males and 40 percent females, a random sample stratified on gender would end up containing six males for every four females.

An example of a stratified random sample is presented in Excerpt 5.5. Notice how the population of schools was first stratified according to three kinds of communities, three kinds of school size, and two kinds of grade levels. This created 18 strata in the population. One of these strata included rural middle schools with an enrollment of 0–599 students, another strata included suburban high schools with an enrollment over 1,000, and so on. Next, a random sample of schools was selected from each strata, with the percentage of schools selected from each strata carefully calculated so that the final sample was "consistent with the overall make-up of schools within Maryland."

EXCERPT 5.5 • *Stratified Random Samples*

A stratified random sample of schools was selected across population density (i.e., urban, suburban, and rural), enrollment (i.e., 0–599, 600–999, 1,000 and greater), and school levels (i.e., middle school, and high school). Percentages of schools across population density and enrollment [and level] were established to maintain a sample consistent with the overall make-up of schools within Maryland.

Source: P. Maccini and J. C. Gagnon. (2002). Perceptions and application of NCTM standards by special and general education teachers. *Exceptional Children, 68*(3), p. 330.

In some studies in which stratified random samples are used, researchers will make the size of the sample associated with one or more of the strata larger than that strata's proportionate slice of the population. This oversampling in certain strata is done for one of three reasons: (1) anticipated difficulty in getting people in certain strata to participate in the study, (2) a desire to make comparisons between strata (in which case there are advantages to having equal strata sizes in the sample, even if those strata differ in size in the population), and (3) a need to update old strata sizes, when using archival data, because of recent changes in the characteristics of the population. In Excerpt 5.6, we see an example of a stratified random sample that involved oversampling for the first of these three reasons.

EXCERPT 5.6 • *"Oversampling" in a Stratified Random Sample*

The first sample used in our study, called the "South Bend sample," was drawn from a stratified random sample of households in Saint Joseph County. . . . In the South Bend sample, we oversampled among poor and minority individuals [because] research has found that telephone survey response rates tend to be lower among lower-income populations because of their distrust of telephone surveys generally and the lack of continuous telephone service.

Source: K. T. Stroupe, E. D. Kinney, and T. J. Kniesner. (2000). Does chronic illness affect the adequacy of health insurance coverage? *Journal of Health Politics, 25*(2), p. 316.

Research
Navigator.com

Systematic
sample

Systematic Samples. A third type of probability sample is called a systematic sample. This type of sample is created when the researcher goes through an ordered list of members of the population and selects, for example, every fifth entry on the list to be in the sample. (Of course, the desired size of the sample and the number of entries on the list determine how many entries are skipped following the selection of each entry to be in the sample.) So long as the starting position on the list is determined randomly, each entry on the full list has an equal chance of ending up in the sample. Thus if the researcher decides to generate a sample by selecting every fifth entry, the first entry selected for the sample should not arbitrarily be the entry at the top of the list (or the one positioned in the fifth slot); instead, a random decision should determine which of the first five entries goes into the sample.

Excerpt 5.7 exemplifies the use of a systematic sample. Notice that the starting point for this systematic sample was chosen at random. That identified the first advertising director to be included in the sample. Then, every 15th advertising director on the list (past that first one) was selected until the sample size of 100 was reached.

EXCERPT 5.7 • *Systematic Samples*

This study is based on a systematic random sample of advertising directors of 100 daily newspapers listed in the Editor & Publisher Yearbook. . . . To ensure that the sample of advertising directors would be representative of all possible ad directors, the sample was chosen by selecting a starting point at random and then choosing every 15th advertising director.

Source: A. D. Fletcher, B. I. Ross, and J. C. Schweitzer. (2002). Newspaper ad directors see political ads as less honest. *Newspaper Research Journal, 23*(1), p. 52.

Cluster Samples.   The last of the four kinds of probability sampling to be discussed here involves what are called cluster samples. When this technique is used to extract a sample from a population, the researcher first develops a list of the clusters in the population. The clusters might be households, schools, litters, car dealerships, or any other groupings of the things that make up the population. Next, a sample of these clusters is randomly selected. Finally, data are collected from each person, animal, or thing that is in each of the clusters that have been randomly selected, or data are collected from a randomly selected subset of the members of each cluster.

In Excerpt 5.8, we see an example of a cluster sample. Actually, this is an example of a multistage cluster sample. Here, there were three stages of the sampling process. First, 52 out of 1,270 geographical areas (called *PSUs*) were randomly selected. Next, 187 high schools within these geographical areas were randomly selected. Finally, one or two intact classrooms within these schools were randomly selected. Besides being a good example of a multistage cluster sample, Excerpt 5.8 illustrates the way the concepts of stratification and oversampling are not restricted to stratified random samples.

EXCERPT 5.8 • *Cluster Samples*

The YRBS [Youth Risk Behavior Surveillance System] employed a three-stage cluster sample design to produce a nationally representative sample of students in grades 9–12. The first-stage sampling frame contained 1,270 primary sampling units (PSUs) consisting of large counties or groups of smaller, adjacent counties. From the 1,270 PSUs, 52 were selected from 16 strata formed on the basis of the degree of urbanization and the relative percentage of Black and Hispanic students in the PSU. PSUs were selected with probability proportional to school enrollment size. At the second sampling stage, 187 schools were selected with probability proportional to school enrollment size. To enable separate analyses of data for Black and Hispanic students, schools with substantial numbers of these students were sampled at higher rates than all other schools. The third stage of sampling consisted of randomly selecting one or two intact classes of a required subject from grades 9–12 at each chosen school. All students in selected classes were eligible to participate in the survey.

Source: H. I. Hall, S. E. Jones, and M. Saraiya. (2001). Prevalence and correlates of sunscreen use among US high school students. *Journal of School Health, 71*(9), p. 453.

Nonprobability Samples

In many research studies, the investigator does *not* begin with a finite group of persons, animals, or objects in which each member has a known, nonzero probability of being plucked out of the population for inclusion in the sample. In such situations, the sample is technically referred to as a **nonprobability sample.** Occasionally, as in Excerpt 5.9, an author will tell us directly that one or more nonprobability samples served as the basis for the inferential process. Few authors do this, however, and so you need to be able to identify this kind of sample from the description of the study's subject pool.

Although inferential statistics can be used with nonprobability samples, extreme care must be used in generalizing results from the sample to the population. From the research write-up, you probably will be able to determine who (or what) was in the sample that provided the empirical data. Determining the larger group to whom such inferential statements legitimately apply is usually a much more difficult task.

We will now consider four of the most frequently seen types of nonprobability samples. These are called purposive samples, convenience samples, quota samples, and snowball samples.

Purposive Samples. In some studies, the researcher starts with a large group of potential subjects. To be included in the sample, however, members of this large group must meet certain criteria established by the researcher because of the nature

EXCERPT 5.9 • *Nonprobability Samples*

A nonprobability sample of 192 male and female undergraduates was recruited in student dining halls, outside the library, and in the student union building on the campus of a northeastern university. Recruitment occurred on different days of the week, excluding weekends, and at different times of day to minimize a selection bias. . . . Recruitment of subjects was accomplished by two female undergraduate students enrolled in an independent study course on consumer dietary behavior taught by a faculty member from the nutrition department.

Source: L. McArthur, R. I. Rosenberg, F. M. Grady, and A. B. Howard. (2002). College students' compliance with food guide pyramid recommendations. *Journal of Family and Consumer Sciences, 94*(2), pp. 30–31.

of the questions to be answered by the investigation. Once these screening criteria are employed to determine which members of the initial group wind up in the sample, the nature of the population at the receiving end of the "inferential arrow" is different from the large group of potential subjects with which the researcher started. The legitimate population associated with the inferential process is either (1) the portion of the initial group that satisfied the screening criteria, presuming that only a subset of these acceptable people (or objects) were actually measured or (2) an abstract population made up of people (or objects) similar to those included in the sample, presuming that each and every "acceptable" person (or object) was measured. These two notions of the population, of course, are meant to parallel the two situations depicted earlier in Figure 5.1.

Excerpt 5.10 illustrates the way researchers will sometimes use and describe their **purposive samples.** In this passage, notice how the researchers set up four criteria for determining whether or not a day-care center was qualified to be in the sample. By describing these criteria (and by using the term *purposive sample*), the researchers help their readers avoid the mistake of generalizing the results of this study to all day-care centers.

In should be noted that the journal article from which Excerpt 5.10 was taken contained a detailed description of the families associated with this study. That description (not shown in this excerpt) focused on several demographic characteristics other than those used as screening criteria. Such descriptions are exceedingly important in studies involving purposive samples, for the relevant populations associated with nonprobability samples are abstract rather than tangible. As pointed out earlier, the nature of an abstract population is determined by who or what is in the sample. Accordingly, if the characteristics of the sample are not known, how can anyone describe the population to which the inference is directed?

EXCERPT 5.10 • *Purposive Samples*

A purposive sample of 11 licensed day care centers serving low-income families of toddlers (2–3 years old) in Chicago participated in a study of the effectiveness of parent training for increasing parenting self-efficacy, reducing child behavior problems, promoting positive parent–child relationships, and reducing parental reliance on harsh discipline strategies. . . . Criteria for day care center selection included centers (a) with over 90% of enrolled families meeting income eligibility requirements for subsidized childcare; (b) that are licensed by the Department of Children and Family Services; (c) that serve families of 2- and 3-year-olds; and (d) that are located in Chicago.

Source: D. Gross, W. Julion, and L. Fogg. (2001). What motivates participation and dropout among low-income urban families of color in a prevention intervention? *Family Relations, 50*(3), p. 247.

Convenience Samples.   In some studies, no special screening criteria are set up by the researchers to make certain that the individuals in the sample possess certain characteristics. Instead, the investigator simply collects data from whoever is available or can be recruited to participate in the study. Such data-providing groups, if they serve as the basis for inferential statements, are called convenience samples.

The population corresponding to any convenience sample is an abstract (i.e., hypothetical) population. It is considered by the researcher to include individuals (or objects) similar to those included in the sample. Therefore, the sample-population relationship brought about by convenience samples is always like that pictured earlier in Figure 5.1b.

Excerpts 5.11 and 5.12 illustrate the use of convenience samples. In these excerpts, the researchers clearly label the kind of sample they used. Not all researchers are so forthright.

It should be noted that the statements presented in Excerpts 5.11 and 5.12 do not constitute the full description of the convenience samples used in these studies. In each case, the researchers provided extremely detailed descriptions of the individuals from whom data were gathered. Unfortunately, many researchers put us in a quandary by not providing such descriptions. Unless we have a good idea of who is in a convenience sample, there is no way to conceptualize the nature of the abstract population toward which the statistical inferences are aimed.

Quota Samples.   The next type of nonprobability sample that we will consider is called a quota sample. Here, the researcher decides that the sample should contain X percent of a certain kind of person (or object), Y percent of a different kind of

EXCERPTS 5.11–5.12 • *Convenience Samples*

A convenience sample of 309 respondents was gathered in Greece.

Source: J. Tsalikis, B. Seaton, and P. Tomaras. (2002). A new perspective on cross-cultural ethical evaluations: The use of conjoint analysis. *Journal of Business Ethics, 35*(4), p. 285.

- -

We also questioned a convenience sample of teens and adults on the street, in local restaurants and stores, and in local businesses.

Source: J. Denner, D. Kirby, K. Coyle, and C. Brindis. (2001). The protective role of social capital and cultural norms in Latino communities: A study of adolescent births. *Hispanic Journal of Behavioral Sciences, 23*(1), p. 8.

person (or object), and so on. Then, the researcher simply continues to hunt for enough people/things to measure within each category until all predetermined sample slots have been filled.

In Excerpt 5.13, we see an example of a quota sample that was used in a study conducted to assess the stress that grandparents have when they are responsible for raising their grandchildren. In this investigation, the researchers wanted approximately 33 of the grandparents they studied to fall into each of four categories: middle-aged African Americans, middle-aged Caucasians, older African Americans, and older Caucasians. These were the quotas. As indicated in the excerpt, they searched diligently for grandparents who met these recruiting criteria, ending up

EXCERPT 5.13 • *Quota Samples*

Quota sampling was used to create approximately equal groups of African American, Caucasian, middle aged and older grandparents. . . . Participants were recruited through public and private schools, social service agencies, churches, pre-schools, Big Brother/Big Sister organizations, grandparent support groups, and other grandparents. The research staff made personal visits to over 50 schools and agencies where they were able to obtain the cooperation of officials who agreed to distribute flyers that described the project and provided a telephone number that potential participants could call. Some organizations called or sent flyers to individuals who were known to be custodial grandparents; others advertised the information in their bulletin or sent flyers home with all school children.

Source: R. G. Sands and R. S. Goldberg-Glen. (2000). Factors associated with stress among grandparents raising their grandchildren. *Family Relations, 49*(1), p. 99.

with what they wanted: 32 African American and 32 Caucasian middle-aged grand-parents, and 34 African American and 31 Caucasian older grandparents.

On the surface, quota samples and stratified random samples seem to be highly similar. There is, however, a big difference. To obtain a stratified random sample, a finite population is first subdivided into sections and then a sample is se-lected randomly from each portion of the population. When combined, those ran-domly selected groups make up the stratified random sample. A quota sample is also made up of different groups of subjects that are combined. Each subgroup, however, is not randomly extracted from a different stratum of the population; rather, the researcher simply takes whoever comes along until all vacant sample slots are occupied. As a consequence, it is often difficult to know to whom the re-sults of a study can be generalized when a quota sample serves as the basis for the inference.

Research
Navigator.c⊛m
Snowball sample

Snowball Samples.　　A snowball sample is like a two-stage convenience or purpo-sive sample. First, the researcher locates a part of the desired sample by turning to a group that is conveniently available or to a set of individuals who possess certain characteristics deemed important by the researcher. Then, those individuals are asked to help complete the sample by going out and recruiting family members, friends, acquaintances, or coworkers who might be interested (and who possess, if a purposive sample is being generated, the needed characteristics). Excerpt 5.14 il-lustrates how this technique of snowballing is sometimes used in research studies.

EXCERPT 5.14 • *Snowball Samples*

A criterion-based snowball, or network, sample was used and was recruited in the following manner. Interviews began with diabetes center personnel and diabetes re-searchers who provided the names of diabetes care providers regarded to be opinion leaders or professionals with extensive knowledge of diabetes and diabetes care in the local practice community. New names were elicited at the end of each interview until they began to repeat, resulting in 56 potential interviewees.

Source: A. C. Larme and J. A. Pugh. (2001). Evidence-based guidelines meet the real world: The case of diabetes care. *Diabetes Care, 24*(10), p. 1729.

The Problems of Low Response Rates,
Refusals to Participate, and Attrition

If the researcher uses a probability sample, there will be little ambiguity about the destination of the inferential statement that is made—as long as the researcher clearly defines the *population* that supplied the study's subjects. Likewise, there will be little ambiguity associated with the target of inferential statements based upon nonprobability samples—as long as the *sample* is fully described. In each case, however, the inferential process becomes murky if data are collected from less than 100 percent of the individuals (or objects) that comprise the sample. In this section, we need to consider three frequently seen situations in which inferences are limited because only a portion of the full sample is measured.

Response Rates

In many studies, the research data are collected by mailing one or more surveys, questionnaires, or tests to members of the sample. Usually, only a portion of the individuals who receive these mailed measurement probes furnish the researcher with the data that was sought. In many cases, the recipient of the survey, questionnaire, or test simply does not take the time to read and answer the questions. In other cases, the questions are answered but the instrument is never sent back to the researcher. In any event, the term **response rate** has been coined to indicate the percentage of sample subjects who send their completed forms back to the researcher.

In Excerpts 5.15, 5.16, and 5.17, we see typical response rates from three studies in which surveys were sent to all members of the defined populations. Because the response rate in each study was far below the optimum value of 100 percent, the

EXCERPTS 5.15–5.17 • *Response Rates*

Surveys were sent to a random sample of 1,069 MBAs and completed surveys were received from 494, for a response rate of 46%.

Source: J. A. Schneer and F. Reitman. (2002). Managerial life without a wife: Family structure and managerial career success. *Journal of Business Ethics, 37*(1), p. 28.

- -

Of the 780 questionnaires distributed, 52.4%, or 409, of the questionnaires were returned.

Source: K. M. Scouller and D. Smith. (2002). Prevention of youth suicide: How well informed are the potential gatekeepers of adolescents in distress? *Suicide and Life-Threatening Behavior, 32*(1), p. 69.

- -

After a pilot study of 15 physicians to refine a questionnaire, the survey was sent to a stratified random sample of 220 physicians in active practice in the county in which our offices are located. . . . The response rate was 62 or 28%.

Source: E. W. Grabois and M. A. Nosek. (2001). The Americans with Disabilities Act and medical providers: Ten years after passage of the act. *Policy Studies Journal, 29*(4), p. 686.

statistical inferences extend only to individuals similar to those who returned completed surveys. Fortunately, the journal articles from which these excerpts were taken also included detailed descriptions of the respondents, thereby clarifying the appropriate abstract population associated with the sample used in each study.

Adequate response rates rarely show up in studies where the researcher simply sits back and waits for responses from people who have been mailed just once a survey, questionnaire, or test. As Excerpts 5.18, 5.19, and 5.20 show, researchers can do certain things both before and after the measuring instrument is mailed in an effort to achieve a high response rate. Researchers (like those associated with these three excerpts) who try to get responses from everyone in the target sample deserve credit for their efforts; on the other hand, you ought to downgrade your evaluation of those studies in which little or nothing is done to head off the problem of ending up with a poor response rate.

Most researchers who collect data through the mail or via the Internet want their findings to generalize to individuals like those in the *full* group to whom the measuring instrument was originally sent, not just individuals like those who send back completed instruments. To get a feel for whether less-than-perfect response rates ought to restrict the desired level of generalizability, researchers sometimes conduct

EXCERPTS 5.18–5.20 • *Working to Get a Good Response Rate*

The nonrespondents were mailed a second copy of the survey packet after three weeks had elapsed.

Source: M. Nelson, B. Herlihy, and J. Oescher. (2002). A survey of counselor attitudes towards sex offenders. *Journal of Mental Health Counseling,* 24(1), pp. 54–55.

To encourage participation, we enclosed a letter from the executive director of The Arc Michigan explaining the importance of this project and invited participants to enter in a lottery for a $200 donation to their chapter.

Source: D. A. Salem, P. G. Foster-Fishman, and J. R. Goodkind. (2002). The adoption of innovation in collective action organizations. *American Journal of Community Psychology,* 30(5), p. 689.

To increase the number of responses, we decided to use questionnaires translated into Spanish and Korean, given that the largest numbers of ethnic business owners belonged to these two groups.

Source: R. Chaganti and P. G. Greene. (2002). Who are ethnic entrepreneurs? A study of entrepreneurs' ethnic involvement and business characteristics. *Journal of Small Business Management,* 40(2), p. 134.

a midstream ministudy to see whether a **nonresponse bias** exists. As indicated in Excerpts 5.21 and 5.22, there are different ways to check on a possible nonresponse bias. The methods exemplified by the first of these excerpts are easier to execute, but they provide the least impressive evidence as to the existence of any nonresponse bias. In contrast, the method illustrated in Excerpt 5.22 is difficult to accomplish; it is, however, the best approach for investigating possible nonresponse bias.

Refusal to Participate

In studies where individuals are asked to participate, some people may decline. Such **refusals to participate** create the same kind of problem that is brought about

EXCERPTS 5.21–5.22 • *Checking for a Nonresponse Bias*

Three checks for nonresponse bias were conducted. First, respondents were compared to nonrespondents to see whether they differed in terms of basic business characteristics such as number of employees, volume of sales, and age of the firm. No significant differences were observed at the .05 level. Second, since surveys arrived over a period of almost eight weeks and involved the mailing of a reminder postcard, one could argue that late respondents more closely resemble nonrespondents, in which case, if a response bias exists, late respondents would differ from early respondents. Accordingly, respondents were grouped by arrival date and the dependent variables were compared using one-way analysis of variance. No significant differences were observed. Finally, respondents had the option to identify themselves and, to the extent that anonymous respondents more closely resemble nonrespondents, if a response bias exists, anonymous respondents would differ from respondents that disclosed their identity. No statistical differences between anonymous and identified respondents were observed.

Source: A. BarNir and K. A. Smith. (2002). Interfirm alliances in the small business: The role of social networks. *Journal of Small Business Management, 40*(3), p. 224.

- -

Additionally, we contacted 20 nonrespondents by telephone and asked them to complete the inventories. All of the individuals agreed to complete the inventories. These individuals were then sent the inventories (if necessary) under the same cover letter detailed above. Comparative analysis on the composite scale scores of each of the inventories . . . revealed that there were no statistically significant differences in the mean responses of respondents and nonrespondents.

Source: J. R. Nelson, A. Maculan, M. L. Roberts, and B. J. Ohlund. (2001). Sources of occupational stress for teachers of students with emotional and behavioral disorders. *Journal of Emotional and Behavioral Disorders, 9*(2), p. 124.

by low response rates. In each case, valid inferences extend only to individuals similar to those who actually supplied data, not to the larger group of individuals who were *asked* to supply data. In Excerpt 5.23, we see a case in which nearly 40 percent of the potential subjects chose not to participate.

EXCERPT 5.23 • *Refusals to Participate*

To be eligible for the study, participants had to be 40–75 years old, live in the local area, have a telephone, read and write English, and be diagnosed with Type 2 diabetes for at least 1 year. . . . Participants were recruited through the practices of 16 primary care physicians who sent letters describing the study to their patients who were purported to have Type 2 diabetes. . . . Of the 265 patients who were eligible, 160 (61%) agreed to participate.

Source: M. Barrera, R. E. Glasgow, H. G. McKay, S. M. Boles, and E. G. Feil. (2002). Do Internet-based support interventions change perceptions of social support? An experimental trial of approaches for supporting diabetes self-management. *American Journal of Community Psychology, 30*(5), pp. 642–643.

Just as some researchers perform a check to see whether a less-than-optimal response rate affects the generalizability of results, certain investigators will compare those who agree to participate with those who decline. If no differences are noted, a stronger case exists for applying inferential statements to the full group of individuals invited to participate (and others who are similar) rather than simply to folks similar to those who supplied data. Researchers who make this kind of comparison in their studies deserve bonus points from you as you critique their investigations. Conversely, you have a right to downgrade your evaluation of a study if the researcher overlooks the possible problems caused by refusals to participate.

Attrition[2]

In many studies, less than 100 percent of the subjects remain in the study from beginning to end. In some instances, such attrition arises because the procedures or data-collection activities of the investigation are aversive, boring, or costly to the participant. In other cases, forgetfulness, schedule changes, or changes in home location explain why certain individuals become dropouts. Regardless of the causal forces that bring about the phenomenon of **attrition,** it should be clear why attrition can affect the inferential process.

---

[2]The problem of attrition is sometimes referred to as *mortality.*

Excerpt 5.24 illustrates the problem that can be caused by attrition. Of the 162 couples who indicated a willingness to participate in this study, 150 showed up when the investigation began (at time 1). By the time the study ended, at time 3, 40 of the 150 couples had dropped out. That is an attrition rate of nearly 27 percent. Perhaps the results of the study would have been different if those 40 couples had remained in the study.

EXCERPT 5.24 • *Attrition*

Participants were 150 married couples residing in California and Illinois. . . . Participants were informed that the study concerned relationships, would require three separate data collections, and would not negatively affect the contact student's grade should they drop out. Initially, 162 couples agreed to participate but 12 would not verify their participation to a research assistant who called after data collection and were eliminated from the study. Because of attrition, the *n* of 150 at Time 1 (T1) dropped to 130 at Time 2 (T2) and 110 at Time 3 (T3).

Source: D. J. Canary, L. Stafford, and B. A. Semic. (2002). A panel study of the associations between maintenance strategies and relational characteristics. *Journal of Marriage and Family, 64*(2), p. 397.

A Few Warnings

As we approach the end of this chapter, I'd like to offer a handful of warnings about the inferential connection between samples and populations. I highly suggest that you become sensitive to these issues, because many professional journals contain articles in which the researcher's conclusions seem to extend far beyond what the inferential process legitimately allows. Unfortunately, more than a few researchers get carried away with the techniques used to analyze their data—and their technical reports suggest that they gave little or no consideration to the nature of their samples and populations.

My first warning has to do with *a possible mismatch between the source of the researcher's data and the destination of the inferential claims.* Throughout this chapter, we have emphasized the importance of a good match between the sample and the population. Be on guard when you read or listen to research reports, because the desired fit between sample and population may leave much to be desired. Consider, for example, the information presented in Excerpt 5.25.

The major concern you ought to have with this study involves the nature of the sample. As pointed out in Excerpt 5.25, the sample was made up solely of adolescent girls recruited from *one* large hospital in Atlanta and *one* of its satellite clin-

random sample is to draw slips of paper from a hat. Random samples can also be produced by flipping coins or rolling dice to determine which members of the population end up in the sample.

Most contemporary researchers do not draw their random samples by rolling dice, flipping coins, or drawing slips of paper from a hat. Instead, they utilize either a printed **table of random numbers** or a set of **computer-generated random numbers.** To identify which members of the population get into the sample, the researcher first assigns unique ID numbers (such as 1, 2, 3, etc.) to the members of the population. Then, the researcher turns to a table of random numbers (or a set of computer-generated random numbers) where the full set of ID numbers will appear in a scrambled order. Finally, the ID numbers that appear at the top of the list (e.g., 27, 4, 9) designate which members of population get into the sample.

In Excerpts 5.29 and 5.30, we see how easy it is for a researcher to indicate that a random sample was selected via a table of random numbers or computer-generated random numbers. These authors deserve credit for clarifying exactly how their random samples were created. All researchers should follow these good examples!

EXCERPTS 5.29–5.30 • *Using a Table of Random Numbers and*
Computer-Generated Random Numbers

During that year [1999] all commercials appearing between 8:00 A.M. and 12:00 A.M. on fifteen randomly-selected days of each month in the year (chosen through a table of random numbers) were videotaped. The videotapes were subsequently played back for content analysis.

Source: R. T. Peterson. (2002). The depiction of African American children's activities in television commercials: An assessment. *Journal of Business Ethics, 36*(4), p. 305.

- -

Using a computer-generated list of random numbers, we randomly selected 30 journals from 107 categorized as general internal medical journals by the Institute for Scientific Information.

Source: K. P. Lee, M. Schotland, P. Bacchetti, and L. A. Bero. (2002). Association of journal quality indicators with methodological quality of clinical research articles *Journal of the American Medical Association, 287*(21), p. 2805.

The final warning I wish to provide is really a repetition of a major concern expressed earlier in this chapter. Simply stated, an empirical investigation that incorporates inferential statistics is worthless unless there is a detailed description of the population or the sample. No matter how carefully the researcher describes the measuring instruments and procedures of the study, and regardless of the levels of appropriateness and sophistication of the statistical techniques used to analyze the data, the results will be meaningless unless we are given a clear indication of the population from which the sample was drawn (in the case of probability samples) or the sample itself (in the case of nonprobability samples). Unfortunately, too many researchers get carried away with their ability to use complex inferential techniques when analyzing their data. I can almost guarantee that you will encounter technical write-ups in which the researchers emphasize their analytical skills to the near exclusion of a clear explanation of where their data came from or to whom the results apply. When you come across such studies, give the authors *high* marks for being able to flex their "data analysis muscles"—but *low* marks for neglecting the basic inferential nature of their investigations.

To see an example of a well-done description of a sample, consider Excerpt 5.31. Given this relatively complete description of the 125 homeless adolescents who formed this study's sample, we have a much better sense of the population to which the statistical inferences can be directed. After reading the material in Excerpt 5.31, go back and take a look at Excerpt 5.2, which describes a sample of college students used in a different study. In which case do you have the best sense of the kind of people included in the sample?

EXCERPT 5.31 • *Detailed Description of a Sample*

Of the 125 homeless adolescents who participated in the study, almost 70% were male. The sample was 37% African American and 42% Caucasian; the remaining 21% were identified as other (either Hispanic, American Indian, or biracial). The participants ranged in age from 14 to 23 years. A large percentage of the respondents indicated their natural parents had divorced (42%) and remarried. Furthermore, approximately, 30% of the participants indicated they had been "thrown out" of these homes, as opposed to running away. Interestingly, 51% of respondents reported staying in touch with their families since becoming homeless. Self-reported factors that may have contributed to family problems included debts (22%), alcohol or drug problems (18%), physical illness (33%), and mental illness (16%).

An overwhelming majority of the respondents (95%) had engaged in sexual intercourse, with 13 years as the median age at first coitus. Respondents were asked if they had ever exchanged sex for money, food, shelter, or drugs. Approximately 36% indicated experience with survival sex for money, and 20% had exchanged sex for food, shelter, or drugs. A significant percentage of the participants reported a forced sexual experience (34%) or having experienced physical abuse (47%).

Source: B. M. Beech, L. Myers, and D. J. Beech. (2002). Hepatitis B and C infections among homeless adolescents. *Family and Community Health, 25*(2), pp. 31–32.

Review Terms

Abstract population
Attrition
Convenience sample
Inferential statistics
Mortality
Nonprobability sample
Parameter
Population
Probability sample
Purposive sample
Quota sample

Refusals to participate
Response rate
Sample
Simple random sample
Statistic
Statistical inference
Statistical focus
Stratified random sample
Table of random numbers
Tangible population

The Best Items in the Companion Website

1. An interactive online quiz (with immediate feedback provided) covering Chapter 5.
2. Ten misconceptions about the content of Chapter 5.
3. An email message sent from the author to his students to help them understand the difference between tangible and abstract populations.
4. A poem about questionnaires (written by a famous statistician).
5. The best passage from Chapter 5 (selected by the author).

Fun Exercises inside Research Navigator

1. **What is the ethnic composition of a national probability sample of children aged 18 to 36 months?**

   In this U.S. study, parents of young children were interviewed concerning the language development of their children. The 278 children who were the focus of this study were carefully selected to be a representative probability sample of all similarly aged children living in the continental United States. Stratified random sampling was used in an effort to achieve this goal, with 94.4 percent of the targeted parents agreeing to participate. As you would guess, the gender split in the sample was quite even (with 51 percent being girls). Focus now, however, on the sample's ethnic composition. There were four ethnic categories: African American, Latino/Hispanic, White, and Other (Asian or mixed). Choose any one of these ethnic categories and guess its percentage "slice" of the sample. To find out how accurate your guess is, locate the PDF version of the research report in the Communication Sciences and Disorders database of ContentSelect and look (on page 736) at Table 1.

   L. Rescoria & T. M. Achenbach. Use of the Language Development Survey (LDS) in a national probability sample of children 18 to 36 months old. *Journal of Speech, Language, and Hearing*

Research. Located in the COMMUNICATION SCIENCES AND DISORDERS database of ContentSelect.

2. **Illicit psychostimulants on the college campus: Who uses them and why?**
   In this study, a sample of college students completed anonymous question-naires through which they provided information about demographic variables, personality variables, and their use or nonuse of illicit drugs. Summarizing their findings in the journal article's "Discussion" section, the authors said this: "The present study suggests that abuse of stimulants, both prescription and illegal, may be a significant problem on U.S. college campuses. Roughly a third of the college students surveyed reported illicit use of prescription am-phetamines." OK. Let's now back up a bit. How many colleges and universi-ties do you think supplied the sample of students used in this study? And what kind of sampling do you think the researchers used? To find out the answers to these two not-so-trivial questions, locate the PDF version of the research report in the Nursing, Health, and Medicine database of ContentSelect and read (on page 284) the section entitled "Participants." You may be quite sur-prised at what you find!

   K. G. Low & A. E. Gendaszek. Illicit use of amphetamines among college students: A prelimi-nary study. *Psychology, Health, and Medicine.* Located in the NURSING, HEALTH, AND MEDICINE database of ContentSelect.

Review Questions and Answers begin on page 516.

6

Estimation

In the previous chapter, we laid the foundation for our consideration of inferential statistics. We did that by considering the key ingredients of this form of statistical thinking and analysis: population, sample, parameter, statistic, and inference. In this chapter, we now turn our attention to one of the two main ways in which researchers use sample statistics to make educated guesses as to the values of population parameters. These procedures fall under the general heading **estimation.**

This chapter is divided into three main sections. First, the logic and techniques of *interval estimation* are presented. Next, we examine a second, slightly different way in which estimation works; this approach is called *point estimation.* Finally, I offer a few tips to keep in mind as you encounter research articles that rely on either of these forms of estimation.

Before beginning my discussion of estimation, I need to point out that the two major approaches to statistical inference—estimation and hypothesis testing—are similar in that the researcher makes an educated guess as to the value of the population parameter. In that sense, both approaches involve a form of guesswork that might be construed to involve estimation. Despite this similarity, the term *estimation* has come to designate just one of the two ways in which researchers go about making their educated guesses about population parameters. The other approach, hypothesis testing, is discussed in Chapters 7 and 8.

Interval Estimation

To understand how **interval estimation** works, you must become familiar with three concepts: sampling errors, standard errors, and confidence intervals. In addition, you must realize that a confidence interval can be used with just about any statistic that is computed on the basis of sample data. To help you acquire these skills, we begin with a consideration of what is arguably the most important concept associated with inferential statistics: sampling error.

Sampling Error

When a sample is extracted from a population, it is conceivable that the value of the computed statistic will be identical to the unknown value of the population parameter. Although such a result is possible, it is far more likely that the statistic will turn out to be different from the parameter. The term **sampling error** refers to the magnitude of this difference.

To see an example of sampling error, flip a coin 20 times, keeping track of the proportion of times the outcome is heads. I'll consider your 20 coin flips to represent a sample of your coin's life history of flips, with that total life history being the population. I will also assume that your coin is unbiased and that your flipping technique does not make a heads outcome more or less likely than a tails outcome. Given these two simple assumptions, I can assert that the parameter value is known to be .50. Now, stop reading, take out a coin, flip it 20 times, and see how many of your flips produce a heads outcome.

I do not know, of course, how your coin-flipping exercise turned out. When *I* flipped my coin (a nickel) 20 times, however, I *do* know what happened. I ended up with 13 heads and 7 tails, for a statistic of .65. The difference between the sample's statistic and the population's parameter is the sampling error. In our case, therefore, the sampling error turned out to be .15.[1]

If you end up observing 10 heads in your 20 coin flips, the sampling error would be equal to zero. Such a result, however, is not likely to occur. Usually, the sample statistic will contain sampling error and fail to mirror exactly the population parameter. Most of the time, of course, the size of the sampling error will be small, thus indicating that the statistic is a reasonably good approximation of the parameter. Occasionally, however, a sample will yield a statistic that is quite discrepant from the population's parameter. That would be the case if you get 19 or 20 heads (or tails) when flipping a coin 20 times.

It should be noted that the term sampling error does *not* indicate that the sample has been extracted improperly from the population or that the sample data have been improperly summarized. (I ended up with a sampling error of .15 even though I took a random sample from the population of interest and even though I carefully summarized my data.) When sampling error exists, it is attributable not to any mistake being made but rather to the natural behavior of samples. Samples generally do not turn out to be small mirror images of their corresponding populations, and statistics usually do not turn out equal to their corresponding parameters. Even with proper sampling techniques and data analysis procedures, sampling error ought to be expected.

In my example dealing with 20 coin flips, we knew what the parameter's value was equal to. In most inferential situations, however, the researcher will know the numerical value of the sample's statistic but not the value of the population's param-

---

[1]I computed the sampling error by subtracting .50 from .65.

eter. This situation makes it impossible for the researcher to compute the precise size of the sampling error associated with any sample, but it does not alter the fact that sampling error should be expected. For example, suppose I gave you a coin that was known *only by me* to be slightly biased. Imagine that it would turn up heads 55 percent of the time over its life history. If I asked you to flip this coin 20 times and then make a guess as to the value of the coin's parameter value, you should expect sampling error to occur. Hence, not knowing the parameter value (and thus not being able to compute the magnitude of any sample's sampling error) should not affect your expectation that the statistic and the parameter are at least slightly unequal.[2]

Sampling Distributions and Standard Errors

Most researchers extract a single sample from any population about which they want to make an educated guess. Earlier, for example, I asked you to take a sample of 20 flips of your coin's coin-flipping life history. It is possible, however, to *imagine* taking more than one sample from any given population. Thus I can imagine taking multiple samples from the coin I flipped that gave us, in the first sample, an outcome of .65 (that is, 65 percent heads).

When I imagine taking multiple samples (each made up of 20 flips) from that same coin, I visualize the results changing from sample to sample. In other words, whereas I obtained a statistic of .65 in my first sample, I would not be surprised to find that the statistic turns out equal to some other value for my second set of 20 flips. If a third sample (of 20 flips) were to be taken, I would not be surprised to discover that the third sample's statistic assumes a value different from the first two samples' statistics. If I continued (in my imagination) to extract samples (of 20 flips) from that same coin, I would eventually find that values of the statistic (1) would begin to repeat, as would be the case if I came across another sample that produced 13 heads, and (2) would form a distribution having tails that extend away from the distribution's modal value.

The distribution of sample statistics alluded to in the preceding paragraph is called a **sampling distribution,** and the standard deviation of the values that make up such a distribution is called a **standard error.** Thus a standard error is nothing more than an index of how variable the sample statistic is when multiple samples of the same size are drawn from the same population. As you recall from Chapter 2, variability can be measured in various ways; the standard error, however, is always conceptualized as being equal to the standard deviation of the sampling

---

[2]If a population is perfectly homogenous, the sampling error will be equal to 0. If the population is heterogeneous but an enormously large sample is drawn, here again the statistic will turn out equal to the parameter once that statistic is rounded to one or two decimal places. Both of these situations, however, are unrealistic. Researchers typically are involved with heterogeneous populations and base their statistical inferences on small samples where $n < 50$.

distribution of the statistic (once we imagine that multiple samples are extracted and summarized).[3]

Figure 6.1 contains the sampling distribution that we would end up with if we took many, many samples (of 20 flips per sample) from a fair coin's population of potential flips, with the statistical focus being the proportion of heads that turn up within each sample. The standard deviation of this sampling distribution is equal to about .11. This standard error provides a numerical index of how much dispersion exists among the values on which the standard deviation is computed; in this case, each of those values corresponds to the proportion of heads associated with one of our imaginary samples.

The standard error indicates the extent to which the statistic fluctuates, from sample to sample, around the value of the parameter. The standard error, therefore, provides a measure of how much sampling error is likely to occur whenever a sample of a particular size is extracted from the population in question. To be more specific, the chances are about 2 out of 3 that the sampling error will be smaller than the size of the standard error (and about 1 in 3 that the sampling error will be larger than the size of the standard error). If the standard error is small, therefore, this would indicate that we should expect the statistic to approximate closely the value of the parameter. On the other hand, a large standard error would indicate that a larger discrepancy between the statistic and parameter is to be anticipated.

Earlier, I said that researchers normally extract only one sample from any given population. Based on my earlier statement to that effect (and now my reiteration of that same point), you may be wondering how it is possible to know what the standard error of the sampling distribution is equal to in light of the fact that the researcher would not actually develop a sampling distribution like that shown in Figure 6.1. The way researchers get around this problem is to use their sample data to estimate the standard error. I will not discuss the actual mechanics that are involved in doing this; rather, I simply want you to accept my claim that it *is* possible to do this.[4]

In my earlier example about a coin being flipped 20 times, the statistical focus was a proportion. Accordingly, the standard error (of .11) illustrated in Figure 6.1 is the standard error *of the proportion.* In some actual studies, the researcher's statistical focus will be a proportion, as has been the case in my coin-flipping example. In many studies, however, the statistical focus is something other than

---

[3]Even though the concepts of standard deviation and standard error are closely related, they are conceptually quite different. A standard deviation indicates the variability inside a single set of actual data points; a standard error, in contrast, indicates how variable the sample statistic is from sample to sample.

[4]For example, when I use my single sample of 20 coin flips (13 heads, 7 tails) to estimate the standard error of the theoretical sampling distribution, I obtain the value of .1067. This estimated standard error of the proportion approximates the true value, .1118, that corresponds to the full sampling distribution shown in Figure 6.1.

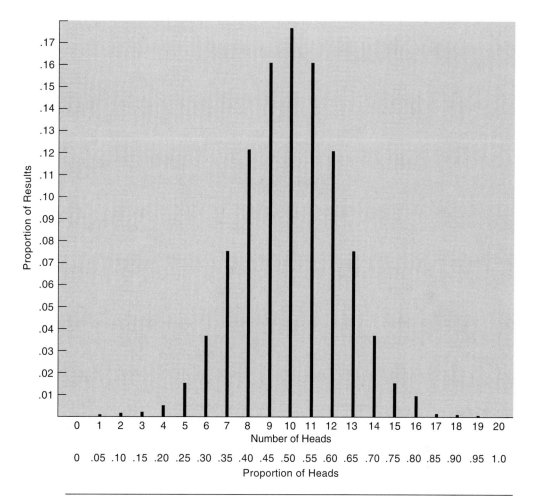

FIGURE 6.1   *Sampling Distribution of Number/Proportion of Heads in 20 Flips of a Fair Coin*

proportion. When reading journal articles, I find that the overwhelming majority of researchers focus their attention on means and correlation coefficients. There are, of course, other ways to "attack" a data set, and I occasionally come across articles in which the median, the variance, or the degree of skewness represents a study's statistical focus. Regardless of the statistical focus selected by the researcher, the standard error concept applies so long as the study involves inferential statistics.

Consider, for example, the short passage contained in Excerpt 6.1. As you can see, several distance runners were recruited for this study. In describing these runners, the researchers provide the sample mean on several characteristics (e.g., age,

EXCERPT 6.1 • *Estimated Standard Error of the Mean*

We recruited 17 highly trained, heat-acclimated distance runners from a college cross-country team and the local running community. . . . The physical characteristics of the subjects (3 women, 14 men) were (mean ± *SEM*) age, 28 ± 2 years; height, 180 ± 2 cm; weight, 68.5 ± 2.1 kg; body fat, 11.2 ± 1.3%; and training volume, 89 ± 10 km/wk.

Source: J. M. Clements, D. J. Casa, J. C. Knight, and J. M. McClung. (2002). Ice-water immersion and cold-water immersion provide similar cooling rates in runners with exercise-induced hyperthermia. *Journal of Athletic Training, 37*(2), p. 147.

height). For each of these variables, the researchers also provide an index of sampling variability. Because the mean is the statistical focus, that index is the standard error of the mean (SEM).

By providing (in Excerpt 6.1) information as to the estimated SEM associated with each variable, the researchers were alerting their readers to the fact that their data allowed them to compute sample statistics, not population parameters. In other words, each SEM in this short passage cautions us not to consider the mean equal to μ. If a different group of distance runners were to be plucked out of the same population that supplied the 17 participants in this study, the mean age for the new group of runners would probably turn out equal to some value other than 28, the mean height would probably turn out equal to some value other than 180 cm, and so on.

Excerpt 6.2 contains another example where information on the standard error of the mean was presented, this time in a table.[5] In the study from which this excerpt was taken, an effort was made to predict ACL knee injuries of male and female Division I collegiate basketball players. The information presented in Excerpt 6.2 was included near the beginning of the results section of the research report simply to provide descriptive data on the two groups of subjects.

In Excerpt 6.2, the presence of SEM values make it clear that the researcher considered the two groups of athletes to be samples. If the researcher had been interested only in the 23 male athletes and 25 female athletes from whom data were gathered, it would have been illogical to compute SEM values. (The fact that the two groups were viewed as samples was also made clear later in the research report when inferential statistics were used to compare the men against the women.)

[5]The term *estimated standard error* should have been used to label these numbers, not *standard error.* In each case, the data from a single sample were used to estimate the true standard error.

EXCERPT 6.2 • *Estimated Standard Error of the Mean in a Table*

TABLE 1 *Subject Characteristics (Mean ± Standard Error of the Mean)*

| | Male | | Female | |
	M	SEM	M	SEM
Variable				
Age	19.75	±0.25	19.63	±0.41
Height (cm)	187.21	±4.64	176.10	±1.91
Weight (kg)	88.01	±5.93	70.80	±2.93
Sum-of-seven skinfolds (mm)	81.88	±15.01	102.69	±6.72

Source: J. L. Moul. (1998). Differences in selected predictors of anterior cruciate ligament tears between male and female NCAA Division I collegiate basketball players. *Journal of Athletic Training, 33*(2), p. 119.

The SEM values in Excerpt 6.2 give us a feel for how much variability we should expect to see if a different sample of male and female Division I basketball players were to be studied (assuming, of course, that these new samples that we now think about are viewed as being pulled out of the same abstract male and female populations as were the two samples actually described in Excerpt 6.2). Consider, for example, the SEM of ±0.25 for the male athletes on the variable of age. This SEM, being relatively small, indicates that another sample of 23 collegiate male basketball players from Division I schools would be expected to have a mean age not too different from 19.75. Comparing the male and female SEM values for the other three variables suggests that the means on height, weight, and skinfolds for additional samples of males would fluctuate more than would comparable means for additional samples of females.

In Excerpt 6.3, we see a case where SEM values are presented graphically in a bar graph. In this excerpt, each bar corresponds to a different sample, with the height of each bar indicating that sample's mean. As you can see, a vertical line protrudes from the top of each bar. The lengths of these lines indicate the samples' SEM values. Since each of the bars for the breastfeeding group (one for grimaces, the other for crying) has a smaller SEM line than do the bars for the control group, this indicates that the means for the breastfeeding group are more stable than are the means for the control group.

Excerpt 6.4 contains the graph showing how four groups of college students performed on an ability test called the Stafford Identical Blocks Test (SIBT). This 15-minute multiple-choice test contained 30 items, each involving a picture of a

EXCERPT 6.3 • *Estimated Standard Error of the Mean in a Bar Graph*

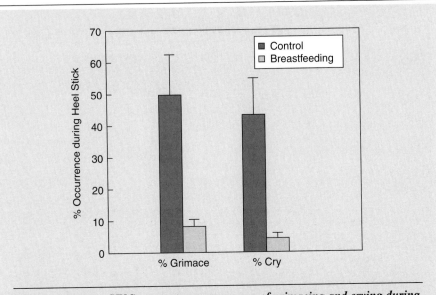

FIG. 1   *Mean (+ SEM) percentage occurrence of grimacing and crying during the heel stick procedure for control newborns and newborns who were breast-feeding before and during the procedure (N = 15/group).*

Source: L. Gary, L. W. Miller, B. L. Philipp, and E. M. Blass. (2002). Breastfeeding is analgesic in healthy newborns. *Pediatrics, 109*(4), p. 592.

"standard" block figure paired with five response options that showed rotated blocks (only one of which corresponded with the standard block). The four groups of students differed in terms of "handedness," with four—rather than just two—groups set up to accommodate individuals who were, to varying degrees, ambidextrous. Groups 1 to 4 contained folks who were totally right-handed, predominantly right-handed, predominantly left-handed, and totally left-handed, respectively.

The graph in Excerpt 6.4 contains means and SEMs to show how each of the four groups performed on the SIBT. The means are represented by the small squares that are positioned inside the rectangular boxes. The heights of those rectangular boxes were determined by adding one SEM to the mean (to get the top of each rectangle) and by subtracting one SEM from the mean (to get the bottom of each rectangle). The visual display of each group's SEM gives us an idea of the range within which we could expect the group means to be located if this study were to be replicated.

In Excerpt 6.5, we see a passage that closely resembles the one presented earlier in Excerpt 6.1. In both cases, several means are presented, each accompanied

EXCERPT 6.4 • *Estimated Standard Error of the Mean in a Graph*

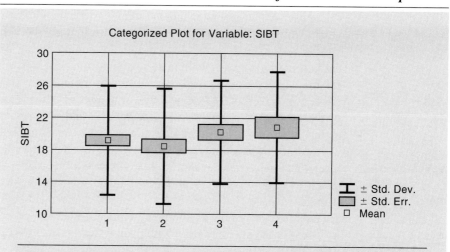

Categorized Plot for Variable: SIBT

FIG 1. *Means, standard errors of the means and standard deviations of the means on the Stafford Identical Blocks Test (SIBT) for hand preference classes (HPREFGRP).*

Source: L. J. Cerone and W. F. McKeever. (1999). Failure to support the right-shift theory's hypothesis of a "heterozygote advantage" for cognitive abilities. *British Journal of Psychology, 90*(1), p. 109.

by an estimated standard error. In the excerpt we looked at earlier, the abbreviation SEM was used to explain the meaning of the numbers (each preceded by a ± sign) that immediately followed each mean. Here, in Excerpt 6.5, the abbreviation SE is used. These two excerpts provide yet another case where different abbreviations or symbols are used by different researchers to refer to the same statistical concept. To understand research reports, you must develop the ability to see through such surface differences.

EXCERPT 6.5 • *Estimated Standard Error of the Mean in the Text*

Participants in all three conditions had equivalent reading ability, as measured by the Nelson-Denny comprehension test. The raw score means were $M = 27.65$, $SE = .79$ for readers of easy texts; $M = 27.39$, $SE = .81$ for readers of standard texts; and $M = 28.25$, $SE = .79$ for readers of difficult texts; maximum score = 36.

Source: L. Lin, K. M. Zabrucky, and D. Moore. (2002). Effects of text difficulty and adults' age on relative calibration of comprehension. *American Journal of Psychology, 115*(2), p. 192.

Confidence Intervals

Researchers who report standard errors along with their computed sample statistics deserve to be commended. This practice helps to underscore the fact that sampling error is very likely to be associated with any sample mean, with any sample standard deviation, with any sample correlation coefficient, and with any other statistical summary of sample data. By presenting the numerical value of the standard error (as in Excerpts 6.1, 6.2, and 6.5) or by putting a line segment through the statistic's position in a graph (as in Excerpts 6.3 and 6.4), researchers help us to remember that they are only making educated *guesses* as to parameters.

Research
Navigator.c⊕m

Confidence
intervals

Although standard errors definitely help us when we try to understand research results, a closely related technique helps us even more. As the title of this section indicates, we now wish to talk about **confidence intervals.** My fourfold objective here is to show what a confidence interval looks like, to explain how confidence intervals are built, to clarify how to interpret confidence intervals properly, and to point out how confidence intervals carry with them a slight advantage over standard errors.

Confidence Intervals: What They Look Like.   A confidence interval is simply a finite interval of score values on the dependent variable. Such an interval is constructed by adding a specific amount to the computed statistic (thereby obtaining the upper limit of the interval) and by subtracting a specific amount from the statistic (thereby obtaining the lower limit of the interval). In addition to specifying the interval's upper and lower limits, researchers will always attach a percent to any interval that is constructed. Most often, this percentage value will be either 95 or 99. Taken together, the interval's length and the percentage value that goes with it form the confidence interval.

In technical research reports, confidence intervals are typically presented in one of three ways. Excerpts 6.6 and 6.7 illustrate how confidence intervals will sometimes be reported within the text of the research report. Although both of these excerpts present 95 percent confidence intervals, notice that these presentations differ in that: (1) the confidence intervals are built around means in one excerpt but percentages in the other and (2) the end points of the confidence intervals are presented in Excerpt 6.6 whereas in Excerpt 6.7 the researchers used a format in which they indicate, for each confidence interval, half the distance between the interval's end points. (In Excerpt 6.7, the first of the two confidence intervals would have an upper end of $67.8 + .09$, or 68.7 percent, and a lower end of $67.8 - .09$, or 66.9 percent; the end points of the second confidence interval would be determined in the similar fashion.)

The second place you will see confidence intervals is in tables. Excerpt 6.8 illustrates this reporting strategy. Notice how the confidence intervals here are wider than the interval you would have if you simply added the standard error to the mean (to get the upper end of the new interval) and subtracted the standard error from the mean (to get the lower end of the new interval). As is the case here, 95 percent

EXCERPTS 6.6–6.7 • *Confidence Intervals Reported in the Text*

Fat consumption is positively correlated with coronary heart disease mortality in men ($r_s = 0.79$; 95% confidence interval 0.70 to 0.86) and inversely associated with coronary heart disease mortality in women (-0.30; -0.49 to -0.08) over this time.

Source: D. A. Lawlor, S. Ebrahim, and G. D. Smith. (2001). Sex matters: Secular and geographical trends in sex differences in coronary heart disease mortality. *British Medical Journal, 323*(7312), p. 541.

- -

National vaccination coverage with ≥ 1 dose of VAR [varicella vaccine] increased from 67.8% (95% confidence interval [CI] = $\pm 0.9\%$) in 2000 to 76.3% (95% CI = $\pm 0.8\%$) in 2001.

Source: Anonymous. (2002). National, state, and urban area vaccination coverage levels among children aged 19–35 months—United States, 2001. *Morbidity and Mortality Weekly Report, 51*(30), p. 664.

EXCERPT 6.8 • *Confidence Intervals Reported in a Table*

Table 3 shows the confidence intervals around the mean for each [blood pressure] measurement.

TABLE 3 *Cell Statistics*

	Mean	Standard Error	95% Confidence Interval	
			Lower	Upper
Systolic, leg uncrossed	143.9	2.3	139.3	148.4
Systolic, leg crossed	145.6	2.3	141.1	150.2
Diastolic, leg uncrossed	79.1	1.7	75.7	82.5
Diastolic, leg crossed	79.4	1.6	76.3	82.5

Source: C. S. Avvampato. (2001). Effect of one leg crossed over the other at the knee on blood pressure in hypertensive patients. *Nephrology Nursing Journal, 28*(3), p. 326. (Adapted slightly for presentation here.)

confidence intervals usually turn out to be about twice as wide as the comparable interval formed by moving 1 standard error above and below the mean.

The third way researchers sometimes report confidence intervals is through a picture. To see an example of this way of presenting information on confidence intervals, take a look at Excerpt 6.9. In this excerpt, the height of each of the four bars indicates a percentage. Extending upwards from the top of each bar is a T-shaped line. For any of the bars, this T-shaped line represents the portion of the confidence interval that lies above that bar's percentage. The other portion of the confidence interval—the part that lies below the percentage—is hidden by the bar. As you can see, the inclusion of information on the confidence intervals allows us to know that

EXCERPT 6.9 • *Confidence Intervals Reported in a Graph*

Figure 1 shows the increase from 1990 to 1999 in the percentage of California indoor workers reporting smoke-free workplaces. In 1990, only 35.0% (95% CI = 33.7, 36.3) of California indoor workers reported working in a clean air environment, but this percentage increased to 93.4% (95% CI = 92.6, 94.2) by 1999.

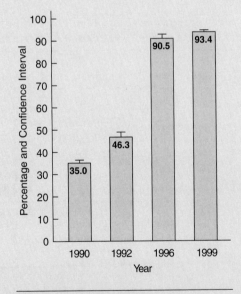

FIGURE 1 *Indoor workers reporting smoke-free workplaces (1990, 1992, 1996, and 1999 California Tobacco Surveys).*

Source: E. A. Gilpin, A. J. Farkas, S. L. Emery, C. F. Ake, and J. P. Pierce. (2002). Clean indoor air: Advances in California, 1990–1999. *American Journal of Public Health, 92*(5), p. 787.

(1) the four percentages correspond to sample statistics, not population parameters, and (2) different samples drawn from the same populations would likely yield percentages very close to the ones shown in Excerpt 6.9.

Before leaving this section, note that the confidence intervals reported in Excerpts 6.6 through 6.9 were constructed to help interpret a variety of sample statistics: means, percentages, and correlation coefficients. These particular excerpts were specifically selected not only because they illustrate different procedures for reporting confidence intervals but also because they help to underscore the point that confidence intervals can be constructed around *any* sample statistic.

The Construction of Confidence Intervals.   The end points of a confidence interval are not selected by the researcher magically making two values appear out of thin air. Rather, the researcher first makes a decision as to the level of confidence that is desired (usually 95 or 99). Then, the end points are computed by means of a joint process that involves the analysis of sample data (so as to obtain the estimated standard error of the statistic) that is then multiplied by a tabled numerical value.[6]

Although you do not need to know the various formulas used to construct confidence intervals, you should be cognizant of the fact that a scientific approach is taken to the creation of any confidence interval. Moreover, you should be aware of three factors that affect the length of any confidence interval. These factors are the level of confidence selected by the researcher, the degree of homogeneity within the sample, and the size of the sample. If other things are held constant, the distance between the end points of a confidence interval will be smaller to the extent that (1) the researcher selects a lower level of confidence, (2) the sample is homogeneous, and (3) the sample is large. Because short (i.e., narrow) intervals that have a high level of confidence associated with them are more helpful in inferential statistics, researchers typically try to base their confidence intervals on large samples.

It should be noted that the length of a confidence interval is also affected by the nature of the statistic computed on the basis of sample data. For example, confidence intervals built around the mean will be shorter than those constructed for the median. The same situation holds true for Pearson's product-moment correlation coefficient as compared with Spearman's rho. This may explain, in part, why $\bar{X}$s and rs are seen so frequently in the published literature.

The Proper Interpretation of Confidence Intervals.   Confidence intervals are often misinterpreted to designate the probability that population parameters lie somewhere between the intervals' upper and lower limits. For example, many people (including more than a few researchers) would look at the end points of the first

---

[6]For example, if we were to build a 95 percent confidence interval around the mean in Excerpt 6.2 that corresponds to the weight of the 23 male athletes, we would multiply the estimated standard error of 5.93 times 2.07, with the second of these numbers coming from a *t*-table. The product, 16.01, would then be added to and subtracted from the mean of 88.01 to establish the "ends" of our confidence interval.

95 percent confidence interval presented in Excerpt 6.6 and conclude that there is a .95 probability (i.e., a 95 percent chance) that the population parameter, p, lies somewhere between 0.70 and 0.86. Confidence intervals should *not* be interpreted in this fashion.

After a sample has been extracted from a population and then measured, the confidence interval around the sample's statistic either will or will not "cover" the value of the parameter. Hence, the probability that the parameter lies between the end points of a confidence interval is either 0 or 1. Because of this fact, a confidence interval should never be considered to specify the chances (or probability) that the parameter is "caught" by the interval.

The proper way to interpret a confidence interval is to *imagine* that (1) many, many samples of the same size are extracted from the same population and (2) a 95 percent confidence interval is constructed separately around the statistic computed from each sample's data set. Some of these intervals would "capture" the parameter—that is, the interval's end points would be such that the parameter would lie within the interval. On the other hand, some of these confidence intervals would *not* capture the parameter. Looked at collectively, it would turn out that 95 percent of these 95 percent confidence intervals contain the parameter. Accordingly, when you see a 95 percent confidence interval, you should consider that the chances are 95 out of 100 that the interval you are looking at is one of those that does, in fact, capture the parameter. Likewise, when you encounter a 99 percent confidence interval, you can say to yourself that the chances are even higher (99 out of 100) that the interval in front of you is one of the many possible intervals that would have caught the parameter.

The Advantage of Confidence Intervals over Estimated Standard Errors. As I indicated in a previous section, a confidence interval is determined by first computing and then using the value of the estimated standard error. Researchers should be commended for providing either one of these inferential aids to their readers, for it is unfortunately true that most researchers supply their readers with neither standard errors nor confidence intervals for any of the sample statistics that are reported. Nevertheless, confidence intervals carry with them a slight advantage that is worth noting.

When a confidence interval is computed, it will be labeled as to its level of confidence. (As exemplified by Excerpts 6.6 through 6.9, researchers usually build 95 percent confidence intervals.) In contrast, standard error intervals rarely are labeled as to their level of confidence. Given the fact that standard error intervals usually have a confidence level of about 68 percent, they are apt to be misinterpreted and thought to be better than they really are.

Consider, for example, the material presented earlier in Excerpt 6.1. If you use the number that follows the $\pm$ symbol to create the ends of an interval, you end up with an interval for the age variable that extends from 26 to 30. That interval, however, is *not* a 95 percent confidence interval. You could come close to having a 95 percent interval by *doubling* the 2 and then adding 4 to 28 (to get the upper end of your interval) and subtracting 4 (to get the lower end). However, doing this only works accurately when the sample size is quite large.

Point Estimation

When engaged in interval estimation, a researcher will (1) select a level of confidence (e.g., 95 percent), (2) analyze the sample data, (3) extract a number out of a statistical table, and (4) scientifically build an interval that surrounds the sample statistic. After completing these four steps, the researcher makes an educated guess as to the unknown value of the population parameter. In making this guess, the researcher ends up saying, "My data-based interval extends from _____ to _____, and the chances are _____ out of 100 that this interval is one of the many possible intervals (each based on a different sample) that would, in fact, contain the parameter between the interval limits."

A second form of estimation is called **point estimation,** and here again an educated guess is made, on the basis of sample data, as to the unknown value of the population parameter. With this second kind of estimation, however, the activities and thinking of the researcher are much simpler. With point estimation, no level of confidence needs to be selected, no statistical table needs to be consulted, and no interval needs to be created. Instead, the researcher simply computes the statistic on the basis of the sample data and then posits that the unknown value of the population parameter is the same. Thus the researcher who uses this guessing technique ends up saying, "Since the sample-based statistic turned out equal to _____, my best guess is that the value of the parameter is also equal to that particular value."

Point estimation, of course, is likely to produce statements that are incorrect. Because of the great likelihood of sampling error, the value of the statistic will rarely match the value of the parameter. For this reason, interval estimation is generally considered to represent a more logical way of making educated guesses as to parameter values than is point estimation.

Despite the fact that point estimation disregards the notion of sampling error, researchers often can be seen making pinpoint guesses as to parameter values. Consider, for example, the material contained in Excerpts 6.10 and 6.11.

In Excerpt 6.10, we are told directly that stated risk (of 1 in 755) is a point estimate. You will occasionally see statements like this where the term *point estimate* is used. However, you are far more likely to see statements that include a point number, based on sample evidence, *without* the researcher using the term point estimate. An example of this common practice appears in Excerpt 6.11. The three percentages cited in this passage undoubtedly came from one or more studies. However, even if those percentages were based on hundreds or thousands of people (or even hundreds of thousands of people), they still are sample statistics, not population parameters.

EXCERPTS 6.10–6.11 • *Point Estimation*

Overall, the point estimate of the risk of a perinatal death associated with a trial of labor is 1 in 775. . . .

Source: G. C. S. Smith, J. P. Pell, A. D. Cameron, and R. Dobbie. (2002). Risk of perinatal death associated with labor after previous cesarean delivery in uncomplicated term pregnancies. *Journal of the American Medical Association, 287*(20), p. 2690.

- -

One reason many Americans do not visit the ER is fear. Twenty-five percent fear having to get stitches, 55% fear infections, and 20% fear not being able to participate in physical activities for extended periods.

Source: Anonymous. (2002). Summer sports injuries not treated because of fear. *AORN Journal, 76*(1), p. 56.

A place where *many* researchers engage in point estimation is in the discussion of the measuring instruments used to collect data. As was indicated in Chapter 4, these discussions often involve the presentation of reliability and validity coefficients.

Give yourself a pat on the back if you recall, within that discussion, my claim that such coefficients are only estimates. If a different sample of examinees were to provide the data for the assessment of reliability and/or validity, the obtained coefficients most likely would fluctuate. Sampling error would account for such fluctuation.

Although it is possible to build confidence intervals around reliability and validity coefficients, researchers rarely do this. Instead, point estimates are typically provided. This is a common practice, even in cases where the researcher recognizes that the computed reliability and/or validity coefficients are only estimates. Consider, for example, Excerpts 6.12 and 6.13.

In each of these excerpts, notice how the researchers point out that the data used to compute the reliability coefficients came from *samples*. Accordingly, the reliability coefficients presented in these two excerpts are point estimates, not parameters. You need to keep these examples in mind when you come across the reliability and validity evidence researchers will include in their journal articles. Such presentations rarely include a statement to the effect that sample data were used to compute the reliability and validity coefficients, and they typically include misleading statements (such as "the internal consistency of the instrument was determined to be .92" or "the concurrent validity of the measuring device was found to be .86") that give the impression that the numerical values being presented are parameters.

EXCERPTS 6.12–6.13 • *Point Estimates of Reliability*

In this sample, Cronbach's alpha (α) for mother and child report of acceptance was .81 and .87, respectively; α for mother and child report of rejection was .79 and .75, respectively.

Source: S. A. Wolchik, J. Tein, I. N. Sandler, and K. W. Doyle. (2002). Fear of abandonment as a mediator of the relations between divorce stressors and mother-child relationship quality and children's adjustment problems. *Journal of Abnormal Child Psychology, 30*(4), p. 406.

- -

Split-half reliability in our sample was .96.

Source: M. A. Evans, D. Shaw, and M. Bell. (2000). Home literacy activities and their influence on early literacy skills. *Canadian Journal of Experimental Psychology, 54*(20), p. 68.

In Excerpts 6.14 and 6.15 we see two cases in which confidence intervals were built around sample-based reliability coefficients. (In these excerpts, notice how the confidence intervals were built around different kinds of reliability estimates, thus revealing once again the generalizability of confidence intervals.) The researchers who conducted these studies deserve high praise for recognizing that their reliability coefficients were sample statistics, not population parameters.

Although the likelihood of sampling error causes the practice of point estimation to seem quite ill-founded, this form of statistical inference deserves to be

EXCERPTS 6.14–6.15 • *Confidence Intervals Built Around*
Reliability Coefficients

Test-retest reliability was $r = .82$ (95% CI = .66 − .91) for boys and $r = .81$ (95% CI = .67 − .90) for girls.

Source: P. Patterson, J. Bennington, and T. De La Rosa. (2001). Psychometric properties of child- and teacher-reported curl-up scores in children ages 10–12 years. *Research Quarterly for Exercise and Sport, 72*(2), p. 120.

- -

This clinical evaluation was chosen because of its good intrarater reliability ($r = 0.79$ [CI 0.68 − 0.87]). . . .

Source: H. Corriveau, F. Prince, R. Hebert, and M. Raiche. (2000). Evaluation of postural stability in elderly with diabetic neuropathy. *Diabetes Care, 23*(8), p. 1187–1188.

respected for two reasons. These two supportive arguments revolve around (1) the role played by point estimation in interval estimation and (2) the reliance on point estimation by more advanced scientific disciplines (such as physics). Let's consider briefly each of these reasons why it would be unwise to look upon point estimation with complete disrespect.

When engaged in interval estimation, the researcher builds a confidence interval that surrounds the sample statistic. Point estimation is relied on in two ways when such intervals are constructed. First of all, the pinpoint value of the sample statistic is used as the best single estimate of the population parameter. The desired interval is formed by adding a certain amount to the statistic and subtracting a certain amount from the statistic. Hence, the value of the statistic, as a *point estimate* of the parameter, serves as the foundation for each and every confidence interval that is constructed.

Interval estimation draws on point estimation in a second manner. To be more specific, the amount that is added to (and subtracted from) the statistic in order to obtain the interval's upper and lower limits is based on a point estimate of the population's variability. For example, when a confidence interval is constructed around a sample mean, the distance between the end points of the interval is contingent on, among other things, a *point estimate* of the population standard deviation. Likewise, whenever a confidence interval is built around a sample proportion, the length of the interval cannot be specified until the researcher first uses *point estimation* to guess how variable the population is.

From a totally different perspective, the practice of point estimation deserves to be respected. Certain well-respected scientists assert that as a discipline advances and becomes more scientifically rigorous, point estimation is turned to with both increased frequency and greater justification.

Warnings Concerning Interval and Point Estimation

As we wrap up this chapter, I would like to provide four cautionary comments concerning the techniques of estimation. The first three of these warnings concern interval estimation while the fourth is relevant to both kinds of estimation techniques: point and interval. You will be a better consumer of the research literature if you will keep these final points in mind.

First of all, be aware that the second of two numbers separated by a plus-and-minus sign can represent any of three things. In other words, if you see the notation 63 ± 8, be careful before you determine what the 8 signifies. It might be the standard deviation, it might be an estimated standard error, or it might be half the distance to the end points of a confidence interval. Excerpts 2.23, 6.1, and 6.7 illustrate these three possibilities. Researchers will almost always clarify the meaning of such statements within a table or figure, or in the text of the research article. Take the time to look and read before jumping to any conclusions!

A second warning concerns the fact that sample data allow a researcher to *estimate* the standard error of the statistic, not to *determine* that standard error in a definitive manner. Excerpts in this chapter illustrate how researchers sometimes forget to use the word *estimated* prior to the phrase *standard error.* Keep in mind that the researcher will never know for sure, based on the sample data, how large the standard error is; it can only be estimated.

The third warning concerns, once again, confidence intervals. The sample statistic, of course, will always be located between the upper and lower limits of the confidence interval—but it will *not* always be located halfway between the interval's end points. When confidence intervals are built around a sample mean, it is true that $\overline{X}$ will turn out to be positioned at the midpoint of the interval. When confidence intervals are constructed for many other statistics (e.g., r, s, and s^2), however, one "side" of the interval will be longer than the other "side."[7] Whenever a confidence interval is built around a proportion (or percent), the same thing will happen unless the value of the statistic is .50 (i.e., 50 percent).

My final warning applies to both interval estimation and point estimation—and this is by far the most important of our end-of-chapter cautionary comments. Simply stated, the entire process of estimation requires that the data used to form the inference come from a *random* sample. For the techniques of estimation to work properly, therefore, there must be a legitimate connection between the sample and population such that either (1) the former is actually extracted, randomly, from the latter (with no refusals to participate, mortality, or response rate problems); or (2) the population, if hypothetical, is conceptualized so as to match closely the nature of the sample. Without such a link between sample and population, neither form of estimation can be expected to function very well.

Review Terms

Confidence interval
Estimation
Interval estimation
Point estimation

Sampling distribution
Sampling error
Standard error

The Best Items in the Companion Website

1. An interactive online quiz (with immediate feedback provided) covering Chapter 6.
2. Ten misconceptions about the content of Chapter 6.
3. An online resource entitled "Sampling Distributions."
4. An email message about a "dead even" political race sent from the author to his students.
5. Two jokes, one about probability and the other about statisticians screwing in light bulbs.

[7]The degree to which such confidence intervals appear to be lopsided is inversely related to sample size. If *n* is large enough, the statistic will be positioned in the middle of the interval.

Fun Exercises inside Research Navigator

1. **How long do surgical implants for back pain last before replacement is needed?**

   This study focused on 70 individuals with severe and chronic back pain. Each of these individuals had a device called a "spinal cord stimulation" (SCS) surgically implanted. The positive finding of this investigation was the fact that most patients reported lower levels of back pain following the implantation of the SCS device. The negative finding was the frequent need for a follow-up surgery to repair or replace the SCS device. The median time from initial implantation to the first revision surgery was 36 months. Because the 70 patients were considered to be a sample rather than a population, a 95 percent confidence interval was placed around this median. This CI extended from 24 to 60 months. Based on the median value and the end points of the CI, what kind of skewness (positive or negative) do you think the time-to-revision data had? To find out, locate the PDF version of the research report in the Nursing, Health, and Medicine database of ContentSelect and look at Figure 3 on page 100.

   A. D. Kay, M. D. McIntyre, W. A. Macrea, & T. R. K. Varma. Spinal cord stimulation—A long-term evaluation in patients with chronic pain. *British Journal of Neurology.* Located in the NURSING, HEALTH, AND MEDICINE database of ContentSelect.

2. **How often do nurses and nurse assistants fail to record children's growth data?**

   In this study, the researchers looked at a random sample of 149 medical charts of children who had been seen at the Yale-New Haven Hospital Primary Care Center. Each chart was examined for several purposes, one of which was to see if the nurse or nurse practitioner (who first saw the child) followed instructions by recording the child's height, weight, and (for very young children) head circumference. On 31 (21%) of the charts, at least one of these three expected growth measurements was unrecorded. A 95 percent confidence interval extended from 14.5 percent to 27.5 percent. Do you think the three measurements—height, weight, and head circumference—were unrecorded at the same rate, or do you think one of them was the main culprit? To find out, locate the PDF version of the research report in the Communication Sciences and Disorders database of ContentSelect, look at Table 2 (on page 100), and examine the unplotted percentages for the overall sample.

   R. S. Chen & R. N. Shiffman. Assessing growth patterns—Routine but sometimes overlooked. *Clinical Pediatrics.* Located in the COMMUNICATION SCIENCES AND DISORDERS database of ContentSelect.

   Review Questions and Answers begin on page 516.

7

Hypothesis Testing

In Chapter 6, we saw how the inferential techniques of estimation can assist researchers when they use sample data to make educated guesses about the unknown value of population parameters. Now, we turn our attention to a second way in which researchers engage in inferential thinking. This procedure is called **hypothesis testing.**

Before we turn our attention to the half-dozen elements of hypothesis testing, I'd like to reiterate something I said near the beginning of Chapter 5. In order for inferential statistics to begin, the researcher must first answer four preliminary questions: (1) What is/are the relevant population(s)? (2) How will a sample be extracted from the population(s) of interest? (3) What characteristic(s) of the sample people, animals, or objects will serve as the target of the measurement process? (4) What is the study's statistical focus—or stated differently, how will the sample data be summarized so as to obtain a statistic that can be used to make an inferential statement concerning the unknown parameter? In the remaining portions of this chapter, I will assume that these four questions have been both raised and answered by the time the researcher starts to apply the hypothesis testing procedure.

To help you understand the six-step version of hypothesis testing, I first will simply list the various steps in their proper order (that is, the order in which a researcher ought to do things when engaged in this form of statistical inference). After presenting an ordered list of the six steps, I then will discuss the function and logic of each step.

An Ordered List of the Six Steps

Whenever researchers use the six-step version of the hypothesis testing procedure, they will

1. State the null hypothesis.
2. State the alternate hypothesis.

3. Select a level of significance.
4. Collect and summarize the sample data.
5. Refer to a criterion for evaluating the sample evidence.
6. Make a decision to discard/retain the null hypothesis.

It should be noted that there is no version of hypothesis testing that involves fewer than six steps. Stated differently, it is outright impossible to eliminate any of these six ingredients and have enough left to test a statistical hypothesis.

A Detailed Look at Each of the Six Steps

As indicated previously, the list of steps we just presented is arranged in an ordered fashion. In discussing these steps, however, we now will look at these six component parts in a somewhat jumbled order: 1, 6, 2, 4, 5, and then 3. My motivation in doing this is not related to sadistic tendencies! Rather, I am convinced that the function and logic of these six steps can be understood far more readily if we purposely chart an unusual path through the hypothesis testing procedure. Please note, however, that the six steps will now be rearranged only for pedagogical reasons. If I were asked to apply these six steps in an actual study, I would use the ordered list as my guide, not the sequence to which we now turn.

Step 1: The Null Hypothesis

Research
Navigator.c⊛m
Null hypothesis

When engaged in hypothesis testing, a researcher begins by stating a **null hypothesis.** If there is just one population involved in the study, the null hypothesis is a pinpoint statement as to the unknown quantitative value of the parameter in the population of interest. To illustrate what this kind of null hypothesis might look like, suppose that (1) we conduct a study in which our population contains all full-time students enrolled in a particular university, (2) our variable of interest is intelligence, and (3) our statistical focus is the mean IQ score. Given this situation, we could set up a null hypothesis to say that $\mu = 100$. This statement deals with a population *parameter,* it is *pinpoint* in nature, and *we* made it.

The symbol for null hypothesis is H_0, and this symbol is usually followed by (1) a colon, (2) the parameter symbol that indicates the researcher's statistical focus, (3) an equal sign, and (4) the pinpoint numerical value that the researcher has selected. Accordingly, we could specify the null hypothesis for our imaginary study by stating H_0: $\mu = 100$.

If our study's statistical focus involved something other than the mean, we would have to change the parameter's symbol so as to make H_0 consistent with the study's focus. For example, if our imaginary study were to be concerned with the variance among students' heights, the null hypothesis would need to contain the symbol σ^2 rather than the symbol μ. Or, if we were concerned with the product-moment correlation between the students' heights and weights, the symbol ρ would have to appear in H_0.

With respect to the pinpoint numerical value that appears in the null hypothesis, researchers have the freedom to select any value that they wish to test. Thus in our example dealing with the mean IQ of university students, the null hypothesis could be set up to say that $\mu = 80$, $\mu = 118$, $\mu = 101$, or $\mu =$ any specific value of our choosing. Likewise, if our study focused on the variance, we could set up H_0, the null hypothesis, to say that $\sigma^2 = 10$ or that $\sigma^2 =$ any other positive number of our choosing. And in a study having Pearson's product-moment correlation coefficient as its statistical focus, the null hypothesis could be set up to say that $\rho = 0.00$ or that $\rho = -.50$ or that $\rho = +.92$ or that $\rho =$ any specific number between -1.00 and $+1.00$.

The only statistical restrictions on the numerical value that appears in H_0 are that it (1) must lie somewhere on the continuum of possible values that correspond to the parameter and (2) cannot be fixed at the upper or lower limit of that continuum, presuming that the parameter has a lowest and/or highest possible value. These restrictions rule out the following null hypotheses:

$$H_0: \sigma^2 = -15 \qquad H_0: \rho = +1.30$$
$$H_0: \sigma^2 = 0 \qquad H_0: \rho = -1.00$$

because the variance has a lower limit of 0 while Pearson's product-moment correlation coefficient has limits of ± 1.00.

Excerpts 7.1 and 7.2 each contain a null hypothesis. In the first of these excerpts, the null hypothesis deals with the notion of relationship, and hence the statistical focus would be a correlation coefficient. If this null hypothesis had been expressed in symbols rather than in words, it would have taken the form $H_0: \rho = 0$, where ρ would represent the correlation within the population of CPA firms between scores of ethical orientation and scores of ethical organizational culture.

In Excerpt 7.2, the statistical focus of the null hypothesis is the mean. That is made clear by the inclusion of the symbol μ. As you can see, there are two μs in this null hypothesis. This is because there were two populations in this study, users and nonusers of distance education. These two groups were compared with respect to 17 attitudinal variables, but the null hypothesis for each of these 17 comparisons took the form of the null hypothesis shown in Excerpt 7.2. Of course, the meaning of μ would not remain constant within all 17 comparisons, because each time it would coincide with a different attitudinal variable.

Earlier, I indicated that every null hypothesis must contain a pinpoint numerical value. If you are wondering why there is no pinpoint number in Excerpt 7.2, I need to point out that it is there, but hidden. If two things are equal, there is no difference between them, and the notion of no difference is equivalent to saying that a zero difference exists. Accordingly, the null hypothesis shown in Excerpt 7.2 could be rewritten as $H_0: \mu_{users} - \mu_{nonusers} = 0$. We can state this same null hypothesis in

EXCERPTS 7.1–7.2 • *The Null Hypothesis*

As we know of no previous study of ethical culture within CPA firms that would provide the specifics necessary to hypothesize the direction of affect, the second hypothesis is stated in the null form:

H_0: Ethical orientation and organizational ethical culture are not related.

Source: P. C. Douglas, R. A. Davidson, and B. N. Schwartz. (2001). The effect of organizational culture and ethical orientation on accountants' ethical judgements. *Journal of Business Ethics, 34*(2), p. 105.

- -

To further explore attitudinal differences between the two groups, a hypothesis test of the difference between the two group means was performed between users and nonusers for each of the seventeen attitudinal variables. The null hypothesis for each variable was that the mean score answers for the two groups were identical:

$$H_0: \mu_{\text{users}} = \mu_{\text{nonusers}}.$$

Source: R. H. Bee and E. E. Usip. (1998). Differing attitudes of economics students about web-based instruction. *College Student Journal, 32*(2), p. 263.

a different way (so as to see a pinpoint numerical value) by remembering that (1) there is no variability between two means that are equal to each other and (2) the variance is equal to 0 whenever there is no variability among the numbers being considered. Hence, the null hypothesis could be rewritten as $H_0: \sigma_\mu^2 = 0$.

Although researchers have the freedom to select any pinpoint number they wish for H_0, a zero is often selected when two or more populations are being compared. When this is done, the null hypothesis becomes a statement that there is no difference between the populations. Because of the popularity of this kind of null hypothesis, people sometimes begin to think that a null hypothesis *must* be set up as a "no difference" statement. This is both unfortunate and wrong. When two populations are compared, the null hypothesis can be set up with any pinpoint value the researcher wishes to use. (For example, in comparing the mean height of men and women, we could set up a legitimate null hypothesis that stated $H_0: \mu_{\text{men}} - \mu_{\text{women}} = 2$ inches.) When the hypothesis testing procedure is used with a single population, the notion of "no difference," applied to parameters, simply doesn't make sense. How could there be a difference, zero or otherwise, when there is only one μ (or only one ρ, or only one σ^2, etc.)?

In Excerpts 7.3 and 7.4, we see null hypotheses that are more complex. In the first of these excerpts, the null hypothesis includes the symbol for beta, and it says

EXCERPTS 7.3–7.4 • *Two Additional Null Hypotheses*

The authors used as independent variables the four measures hypothesized to have a quantitative effect on the quality of service learning (i.e., duration, location, personal contact, and project focus). The five areas measured by the student attitudinal survey were the dependent variables. Five multiple regression analyses were conducted to test for the hypothesis:

$$H_0: \beta_1 = \beta_2 = \beta_3 = \beta_4 = 0.$$

Source: K. P. Moore and J. H. Sandholtz. (1999). Designing successful service learning projects for urban schools. *Urban Education, 34*(4), p. 486.

- -

The hypothesis being tested is that the population means for the five geographical categories are the same for all three types of service use (hospital days, home health visits, and office visits). The dependent variables are hospital days, home health days, and physician office visits.

Source: K. H. Dansky. (1998). Profile of hospitals, physicians, and home health service use by older persons in rural areas. *The Gerontologist, 38*(3), p. 324.

that the four different βs are not only equal to each other but also equal to zero.[1] This null hypothesis was actually set up five different times, once for each of the five areas measured by the student attitudinal survey.

In Excerpt 7.4, we see that the null hypothesis involved five population means, one for each of the geographical areas. Had this null hypothesis been stated symbolically, it would have taken the form $H_0: \mu_1 = \mu_2 = \mu_3 = \mu_4 = \mu_5$. However, this null hypothesis was set up three different times, once for each of the dependent variables mentioned. Therefore, in the first H_0, each μ would stand for hospital days, in the second H_0, each μ would stand for home health visits, and in the third H_0, each μ would stand for office visits.

Before we leave our discussion of the null hypothesis, it should be noted that H_0 does *not* always represent the researcher's personal belief, or hunch, as to the true state of affairs in the population(s) of interest. In fact, the vast majority of null hypotheses are set up by researchers in such a way as to *disagree* with what they actually believe to be the case. We will return to this point later (when we formally consider the research hypothesis). For now, however, all I want to do is alert you to

---

[1]In a later chapter dealing with regression, the meaning of β will be clarified.

the fact that the H_0 associated with any given study probably is *not* an articulation of the researcher's honest belief concerning the population(s) being studied.

Step 6: The Decision Regarding H_0

At the end of the hypothesis testing procedure, the researcher will do one of two things with H_0. One option is for the researcher to take the position that the null hypothesis is probably false. In this case, the researcher **rejects** H_0. The other option available to the researcher is to refrain from asserting that H_0 is probably false. In this case, a **fail-to-reject** decision is made.

If, at the end of the hypothesis testing procedure, a conclusion is reached that H_0 is probably false, the researcher will communicate this decision by saying one of four things: that H_0 was rejected, that a statistically significant finding was obtained, that a reliable difference was observed, or that p is less than a small decimal value (e.g., $p < .05$). In Excerpts 7.5 through 7.7, we see examples of how researchers will sometimes communicate their decision to disbelieve H_0.

Just as there are different ways for a researcher to tell us that H_0 is considered to be false, there are various mechanisms for expressing the other possible decision

EXCERPTS 7.5–7.7 • *Rejecting the Null Hypothesis*

Therefore, the null hypothesis was rejected.

Source: C. J. Coles, A. F. Greene, and H. O. Braithwaite. (2002). The relationship between personality, anger expression, and perceived family control among incarcerated male juveniles. *Adolescence, 37*(146), p. 400.

- -

Chi-square analysis confirmed a significant difference in activity levels of male versus female, suggesting that among the sample group male subjects had a significantly higher rate of participation in regular exercise than females.

Source: L. Grubbs and J. Carter. (2002). The relationship of perceived benefits and barriers to reported exercise behaviors in college undergraduates. *Family and Community Health, 25*(2), p. 324.

- -

Grade level was correlated with the frequency of family hassles ($r = -.20, p < .05$), with adolescents in higher grades less likely to report family hassles than adolescents in lower grades.

Source: A. Vinokurov, E. J. Trickett, and D. Birman. (2002). Acculturative hassles and immigrant adolescents: A life-domain assessment for Soviet Jewish refugees. *Journal of Social Psychology, 142*(4), p. 436.

concerning the null hypothesis. Instead of saying that a fail-to-reject decision has been reached, the researcher may tell us that H_0 was tenable, that H_0 was accepted, that no reliable differences were observed, that no significant difference was found, that the result was not significant (often abbreviated as *ns* or *NS*), or that *p* is greater than a small decimal value (e.g., *p* > .05). Excerpts 7.8 through 7.11 illustrate these different ways of communicating a fail-to-reject decision.

It is especially important to be able to decipher the language and notation used by researchers to indicate the decision made concerning H_0. This is because most researchers neither articulate their null hypotheses nor clearly state that they used the hypothesis testing procedure. Often, the only way to tell that a researcher has used this kind of inferential technique is by noting what happened to the null hypothesis.

EXCERPTS 7.8–7.11 • *Failing to Reject the Null Hypothesis*

No significant correlations between the fall in PGC and percent reduction in ACR or between changes in mean arterial pressure and ERPF were detected.

Source: C. A. Houlihan, T. J. Allen, A. L. Baxter, and S. Panangiotopoulos. (2002). A low-sodium diet potentiates the effects of losartan in type 2 diabetes. *Diabetes Care, 25*(4), p. 668.

- -

We accepted the null hypothesis. . . .

Source: J. S. Brook, M. Whiteman, S. Finch, and P. Cohen. (2000). Longitudinally foretelling drug use in the late twenties: Adolescent personality and social-environmental antecedents. *Journal of Genetic Psychology, 161*(1), p. 48.

- -

Buyer collectivism, however, is not associated with the buyers' asking for information ($r = -.09$, *ns*).

Source: D. A. Cai, S. R. Wilson, and L. E. Drake. (2000). Culture in the context of intercultural negotiation: Individualism-collectivism and paths to integrative agreements. *Human Communication Research, 24*(4), p. 608.

- -

The data showed no differences between the longhand, $M = 4.9$, and word processor, $M = 4.9$, conditions in terms of content quality. These ratings also failed to vary reliably between narrative ($M = 4.9$), persuasive ($M = 4.8$), and descriptive ($M = 4.9$) texts.

Source: D. A. Cai, S. R. Wilson, and L. E. Drake. (2001). Competition for working memory among writing processes. *The American Journal of Psychology, 114*(2), p. 184.

Step 2: The Alternative Hypothesis

Near the beginning of the hypothesis testing procedure, the researcher must state an **alternative hypothesis.** Referred to as H_a (or as H_1), the alternative hypothesis takes the same form as the null hypothesis. For example, if the null hypothesis deals with the possible value of Pearson's product-moment correlation in a single population (e.g., H_0: $\rho = +.50$), then the alternative hypothesis must also deal with the possible value of Pearson's correlation in a single population. Or, if the null hypothesis deals with the difference between the means of two populations (perhaps indicating that $\mu_1 = \mu_2$), then the alternative hypothesis must also say something about the difference between those populations' means. In general, therefore, H_a and H_0 are identical in that they must (1) deal with the same number of populations, (2) have the same statistical focus, and (3) involve the same variable(s).

The only difference between the null and alternative hypothesis is that the possible value of the population parameter included within H_a will always differ from what is specified in H_0. If the null hypothesis is set up so as to say H_0: $\rho = +.50$, then the alternative hypothesis might be set up to say H_a: $\rho \neq +.50$; or, if a researcher specifies, in Step 1, that H_0: $\mu_1 = \mu_2$, we might find that the alternative hypothesis is set up to say H_a: $\mu_1 \neq \mu_2$.

Excerpt 7.12 contains an alternative hypothesis, labeled H_a, as well as the null hypothesis with which it was paired. Notice that both H_0 and H_a deal with the same population and have the same statistical focus (the mean). If expressed symbolically, these two hypotheses would have looked identical to the H_0 and H_a shown in the final sentence of the previous paragraph. Expressed in that manner, the μs appearing in both H_0 and H_a would be representing admission rates.

As was indicated in the previous section, the hypothesis testing procedure terminates (in Step 6) with a decision to either reject or fail to reject the null hypothesis. In the event that H_0 is rejected, H_a represents the state of affairs that the researcher will consider to be probable. In other words, H_0 and H_a always represent two opposing statements as to the possible value of the parameter in the population(s) of interest. If, in Step 6, H_0 is rejected, then belief shifts *from H_0 to H_a.* Stated differently, if a reject decision is made at the end of the hypothesis testing procedure, the researcher will reject H_0 *in favor of H_a.*

EXCERPT 7.12 • *The Alternative Hypothesis*

H_0 = no difference between the mean reductions in admission rates of the two populations
H_a = the population means are different

Source: R. B. Smith. (2001). Gatekeepers and sentinels: Their consolidated effects on inpatient medical care. *Evaluation Review, 25*(3), p. 293.

Although researchers have flexibility in the way they set up alternative hypotheses, they normally will set up H_a either in a **directional** fashion or in a **nondirectional** fashion.[2] To clarify the distinction between these options for the alternative hypothesis, let's imagine that a researcher conducts a study to compare men and women in terms of intelligence. Further suppose that the statistical focus of this hypothetical study is on the mean, with the null hypothesis asserting that H_0: $\mu_{men} = \mu_{women}$. Now, if the alternative hypothesis is set up in a nondirectional fashion, the researcher will simply state H_a: $\mu_{men} \neq \mu_{women}$. If, on the other hand, the alternative hypothesis is stated in a directional fashion, the researcher will specify a direction in H_a. This could be done by asserting H_a: $\mu_{men} > \mu_{women}$ *or* by asserting H_a: $\mu_{men} < \mu_{women}$.

The directional/nondirectional nature of H_a is highly important within the hypothesis testing procedure. The researcher will need to know whether H_a was set up in a directional or nondirectional manner in order to decide whether to reject (or to fail to reject) the null hypothesis. No decision can be made about H_0 unless the directional/nondirectional character of H_a is clarified.

In most empirical studies, the alternative hypothesis is set up in a nondirectional fashion. Thus if I had to guess what H_a would say in studies containing the null hypotheses presented here on the left, I would bet that the researchers had set up their alternative hypotheses as indicated on the right.

	Corresponding nondirectional H_a
Possible H_0	
H_0: $\mu = 100$	H_a: $\mu \neq 100$
H_0: $\rho = +.20$	H_a: $\rho \neq +.20$
H_0: $\sigma^2 = 4$	H_a: $\sigma^2 \neq 4$
H_0: $\mu_1 - \mu_2 = 0$	H_a: $\mu_1 - \mu_2 \neq 0$

Researchers typically set up H_a in a nondirectional fashion because they do not know whether the pinpoint number in H_0 is too large or too small. By specifying a nondirectional H_a, the researcher permits the data to point one way or the other in the event that H_0 is rejected. Hence, in our hypothetical study comparing men and women in terms of intelligence, a nondirectional alternative hypothesis would allow us to argue that μ_{women} is probably higher than μ_{men} (in the event that we reject the H_0 because $\overline{X}_{women} > \overline{X}_{men}$); or such an alternative hypothesis would allow us to argue that μ_{men} is probably higher than μ_{women} (if we reject H_0 because $\overline{X}_{men} > \overline{X}_{women}$).

---

[2]A directional H_a is occasionally referred to as a *one-sided* H_a; likewise, a nondirectional H_a is sometimes referred to as a *two-sided* H_a.

Occasionally, a researcher will feel so strongly (based on theoretical consideration or previous research) that the true state of affairs falls on one side of H_0's pinpoint number that H_a is set up in a directional fashion. So long as the researcher makes this decision prior to looking at the data, such a decision is fully legitimate. It is, however, totally inappropriate for the researcher to look at the data first and then subsequently decide to set up H_a in a directional manner. Although a decision to reject or fail to reject H_0 could still be made after first examining the data and then articulating a directional H_a, such a sequence of events would sabotage the fundamental logic and practice of hypothesis testing. Simply stated, decisions concerning how to state H_a (and how to state H_0) must be made without peeking at any data.

Research Navigator.c⊛m

One-tailed test
Two-tailed test

When the alternative hypothesis is set up in a nondirectional fashion, researchers sometimes use the phrase **two-tailed test** to describe their specific application of the hypothesis testing procedure. In contrast, directional H_as lead to what researchers sometimes refer to as **one-tailed tests.** Inasmuch as researchers rarely specify the alternative hypothesis in their technical write-ups, the terms *one-tailed* and *two-tailed* help us to know exactly how H_a was set up. For example, consider Excerpts 7.13 and 7.14. Here, we see how researchers sometimes use the term *two-tailed* or *one-tailed* to communicate their decisions to set up H_a in a nondirectional or directional fashion.

EXCERPTS 7.13–7.14 • *Two-Tailed and One-Tailed Tests*

Two-tailed tests of significance were used in all analyses.

Source: C. Barrowclough, G. Haddock, N. Tarrier, and S. W. Lewis. (2001). Randomized controlled trial of motivational interviewing, cognitive behavior therapy, and family intervention for patients with comorbid schizophrenia and substance use disorders. *American Journal of Psychiatry, 158*(10), p. 1709.

- -

A one-tailed test was used to test for significance because of the proposed directional hypothesis.

Source: J. D. Kaufman, C. L. Stamper, and P. E. Tesluk. (2001). Do supportive organizations make for good corporate citizens? *Journal of Managerial Issues, 13*(4), p. 441.

If H_a is set up in a directional manner, the null hypothesis can be expressed as an **inexact H_0.** This type of null hypothesis functions exactly like the kind of H_0 we have been considering, so it really does not matter whether H_0 takes the form of an inexact statement or an exact statement. Nonetheless, I feel it necessary to illustrate what an inexact H_0 looks like so you are not thrown into a tizzy if you ever see one in a research report.

Suppose a researcher wants to compare a sample of high school students against a sample of college students in terms of their vocabulary. Further suppose that our hypothetical researcher can look ahead into the hypothesis testing procedure and knows that the alternative hypothesis in Step 2 will be set up in a directional manner to say H_a: $\mu_{college} > \mu_{high\ school}$. If the researcher knows from the beginning that H_a will be directional, then the null hypothesis (in Step 1) could be set up to say H_0: $\mu_{college} \leq \mu_{high\ school}$. This null hypothesis is inexact because it does not contain a pinpoint numerical value for the population parameter (as would be the case if the null hypothesis were to be set up to say H_0: $\mu_{college} - \mu_{high\ school} = 0$). Instead, this inexact H_0 says that the mean vocabulary among college students is equal to or lower than the mean vocabulary among high school students, with lower being anything from a tiny amount to an enormous difference.

Excerpt 7.15 provides an illustration of an inexact null hypothesis. If this H_0 had been expressed symbolically, it would have taken the form H_0: $\rho \leq 0.00$. It is worth noting that the null hypothesis, when set up to be inexact, does not overlap whatsoever with the alternative hypothesis. This is due to the general requirement that H_0 and H_a be mutually exclusive.

EXCERPT 7.15 • *An Inexact Null Hypothesis (and Its Alternative Hypothesis)*

H_0: The relationship between social performance and financial performance in the commercial banking industry is either zero or negative.
H_a: The relationship between social performance and financial performance in the commercial banking industry is positive.

Source: W. G. Simpson and T. Kohers. (2002). The link between corporate social and financial performance: Evidence from the banking industry. *Journal of Business Ethics, 35*(2), p. 102.

In terms of the ultimate reject or fail-to-reject decision reached by the researcher, it makes absolutely no difference whether the null hypothesis is set up to be exact or inexact. I prefer to articulate any null hypothesis as an exact H_0, for this is consistent with the notion that the null hypothesis is a *point* on a numerical continuum, with the alternative hypothesis represented by either (1) the rest of that continuum, both above and below the null point, if H_a is nondirectional, or (2) the segment of the continuum that lies on just one side of the null point, if H_a is directional. Certain authors have a preference for conceptualizing H_0 in an inexact manner, thereby equating H_0 to one of those two segments. It really doesn't matter which definition of H_0 is used. (If H_a is nondirectional, however, there is no option. In that more common situation, H_0 must be exact.)

Step 4: Collection and Analysis of Sample Data

So far, we have covered Steps 1, 2, and 6 of the hypothesis testing procedure. In the first two steps, the researcher states the null and alternative hypotheses. In Step 6, the researcher will either (1) reject H_0 in favor of H_a or (2) fail to reject H_0. We now turn our attention to the principal stepping-stone that is used to move from the beginning points of the hypothesis testing procedure to the final decision.

Inasmuch as the hypothesis testing procedure is, by its very nature, an empirical strategy, it should come as no surprise that the researcher's ultimate decision to reject or to retain H_0 is based on the collection and analysis of sample data. No crystal ball is used, no Ouija board is relied on, and no eloquent argumentation is permitted. Once H_0 and H_a are fixed, only scientific evidence is allowed to affect the disposition of H_0.

The fundamental logic of the hypothesis testing procedure can now be laid bare because the connections between H_0, the data, and the final decision are as straightforward as what exists between the speed of a car, a traffic light at a busy intersection, and a lawful driver's decision as the car approaches the intersection. Just as the driver's decision to stop or to pass through the intersection is made after observing the color of the traffic light, the researcher's decision to reject or to retain H_0 is made after observing the sample data. To carry this analogy one step further, the researcher will look at the data and ask, "Is the empirical evidence inconsistent with what one would expect if H_0 were true?" If the answer to this question is yes, then the researcher has a green light and will reject H_0. On the other hand, if the data turn out to be consistent with H_0, then the data set serves as a red light telling the researcher not to discard H_0.

Because the logic of hypothesis testing is so important, let us briefly consider a hypothetical example. Suppose a valid intelligence test is given to a random sample of 100 males and a random sample of 100 females attending the same university. If the null hypothesis had first been set up to say H_0: $\mu_{male} = \mu_{female}$ and if the data reveal that the two sample means (of IQ scores) differ by only two points, the sample data would be consistent with what we expect to happen when two samples are selected from populations having identical means. Clearly, the notion of sampling error could fully explain why the two $\overline{X}$s might differ by two IQ points even if $\mu_{male} = \mu_{female}$. In this situation, no empirical grounds exist for making the data-based claim that males at our hypothetical university have a different IQ, on the average, than do their female classmates.

Now, let's consider what would happen if the difference between the two sample means turns out to be equal to 40 (rather than 2) IQ points. If the empirical evidence turns out like this, we would have a situation where the data are inconsistent with what one would expect, if H_0 were to be true. Although the concept of sampling error strongly suggests that neither sample mean will turn out exactly equal to its population parameter, the difference of 40 IQ points between $\overline{X}_{males}$ and $\overline{X}_{females}$ is quite improbable if, in fact, μ_{males} and $\mu_{females}$ are equal. With results such as this, the researcher would reject the arbitrarily selected null hypothesis.

To help drive home the point I am trying to make about the way sample data influence the researcher's decision concerning H_0, let's shift our attention to a real study that had Pearson's correlation as its statistical focus. In Excerpt 7.16, we see a single sentence drawn from a study of daily well-being. Based on undergraduate students' statements contained in a 14-day diary, the researchers computed three scores for each participant: competence, autonomy, and relatedness (i.e., involvement with others). One bivariate correlation was computed between autonomy and competence; a second bivariate correlation was computed between competence and relatedness.

EXCERPT 7.16 • *Rejecting H_0 When the Sample Data Are Inconsistent with H_0*

The autonomy-competence correlation was significant, $r = .30$, $p < .05$, but relatedness and autonomy were not significantly related, $r = .13$, *ns.*

Source: H. T. Reis, K. M. Sheldon, S. L. Gable, J. Roscoe, and R. M. Ryan. (2000). Daily well-being: The role of autonomy, competence, and relatedness. *Personality and Social Psychology Bulletin, 26*(4), pp. 424–425.

In the study from which Excerpt 7.16 was taken, the hypothesis testing procedure was used separately to evaluate each of the two sample rs. In each case, the null hypothesis stated H_0: $\rho = 0.00$. The sample data, once analyzed, yielded correlations of .30 and .13. The first of these rs was found to be so inconsistent with H_0 that sampling error alone was considered to be an inadequate explanation for the observed discrepancy between the pinpoint number in H_0, 0.00, and the data-based r of .30. Accordingly, the null hypotheses connected to the autonomy-competence correlation were rejected, as indicated by the notation $p < .05$. The second sample correlation ($r = .13$), however, did not end up as far away from 0.00. In this instance, sampling error *was* considered to be a plausible explanation for the difference between 0.00 and .13. Accordingly, the null hypothesis concerning the relatedness-autonomy correlation was not rejected, as indicated by the notation *ns.*

In Step 4 of the hypothesis testing procedure, the summary of the sample data will always lead to a single numerical value. Being based on the data, this number is technically referred to as the **calculated value.** (It is also called the **test statistic.**)

Occasionally, the researcher's task in obtaining the calculated value involves nothing more than computing a value that corresponds to the study's statistical focus. This was the case in Excerpt 7.16, where the statistical focus was Pearson's correlation coefficient and where the researcher needed to do nothing more than compute a value for r.

In most applications of the hypothesis testing procedure, the sample data are summarized in such a way that the statistical focus becomes hidden from view. For example, consider Excerpts 7.17 and 7.18 in which we see that the calculated values turned out equal to 5.868 and 2.08.

EXCERPTS 7.17–7.18 • *The Calculated Value*

There was a significant difference in the average rating as a fan of a specific basketball team ($F = 5.868$, $p < .05$). Males ($M = 7.27$) rated themselves more highly as fans of a specific team relative to females ($M = 6.92$), though both groups reported being fans of the respective teams.

Source: J. D. James and L. L. Ridinger. (2002). Female and male sport fans: A comparison of sport consumption motives. *Journal of Sport Behavior, 25*(3), p. 267.

- -

In terms of perspective of instructional planning, a post hoc independent t test revealed that low performers tended to have a change in perspective more than the high performers, ($M = .69$ vs. $M = .45$), $t = 2.08$, $p < .05$.

Source: A. L. Baylor. (2002). Expanding preservice teachers' metacognitive awareness of instructional planning through pedagogical agents. *Educational Technology, Research and Development, 5*(2), p. 17.

In each of these excerpts, two means were compared. Within each study, the researchers put their data into a formula that produced the calculated value. In Excerpt 7.17, an F-test was used to compare the two means, with the calculated value turning out equal to 5.868. In Excerpt 7.18, the researcher chose to compare the two means via a t-test; here, the calculated value turned out equal to 2.08. The important thing to notice about these two excerpts is that in neither case does the calculated value equal the difference between the two means being compared. In later chapters, you will learn about F-tests and t-tests, so you should not worry if you do not currently comprehend everything that is presented in these excerpts. They are shown solely to illustrate the typical situation in which the statistical focus of a study is *not* reflected directly in the calculated value.

Before computers were invented, researchers would always have a single goal in mind when they turned to Step 4 of the hypothesis testing procedure. That goal was the computation of the data-based calculated value. Now that computers are widely available, researchers still are interested in the magnitude of the calculated value derived from the data analysis. Contemporary researchers, however, are also interested in a second piece of information generated by the computer. This second item is the data-based *p*-value.

Whenever researchers use a computer to perform the data analysis, they will either (1) tell the computer what the null hypothesis is going to be or (2) accept the computer's built-in default version of H_0. The researcher will also specify whether H_a is directional or nondirectional in nature. Once the computer knows what the researcher's H_0 and H_a are, it can easily analyze the sample data and compute the probability of having a data set that deviates as much or more from H_0 as does the data set being analyzed. The computer informs the researcher as to this probability by means of a statement that takes the form $p =$ _____, with the blank being filled by a single decimal value somewhere between 0 and 1.

Excerpts 7.19 and 7.20 illustrate nicely how a *p*-value is like a calculated value in that either one can be used as a single-number summary of the sample data. In each of these excerpts, two groups were compared in terms of the percentage of group members who did what they were supposed to do. In each study, the researchers used a *p*-value to assess the likelihood, under the null hypothesis, of getting two percentages that differed as much or more than the two percentages actually observed. With the null hypothesis being that the two groups were equivalent in terms of compliance, each *p* functioned as a measure of how inconsistent the sample data were with the null hypothesis.

EXCERPTS 7.19–7.20 • *Using p as the Calculated Value*

Compliance with the recommended duration of hand hygiene was poor in both protocols but was significantly better in the hand-rubbing group than in the hand-scrubbing group (44% vs. 28%, respectively; $p = .008$).

Source: J. J. Parienti, P. Thibon, R. Heller, and Y. Le Roux. (2002). Hand-rubbing with an aqueous alcoholic solution vs traditional surgical hand-scrubbing and 30-day surgical site infection rates: A randomized equivalence study. *Journal of the American Medical Association, 288*(6), p. 725.

93 (96%) patients in the azithromycin group and 87 (95%) in the vitamin C group reported taking at least five of the six study drug capsules ($p = 0.70$).

Source: A. T. Evans, S. Husain, L. Durairaj, and L. S. Sadowski. (2002). Azithromycin for acute bronchitis: A randomised, double-blind controlled trial. *The Lancet, 359*(9318), p. 1651.

Be sure to note that there is an *inverse* relationship between the size of *p* and the degree to which the sample data deviate from the null hypothesis. In Excerpt 7.19, if the two percentages had been closer together, the *p*-value would have been *larger* than .008. In Excerpt 7.20, if the two percentages had been further apart, the *p*-value would have been *smaller* than .70.

Step 5: The Criterion for Evaluating the Sample Evidence

After the researcher has summarized the study's data, the next task involves asking the question "Are the sample data inconsistent with what would likely occur if the null hypothesis were true?" If the answer to this question is "yes," then H_0 will be rejected; on the other hand, a negative response to this query will bring forth a fail-to-reject decision. Thus as soon as the sample data can be tagged as consistent or inconsistent (with H_0), the decision in Step 6 is easily made. "But how," you might ask, "does the researcher decide which of these labels should be attached to the sample data?"

If the data from the sample(s) are in perfect agreement with the pinpoint numerical value specified in H_0, then it is obvious that the sample data are consistent with H_0. (This would be the case if the sample mean turned out equal to 100 when testing H_0: $\mu = 100$, if the sample correlation coefficient turned out equal to 0.00 when testing H_0: $\rho = 0.00$, etc.) Such a situation, however, is unlikely. Almost always, there will be a discrepancy between H_0's parameter value and the corresponding sample statistic.

In light of the fact that the sample statistic (produced by Step 4) is almost certain to be different from H_0's pinpoint number (specified in Step 1), the concern over whether the sample data are inconsistent with H_0 actually boils down to the question "Should the observed difference between the sample evidence and the null hypothesis be considered to be a big difference or a small difference?" If this difference (between the data and H_0) is judged to be large, then the sample data will be looked on as being inconsistent with H_0 and, as a consequence, H_0 will be rejected. If, on the other hand, this difference is judged to be small, the data and H_0 will be looked on as consistent with each other and, therefore, H_0 will not be rejected.

To answer the question about the sample data's being either consistent or inconsistent with what one would expect if H_0 were true, a researcher can use either of two simple procedures. As you will see, both of these procedures involve comparing a single-number summary of the sample evidence against a criterion number. The single-number summary of the data can be either the calculated value or the *p*-value. Our job now is to consider what each of these data-based indices is compared against and what kind of result forces researchers to consider their samples as representing a large or a small deviation from H_0.

One available procedure for evaluating the sample data involves comparing the calculated value against something called the **critical value.** The critical value is nothing more than a number extracted from one of many statistical tables developed by mathematical statisticians. Applied researchers, of course, do not close their eyes and point to just any entry in a randomly selected table of critical values. Instead, they must learn which table of critical values is appropriate for their studies and also how to locate the single number within the table that constitutes the correct critical value.

As a reader of research reports, you do not have to learn how to locate the proper table that contains the critical value for any given statistical test, nor do you have to locate, within the table, the single number that allows the sample data to be labeled as being consistent or inconsistent with H_0. The researcher will do these things. Occasionally, the critical value will be included in the research report, as exemplified in Excerpts 7.21 through 7.23.

EXCERPTS 7.21–7.23 • *The Critical Value and the Decision Rule*

When conducting a one-tailed test using a sample as large as the one here, *t* values exceeding 1.645 are statistically significant.

Source: J. A. Johnson and P. M. Roman. (2002). Predicting closure of private substance abuse treatment facilities. *Journal of Behavioral Health Services and Research, 29*(2), p. 120.

The test of the null hypothesis is based on a comparison of the calculated *F* value with the critical *F* value [and] in this case, the calculated *F* value = 586.80 which is higher than the critical value of 6.63. Therefore, we reject the null. . . .

Source: Q. Shen. (2000). Spatial and social dimensions of commuting. *Journal of the American Planning Association, 66*(1), pp. 80–81.

The minimum *Z*-score necessary to reject the null hypothesis is 2.32.

Source: C. P. Fulford and G. Sakaguchi. (2002). Validating a taxonomy of interaction strategies for two-way interactive distance education television. *International Journal of Instructional Media, 29*(1), p. 83.

Once the critical value is located, the researcher will compare the data-based summary of the sample data against the scientific dividing line that has been extracted from a statistical table. The simple question being asked at this point is whether the calculated value is larger or smaller than the critical value. With most tests (such as *t, F,* chi-square, and tests of correlation coefficients), the researcher will follow a decision rule that says to reject H_0 if the calculated value is at least as large as the critical value. With a few tests (such as *U* or *W*), the decision rule tells the researcher to reject H_0 if the calculated value is smaller than the critical value. You do not need to worry about which way the decision rule works for any given test because this is the responsibility of the individual who performs the data analysis. The only things you need to know about the comparison of calculated and critical values are (1) that this comparison allows the researcher to decide easily whether to reject or fail to reject H_0 and (2) that some tests use a decision rule that says to reject H_0 if the calculated value is larger than the critical value, whereas other tests involve a decision rule that says to reject H_0 if the calculated value is smaller than the critical value.

The researchers associated with Excerpts 7.21, 7.22, and 7.23 helped the readers of their research reports by specifying not only the critical value but also the nature of the decision rule that was used when the calculated value was compared against the critical value. In most research reports, you will not see either of these things; instead, you will only be given the calculated value. (On rare occasions, you won't even see the calculated value.) As indicated previously, however, you should not be concerned about this because it is the researcher's responsibility to obtain the critical value and to know which way the decision rule operates. When reading most research reports, all you can do is trust that the researcher did these two things properly.

Research
Navigator.c⊕m

Level of
significance

The second way a researcher can evaluate the sample evidence is to compare the data-based *p*-value against a preset point on the 0-to-1 scale on which the *p* must fall. This criterion is called the **level of significance,** and it functions much as does the critical value in the first procedure for evaluating sample evidence. Simply stated, the researcher compares his or her data-based *p*-value against the criterion point along the 0-to-1 continuum so as to decide whether the sample evidence ought to be considered consistent or inconsistent with H_0. The decision rule used in this second procedure is always the same: If the data-based *p*-value is equal to or smaller than the criterion, the sample is viewed as being *in*consistent with H_0; if, on the other hand, *p* is larger than the criterion, the data are looked on as being consistent with H_0.

I will discuss the level of significance in more depth in the next section, since it is a concept that must be dealt with by the researcher no matter which of the two procedures is used to evaluate the sample data. (With the second procedure, the level of significance *is* the criterion against which the data-based *p*-value is compared; with the first procedure, the level of significance influences the size of the critical value against which the calculated value is compared.) Before we leave this section, however, I need to point out that the same decision will be reached regarding H_0 no matter which of the two procedures is used in Step 5 of the hypothesis testing procedure. For example, suppose a researcher conducts an *F*-test and rejects H_0 because the calculated value is larger than the critical value. If that researcher were to compare the data-based *p* against the level of significance, it would be found that the former is smaller than the latter, and the same decision about H_0 would be made. Or, suppose a researcher conducts a *t*-test and fails to reject H_0 because the calculated value is smaller than the critical value. If that researcher were to compare the data-based p against the level of significance, it would be found that the former is larger than the latter, and the same fail-to-reject decision would be made.

Step 3: Selecting a Level of Significance

After the data of a study are collected and summarized, the six-step hypothesis testing procedure allows absolutely no subjectivity to influence, or bias, the ultimate decision that is made concerning the null hypothesis. This goal is accomplished by reliance on a scientific cutoff point to determine whether the sample data are consistent or inconsistent with H_0. By referring (in Step 5) to a numerical criterion, it becomes clear whether or not sampling error provides, by itself, a sufficient explanation for the observed difference between the single-number summary of the researcher's data (computed in Step 4) and H_0's pinpoint numerical value (articulated in Step 1). If the single-number summary of the data is found to lie on H_a's side of the criterion number (or if the data-based p lands on H_a's side of the level of significance), a decision (in Step 6) is made to reject H_0 in favor of H_a (set forth in Step 2); on the other hand, if the calculated value lands on H_0's side of the critical value (or if the data-based p lands on H_0's side of the level of significance), a fail-to-reject decision is made.

Either the critical value or the level of significance serves as a scientific cutoff point that determines what decision will be made concerning the null hypothesis. The six-step hypothesis testing procedure not only allows the researcher to do something that affects the magnitude of this criterion—*it actually forces the researcher to become involved in determining how rigorous the criterion will be.* The researcher should not, as I have pointed out, do anything like this after the data have been collected and summarized. However, the researcher *must* do something prior to collecting data that has an impact on how large or small the criterion number will be.

After the null and alternative hypotheses have been set up, but before any data are collected, the researcher must select a level of significance. This third step of the hypothesis testing procedure simply asks the researcher to select a positive decimal value of the researcher's choosing. Although the researcher has the freedom to select any value between 0 and 1 for the level of significance, most researchers select a small number such as .10, .05, or .01. The most frequently selected number is .05.

Before explaining how the researcher-selected level of significance influences the size of the critical value, I need to alert you to the fact that not all researchers use the phrase *level of significance* to designate the decimal number that must be specified in Step 3. Instead of indicating, for example, that the level of significance is set equal to .05, some researchers will state that "the **alpha level** (α) is set equal to .05," others will assert that "$p = .05$," and still others will indicate that "H_0 will be rejected if $p < .05$." Likewise, a decision to use the .01 level of significance might be expressed using statements such as "alpha = .01," "$\alpha = .01$," or "results will be considered significant if $p < .01$."

In Excerpts 7.24 through 7.28, we see different ways in which researchers report what level of significance was selected within their studies.

EXCERPTS 7.24–7.28 • *The Level of Significance*

A significance level of 0.05 was used.

Source: Y. Ropert-Caudert, A. Kato, R. P. Wilson, and M. Kurita. (2002). Women's perception of physicians' influence of weight gain during pregnancy. *Journal of Family and Consumer Sciences, 94*(2), p. 19.

A two-tailed alpha level of .05 was fixed for testing these coefficients.

Source: V. Lee and H. Wagner. (2002). The effect of social presence on the facial and verbal expression of emotion and the interrelationships among emotion components. *Journal of Nonverbal Behavior, 26*(1), p. 15.

Statistical significance was defined at the two tailed $p = 0.05$ level.

Source: I. A. Bernstein, O. Webber, and R. Woledge. (2002). An ergonomic comparison of rowing machine designs: Possible implications for safety. *British Journal of Sports Medicine, 36*(2), p. 109.

All tests were 2-sided and were considered significant at $\alpha = .05$.

Source: M. D. Klinnert, M. R. Price, A. H. Liu, and J. L. Robinson. (2002). Unraveling the ecology of risks for early childhood asthma among ethnically diverse families in the Southwest. *American Journal of Public Health, 92*(5), p. 793.

For all tests, the statistical threshold was 0.05.

Source: Y. Ropert-Caudert, A. Kato, R. P. Wilson, and M. Kurita. (2002). Short underwater opening of the beak following immersion in seven penguin species. *The Condor, 104*(2), p. 445.

If the single-number summary of the sample data is a *p*-value, the pragmatic value of the level of significance is clear. In this situation, *p* is compared directly against α to determine whether or not H_0 should be rejected. But even if the single-number summary of the sample data is a calculated value, the level of significance still performs a valuable, pragmatic function. This is because a critical value cannot be located (in Step 5) unless the level of significance has first been set. As indicated in our earlier discussion of Step 4, there are many tables of critical values. Once the proper table is located, the researcher still has the task of locating the single number within the table that will serve as the critical value. The task of locating the critical value is easy, so long as the level of significance has been specified.[3]

Although the level of significance plays an important pragmatic role within the six-step hypothesis testing procedure, the decimal number selected in Step 3 is even more important from a different perspective. When I introduced the concept of the null hypothesis and when I talked about the reject or fail-to-reject decision that researchers will make regarding the null hypothesis, I was careful to use language that did *not* suggest that H_0 is ever *proven* to be true or false by means of hypothesis testing. Regardless of the decision made about H_0 after the calculated and critical values (or p and α) are compared, it is possible that the wrong decision will be reached. If H_0 is rejected in Step 6, it is conceivable that this action represents a mistake, since H_0 may actually be true. Or, if H_0 is not rejected, it is conceivable that *this* action represents a mistake, since H_0 may actually be an inaccurate statement about the value of the parameter in the population(s).

In light of the fact that a mistake can conceivably occur regardless of what decision is made at the end of the hypothesis testing procedure, two technical terms have been coined to distinguish between these potentially wrong decisions. A **Type I error** designates the mistake of rejecting H_0 when the null hypothesis is actually true. A **Type II error,** on the other hand, designates the kind of mistake that is made if H_0 is not rejected when the null hypothesis is actually false. The following chart may help to clarify the meaning of these possible errors.

		Is H_0 Really True?	
		Yes	**No**
	Reject H_0	Type I Error	Correct Decision
Researcher's Decision			
	Fail-to-Reject H_0	Correct Decision	Type II Error

Beyond its pragmatic utility in helping the researcher locate the critical value (or in serving as the criterion against which the data-based p is compared), the level of significance is important because it establishes the probability of a Type I error. In other words, the selected alpha level determines the likelihood that a true null hypothesis will be rejected. If the researcher specifies, in Step 3, that $\alpha = .05$, then the

---

[3]With certain tests, researchers cannot locate the critical value unless they also know (1) whether their test is one- or two-tailed in nature and (2) how many degrees of freedom are connected with the sample data. I will discuss the concept of degrees of freedom in later chapters.

chances of rejecting a true null hypothesis become equal to 5 out of 100. If, on the other hand, the alpha level is set equal to .01 (rather than .05), then the chances of rejecting a true null hypothesis would become equal to 1 out of 100. The alpha level, therefore, directly determines the probability that a Type I error will be committed.[4]

After realizing that the researcher can fully control the likelihood of a Type I error, you may be wondering why the researcher does not select an alpha level that would dramatically reduce the possibility that a true H_0 will be rejected. To be more specific, you may be inclined to ask why the alpha level is not set equal to .001 (where the chance of a Type I error becomes equal to 1 out of 1,000), equal to .00001 (where the chance of Type I error becomes equal to 1 out of 100,000), or even equal to some smaller decimal value. To answer this legitimate question, we must consider the way in which a change in the alpha level has an effect on both Type I error risk *and* Type II error risk.

If the alpha level is changed, it's as if there is an apothecary scale in which the two pans hanging from opposite ends of the balance beam contain, respectively, Type I error risk and Type II error risk. The alpha level of a study could be changed so as to decrease the likelihood of a Type I error, but this change in alpha will simultaneously have an opposite effect on the likelihood of a Type II error. Hence, researchers rarely move alpha from the more traditional levels of .05 or .01 to levels that would greatly protect against Type I errors (such as .0001) because such a change in the alpha level would serve to make the chances of a Type II error unacceptably high.

In Excerpts 7.29, 7.30, and 7.31, we see three cases where a connection is drawn between the selected level of significance and the likelihood of a Type I error and/or a Type II error. The second and third group of researchers deserve your respect for having explained why they chose the levels of significance they did. Far too many researchers, without thinking, set alpha equal to .05 simply because this is the most popular level of significance. If they weighed the risks of Type I and Type II errors in their own studies, they might choose some level of significance other than .05.

Near the beginning of this chapter, I pointed out that H_0 is normally set up so as to disagree with the researcher's personal hunch regarding the population parameter(s) focused on in the study. For example, if a researcher thinks that a new pill will reduce the mean stress level among students preparing to take their final examinations, a study might be set up involving an experimental group and a placebo group. Within this study, the researcher's null hypothesis would probably be set up to say that the pill has no effect on stress (i.e., H_0: $\mu_{experimental} = \mu_{placebo}$).

In light of the fact that researchers typically like to reject H_0 to gain empirical support for their honest hunches, and in light of the fact that a change in the level

---

[4]As you will see later, the alpha level defines the probability of a Type I error only if (1) important assumptions underlying the statistical test are valid and (2) the hypothesis testing procedure is used to evaluate only *one* null hypothesis.

EXCERPTS 7.29–7.31 • *The Alpha Level and the Risk of Type I and II Errors*

The probability of Type I error (alpha) was set at .05 in all statistical analyses.

Source: M. Hojat, R. Shapurian, D. Foroughi, and H. Nayerahmadi. (2000). Gender differences in traditional attitudes toward marriage and the family. *Journal of Family Issues, 21*(4), p. 428.

We [used] a strategy that reduces Type II statistical errors at the expense of making an increased number of Type I statistical errors. . . . The strategy was implemented by conducting unpaired *t* tests (alpha = $P \leq 0.2$).

Source: H. Shi, K. E. Vigneau-Callahan, A. I. Shestopalov, and P. E. Milbury. (2002). Characterization of diet-dependent metabolic serotypes: Proof of principle in female and male rats. *Journal of Nutrition, 132*(2), p. 1032.

Continuous baseline variables were compared by analysis of variance and considered significant if different at the $p < 0.15$ level; a liberal significance level was employed to minimize type II error.

Source: P. J. McGrath, J. W. Stewart, M. N. Janal, and E. Petkova. (2000). A placebo-controlled study of fluoxetine versus imipramine in the acute treatment of atypical depression. *American Journal of Psychiatry, 157*(3), p. 346.

of significance has an impact on the likelihood of Type II errors, you now may be wondering why the researcher does not move alpha in the opposite direction. It is true that a researcher would decrease the chance of a Type II error by changing alpha—for example, from .05 to .40—since such a change would make it more likely that H_0 would be rejected. Researchers do not use such high levels of significance simply because the scientific community generally considers Type I errors to be more dangerous than Type II errors. In most disciplines, few people would pay attention to researchers who reject null hypotheses at alpha levels higher than .20, because such levels of significance are considered to be too lenient (i.e., too likely to yield reject decisions that are Type I errors).

The most frequently seen level of significance, as illustrated earlier in Excerpts 7.24 through 7.28, is .05. This alpha level is considered to represent a happy medium between the two error possibilities associated with any application of the six-step hypothesis testing procedure. If, however, a researcher feels that it is more important to guard against the possibility of a Type I error, a lower alpha level (such as .01 or .001) will be selected. On the other hand, if it is felt that a Type II error would be more dangerous than a Type I error, then a higher alpha level (such as .10

or .15) will be selected. Excerpts 7.32 and 7.33 illustrate such situations. In Excerpt 7.32, the researchers wanted to guard against making a Type II error. In Excerpt 7.33 it was a Type I error that the researchers were most worried about.

EXCERPTS 7.32–7.33 • *Reasons for Using Alpha Levels Other Than .05*

Given that weak to moderate relationships could be expected due to the large amount of variation that typically exists in heterogeneous cross-sectional data, we accepted $P \leq .10$ as an indication of statistical significance.

Source: O. Clapps, L. Cleveland, and J. Park. (2002). Dietary behaviors associated with total fat and saturated fat intake. *Journal of the American Dietetic Association, 102*(4), p. 494.

- -

Because of the relatively small number of respondents, it was decided to accept a probability level of $p < .01$ as significant for this study.

Source: J. Kear-Colwell and G. A. Sawle. (2001). Coping strategies and attachment in pedophiles: Implications for treatment. *International Journal of Offender Therapy and Comparative Criminology, 45*(2), p. 175.

Before concluding our discussion of the level of significance, I need to clarify two points of potential confusion. To accomplish this goal, I want to raise and then answer two questions: "Does the alpha level somehow determine the likelihood of a Type II error?" and "If H_0 is rejected, does the alpha level indicate the probability that H_0 is true?"

The first point of potential confusion concerns the relationship between alpha and Type II error risk. Since alpha does, in fact, determine the likelihood that the researcher will end up rejecting a true H_0, and since it is true that a change in alpha affects the chance of a Type I error *and* the chance of a Type II error (with one increasing, the other decreasing), you may be tempted to expect the level of significance to dictate Type II error risk. Unfortunately, this is not the case. The alpha level specified in Step 3 does influence Type II error risk, but so do other features of a study such as sample size, population variability, and the reliability of the measuring instrument used to collect data.

The second point of potential confusion about the alpha level again concerns the decision reached at the end of the hypothesis testing procedure. If a study's H_0 is rejected in Step 6, it is *not* proper to look back to see what alpha level was specified in Step 3 and then interpret that alpha level as indicating the probability that H_0 is true. For example, if a researcher ends up rejecting H_0 after having set the level of significance equal to .05, you cannot legitimately conclude that the chances of H_0 being true are less than 5 out of 100. The alpha level in any study indicates only what the chances are that the forthcoming decision will be a Type I error. If alpha is set equal to .05, then the chances are 5 out of 100 that H_0 will be rejected *if H_0 is actually true.* Statisticians sometimes try to clarify this distinction by pointing out that the level of significance specifies "the probability of a reject decision, given a true H_0" and *not* "the probability of H_0 being true, given a reject decision."

Results That Are Highly Significant and Near Misses

As indicated earlier, the level of significance plays a highly important role in hypothesis testing. In a very real sense, it functions as a dividing line. Statistical significance is positioned on one side of that line, the lack of statistical significance on the other. That dividing line is clearly visible if the researcher decides to reject or fail-to-reject H_0 by comparing the data-based p against the level of significance. But even when the procedure for deciding H_0's fate involves comparing the data-based calculated value against a tabled critical value, the level of significance is still involved. That's because α influences the size of the critical value.

Because the level of significance plays such an important role—both pragmatically and conceptually—in hypothesis testing, it often is included when the decision about H_0 is declared. With the level of significance set at .05 (the most popular α-level), a decision to reject H_0 is often summarized by the notation $p <$ .05, while a decision not to reject H_0 is summarized by the notation $p >$ .05. Earlier, you saw such notational summaries in Excerpts 7.7, 7.16, 7.17, and 7.18.

Many researchers do not like to summarize their results by reporting simply that the null hypothesis either was or was not rejected. Instead, they want their readers to know how much of a discrepancy existed between the data-based p and the level of significance (or between the data-based critical value and the critical value). In doing this, the researcher's goal is to provide evidence as to how strongly the data challenge H_0. In other words, these researchers want you to know if they beat the level of significance by a wide margin (presuming that H_0 was rejected) or if they just missed beating α (presuming that H_0 was retained).

Consider Excerpts 7.34 and 7.35. In the first of these excerpts, the researchers report that their data-based p turned out to be smaller than .0000001. Their motivation for giving us this information, I think, was to show that they beat the .05 level of significance "by a mile." In Excerpt 7.35, the researcher did two things: (1) she used the phrase **highly significant,** and (2) she pointed out that her data-based p was not just small enough to beat the .05 criterion, but rather so very small that her sample data would have been significant if alpha had been set equal to .001.

As exemplified by Excerpt 7.35, research reports contain statements indicating that the researchers' data-based p turned out smaller than some small number other than .05. You regularly will see $p < .01$, you will come across $p < .001$ quite often,

Research Navigator.com

Highly significant

EXCERPTS 7.34–7.35 • *Rejecting the Null Hypothesis with Room to Spare*

For the entire group, the correlation was $r = 0.86$, $p < 0.0000001$.

Source: M. L. Shuer, A. L. Hoff, W. S. Kremen, and M. H. Wieneke. (2002). Neuropsychiatric testing and the menstrual cycle/Dr. Hoff and colleagues reply. *American Journal of Psychiatry, 159*(4), p. 680.

- -

Highly significant differences ($P < .001$) between White and non-White women enrolled during the new campaign were found in 2 categories. . . .

Source: J. L. Rogers. (2002). Effectiveness of media strategies to increase enrollment and diversity in the women's health registry. *American Journal of Public Health, 92*(4), p. 613.

and you will see $p < .0001$ every now and then. Such statements do *not* indicate that the researcher initially set the level of significance equal to .01, .001, or .0001!

Many researchers use an approach to hypothesis testing that involves reporting the most impressive *p*-statement that honestly describes their data. They first check to see they have statistical significance at the .05 level. If they do, then they know they at least can say $p < .05$. They next check to see if the sample data would have been significant at the .01 level, had this been the selected alpha level. If the answer is yes, they then check again, this time to see if the data are significant at the .001 level. This process continues until either (1) the data cannot beat a more rigorous level of significance or (2) the researcher does not want to check further to see if p might beat an even more impressive α. It is clear that this approach to hypothesis testing was used in Excerpt 7.36.

Researchers often test more than one null hypothesis in the same study. In the research reports for these investigations, it is usually the case that certain results are

EXCERPT 7.36 • *Reporting p $<.0001$ in Conjunction with a .05 Alpha Level*

Planned comparisons were performed with an alpha of .05, and showed that verbal expression of negative emotion was greater in negative than in positive talks, $t(53) = 11.52$, $p < .0001$.

Source: V. Lee and H. Wagner. (2002). The effect of social presence on the facial and verbal expression of emotion and the interrelationships among emotion components. *Journal of Nonverbal Behavior, 26*(1), pp. 12–13.

summarized via the statement $p < .05$, other results are summarized via the statement $p < .01$, and still other results are summarized via the statement $p < .001$. (Recently, I read a research report in which four different p-statements—$p < .05$, $p < .01$, $p < .005$, and $p < .001$—were connected to the results presented in a single table!) In any one of these studies, it is highly unlikely that the researcher decided at the outset to use different alpha levels with the different null hypotheses being tested. Rather, it's far more probable that all H_0s were initially tested with α set equal to .05, with the researcher then revising α (as indicated in the previous paragraph) so that more impressive p-statements could be presented.

Now, let us shift gears and consider what happens if the data-based p is larger than the initially specified level of significance. If p is much larger than α, the situation is clear: the null hypothesis cannot be rejected. At times, however, p turns out to be just slightly larger than α. For example, p might turn out equal to .07 when α is set at .05. Many researchers consider this to be a near miss, and they will communicate this observation via certain commonly seen phrases. When p fails to beat α by a small amount, researchers often say that they achieved **marginal significance,** that their findings **approached significance,** that there was a **trend toward significance,** or that the results indicate **borderline significance.** In Excerpts 7.37 and 7.38, we see two examples of this.

It should be noted that some researchers use an approach to hypothesis testing that has two clear rules: (1) choose the level of significance at the beginning of the study and then never change it, and (2) consider any result, summarized by p, to lie on one side or the other side of α, with it making no difference whatsoever whether p is a smidgen or a mile away from α. According to this school of thought, the *only* thing that matters is whether p is larger or smaller than the level of significance.

EXCERPTS 7.37–7.38 • *Just Barely Failing to Reject the Null Hypothesis*

The interaction of the two experimental factors attained marginal significance ($F(1, 134) = 3.58, p < .07$).

Source: J. Sengupta and G. V. Johar. (2002). Effects of inconsistent attribute information on the predictive value of product attitudes: Toward a resolution of opposing perspectives. *Journal of Consumer Research, 29*(2), p. 46.

- -

The performance difference between semantically misleading and semantically neutral relative sentences was only of borderline significance ($p = .06$).

Source: M. L. Morrisette and J. A. Gierut. (2002). Syntactic and semantic processing in Hebrew readers with prelingual deafness. *American Annals of the Deaf, 145*(5), p. 444.

Consider, for example, Excerpts 7.39 and 7.40. The data-based ps in this study turned out equal to .052 and .048, respectively. Even though each p was extremely close to the common α level used in both studies, .05, notice that the result in the first study was declared not significant whereas the result in the second study was referred to as being significant.

EXCERPTS 7.39–7.40 • *An All-or-Nothing Approach to Hypothesis Testing*

Slightly over 37% of the athletes reported smoking marijuana in the last year as opposed to about 43% of the nonathletes. This is similar to the pattern for cigarette smoking, although the difference between athletes and nonathletes for marijuana was not significant ($p = .052$).

Source: A. H. Naylor, D. Gardner, and L. Zaichkowsky. (2001). Drug use patterns among high school athletes and nonathletes. *Adolescence, 36*(144), p. 634.

There was a significant main group effect on mean visual response latency, $F(2, 35)$ = 3.32, $p = .048$.

Source: M. Gang and L. S. Siegel. (2002). Sound-symbol learning in children with dyslexia. *Journal of Learning Disabilities, 35*(2), p. 144.

A Few Cautions

Now that you have considered the six-step hypothesis testing procedure from the standpoint of its various elements and its underlying rationale, you may be tempted to think that it will be easy to decipher and critique any research report in your field that has employed this particular approach to inferential statistics. I hope, of course, that this chapter has helped you become more confident about making sense out of statements such as these: "A two-tailed test was used," "A rigorous alpha level was employed to protect against the possibility of a Type I error," and "The results were significant ($p < .01$)." Before I conclude this chapter, however, it is important that I alert you to a few places where misinterpretations can easily be made by the consumers of research literature (and by researchers themselves).

Alpha

The word *alpha* (or its symbol α) refers to two different concepts. Within the hypothesis testing procedure, alpha designates the level of significance selected by the researcher. In discussions of measuring instruments, alpha means something entirely different. In this context, alpha refers to the estimated internal consistency of the questionnaire, inventory, or test being discussed. Note that alpha must be a *small* decimal number in hypothesis testing in order to accomplish the task of protecting against Type I errors. In contrast, alpha must be a *large* decimal number in order to document high reliability.

The Importance of H_0

Earlier in this chapter, I presented excerpts from various journal articles wherein the null hypothesis was clearly specified. Unfortunately, most researchers do not take the time or space to indicate publicly the precise nature of H_0. They don't do this because they presume that their readers will understand what the null hypothesis was in light of the number of samples involved in the study, the nature of the measurements collected, and the kind of statistical test used to analyze the data.

Right now, you may feel that you will never be able to discern H_0 unless it is specifically articulated. However, after becoming familiar with the various statistical tests used to analyze data, you will find that you can make accurate guesses as to the unstated null hypotheses you encounter. Many of the chapters in this book, beginning with Chapter 9, will help you acquire this skill.

This skill is important to have because the final decision of the hypothesis testing procedure always has reference to the point of departure. Researchers never end up by rejecting (or failing to reject) in the abstract; instead, they *always* will terminate the hypothesis testing procedure by rejecting (or failing to reject) a *specific* H_0. Accordingly, no decision to reject should be viewed as important unless we consider what specifically has been rejected.

On occasion, the hypothesis testing procedure is used to evaluate a null hypothesis that could have been rejected from the very beginning, strictly on the basis of common sense. Although it is statistically possible to test such an H_0, no real discovery is made by rejecting something that was known to be false from the outset. To illustrate, consider Excerpt 7.41.

In the study from which Excerpt 7.41 was taken, 120 individuals were first given a battery of personality tests, with the results used to secretly classify each

EXCERPT 7.41 • *Rejecting an Unimportant H_0*

A *t* test showed that the shy group received significantly higher shyness ratings than the nonshy group both at Time 1, $t(116) = 3.06$, $p < .01$, and Time 2, $t(114) = 2.93$, $p < .01$ (both tests two-tailed).

Source: D. L. Paulhus and P. D. Trapnell. (1998). Typological measures of shyness: Additive, interactive, and categorical. *Journal of Research in Personality, 32,* p. 191.

participant as being either above- or below-average in terms of shyness. These individuals then met in small weekly discussion groups. After the second and seventh meetings, each participant rated the other group members on shyness. Using these ratings, the researchers compared those who had been identified as shy by the personality tests with those whose test scores indicated that they were not shy. Not surprisingly, results indicated that the shy group, on the average, received higher shyness ratings.

I cannot exaggerate the importance of the null hypothesis to the potential meaningfulness of results that come from someone using the hypothesis testing procedure. Remember that a reject decision, by itself, is not indicative of a useful finding. Such a result could be easily brought about simply by setting up, in Step 1, an outrageous H_0. Consequently, you should always be interested in not only the ultimate decision reached at the end of the hypothesis testing procedure but also the target of that decision—H_0.

The Ambiguity of the Word Hypothesis

In discussing the outcomes of their data analyses, researchers will sometimes assert that their results support the hypothesis (or that the results do not support the hypothesis). But which hypothesis is being referred to?

As you now know, the hypothesis testing procedure involves two formal hypotheses, H_0 and H_a. In addition, the person conducting the study may have a hunch (i.e., prediction) as to how things will turn out. Many researchers refer to such hunches as their *hypotheses*. Thus, within a single study, there can be three different hypotheses![5] Usually, the full context of the research report will help to make clear which of these three hypotheses stands behind any statement about the hypothesis. At times, however, you will need to read very carefully to accurately understand what the researcher found.

To illustrate why I offer this caution, consider the single sentence in Excerpt 7.42. As you can see, the final word in this sentence is *hypothesis*. But which hypothesis is it: the null hypothesis, the alternative hypothesis, or the researchers' hunch (i.e., the **research hypothesis**)? After reading Chapter 9, you will be in a position to guess, with a high degree of confidence, that it is not the null hypothesis. Now, we're down to two choices, the alternative hypothesis and the research hypothesis. Because the tests of the correlation coefficients were conducted in a two-tailed fashion, the hypothesis that was supported was not H_a but instead was the researchers' hunch. The point of this little guessing game was simply to point out that you must be careful when you come across the word *hypothesis*. It does *not* always mean the same thing!

---

[5]The researcher's hunch will differ from *both* H_0 and H_a if the alternative hypothesis is set up to be nondirectional even though the researcher's prediction is directional. This situation is not uncommon. Many researchers have been taught to conduct two-tailed tests—even though they have a directional hunch—in order to allow the data to suggest that reality is on the flip side of their hunch. (In using a one-tailed test, this could never happen.)

EXCERPT 7.42 • *The Ambiguity of the Word* Hypothesis

Also, a significant negative correlation between relational length and openness was found, providing support for the hypothesis.

Source: M. Dainton and B. Aylor. (2002). Routine and strategic maintenance efforts: Behavioral patterns, variations associated with relational length, and the prediction of relational characteristics. *Communication Monographs, 69*(1), p. 59.

When p Is Reported to Be Equal to or Less Than Zero

Whenever sample data are analyzed by a computer for the purpose of evaluating a null hypothesis, a *p*-value will be produced. This *p* is a probability, and it can end up being any number between 0 and 1. As you now know, a small value of *p* causes H_0 to be rejected. The researcher takes that action because a small *p* signifies that a true H_0 population situation would not likely produce a randomly selected data set that, when summarized, is at least as far away from H_0's pinpoint number as is the researcher's actual data set. In most of the excerpts of this chapter, the *p* turned out to be very low. In one case, *p* was equal to .048; in another, *p* was reported to be less than .008. We even saw one instance where *p* turned out to be smaller than .0000001.

Occasionally, as illustrated in Excerpts 7.43 and 7.44, you will encounter cases where the reported *p*-value is equal to or less than zero. Such *ps* are misleading, for they do not mean that an imaginary population defined by H_0 had no chance whatsoever (or less than no chance) to produce sample data like that obtained by the researcher. Rather, such *p*-statements are created when exceedingly small computer-generated *p*-values (e.g., *p* = .00003) are rounded off to a smaller number of

EXCERPTS 7.43–7.44 • *ps Reported to Be Equal to or Less Than Zero*

This difference was large enough to be statistically significant ($t = 14.82, p = .00$).

Source: M. Nelson, B. Herlihy, and J. Oescher. (2002). A survey of counselor attitudes towards sex offenders. *Journal of Mental Health Counseling, 24*(1), p. 57.

- -

A Pearson correlation ($r = .92, p < .000$) indicated that the participants had adequately reported their grades.

Source: R. Bogler and A. Somech. (2002). Motives to study and socialization tactics among university students. *Journal of Social Psychology, 142*(2), p. 239.

decimal places. It's important to know this to avoid falling into the trap of thinking that H_0 is proven to be wrong in those cases where p is reported to be zero or less than zero.

The Meaning of Significant

If the null hypothesis is rejected, the researcher may assert that the results are **significant.** Since the word *significant* means something different when used in casual everyday discussions than when it is used in conjunction with the hypothesis testing procedure, it is crucial that you recognize the statistical meaning of this frequently seen term. Simply stated, a statistically significant finding may not be very significant at all.

In our everyday language, the term *significant* means important or noteworthy. In the context of hypothesis testing, however, the term *significant* has a totally different meaning. Within this inferential context, a significant finding is simply one that is not likely to have occurred if H_0 is true. So long as the sample data are inconsistent with what one would expect from a true null situation, the statistical claim can be made that the results are significant. Accordingly, a researcher's statement to the effect that the results are significant simply means that the null hypothesis being tested has been rejected. It does *not* necessarily mean that the results are *important* or that the absolute difference between the sample data and H_0 was found to be *large.*

Whether or not a statistically significant result constitutes an important result is influenced by (1) the quality of the research question that provides the impetus for the empirical investigation and (2) the quality of the research design that guides the collection of data. I have come across journal articles that summarized carefully conducted empirical investigations leading to statistically significant results, yet the studies seemed to be quite insignificant. Clearly, to yield important findings, a study must be dealing with an important issue.

But what if statistically significant results *are* produced by a study that focuses on an important question? Does this situation mean that the research findings are important and noteworthy? The answer, unfortunately, is no. As you will see in the next chapter, it is possible for a study to yield statistically significant results even though there is a tiny difference between the data and the null hypothesis. For example, in a recent study reported in the *Journal of Applied Psychology,* the researcher tested H_0: $\rho = 0$ within the context of a study dealing with correlation. After collecting and analyzing the sample data, this null hypothesis was rejected, with the report indicating that the result was "significant at the .001 level." The sample value that produced this finding was $-.03$!

Even if the issue being investigated is crucial, I cannot consider a correlation of $-.03$ to be very different in any meaningful way from the null value of 0. (With $r = -.03$, the proportion of explained variance is equal to .0009.) As you will soon learn, a large sample can sometimes cause a trivial difference to end up being statistically significant—and that is precisely what happened in the correlational study to which I am referring. In that investigation, there were 21,646 individuals in the sample. Because of the gigantic sample, a tiny correlation turned out to be statistically significant. Although significant in a statistical sense, the r of $-.03$ was clearly insignificant in terms of its importance.

Review Terms

Accept	Reliable difference
Alpha	Research hypothesis
Alternative hypothesis	Significant
Calculated value	Test statistic
Critical value	Two-tailed test
Directional	Type I error
Fail to reject	Type II error
Hypothesis testing	α
Level of significance	H_0
Nondirectional	H_a
Null hypothesis	ns
One-tailed test	p
Reject	.05

The Best Items in the Companion Website

1. An email message sent from the author to his students entitled "Learning about Hypothesis Testing Is NOT Easy!"
2. An interactive online quiz (with immediate feedback provided) covering Chapter 7.
3. Ten misconceptions about the content of Chapter 7.
4. Chapter 7's best passage (selected by the author).
5. An interactive online resource called "Type I Errors."

Fun Exercises inside Research Navigator

1. **Are college students more aggressive if they listen to more music?**

   In this study, 243 undergraduate college students were measured in terms of two music variables (what kind they liked and how often they listened) and several personality variables (such as aggression). In one set of their analyses, the researchers computed five separate Pearson rs, correlating frequency of listening with five personality variables (aggression, trust, self-esteem, attitudes toward women, and assault). Each of these sample correlation coefficients was evaluated using the hypothesis testing procedure. (As is usually the case, the researchers who conducted these five tests did not specify the null hypothesis; instead, they are counting on you to know that in each case H_0 specified a zero correlation in the population.) How do you think these five tests turned out? Do you think all five null hypotheses were rejected, just some of them, or none of them? To find out, locate the PDF version of the research report in the Communication database of ContentSelect and read the last paragraph on page 33.

A. M. Rubin, D. V. West, & W. S. Mitchell. Differences in aggression, attitudes toward women, and distrust as reflected in popular music preferences. *Media Psychology.* Located in the COM-MUNICATION database of ContentSelect.

2. Are smokers or nonsmokers better workers?

To see whether smokers differ from nonsmokers in work quality, the researchers of this study collected job performance and discipline data on 136 hotel employees. Using a *t*-test, they applied the hypothesis testing procedure nine times to compare the smokers ($n = 65$) versus the nonsmokers ($n = 71$) on each of the study's nine dependent variables: job knowledge, work quality, tardiness, and so on. Though not articulated in the research report, the null hypothesis in each of these *t*-tests stated that the population mean for the smoking group was equal to the population mean for the nonsmoking group. (We know that the alternative hypothesis was nondirectional because the researchers pointed out that their tests were "two-tailed.") Do you think any of the nine null hypotheses was rejected? If so, which of the comparison groups—smokers or nonsmokers—do you think had the better sample mean? To find out, locate the PDF version of the research report in the Psychology database of ContentSelect, look at Table 1, and then read (on page 344) the two paragraphs in the "Results" section.

P. C. Morrow & T. Leedle. A comparison of job performance and disciplinary records of smokers and nonsmokers. *Journal of Psychology.* Located in the PSYCHOLOGY database of ContentSelect.

Review Questions and Answers begin on page 516.

8

Effect Size, Power, CIs, and Bonferroni

In Chapter 7, we considered the basic six-step version of hypothesis testing procedure. Although many researchers use that version of hypothesis testing, there is a definite trend toward using a seven-step or nine-step procedure when testing null hypotheses. In this chapter, we will consider the extra step(s) associated with these approaches to hypothesis testing. In addition, this chapter includes two related topics: the connection between hypothesis testing and confidence intervals, and the problem of an inflated Type I error rate brought about by multiple tests conducted simultaneously.

The Seven-Step Version of Hypothesis Testing

As you will recall from the previous chapter, the elements of the simplest version of hypothesis testing are as follows:

1. State the null hypothesis (H_0).
2. State the alternative hypothesis (H_a).
3. Select a level of significance (α).
4. Collect and analyze the sample data.
5. Refer to a criterion for evaluating the sample evidence.
6. Reject or fail to reject H_0.

To these six steps, many researchers add a seventh step. Instead of ending the hypothesis testing procedure with a statement about H_0, these researchers return to their sample data and perform one of three additional analyses. Regardless of which specific analysis is applied to the data, the purpose of the seventh step is the same:

to go beyond the decision made about H_0 and say something about the *degree* to which the sample data turned out to be incompatible with the null hypothesis.

Before discussing what researchers do when they return to their data in Step 7 of this (slightly expanded) version of hypothesis testing, I want to explain why competent researchers take the time to do this. Simply stated, they do this because a result that is deemed to be statistically significant can be, at the same time, completely devoid of *any* practical significance whatsoever. This is because there is a direct relationship between the size of the sample(s) and the probability of rejecting a false null hypothesis. If the pinpoint number in H_0 is wrong, large samples increase the likelihood that the result will be statistically significant—even if H_0 is very, very close to being true. In such situations, a decision to reject H_0 in favor of H_a is no great accomplishment due to the fact that H_0 is "off" by such a small amount.

In Excerpts 8.1 and 8.2, this critically important distinction between **statistical significance** and **practical significance** is discussed.[1] Considered jointly, the authors of these passages are asserting that the findings of many studies in their disciplines contain results that are trivial in terms of practical implications. This same assertion undoubtedly holds true for research studies conducted in other disciplines. Unfortunately, applied researchers either don't know or don't heed the warning contained in this excerpt's second sentence: Large sample sizes can produce a statisti-

EXCERPTS 8.1–8.2 • *Statistical Significance versus Practical Significance*

Further, studies documenting the practical significance, as opposed to the statistical significance, of noted changes must be a high priority. . . .

Source: R. D. Mattes. (2002). The chemical senses and nutrition in aging: Challenging old assumptions. *Journal of the American Dietetic Association, 102*(2), p. 193.

- -

It is also important to note the difference between statistical significance and clinical significance. While there may be a statistical difference between a 1-year transplant survival of 96% and 98%, when analyzing 10,000 renal transplants, there is no clinical difference.

Source: R. Huizinga. (2002). Update in immunosuppression. *Nephrology Nursing Journal, 29*(3), p. 261.

[1]As indicated in Excerpt 8.2, the term *clinical significance,* used frequently within medical research, means the same thing as practical significance.

cally significant result even though there is limited or no practical importance associated with the finding.

We now turn to three ways in which a researcher can perform the seventh step of the seven-step version of hypothesis testing. These options include (1) computing a strength-of-association index, (2) estimating the effect size, and (3) assessing the statistical power of the test used to make a decision about H_0.

Step 7a: Computing a Strength-of-Association Index

In our earlier discussion of bivariate correlation (see Chapter 4), we saw that researchers often report the value of r^2 along with or instead of the value of r. The square of the correlation coefficient indicates the proportion of variability in one variable that is explained by or associated with variability in the other variable, and because of this fact r^2 (but not r) is considered to be an index of the "strength of association" in the data.

When engaged in hypothesis testing, researchers can compute a **strength-of-association index** after making a decision to reject H_0. By so doing, they give us information as to the *degree* to which the sample data were found to be incompatible with H_0. Various strength-of-association indices have been developed, but they are similar in that they indicate the proportion of variance in the dependent variable that is explained by the study's independent variable. Such information is conveyed by means of a decimal number between 0 and 1.00.

Along with r^2, the two most frequently seen strength-of-association indices are **eta squared** and **omega squared.** When expressed as symbols, these two indices appear as η^2 and ω^2, respectively. In Excerpts 8.3, 8.4, and 8.5 we see cases where r^2, eta squared, and omega squared were used in an effort to probe the practical significance of the researchers' findings. The researchers who computed these strength-of-association indices deserve high marks for attending to the issue of practical significance in addition to evaluating whether or not there was statistical significance.

Research
Navigator.com
Eta squared

Step 7b: Estimating the Effect Size

Instead of computing a strength-of-association index after H_0 is rejected, a researcher may choose to examine the sample data so as to estimate the actual degree to which the null hypothesis is false. When doing this, most researchers utilize a procedure that yields estimates that are standardized in the sense that they take into consideration the amount of variability in the data. An estimate so derived will usually turn out equal to a decimal value between 0 and 1.0, but it is possible for the effect size to end up larger than 1.0 if there is a giant discrepancy between the sample evidence and H_0.

EXCERPTS 8.3–8.5 • *Strength of Association Indices*

There was a significant correlation between self-rated level of involvement and the total number of barriers ($r = .71$; $p < .001$). Therefore, those nurse practitioners who were more active in public policy change also rated their involvement in public policy activities higher than those who were less involved. This variable explained 50% ($r^2 = .50$) of the variance in public policy activities.

Source: L. S. Oden, J. H. Price, R. Alteneder, D. Boardley, and S. E. Ubokudom. (2000). Public policy involvement by nurse practitioners. *Journal of Community Health, 25*(2), p. 146.

- -

For all F tests, eta squared (η^2) is included as a measure of effect size. The η^2 reflects the proportion of variance in the dependent variable explained by the independent variable; it is similar in concept to the coefficient of determination, r^2.

Source: D. S. Kreiner, S. D. Schnakenberg, A. G. Green, M. J. Costello, and A. F. McClin. (2002). Effects of spelling errors on the perception of writers. *Journal of General Psychology, 129*(1), p. 9.

- -

Substantial, moderate, and no changes in PSDQ scales were defined based on Omega^2 (ω^2) as an estimate of effect size: Substantial $\geq .15$; Moderate $\geq .06$ and $< .15$; and None $< .06$ (Keppel, 1991).

Source: J. G. Van Vorst, J. Buckworth, and C. Mattern. (2002). Physical self-concept and strength changes in college weight training classes. *Research Quarterly for Exercise and Sport, 73*(1), p. 114.

In Excerpt 8.6, we see a case in which estimated **effect sizes** are presented for two statistical comparisons that were made. With each test, the null hypothesis was H_0: $\mu_{whites} = \mu_{minorities}$, and in each case it was rejected. After discovering that the two sample means in each comparison were statistically significant, the authors used estimated effect sizes to answer the exceedingly good question, "But is this of practical significance?"

When interpreting effect size indices (like the values of 0.1934 and 1.480 shown in Excerpt 8.6), researchers utilize criteria established by Jacob Cohen, who is cited in the excerpt. For the kind of statistical test used in Excerpt 8.6, these criteria say that estimated effect sizes of .20, .50, and .80 indicate small, medium, and large differences between the two sample means being compared. These criteria for evaluating effect sizes have become quite popular and are now used in many disciplines.

In Excerpt 8.7, we see a passage from a different study in which practical significance was assessed via effect size indices. In this excerpt, notice that the esti-

EXCERPT 8.6 • *Estimated Effect Size*

Another issue is whether statistically significant differences are also of practical significance. On the job-satisfaction measure, the mean score on a 7-point scale was 5.75 (SD = 1.29) for minorities and 5.98 (SD = 1.10) for Whites. The former is obviously lower, but is this of practical significance? We computed an effect size of 0.1934 with respect to the difference in minority and White mean scores on job satisfaction (Cohen, 1988). On the basis of Cohen, an effect size of 0.19 would be considered trivial or small. Also, we computed an effect size of 1.1480 with respect to the difference in minority and White scores on feelings of distinctiveness. That effect size indicates that the difference in the means between minority and White scores was substantial.

Source: J. Ofori-Dankwa and A. Tierman. (2002). The effect of researchers' focus on interpretation of diversity data. *Journal of Social Psychology, 142*(3), p. 283.

mated effect size for each of the comparisons is symbolized as *d*. Also notice that these two *d*s were evaluated against the criteria mentioned in the previous paragraph. Using these criteria, we can evaluate the first test in Excerpt 8.7 as revealing a large difference between the two sample means. The second test also yielded a statistically significant difference, but we can see (because this *d* = .70) that we should evaluate the difference between the sample means as being medium to large.

EXCERPT 8.7 • *Estimated Effect Size Symbolized as d*

Effect sizes also were calculated for each comparison using a common index, the *d* statistic (Rosnow & Rosenthal, 1989). With regard to the interpretation of this index, *d* of .20 is a small effect, *d* of .50 is a moderate effect, and *d* of .80 or greater is a large effect (Cohen, 1988; Rosnow & Rosenthal). . . . Fathers reported being significantly more accommodating (*M* = 3.8, *SD* = 1.16) than mothers reported them to be (*M* = 2.7, *SD* = 1.32), *t*(55) = 5.68, *p* < .001, *d* = .89. When mothers' and fathers' perceptions of mothers' accommodation were compared, a similar pattern was found: Mothers also perceived themselves to be more accommodating (*M* = 3.8, *SD* = .97) than fathers perceived mothers to be (*M* = 3.0, SD = 1.31), *t*(55) = −3.16, *p* < .005, *d* = .70.

Source: D. A. Madden-Derdich and S. A. Leonard. (2002). Shared experiences, unique realities: Formerly married mothers' and fathers' perceptions of parenting and custody after divorce. *Family Relations, 51*(1), p. 40.

Step 7c: Computing the Statistical Test's Power

As was pointed out earlier in this chapter, the sample size used by a researcher is one of the factors that influences whether or not a false null hypothesis will be rejected. With large samples, it is possible that a false H_0 will be rejected—even if there is little or no practical significance associated with the findings. As proof that this can happen, I briefly summarized, near the end of Chapter 7, a study in which a tiny correlation coefficient ($-.03$) ended up being statistically significant. In that study, the sample size was 21,646.

The sample size, if too large, will make the statistical test too powerful in the sense that null hypotheses that are false by a trivial amount will be declared statistically significant. Such a finding has statistical significance but no practical significance. As we have seen, a small strength-of-association index or an observed effect size provides a red flag that serves to alert the researcher and you that an *unimportant* finding has been declared statistically significant because of a large sample size.

The sample size, on the other hand, can be too small and, as a consequence, cause the findings to be misleading. Due to the fact that there is a direct relationship between the sample size and the probability of rejecting a false H_0, a statistical test based on an insufficient amount of data will likely lead to a fail-to-reject decision—even if the discrepancy between the arbitrary null hypothesis, on the one hand, and the reality of the population(s), on the other hand, is so large as to deserve the label *important* or *noteworthy*. If a researcher doesn't reach a reject decision when H_0 is off target by a wide margin, then a major Type II error is committed.

After conducting a statistical test and reaching a fail-to-reject decision, researchers can assess the likelihood that their test would reject H_0. To do this, the researcher not only has the opportunity but is required to specify the point on a continuum that shows how false the null hypothesis must be before it ceases to be false by only a small, unimportant, trivial amount and begins to be false by a large, important, and noteworthy amount. The term **statistical power** denotes the likelihood of rejecting a false H_0 that is false to the degree specified by this point, and its complement is the probability of a Type II error. Researchers want to use sample sizes that are sufficiently large to give their tests adequate power; conversely, they don't want to use sample sizes that are so small as to make the probability of rejecting a grossly false H_0 too low.

After reaching a fail-to-reject decision, researchers will sometimes compute the power of the statistical test in an effort to find out whether the amount of sample data was sufficient to make the test sensitive to important deviations from the null. If the reported power turns out to be high enough (say .80 or higher), this would indicate that the researcher's test was likely to reject H_0—if the discrepancy between H_0 and the actual state of affairs in the population(s) is big, important, and noteworthy. When a fail-to-reject decision is supplemented by a power analysis that yields a value close to 1.0 for the test's power, researchers are simply saying that they had large enough sample sizes so as to make it unlikely that an important finding was missed due to a Type II error.

Excerpt 8.8 illustrates the manner in which a researcher can add a seventh step to the six basic steps of hypothesis testing outlined in Chapter 7. Here again, as was the case in Steps 7a or 7b, the researcher returns to the data and performs some additional computation designed to address the legitimate concern as to the likely degree to which H_0 is off target.

EXCERPT 8.8 • *Adequate Statistical Power*

As noted in Table 3 [not shown here], none of the correlations reached significance. . . . A power analysis (Cohen, 1988) indicated that, based on our sample size and alpha level, we had sufficient power (.80) to reject the null hypothesis of $\rho = 0$ if the population correlation coefficient was approximately .35.

Source: M. Lahey, J. Edwards, and B. Munson. (2001). Is processing speed related to severity of language impairment? *Journal of Speech, Language, and Hearing Research, 44*(6), p. 1358.

In this excerpt, the researchers indicate that they tested each of several correlation coefficients to see if any of them was significantly different from zero. None was. Returning to their data, the researchers conducted a power analysis. They did this to see if their statistical tests had sufficient power to reject the null hypothesis, presuming that the population correlation (associated with each test) was equal to something *other than* zero. This power analysis indicated that the researchers' sample size was of such a size that they had an 80 percent chance of detecting a false null situation (i.e., of achieving statistical significance) if ρ, the population correlation, was equal to .35. (If ρ happened to be higher, they would have had an even *better* chance of rejecting H_0.) Thus, the chances were slim that the researchers failed to detect a *meaningful* false null situation.

Whenever the hypothesis testing procedure is used, there is an inverse relationship between the power of the test and the probability of a Type II error. If power is high, the chances of not rejecting a false null hypothesis are low; conversely, when power is low, there is a high probability that a fail-to-reject decision will be made. In Excerpt 8.9, we see a case in which the researchers admit that their low power may have caused them to commit a Type II error.

In the study connected to Excerpt 8.9, there were four groups of children created by a combination of factors: the child's language (either typical or impaired) and the kind of treatment intervention (enrichment or play). Two of these groups had a sample size of 8; the other two had a sample size of 9. In one of the researcher's statistical comparisons, the two enrichment groups were pooled together and compared with the combined plays groups. Contrary to what the researchers expected, the null hypothesis (of the two treatments being equivalent) could not be rejected.

EXCERPT 8.9 • *Insufficient Statistical Power*

A post hoc power analysis, however, showed that, even with the two-way alpha set at .10, this test had power of only .52. This indicates that it would have been capable of detecting an effect only approximately half the time, if one actually were present. Approximately 35 subjects per group would have been necessary to achieve the commonly accepted power of .80 with an effect of this size. Thus, it remains possible that we missed a significant finding that the Enrichment group did differ from the Play group in some way.

Source: M. E. Fey and D. F. Loeb. (2002). An evaluation of the facilitative effects of inverted yes-no questions on the acquisition of auxiliary verbs. *Journal of Speech, Language, and Hearing Research, 45*(1), pp. 166–167.

In the third sentence of Excerpt 8.9, notice what the researchers say about power and sample size. Whereas they actually had sample sizes of 8 or 9, their power analysis indicated that they would have needed 35 children in each of their four subgroups in order to have a power of .80. With that level of power, they would have had an 80 percent chance to reject the null hypothesis, presuming the true difference between the two interventions equals what was seen in the sample data.

Such discussions of power and Type II errors usually crop up in two situations, both of which involve null hypotheses that are *not* rejected. Sometimes, when large amounts of sample data have been analyzed, the post hoc power analysis will reveal that the analysis had sufficient sensitivity to reveal any differences that really exist. Here, the nonsignificant results in the presence of high power will usually be interpreted to mean that the null hypothesis either is true or is false to only a trivial degree. On other occasions, a post hoc power analysis is conducted because the researcher is hesitant to discard his or her personal belief (hope?) that the null hypothesis is wrong; the power analysis is executed in an effort to show that the study didn't have much of a chance to detect a false null situation. Since it is the researcher who can control, to a large degree, the power associated with his or her analysis, it is fair to ask any researcher who tries to blame low power for a nonsignificant result, "Why didn't you design your study so it would possess adequate power?"

The Nine-Step Version of Hypothesis Testing

Although many researchers still utilize the six-step and seven-step versions of hypothesis testing, there is a definite trend toward using a nine-step approach. Six of the steps of this more elaborate version of hypothesis testing are identical to the six basic elements considered in Chapter 7, while the other three steps are related to the concepts of effect size, power, and sample size considered in the earlier portion of this chapter. Listed in the order in which the researcher will deal with them, the various elements of the nine-step version of hypothesis testing are as follows:

        1. State the null hypothesis, H_0.
        2. State the alternative hypothesis, H_a.
        3. Specify the desired level of significance, α.
(new) **4.** Specify the effect size, ES.
(new) **5.** Specify the desired level of power.
(new) **6.** Determine the proper size of the sample(s).
        7. Collect and analyze the sample data.
        8. Refer to a criterion for assessing the sample evidence.
        9. Make a decision to discard/retain H_0.

The steps in the first third and final third of this nine-step version of hypothesis testing are identical to the six steps we discussed in Chapter 7. We will focus here only on Steps 4, 5, and 6. Although our discussion of these three steps will, in some ways, seem redundant considering the material presented earlier in this chapter, there is an important way in which the seven- and nine-step versions of hypothesis testing differ. In the seven-step approach considered earlier in this chapter, the researcher executes the six basic steps and then adds a seventh step. That seventh step—regardless of whether it involves computing a strength-of-association index, estimating effect size, or assessing the statistical test's power—involves returning to the sample data *after* the reject/retain decision has been made. In contrast, the nine-step version of hypothesis testing requires that the researcher specify the effect size, specify the desired power, and then determine the size of the sample(s) *before* any data are collected.

Step 4: Specification of the Effect Size

In discussing Step 7c of the seven-step version of hypothesis testing, I pointed out the option of following up a reject/fail-to-reject decision with a computation of the statistical test's power. As you will recall, such a procedure requires that the researcher specify a point that divides a hypothetical continuum of non-null effects into two segments: (1) a segment that contains all non-null possibilities that are considered, by the researcher, to be only trivial deviations from the situation articulated in H_0, and (2) a segment that contains all non-null possibilities that are judged to be important deviations from the null case. This numerical value, selected arbitrarily by the researcher, is technically referred to as the **effect size.**

    To illustrate what an effect size is and how it gets selected, suppose a researcher uses the hypothesis testing procedure in a study where there is one population, where the data are IQ scores, where the statistical focus is on the mean, and where the null and alternative hypotheses are H_0: $\mu = 100$ and H_a: $\mu = 100$, respectively. In this hypothetical study, the continuum of possible false null cases, as specified by H_a, extends from a value that is just slightly greater than 100 (say, 100.1) to whatever the maximum earnable IQ score is (say 300). The researcher might decide to set 110 as the effect size. By so doing, the researcher would be declaring that (1) the true μ is judged to be only trivially different from 100 if it lies anywhere between 100 and 110, while (2) the difference between the true μ and 100 is considered to be important so long as the former is at least 10 points greater than H_0's pinpoint value of 100.

Most researchers convert their **raw effect sizes** into **standardized effect sizes** by dividing the raw effect size by the estimated standard deviation in the population. Since IQ scores are considered to have a standard deviation of about 15 points, the standardized effect size in the previous example would be equal to 10/15, or .67. Note that the resulting standardized effect size is influenced greatly by the researcher's initial judgment as to what point separates trivial from important deviations from the null case. If our hypothetical researcher had specified 105 (rather than 110) as this point, the standardized effect size would have turned out equal to .33. If 115 had been specified, the standardized effect size would have become equal to 1.00.

In many situations, a researcher will be unable to posit a reasonable guess as to the value of the standard deviation in the population. There may be no previous research relevant to the researcher's study because the researcher's study involves a new measuring instrument, a new procedure, or a different kind of participant than was used by earlier researchers. In any event, a statistician by the name of Jacob Cohen has argued that researchers can arbitrarily set the standardized effect size equal to .20, .50, or .80 depending on whether they are interested in detecting a **small, medium,** or **large** deviation from the null case. When applied to our hypothetical study involving IQ scores, these standardized effect sizes translate into points along the H_a continuum of 103 (for a small effect), 107.5 (for a medium effect), and 112 (for a large effect).[2]

In Excerpts 8.10 and 8.11, we see two examples in which the effect size was specified within the nine-step version of hypothesis testing. In the first of these excerpts, the effect size is clearly in view, with the researchers selecting a standardized effect size of .75. In Excerpt 8.11, the effect size might not be so visible because there are six numbers, with none of them labeled as the effect size. In this passage, it is the first number, 0.3 percent, that is the researchers' choice for the effect size. As should be obvious, this particular effect size is not of the standardized variety; instead, it is positioned within the raw score units of data collected by the researchers. (HbA_{1c} is a component of our blood that is related to diabetes.)

---

[2]Although it is quite easy for a researcher to select one of Cohen's standardized effect size values of .20, .50, or .80, Cohen strongly urges researchers to determine the effect size by making a judgment as to where the trivial and meaningful sections lie along the H_a continuum, and then by dividing the point of separation by a reasonable guess as to the value of σ.

EXCERPTS 8.10–8.11 • A Priori *Specification of Effect Size*

Prior to conducting this study, a power analysis indicated that at least 25 dyads should be assessed for this study to achieve a minimum power level of .80, with alpha = .05 and an effect size of .75.

Source: L. S. Bethea. (2002). The impact of an older adult parent on communicative satisfaction and dyadic adjustment in the long-term marital relationship: Adult-children and spouses; retrospective accounts. *Journal of Applied Communication Research, 30*(2), p. 112.

- -

To detect a significant and clinically relevant intraindividual HbA_{1c} difference of 0.3% with a statistical power of 0.8 (beta = 0.2) and a two-sided alpha of 0.05, and assuming a correlation of 0.5 between the paired values, 106 patients were needed.

Source: A. M. E. Stades, J. B. L. Hoekstra, I. Van den Tweel, D. W. Erkelens, and F. Holleman. (2002). Additional lunchtime basal insulin during insulin lispro intensive therapy in a randomized, multicenter, crossover study in adults: A real-life design. *Diabetes Care, 25*(4), p. 713.

Step 5: *Specification of the Desired Level of Power*

The researcher's next task within the nine-step hypothesis testing procedure is to specify the level of power that is desired for rejecting H_0 if H_0 is off by an amount equal to the previously established effect size. Power is a probability value and can range from 0 to 1.0. Only high values are considered, however, because the complement of power is the probability of a Type II error.

The researcher does not know, of course, exactly how far off-target the null hypothesis is (or even if it is wrong at all). The specified effect size is simply the researcher's judgment as to what would or wouldn't constitute a meaningful deviation from the null case. Note, however, that if the null hypothesis is wrong by an amount that is greater than the specified effect size, then the actual probability of rejecting H_0 will be larger than the specified power level. Thus the power level selected in Step 5 represents the lowest acceptable power for any of the potentially true H_a conditions that are considered to be meaningfully different from H_0.

To see illustrations of how researchers report desired levels of power, take another look at Excerpts 8.10 and 8.11. In the first of these excerpts, they set up their hypothesis testing procedure such that they would have an 80 percent chance of rejecting H_0, presuming that their H_0 was false and that the reality of the population being studied corresponded to a standardized effect size of .75. Note that the power of .80 cited in Excerpt 8.10 was not computed; rather, it was specified by the researchers prior to the collection of any data. (Likewise, the effect size of .75 was not computed but rather selected by the researchers for their power analysis.)

In Excerpt 8.11, the researcher also selected a power level of .80 (although it is shown as 0.8). It is worth noting what immediately follows, in parentheses, this specification of power. (It says beta = 0.2.) **Beta** is simply the probability of a Type II error. Since power and Type II error risk are complementary and must add up to 1.00, beta becomes fixed as soon as a statement is made as to the desired power level. Thus, there was a 20 percent chance of a Type II error, or **beta error,** in Excerpt 8.10 as well as in Excerpt 8.11, because a power level of .80 was specified in both studies.

Before leaving our discussion of statistical power, we need to address a question that you may have formulated. Inasmuch as power is a good thing to have for trying to detect situations where H_0 is false by an amount at least equal to the effect size, why doesn't the researcher specify a power equal to .95 or .99 or even .999? There are two reasons why such high power values are rarely seen in applied research studies. First, they would place unreasonable demands on researchers when they move to Step 6 and compute the sample size required to provide the desired power. Second, extremely high power increases the probability that trivial deviations from H_0 will be labeled as statistically significant. For these two reasons, power levels higher than .90 are rarely seen.

Step 6: Determination of the Needed Sample Size

After stating H_0 and H_a, after selecting a level of significance, and after specifying the effect size and the desired power, the researcher then uses a formula, a specially prepared table, or a computer program to determine the size of the sample(s) needed in the study. No judgment or decision making comes into play at this point in the nine-step version of hypothesis testing, since the researcher simply calculates or looks up the answer to a very pragmatic question: How large should the sample be? At this point (and also in Steps 7–9), the researcher functions like a robot who performs tasks in a routine fashion without using much brain power.

To see the kind of things researchers say when they talk about having computed their sample sizes, take another look at Excerpts 8.10 and 8.11. As you will see, the researcher associated with Excerpt 8.10 found out that a total of 25 dyads were needed in her study, while the team of researchers associated with Excerpt 8.11 determined that 106 patients were needed for their study. These excerpts are worth looking at closely because they illustrate how researchers will usually indicate the main ingredients that went into the determination of their needed sample sizes. Note that both excerpts contain an indication of (1) the selected level of significance, (2) the desired statistical power, and (3) the chosen effect size.

Excerpts 8.10 and 8.11 are instructive because they help to reveal the interconnectedness between alpha, the effect size, power, Type II error risk, and sample size. In these excerpts, we are not told what procedure the researchers used to determine how large their samples needed to be. Most likely, they used a computer program or a published table. The computer or the table took in the researchers' decisions regarding α, the effect size, and power (or beta), and then it spit out the proper *n* for them to use.

On occasion, researchers will be forced to use a limited number of people or animals in their studies. For example, time and/or money may dictate that a fixed number of animals be used. Sometimes only a fixed number of individuals may volunteer to participate. In other studies, researchers cannot use more than the number of people that are at the site to which they have been given access. For any of these or other reasons, researchers who want to use the nine-step version of hypothesis testing must sometimes slightly adjust the nature and order of the step dealing with the size of the sample.

When the sample size is a given due to the pragmatic contingencies of the study being conducted, Steps 5 and 6 of the nine-step approach to hypothesis testing become the following:

Step 5: Specify the fixed number of available subjects.
Step 6: Determine and assess the statistical power of the planned test.

After stating H_0 and H_a, after specifying the desired level of significance and effect size, and after taking account of the available sample size, the researcher then uses a formula or a specially designed table to determine the level of statistical power associated with the intended analysis of the data. If the resulting power (i.e., the probability of detecting meaningful deviations from H_0) is sufficiently high, then the researcher will proceed to collect and evaluate the study's data. On the other hand, if the power analysis yields a value that is too low, the researcher will either (1) change one or more of the initial decisions (e.g., the alpha level) in an effort to boost the study's power or (2) put the study on hold until a larger number of people or animals becomes available.

In Excerpt 8.12, we see an example of the nine-step version of hypothesis testing wherein the power of the statistical test was determined (in Step 6) for a fixed sample size. Notice that the computed power in this study turned out to be .91. This level was higher than .80, the minimum power level recommended by Cohen. Because of this, the researchers went ahead with their study, knowing that the chances were high (91 percent) that they would reject H_0 if the effect in the population was equal to or greater than .4. Stated differently, they had only a 9 percent chance of making a Type II error by missing an effect this large.

As we finish our discussion of the nine-step version of hypothesis testing, I want to underscore the primary advantage of this approach to evaluating any null hypothesis. The eventual results of the statistical test become easier to interpret after the researcher has successfully wrestled with the issue of what ought to be viewed as a meaningful deviation from H_0, and after the sample size has been computed so as to create the desired level of power (or the power computed on the basis of the available sample). In contrast, the six-step version of hypothesis testing can lead to a highly ambiguous finding.

EXCERPT 8.12 • *Power Computed for a Fixed Sample Size*

The sample consisted of 95 adult subjects selected from an outpatient hemodialysis center at the University of Miami School of Medicine/Jackson Memorial Hospital in Miami, Fla. . . . Each patient had a diagnosis of end-stage renal disease (ESRD) and was receiving hemodialysis treatment. . . . An a priori power analysis was conducted. Assuming a large effect size of 0.4 and an alpha level of .05, the 95 subjects yielded a minimum power rating of 0.91.

Source: W. J. Matthews, J. M. Conti, and S. G. Sireci. (2001). The effects of intercessory prayer, positive visualization, and expectancy on the well-being of kidney dialysis patients. *Alternative Therapies in Health and Medicine, 7*(5), pp. 43–44.

If no consideration is given to the concepts of effect size and power, the researcher may end up very much in the dark as to whether (1) a fail-to-reject decision is attributable to a trivial (or zero) deviation from H_0 *or* is attributable to the test's insensitivity to detect important non-null cases due to a small sample size, or (2) a reject decision is attributable to H_0 being false by a nontrivial amount *or* is attributable to an unimportant non-null case being labeled *significant* simply because the sample size was so large. In Excerpts 8.13 and 8.14, we see examples of how murky results can be produced when the six-step approach to hypothesis testing is used. In Excerpt 8.13, the researchers tell us, in essence, that the statistically insignificant results may have been caused by insufficient power. In Excerpt 8.14, we see a research team that obtained statistically significant results but admits, in essence, that the initial findings may have been caused by an overly large sample size making the statistical tests too sensitive.

The advantage of the nine-step (or seven-step) approach to hypothesis testing is *not* that the researcher will be able to know whether the decision reached about H_0 is right or wrong. Regardless of the approach used, a reject decision might be correct or it might constitute a Type I error, and similarly a fail-to-reject decision might be correct or it might be a Type II error. The advantage of having effect size and power built into the hypothesis testing procedure is twofold: On the one hand, the researchers know and control, on an *a priori* basis, the probability of making a Type II error, and on the other hand, they set up the study so that no critic can allege that a significant result, if found, was brought about by an overly sensitive test (or that a nonsignificant result, if found, was produced by an overly insensitive test).[3]

---

[3]In saying this, I assume that the hypothetical critic agrees with the researcher's decisions about H_0, H_a, alpha, and the effect size.

EXCERPTS 8.13–8.14 • *Problems Caused by Small and Large Samples*

Limitations of this study include the low number of women using oral contraceptives ($N = 14$). A larger number would have been more desirable because the statistical analysis shows that the power is too low to draw meaningful conclusions from this group (beta = 0.47).

Source: E. M. Wojtys, L. J. Huston, M. D. Boynton, K. P. Spindler, and T. N. Lindenfeld. (2002). The effect of the menstrual cycle on anterior cruciate ligament injuries in women as determined by hormone levels. *American Journal of Sports Medicine, 30*(2), p. 187.

- -

Respondents to the survey were asked about violence in both current and previous marital unions. Within current unions, five-year rates of violence were comparable for men and women: 4.3% of men and 3.7% of women experienced at least one act of violence by a current marital partner. Due to the very large sample size, this small difference in rates of violence between men and women is statistically significant but for policy purposes is unlikely to be considered substantially important.

Source: H. Johnson and V. P. Bunge. (2001). Prevalence and consequences of spousal assault in Canada. *Canadian Journal of Criminology, 43*(1), p. 32.

Hypothesis Testing Using Confidence Intervals

Researchers can, if they wish, engage in hypothesis testing by means of using one or more confidence intervals, rather than by comparing a calculated value against a critical value or by comparing a *p*-level against α. Although this approach to hypothesis testing is not used as often as the approaches discussed in Chapter 7, it is important for you to understand what is going on when a researcher uses confidence intervals within the context of hypothesis testing.

Whenever confidence intervals are used in this manner, it should be noted that everything about the hypothesis testing procedure remains the same except the way the sample data are analyzed and evaluated. To be more specific, this alternative approach to hypothesis testing involves the specification of H_0, H_a, and alpha, and the final step will involve a reject or fail-to-reject decision regarding H_0. The concepts of Type I and Type II errors are still relevant, as are the opportunities to specify effect size and power and to compute the proper sample size if the nine-step version of hypothesis testing is being used.

As indicated in Chapter 7, calculated and critical values usually are numerical values that are metric-free. Such calculated and critical values have no meaningful connection to the measurement scale associated with the data. Although it is advantageous for the researcher to use metric-free calculated and critical values, such values provide little insight as to why H_0 ultimately is rejected or not rejected. The advantage of confidence intervals is that they help to provide that insight.

The way confidence intervals are used within hypothesis testing is easy to explain. If there is just a single sample involved in the study, the researcher will take the sample data and build a confidence interval around the sample statistic. Instead of computing a calculated value, the researcher computes an interval, with the previously specified alpha level dictating the level of confidence associated with the interval (an α of .05 calls for a 95 percent interval, an α of .01 calls for a 99 percent interval, etc.). Instead of then turning to a critical value, the researcher turns to the null hypothesis and compares the confidence interval against the pinpoint number contained in H_0. The decision rule for the final step is straightforward: If the null number is outside the confidence interval, H_0 can be rejected; otherwise, H_0 must be retained.

Excerpt 8.15 illustrates the confidence interval approach to hypothesis testing. In this study, two sets of measurements (on a sample of diabetics) were correlated. The null hypothesis that was tested said H_0: $\rho = 0$, where ρ was the correlation in the population. As you can see, the sample correlation coefficient turned out equal to $-.6$. The ends of the confidence interval extended from $-.11$ to $-.86$. Since 0, the pinpoint number from H_0, is not included within this interval, the null hypothesis was rejected.

EXCERPT 8.15 • *A Confidence Interval Approach to Hypothesis Testing*

There was a significant negative correlation between frequency of hypoglycemic episodes and peak tremor ($r = -0.6$; 95% CI, -0.11 to -0.86; $P < 0.02$).

Source: N. D. Harris, I. A. Macdonald, R. R. Holman, and S. R. Heller. (2000). Does the choice of treatment for type 2 diabetes affect the physiological response to hypoglycemia? *Diabetes Care, 23*(7), p. 1022.

A confidence interval can also be used to determine whether two samples differ sufficiently to allow the researcher to reject a null hypothesis that says the corresponding populations have the same parameter value. To illustrate, consider Excerpt 8.16. In this excerpt, there were two samples of data, with both sets of data coming from a single group of individuals who were interviewed on two occasions. The mean number of cardinal problems during the first interview was 8.5; the mean during the second interview was 2.9. The difference between these means was 5.6, with a confidence interval (for the difference between means) that extended from

EXCERPT 8.16 • *Using a Confidence Interval to Compare Two Groups*

After admission to secure care there was a significant reduction in the overall amount of problems. For example, the mean number of cardinal problems (i.e., problems for which some form of intervention is worth offering) per individual at the first interview was 8.5 (*SD* 2.9), whereas at the second interview it was 2.9 (*SD* 2.4, mean difference 5.6, 95% *CI* 5.0−6.3).

Source: L. Kroll, J. Rothwell, D. Bradley, P. Shah, S. Bailey, and R. C. Harrington. (2002). Mental health needs of boys in secure care for serious or persistent offending: A prospective, longitudinal study. *The Lancet, 359*(9322), p. 1977.

5.0 to 6.3. The null hypothesis was H_0: $\mu_{1st} = \mu_{2nd}$, which could be rewritten as H_0: $\mu_{1st} - \mu_{2nd} = 0$. If the confidence interval had ended up with one end being a positive number and one end being a negative number, it would have overlapped the null point of 0. Had that been the result, the null hypothesis would have been retained. In reality, the CI did not overlap 0, and the researchers were able to claim that a statistically significant difference existed between the two sample means.

Before completing our discussion of the confidence-interval approach to hypothesis testing, we need to alert you (once again) to the difference between a confidence interval and a standard error interval.[4] Many researchers who compute calculated and critical values within one of the more traditional approaches to hypothesis testing will summarize their sample data in terms of values of the statistic plus or minus the standard error of the statistic. Intervals formed by adding and subtracting the standard error to the sample statistic do *not* produce alpha-driven confidence intervals. Instead, the result is a 68 percent interval. (Alpha-driven confidence intervals will typically be 95 percent intervals.)

To illustrate the difference between true confidence intervals and standard error intervals, consider Excerpt 8.17. The intervals based on 217.8 ± 19.2 and 170.3 ± 12.9 extend from 198.6 to 237.0 and 157.4 to 183.2, respectively. Although these intervals do not overlap, the null hypothesis (of no difference between the population means) was not rejected. This potentially confusing set of results is attributable to the intervals being standard error intervals, which are approximately equivalent to 68 percent confidence intervals. If 95 percent confidence intervals had been reported, each one would have been wider, they would have overlapped each other, and the "NS" result would have been immediately understandable.

---

[4]The difference between confidence intervals and standard errors was first covered in Chapter 6.

EXCERPT 8.17 • *Standard Error Intervals versus Confidence Intervals*

Results are expressed as means (SEM). . . . Levels of serum cortisol at t_0 [baseline] and t_1 [after 1 week of cycling] did not vary significantly (217.8 (19.2) and 170.3 (12.9) mIU/ml respectively; $p > 0.05$). . . .

Source: J. L. Chicharro, A. Lopez-Calderon, J. Hoyos, and A. I. Martin-Valesco. (2001). Effects of an endurance cycling competition on resting serum insulin-like growth factor I (IGF-I) and its binding proteins IGFB-1 and IGFBP-3. *British Journal of Sports Medicine, 35*(5), p. 305.

Adjusting for an Inflated Type I Error Rate

In Chapter 7, I indicated that the researchers have direct control over the probability that they will make a Type I error when making a judgment about H_0. (Type I errors, you will recall, occur when true null hypotheses are rejected.) This control is exerted when the researcher selects the level of significance. As long as the underlying assumptions of the researcher's statistical test are tenable, the alpha level selected in Step 3 of the hypothesis testing procedure instantly and accurately establishes the probability that a true H_0 will be rejected.

The fact that α dictates Type I error risk holds true *only* for situations where researchers use the hypothesis testing procedure just once within any given study. In many studies, however, more than one H_0 is tested. In Excerpt 8.18, we see an illustration of this common practice of applying the hypothesis testing procedure multiple times within the same study. As you can see, six correlation coefficients appear in this excerpt. The *p*-value, presented for each of the computed *r*s, indicates that the hypothesis testing procedure was used here six times, once for each *r*.

When the hypothesis testing procedure is applied multiple times within the same study, the alpha level used within each of these separate tests specifies the

EXCERPT 8.18 • *Hypothesis Testing Used More Than Once*

Dimension 1 for female voices produced significant bivariate correlations with CPP ($r = -0.73, p = 0.016$), RPK ($r = -0.64, p = 0.045$), abnormality ($r = 0.80, p = 0.001$), and rough ($r = 0.71, p = 0.001$). Dimension 2 correlated significantly with BRI ($r = -0.87, p = 0.001$) and PSR ($r = -0.77, p = 0.009$).

Source: V. I. Wolfe, D. P. Martin, C. I. Palmer. (2000). Perception of dysphonic voice quality by naive listeners. *Journal of Speech, Language, and Hearing Research, 43*(3), p. 701.

Type I error risk that would exist if that particular test were the only one being conducted. However, with multiple tests being conducted in the study, the actual probability of making a Type I error somewhere within the set of tests *exceeds* the alpha level used within any given test. The term **inflated Type I error risk** is used to refer to this situation where the alpha level used within each of two or more separate tests understates the likelihood that at least one of the tests will cause the researcher to reject a true H_0.

A simple example may help to illustrate the problem of an inflated Type I error rate. Suppose you were given a fair die and told to roll it on the table. Before you toss the die, also suppose that the person running this little game tells you that you will win $10 if your rolled die turns out to be anything but a six. If you get a six, however, you must fork over $50. With an unloaded die, this would be a fair bet, for your chances of winning would be 5/6 while the chances of losing would be 1/6.

But what if you were handed a pair of fair dice and asked to roll both members of the pair simultaneously, with the rule being that you would win $10 if you can avoid throwing an evil six but lose $50 if your roll of the dice produces a bad outcome. This would not be a fair bet for you, for the chances of avoiding a six are $5/6 \times 5/6 = 25/36$, a result that is lower than the 5/6 value needed to make the wager an even bet in light of the stakes ($10 versus $50). If you were handed five pairs of dice and were asked to roll them simultaneously, with the same payoff arrangement in operation (i.e., win $10 if you avoid a six, otherwise lose $50), you would be at a terrific disadvantage. With 10 of the six-sided cubes being rolled, the probability of your winning the bet by avoiding a six anywhere in the full set of results is equal to approximately .16. You would have a 16 percent chance of winning $10 versus an 84 percent chance of losing $50. That would be a very good arrangement for your opponent!

As should be obvious, the chances of having an evil six show up at least once increase as the number of dice being thrown increases. With multiple dice involved in our hypothetical game, there would be two ways to adjust things to make the wager equally fair to both parties. One adjustment would involve changing the stakes. For example, with two dice being rolled, the wager could be altered so you would win $11 if you avoid a six or lose $25 if you don't. The other kind of adjustment would involve tampering with the two little cubes so as to produce a pair of loaded dice. With this strategy, each die would be weighted such that its chances of ending up as something other than a six would be equal to a tad more than 10/11. This would allow two dice to be used, in a fair manner, with the original stakes in operation ($10 versus $50).

When researchers use the hypothesis testing procedure multiple times, an adjustment must be made somewhere in the process to account for the fact that at least one Type I error somewhere in the set of results increases rapidly as the number of tests increases. Although there are different ways to effect such an adjustment, the most popular method is to change the level of significance used in conjunction with the statistical assessment of each H_0. If the researcher wants to have a certain level of protection against a Type I error anywhere within his or her full set of results, then he or she would make the alpha level more rigorous within each of the individual tests. By so doing, it's as if the researcher is setting up a fair wager in that the claimed alpha level will truly match the study's likelihood of yielding a Type I error.

The most frequently used procedure for adjusting the alpha level is called the **Bonferroni technique,** and it is quite simple for the researcher to apply or for consumers of research to understand. When there is a desire on the part of the researcher to hold the Type I error in the full study equal to a selected value, the alpha levels for the various tests being conducted must be chosen such that the sum of the individual alpha levels is equivalent to the full-study alpha criterion. This is usually accomplished by simply dividing the desired Type I error risk for the full study by the number of times the hypothesis testing procedure is going to be used. Excerpt 8.19 illustrates nicely how the Bonferroni technique works.

EXCERPT 8.19 • *The Bonferroni Adjustment Procedure*

Because seven separate analyses were conducted, increasing the probability of a Type I error, Bonferroni's procedure was used and resulted in an operational alpha level of .007 (.05/7).

Source: B. E. Bride. (2001). Single-gender treatment of substance abuse: Effect on treatment retention and completion. *Social Work Research, 25*(4), p. 227.

When using the Bonferroni technique, researchers typically indicate the size of the adjusted alpha used to evaluate each null hypothesis that was set up and tested. As you now know, that adjusted alpha is computed in a simple fashion by dividing the desired overall Type I error risk by the number of tests being conducted. The term **experimentwise error rate** refers to this desired study-wide Type I error risk. In Excerpt 8.20, we see this term being used in a study where the researchers used an experimentwise alpha level of .016.

Since the Bonferroni technique leads to a more rigorous alpha level for each of the separate tests being conducted, each of those tests becomes more demanding. In other words, Bonferroni-adjusted alpha levels (as compared with an unadjusted level of significance) create a situation wherein the sample data must be even more inconsistent with null expectations before the researcher is permitted to reject H_0. If the researcher makes a decision about H_0 by comparing the data-based *p*-value against the adjusted alpha, that alpha criterion will be smaller and therefore harder to beat. Or, if each test's calculated value is compared against a critical value, the researcher will find that the Bonferroni technique has created a more stringent

Research Navigator.c⊕m

Bonferroni technique

EXCERPT 8.20 • *Experimentwise Error Rate*

Additionally, as there were 3 dependent variables in this study, and in an effort to minimize the experimentwise-error rate, α was adjusted using the Bonferroni technique (i.e., $P < .05/3 = P < .016$). Thus, $P < .016$ was the criterion α level used to determine statistical significance.

Source: B. J. Cardinal and H. J. Engels. (2001). Ginseng does not enhance psychological well-being in healthy, young adults: Results of a double-blind, placebo-controlled, randomized clinical trial. *Journal of the American Dietetic Association, 101*(6), p. 657.

criterion. Thus it does not make any difference which of these two paths the researcher takes in moving from the sample data to the ultimate decision about the null hypothesis. Either way, more protection against Type I errors is brought about by making it harder for the researcher to reject H_0.

Excerpts 8.21 and 8.22 illustrate nicely how the Bonferroni technique brings about a more demanding assessment of each of the various correlational null hypotheses that is tested. In the first of these excerpts, notice how the *p*-level needed to achieve statistical significance changed from .05 to .01 because five separate tests were conducted. Here, the Bonferroni adjustment made it harder for the researchers to reject their null hypotheses because the alpha criterion became smaller. In Excerpt 8.22, the Bonferroni adjustment created a more stringent criterion because the critical value became larger. At the .05 level of significance, the critical value for the *F*-test used in this study would have been 5.32, and the first test would have been significant. However, the critical value became 11.3 because of the Bonferroni adjustment, thus meaning that the calculated value of 5.52 was not significant (because an *F*-test's calculated value, to reject H_0, must equal or exceed the critical value).

It may seem odd that researchers who want to reject their null hypothesis choose to apply the Bonferroni technique and thereby make it more difficult to accomplish their goal. However, researchers who use the Bonferroni technique are not doing something stupid, self-defeating, or inconsistent with their own objectives. Although the Bonferroni technique does, in fact, create a more demanding situation for the researcher, it does not function to pull something legitimate out of reach. Instead, this technique serves the purpose of helping the researcher pull in the reins so he or she is less likely to reach out and grab something that, in reality, is nothing at all. The Bonferroni technique, of course, does not completely eliminate the chance that a Type I error will be made. But it does eliminate the problem of an *inflated* Type I error risk.

Although the Bonferroni procedure is the most frequently used technique for dealing with the inflated Type I error problem, other procedures have been developed to accomplish the same general procedure. One of these is formally called the

EXCERPTS 8.21–8.22 • *Why Bonferroni Makes It Harder to Reject H_0*

A *p* value of 0.05, two tailed, was used to determine statistical significance when rejecting null hypotheses. However, since five tests of association were performed, a *p* value of 0.01 was required after Bonferroni correction to reject the null hypotheses.

Source: M. C. Rosario-Campos, J. F. Leckman, M. T. Mercadante, and R. G. Shavitt. (2001). Adults with early-onset obsessive-compulsive disorder. *American Journal of Psychiatry, 158*(11), p. 1900.

- -

An alpha level of 0.05 was considered statistically significant. . . . Examination of data from the first trial failed to reveal a reliable effect of cube size on peak grip force rate, $F(1,8) = 5.52$, $p > .01$ or peak load force rate, $F(1,8) = 2.16$, $p > .01$. (With a Bonferroni correction, the required significance level reduces from .05 to .01 because there were five trials in the block and thus five possible comparisons.)

Source: J. Randall Flanagan, Sara King, Daniel M. Wolpert, and Roland S. Johansson. (2001). Sensorimotor prediction and memory in object manipulation. *Canadian Journal of Experimental Psychology, 55*(2), pp. 90, 92.

Sidak modification of Dunn's procedure. If you come across a research report in which it has been used, you are likely to see it referred to by its "nickname," the **Dunn-Sidak modification.**

A Few Cautions

As we come to the close of our two-chapter treatment of hypothesis testing, I want to offer a few more cautions that should assist you as you attempt to make sense out of the technical write-ups of empirical investigations. These tips (or warnings!) are different from the ones provided at the end of Chapter 7, so you may profit from a review of what I said there. In any event, here are four more things to keep in mind when you come across statistical inferences based on the hypothesis testing procedure.

Two Meanings of the Term **Effect Size**

When the seven-step approach to hypothesis testing is used, the researcher may opt (in Step 7) to compute the effect size. We saw an example of this in Excerpt 8.6. In that study, the computed effect size turned out equal to .19 (which was rounded off from .1934). Note that this kind of effect size is based entirely on a comparison of the sample evidence and the pinpoint value specified in H_0. If the data closely approximate H_0, the estimated effect size will turn out to be small. On the other hand, a large discrepancy between the sample evidence and H_0 will cause the estimated effect size to be large.

When the nine-step version of hypothesis testing is employed, a different kind of effect size comes into play. Within this strategy, researchers *specify* (rather than compute) the effect size, and this is done prior to the collection and examination of any data. When researchers specify the effect size in Step 4 of the nine-step version of hypothesis testing, they are not making a predictive statement as to the magnitude of the effect that will be found once the data are analyzed. Rather, they are indicating through Step 4 the minimum size of an effect that they consider to have practical significance. Most researchers hope that the magnitude of the true effect size will exceed the effect size specified prior to the collection of any data.

It is unfortunate that the same term—effect size—is used by researchers to refer to two different things. However, a careful consideration of context ought to clarify which kind of effect size is being discussed. If reference is made to the effect size within the research report's method section (and specifically when the sample size is being discussed), then it is likely that the nine-step version of hypothesis testing was used, with the effect size being a judgment call as to the dividing line between trivial and important findings. If, on the other hand, reference is made to the effect size during a presentation of the obtained results, that effect size is probably a data-based measure of how false the null hypothesis seems to be.

Cohen's Effect Size Values of .2, .5, and .8

When doing a power analysis within the nine-step version of hypothesis testing, the researcher must specify an effect size. If the study involves one or two groups and if the study's statistical focus is on the mean, many researchers choose one of Cohen's popular values of .2, .5, or .8 to indicate their decision to specify a small, medium, or large effect size, respectively. This is very easy for the researcher to do. However, even Cohen himself argues that it is always better for the researcher to specify the effect size by thinking about the particular study being conducted rather than to use one of the accepted values cited earlier in this paragraph. In other words, it is preferable for the researcher to think about the data to be collected and to specify what distinguishes trivial from meaningful deviations from H_0 *in terms of the raw units associated with the measuring instrument.* (For example, a researcher investigating a new diet might assert that a nontrivial effect exists if the diet brings about a mean weight loss of at least five pounds.) Although this is not typically a difficult task by itself, the researcher who does this must also be able to estimate how much variability exists in the population(s) to which the statistical inference is intended. In many studies, it is difficult to estimate σ.

Researchers who perform a power analysis within the nine-step version of hypothesis testing should be given high marks for doing something that helps to make their investigations superior to those that are based on the simpler six-step or seven-step versions. However, you should give them even higher marks when they follow Cohen's recommendation to avoid selecting .2, .5, or .8 as the value for the effect size and instead specify it after (1) deciding what is and isn't significant in a practical sense and (2) estimating the variability in the population. Excerpt 8.23 comes from such a study.

EXCERPT 8.23 • *Defining Effect Size in the Metric of the Dependent Variable*

The primary outcome measure was the Rivermead mobility index, in which scores range from 0 to 15, with higher scores indicating greater mobility. . . . We defined a substantial improvement in mobility as an increase of three Rivermead mobility index scale points. In the sample size calculation we used an SD of 4.7 index points [based on previous research] and obtained a sample size of 100–150 for 90% power with $p = 0.05$–0.01.

Source: J. Green, A. Forster, S. Bogle, and J. Young. (2002). Physiotherapy for patients with mobility problems more than 1 year after stroke: A randomized controlled trial. *The Lancet, 359*(9302), pp. 199–200.

The Simplistic Nature of the Six-Step Version of Hypothesis Testing

Most researchers test null hypotheses with the six-step version of the hypothesis testing procedure. This is unfortunate because the important distinction between statistical and practical significance is not addressed in any way whatsoever by this simplistic approach to testing null hypotheses. Consequently, the outcome is ambiguous no matter what decision is reached about H_0. A reject decision may have been caused by a big difference between the single-number summary of the sample evidence and the pinpoint number in H_0; however, that same decision may have come about by a small difference being magnified by a giant sample size. Likewise, a fail-to-reject decision might be the result of a small difference between the sample evidence and the null hypothesis; however, the researcher's decision not to reject H_0 may have resulted from a big difference that was camouflaged by a small sample size.

To see an example in which a small sample size created a problem, take another look at Excerpt 8.9. In that excerpt, the researchers seem to be apologizing for having used a sample size that was too small, and they admit that the low power of their test may have caused them to miss something important. To see an example of the opposite kind of problem, consider Excerpt 8.24. All 12 of the correlations referred to in this excerpt turned out to be statistically significant, with $p < .05$ in each case. Are you impressed? If so, would you still be impressed if I told you that none of the sample rs was larger than .45, that five of them were smaller than .15, and that two of these significant correlation coefficients were equal to .06 and .04? (If you're *still* of the opinion that a significant correlation always reveals something important, please concentrate on the two smallest of those 12 correlations and figure out, for each one, the coefficient of determination!)

EXCERPT 8.24 • *The Danger of Interpreting Significant to Mean Big*

Pearson correlations were computed between the proximity ratings, similarity-to-self ratings, category typicality ratings, and group status (ingroup or outgroup) of category in separate analyses for both the object and person conditions. . . . The results of the correlational analysis indicated significant positive correlations between all variables [in both the object and person conditions].

Source: J. B. Worthen, R. P. McGlynn, L. Y. Solis, and S. Coats. (2002). Proximity attitudes toward objects and people: Reference to a category and a self-representation? *American Journal of Psychology, 115*(2), p. 241.

With the seven-step and nine-step versions of hypothesis testing, there is less ambiguity associated with the ultimate decision to reject or retain the null hypothesis. This fact is illustrated nicely by Excerpt 8.25. The researchers who conducted this study computed effect sizes after several null hypotheses were rejected. Hence, they were applying the seven-step version of hypothesis testing. Notice how the end of the first sentence in this excerpt brings a sense of clarity to their statistical decision.

If all researchers used the seven-step or nine-step versions of hypothesis testing, it would be easier for you and others to make sense out of statistically based researcher reports. Unfortunately, most researchers use the six-step approach to testing null hypotheses. Whenever you encounter a researcher who has used this more simplistic version of hypothesis testing, *you* will have to be the one who applies the important seventh step. Although you probably will not be able to conduct a post hoc power analysis or compute certain of the strength-of-association indices (such as eta squared or omega squared), there are certain things you *can* do.

If a correlation coefficient is reported to be statistically significant, look at the size of the r and ask yourself what kind of relationship (weak, moderate, or strong) was revealed by the researcher's data. Better yet, square the r and then convert the

EXCERPT 8.25 • *The Advantage of Moving beyond the Six-Step Version of Hypothesis Testing*

Although the self-ratings of general practitioners ($M = 2.80$, $SD = 0.79$) with respect to their level of knowledge about adolescent suicide were significantly higher than those of teachers, ($M = 2.64$, $SD = 0.92$), $t(847) = 2.77$, $p < .01$, $d = .23$, the effect size is small and not clinically meaningful. Both professions rated their level of knowledge as within the moderate range [on the 1-to-5 scale].

Source: K. M. Scouller and D. I. Smith. (2002). Prevention of youth suicide: How well informed are the potential gatekeepers of adolescents in distress? *Suicide and Life-Threatening Behavior, 32*(1), p. 73.

resulting coefficient of determination into a percentage; then make your own judgment as to whether a small or large amount of variability in one variable is being explained by variability in the other variable. If the study focuses on means rather than correlations, look carefully at the computed means. Ask yourself whether the observed difference between two means represents a finding that has practical significance.

I cannot overemphasize my warning that you can be (and will be) misled by many research claims if you look only at *p* statements when trying to assess whether results are important. Most researchers use the simple six-step version of hypothesis testing, and the only thing revealed by this procedure is a yes or no answer to the question, "Do the sample data deviate from H_0 more than we would expect by chance?" Even if a result is statistically significant with $p < .0001$, it may be the case that the finding is completely devoid of *any* practical significance!

Inflated Type I Error Rates

My final caution is simply a reiteration of something I said earlier in this chapter. This has to do with the heightened chance of a Type I error when multiple tests are conducted simultaneously. This is a serious problem in scientific research, and this caution deserves to be reiterated.

Suppose a researcher measures each of several people on seven variables. Also suppose that the true correlation between each pair of these variables is exactly 0.00 in the population associated with the researcher's sample. Finally, suppose our researcher computes a value for *r* for each pair of variables, tests each *r* to see if it is significantly different from 0.00, and then puts the results into a correlation matrix. If the .05 level of significance is used in conjunction with the evaluation of each r, the chances are greater than 50–50 that at least one of the rs will turn out to be significant. In other words, even though the alpha level is set equal to .05 for each separate test that is conducted, the collective Type I error risk has ballooned to over .50 due to the fact that 21 separate tests are conducted.

My caution here is simple. Be wary of any researcher's conclusions if a big deal is made out of an unreplicated single finding of significance when the hypothesis testing procedure is used simultaneously to evaluate many null hypotheses. In contrast, give researchers extra credit when they apply the Bonferroni technique to hold down their study-wide Type I error risk.

Review Terms

Alpha error	Medium standardized effect size
Beta error	Omega squared
Bonferroni technique	Power
Dunn-Sidak modification	Practical significance
Effect size (raw and standardized)	Sample size determination
Eta squared	Small standardized effect size
Inflated Type I error risk	Statistical significance
Intraclass correlation	Strength-of-association index
Large standardized effect size	Type II error risk

The Best Items in the Companion Website

1. An email message sent from the author to his students entitled "Binoculars and Significance."
2. An interactive online quiz (with immediate feedback provided) covering Chapter 8.
3. Ten misconceptions about the content of Chapter 8.
4. An email message sent by the author to his students concerning the seven-step and nine-step versions of hypothesis testing.
5. An interactive online resource called "Statistical Power."

Fun Exercises inside Research Navigator

1. Does "strategy training" help stroke patients with daily living activities?

A stroke patient with apraxia either doesn't know what to do or knows what do but not how to do it. To see whether a new treatment might help such patients, the researchers randomly assigned 113 stroke patients to two groups.

Those in one group received traditional occupational therapy, in which the focus was on improving motor behavior skills. Those in the other group received cognitive "strategy training" in addition to the usual occupational therapy. Data on the main dependent variable in this study came from observers who assessed each patient's ability to perform four tasks (e.g., put on a shirt or blouse). After computing the effect size (*d*) to contrast the two groups' improvement over the eight-week period of the study, the researchers reported that the strategy training had "a small to medium" effect. How large do you think their computed *d* was? To find out, locate the PDF version of the research report in the Nursing, Health, and Medicine database of ContentSelect, go to page 559, and read the first paragraph in the section entitled "Outcome."

M. Donkervoort, J. Dekker, F. C. Stehmann-Saris, & B. G. Deelman. Efficacy of strategy training in left hemisphere stroke patients with apraxia: A randomised clinical trial. *Neuropsychological Rehabilitation*. Located in the NURSING, HEALTH, AND MEDICINE database of ContentSelect.

2. **Comparing males versus females (on a spatial abilities task) and BESD versus *d* (as an index of practical significance).**

In this study, males and females were compared in terms of their ability to perform a paper-and-pencil spatial task. Gender groups were compared at each of three age levels: 9, 13, and 21 to 35. At each age level, there was a statistically significant difference between males and females in their mean rate of correct responding. To see if each of these gender differences was also significant in a practical sense, the researchers computed two measures of effect size: Cohen's *d* and something called BESD. (This latter measure is computed as the simple difference between the percentage of each group located above the combined median of the two groups pooled together.) To find out (1) which gender group was superior at each age level and (2) whether *d* and BESD indicated the same thing, locate the PDF version of the research report in the Biology database of ContentSelect, read bottom two paragraphs on page 214, and look at Tables 2 and 3.

E. Govier & G. Salisbury. Age-related sex differences in performance on a side-naming spatial task. *Psychology, Evolution, and Gender*. Located in the BIOLOGY database of ContentSelect.

Review Questions and Answers begin on page 516.

9

Statistical Inferences Concerning Bivariate Correlation Coefficients

In Chapter 3, we considered several descriptive techniques used by researchers to summarize the degree of relationship that exists between two sets of scores. In this chapter we will examine how researchers deal with their correlation coefficients inferentially. Stated differently, the techniques to be considered here are the ones used when researchers have access only to sample data but wish to make educated guesses as to the nature of the population(s) associated with the sample(s). As you will see shortly, the techniques used most frequently to do this involve hypothesis testing. Occasionally, however, inferential guesses are made through the use of confidence intervals.

We begin this chapter with a consideration of the statistical tests applied to various bivariate correlation coefficients, along with an examination of the typical ways researchers communicate the results of their analyses. I will also point out how the Bonferroni technique is used in conjunction with tests on correlation coefficients, how researchers compare two (or more) correlation coefficients to see if they are significantly different, and how statistical tests can be applied to reliability and validity coefficients. Finally, I will provide a few tips designed to help you become a more discerning consumer of research claims that emanate from studies wherein inferential statistics are applied to correlation coefficients.

Statistical Tests Involving a Single Correlation Coefficient

Later in this chapter, we will consider the situation in which data are analyzed to see if a significant difference exists between two or more correlation coefficients.

Before doing that, however, we need to consider the simpler situation where the researcher has a single sample and a single correlation coefficient. Although simple in nature because only one sample is involved, the inferential techniques focused on in the first part of this chapter are used far more frequently than the ones that involve comparisons between/among correlation coefficients.

The Inferential Purpose

Figure 9.1 has been constructed to help clarify what researchers are trying to do when they apply an inferential test to a correlation coefficient. I have set up this picture to make it consistent with a hypothetical study involving Pearson's product-moment correlation. However, by changing the symbols that are included, we could make our picture relevant to a study wherein any other bivariate correlation coefficient is tested.

As Fig. 9.1 shows, a correlation coefficient is computed on the basis of data collected from a sample. Although the sample-based value of the correlation coefficient is easy to obtain, the researcher's primary interest lies in the corresponding value of the correlation in the population from which the sample has been drawn. However, the researcher cannot compute the value of the correlation coefficient in the population because only the objects (or persons) in the sample can be measured. Accordingly, an inference (i.e., educated guess) about the parameter value of the correlation is made on the basis of the known value of the statistic.

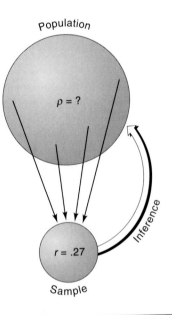

FIGURE 9.1   *The Inferential Purpose of a Test on a Correlation Coefficient*

The nature of the inference that extends from the sample to the population could take one of two forms depending on whether the researcher wishes to use the techniques of estimation or to set up and evaluate a null hypothesis. Near the end of the chapter, we will examine the way confidence intervals are sometimes used to make inferences about correlation coefficients. We first turn our attention to the way researchers set up, evaluate, and report what happens to correlational null hypotheses.

The Null Hypothesis

When researchers are concerned about the relationship between two variables in a single population but can collect data only from a sample taken from that population, they are likely to attack their inferential question by means of hypothesis testing. In doing this, a null hypothesis serves as the hub around which all other statistical elements revolve.

In dealing with a single correlation, the null hypothesis will simply be a pinpoint statement as to a possible value of the correlation in the population. Although researchers have the freedom to choose any value between -1.00 and $+1.00$ for inclusion in H_0, typical researchers will set up their correlational null hypothesis to say that there is, in the relevant population, a zero correlation between the two variables of interest. In Excerpt 9.1, we see an example where the notion of no relationship appeared in a stated null hypothesis.

EXCERPT 9.1 • *The Notion of a Zero Correlation in the Stated H_0*

With no controls for family size, the null hypothesis is that no relationship exists between proportion of sons and household characteristics.

Source: S. Clark. (2000). Son preference and sex composition of children: Evidence from India. *Demography, 37*(1), p. 101.

In Excerpts 9.2 and 9.3, we see two cases where the researchers alluded to the correlational null hypothesis after conducting their data analyses. They did that by saying "significantly different from zero" and "null hypothesis of no relationship." Had the null hypothesis in Excerpt 9.2 been stated explicitly, it would have taken the form H_0: $\rho = 0.00$. In contrast, the null hypothesis in Excerpt 9.3, being inexact in nature, would have the form H_0: $\rho \leq 0.00$.

Because the correlational null hypothesis is usually set up to say that a zero correlation exists in the population, most researchers do not explicitly state the H_0 that is tested but rather take for granted that recipients of their research reports will

EXCERPTS 9.2–9.3 • *Indication in Results That H_0 Specified a Zero Correlation*

All the correlation coefficients are significantly different from zero.

Source: R. A. Kerber, E. O'Brien, K. R. Smith, and R. M. Cawthon. (2001). Familial excess longevity in Utah genealogies. *The Journals of Gerontology, 56A(3),* p. B135.

- -

The null hypothesis of no relationship or a negative relationship between the CRA rating and return on assets was rejected. . . .

Source: W. G. Simpson and T. Kohers. (2002). The link between corporate social and financial performance: Evidence from the banking industry. *Journal of Business Ethics, 35(2),* p. 105.

know that the inferential conclusions refer to a null hypothesis of no relationship. Consider, for example, Excerpts 9.4 and 9.5. In each case, the sample r presented in the report was compared against the null value of zero—even though the tested H_0 never appeared in the technical write-ups.

In light of the fact that very few researchers either state the null hypothesis when applying a test to a sample correlation coefficient or refer to H_0's pinpoint number when discussing their results, you frequently will be forced into the position of having to guess what a researcher's H_0 was. In these situations, a safe bet is that H_0 was a statement of no relationship in the population. If researchers set up a

EXCERPTS 9.4–9.5 • *Tests on r without Any Reference to the Null Hypothesis*

Correlation between the two items is high and significant ($r = .81, p < .05$).

Source: H. Kwak, R. J. Fox, and G. M. Zinkhan. (2002). What products can be successfully promoted and sold via the Internet? *Journal of Advertising Research, 42(1),* p. 26.

- -

The correlation between the importance of online media and television in meeting entertainment needs was not significant ($r = .19, p > .05$).

Source: J. M. Kayany and P. Yelsma. (2000). Displacement effects of online media in the socio-technical contexts of households. *Journal of Broadcasting and Electronic Media, 44(2),* p. 226.

null hypothesis that specifies a population correlation different from zero, I am confident that they will specify H_0's pinpoint number.

The Calculated Value, Critical Value, and Sample Size

In conducting a statistical test on a single correlation coefficient, researchers usually compute a sample-based calculated value that is nothing more than a correlation coefficient. If you review Excerpts 9.4 and 9.5, you will see examples of this. Many researchers (when assessing a no relationship H_0) follow this procedure of letting the computed correlation serve as the calculated value because tables of critical values have been developed that contain, as entries, values of the correlation coefficient.

When the sample value of r is considered to be the calculated value, there are two ways to determine whether it is statistically significant. If the data have been analyzed on a computer or Internet website, then the data-based value of p can be compared against the level of significance. If p is equal to or smaller than α, the null hypothesis will be rejected. In Excerpt 9.6, you can see this decision-making approach in operation. (Although the level of significance is not specified in Excerpt 9.6, an alpha level of .05 was used.)

Excerpt 9.7 illustrates the second method for determining whether a sample r is statistically significant. If the data have not been analyzed such that a data-based p is available, the researcher can compare the sample value of r against a tabled critical value. If the former equals or exceeds the latter, H_0 will be rejected. On

EXCERPTS 9.6–9.7 • *Two Ways to Decide Whether r Is Statistically Significant*

At 5 years of age, there was a [significant] positive relationship between PAL and body weight ($r = 0.19$, $P = .03$) but not with percentage of body fat ($r = -0.05$, $P = .55$).

Source: A. D. Salbe, C. Weyer, I. Harper, and R. S. Lindsay. (2002). Assessing risk factors for obesity between childhood and adolescence: II. Energy metabolism and physical activity. *Pediatrics, 110*(2), p. 309.

- -

As expected, the oldest article contained the largest percentage of expired URLs and a statistically significant positive correlation (r critical value $= 0.4971$) was observed between the age of an article and the percentage of inactive URLs. Correlation coefficients of 0.55 and 0.52 were noted in October and May.

Source: M. K. Taylor and D. Hudson. (2000). "Linkrot" and the usefulness of Web site bibliographies. *Reference and User Services Quarterly, 39*(3), p. 274.

occasion (but not often), you will come across a research report that includes the tabled critical value. An example of such a situation is presented in Excerpt 9.7. In this excerpt, each of the two sample correlation coefficients, 0.55 and 0.52, involved the same two variables, and they differ only in terms of the month in which the data were gathered. To see if each *r* was significantly different from zero, it was compared against the critical value of .4971. Because both *r*s were larger than the critical value, each was declared to be a statistically significant positive correlation.

Occasionally, researchers will use a *t*-test to evaluate the null hypothesis associated with their correlational study. When this is done, the data-based correlation coefficient is put into a *t*-formula that yields a calculated value referred to as *t*. To determine whether H_0 should be rejected, the researchers then take the calculated *t* and compare it against the appropriate critical *t* located in a *t*-table. H_0 will be rejected if the computed *t* is equal to or larger than the critical value. Otherwise, a fail-to-reject decision will be made.

To see an example where a *t*-test was used within a correlational study, consider Excerpt 9.8. In this study, the data-based correlation coefficient of .61 was put into a formula that resulted in a calculated *t*-value of 4.48. The critical value against which this calculated value was compared did not appear in the article from which Excerpt 9.8 was taken, but you can confidently guess that it was smaller than 4.48 since the notation "$p < .001$" signifies that the null hypothesis—of a zero correlation in the population—was rejected. (Such a guess would be correct, for the actual critical value was equal to 2.032.)

EXCERPT 9.8 • *Using a t-Test to Evaluate a Correlation Coefficient*

A correlation was performed using each participant's prime and target time means. As was expected, this correlation was significant, $r = .61$, $t(34) = 4.48$, $p < .001$. People who were slow to respond to the prime tended to be slow to respond to the target.

Source: A. L. Beer and V. A. Diehl. (2001). The role of short-term memory in semantic priming. *Journal of General Psychology, 128*(3), p. 340.

With respect to the use of a *t*-test to evaluate a correlation coefficient, two points are worth noting. First, the conclusion reached using the *t*-test will be identical to the decision about H_0 that would be made if the computed correlation coefficient serves as the calculated value (and is compared against a correlation-coefficient-type critical value). Thus if the *t*-test used in Excerpt 9.8 had been bypassed, with the computed correlation of .61 compared against the appropriate critical value, the same decision would have been made to reject the null hypothesis of a zero correlation in the population. Thus the *t*-test applied in this situation is really an extra step that is not necessary.

My second comment about the use of a *t*-test to evaluate a correlation coefficient concerns the nondecimal number that typically is reported next to the letter *t*. In Excerpt 9.8, this number is 34. This reported value signifies the "degrees of freedom" associated with the *t*-test, and it is equal to the sample size less 2 (i.e., $n - 2$). It is a useful number because we can quickly determine the sample size from which the correlation coefficient was computed by adding 2 to the *t*-test's degrees of freedom. Hence, Excerpt 9.8 reveals that there were 36 participants involved in the study, each of whom was timed as he or she responded to the prime and to the target.

Later in this chapter, we will return to the issue of sample size as it affects tests of correlational null hypotheses. For now, all I want to do is indicate that it is helpful to know the size of the sample when inferences are made concerning a correlation coefficient. When the *t*-test is not used, however, a researcher can still give us information about the sample size. As exemplified in Excerpt 9.9, the disclosure of the sample size doesn't take up very much room in the research report!

EXCERPT 9.9 • *Indication of the Sample Size*

Participants who reported higher spirituality before the retreat tended to report greater changes in spirituality ($r = .43, P < .001, n = 70$).

Source: J. E. Kennedy, R. A. Abbott, and B. S. Rosenberg. (2002). Changes in spirituality and well-being in a retreat program for cardiac patients. *Alternative Therapies in Health and Medicine, 8*(4), p. 69.

Tests on Specific Kinds of Correlation

Up until this point, we have been discussing tests of correlation coefficients in the generic sense. However, there is no such thing as a generic correlation. When correlating two sets of data, a specific correlational procedure must be used, with the choice usually being influenced by the nature of variables and/or the level of measurement of the researcher's instruments. As you will recall from Chapter 3, there are many different kinds of bivariate correlations: Pearson's, Spearman's, biserial, point biserial, phi, tetrachoric, and so on.

With any of the various correlation procedures, a researcher can apply the hypothesis testing procedure. When researchers report having tested *r* without specifying the type of correlation that was computed, you should presume that *r* represents Pearson's product-moment correlation. Thus, it's a good guess that the correlations you saw in Excerpts 9.4 through 9.9 were all Pearson *r*s. In Excerpts 9.10 through 9.13, we now see illustrations of other kinds of bivariate correlation coefficients being subjected to inferential testing.

EXCERPTS 9.10–9.13 • *Tests on Specific Kinds of Correlation*

A positive correlation existed between the number of carcasses collected and yearly cumulative snowfall (rho = 0.69, $n = 8$, $P = 0.028$, one-tailed test).

Source: G. Gonzalez and J. Crampe. (2001). Mortality patterns in a protected population of isards (Rupicapra pyrenaica). *Canadian Journal of Zoology, 79*(11), p. 2075.

We found a significant correlation between time of birth and whether one was identified as a day person or as a night person, $r_{pb} = .33$, p < .01.

Source: B. Wallace and L. E. Fisher. (2001). Day persons, night persons, and time of birth: Preliminary findings. *Journal of Social Psychology, 141*(1), p. 113.

Welfare status at follow-up and employment status at follow-up were also correlated (Phi = −.23, p < .05).

Source: N. P. Messina, E. D. Wish, S. Nemes, and B. Wraight. (2000). Correlates of underreporting of post-discharge cocaine use among therapeutic community clients. *Journal of Drug Issues, 30*(1), p. 1027.

We assessed the degree of similarity between paternal alcohol dependence and significant drinking history by means of a tetrachoric correlation, assuming a normal liability distribution underlying each. The resulting correlation was highly significant (tetrachoric $r = 0.57$, $P < .001$).

Source: W. G. Iacono, S. R. Carlson, S. M. Malone, and M. McGue. (2002). P3 event-related potential amplitude and the risk for disinhibitory disorders in adolescent boys. *Archives of General Psychiatry, 59*(8), p. 753.

Tests on Many Correlation Coefficients (Each of Which Is Treated Separately)

In most of the excerpts presented so far in this chapter, inferential interest was focused upon a single correlation coefficient. Although some researchers set up only one correlational null hypothesis (because each of their studies involves only one correlation coefficient), most researchers have two or more correlations that are inferentially tested in the same study. Our objective now is to consider the various ways in which such researchers present their results, to clarify the fact that a separate H_0 is associated with each correlation coefficient that is computed, and to consider the way in which the Bonferroni adjustment technique can help the researcher avoid the problem of an inflated Type I error risk.

Research
Navigator.com
Correlation matrix

Tests on the Entries of a Correlation Matrix

As we saw in Chapter 3, a **correlation matrix** is an efficient way to present the results of a correlational study in which there are three or more variables and a correlation coefficient is computed between each possible pair of variables.[1] Typically, each of the entries within the correlation matrix will be subjected to an inferential test. In Excerpt 9.14, we see an illustration of this situation.

EXCERPT 9.14 • *Tests of Many rs in a Correlation Matrix*

TABLE 2.   *Correlations for the Total Sample (N = 100)*

	1	2	3	4	5	6
1. Affect: Mother	—					
2. Affect: Father	.24*	—				
3. Autonomy: Mother	.66**	.08	—			
4. Autonomy: Father	.15	.71**	.28*	—		
5. Depressive Syptoms	.02	−.44*	−.09	−.40*	—	
6. Grade Point Average	.26*	.11	.08	.06	.00	—

Note: *p < .05; **p < .001

Source: M. E. Kenny, L. A. Gallagher, R. Alvarez-Salvat, and J. Silsby. (2002). Sources of support and psychological distress among academically successful inner-city youth. *Adolescence,* 37(145), p. 167.

[1] Whenever a correlation coefficient is computed, it is really not the variables per se that are being correlated. Rather, it is the measurements of one variable that are correlated with the measurements of the other variable. This distinction is not a trivial one because it is possible for a low correlation coefficient to grossly underestimate a strong relationship that truly exists between the two variables of interest. Poor measuring instruments could create this anomaly.

In Excerpt 9.14, the correlation matrix presents the 15 bivariate correlations that were computed among the six variables. Each of the resulting rs was subjected to a separate statistical test. And in each case, the null hypothesis was a no-relationship statement about the population associated with the single sample of participants used in the investigation. If the unnamed correlation coefficients are Pearson's rs, as I think is the case, then each of the 15 null hypotheses could be written as $H_0: \rho = 0.00$. There would be 15 null hypotheses rather than just one because each of the rs that was tested involved a different pair of variables.

Tests on Correlation Coefficients in a Table That Is Not a Correlation Matrix

At times, researchers will summarize the results of their correlational studies by means of a table that is not a true correlation matrix. Consider, for example, Excerpt 9.15. In the study associated with this excerpt, three different assessment devices—the MMSE, the SBR-15, and the BNT—were used to measure dementia (i.e., cognitive deterioration) in a sample of 78 elderly people. Those elders were also

EXCERPT 9.15 • *Tests of Many rs in a Table That Is Not a Correlation Matrix*

TABLE 5. *Bivariate Correlations between the SBV-15, the BNT, and Cognitive Tests Used to Assess the Degree of Cognitive Deterioration*

Test	MMSE	SBV-15	BNT
Benton Visual Retention	0.597**	0.597**	0.660**
BNT	0.685**	0.834**	1.000
Block Design	0.657**	0.658**	0.729**
Digit Span	0.503**	0.420**	0.420**
Age	−0.383**	−0.389**	−0.341**
Education	0.369**	0.361**	0.199
Verbal Fluency	0.358*	0.283**	0.420**
MMSE	1.000	0.651**	0.685**
Luria Motor	0.528**	0.441**	0.577**
REY Verbal Learning	0.534**	0.350**	0.525**

Notes: MMSE = Mini-Mental State Examination; SBV-15 = Shortened Boston Version-15; BNT = Boston Naming Test.

$*p < .05; **p < .01.$

Source: M. D. Calero, M. L. Arnedo, E. Navarro, M. Ruiz-Pedrosa, and C. Carnero. (2002). Usefulness of a 15-item version of the Boston Naming Test in neuropsychological assessment of low-educational elders with dementia. *The Journals of Gerontology, 57B*(2), p. P190.

measured in terms of age, educational level, verbal fluency, and ability to perform certain tasks (e.g., "block design" and "digit span") extracted from standard intelligence tests. Each of the correlation coefficients shown in Excerpt 9.15 was tested to see if it was significantly different from zero. In every case except one, the null hypothesis was rejected.

Tests on Several Correlation Coefficients Reported in the Text

Research write-ups often present the results of tests on many correlation coefficients in the text of the article rather than in a table. Excerpt 9.16 illustrates this approach to revealing how the outcome of inferential tests on several correlation coefficients can be summarized.

EXCERPT 9.16 • *Tests on Several rs with Results in the Text*

The correlation patterns evinced consistent intercorrelations among the three motives and among the three socialization tactics. The intercorrelations among the three motives revealed a positive correlation between the scholastic motive and the instrumental motive ($r = .14$, $p < .05$) and no significant relation between the collegiate motive and the two other motives ($p > .05$). The intercorrelations among the three socialization tactics revealed a positive relation between scholastic socialization and instrumental socialization ($r = .22$, $p < .05$) and no significant relation between collegiate socialization and the two other socialization tactics ($p > .05$).

Source: R. Bogler and A. Somech. (2002). Motives to study and socialization tactics among university students. *Journal of Social Psychology, 142*(2), p. 239.

In Excerpt 9.16, we see what happened when each of six correlation coefficients was tested for significance. Even though we are not told these things directly, I would guess that (1) each of the six correlations was a Pearson's r, (2) the null hypothesis for each test took the form H_0: $\rho = 0.00$, (3) each alternative hypothesis was nondirectional, (4) the critical value used to make the decision about each H_0 was equal to .14 or something smaller than this, and (5) the sample size was quite large.

The Bonferroni Adjustment Technique

In Chapter 8, I explained why researchers will sometimes use the **Bonferroni technique** to adjust their level of significance. As you will recall, the purpose of doing this is to hold down the chances of a Type I error when multiple tests are conducted. I also hope that you remember the simple mechanics of the Bonferroni technique:

Simply divide the desired study-wide Type I error risk by the number of tests being conducted.

In Excerpts 9.17 and 9.18, we see two examples in which the Bonferroni technique was used in conjunction with correlation coefficients. Both of these excerpts are worth considering.

EXCERPTS 9.17–9.18 • *Use of the Bonferroni Correction with Tests on Several Correlation Coefficients*

Using the Bonferroni approach to control for Type I error across the four correlations, a *p*-value of less than .0125 (.05/4) was required for significance.

Source: S. Maier. (2002). Getting it right? Not in 59 percent of stories. *Newspaper Research Journal, 23*(1), p. 24.

- -

Although none of the presented correlations survived a Bonferroni correction, and a large number of correlations may lead to a higher chance of finding spuriously significant associations, the correlations between 5-HT$_{1A}$ receptor binding potential and anxiety as measured by the Revised NEO Personality Inventory (correlation range = −0.49 to −0.60) may be regarded as large.

Source: J. Tauscher, R. M. Bagby, M. Javanmard, and B. K. Christensen. (2001). Inverse relationship between serotonin 5-HT$_{1A}$ receptor binding and anxiety: A[11C]WAY-100635 PET investigation in healthy volunteers. *American Journal of Psychiatry, 158*(8), p. 1328.

Excerpt 9.17 provides a nice review as to why the Bonferroni technique is used and how it works. In Excerpt 9.18, we see a case in which a team of researchers used the Bonferroni technique but did not become slaves to it. These researchers ended up with 56 *r*s generated by correlating each of 14 paper-and-pencil measures of anxiety with each of four locations of brain activity. As the researchers report, none of their 56 correlations survived the Bonferroni correction (which changed the level of significance from .05 to .0009). However, these researchers noticed that the four largest correlations all involved one of the 14 paper-and-pencil measures of anxiety. Believing that pure chance was unlikely to cause four correlations to be grouped together on one of the 14 rows in the table of 56 correlation coefficients, the researchers overruled the Bonferroni-adjusted results and stated that those four correlations "may be regarded as large."

When you come across the report of a study that presents the results of inferential tests applied to several correlation coefficients, try to remember that the conclusions drawn can be radically different depending on whether or not some form of

Bonferroni adjustment technique is used. For example, consider once again Excerpt 9.14. In this excerpt, we saw that 15 correlations were tested for significance, with results allowing the researchers to put a single asterisk (signifying $p < .05$) next to five of the rs, and a double asterisk (signifying $p < .001$) next to two other rs. If the Bonferroni technique had been applied, however, the null hypotheses associated with the rs of .24, .26, and .28 would have been retained rather than rejected.

Tests of Reliability and Validity Coefficients

As indicated in Chapter 4, many of the techniques for estimating reliability and validity rely totally or partially on one or more correlation coefficients. After computing these indices of instrument quality, researchers often apply a statistical test to determine whether or not their reliability and validity coefficients are significant. Excerpts 9.19 and 9.20 illustrate such tests.

EXCERPTS 9.19–9.20 • *Tests of Reliability and Validity Coefficients*

Intra-listener reliability was established with 43% of participants participating in a test-retest format, with a second response session to the same stimulus after approximately 2 weeks. Pearson Product-Moment Correlations were computed, with overall test-retest reliability $r = .89$ ($p < .05$).

Source: D. Misenhelter and H. E. Price. (2001). An examination of music and nonmusic majors' response to selected excerpts from Stravinsky's Le Sacre du Printemps. *Journal of Research in Music Education, 49*(4), p. 325.

- -

This construct had significant convergent validity for parent and youth reports ($r = .40$, $p < .005$).

Source: B. M. Bullock and T. J. Dishion. (2002). Sibling collusion and problem behavior in early adolescence: Toward a process model for family mutuality. *Journal of Abnormal Child Psychology, 30*(2), p. 147.

When you come across a research report in which reliability and validity coefficients are tested for significance, be careful to focus your attention on the size of the coefficient (which should be large) as well as the reported p-level (which may be quite small). For example, in Excerpt 9.19, it is nice to know that the reported test-retest reliability coefficient turned out to be significantly different from zero (with $p < .05$); however, what's also important is the size of the stability coefficient, which in this case is quite high at .89. Look at what happens, however, when we consider both p and r in Excerpt 9.20. Here, the p looks good (since it is less than .005) but the validity coefficient of .40 appears quite inadequate. This result provides proof that it is possible for a reliability or validity coefficient to end up being statistically significant even though it is unimpressive in terms of its absolute size.

Statistically Comparing Two Correlation Coefficients

At times, researchers will have two correlation coefficients that they wish to compare. The purpose of such a comparison is to determine whether a significant difference exists between the two *r*s, with the null hypothesis being a statement of no difference between the two correlations in the population(s) associated with the study. For such tests, a no-difference H_0 is fully appropriate.

Figure 9.2 is designed to help you distinguish between two similar but different situations where a pair of correlation coefficients is compared. In Figure 9.2(a), we see that a sample is drawn from each of two populations, with a bivariate correlation coefficient computed, in each sample, between the same pair of variables. In this picture, I have labeled these variables as X and Y; the two variables might be height and weight, running speed and swimming speed, or any other pair of variables. The null hypothesis is that correlation between X and Y has the same value in each of the two populations. Notice that the single inference here is based on both groups of sample data and is directed toward the *set* of populations associated with the study.

In Fig. 9.2(b), we see that a single sample is drawn from one population, but two correlation coefficients are computed on the basis of the sample data. One correlation addresses the relationship between variables X and Y while the other correlation is concerned with the relationship between variables X and Z. The null hypothesis in this kind of study is that the parameter value of the correlation between X and Y is equal to the parameter value of the correlation between X and Z. Based on the sample's pair of correlation coefficients, a single inference is directed toward the unknown values of the pair of correlations in the population.

Excerpt 9.21 nicely illustrates both of the situations depicted in Fig. 9.2. In the study from which this excerpt was taken, the researchers had 74 men and 153 women fill out three questionnaires: the BIASS, the ATH, and the MPS. After scoring the questionnaires, the data from the men were used to obtain three bivariate correlations among the questionnaires. In a similar fashion, the three questionnaires were correlated using the data gathered from the women.

In Excerpt 9.21, the first sentence illustrates the type of comparison shown in Figure 9.2(a). The second and third sentences, however, each illustrate the type of comparison shown in Figure 9.2(b). Throughout this excerpt, note that the letter z is used in conjunction with each of the three comparisons that were made. This

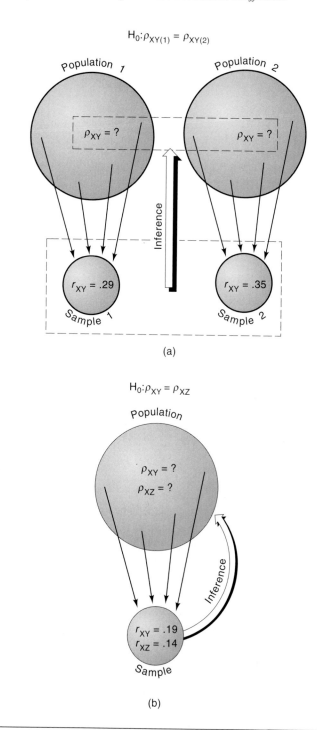

FIGURE 9.2 *Two Kinds of Inferential Situations Involving Two Correlations*

EXCERPT 9.21 • *Statistical Comparison of Two Correlation Coefficients*

The difference in correlations between the BIASS and the MPS for the men ($r = -.06$) and women ($r = .19$) approached statistical significance ($z = -1.75, p < .10$, two-tailed). The difference in the male participants' correlations between the BIASS and the MPS ($r = -.06$) and the ATH ($r = .31$) was statistically significant ($z = 2.27, p < .05$, two-tailed). The difference in the female participants' correlations between the BIASS and the ATH ($r = .38$) and the MPS ($r = .19$) approached statistical significance ($z = 1.80, p < .10$, two-tailed).

Source: K. M. Wilson and J. L. Huff. (2001). Scaling Satan. *Journal of Psychology, 135*(3), pp. 295–296.

simply indicates that a *z*-test was used. This test procedure operates much like the *t*-test discussed earlier in this chapter except that (1) the null hypothesis of the *z*-test is that no difference exists between two ρs (whereas the *t*-test's null hypothesis usually says that ρ is 0.00), and (2) the *z*-test does not have degrees of freedom associated with it (whereas the *t*-test's degrees of freedom are equal to 2 less than the number of pairs of scores).

The Use of Confidence Intervals around Correlation Coefficients

When researchers subject a data-based correlation coefficient to an inferential statistical procedure, they will probably do so via hypothesis testing. All of the excerpts presented so far in this chapter have been taken from studies in which this testing strategy was used. It is possible, however, for a researcher to deal inferentially with a correlation coefficient simply by placing a confidence interval around the sample value of *r*. Oddly, few researchers do this.

As was indicated previously, confidence intervals can be used *within* the context of hypothesis testing. In applying inferential tests to correlation coefficients, most researchers do not place confidence intervals around their sample values of *r*, but a few do. We see an illustration of this use of confidence intervals in Excerpt 9.22.

In Excerpt 9.22, notice that the first confidence interval extends from 0.25 to 0.61 whereas the second CI extends from 0.03 to 0.46. In each case, the entire CI is positioned on the positive side of 0.00, the pinpoint number contained in the null hypothesis that was being tested. Since neither CI overlapped 0.00, the researchers rejected each H_0. The fact that hypothesis testing was used here is made clear by the use of the term *significantly correlated* and by the inclusion of the notational statements "$P < .001$" and "$P = .02$."

EXCERPT 9.22 • *Use of Confidence Intervals to Test a Correlational* H_0

We searched MEDLINE and PsychLit for all controlled trials published in English between January 1981 and December 2000 in which adult outpatients with MDD were randomly assigned to receive medication or placebo. Seventy-five trials met our criteria for inclusion. . . . Both the proportion of patients responding to placebo and the proportion responding to medication were significantly positively correlated with the year of publication (for placebo: $n = 75$; $r = 0.45$; 95% confidence interval [CI], 0.25–0.61; $P < .001$; for medication: $n = 75$; $r = 0.26$; 95% CI, 0.03–0.46; $P = .02$).

Source: B. T. Walsh, S. N. Seidman, R. Sysko, and M. Gould. (2002). Placebo response in studies of major depression: Variable, substantial, and growing. *Journal of the American Medical Association, 287*(14), p. 1840.

Cautions

I feel obligated to end this chapter by suggesting a few cautions that you should keep in mind when trying to decipher (and critique) research reports based on correlation coefficients. As you will see, my comments here constitute a reiteration of some of the points presented at the end of Chapter 3 as well as some of the points offered at the conclusions of Chapters 7 and 8.

Relationship Strength, Effect Size, and Power

Many researchers seem to get carried away with the *p*-levels associated with their correlation coefficients and thus seem to forget that the estimated strength of a relationship is best assessed by squaring the sample value of *r*. Discovering that a correlation coefficient is significant may not really be very important—even if the results indicate $p < .01$ or $p < .001$—unless the value of r^2 is reasonably high. The result may be significant in a statistical sense (thus indicating that the sample data are not likely to have come from a population characterized by H_0), but it may be quite insignificant in a practical sense.

Consider Excerpt 9.23. A correlation of .58 certainly does not signify "a very strong relationship," even if you *fail* to convert it into a coefficient of determination. Here, we have a good example in which the researchers looked at and were impressed by *p*, with little regard for the size of *r*.

To see an example where the important distinction between statistical significance and practical significance *was* kept in mind, take a look at Excerpts 9.24 and 9.25. In these excerpts, notice the presence of the phrases "although significant" and "in spite of the observed statistical significance." Both sets of researchers deserve high praise for warning readers to be careful when evaluating their significant *r*s.

EXCERPT 9.23 • *Incorrect Focus on p Rather Than r*

As predicted, this analysis indicated a very strong relationship ($r = 0.58$, $df = 70$, $p < 0.001$) between severity of borderline personality disorder and the second factor, painful incoherence. . . .

Source: T. Wilkinson-Ryan and D. Westen. (2000). Identity disturbance in borderline personality disorder: An empirical investigation. *American Journal of Psychiatry, 157*(4), p. 537.

EXCERPTS 9.24–9.25 • *Expressed Concern for the Strength of Statistically Significant Correlations*

A significant positive correlation ($r_{pb} = .22$, $P = .01$) was found between patient satisfaction and the use of computers in hospital A, although it explained only 4% of the variance. . . . Although significant, the strength of this relationship was weak.

Source: E. Yellen and G. Davis. (2001). Patient satisfaction in ambulatory surgery. *AORN Journal, 74*(4), p. 493.

- -

However, in spite of the observed statistical significance, from a practical standpoint the likelihood of attaining a doctoral school placement is only weakly associated with faculty gender. Specifically, the phi coefficient for the tabled data is only -0.053, indicating a low degree of association.

Source: D. L. Collins, A. Reitenga, A. B. Collins, and S. Lane. (2000). "Glass walls" in academic accounting? The role of gender in initial employment position. *Issues in Accounting Education, 15*(3), p. 380.

In Chapter 8, I pointed out how researchers can apply a seven-step version of hypothesis testing by computing a strength-of-association index, by estimating effect size, or by conducting a post hoc power analysis. These three strategies can be used with correlation coefficients. In fact, we saw the first of these three things done in Excerpt 9.24, where the researchers moved beyond the raw correlation coefficient and focused on the percent of variance explained.

To see how effect sizes can be useful when interpreting correlation coefficients, consider Excerpt 9.26. In the note beneath the table, the researchers provide a set of criteria for evaluating the entries in the correlation matrix. Notice how they allow us to evaluate the correlations of .24 and .28 as small (even though they have an asterisk that indicates $p < .05$) and to evaluate the correlation of .36 as medium (even though it has an asterisk that indicates $p < .01$).

EXCERPT 9.26 • *Effect Size Criteria*

TABLE 2. *Correlations among IAT, Discrepancy, Should, Would, and MRS Scores*

	1.	2.	3.	4.	5.
1. IAT scores	—				
2. Discrepancy	.17	—			
3. Should	.19	.04	—		
4. Would	.24*	.52**	.62**	—	
5. MRS	.28*	.17	.44**	.36**	—

Note. $*p < .05$, $**p < .01$. $N = 79$. Conventional effect sizes for r: $.10 =$ small; $.30 =$ medium; $.50 =$ large.

Source: M. J. Monteith, C. I. Voils, and L. Ashburn-Nardo. (2001). Taking a look underground: Detecting, interpreting, and reacting to implicit racial biases. *Social Cognition, 19*(4), p. 409.

The third strategy, involving a post hoc power analysis, is illustrated in Excerpt 9.27. In the second and third sentences of this excerpt, the researchers indicate that their computed correlations turned out to be nonsignificant. In the last sentence, they point out that their study had above-average power to detect population correlations as small as .40. Thus, the researchers are using the results of their post hoc power analysis to argue that they most likely did *not* make a Type II error when they failed to reject the null hypothesis.

EXCERPT 9.27 • *A Post Hoc Power Analysis within a Correlational Study*

We also conducted analyses restricted to the soccer athletes to investigate potential relationships between cumulative exposure to soccer and performance on the selected tests. With the exception of the Wechsler Digit Span Test (digits backward), Pearson's correlation coefficients revealed no evidence of a significant relationship between exposure to soccer and neurocognitive performance. Likewise, there was no significant relationship between exposure to soccer and Scholastic Aptitude Test scores. . . . For the soccer history characteristics, the study had 90% power to detect correlations as low as 0.40. . . .

Source: K. M. Guskiewicz, S. W. Marshall, S. P. Broglio, R. C. Cantu, and D. T. Kirkendall. (2002). No evidence of impaired neurocognitive performance in collegiate soccer players. *American Journal of Sports Medicine, 30*(2), pp. 159–160.

Although researchers can demonstrate a concern for relationship strength, effect size, or power as illustrated in the excerpts we have considered, they do an even better job if they utilize the nine-step version of hypothesis testing. As I hope you recall from Chapter 8, this involves setting up the study so that it will have the desired level of power and the right sample size. When a researcher's study is focused on one or more correlation coefficients, it is quite easy to add these extra tasks to the basic six-step version of hypothesis testing.

When you come across a study in which the appropriate sample size was determined prior to the collection of any data, give the researcher some bonus points for taking the time to set up the study with sensitivity to both Type I *and* Type II errors. When you come across a study in which the power associated with the test(s) conducted on the correlation coefficient(s) is computed in a post hoc sense, give the researcher only a few bonus points. And when you come across a study in which there is no mention whatsoever of statistical power, award *yourself* some bonus points for detecting a study that could have been conducted better than it was.

Linearity and Homoscedasticity

Tests on Pearson's *r* are conducted more frequently than tests on any other kind of correlation coefficient. Whenever tests on Pearson's *r* are conducted, two important assumptions about the population must hold true in order for the test to function as it was designed. One of these important prerequisite conditions is referred to as the linearity assumption. The other is referred to as the equal variance assumption (or, alternatively, as the assumption of homoscedasticity).

The assumption of **linearity** states that the relationship in the population between the two variables of interest must be such that the bivariate means fall on a straight line. The assumption of **homoscedasticity** states that (1) the variance of the *Y* variable around μ_y is the same regardless of the value of *X* being considered and (2) the variance of the *X* variable around μ_x is constant regardless of the value of *Y* being considered. If a population is characterized by a curvilinear relationship between *X* and *Y* and/or characterized by heteroscedasticity, the inferential test on Pearson's *r* will provide misleading information concerning the existence and strength of the relationship in the population.

The easiest way for a researcher to check on these two assumptions is to look at a scatter diagram of the sample data. If the data in the sample appear to conform to the linearity and equal variance assumptions, then the researcher can make an informed guess that linearity and homoscedasticity are also characteristics of the population. In that situation, the test on *r* can then be performed. If a plot of the data suggests, however, that either of the assumptions is untenable, then the regular test on *r* should be bypassed in favor of one designed for curvilinear or unequal variance conditions.

As a reader of the research literature, my preference is to be able to look at scatter diagrams so I can judge for myself whether researchers' data sets appear to meet the assumptions that underlie tests on r. Because of space limitations, however, technical journals rarely permit such visual displays of the data to be included. If scatter diagrams cannot be shown, then it is my feeling that researchers should communicate in words what *they* saw when they looked at their scatter diagrams.

Consider Excerpts 9.28 and 9.29. In the first of these excerpts, the researchers report having looked at a scatterplot and observed that the relationship was not linear, thus calling into question the validity of the computed correlation. In Excerpt 9.29, we see a second example where a scatterplot was examined, this time with an eye toward the assumption of normality that's associated with Pearson's correlation.

I feel that too many researchers move too quickly from collecting their data to testing their rs to drawing conclusions based upon the results of their tests. Few take the time to look at a scatter diagram as a safety maneuver to avoid misinterpretations caused by curvilinearity or heteroscedasticity. I applaud the small number of researchers who take the time to perform this extra step.

EXCERPTS 9.28–9.29 • *Expressed Concern for Linearity and Normality*

Figure 5a [not shown here] shows a scatterplot of the real data for the 576 English registration districts, with church attendance plotted against pluralism. . . . Although the correlation across all English districts is close to zero (.027), the results do not follow a linear pattern.

Source: D. Voas, A. Crockett, and D. V. A. Olson. (2002). Religious pluralism and participation: Why previous research is wrong. *American Sociological Review, 67*(2), p. 222.

The correlations shown in Table 1 [not shown here] are Pearson correlations, which generally presume normally distributed data. . . . There appeared to be several potential outliers in the scatterplot of these data, most notably for Romania, Turkey, and Venezuela, so the analysis was repeated removing each (and eventually all) of these countries from the data set.

Source: K. A. Getz and R. J. Volkema. (2001). Culture, perceived corruption, and economics. *Business and Society, 40*(1), p. 20.

Causality

When we initially looked at correlation from a descriptive standpoint in Chapter 3, I pointed out that a correlation coefficient usually should not be interpreted to mean that one variable has a causal impact on the other variable. Now that we have considered correlation from an inferential standpoint, I want to embellish that earlier point by saying that a correlation coefficient, even if found to be significant at an impressive alpha level, normally should not be viewed as addressing any cause-and-effect question.

In Excerpt 9.30, the researchers do two nice things. First, they point out that correlation does not necessarily imply causality. Second, they offer a reason, connected to a plausible "third variable," as to why their correlations turned out as they did. Not all researchers would have said these things. Many would have looked at the computed rs (all nine of which were significant, with seven having ps smaller than .001) and been swept away into thinking that causal relationships were being revealed.

EXCERPT 9.30 • *Correlation and Causality*

To assess which of these two situations dominated, we calculated simple correlation coefficients for the correlation between the number of bonus points awarded to a particular student and the scores he or she made on quizzes or exams. In Table 1 [not shown here], we provide the correlation coefficients and their t statistics for both semesters in which the technology was employed. In all cases, the correlation coefficients were positive, indicating that those students with the most bonus points also did the best on quizzes and exams. The t statistics also allow us generally to reject the hypothesis that these estimates are not different from zero, at traditional levels of significance. Of course, correlation does not imply causality. It could be the case that the brightest students are the ones most comfortable with this new technology.

Source: S. E. Hein and K. A. Austin. (2001). Using World Wide Web utilities to engage students in money, banking, and credit. *Journal of Education for Business, 76*(3), p. 170.

Attenuation

The inferential procedures covered in this chapter assume that the two variables being correlated are each measured without error. In other words, these procedures are designed for the case where each variable is measured with an instrument that has perfect reliability. While this assumption may have full justification in a theoretical sense, it certainly does not match the reality of the world in which we live. To the best of my knowledge, no researcher has ever measured two continuous variables and ended up with data that were perfectly reliable.

When two variables are measured such that the data have less than perfect reliability, the measured relationship in the sample data will systematically underestimate the strength of the relationship in the population. In other words, the computed correlation coefficient will be a **biased estimate** of the parameter if either or both of the variables are measured without error-free instruments. The term **attenuation** has been coined to describe this situation, where, using the product-moment correlation as an example, measurement error causes r to systematically underestimate ρ.

Once you come to understand the meaning (and likely occurrence) of attenuation, you should be able to see why statistical tests that yield fail-to-reject decisions are problematic in terms of interpretation. If, for example, a researcher computes Pearson's r and ends up not rejecting H_0: $\rho = 0.00$, this outcome *may* have come about because there is a very weak (or possibly no) relationship between the two variables in the population. On the other hand, the decision not to reject H_0 *may* have been caused by attenuation masking a strong relationship in the population.

In Chapter 4, we spent a great deal of time considering various techniques used by researchers to estimate the reliability of their measuring instruments. That discussion now becomes relevant to our consideration of inferential reports on correlation coefficients. If a researcher's data possess only trivial amounts of measurement error, then attenuation becomes only a small concern. On the other hand, reports of only moderate reliability coupled with correlational results that turn out nonsignificant leave us in a quandary as to knowing anything about the relationship in the population.

If researchers have information concerning the reliabilities associated with the measuring instruments used to collect data on the two variables being correlated, they can use a formula that adjusts the correlation coefficient to account for the suspected amount of unreliability. When applied, this **correction-for-attenuation** formula will always yield an adjusted r that is higher than the uncorrected, raw r. In Excerpt 9.31, we see an example where a group of researchers conducted a correlational study and used the correction-for-attenuation formula.

Research
Navigator.c⊛m

Correction-for-
attenuation

EXCERPT 9.31 • *Correlation Coefficients and Attenuation*

All of the obtained correlations were statistically significant. . . . The mean correlation between wives' and husbands' descriptions of wives' marital behavior was .42, and the mean attenuation-corrected correlation (correcting for both internal consistency reliability and retest reliability) was .59. . . . The strongest validity correlation for descriptions of wives was that for anger/aggression ($r = .68$; attenuation-corrected $r = .84$), and the weakest validity correlation was that for projective mystification ($r = .16$; attenuation-corrected $r = .33$).

Source: P. D. Werner, R. J. Green, J. Greenberg, T. L. Browne, and T. E. McKenna. (2001). Beyond enmeshment: Evidence for the independence of intrusiveness and closeness-caregiving in married couples. *Journal of Marital and Family Therapy, 27*(4), p. 463.

Attenuation, of course, is not the only thing to consider when trying to make sense out of a correlation-based research report. Several of these other relevant considerations have been addressed within our general discussion of cautions. Two points are worth reiterating, each now connected to the concept of reliability. First, it is possible that a correlation coefficient will turn out to be statistically significant even though H_0 is true and even though highly reliable instruments are used to collect the sample data; do not forget that Type I errors *do* occur. Second, it is possible that a correlation coefficient will turn out to be nonsignificant even when H_0 is false and even when highly reliable data have been collected; do not forget about the notion of Type II errors and power.

Fisher's r-to-z Transformation

When researchers report on how they dealt inferentially with one or more correlation coefficients, they may make reference to their use of **Fisher's *r*-to-*z* transformation.** This transformation is part of the data analysis procedures that researchers use when dealing with their sample data, and you do not need to understand how this transformation operates in order to understand and critique the researchers' findings. My only reason for mentioning it here is to point out that you should not be thrown for a loop when you come across this phase.

In Excerpts 9.32 and 9.33, we see two cases where Fisher's *r*-to-*z* transformation was used. In the first of these excerpts, it was used when a single correlation was tested for significance. In the second excerpt, Fisher's transformation was used to compare two correlations to see if they were significantly different.

EXCERPTS 9.32–9.33 • *Fisher's* r-to-z *Transformation*

Furthermore, to determine whether the correlation coefficient was statistically different from 0, Fisher's *r*-to-*z* transformation was performed on the correlation.

Source: S. Jakob, R. Zabielski, R. Mosenthin, and J. L. V. Piedra. (2001). Influence of intraduodenally infused olive and coconut oil on postprandial exocrine pancreatic secretions of growing pigs. *Journal of Animal Science, 79*(2), p. 479.

- -

According to Fisher's Z test, the difference in correlations was significant (Fisher's $Z = -5.13, p < 0.001$).

Source: L. Keltikangas-Jarvinen. (2002). Aggressive problem-solving strategies, aggressive behavior, and social acceptance in early and late adolescence. *Journal of Youth and Adolescence, 31*(4), p. 284.

Review Terms

Attenuation   Correlation matrix
Biased estimate   Fisher's r-to-z transformation
Bonferroni technique   Homoscedasticity
Correction for attenuation   Linearity

The Best Items in the Companion Website

1. An interactive online quiz (with immediate feedback provided) covering Chapter 9.
2. Nine misconceptions about the content of Chapter 9.
3. An email message sent from the author to his students entitled "Significant Correlations."
4. Four e-articles illustrating the use of hypothesis testing with correlations.
5. A delightful poem "A Word on Statistics."

Fun Exercises inside Research Navigator

1. **Are attractive people more "socially connected"?**

   In this study, each of 125 college students submitted 20 photos to answer the question "Who are you?" For the central part of the study, each participant's photos were rated by a set of judges so as to determine two scores for the participant: (1) his or her physical attractiveness and (2) his or her social connectedness. (Social connectedness was rated high if a photo showed the participant with others, if people were smiling, and so on; social attractiveness was rated low if the photo showed the participant alone, if no people were in the photo, or if there were two or more people who looked unhappy.) These two sets of scores were correlated, and the resulting r was tested for significance. If you had to guess the value of r and also guess whether it turned out to be statistically significant, what would your guesses be? To find out if your guesses are good ones, locate the PDF version of the research report in the Psychology database of ContentSelect and read the second paragraph of the "Results and Discussion" section.

   S. J. Dollinger. Physical attractiveness, social connectedness, and individuality: An autophotographic study. *Journal of Psychology.* Located in the PSYCHOLOGY database of ContentSelect.

2. **Who eats more: those who do or don't have their lower-level needs met?**

   A group of adults ranging in age from 21 to 79 years old filled out two questionnaires. One of these, the *Basic Need Satisfaction Inventory* (BNSI), measures people's perceived satisfaction with meeting different kinds of needs: basic physiological needs, safety/security, love and belonging, self-esteem, and self-actualization. (As you may have noticed, these needs correspond with Maslow's hierarchy of needs.) The other questionnaire, the *Emotional Eating Scale* (EES), measures the degree to which people eat as a response to emotional states. The main finding of this study was connected to the statistically significant correlation between the composite scores of these two measures. Do you think it was a positive or negative correlation? To find out, locate the PDF version of the research report in the Nursing, Health, and Medicine database of ContentSelect and read the last full sentence on page 697.

G. M. Timmerman & G. J. Acton. The relationship between basic need satisfaction and emotional eating. *Issues in Mental Health Nursing.* Located in the NURSING, HEALTH, AND MEDICINE database of ContentSelect.

Review Questions and Answers begin on page 516.

10

Inferences Concerning One or Two Means

In the previous chapter, we saw how inferential statistical techniques can be used with correlation coefficients. Now, we turn our attention to the procedures used to make inferences with means. A variety of techniques are used by applied researchers to deal with their sample means, and we will consider many of these inferential procedures here and in several of the following chapters. Multiple chapters are needed to deal with this broad topic because the inferential procedures used by researchers vary according to (1) how many groups of scores are involved, (2) whether underlying assumptions seem tenable, (3) how many independent variables come into play, (4) whether data on concomitant variables are used to increase power, and (5) whether people are measured under more than one condition of the investigation.

In this introductory chapter on inferences concerning means, we will restrict our focus to the cases where the researcher has computed either just one sample mean or two sample means. I will illustrate how statistical tests are used in studies where interest lies in one or two means and the way interval estimation is sometimes used in such studies. Near the end of this chapter, we will consider the assumptions that underlie the inferential procedures covered in this chapter, and we will also examine the concept of "overlapping distributions." With this overview now under your belt, let us turn to the simplest inferential situation involving means: the case where there is a single mean.

Inferences Concerning a Single Mean

If researchers have collected data from a single sample and if they wish to focus on $\bar{X}$ in an inferential manner, one (or both) of two statistical strategies will be implemented. On the one hand, a confidence interval can be built around the sample mean. On the other hand, a null hypothesis can be set up and then evaluated by means of the hypothesis testing procedure.

The Inferential Purpose

Figure 10.1 has been constructed to help clarify what researchers are trying to do when they use the mean of a sample as the basis for building a confidence interval or for assessing a null hypothesis. As this figure shows, $\overline{X}$ is computed on the basis of data collected from the sample. Although the sample-based value of the mean is easy to obtain, primary interest lies in the corresponding value of μ, the population mean.[1] However, the researcher cannot compute the value of μ because only the objects in the sample can be measured. Accordingly, an inference (i.e., educated guess) about the unknown value of the population parameter, μ, is made on the basis of the known value of the sample statistic, $\overline{X}$.

In summarizing their empirical investigations, many researchers discuss their findings in such a way that the exclusive focus seems to be on the sample data. The thick arrow in Fig. 10.1 will help you remember that the different inferential techniques to which we now turn our attention are designed to allow a researcher to say something about the *population* involved in the study, not the sample. If concern rested with the sample, no inferential techniques would be necessary.

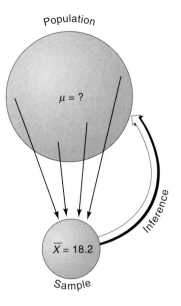

FIGURE 10.1   *The Inferential Purpose When One Sample's Mean Is Computed*

---

[1]If the researcher's data come from a probability sample, then μ represents the mean of the study's *tangible* population. On the other hand, if the data come from a convenience or purposive sample (or some other form of nonprobability sample), then μ represents the mean of the study's abstract population.

Interval Estimation

Of the two basic ways of applying inferential statistics to a sample mean, the **confidence interval** procedure is simpler. All the researcher will do in implementing this inferential strategy is (1) make a decision as to the level of confidence that will be associated with the interval to be built and (2) build the interval around $\bar{X}$ by using a formula that incorporates information from the sample (e.g., $\bar{X}$, *SD*, and *n*) as well as a numerical value extracted from a statistical table. The result will be an interval that extends equally far above and below the sample value of $\bar{X}$.

In Excerpt 10.1, we see a case in which confidence intervals were placed around two sample means. The first CI extended from 0.3 to 3.1, whereas the second CI extended from 7.1 to 10.7. Each of these was a 95% CI. Each CI gives us a sense for how trustworthy the sample mean is. If the study were to be replicated, we would expect sampling error to cause the mean in the replicated study to be different from the original mean. But how much variation should we expect? The CI gives us a range within which we would expect to find that next sample mean.

EXCERPT 10.1 • *Confidence Intervals around a Single Mean*

Childhood sexual abuse onset predated that of social fears by a mean of 1.7 years (95% CI, 0.3–3.1) and suicide attempt by a mean of 8.9 years (95% CI, 7.1–10.7).

Source: E. C. Nelson, A. C. Heath, P. A. F. Madden, and M. L. Cooper. (2002). Association between self-reported childhood sexual abuse and adverse psychosocial outcomes: Results from a twin study. *Archives of General Psychiatry, 59*(2), p. 141.

As you may recall from Chapter 8, it is technically wrong to interpret these (or other) CIs by saying or thinking that there is a 95% chance that the population mean lies somewhere between the end points of the CI. Instead, you need to imagine (1) that many samples are drawn randomly from the same population, (2) that a separate CI is built for each sample, and (3) that each CI is examined to see if it has captured the population mean. With these three things in mind, the correct way to interpret a 95% CI is to say or think that it is one of many (actually 95%) CIs that would, in fact, overlap μ rather than one of the few (actually 5%) that would not.

Excerpt 10.2 again illustrates how researchers build confidence intervals around means, except here the results are presented in a table. In this excerpt, notice that the sample sizes for three groups of children were not the same. Next, notice that the widths of the CIs for the ABC measure are not the same. (For example, the CI for the nonfluent group, extending from 56.8 to 75.1, is not as wide as the CI for the fluent group, which extends from 33.6 to 58.0.) These CIs illustrate the fact that if other things are held constant, there is an inverse relationship between interval

EXCERPT 10.2 • *Confidence Intervals around Means*

TABLE 3   *Scores for Autistic Symptoms and Socialization of Children 6–8 Years Old with Autism Who Were or Were Not Verbally Fluent at 2-Year Follow-Up and Scores of Children 4–6 Years Old with Asperger's Syndrome at Study Enrollment*

	Score of Children with Autism at 2-Year Follow-Up				Score of Children with Asperger's Syndrome at Study Enrollment (N = 21)	
	Nonfluent (N = 26)		Fluent (N = 18)			
Measure	*Mean*	*95% CI*	*Mean*	*95% CI*	*Mean*	*95% CI*
ABC[a]	66.0	56.8–75.1	45.8	33.6–58.0	49.7	38.5–61.0
VABS-S[b]	48.8	43.0–54.5	69.8	62.7–76.9	64.3	58.2–70.5

[a]Autism Behavior Checklist
[b]Raw score from Vineland Adaptive Behavior Scales socialization scale

Source: P. Szatmari, S. E. Bryson, D. L. Streiner, and F. Wilson. (2000). Two-year outcome of preschool children with autism or Asperger's Syndrome. *American Journal of Psychiatry,* 157(12), p. 1984. [Adapted slightly for presentation here.]

width and sample size. If you look at the CIs for the VABS-S measure, once again you will see that the shortest CI has been built around the mean of the largest sample, whereas the widest CI has been built around the mean of the smallest sample.

Tests Concerning a Null Hypothesis

When researchers have a single sample (and thus a single population) and have inferential interest in the mean, they can approach the data by means of the hypothesis testing procedure. When this strategy is used, a null hypothesis must be articulated. In this kind of research situation, the null hypothesis will take the form

$$H_0: \mu = a$$

where *a* stands for a pinpoint numerical value selected by the researcher.

After specifying H_0, researchers will proceed to apply the various steps of the inferential testing strategy they have decided to follow. Regardless of which strategy is used, researchers assess the discrepancy between the sample mean and H_0's pinpoint value; if the difference between $\overline{X}$ and H_0's μ-value is large enough, H_0

will be rejected and viewed as not likely to be true due to the small value of p associated with the sample data.

There are several available test procedures that can be used to analyze the data of a one-sample study wherein the statistical focus is the mean. The two most popular of these test procedures are the **t-test** and the **z-test.** These two ways of testing the discrepancy between $\overline{X}$ and H_0's μ-value are identical in logic and have the same decision rule when comparing the calculated value against the critical value.[2] The only difference between the two tests is that the z-test yields a calculated value that is slightly larger than it ought to be (and a p-value that is slightly smaller than it ought to be). However, the amount of the bias is trivial when the sample size is at least 30.

Excerpts 10.3 and 10.4 illustrate how researchers will often present their results when they have a single sample and conduct a z-test or a t-test to evaluate a null hypothesis of the form H_0: μ = a. In the first of these excerpts, the pinpoint number from the null hypothesis is not shown. However, it was equal to the mean score on the norms. In Excerpt 10.4, the null hypothesis took the form H_0: $\mu = 3.0$,

EXCERPTS 10.3–10.4 • *Use of z or t to Test the Mean of a*
Single Sample

Comparisons of a group mean with a population mean used a one-sample z test. . . . Subjects were significantly impaired compared with the norms on all dimensions [e.g., $z = 3.2$ for Bodily Health], although impairment on emotional dimensions was most marked [e.g., $z = 26.8$ for Social Role].

Source: P. J. McGrath, J. W. Stewart, M. N. Janal, and E. Petkova. (2000). A placebo-controlled study of fluoxetine versus imipramine in the acute treatment of atypical depression. *American Journal of Psychiatry, 157*(3), p. 346.

- -

In the first analysis it was predicted that counselors' attitudes toward sex offenders would be positive. This was tested by comparing the total mean score on the ATS ($M = 3.34$) to that of the neutral value for the underlying scale ($M = 3.00$) using a one-sample t test. The mean score fell approximately one third of a point above the neutral value on a 5-point scale. This difference was large enough to be statistically significant ($t = 14.82$, $df = 436$, $p = .00$).

Source: M. Nelson, B. Herlihy, and J. Oescher. (2002). A survey of counselor attitudes towards sex offenders. *Journal of Mental Health Counseling, 24*(1), p. 57.

[2]This decision rule says to reject H_0 if the calculated value is as large as or larger than the critical value; otherwise, the null hypothesis should not be rejected.

with 3.0 chosen as the null point because it represented the neutral point on a 5-point rating scale.

Near the end of Excerpt 10.4, notice that a number labeled *df* is presented immediately after the calculated value of $t = 14.82$. This number, which here is 436, is technically referred to as the **degrees of freedom,** or *df,* for the *t*-test that was performed.[3] If you add 1 to the *df* number, you can determine how large the sample was. Knowing this, you can determine that 437 counselors were involved in this study.

Inferences Concerning Two Means

If researchers want to compare, using inferential statistics, two samples in terms of the mean scores, they can utilize a confidence interval approach to the data or an approach that involves setting up and testing a null hypothesis. We will consider the way in which estimation can be used with two means after we examine the way in which two means can be compared through a tested H_0. Before we do either of these things, however, I must draw a distinction between two 2-group situations: those that involve independent samples and those that involve correlated samples.

Independent versus Correlated Samples

Whether two samples are considered to be independent or correlated is tied to the issue of the nature of the groups *before* data are collected on the study's dependent variable. If the two groups have been assembled in such a way that a logical relationship exists between each member of the first sample and one and only one member of the second sample, then the two samples are **correlated samples.** On the other hand, if no such relationship exists, the two samples are **independent samples.**

Correlated samples come into existence in one of three ways. If a single group of people is measured twice (e.g., to provide pretest and posttest data), then a relationship exists in the data because each of the pretest scores goes with one and only one of the posttest scores, since both come from measuring the same research participant. A second situation that produces correlated samples is **matching.** Here, each person in the second group is recruited for the study because he or she is a good match for a particular individual in the first group. The matching could be done in terms of height, IQ, running speed, or any of a multitude of possible matching variables. The matching variable, however, is never the same as the dependent variable that will be measured and then used to compare the two samples. The third situation that produces correlated samples occurs when biological twins are split up,

Research
Navigator.c⊕m
Independent
samples

---

[3]There is no *df* value in Excerpt 10.3 because *z*-tests do not utilize the *df* concept.

with one member of each pair going into the first sample and the other member going into the second group. Here, the obvious connection that ties together the two samples is genetic similarity.

When people, animals, or things are measured twice or when twin pairs are split up, it is fairly easy to sense which scores are paired together and why such pairing exists. When a study involves matching, however, things are slightly more complicated. That is because two data-based variables are involved. The data on one or more of these variables are used to create pairs of people such that the two members of any pair are as similar as possible on matching variables. Once the matched pairs are formed, then new data are examined on the dependent variable of interest to see if the two groups of individuals differ *on the dependent variable.* For example, a researcher might create matched pairs of students who have low academic self-concept, randomly split up the pairs to form an experimental group (that receives tutoring) and a control group (that does not), and then compare the two groups in terms of how they perform at the end of the term on a final course examination. In this hypothetical study, the matching variable would be academic self-concept (with these scores discarded after being used to form matched pairs); the scores of primary interest—that is, the scores corresponding to the dependent variable—would come from the final course examination.

Excerpt 10.5 ought to clarify the distinction between matching and dependent variables. This excerpt comes from a study in which 11 college students known to have learning disabilities (LD) were compared with 11 of their peers who did not have learning disabilities (NLD). These two groups were compared in terms of several dependent variables of interest, one of which was the ability to find words (i.e., retrieve them from memory) after having heard them in sentences.

In the study associated with Excerpt 10.5, there were two matching variables, age and IQ. The study's dependent variable is represented by the scores in the two columns at the right. These data at the right, which indicate how well each individual performed on the word-finding task, should be thought of as correlated samples.

The term *correlated,* as used in this context, should *not* be interpreted to mean that the researcher is concerned about correlation. (Excerpt 10.5 is a case in point, for here the researchers want to compare the mean word-finding scores of the LD and NLD groups.) Rather, it simply means that scores on the dependent variable are logically connected across the two samples. This connection is not based on the size of the scores but rather on a consideration of where the data came from. For example, the two word-finding scores of 116 go together not because of their size but rather because these scores came from two matched participants (LD #7 and NLD #10).

If the two groups of scores being compared do not represent one of these three situations (pre–post, matched pairs, or twins), then they are considered to be independent samples. Such samples can come about in any number of ways. People might be assigned to one of two groups using the method of simple randomization, or possibly they end up in one or the other of two groups because they possess a

EXCERPT 10.5 • *Data on the Matching and Dependent Variables*

Participant		Age (Years)		IQ Score		Word-Finding Composite Score	
LD	NLD	LD	NLD	LD	NLD	LD	NLD
1	4	21	20	109	102	106	86
2	2	21	21	98	96	90	111
3	3	20	21	91	96	129	102
4	8	21	20	110	108	102	106
5	5	19	20	109	104	92	126
6	6	20	20	110	108	129	90
7	10	20	21	105	105	116	116
8	11	19	20	102	98	102	94
9	7	21	21	108	105	94	118
10	1	18	19	102	98	140	106
11	9	20	21	109	111	129	92
	M =	21	20	103	105	111.636	104.272

Note: LD = participant with learning disabilities; NLD = matched participant without learning disabilities.

Source: S. S. Rubin and C. M. Johnson. (2002). Lexical access in college students with learning disabilities: An electrophysiological and performance-based investigation. *Journal of Learning Disabilities, 35*(3), pp. 260–261. [Adapted slightly for presentation here.]

characteristic that coincides with the thing that distinguishes the two groups. This second situation is exemplified by the multitude of studies that compare males against females, students who graduate against those who don't graduate, people who die of a heart attack versus those who don't, and so on. Or, maybe one of the two groups is formed by those who volunteer to undergo some form of treatment whereas the other group is made up of folks who choose not to volunteer. A final example (of the ones to be mentioned) would be created if the researchers simply designate one of two intact groups to be their first sample, which receives something that might help them, while the second intact group is provided with nothing at all or maybe a placebo.

In Excerpts 10.6 and 10.7, we see descriptions of data sets that represent independent and correlation samples. It's easy to tell that the data in the first of these studies should be thought of as independent samples due to the fact that the sample sizes are different. (Whenever n_1 is different from n_1, it's impossible to have each score in one of the data sets paired logically with one of the scores in the second data set.) The two data sets in Excerpt 10.7 were correlated because of the pretest versus posttest nature of the questionnaire scores.

EXCERPTS 10.6–10.7 • *Independent and Correlated Samples*

The sample consisted of 57 subjects, 32 of whom were randomly assigned to the control group (i.e., no insider information treatment), while the remaining 25 students were in the insider information treatment group.

Source: M. Abdolmohammadi and J. Sultan. (2002). Ethical reasoning and the use of insider information in stock trading. *Journal of Business Ethics, 37*(2), p. 169.

- -

Patients with low back pain completed the questionnaires during initial consultation with a physical therapist and again 6 weeks later ($n = 106$).

Source: M. Davidson and J. L. Keating. (2002). A comparison of five low back disability questionnaires: Reliability and responsiveness. *Physical Therapy, 82*(1), p. 8.

Research Navigator.c⊕m
Matched samples
Paired samples

Although this was not done in either of the two excerpts we have just considered, researchers sometimes indicate explicitly that their data came from independent samples or correlated samples. When they do so, you will have no trouble knowing what kind of samples were used. However, they may use terms other than independent samples and correlated samples. Correlated samples are sometimes referred to as **paired samples, matched samples, dependent samples,** or **within samples,** while independent samples are sometimes called **unpaired samples, unmatched samples,** or **uncorrelated samples.**

To understand exactly what researchers did in comparing their two groups, you must develop the ability to distinguish between correlated samples and independent samples. The language used by the researchers will help to indicate what kind of samples were involved in the study. If a descriptive adjective is not used, you will have to make a judgment based on the description of how the two samples were formed.

The Inferential Purpose

Before we turn our attention to the way researchers typically summarize studies that focus on two sample means, I want to underscore the fact that these comparisons of means are inferential in nature. Figure 10.2 is designed to help you visualize this important point.

Panel A in Figure 10.2 represents the case where the means of two independent samples are compared. Panel B represents the case where two correlated samples of data are compared in terms of means. (In panel B, the dotted chains that extend from population 1 to population 2 are meant to denote the pairing or matching that is characteristic of correlated samples.)

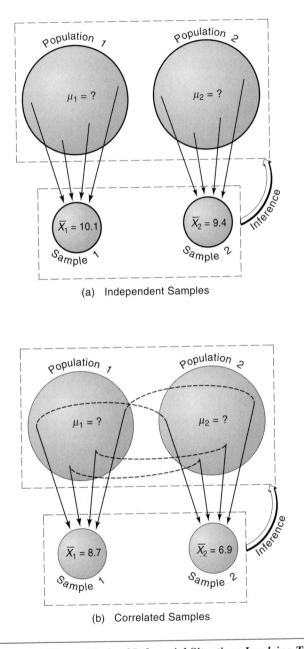

(a) Independent Samples

(b) Correlated Samples

FIGURE 10.2   *Two Different Kinds of Inferential Situations Involving Two Means*

    Two points about Figure 10.2 need to be highlighted. First, in both the independent-samples situation and in the correlated-samples situation, inferential statements are made about populations, not samples. Unfortunately, researchers often discuss their results as if the samples were the total focus of their investigations. If you keep Figure 10.2 in mind when you are dealing with these research summaries, you can (and should) correct the discussion by having all conclusions apply to the study's populations.

My second point regarding Figure 10.2 concerns the fact that the statistical inference, in panel A and in panel B, extends from the full set of sample data to the study's *pair* of populations. Separate inferences are not made from each sample to its corresponding population because the purpose is to make a comparison between two things. The focus here is on how μ_1 compares with μ_2, and thus the inferential arrow in each picture points to the dotted box surrounding both populations involved in the study.

Setting Up and Testing a Null Hypothesis

The null hypothesis for the two-sample case having a focus on means can be expressed in the same form regardless of whether the samples are independent or correlated. The most general way to write the null hypothesis is to state

$$H_0: \mu_1 - \mu_2 = a$$

where a represents any pinpoint number the researcher wishes to use in H_0. In most studies, researchers decide to set up a no-difference null hypothesis, and they accomplish this goal by saying $H_0: \mu_1 - \mu_2 = 0$. An alternative way to express the notion of no difference is to say $H_0: \mu_1 = \mu_2$.

Unfortunately, the null hypothesis is rarely stated in studies where two means are inferentially compared using a statistical test (or in other studies, for that matter). Evidently, most researchers assume that their readers will be able to discern the null hypothesis from the discussion of the research hypothesis and/or the way the sample data are summarized. A good rule of thumb to use when trying to decipher research reports is to presume that a test of two means revolved around a no-difference H_0 unless it is explicitly stated that some other kind of null hypothesis was set up.

After the sample data are collected, summarized, and analyzed, the results of the statistical comparison of the two $\overline{X}$s will be presented within the text of the report and/or in a table. Excerpts 10.8 and 10.9 illustrate the way results are typically presented, with the first and second studies involving independent and correlated samples, respectively. In both of these excerpts, the two sample means being compared were far enough apart to permit the null hypothesis to be rejected. In each case, the null hypothesis could be expressed by $H_0: \mu_1 = \mu_2$. Of course, the μs in this symbolic expression of H_0 would not represent the same variable in these two excerpts. In Excerpt 10.8, the μs would correspond with the widows' age while in Excerpt 10.9 they would represent VP complexity.

In Excerpts 10.8 and 10.9, we see that the data from each study were analyzed by a t-test. As we saw in Chapter 9, t-tests can be used in conjunction with inferential tests on correlation coefficients; moreover, t-tests can be used when a study's statistical focus is on a variety of other things (e.g., proportions and regression

EXCERPTS 10.8–10.9 • *Comparison of Two Sample Means Using a t-Test*

At the time of their partners' deaths, the respondents who fully participated were approximately 73 years old ($SD = 8.4$). The women ($n = 68$) were widowed at an earlier age than the men ($n = 43$), $M_{women} = 70.6$, $M_{men} = 76.9$; $t(109) = 4.14$, $p < .001$.

Source: B. V. Baarsen. (2002). Theories on coping with loss: The impact of social support and self-esteem on adjustment to emotional and social loneliness following a partner's death in later life. *The Journals of Gerontology, 57B*(1), p. S35.

We performed a paired-samples t test to test whether the average VP complexity of the disrupted sentences was significantly different from that of the fluent sentences. The t test confirmed a significant difference [$t(25) = 4.15$, $p < .01$].

Source: M. Rispoli and P. Hadley. (2001). The leading-edge: The significance of sentence disruptions in the development of grammar. *Journal of Speech, Language, and Hearing Research, 44*(5), p. 1138.

coefficients). Nevertheless, t-tests probably are used more often with means than anything else.

Note that the authors of Excerpts 10.8 and 10.9, in reporting their t-test results, provide information as to the degrees of freedom associated with the tests that were conducted. These *df* values are useful because they allow us to know how much data each t was based on. When t-tests are conducted to compare the means of two independent samples, the total amount of data can be determined by adding 2 to the t-test's *df.* When t-tests are used to see if a significant difference exists between the means of two correlated samples of data, you can determine how many pairs of data were used by adding 1 to the t-test's *df.* Armed with this knowledge, we can verify that there were a total of 111 individuals involved in the study associated with Excerpt 10.8, and we can determine (on our own) that there were 26 individuals involved in the study from which Excerpt 10.9 was drawn.

Although a statistical test comparing two means can be conducted using a t-test, it can also be accomplished by means of a **z-test** or an **F-test.** The z-test provides a result that is slightly biased in the sense that its probability of resulting in a Type I error is greater than the level of significance (with this bias being more pronounced when the sample sizes are small). The F-test, on the other hand, is not biased. The F-test's conclusion regarding H_0 will always be identical to the conclusion reached by a t-test. Hence, it really doesn't matter whether researchers compare their two means using a t-test or an F-test.

In light of the fact that (1) some researchers opt to use an *F*-test when comparing two means and (2) the results of an *F*-test are typically presented in a way that requires an understanding of concepts not yet addressed, I feel obliged to comment briefly about *F*-test results. Here I will focus attention exclusively on the use of *F*-tests to compare the means of two independent samples. In a later chapter, I will show how *F*-tests can be used with correlated samples.

To begin our discussion of *F*-tests applied to the means of two independent samples, consider the material in Excerpt 10.10. In this excerpt, note that there were two groups being compared, that the focus was on the mean age for those who attempted (31.80) and did not attempt (34.49) suicide, and that a statistically significant difference was found between these sample means, as indicated by the notation $p < .05$ at the end of the excerpt. Also note that the calculated value turned out equal to 4.18 and that this value is referred to as *F*.

EXCERPT 10.10 • *Comparison of Means from Two Independent Samples Using an F-Test*

Respondents who reported suicide attempts were younger ($M = 31.80$) compared to respondents without suicide attempts ($M = 34.49$), $F(1, 482) = 4.18, p < .05$.

Source: S. E. Ullman and L. R. Brecklin. (2002). Sexual assault history and suicidal behavior in a national sample of women. *Suicide and Life-Threatening Behavior, 32*(2), p. 125.

In Excerpt 10.10, also note that there are two degrees of freedom values presented along with the calculated value. The *df*s appear within a set of parentheses immediately to the right of the *F*, and they are separated by a comma. *F*-tests always have a pair of *df* values associated with them, and in this case the *df* values are equal to 1 and 482.

The *df* values presented along with the results of an *F*-test can be used to discern the amount of data used to make the statistical comparison. When an *F*-test is used as in Excerpt 10.10 to compare the means of two independent samples, all you need to do to determine the amount of data used is add the two *df* values together and then add 1 to the resulting sum. Thus in this study the calculated value of 4.18 was based on a total of 484 pieces of data. Since each piece of data corresponded to a particular person and her age, we know that there were 484 people involved in this study.

Sometimes, a table will be used to present the results of the kind of *F*-test we have been discussing. An example of such a table is contained in Excerpt 10.11. The first thing to note about this excerpt is the researcher's use of the acronym **ANOVA**

EXCERPT 10.11 • F-*Test Comparison of Two Sample Means with Results Presented in an Analysis of Variance Summary Table*

Hypothesis 1a posited lower ethical reasoning in community practitioners than in first-year pharmacy students. A one-way ANOVA was used to assess this hypothesis, and reveals that first year pharmacy students score significantly higher on moral reasoning than did their community pharmacy counterparts (Table II). This difference was significant at the 0.01 level ($p = 0.004$).

TABLE II *Relationship between Students and Practitioners on Ethical Reasoning*

	Practitioner Group	Student Group
Mean	36.40	42.47
SD	14.01	14.19
N	113	77

Source	df	SS	MS	F	p
Between groups	1	1686.92	1686.92	8.50	0.004**
Within groups	188	37302.2	198.42		

**Significant at the .01 alpha level

Source: D. A. Latif. (2000). Ethical cognition and selection-socialization in retail pharmacy. *Journal of Business Ethics, 25*(4), p. 352. [Adapted slightly for presentation here.]

in reference to the statistical analysis that was conducted. This acronym stands for the phrase **analysis of variance.** This phrase is misleading, for it probably would lead an uninformed reader to think that the statistical focus was on variances. However, as you will see, the analysis of variance focuses on *means.*

The main thing going on in Excerpt 10.11 is a statistical comparison of the two means (36.40 and 42.47) shown in the top half of the table. Based on what the researcher has said in the text and in the table's title, it seems reasonable to guess that each of the means represents the average amount of ethical reasoning exhibited (most likely on a questionnaire) by two samples: a practitioner group and a student group. The numbers beneath each of the two sample means provide descriptive information concerning the number of people in each group and the variability within each group's set of ethical reasoning scores.

The outcome of the inferential test comparing two means is presented in the lower half of the table. The calculated value is presented at the far right in the column labeled *F*. This data-based value, 8.50, turned out to be significant, as indicated by the *p*-value and the note beneath the table. Thus, the two sample means differed by an amount that was beyond the limits of chance sampling, presuming that $\mu_{practitioners}$ and $\mu_{students}$ were equal. The null hypothesis, therefore, was rejected.

There are two *df* values presented in the analysis of variance table. On the row labeled "Between groups," the *df* value is equal to 1; this will always be the case when two sample means are being compared. The *df* value on the row labeled "Within groups" is found first by subtracting 1 from each sample size and then by adding the resulting figures [$(113 - 1) + (77 - 1) = 188$]. Note that the sum of the *df*s for the "Between groups" and "Within groups" rows is equal to 189, one less than the total number of people used in the analysis.

The numbers in the *SS* column are the *sums of squares*. These numbers come from a statistical analysis of the sample data, and there is really no way to make sense out of this column of the analysis of variance table. The next column is labeled *MS* for *mean squares*. The first of these values was found by dividing the first row's *SS* by that row's *df* ($1686.92 \div 1 = 1686.92$). In a similar fashion, the second row's *MS* was found by dividing 37302.2 by 188. Finally, the calculated value for the *F* column was computed by dividing the "between groups" *MS* by the "within groups" *MS* ($1686.92 \div 198.42 = 8.50$).

In one sense, all of the numbers in the *df, SS,* and *MS* columns of the analysis of variance table are used solely as stepping stones to obtain the calculated value. The two *df* values are especially important, however, because the researcher must use both of these numbers (along with the selected level of significance) to locate the critical value. Accordingly, the three most important numbers in the table are the two values in the *df* column and the single number in the *F* column.

Interval Estimation with Two Means

As noted in Chapter 6, confidence intervals can be used to deal with a null hypothesis that a researcher wishes to test. Or, the confidence interval can be set up in studies where no test is being conducted on any H_0, with interest instead residing strictly in the process of interval estimation. Regardless of the researcher's objective, it is important to be able to decipher the results of a study in which the results are presented using a confidence interval around the difference between two means.

Consider Excerpt 10.12. Within this excerpt, notice how there is just one confidence interval, not two. Instead of building a separate CI around the two sample means (0.10 and −0.88), a single CI was built around 0.98, the *difference* between the two means. Because this CI did not overlap 0, the researchers were able to say that a significant difference existed in the change in depression that occurred during pregnancy as compared with the change that occurred after childbirth. The null hypothesis—of equal amounts of change during these two periods—was rejected.

EXCERPT 10.12 • *Using a Confidence Interval to Do Hypothesis Testing with Two Means*

There was a small rise in depression symptom score during pregnancy (mean change 0.10; *SE* 0.043) and a small drop after childbirth (−0.88; 0.047). These changes were significantly different (difference 0.98, 95% confidence interval 0.83 to 1.13; $P < 0.001$).

Source: J. Evans, J. Heron, H. Francomb, S. Oke, and J. Golding. (2001). Cohort study of depressed mood during pregnancy and after childbirth. *British Medical Journal, 323*(7307), p. 256.

Multiple Dependent Variables

If data are collected from one or two samples on two or more dependent variables, researchers with inferential interest in their data may build several confidence intervals or set up and test several null hypotheses, one for each dependent variable. A quick look at a few excerpts from recent studies will illustrate how researchers often talk about such analyses.

Results Presented in the Text

In Excerpts 10.13 and 10.14, we see two examples of how researchers often discuss what they discovered when they compared two groups on multiple dependent variables. While both studies involved two means per comparison, note how a *t*-test was used in Excerpt 10.13 in conjunction with correlated samples, whereas an *F*-test was used in Excerpt 10.14 in conjunction with that study's independent samples.

Results Presented in a Table

Excerpt 10.15 illustrates how a table can be used to convey the results of a two-sample comparison of means on several dependent variables. The numerical values in the *t*-test column are the calculated values that resulted from a comparison of the two means on each row. Hence, the first calculated value of 1.13 came from a comparison of 28.48 and 25.67. As you can see, one of these calculated values has a single asterisk next to it, while a double asterisk is positioned next to two other calculated values. As indicated in the note beneath the table, the single-asterisk calculated value achieved statistical significance at the .05 level, whereas the double-asterisk calculated values achieved statistical significance at the .01 level.

When reading research reports, try to remember that you can use the reported *df* numbers to help you understand the way the study was structured, how many

EXCERPTS 10.13–10.14 • *Comparing Two Means on Multiple Dependent Variables*

Prior to testing study hypotheses, we used paired *t* tests to determine which variables actually changed from pre- to postintervention. Results revealed significant increases from pretest to posttest for condom use self-efficacy, both the mechanics, $t(84) = -6.05, p < .001$; pretest $M = 4.01, SD = .75$; posttest $M = 4.39, SD = .64$, and communication subscales, $t(84) = -3.18, p < .01$; pretest $M = 4.18, SD = .71$; posttest $M = 4.40, SD - .57$.

Source: D. M. Huebner, M. C. Davis, C. J. Nemeroff, and Leona S. Aiken. (2002). The impact of internalized homophobia on HIV preventive interventions. *American Journal of Community Psychology, 30*(3), p. 340.

There was no significant difference at Time 1 between the intervention and the control sites on the pretest videotaped vignette measure, $F(1, 28) = 1.7$, *ns,* and on the pretest written measure, $F(1, 28) = 1.1$, *ns*.

Source: S. Wood, J. L. Cummings, B. Schnelle, and M. Stephens. (2002). A videotape-based training method for improving the detection of depression in residents of long-term care facilities. *The Gerontologist, 42*(1), p. 117.

groups got compared, and how many participants were involved. For example, consider Excerpt 10.15. Here, we do not need the *df* information to help us figure out how many people were in the study or in each of the two groups. That information is presented in the table's title and next to group names used to label the columns of means and standard deviations. But what if someone asked you whether the 21 individuals in the traditional group were matched with the 21 individuals in the nontraditional group? You could answer that question by using your knowledge of how degrees of freedom work. As indicated earlier, if two samples are correlated, $df + 1 =$ the number of pairs of scores; however, if two samples are independent, $df + 2 =$ the total number of scores in both groups combined. Knowing these two things, you ought to be able to determine quickly (and confidently) that the two groups in Excerpt 10.15 were independent rather than correlated samples.

Knowing how to use *df* numbers, of course, is not the most important skill to have when it comes to *t*- or *F*-tests. Clearly, it's more important for you to know what these tests compare, what the null hypothesis is, and what kind of inferential error might be made. Even though *df* numbers are *not* of critical importance, it's worth the effort to learn how to use them as an aid to interpreting what went on in the studies you read.

EXCERPT 10.15 • *Results of a Two-Group Comparison on Seven Dependent Variables Presented in a Table*

TABLE 1   *Means and Standard Deviations for Grade Point Averages, Psychological Functioning, and Support Scores with t-test Results for Traditional and Nontraditional Groups (N = 42)*

Variable	Traditional (n = 21)		Nontraditional (n = 21)		t test	df
	M	SD	M	SD		
Depression score	28.48	8.74	25.67	7.31	1.13	40
Anxiety score	12.91	9.51	9.14	6.80	1.47	40
Average GPA[a]	76.36	8.59	83.76	4.33	−2.95**	31
Emotional quantity score	5.12	1.93	3.77	1.62	2.47*	40
Emotional quality score	5.19	0.65	4.91	1.16	0.98	40
Instrumental quantity score	2.38	0.95	1.40	0.90	3.46**	40
Instrumental quality score	4.97	0.83	4.36	1.34	1.72	40

a. Average GPA = grade point average of GPA 1, GPA 2, and GPA 3.

$*p < .05. **p < .01.$

Source: S. Carney-Crompton and J. Tan. (2002). Support systems, psychological functioning, and academic performance of nontraditional female students. *Adult Education Quarterly,* *52*(2), p. 145.

Use of the Bonferroni Adjustment Technique

When a researcher sets up and tests several null hypotheses, each corresponding to a different dependent variable, the probability of having at least one Type I error pop up somewhere in the set of tests will be higher than indicated by the level of significance used in making the individual tests. As indicated in Chapter 8, this problem is referred to as the *inflated Type I error problem*. There are many ways to deal with this problem, but the most common strategy is the application of the **Bonferroni adjustment technique.**

In Excerpts 10.16 and 10.17, we see two examples of the Bonferroni adjustment technique. Even though *t*-tests were used in the first of these studies whereas *F*-tests were used in the second study, these two passages are identical in two important ways. First, they demonstrate *how* the Bonferroni adjustment procedure works; second, they explain *why* this adjustment is made.

In Excerpts 10.16 and 10.17, each of the *t*- and ANOVA *F*-tests compared two means. It should be noted that the Bonferroni technique can be used in studies

EXCERPTS 10.16–10.17 • *Use of the Bonferroni Adjustment Technique*

A series of matched *t* tests were conducted to compare mothers' and fathers' assessments in the areas of interest, namely, parenting and custody satisfaction. Because of an inflated Type I error rate resulting from the use of multiple tests, a Bonferroni adjustment was performed (.05/number of comparisons), and the alpha was established at .005.

Source: D. A. Madden-Derdich and S. A. Leonard. (2002). Shared experiences, unique realities: Formerly married mothers' and fathers' perceptions of parenting and custody after divorce. *Journal of Family Relations, 51*(1), p. 40.

Means and standard deviations for social connectedness, social appraisal, and perceived stress are presented in Table 1 [not shown here] for comparison by gender. [W]e performed a one-way analysis of variance on each measure with gender as the independent variable. The alpha level for these analyses was adjusted to .017 (.05 ÷ 3) using the Bonferroni procedure to reduce the likelihood of Type I error due to multiple analyses.

Source: R. M. Lee, K. A. Keough, and J. D. Sexton. (2002). Social connectedness, social appraisal, and perceived stress in college women and men. *Journal of Counseling and Development, 80*(3), p. 357.

where hypothesis testing is used with a single sample, if a separate H_0 is evaluated for each of two or more dependent variables. Moreover, this procedure for handling the inflated Type I error problem can be used regardless of the statistical test (z, t, or F) used to analyze the study's data.

A Pseudo-Bonferroni Adjustment

Some researchers who have multiple dependent variables attempt to hold down their total Type I error risk by using a crude technique referred to here as the **pseudo-Bonferroni adjustment procedure.** This procedure works as follows: The researchers take the normal level of significance and change it to a popular but more rigorous level. For example, researchers who normally would set alpha equal to .05 if there were just one dependent variable might decide to use an alpha level of .01 to compensate for the inflated Type I error risk caused by multiple dependent variables.

Excerpt 10.18 illustrates the use of the pseudo-Bonferroni technique. In this passage, note that the researchers say that a conservative alpha level of .01 was used because of the "multiplicity." The multiplicity to which they refer came about because they conducted 30 statistical tests involving means: eight *t*-tests in which a

EXCERPT 10.18 • *A Pseudo-Bonferroni Adjustment*

In the absence of a control group, we hypothesized that the depressed sample would show lower QOL [quality of life] than norms on mental health, social functioning, and vitality QOL measures. We also hypothesized that, despite similar levels of physical functioning, depressed subjects would rate themselves lower on their general health perception . . . that women would rate themselves lower on QOL [and] that older subjects would rate themselves lower on physical QOL measures. Because of multiplicity, a more conservative alpha of 0.01 was used to test significance for all analyses pertaining to QOL.

Source: P. M. Doraiswamy, Z. M. Khan, R. M. J. Donahue, and N. E. Richard. (2002). The spectrum of quality-of-life impairments in recurrent geriatric depression. *The Journals of Gerontology, 57A*(2), p. M135.

single depressed sample was compared against a set of norms, 11 *F*-tests in which males were compared against females, and 11 additional *F*-tests in which individuals over 70 years old were compared with those under 70.

When multiple tests are conducted, a change in the alpha level (e.g., from .05 to .01) does bring about greater control of Type I errors. I refer to it as a pseudo-Bonferroni technique, however, because the study-wide risk of falsely rejecting one or more true null hypotheses rarely will be equal to the desired (in most cases) .05 level.

Power Analysis and Strength-of-Effect Estimation

When dealing with one or two means using hypothesis testing, many researchers give no evidence that they are aware of the important distinction between statistical significance and practical significance. Those researchers seem content simply to reject or to fail to reject the null hypotheses that they assess, with impressive *p*-levels sometimes reported along with calculated values when the sample data "beat" the conventional .05 alpha level by a wide margin. A few researchers, however, make an effort to provide insight into their results or to set up their studies with systematic control over the probability of Type II errors. In Chapter 8, I discussed in general terms the way researchers can accomplish these goals. Now, I wish to illustrate how researchers actually do these things in studies where there is inferential interest in one or two means.

In Excerpt 10.19, we see a case where a researcher computed an **effect size** index, *d*, for the *t*-test that had revealed a statistically significant difference between the means of two samples. This illustrates one way in which researchers can exe-

Research
Navigator.c⊛m
Effect size

EXCERPT 10.19 • *Computation of an Effect Size (d)*

Although the self-ratings of general practitioners ($M = 2.80$, $SD = 0.79$) with respect to their level of knowledge about adolescent suicide were significantly higher than those of teachers, ($M = 2.64$, $SD = 0.92$), $t(847) = 2.77$, p $<$ .01, $d = .23$, the effect size is small and not clinically meaningful.

Source: K. M. Scouller and D. I. Smith. (2002). Prevention of youth suicide: How well informed are the potential gatekeepers of adolescents in distress? *Suicide and Life-Threatening Behavior, 32*(1), p. 73.

**Research
Navigator.c⊛m**

Eta squared

cute the seven-step version of hypothesis testing. Notice that the researchers say that their effect size turned out to be "small and not clinically meaningful." That interpretation was based on Cohen's criteria for *d,* where .20 is said to be small, .50 is considered to be medium, and .80 is viewed as being large.

Excerpts 10.20 and 10.21 show how researchers can compute strength-of-association measures in an effort to see whether statistically significant results are also significant in a practical sense. As you can see, the techniques used to do this were **eta squared** and **omega squared.** As indicated in Chapter 8, the criteria for

EXCERPTS 10.20–10.21 • *Eta Squared and Omega Squared*

ANOVA results revealed that those men exposed to the narrative monologue message ($M = 4.88$, $SD = 1.21$) reported more message minimization (i.e., the narrative message was perceived to be more boring, overblown, exaggerated, overstated, and distorted) than men exposed to the fact-based message ($M = 5.60$, $SD = .86$), $F(1, 79) = 9.30$, $p = .003$, eta squared = .11.

Source: M. T. Mormon. (2000). The influence of fear appeals, message design, and masculinity on men's motivation to perform the testicular self-exam. *Journal of Applied Communication Research, 28*(2), p. 103.

- -

On the other hand, for the knee joint angle of 162 deg, the average maximal voluntary isometric torque measurement following the stretching exercises was a significant, $t(54) = 3.23$, $p < .010$, $\omega^2 = .15$, 7% less than the prestretch value.

Source: A. G. Nelson, J. D. Allen, and A. Cornwell. (2001). Inhibition of maximal voluntary isometric torque production by acute stretching is joint-angle specific. *Research Quarterly for Exercise and Sport, 72*(1), pp. 69–70.

Research
Navigator.c⊕m

Power analysis

interpreting these are as follows: less than .06 is small, .06 to .15 is medium, and greater than .15 is large.

After failing to reject the null hypothesis, some researchers conduct a post hoc **power analysis.** In doing this, they enter the known facts about their study (e.g., sample sizes, level of significance, means, and *SD*s) into a formula that determines how much power there was to detect differences as large as or larger than the observed effect size. In Excerpt 10.22, we see a case where this was done. In the second sentence of this passage, the researchers are saying that their statistical test had a 95 percent chance (i.e., a power of .95) to yield a statistically significant difference between the two groups *if* the two population means differed as much as the two sample means (2.9 and 6.0). This power value—95 percent—is not mentioned in Excerpt 10.22, but it comes from our knowledge that power and Type II error risk are complementary and must add up to 1.0.

EXCERPT 10.22 • *Post Hoc Computation of Power*

The preoperative AP laxity values [mean ± standard error] were not significantly different between group 1 (2.9 ± 1.4 mm) and group 2 (6.0 ± 1.2 mm). A post hoc power analysis revealed that we had a 5% chance that the laxity values were different (a 0.05 probability of committing a type II error).

Source: B. D. Beynnon, B. S. Uh, R. J. Johnson, and B. C. Fleming. (2001). The elongation behavior of the anterior cruciate ligament graft in vivo. *American Journal of Sports Medicine, 29*(2), p. 165.

In the four excerpts we have just considered, the researchers' computation of effect size indices, of strength-of-association measures, and of power were all performed *after* the data in each study had been gathered. As pointed out in Chapter 8, however, it is possible to conduct a power analysis *before* any data are collected. The purpose of such an analysis is to determine how large the sample(s) should be so as to have a known probability of rejecting H_0 when H_0 is false by an amount at least as large as the researcher-specified effect size.

In Excerpt 10.23, we see how a power analysis was conducted in a study involving two kinds of formula fed to preterm infants. In doing this power analysis, the researchers first decided that their statistical focus would be the mean, that they would compare their two sample means with a *t*-test, that they would use the .05 level of significance, that they wanted to detect a difference between the population means if that difference was equal to or larger than four-tenths of a standard deviation, and

EXCERPT 10.23 • *A Power Analysis Used to Determine Sample Sizes*

> The calculated sample size (100 infants per randomized group) permitted detection of a 0.4 standard deviation (SD) difference between diet groups with 80% power at 5% significance. . . . Data for [these] randomized groups were compared using Student's t test. . . .
>
> *Source:* M. S. Fewtrell, R. Morley, R. A. Abbott, and A. Singhal. (2002). Double-blind, randomized trial of long-chain polyunsaturated fatty acid supplementation in formula fed to preterm infants. *Pediatrics, 110*(1), p. 74.

that they wanted to have an 80 percent chance of rejecting H_0. After making these decisions, the researchers then used a formula or a computer program that told them that data would be needed from 100 infants in each of the two diet groups.

Underlying Assumptions

When a statistical inference concerning one or two means is made using a confidence interval or a *t*-, *F*-, or *z*-test, certain assumptions about the sample(s) and population(s) are typically associated with the statistical technique applied to the data. If one or more of these assumptions are violated, then the probability statements attached to the statistical results may be invalid. For this reason, well-trained researchers (1) are familiar with the assumptions associated with the techniques used to analyze their data and (2) take the time to check out important assumptions before making inferences from the sample mean(s).

For the statistical techniques covered thus far in this chapter, there are four underlying assumptions. First, each sample should be a random subset of the population it represents. Second, there should be "independence of observations" (meaning that a particular person's score is not influenced by what happens to any other person during the study). Third, each population should be normally distributed in terms of the dependent variable being focused on in the study. And fourth, the two populations associated with studies involving two independent samples or two correlated samples should each have the same degree of variability relative to the dependent variable.

The assumptions dealing with the randomness and independence of observations are methodological concerns, and researchers rarely talk about either of these assumptions in their research reports. The other two assumptions, however, are often discussed by researchers. To be a discerning consumer of the research literature, you will need to know when the **normality assumption** and **equal variance**

assumption should be considered, what is going on when the normality and equal variance assumptions are tested, what researchers will do if they find that their data violate these assumptions, and under what conditions a statistical test will be "robust" to violations of the normality or equal variance assumption. This section is intended to provide you with this knowledge.

Researchers should consider the normality and equal variance assumptions *before* they evaluate their study's primary H_0. Assumptions should be considered first because the statistical test used to evaluate the study's H_0 may not function the way it is supposed to function if the assumptions are violated. In a sense, then, checking on the assumptions is like checking to see if there are holes in a canoe (or whether your companion has attached an outboard motor) before getting in and paddling out to the middle of a lake. Your canoe simply won't function the way it is supposed to if it has holes or has been turned into a motorboat.

When the normality or equal variance assumption is examined, the researcher will use the sample data to make an inference from the study's sample(s) to its population(s). This inference is similar to the one that the researcher wishes to make concerning the study's primary H_0, except that assumptions do not deal with the mean of the population(s). As their names suggest, the normality assumption deals with distributional shape whereas the equal variance assumption is concerned with variability. Often, the sample data will be used to test these assumptions. In such cases the researcher will apply all of the steps of the hypothesis testing procedure, starting with the articulation of a null hypothesis and ending with a reject or fail-to-reject decision. In performing such tests, researchers will hope that the null hypothesis of normality or of equal variance will *not* be rejected, for then they will be able to move ahead and test the study's main null hypothesis concerning the mean(s) of interest.

Excerpts 10.24 and 10.25 illustrate how the normality and equal variance assumptions are sometimes tested by applied researchers.[4] In each of these excerpts, notice that the null hypothesis for the assumption was not rejected. That was the desired result, for the researchers were then permitted to move to do what they were really interested in, a comparison of their two sample *means*.

The assumption of equal variances is often referred to as the **homogeneity of variance assumption.** This term is somewhat misleading, however, since it may cause you to think that the assumption specifies homogeneity *within* each population in terms of the dependent variable. That is not what the assumption means. The null hypothesis associated with the equal variance assumption says that $\sigma_1^2 = \sigma_2^2$. This assumption can be true even when there is a large degree of variability within

![Research Navigator.com logo]

Research
Navigator.c⊕m

Homogeneity
of variance

---

[4]In Excerpt 10.24, the researcher used the Kolmogorov–Smirnof test to check on the normality assumption. Other tests that are sometimes used to do the same thing are the chi-squared goodness-of-fit test and Lilliefor's test. In Excerpt 10.25, Levene's test was used to check on the equal variance assumption; other test procedures frequently used to check on the equal variance assumption include *F,* Hartley's *F*-max, Cochran's *C,* and Bartlett's chi-squared test.

EXCERPTS 10.24–10.25 • *Testing the Normality and Equal Variance Assumptions*

The 2 treatment groups differed in the type of isotonic resistance training used for their hip and knee extensors. . . . The Kolmogorov-Smirnov test was used to confirm that the values for each of the outcome variables were normally distributed ($P \geq$ .05). We assessed normality because it is an underlying assumption that needs to be met when using parametric analysis.

Source: M. C. Morrissey, W. I. Drechsler, D. Morrissey, and P. R. Knight. (2002). Effects of distally fixated versus nondistally fixated leg extensor resistance training on knee pain in the early period after anterior cruciate ligament reconstruction. *Physical Therapy, 82*(1), p. 40.

Independent sample t-tests were completed to examine the differences on the CTI Total score and the three subscales for the two groups of participants. . . . Levene's Test for Equity of Variances was computed with no significant differences being found. Therefore homogeneity of variance was assumed.

Source: D. R. Strauser, D. C. Lustig, J. Keim, K. Ketz, and A. Malesky. (2002). Analyzing the differences in career thoughts based on disability status. *Journal of Rehabilitation, 68*(1), p. 29.

each population. "Homogeneity of variance" exists if σ_1^2 is equal to σ_2^2, regardless of how large or small the common value of σ^2.

If a researcher conducts a test to see if the normality or equal variance assumption is tenable, it may turn out that the sample data do not argue against the desired characteristics of the study's populations. That was the case in Excerpts 10.24 and 10.25. But what happens if the test of an assumption suggests that the assumption is not tenable?

In the situation where the sample data suggest that the population data do not conform with the normality and/or equal variance assumptions, there are three options available to the researcher. These options include (1) using a special formula in the study's main test so as to "compensate" for the observed lack of normality or heterogeneity of variance, (2) changing each raw score by means of a data transformation designed to reduce the degree of nonnormality or heterogeneity of variance, thereby permitting the regular *t*-test, *F*-test, or *z*-test to be used when the study's main test focuses on the study's mean(s), or (3) using a test procedure other than *t*, *F*, or *z*—one that does not involve such rigorous assumptions about the populations. Excerpts 10.26, 10.27, and 10.28 illustrate these three options.

Excerpt 10.26 represents option 1, for a special version of the *t*-test (called the *t-test with unequal variances*) has built-in protection against violations of the equal

EXCERPTS 10.26–10.28 • *Options When Assumptions Seem Untenable*

A significant Levene's test, $F = 6.71$, $p < .05$, indicated the variances between experimental and control group scores were unequal. An independent groups *t*-test with equal variances not assumed revealed. . . .

Source: M. V. Jones, R. D. Mace, S. R. Bray, A. W. MacRae, and Claire Stockbridge. (2002). The impact of motivational imagery on the emotional state and self-efficacy levels of novice climbers. *Journal of Sport Behavior, 25*(1), p. 67.

The scale scores of the Intention to Use AD Scale were square root transformed [before the *t*-test was applied] because the data were skewed to the right.

Source: M. Roelands, P. Van Oost, A. M. Depoorter, and A. Buysse. (2002). A social-cognitive model to predict the use of assistive devices for mobility and self-care in elderly people. *The Gerontologist, 42*(1), pp. 42–43.

Other comparisons between surviving and nonsurviving populations were performed with Student *t* test for normally distributed variables, and Mann-Whitney test for nonnormally distributed variables.

Source: W. Meadow, L. Frain, Y. Ren, and G. Lee. (2002). Serial assessment of mortality in the neonatal intensive care unit by algorithm and intuition: Certainty, uncertainty, and informed consent. *Pediatrics, 109*(5), p. 880.

variance assumption. Excerpt 10.27 shows option 2, the strategy of transforming the data and then using the regular test procedure to compare the group means. Here, a square root transformation was used. In Excerpt 10.28, the researchers chose option 3; they turned to an entirely different test procedure, one that lacks the same rigorous assumptions that characterize *z*-, *t*-, and *F*-tests.

As illustrated by Excerpt 10.27, **data transformations** are sometimes used by researchers in an effort to make variances more similar or to create data sets that more closely approximate the normal distribution. Many transformations have been designed to help researchers accomplish these goals. In Excerpt 10.28, for example, the square root transformation was used. In Excerpt 10.29, we see two histograms that show how nicely the square root transformation can accomplish the goal of converting a highly skewed distribution of raw scores into a transformed data set that looks fairly normal.

When researchers are interested in comparing the means of two groups, they will often bypass testing the assumption of equal variances if the two samples are

The distribution of hCG concentrations from the athletes' urine specimen is shown in Fig. 1. . . . Fig. 2 represents the histogram of the square root of the dataset excepting the zero values. These adjustments allow for the data to adapt into a Gaussian form.

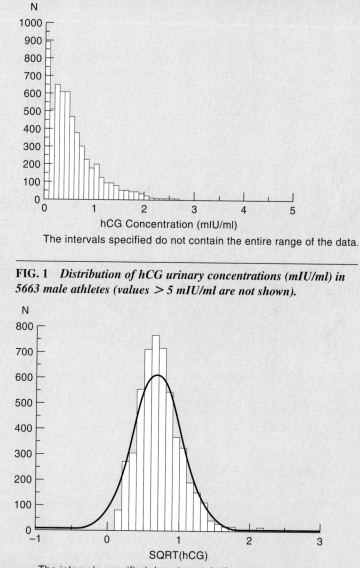

The intervals specified do not contain the entire range of the data.

FIG. 1 *Distribution of hCG urinary concentrations (mIU/ml) in 5663 male athletes (values > 5 mIU/ml are not shown).*

The intervals specified do not contain the entire range of the data.

FIG. 2 *Histogram of the transformed (square root) urinary concentrations of hCG greater than 0 mIU/ml.*

Source: F. T. Delbeke, P. Van Eenoo, and P. DeBacker. (1998). Detection of human chorionic gonadotrophin misuse in sports. *International Journal of Sports Medicine, 19,* p. 288.

equally big. This is done because studies in theoretical statistics have shown that a test on means will function very much as it should even if the two populations have unequal amounts of variability, as long as $n_1 = n_2$. In other words, t-, F-, and z-tests are strong enough to withstand a violation of the equal variance assumption if the sample sizes are equal. Stated in statistical "jargoneze," equal ns make these tests **robust** to violations of the homogeneity of variance assumption.

Excerpt 10.30 illustrates how some researchers will bypass worrying about the normality and equal variance assumptions when their sample sizes are equal. As this particular passage suggests, some researchers will even work hard to generate equal ns solely because of their desire to test null hypotheses with robust tests. If a researcher expends a little extra time or energy to increase the smallest of the ns so as to have equal sample sizes, he or she deserves a pat on the back. However, I have seen cases where a researcher has been so concerned about having equal ns that some of the data in the larger of the two samples was thrown away in order to make the bigger sample the same size as the smaller sample. This most definitely is *not* a good practice, for statistical power is reduced when data are discarded.

EXCERPT 10.30 • *Equal Sample Sizes and Robustness*

Using equal numbers of men and women was important for the statistical tests of our predictions because the F-test is robust to violations of assumptions of normality and homogeneity of variance when sample sizes are equal (Kirk, 1982).

Source: S. A. Meyers and E. Berscheid. (1997). The language of love: The difference a preposition makes. *Personality and Social Psychology Bulletin, 23*(4), p. 347.

Comments

Before concluding our consideration of inferences regarding one or two means, I want to offer five warnings that will, if you heed them, cause you to be a more informed recipient of research results. These warnings are concerned with (1) outcomes where the null hypothesis is not rejected, (2) outcomes where H_0 is rejected, (3) the typical use of t-tests, (4) practical significance, and (5) research claims that seem to neglect the possibility of a Type I or a Type II error.

A Nonsignificant Result Does Not Mean H_0 Is True

In Chapter 7, I indicated that a null hypothesis should *not* be considered to be true simply because it is not rejected. Researchers sometimes forget this important point, especially when they compare groups in terms of pretest means. In making this kind of comparison, researchers usually hope that the null hypothesis will *not* be rejected, for then they can consider the comparison groups to have been the same at the beginning of the study. I'd like to mention three reasons why it's dangerous to think that H_0 is true if it's not rejected.

The context for my three comments is a hypothetical study. Imagine that we have two groups, E and C (experimental and control), with pretest data available on each person in each group. Let's also imagine that the sample means, $\overline{X}_E$ and $\overline{X}_C$, turn out equal to 16 and 14, respectively. Finally, imagine that a *t*-test or *F*-test is used to compare the two $\overline{X}$s, with the result being that the null hypothesis (H_0: $\mu_E = \mu_C$) is not rejected because $p_{\text{two-tailed}} > .05$.

The first reason for not accepting H_0 in this hypothetical study is purely logical in nature. If the null hypothesis had been set up to say that H_0: $\mu_E - \mu_C = 1$, a fail-to-reject decision also would have been reached. That is also what would have happened if H_0's pinpoint number had been set equal to any other value between 0 and $+4.0$. Since the data support multiple null hypotheses that could have been set up (and that are in conflict with each other), there is no scientific justification for believing that any one of them is right while the others are wrong.

The second reason for not accepting H_0 concerns data quality. In Chapter 9, I discussed attenuation and pointed out how measuring instruments that have less than perfect reliability can function to mask a true nonzero relationship that exists between two variables. The same principle applies to inferential tests that focus on things other than correlation coefficients, such as means. In our hypothetical study, data produced by a measuring instrument with low reliability could lead to a fail-to-reject decision; with a more reliable instrument, the sample means—even if they again turn out equal to 16 and 14—might end up producing a p that's lower than .05! Thus, our hypothetical study may have produced a nonsignificant finding because of unreliability in the data, not because H_0: $\mu_E = \mu_C$.

A final consideration that mitigates against concluding that $\mu_E = \mu_C$ when H_0 is retained has to do with statistical power. As I have pointed out on several occasions, there is a direct relationship between sample size and the probability of detecting a situation in which H_0 is false. Thus, the failure to find a statistically significant finding in our hypothetical study may have been caused by *n*s that were too small. Perhaps μ_E and μ_C differ greatly, but our study simply lacked the statistical sensitivity to illuminate that situation.

For these three reasons (logic, reliability, and statistical power), be on guard for unjustified claims that H_0 is true following a decision not to reject H_0.

Overlapping Distributions

Suppose a researcher compares two groups of scores and finds that there is a statistically significant difference between $\overline{X}_1$ and $\overline{X}_2$. Notice that the significant difference exists between the *means* of the two groups. Be on guard for research reports in which the results are discussed without reference to the group means, thus creating the impression that every score in one group is higher than every score in the second group. Such a situation is *very* unlikely.

To illustrate what I mean by overlapping distributions, consider once again the information presented in Excerpt 10.11. In that excerpt, we saw that the mean score on ethical reasoning of 113 members of the practitioner group was found to be significantly different (with $p = .004$) from the mean score of 77 members of the student group. The means being compared were 36.40 and 42.47, respectively.

Did all members of the student group have higher scores than anyone in the practitioner group? The evidence in Excerpt 10.11 suggests not. The two standard deviations were each slightly larger than 14. Thus, there had to be some members of the practitioner group who had higher ethical reasoning scores than some of the members of the student group. If each group of scores had an approximate normal distribution, then more than one-sixth of the practitioner group would have had higher scores than the mean of the student group, and more than one-sixth of the student group would have had lower scores than the mean of the practitioner group. That would constitute a clear case of overlapping groups.

Be on guard for researchers who make a comparison between two different groups (or between a single group that's measured twice), who reject the null hypothesis, and who then summarize their findings by saying something like "girls outperformed boys" or "the treatment produced higher scores than did the control" or "participants improved between pretest and posttest." Such statements are often seen in the abstracts of research reports. When you see these phrases, be sure to insert the three words "on the average" at the beginning of the researcher's summary. Also keep in mind that overlapping distributions are the rule, not the exception, in research investigations.

The Typical Use of t-Tests

In the previous chapter, we saw how a *t*-test can be used to assess a null hypothesis that focuses on a correlation coefficient. In this chapter, we saw how a *t*-test can be used to evaluate a null hypothesis dealing with one or two means. You will discover that *t*-tests can also be used when the researcher's statistical focus is on things other than correlation coefficients and means. For this reason, it is best to consider a *t*-test to be a general tool that can be used to accomplish a variety of inferential goals.

Although a *t*-test can focus on many things, it is used most often when the researcher is concerned with one or two means. In fact, *t*-tests are used so frequently to deal with means that many researchers equate the term *t-test* with the notion of a test focusing on the mean(s). These researchers use a modifying phrase to clarify how many means are involved and the nature of the samples, thus leading to the terms *one-sample t-test, independent-samples t-test, correlated-samples t-test, matched t-test, dependent-samples t-test,* and *paired t-test.* When any of these terms is used, a safe bet is that the *t*-test being referred to had the concept of mean as its statistical focus.

Practical Significance versus Statistical Significance

Earlier in this chapter, you saw how researchers can do certain things in an effort to see whether a statistically significant finding is also meaningful in a practical sense. Unfortunately, many researchers do not rely on computed effect size indices, strength-of-association measures, or power analyses to help them avoid the mistake of "making a mountain out of a molehill." They simply use the six-step version of hypothesis testing and then get excited if the results are statistically significant.

Having results turn out to be statistically significant can cause researchers to go into a trance in which they willingly allow the tail to wag the dog. That's what happened, I think, to the researchers who conducted a study comparing the attitudes of two groups of women. In their technical report, they first indicated that the means turned out equal to 67.88 and 71.24 (on a scale that ranged from 17 to 85) and then stated "despite the small difference in means, there was a significant difference."

To me, the final 11 words of the previous paragraph conjure up the image of statistical procedures functioning as some kind of magic powder that can be sprinkled on one's data and transform a molehill of a mean difference into a mountain that deserves others' attention. However, statistical analyses lack that kind of magical power! Had the researchers who obtained those means of 67.88 and 71.24 not been blinded by the allure of statistical significance, they would have focused their attention on the small difference and not the significant difference. And had they done this, their 11 words would have been "although there was a significant difference, the difference in means was small."

Type I and Type II Errors

My final comment concerns the conclusion reached whenever the hypothesis testing procedure is used. Because the decision to reject or fail to reject H_0 is fully inferential in nature (being based on sample data), there is *always* the possibility that a Type I or Type II error will be committed. You need to keep this in mind as you read technical research reports, as most researchers do not allude to the possibility of inferential error as they present their results or discuss their findings. In certain cases, the researcher simply presumes that you know that a Type I or Type II error may occur whenever a null hypothesis is tested. In other cases, the researcher unfortunately may have overlooked this possibility in the excitement of seeing that the statistical results were congruent with his or her research hypothesis.

Consider Excerpts 10.31 and 10.32. The researchers associated with these studies deserve high praise for indicating that their findings may have been the result of inferential error. Frankly, I wish there were some sort of law that forced researchers to follow the examples shown here.

When reading research reports, you will encounter many articles in which the researchers will talk as if they have discovered something definitive. The researchers'

EXCERPTS 10.31–10.32 • *The Possibility of Inferential Error*

[The] only statistically significant difference between the groups was found in the angle of the knee at the onset of stance during stair ascent. This finding might suggest that open kinetic chain exercises offered a faster return of functional range of motion, but it may also be the result of a type I error.

Source: D. M. Hooper, M. C. Morrissey, W. Drechsler, D. Morrissey, and J. King. (2001). Open and closed kinetic chain exercises in the early period after anterior cruciate ligament reconstruction. *American Journal of Sports Medicine, 29*(2), p. 172.

The lack of significant differences in salivary cortisol levels between groups could be the result of a Type II error. . . .

Source: C. B. Hicks and A. M. Tharpe. (2002). Listening effort and fatigue in school-age children with and without hearing loss. *Journal of Speech, Language, and Hearing Research, 45*(3), p. 581.

assertions typically reduce to the claim that "the data confirm our expectations, so now we have proof that our research hypotheses were correct." Resist the temptation to bow down in front of such researchers and accept everything and anything they might say, simply because they have used fancy statistical techniques when analyzing their data. Remember that *inferences* are *always* involved whenever (1) confidence intervals are placed around means or differences between means and (2) null hypotheses involving one or two means are evaluated. Nothing is *proven* by any of these techniques, regardless of how bold the researchers' claims might be.

Review Terms

Analysis of variance
Confidence interval
Correlated samples
Dependent samples
df
F-test
Homogeneity of variance
  assumption
Independent samples
Matched samples

MS
Overlapping distributions
Paired samples
Pseudo-Bonferroni adjustment
  procedure
Robust
SS
t-test
z-test

The Best Items in the Companion Website

1. An interactive online quiz (with immediate feedback provided) covering Chapter 10.
2. Nine misconceptions about the content of Chapter 10.
3. An email message sent from the author to his students entitled "A Little *t*-Test Puzzle."
4. One of Chapter 10's best passages: "Inference and Proof."
5. Two good jokes about statistics.

Fun Exercises inside Research Navigator

1. **Do men with high or low sperm counts engage in more "active coping" behavior?**

   A group of 55 infertile men in Germany provided data on this study's two variables: sperm concentrations and "active coping style." The data on coping style came from a questionnaire that dealt with such issues as accepting responsibility, seeking social support, and problem solving. The data on sperm concentration came from semen analyses. For one of their analyses, the researchers first created high and low subgroups on the basis of sperm count, and then they used an ANOVA *F*-test to compare these subgroups with respect to their mean scores on active coping. What do you think this *F*-test revealed? To find out, locate the PDF version of the research report in the Nursing, Health, and Medicine database of ContentSelect and take a look (near the top of page 251) at the middle row of Table 1.

   M. Pook, W. K. Rause, & B. Rohrle. A validation study on the negative association between an active coping style and sperm concentration. *Journal of Reproductive & Infant Psychology.* Located in the NURSING, HEALTH, AND MEDICINE database of ContentSelect.

2. **What do college men and women think about housewives and househusbands?**

   In this study, 328 female and 196 male college students took a questionnaire about housewives and househusbands. The questionnaire contained 35 statements such as "Men who are househusbands are not 'real' men." The students responded to each statement on a five-point Likert-type scale ranging from *strongly disagree* (1) to *strongly agree* (5). Five scores were derived from each student's responses to the questionnaire, one each for the four subscales (negative perceptions of househusbands, negative effect on spousal relationships, negative perceptions of housewives, and psychological effects) and one based on the full instrument. A separate *t*-test was used to compare the mean scores for men and women on each of the four subscales and on the composite score. As you would probably guess, most of these *t*-tests revealed a statistically significant difference, with the male mean always reflecting a more traditional perspective. Let's focus on one of those significant results, the one dealing with negative effect on spousal relations. On the 1-to-5 scale, how far apart do you think the male and female means were? After making a guess, locate the PDF version of the research report in the Psychology database of ContentSelect and take a look (on page 648) at Table 2. You may be quite surprised at what you see!

D. K. Wentworth & R. M. Chell. The role of househusband and housewife as perceived by a college population. *Journal of Psychology.* Located in the PSYCHOLOGY database of ContentSelect.

Review Questions and Answers begin on page 516.

11

Tests on Three or More Means Using a One-Way ANOVA

In Chapter 10, we considered various techniques used by researchers when they apply inferential statistics within studies focusing on one or two means. I now wish to extend that discussion by considering the main inferential technique used by researchers when their studies involve three or more means. The popular technique used in these situations is called analysis of variance and it is abbreviated **ANOVA.**

As I pointed out in the preceding chapter, the analysis of variance can be used to see if there is a significant difference between two sample means. Hence, this particular statistical technique is quite versatile. It can be used when a researcher wants to compare two means, three means, or any number of means. It is also versatile in ways that will become apparent in later chapters.

The analysis of variance is an inferential tool that is widely used in many disciplines. Although a variety of statistical techniques have been developed to help applied researchers deal with three or more means, ANOVA ranks first in popularity. Moreover, there is a big gap between ANOVA and whatever ranks second!

In the current chapter, we will focus our attention on the simplest version of ANOVA, something called a one-way analysis of variance. I will begin with a discussion of the statistical purpose of a one-way ANOVA, followed by a clarification of how a one-way ANOVA differs from other kinds of ANOVA. Then, we will turn our attention to the way researchers present the results of their one-way ANOVAs, with examples to show how the Bonferroni adjustment technique is used in conjunction with one-way ANOVAs, how the assumptions underlying a one-way ANOVA are occasionally tested, and how researchers sometimes concern themselves with power analyses, measures of association, and effect size. Finally, I will offer a few tips that should serve to make you better able to decipher and critique the results of one-way ANOVAs.

The Purpose of a One-Way ANOVA

When a study has been conducted in which the focus is centered on three or more groups of scores, a **one-way ANOVA** permits the researcher to use the data in the samples for the purpose of making a single inferential statement concerning the means of the study's populations. Regardless of how many samples are involved, there is just one inference that extends from the set of samples to the set of populations. This single inference deals with the question, "Are the means of the various populations equal to one another?"

In Figure 11.1 I have tried to illustrate what is going on in a one-way ANOVA. There are three things to notice about this picture. First, I have drawn our picture for the specific situation where there are three comparison groups in the study; additional samples and populations can be added to parallel studies that have four, five, or more comparison groups. Second, there is a single inference made from the full set of sample data to the group of populations. Finally, the focus of the inference is on the population means, even though each sample is described in terms of $\overline{X}$, *SD,* and *n.*

Although you will never come across a journal article that contains a picture like that presented in Figure 11.1, I hope that my picture will help you to understand what is going on when researchers talk about having applied a one-way ANOVA to their data. Consider, for example, Excerpt 11.1, which comes from a

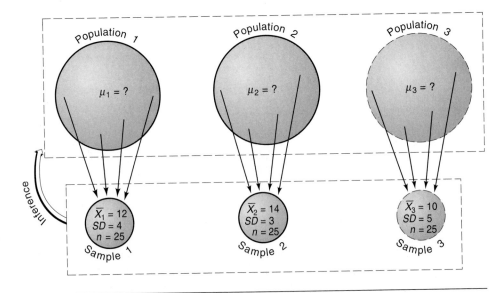

FIGURE 11.1   *Illustration of a One-Way ANOVA's Inferential Objective*

EXCERPT 11.1 • *Sample Data Used in a One-Way ANOVA*

We used one-way analysis of variance procedures to [compare mean DITP scores of] the cross cultural status groups. . . .

TABLE 3   *Mean DITP Scores by Status*

Cross Cultural Status Group	N	Mean DITP Scores	Standard Deviation
Indian business professionals	27	23.1	15.9
Indian prof/prac. currently going to graduate school	9	30.6	14.7
Indian graduate business students	55	41.3	11.5
United States business professionals	27	33.1	11.1
United States prof/prac. currently going to graduate school	21	42.1	13.6
United States graduate business students	9	38.5	18.5

Source: B. Kracher, A. Chatterjee, and A. R. Lundquist. (2002). Factors related to the cognitive moral development of business students and business professionals in India and the United States: Nationality, education, sex and gender. *Journal of Business Ethics, 35*(42), p. 262.

study focused on moral reasoning. In this investigation, individuals in each of three categories (business professional, graduate student, or both) from two countries (India and the United States) were sent a survey that asked them to evaluate moral dilemmas. Based on each person's responses, the researchers computed a DITP score.

After looking at our picture (Figure 11.1), you should be able to look at Excerpt 11.1 and discern what the researchers were trying to accomplish by using a one-way ANOVA. Each row of data in this excerpt, of course, corresponds to one of the six samples involved in this study. Connected to each of these samples was an abstract population (i.e., a larger group of individuals who we imagine filling out the survey). The researchers' goal was to use the data from all six samples to make a single inference concerning the means of those populations. The statistical question dealt with by the one-way ANOVA could be stated as: "In light of the empirical information available in the samples, is it reasonable to think that the mean DITP scores would be the same in these six imaginary populations."

As you can see, the sample means in Excerpt 11.1 turned out to be different from each other. Based on the fact that the $\overline{X}$s in this study were dissimilar, you might be tempted to think that there was an easy answer to the inferential question being posed. However, the concept of sampling error makes it *impossible* to simply look at the sample means, see differences, and then conclude that the population means are also different. Possibly, the population means are identical, with the sample means being dissimilar simply because of sampling error. Or, maybe the discrepancy between the $\bar{X}$s *is* attributable to dissimilarities among the population means. A one-way ANOVA helps researchers to decide, in a scientific manner, whether the sample means are far enough apart to place their eggs into the second of these two possible baskets.

The Distinction between a One-Way ANOVA and Other Kinds of ANOVA

In this chapter we are focusing our attention on the simplest kind of ANOVA, the kind that is referred to as a **one-way ANOVA,** as a **one-factor ANOVA,** or as a **simple ANOVA.** Since there are many different kinds of analysis variance, it is important to clarify the difference between the kind that we are considering in this chapter and the more complex kinds of ANOVA that will be discussed in later chapters. (Some of the more complex kinds of analysis of variance have the labels "two-way ANOVA," "randomized blocks ANOVA," "repeated measures ANOVA," and "multivariate ANOVA.")

Although all ANOVAs are alike in that they focus on means, they differ in three main respects: the number of independent variables, the number of dependent variables, and whether the samples are independent or correlated. In terms of these distinguishing characteristics, a one-way ANOVA has *one* independent variable, it focuses on *one* dependent variable, and it involves samples that are *independent*. It is worthwhile to consider each of these defining elements of a one-way ANOVA because researchers sometimes use the term *ANOVA* by itself without the clarifying adjective *one-way*.

When we say that there is just one independent variable, this means that the comparison groups differ from one another, prior to the collection and analysis of any data, in one manner that is important to the researcher. The comparison groups can differ in terms of a qualitative variable (e.g., favorite TV show) or in terms of a quantitative variable (e.g., number of siblings) but there can be only one characteristic that defines how the comparison groups differ. Since the terms **factor** and **independent variable** mean the same thing within the context of analysis of variance, this first way in which a one-way ANOVA differs from other ANOVAs can be summed up in this manner: A one-way ANOVA has a single factor, that is, one independent variable.

Excerpt 11.2 comes from a study in which 160 black college students filled out a survey designed to measure self-esteem. In addition, each of these students self-identified him/herself as belonging to one of three black ethnic groups: African,

EXCERPT 11.2 • *The Independent Variable of a One-Way ANOVA*

To determine if differences existed among the groups on self-esteem, a one-way ANOVA was conducted. Ethnic group served as the independent variable, and self-esteem was the dependent variable.

Source: R. E. Phelps, J. D. Taylor, and P. A. Gerard. (2001). Cultural mistrust, ethnic identity, racial identity, and self-esteem among ethnically diverse black university students. *Journal of Counseling and Development, 79*(2), p. 213.

African American, or West Indian/Caribbean. A one-way ANOVA was used to analyze the self-esteem data to see if differences existed among the three ethnic groups. The students claiming the same ethnic identity were grouped together to form each of the study's three samples. Accordingly, the independent variable was ethnic group.

As illustrated by Excerpt 11.2, some researchers will identify explicitly the independent variable associated with their one-way ANOVA. However, many researchers choose not to do this and instead presume that their readers can figure out what the independent variable was based on a description of samples used in the study. By the end of this chapter, I feel confident that you'll have little difficulty identifying the independent variable in any one-way ANOVA you encounter.

As you might suspect, a two-way ANOVA has two independent variables, a three-way ANOVA has three independent variables, and so on. In later chapters, we will consider some of these more complex ANOVAs. In this chapter, however, we will restrict our focus to the kind of ANOVA that has a single independent variable.

Usually, it is easy to discern how many independent variables are involved in a study. On rare occasions, you will come across a study in which the researcher used a one-way ANOVA even though there appears to have been two independent variables. Consider again Excerpt 11.1. On first glance, I thought that this study had two separate independent variables: culture and status. However, since independent variables constitute the building blocks of an ANOVA, we can go backward and let the ANOVA tell us how many independent variables there were. Thus, I finally realized that culture and status had been combined into a single six-group independent variable *because* the researchers used a one-way ANOVA (and not a two-way ANOVA) to compare the groups' mean scores.

Even if there is just one independent variable within a study in which the analysis of variance is applied, the ANOVA may or may not be a one-way ANOVA. The second criterion that distinguishes one-way ANOVAs from many other kinds of ANOVAs has to do with the number of dependent variables involved in the analysis. With a one-way ANOVA, there is always just one dependent variable. (If there are two or more dependent variables involved in the same analysis, then you are likely to see the analysis described as a multivariate ANOVA, or MANOVA.)

The **dependent variable** corresponds to the measured characteristic of people, animals, or things from whom or from which data are gathered. For example, in the study from which Excerpt 11.1 was taken, the dependent variable was moral reasoning as measured by the DITP inventory. In that excerpt, the table's title and the label for the middle column of numbers let us know that the dependent variable was connected to the DITP. In Excerpt 11.2, the researchers came right out and told us what their dependent variable was.

The third distinguishing feature of a one-way ANOVA concerns the fact that the comparison groups are independent (rather than correlated) in nature. As you will recall from the discussion in Chapter 10 of independent versus correlated samples, this means that (1) the people or animals who provide the scores in any given group are different from those who provide data in any other comparison group and (2) there is no connection across comparison groups because of matching or because several triplets or litters were split up (with one member of each family being put into each of the comparison groups). It is possible for an ANOVA to be applied to the data that come from correlated samples, but I will delay my discussion of that form of analysis until later in the book.

In Excerpt 11.3, we see a case where the researchers refer to their study's independent variable as being the **between-subjects variable.** The adjective *between subjects* is used by researchers when they want to clarify that comparisons are being made with data that have come from independent samples. (In Chapter 14, you will encounter one-way ANOVAs used in studies where the data come from correlated samples, and you'll see that the independent variables in those studies are considered to be *within subjects* in nature.) Since each of the one-way ANOVAs discussed in this chapter involves data collected from separate groups of individuals who have not been matched in any way, every independent variable we encounter here could be considered to be a between-subjects independent variable.

Now, we turn our attention to the specific components of a one-way ANOVA. We begin that effort with a consideration of the one-way ANOVA's null and alternative hypotheses.

EXCERPT 11.3 • *A Between-Subjects Variable*

A one-way ANOVA was then conducted on the target emotion terms (amusement and happiness) with treatment condition as the between-subjects variable.

Source: P. G. Devereux and G. P. Ginsburg. (2001). Sociality effects on the production of laughter. *Journal of General Psychology, 128*(2), p. 235.

The One-Way ANOVA's Null and Alternative Hypotheses

The null hypothesis of a one-way ANOVA is always set up to say that the mean score on the dependent variable is the same in each of the populations associated with the study. The null hypothesis is usually written by putting equal signs between a set of μs, with each μ representing the mean score within one of the populations. For example, if there were four comparison groups in the study, the null hypothesis would be H_0: $\mu_1 = \mu_2 = \mu_3 = \mu_4$.

If you recall my claim (in Chapter 7) that every null hypothesis must contain a pinpoint parameter, you may now be wondering how the symbolic statement at the end of the preceding paragraph qualifies as a legitimate null hypothesis since it doesn't contain any pinpoint number. In reality, there is a pinpoint number contained in that H_0 but it is simply hidden from view. If the population means are all equal to one another, then there is no variability among those means. Therefore, we can bring H_0's pinpoint number into plain view by rewriting the null hypothesis as H_0: $\sigma_\mu^2 = 0$. As we said earlier, however, you are more likely to see H_0 written with Greek mus and equal signs and no pinpoint number (e.g., H_0: $\mu_1 = \mu_2 = \mu_3$) rather than with a sigma squared set equal to zero.

In Excerpts 11.4 and 11.5, we see examples of one-way ANOVA null hypotheses that have appeared in research summaries. Notice that these two excerpts are similar in that each null hypothesis deals with its study's population means. Moreover, both null hypotheses have been set up to say that there are no differences among the population means.

The researchers associated with Excerpts 11.4 and 11.5 deserve high praise for taking the time to articulate the null hypothesis associated with their one-way ANOVAs. The vast majority of researchers do not do this. They tell us about the data they collected and what happened in terms of results, but they skip over the

EXCERPTS 11.4–11.5 • *The Null Hypothesis in a One-Way ANOVA*

H_0: $\mu_{\text{Seniors}} = \mu_{\text{Juniors}} = \mu_{\text{Sophomores}}$

Source: F. E. Ede, B. Panigrahi, and S. E. Calcich. (1998). African American students' attitudes toward entrepreneurship education. *Journal of Education for Business, 73*(5), p. 294.

- -

A one-way ANOVA was performed [and] indicated that the null hypothesis of equal population means cannot be rejected.

Source: G. Prendergast, Y. Shi, and D. West. (2001). Organizational buying and advertising agency-client relationships in China. *Journal of Advertising, 30*(2), p. 66.

important first step of hypothesis testing. Perhaps they assume that readers will know what the null hypothesis was.

In hypothesis testing, of course, the null hypothesis must be accompanied by an alternative hypothesis. This H_a will always say that at least two of the population means differ. Using symbols to express this thought, we get $H_a: \sigma_\mu^2 \neq 0$. Unfortunately, the alternative hypothesis is rarely included in technical discussions of research studies. Again, researchers evidently presume that their readers are familiar enough with the testing procedure being applied and familiar enough with what goes on in a one-way ANOVA to know what H_a is without being told.

Presentation of Results

The outcome of a one-way ANOVA is presented in one of two ways. Researchers may elect to talk about the results within the text of their report and to present an ANOVA **summary table.** On the other hand, they may opt to exclude the table from the report and simply describe the outcome in a sentence or two of the text. (At times, a researcher wants to include the table in the report but is told by the journal editor to delete it due to limitations of space.)

Once you become skilled at deciphering the way results are presented within an ANOVA summary table, I am confident that you will have no difficulty interpreting results presented within a "tableless" report. For this reason, I begin each of the next two sections with a consideration of how the results of one-way ANOVAs are typically presented in tables. I have divided this discussion into two sections because some reports contain the results of a single one-way ANOVA while other reports present the results of many one-way ANOVAs.

Results of a Single One-Way ANOVA

In Excerpt 11.6, we see a pair of sentences and a table, both of which relate to a study characterized by a single independent variable, a single dependent variable, four independent samples, and a focus on means. In this excerpt, the number 7.93 is the calculated value, and it is positioned in the column labeled **F Ratio.** That calculated value was obtained by dividing the **mean square** (*MS*) on the "between groups" row of the table (7.30) by the mean square on the "within groups" row of the table (.92). Each row's **MS** value was derived by dividing that row's sum of squares (*SS*) value by its *df* value.[1] Those *SS* values came from an analysis of the sample data. The *df* values, on the other hand, came from simply counting the num-

---

[1]A mean square is never computed for the total row of a one-way ANOVA or for the total row of any other kind of ANOVA.

EXCERPT 11.6 • *Results of a One-Way ANOVA Presented via Text and Table*

Analysis was conducted using subjects' dominant learning style as an indicator of achievement. Results from the one-way ANOVA appear in Table 1.

TABLE 1 *ANOVA Summary Table for Dominant Learning-Style Group by Learning Outcome in CPSC 203*

Source	df	Sum of Squares	Mean Square	F Ratio	F Prob
Between groups	3	21.91	7.30	7.93	.00001
Within groups	801	737.33	.92		
Total	804	759.24			

Source: J. L. Ross, M. T. B. Drysdale, and R. A. Schulz. (2001). Cognitive learning styles and academic performance in two postsecondary computer application courses. *Journal of Research on Computing in Education, 33*(4), p. 407.

ber of groups, the number of people within each group, and the total number of participants—with 1 subtracted from each number to obtain the *df* values presented in the table.[2]

The first two *df* values were used by the researcher to locate (in the back of a statistics book) the critical value against which 7.93 was compared. (The researchers did not indicate how large that critical value was, but it must have been smaller than 7.93 because the ANOVA *F* turned out to be significant.) Whereas the researchers needed to use the first two *df* values, you can use the first and the third *df* values (3 and 804) to help you understand the structure of the study. By adding 1 to the between groups *df,* you can determine, or verify, that four groups were involved in this study. And by adding 1 to the total *df,* you can figure out that learning outcome scores were collected from a total of 805 students.

One other feature of Excerpt 11.6 is worth noting. In the far right-hand column, the researchers report that the probability associated with their calculated *F* value was .00001. This small decimal number was *not* the researchers' level of significance. In their article, the researchers stated that "for all statistical tests, the level

[2]The within *df* was computed first by subtracting 1 from each of the four sample sizes, and then by adding the four $n - 1$ values.

of significance was set at the .05 level." With $\alpha = .05$, the researchers could have stated, in the final column or in a note beneath the table, that "$p < .05$." However, they followed the practice (discussed earlier in Chapter 8) of reporting *p*-levels that are precise and that show the degree to which the sample data are inconsistent with the null hypothesis. In this particular case, the four population means, if identical, would have been *very* unlikely to yield sample means as dissimilar as those actually associated with this study's four comparison groups.

In Excerpt 11.7, we see two tables from a different research report, one with the mean, sample size, and standard deviation for each of the five comparison groups, and the other with the one-way ANOVA summary table. The ANOVA summary table here resembles the one you saw in Excerpt 11.6, except here the column of *df* values is positioned as the second (rather than the first) column of numbers. Also note that no row for "total" appears at the bottom of the table. Consequently, if the *N*s had not been included in Table 2a and you wanted to determine how many people were involved as participants, you would need to add together the *df* values

EXCERPT 11.7 • *Another One-Way ANOVA Summary Table*

TABLE 2A   *Mean Scores of Methods Used to Manage ADHD Behaviors in the Classroom by Years of Experience*

Experience	Mean	N	Std. Deviation
0–5 years	24.6607	56	3.1234
6–10 years	25.4697	66	3.1731
11–15 years	25.5806	31	3.2840
16–20 years	25.7391	23	2.9421
Over 20 years	26.3673	49	2.8918

TABLE 2B   *Analysis of Variance*

Source	Sum of Squares	df	Mean Square	F	Prob.
Between Groups	77.876	4	19.469	2.033	.091
Within Groups	2106.364	220	9.574		

Source: C. S. Glass. (2001). Factors influencing teaching strategies used with children who display attention deficit hyperactivity disorder characteristics. *Education, 122*(1), p. 75.

for the between groups and within groups rows ($4 + 220 = 224$ total *df*) and then add 1 ($224 + 1 = 225$ participants).

In the two ANOVA summary tables displayed in Excerpts 11.6 and 11.7, the second row of numbers was labeled "within groups." I would be remiss if I did not warn you that a variety of terms are used by different researchers to label this row of a one-way ANOVA summary table. On occasion, you are likely to see this row referred to as *within, error,* or *residual.* Do not let these alternative labels throw you for a loop. If everything else about the table is similar to the two tables we have just examined, then you should presume that the table you are looking at is a one-way ANOVA summary table.

Because the calculated *F*-value and the *p*-value are the two most important numbers in a one-way ANOVA summary table, researchers will sometimes pull them out of the summary table and include them in a table of the comparison group means and standard deviations. By doing this, spaced is saved in the research report because only one table is needed rather than two. Had this been done in Excerpt 11.7, a note might have appeared beneath Table 2a saying "$F(4, 220) = 2.033, p = .091$." Since this note indicates the *df* for between groups and within groups, you could use these numbers to determine how many people were involved in the study if the sample sizes are not included in the table. A note like this will not contain *SS* or *MS* values, but you really don't need them to understand the study's structure or its results.

Although the results of a one-way ANOVA are sometimes presented in a table similar to those we have just considered, more often the outcome of the statistical analysis simply will be talked about in the text of the report, with no table included. In Excerpts 11.8 and 11.9, we see two illustrations of a one-way ANOVA being summarized in one or two sentences.

In the first of these excerpts, enough information is provided so we can tell that the independent variable was sexual orientation while the dependent variable was age. In Excerpt 11.9, however, no clues appear that would allow us to guess the independent and dependent variables. Despite this difference, the two excerpts are the same in that we are told, through words and *p*s, what happened to the null hypothesis. And in both of these excerpts, the researchers included the calculated value.

In Excerpts 11.8 and 11.9, note that two numbers appear in parentheses next to each *F*. These are the *df* values taken from the between groups and within groups rows of the one-way ANOVA summary table. By adding 1 to the first of these *df* values, you can verify or determine how many groups were compared. To figure out or verify how many people were involved in each study, you must add the two *df* values together and then add 1 to the sum. Thus the studies associated with these two excerpts were based on 397 and 92 individuals, respectively.

Near the end of Excerpt 11.9, the researchers indicate that *MSE* = 5.65. This is the value of the mean square from the middle row of the one-way ANOVA

EXCERPTS 11.8–11.9 • *Presentation of One-Way ANOVA Results without a Table*

As expected, in our sample, age showed the typical gradient for male transsexual subjects (Homosexual mean age: $M = 33.25$, $SD = 8.81$, years, $n = 107$: Bisexual mean age: $M = 38.70$, $SD = 9.20$, years, $n = 153$: Heterosexual mean age: $M = 43.22$, $SD = 9.95$, years, $n = 137$). There was a significant overall difference between groups in age, one-way ANOVA $F(2, 394) = 34.10$, $p < 0.001$.

Source: R. Green and R. Young. (2001). Hand preference, sexual preference, and transsexualism. *Archives of Sexual Behavior, 30*(6), pp. 570–571.

- -

Education levels were found to not differ significantly across age groups on a one-way analysis of variance, $F(4, 87) = 2.03$, $MSE = 5.65$.

Source: C. C. Persad, N. Abeles, R. T. Zacks, and N. L. Denberg. (2002) Inhibitory changes after age 60 and their relationship to measures of attention and memory. *The Journals of Gerontology, 57B*(3), p. P226.

summary table (i.e., the row that is called *error* or *within groups*.) When this value is provided along with the calculated F value and the two *df* numbers, it makes it possible for you to reconstruct the full ANOVA summary table.[3]

Results of Two or More One-Way ANOVAs

Data are often collected on two or more dependent variables in studies characterized by at least three comparison groups, a concern for means, and a single independent variable. Although such data sets can be analyzed in various ways, many researchers choose to conduct a separate one-way ANOVA for each of the multiple dependent variables. Accordingly, we ought to look at some of the different ways researchers present their results when more than one one-way ANOVA has been conducted.

In Excerpt 11.10, we see a table that contains the results of four separate one-way ANOVAs. Since the column headings in this table are identical to those you saw earlier in Excerpts 11.6 and 11.7, and since the row labels for each of these four ANOVAs are also familiar (between groups and within groups), you ought to have

---

[3]Since $F = MS_{\text{between}} \div MS_{\text{error}}$ and since you're given F and MS_{error}, you can determine MS_{between}. Knowing the *df* and *MS* for the summary table's first and second rows allows you to determine the *SS* for each of these rows. Finally, you can determine the entries needed for the bottom row of the summary table by adding the first two rows' *df* values (to obtain df_{total}) and *SS* values (to obtain SS_{total}).

EXCERPT 11.10 • *Results of Four One-Way ANOVAs Combined in One Table*

TABLE 4   *Analysis of Variance Table for Rate-Pressure Product across Groups and Repetitions*

Variable	Source	df	SS	MS	F	P
Baseline	Between groups	3	287.03	95.68	1.11	.348
	Within groups	96	8262.20	86.07		
After 10	Between groups	3	5414.82	1804.94	8.79	.000
repetitions	Within groups	96	19719.29	205.41		
After 15	Between groups	3	34159.93	11386.64	40.09	.000
repetitions	Within groups	96	27267.19	284.03		
After 20	Between groups	3	232147.00	77382.34	339.97	.000
repetitions	Within groups	96	21851.00	227.61		

Source: S. Al-Obaidi, J. Anthony, E. Dean, and N. Al-Shuwai. (2001). Cardiovascular responses to repetitive McKenzie lumbar spine exercises. *Physical Therapy, 81*(9), p. 1532.

little or no difficulty determining that (1) the means of four samples were compared in each of these ANOVAs and (2) 100 individuals supplied the data for each analysis. The text of the article clarified that the data for this study came from college students aged 22 to 44.

Before leaving Excerpt 11.10, we need to point out something important that holds true for any presentation of results that contains the statistical outcome of two or more statistical tests. In such a presentation, a distinct null hypothesis is associated with each outcome that turned out to be either statistically significant or statistically nonsignificant. Hence, four null hypotheses were connected to Excerpt 11.10. Each H_0 would look the same on the surface: $H_0: \mu_1 = \mu_2 = \mu_3 = \mu_4$. They differ, however, with respect to the data represented by the μs. The first of these ANOVAs compared the four samples in terms of a cardiovascular index prior to the time the research participants began their prescribed exercise activity (which varied across the four groups). Each of the remaining three ANOVAs compared these same four samples at different points during the exercise routine.

Now consider Excerpt 11.11. Although I have included in this excerpt some of the text from the research report, as well as a table displaying the ANOVA results, I hope you can decipher what is going on in the table without reading the researchers' explanation. Most importantly, I want to call your attention to the fact that the hypothesis testing procedure was used here three times, once in conjunction with each

EXCERPT 11.11 • *A Table Containing Just the F-Values from Three One-Way ANOVAs*

Our second hypothesis (H_2) regarding a positive relationship between the degree of strategic planning and the venture's performance was tested by means of one-way analysis of variance. Table 2 compares the mean scores for no planning (reactiveness), short-term planning (in-between) and long-term planning (proactiveness). As Table 2 shows, the results support the hypothesis, showing a clear relationship between planning and the three measures of performance (sales volume, owner income, and number of employees).

TABLE 2 *One-Way Analysis of Performance with Strategic Planning*

Performance Variables	No Planning (mean score)	Short-Term Planning (mean score)	Long-Term Planning (mean score)	F	p
Sales Volume	3.7	6.4	6.6	14.2	.00
Income of Owner	45.7	69.4	61.4	2.6	.08
No. of Employees	2.5	12.4	27.3	6.9	.00

Source: M. Lerner and T. Almor. (2002). Relationships among strategic capabilities and the performance of women-owned small ventures. *Journal of Small Business Management, 40*(2), p. 118.

of the performance variables. In each case, H_0 said that the three planning strategies had identical population means.

In many research reports, the results of more than one one-way ANOVA are presented without any ANOVA summary table(s). We now turn our attention to an example where multiple one-way ANOVA results are discussed in the text of the report. Excerpt 11.12 illustrates this common reporting technique. As you read through this passage, you ought to be able to determine (1) how many null hypotheses were tested, (2) what decision was made regarding each H_0, (3) what the dependent variables were, (4) how many comparison groups were involved in each analysis, and (5) how many individuals were in the study.

The Bonferroni Adjustment Technique

In the preceding section, we looked at three examples where separate one-way ANOVAs were used to assess the data from multiple dependent variables. When a researcher has a situation such as this, there will be an inflated Type I error risk un-

EXCERPT 11.12 • *Results of Several One-Way ANOVAs Presented in the Text*

We analyzed the potential moderating effects of suicide history on patients' views of no-suicide agreements. One-way ANOVAs contrasting groups of no prior attempts, one attempt, and more than one attempt revealed no significant differences among means for Coercive Features ($F = 2.41$; $df = 2, 132$) or Detached Features ($F = 2.51$; $df = 2, 132$). The means of Therapeutic Features for no prior attempts ($M = 5.71$; $SD = 1.19$), one attempt ($M = 5.51$; $SD = 1.15$), and more than one attempt ($M = 4.87$; $SD = 1.32$) groups were significantly different ($F = 6.00$; $df = 2, 132$; $p < .003$).

Source: S. E. Davis, I. S. Williams, and L. W. Hays. (2002). Psychiatric inpatients' perceptions of written no-suicide agreements: An exploratory study. *Suicide and Life-Threatening Behavior, 32*(1), p. 60.

less something is done to compensate for the fact that multiple tests are being conducted. In other words, if the data associated with each of several dependent variables are analyzed separately by means of a one-way ANOVA, the probability of incorrectly rejecting at least one of the null hypotheses is greater than the common alpha level used across the set of tests.

Several statistical techniques are available for dealing with the problem of an inflated Type I error risk. Among these, the **Bonferroni adjustment procedure** appears to be the most popular choice among applied researchers. As you will recall from our earlier consideration of this procedure, the researcher compensates for the fact that multiple tests are being conducted by making the alpha level more rigorous on each of the separate tests.

In Excerpt 11.13, we see an example of the Bonferroni technique being used in a study where 15 one-way ANOVAs were used, one for each of the different dependent variables involved in the study. In this excerpt, the researchers explain why and how they applied the Bonferroni adjustment.

In Excerpt 11.13 and in most other applications of the Bonferroni adjustment, the desired study-wide alpha level is divided by the number of tests being conducted, and then that revised alpha becomes the common criterion against which each test's p is compared. In Excerpt 11.13, that common criterion was .003. Most researchers use the Bonferroni procedure in this fashion.

If a researcher considers certain of the study's dependent variables to be of primary concern while other dependent variables are viewed as being of secondary concern, the Bonferroni procedure may be used with a slight twist. Instead of using the same reduced alpha level to evaluate the results of all tests, the researcher has the option of varying the degree to which the alpha level is reduced for

EXCERPT 11.13 • *The Bonferroni Adjustment Used in Conjunction with a One-Way ANOVA*

We conducted the first set of analyses to contrast the three drug-stage comparison groups. First we ran 15 one-way analyses of variance (ANOVAs) to statistically compare the mean scores of the three comparison groups on each of the psychosocial variables within the personality, parental, peer, and self-drug-use domains. We corrected for the increased probability of occurrence of a Type I error that results when conducting multiple comparisons by using a more conservative level of alpha than .05. With a Bonferroni correction approach, the alpha level used was .003, which was calculated by dividing alpha (i.e., .05) by the number of comparisons (i.e., 15).

Source: N. K. Morojele and J. S. Brook. (2001). Adolescent precursors of intensity of marijuana and other illicit drug use among adult initiators. *Journal of Genetic Psychology, 162*(4), p. 438.

the different tests being conducted. Suppose, for example, that a researcher conducts a study in which a one-way ANOVA is applied separately to each of four dependent variables. Instead of setting alpha at .0125 for each of these tests, the researcher could conduct the two primary tests with $\alpha = .02$ and conduct the two secondary tests with $\alpha = .005$. (Using this varying-alpha version of the Bonferroni procedure gives the researcher more power on those tests deemed to be of greater importance.) Any combination of alphas is permitted so long as the sum of the separate alphas does not exceed the desired study-wide Type I error risk.

There is no law, of course, that directs all researchers to deal with the problem of an inflated Type I error risk when multiple one-way ANOVAs are used, each with a different dependent variable. Furthermore, there are circumstances where it would be unwise to take any form of corrective action. Nevertheless, I believe that you should value more highly those reports wherein the researcher either (1) does something (e.g., uses the Bonferroni procedure) to hold down the chances of a Type I error when multiple tests are conducted or (2) explains why nothing was done to deal with the inflated Type I error risk. If neither of these things is done, you have a right to downgrade your evaluation of the study.

Assumptions of a One-Way ANOVA

In Chapter 10, we considered the four main assumptions associated with *t*-tests, *F*-tests, and *z*-tests: independence, randomness, normality, and homogeneity of variance. My earlier comments apply as much now to cases where a one-way ANOVA is used to compare three or more means as they did to cases where two means are compared using a t-, F-, or z-test. In particular, I hope you recall the meaning of these four assumptions and my point about how these tests are robust to the equal variance assumption when the sample sizes of the various comparison groups are equal.

Many researchers who use a one-way ANOVA seem to pay little or no attention to the assumptions that underlie the F-test comparison of their sample means. Consequently, I encourage you to feel better about research reports that (1) contain discussions of the assumptions, (2) present results of tests that were conducted to check on the testable assumptions, (3) explain what efforts were made to get the data in line with the assumptions, and/or (4) point out that an alternative test having fewer assumptions than a regular one-way ANOVA F-test was used. Conversely, I encourage you to lower your evaluation of research reports that do none of these things.

Take a look at Excerpt 11.14. In this study, the researchers used a one-way ANOVA. Before doing so, however, they screened their data in to see if the normality assumption was tenable. Because there were no outliers and because the skewness and kurtosis indices were close to zero, the researchers concluded that it was permissible to proceed with their main analysis, a one-way ANOVA to compare the group means. These researchers set a good example by demonstrating a concern for the normality of their populations. Unfortunately, most researchers give no indication that they thought about the **normality assumption.** Perhaps they are under the mistaken belief that the F-test is always robust to violations of this assumption. Or perhaps they simply are unaware of the assumption. In any event, I salute the researchers associated with Excerpt 11.14 for checking their data before conducting a one-way ANOVA.

Excerpt 11.15 illustrates how the **homogeneity of variance assumption** can be tested. Notice that the results of this probe were nonsignificant. This is what the researchers were hoping would happen when they tested this assumption. They

Research Navigator.com

Homogeneity of variance

EXCERPT 11.14 • *Testing for Normality before Using a One-Way ANOVA*

To provide the fullest possible context for the inter- and subcultural comparisons, the three groups (European families, high-acculturated Chinese families, and low-acculturated Chinese families) were treated jointly as a between-subjects variable in a one-way analysis of variance (ANOVA) design. . . . Prior to the main data analyses, the data were screened for outliers and normality of distribution. There were no obvious outliers, and both kurtosis and skewness tests indicated no serious departure from normality (all tests resulted in absolute values of less than 1).

Source: S. H. Ng, A. P. He, J. H. Liu, A. Weatherall, and C. S. F. Long. (2000). Communication correlates of individualism and collectivism: Talk directed at one or more addressees in family conversations. *Journal of Language and Social Psychology, 19*(1), pp. 32–33.

**EXCERPT 11.15 • *Testing the Equal Variance Assumption before Using
a One-Way ANOVA***

Specific activities were compared among diet groups by one-way analysis of variance (ANOVA). . . . Bartlett tests for homogeneity of group variances were all non-significant.

Source: M. E. Ciminari, D. Afik, W. Karasov, and E. Caviedes-Vidal. (2001). Is diet-shifting facilitated by modulation of pancreatic enzymes? Test of an adaptational hypothesis in yellow-rumped Warblers. *The Auk, 118*(4), p. 1103.

wanted to retain the null hypothesis of equal population variances so they could move forward and compare their sample means with a one-way ANOVA.

Sometimes, preliminary checks on normality and the equal variance assumption suggest that the populations are not normal and/or have unequal variances. When this happens, researchers have three options. They can (1) identify and eliminate outliers, presuming that such scores are the source of the problem, (2) transform their sample data in an effort to reduce nonnormality and/or stabilize the variances, or (3) switch from the one-way ANOVA *F*-test to some other test that

**EXCERPTS 11.16–11.17 • *Options when Underlying Assumptions
Appear to Be Untenable***

This analysis was done with one-way analysis of variance. Because the variances were unequal for aminopeptidase P, we log transformed data.

Source: A. Adam, M. Cugno, G. Molinaro, and M. Perez. (2002). Aminopeptidase P in individuals with a history of angio-oedema on ACE inhibitors. *The Lancet, 359*(9323), p. 2088.

- -

Mean responses were compared by one-way analysis of variance (ANOVA) unless variances did not pass Bartlett's test of homogeneity, in which case means were compared using nonparametric ANOVA (Kruskal-Wallis KW statistic).

Source: J. A. Pechenik, W. Li, and D. E. Cochrane. (2002). Timing is everything: The effects of putative dopamine antagonists on metamorphosis vary with larval age and experimental duration in the prosobranch gastropod Crepidula fornicata. *The Biological Bulletin, 202*(2), p. 140.

does not have such rigorous assumptions. In Excerpts 11.16 and 11.17, we see cases in which researchers employed the second and third of these options, respectively.

Of the four assumptions associated with a one-way ANOVA, the one that is neglected most often is the **independence assumption.** In essence, this assumption says that a particular person's score should not be influenced by the measurement of any other people or by what happens to others in the execution phase of the study. This assumption would be violated if different groups of students (perhaps different intact classrooms) are taught differently, with each student's exam score being used in the analysis.

**Research
Navigator.c⊕m**

Unit of analysis

In studies where groups are a necessary feature of the investigation, the recommended way to adhere to the independence assumption is to have the **unit of analysis** (i.e., the scores that are analyzed) be each group's mean rather than the scores from the individuals in the group. In Excerpt 11.18, we see a case in which a team of researchers used the group mean as the unit of analysis. Notice that they did this because their study's procedures did not conform to the independent assumption.

**EXCERPT 11.18 • *Expressed Concern for the Assumption
of Independence***

Group means were calculated for use in these ANOVAs because of the violation of the assumption of independence when gathering data from interacting groups.

Source: A. K. Rantilla. (2000). Collective task responsibility allocation: Revisiting the group-serving bias. *Small Group Research, 31*(6), p. 748.

Statistical Significance versus Practical Significance

Researchers who use a one-way ANOVA to compare three or more means can do one of four things in an effort to avoid ending up with a result that is insignificant in any practical sense even though it is statistically significant. One option is to conduct a **power analysis** before any data are collected, with the outcome of the power analysis dictating how large the sample sizes should be. A second option is to estimate the **strength of association** (between the independent and dependent variables) after the sample data have been collected and analyzed to obtain the *F*-ratio. The third option is to compute the **effect size** on the basis of the sample data that have been collected. The final option is to compute a **post hoc estimate of the power** associated with the completed analysis.

Unfortunately, only a minority of the researchers who use a one-way ANOVA take the time to perform any form of analysis designed to address the issue of **practical versus statistical significance.** In my opinion, too many researchers simply use the simplest version of hypothesis testing to test their one-way ANOVA's H_0. They collect the amount of data that time, money, or energy will allow, and then they anxiously await the outcome of the analysis. If their *F*-ratios turn out significant, these researchers quickly summarize their studies, with emphasis put on the fact that "significant findings" have been obtained.

I encourage you to upgrade your evaluation of those one-way ANOVA research reports in which the researchers demonstrate that they were concerned about practical significance as well as statistical significance. Examples of such concern appear in Excerpts 11.19 and 11.20. In the first of these excerpts, eta squared—a strength-of-association index—was computed. In Excerpt 11.20, the researchers computed omega squared, another kind of measure of association. Notice that criteria are provided, in Excerpt 11.20, for interpreting omega squared.

In Excerpts 11.21 and 11.22, we see illustrations of the two other ways researchers can examine their results to see if a statistically significant result also signifies significance in a practical (or clinical) sense. In the first of these excerpts, the researchers conducted a post hoc power analysis following their one-way ANOVA.

EXCERPTS 11.19–11.20 • *Eta Squared and Omega Squared*

The three groups were compared using a one-way ANOVA. . . . The comparison of the three groups for total MSQ score showed a significant between-group difference, $F(2, 65) = 4.18$, $p < .05$, $\eta^2 = .05$, with a moderate effect size.

Source: F. E. Ede, B. Panigrahi, and S. E. Calcich. (2002). Sleep disturbances in adolescents with symptoms of attention-deficit/hyperactivity disorder. *Journal of Learning Disabilities*, *35*(3), p. 271.

Univariate analyses of variance (ANOVAs) were performed [to compare the three groups on each dependent variable]. . . . Effect sizes were calculated to see how meaningful the differences in the group means were. This was done using omega squared. . . . In the behavioral and social sciences, the range for effect sizes are .01 for small, .06 for medium, and .15 for large (Cohen, 1977).

Source: R. E. Phelps, J. D. Taylor, and P. A. Gerard. (2001). Cultural mistrust, ethnic identity, racial identity, and self-esteem among ethnically diverse black university students. *Journal of Counseling and Development*, *79*(2), pp. 212–213.

EXCERPTS 11.21–11.22 • *Post Hoc Assessment of Power and Effect Size*

No significant differences [from the one-way ANOVA] were found in levels of state anxiety, $F(2, 88)$, *n.s.*, though care should be taken in interpretation of this finding given the level of statistical power (.55 anticipating a medium or .93 anticipating a large effect size, Cohen, 1988, p. 313).

Source: P. E. King, M. J. Young, and R. R. Behnke. (2000). Public speaking performance improvement as a function of information processing in immediate and delayed feedback interventions. *Communication Education, 49*(4), p. 371.

To compare the magnitude of group differences for the impulsivity variables of interest, estimates of effect sizes were calculated as Cohen's f (Cohen, 1988). These estimates are useful when comparing measurement techniques because, unlike p values, the effect size conveys the magnitude of the phenomenon of interest (Cohen, 1990). For one-way analyses of variance, f scores of .10, .25, and .40 are conventional definitions of small, medium, and large effect sizes (respectively) (Cohen, 1992).

Source: C. W. Mathias, D. M. Dougherty, D. M. Marsh, and F. G. Moeller. (2002). Laboratory measures of impulsivity: A comparison of women with or without childhood aggression. *Psychological Record, 52*(3), p. 295.

In Excerpt 11.22, the researchers computed Cohen's f, an index of effect size. As indicated in this excerpt, the criteria for evaluating f are .10 (small), .25 (medium), and .40 (large). These criteria differ from those used with the d measure of effect size—for which small, medium, and large are defined as .20, .50, and .80, respectively—because f was designed to be flexible so it could be used with any number of means whereas d is appropriate only when there are two means.

The strategies used in Excerpts 11.19 through 11.22 all represent a post hoc effort at dealing with the issue of statistical versus practical significance. Thus, they illustrate the use of the seven-step version of hypothesis testing as applied to a one-way ANOVA. Although the researchers associated with those studies deserve credit for taking this seventh step, even more credit ought to be directed to those researchers who use the nine-step version of hypothesis testing. As I hope you recall (from what was presented in Chapter 8), the nine-step version of hypothesis testing involves doing an *a priori* power analysis for the purpose of determining the proper sample size.

In Excerpt 11.23, we see a case in which a team of researchers performed a power analysis to figure out the optimal sample size for their one-way ANOVA. In this excerpt, notice that the researcher had to specify an effect size (.30) and a desired power level (.80) in order to determine the sample size (120). These three

EXCERPT 11.23 • *A Power Analysis Used to Determine the Sample Size*

Based on a Cohen's medium effect size of 0.30, a level of significance of .05, and a power of 80%, a sample size of 120 participants was required in order to detect a difference of 5 degrees in knee ROM [range of motion in knee flexion] among the [three] groups. . . . Active knee flexion measurements were analyzed with a one-way analysis of variance (ANOVA). . . .

Source: L. A. Beaupre, D. M. Davies, C. A. Jones, and J. G. Cinats. (2001). Exercise combined with continuous passive motion or slider board therapy compared with exercise only: A randomized controlled trial of patients following total knee arthroplasty. *Physical Therapy, 81*(4), p. 1034.

numbers, in this study, were the output of steps 4, 5, and 6 of the nine-step version of the hypothesis testing procedure.

Cautions

Before concluding this chapter, I want to offer a few tips that will increase your skills at deciphering and critiquing research reports based on one-way ANOVAs.

Significant and Nonsignificant Results from One-Way ANOVAs

When researchers say that they have obtained a statistically significant result from a one-way ANOVA, this means that they have rejected the null hypothesis. Because you are unlikely to see the researchers articulate the study's H_0 (in words or symbols) or even see them use the term *null hypothesis* in discussing the results, it is especially important for you to remember (1) that a significant *F* means H_0 has been rejected, (2) what the one-way ANOVA H_0 stipulates, and (3) how to interpret correctly the decision to reject H_0.

Although a one-way ANOVA can be used to compare the means of two groups, this chapter has focused on the use of one-way ANOVAs to compare three or more means. If the data lead to a significant finding when more than two means have been contrasted, it means that the sample data are not likely to have come from populations having the same μ. This one-way ANOVA result does not provide any information as to how many of the μ values are likely to be dissimilar, nor does it provide any information as to whether any specific pair of populations are likely to have different μ values. The only thing that a significant result indicates is that the variability among the full set of sample means is larger than would be expected if all population means were identical.

Usually, a researcher wants to know more about the likely state of the population means than is revealed by a one-way ANOVA. To be more specific, the typical researcher wants to be able to make comparative statements about pairs of population means, such as "μ_1 is likely to be larger than μ_2 but μ_2 and μ_3 cannot be looked on as different based on the sample data." To address these concerns, the researcher must move past the significant ANOVA F and apply a subsequent analysis. In the next chapter, we will consider such analyses, which are called, understandably, post hoc or follow-up tests.

Since you probably will be given information regarding the means that were compared by the one-way ANOVA, you may be tempted, if a significant result has been obtained, to consider each mean to be significantly different from every other mean. Refrain!

To gain an understanding of this very important point, consider once again Excerpt 11.11. In that excerpt, the results of three one-way ANOVAs are presented along with the three sample means compared by each ANOVA. The three means compared in the first one-way ANOVA were 3.7, 6.4, and 6.6, and the F-test yielded statistical significance. This result indicates that the null hypothesis of equal population means was rejected. Hence, it is legitimate to think that $H_0: \mu_1 = \mu_2 = \mu_3$, where each μ corresponds to sales volume. However, it is *not* legitimate to look at the first row of results in Excerpt 11.11 and think that the mean of 3.7 is significantly different from 6.4, or to think that the mean of 3.7 is significantly different from 6.6. A one-way ANOVA simply does not provide such information.[4]

You must also be on guard when it comes to one-way ANOVAs that yield nonsignificant Fs. As I have pointed out now on several occasions, a fail-to-reject decision should not be interpreted to mean that H_0 is true. Unfortunately, many researchers make this inferential mistake when comparison groups are compared in terms of mean scores on a pretest. The researchers' goal is to see whether the comparison groups are equal to one another at the beginning of their studies, and they mistakenly interpret a nonsignificant F-test to mean that no group began with an advantage or a disadvantage.

One-way ANOVAs, of course, can produce a nonsignificant F-value when groups are compared on things other than a pretest. Consider once again Excerpt 11.11. On the second row of the table, we see that the three sample means were 45.7, 69.4, and 61.4. In light of the fact that the p on this row turned out equal to .08, many researchers would make a decision to retain the null hypothesis. Such a

---

[4]Surprisingly, a significant F does not necessarily indicate that a statistically significant difference exists between the largest and smallest sample means.

decision should *not* be interpreted—by you or the researcher—to mean that the three μs (regarding owner income) are likely to be equal. A one-way ANOVA, if nonsignificant, cannot be used to justify such an inference.

Confidence Intervals

In Chapter 10, you saw how a confidence interval can be placed around the difference between two sample means. You also saw how such confidence intervals can be used to test a null hypothesis, with H_0 rejected if the null's pinpoint numerical value lies beyond the limits of the interval. As we now conclude our consideration of how researchers compare three or more means with a one-way ANOVA, you may be wondering why I haven't said anything in this chapter about the techniques of estimation.

When a study's focus is on three or more means, researchers will occasionally build a confidence interval around each of the separate sample means. This is done in situations where (1) there is no interest in comparing all the means together at one time or (2) there is a desire to probe the data in a more specific fashion after the null hypothesis of equal population means has been rejected. Whereas researchers sometimes use interval estimation (on individual means) in lieu of or as a complement to a test of the hypothesis that all μs are equal, they do not use interval estimation as an alternative strategy for testing the one-way ANOVA null hypothesis. Stated differently, you are not likely to come across research studies where a confidence interval is put around the variance of the sample means in order to test $H_0: \sigma_\mu^2 = 0$.

Other Things to Keep in Mind

If we momentarily lump together the current chapter with the ones that preceded it, it is clear that you have been given a slew of tips or warnings designed to help you become a more discerning recipient of research-based claims. Several of the points are important enough to repeat here.

1. The mean is focused on in research studies more than any other statistical concept. In many studies, however, a focus on means does not allow the research question to be answered because the question deals with something other than central tendency.

2. If the researcher's interest resides exclusively in the group(s) from which data are collected, only descriptive statistics should be used in analyzing the data.

3. The reliability and validity of the researcher's data are worth considering. To the extent that reliability is lacking, it is difficult to reject H_0 even when H_0 is false. To the extent that validity is lacking, the conclusions drawn will be unwarranted because of a mismatch between what is truly being measured and what the researcher thinks is being measured with a one-way ANOVA.

4. With a one-way ANOVA, nothing is proven regardless of what the researcher concludes after analyzing the data. Either a Type I error or a Type II error always will be possible no matter what decision is made about H_0.

5. The purpose of a one-way ANOVA is to gain an insight into the population means, not the sample means.

6. Those researchers who talk about (and possibly test) the assumptions underlying a one-way ANOVA deserve credit for being careful in their utilization of this inferential technique.

7. A decision not to reject the one-way ANOVA's H_0 does not mean that all population means should be considered equal.

8. Those researchers who perform a power analysis (either before or after conducting their one-way ANOVAs) or compute strength of association or effect size indices (following the application of a one-way ANOVA) are doing a more conscientious job than are those researchers who fail to do anything to help distinguish between statistical significance and practical significance.

9. The Bonferroni procedure helps to control the risk of Type I errors in studies where one-way ANOVAs are conducted on two or more dependent variables.

10. The *df* values associated with a one-way ANOVA (whether presented in an ANOVA summary table or positioned next to the calculated *F*-value in the text of the research report) can be used to determine the number of groups and the total number of subjects involved in the study.

A Final Comment

We have covered a lot of ground in this chapter. We've looked at the basic ingredients that go into any one-way ANOVA, seen different formats for showing what pops out of this kind of statistical analysis, considered underlying assumptions, and observed how conscientious researchers will make an effort to discuss practical significance as well as statistical significance. You may have assimilated everything presented in this chapter, you may have assimilated only the highlights (with a review perhaps in order), or you may be somewhere between these two extremes. Regardless of how well you can decipher research reports based on one-way ANOVAs at this point, you need to leave this chapter with a crystal clear understanding of one exceedingly important point. Unless you heed the advice embodied in this final comment, you're likely to lose sight of the forest for all the trees.

A one-way ANOVA (like any other statistical analysis) cannot magically transform a flawed study into a sound one. And where can a study be flawed the most? The answer to this question is unrelated to *F*-tests, equal variance assumptions, effect size indices, or Bonferroni adjustments. That's because the potential worth of any study is connected, first and foremost, to the research question that sets the data collection and analysis wheels in motion. If the research question is silly or irrelevant, a one-way ANOVA cannot make the study worthwhile. Hence, don't be impressed by researchers who use one-way ANOVAs *until* you have first considered the merits of the research questions being addressed.

If you would like to see an example of a silly one-way ANOVA, consider Excerpt 11.24. As indicated in this excerpt, a one-way ANOVA was used to compare three groups of individuals. The independent variable concerned the kind of people in each group. One group was made up of children who had a specific language impairment (SLI), the second group was made up of children with Down syndrome (DS), and the third group of was made up of children with typical language development (TL). The final two sentences of this excerpt indicate that a one-way ANOVA was used to compare these three groups in terms of MLU, a measure of speech that was operationally defined as the mean length of utterances.

However, consider closely how the three comparison groups were formed. As indicated in Excerpt 11.24, the three groups were matched on MLU. The success of this matching is evident in the similarity of the MLU means: 3.83, 3.95, and 4.07. Although other parts of this research report may have dealt with interesting issues, two obvious questions must be asked relative to the one-way ANOVA summarized in Excerpt 11.24. Because of the matching strategy used to form the three groups, wasn't it known from the very beginning that the three groups did not differ in terms

EXCERPT 11.24 • *An Unnecessary One-Way ANOVA*

In the present investigation, we compared the morphosyntactic productions of a group of children with SLI, an older MLU-matched group of children with DS, and an MLU-matched group of younger children developing language typically. . . . Mean values for MLU across the three groups were 4.07 morphemes for the TL group, 3.83 morphemes for the DS group, and 3.95 morphemes for the SLI group. A one-way ANOVA was used to detect differences between the groups on MLU. No significant differences between the groups were found, $F(2, 26) = 1.81$, $p = .18$.

Source: P. A. Eadie, M. E. Fey, J. M. Douglas, and C. L. Parsons. (2002). Profiles of grammatical morphology and sentence imitation in children with specific language impairment and Down syndrome. *Journal of Speech, Language, and Hearing Research, 45*(2), pp. 722–723.

of MLU, the variable used to do the matching? If so, wasn't the one-way ANOVA completely unnecessary?

Review Terms

ANOVA
Between groups
Bonferroni adjustment procedure
Dependent variable
df
Error
Factor
f
F
Homogeneity of variance
Independent variable
Mean square
Normality

One-factor ANOVA
One-way ANOVA
Power analysis
Practical significance
    versus statistical significance
Simple ANOVA
Source
Source of variation
Strength-of-association index
Sum of squares
Summary table
Unit of analysis
Within groups

The Best Items in the Companion Website

1. An interactive online quiz (with immediate feedback provided) covering Chapter 11.
2. Eight misconceptions about the content of Chapter 11.
3. An email message sent from the author to his students entitled "A Closed Hydraulic System."
4. The author-selected best passage from Chapter 11: "One-Way ANOVAs and What's Really Important."
5. An interactive online resource entitled "One-Way ANOVA (a)."

Fun Exercises inside Research Navigator

1. **Are college sophomores, juniors, or seniors more confident about their problem-solving abilities?**

   In this Canadian study, 158 college students majoring in physiotherapy completed the *Heppner Problem Solving Inventory* (PSI) during the first week of the academic year. This instrument does not measure problem-solving ability; rather, it evaluates one's *confidence* in being successful when engaged in problem-solving tasks. After scoring the PSI, the researchers used a one-way ANOVA to compare the mean scores of the sophomore ($n = 56$), junior ($n = 53$), and senior ($n = 49$) participants. Four one-way ANOVAs were conducted, one on the PSI total scores and one on each of its three subscales. What do you think these ANOVAs revealed? After you formulate your guess, locate the PDF version of the research report in the Nursing, Health, and Medicine database of ContentSelect, look at Figure 3 (on page 21), and then read (on page 20) the second paragraph of the research report's "Results" section.

J. Wessel, J. Loomis, S. Rennie, P. Brook, J. Hoddinott, & M. Aherne. Learning styles and perceived problem-solving ability of students in a baccalaureate physiotherapy programme. *Physiotherapy Theory and Practice.* Located in the NURSING, HEALTH, AND MEDICINE database of ContentSelect.

2. Do better Sumo wrestlers have different kinds of bodies?

In this study, the physical characteristics of four different groups of professional Sumo wrestlers were compared. These four groups were drawn from different competitive "leagues" of the sport, with the first group ($n = 7$) from the top two leagues, the second group ($n = 12$) from the third-ranked league, the third group ($n = 12$) from the fourth- and fifth-ranked leagues, and the fourth group ($n = 5$) from the bottom two leagues. A one-way ANOVA compared the means of these four samples on each of several dependent variables, including height, weight, and percent body fat. Regarding these three variables, two of the *F*-tests were nonsignificant while one turned out $p < .01$. On which variable—height, weight, or percent body fat—do you think the ANOVA null hypothesis was rejected? After making your guess, locate the PDF version of the research report in the Biology database of ContentSelect and then look at Table 2 at the top of page 181.

K. Hattori, K. Kondo, T. Abe, S. Tanake, & F. Fukunaga. Hierarchical differences in body composition of professional Sumo wrestlers. *Annals of Human Biology.* Located in the BIOLOGY database of ContentSelect.

Review Questions and Answers begin on page 516.

12

Post Hoc and Planned Comparisons

In the previous chapter, we examined the setting, purpose, assumptions, and outcome of a one-way analysis of variance that compares three or more groups. In this chapter, we turn our attention to two categories of inferential procedures that are closely related to the one-way ANOVA. As with a one-way ANOVA, the procedures looked at in this chapter involve one independent variable, one dependent variable, no repeated measures, and a focus on means.

The two classes of procedures considered here are called **post hoc comparisons** and **planned comparisons.** One set of these procedures—the post hoc kind—was developed because a one-way ANOVA *F,* if significant, does not provide any specific insight into what caused the null hypothesis to be rejected. To know that all population means are probably not equal to one another is helpful, but differing scenarios fit the general statement that not all μs are identical. For example, with three comparison groups, it might be that two μs are equal but the third is higher, or maybe two μs are equal but the third is lower, or it could be that all three μs are different. By using a post hoc procedure, the researcher attempts to probe the data to find out which of the possible non-null scenarios is most likely to be true.

The second class of procedures considered in this chapter involves planned comparisons. These procedures were developed because researchers sometimes pose questions that cannot be answered by rejecting or failing to reject the null hypothesis of the more general one-way ANOVA H_0. For example, a researcher might wonder whether a specific pair of μs is different, or whether the average of two μs is different from a third μ. In addition to allowing researchers to answer specific questions about the population means, planned comparisons have another desirable characteristic. Simply stated, the statistical power of the tests used to answer specific, preplanned questions is higher than is the power of the more generic *F*-test from a one-way ANOVA. In other words, planned comparisons allow a researcher to deal with specific, *a priori* questions with less risk of a Type II error than does a two-step approach involving an ANOVA *F*-test followed by post hoc comparisons.

Researchers use post hoc comparisons more often than they do planned comparisons. For this reason, we will first consider the different test procedures and reporting schemes used when a one-way ANOVA yields a significant *F* and is followed by a post hoc investigation. We then will turn our attention to what researchers do when they initially set up and test planned comparisons instead of following the two-step strategy of conducting a one-way ANOVA followed by a post hoc analysis. Finally, we will look at the unusual situation where planned comparisons are conducted along with a one-way ANOVA, with no post hoc investigation conducted to help explain what caused the ANOVA *F* to turn out significant.

Post Hoc Comparisons

Definition and Purpose

There is confusion among researchers as to what is or is not a post hoc test. I have come across examples where researchers conducted a post hoc investigation but used the term *planned comparisons* to describe what they did. I have also come across research reports where planned comparisons were conducted by means of a test procedure that many researchers consider to be post hoc in nature. To help you avoid getting confused when you read research reports, I want to clarify what does and does not qualify as a post hoc investigation.

If a researcher conducts a one-way ANOVA and uses the outcome of the *F*-test to determine whether additional specific tests should be conducted, then I will refer to the additional tests as being **post hoc** in nature. As this definition makes clear, the defining criterion of a post hoc investigation has nothing to do with the name of the test procedure employed, with the number of tests conducted, or with the nature of the comparisons made. The only thing that matters is whether the ANOVA *F*-test must first be checked to see if further analysis of the data set is needed.

In turning to a post hoc investigation, the researcher's objective is to better understand why the ANOVA yielded a significant *F*. Stated differently, a post hoc investigation helps the researcher understand why the ANOVA H_0 was rejected. Since the H_0 specifies equality among all population means, you might say that a set of post hoc comparisons is designed to help the researcher gain insight into the pattern of μs. As we indicated at the outset of this chapter, the ANOVA *F* can turn out to be significant for different reasons—that is, because of different possible patterns of μs. The post hoc analysis helps researchers in their efforts to understand the true pattern of the population means.

In light of the fact that empirical studies are usually driven by research hypotheses, it is not surprising to find that post hoc investigations are typically conducted to find out whether such hypotheses are likely to be true. Furthermore, it should not be surprising that differences in research hypotheses lead researchers to do different things in their post hoc investigations. Sometimes, for example, researchers set up their post hoc investigations to compare each sample mean against every other sample mean. On other occasions they use their post hoc tests to compare the mean associated with each of several experimental groups against a control group's mean, with no comparisons made among the experimental groups. On rare occasions, a post hoc investigation is implemented to compare the mean of one of the comparison groups against the average of the means of two or more of the remaining groups. I will illustrate each of these post hoc comparisons later in the chapter.

Terminology

Various terms are used in a synonymous fashion to mean the same thing as the term **post hoc test.** The three synonyms that show up most often in the published literature are **follow-up test, multiple comparison test,** and *a posteriori* **test.** Excerpts 12.1 through 12.4 show how some of these terms have been used.

You may come across a research report in which the term *contrast* appears. The word **contrast** is synonymous with the term **comparison.** Hence, post hoc contrasts are nothing more than post hoc comparisons. Follow-up contrasts are nothing more than follow-up comparisons. *A posteriori* contrasts are nothing more than *a posteriori* comparisons.

It is also worth noting that the *F*-test used in the preliminary ANOVA is sometimes referred to as the **omnibus *F*-test.** This term seems appropriate because the ANOVA's H_0 involves *all* of the population means. Since post hoc (and planned) investigations often use *F*-tests to accomplish their objectives, it is helpful when researchers use the term *omnibus* (when referring to the ANOVA *F*) to clarify which *F* is being discussed. Excerpt 12.5 illustrates the use of this term.

Finally, the terms *pairwise* and *nonpairwise* often pop up in discussions of post hoc (and planned) comparisons. The term **pairwise** simply means that groups are being compared two at a time. For example, pairwise comparisons among three groups labeled A, B, and C would involve comparisons of A versus B, A versus C, and B versus C. With four groups in the study, a total of six pairwise comparisons would be possible.

A **nonpairwise** (or **complex**) **comparison** involves three or more groups, with these comparison groups divided into two subsets. The mean score for the data in each subset is then computed and compared. For example, suppose there are four comparison groups in a study: A, B, C, and D. The researcher might be interested in comparing the average of groups A and B against the average of groups C and D. This would be a nonpairwise comparison, as would a comparison between the first group and the average of the final two groups (with the second group omitted from the comparison).

EXCERPTS 12.1–12.4 • *The Term* Post Hoc *and Its Synonyms*

Statistical analysis of the data was performed using one-factor analysis of variance (P < 0.05) and a post hoc test. . . .

Source: Y. Takeda, S. Kashiwaguchi, K. Endo, T. Matsuura, and T. Sasa. (2002). The most effective exercise for strengthening the supraspinatus muscle: Evaluation by magnetic resonance imaging. *American Journal of Sports Medicine, 30*(3), p. 376.

- -

Comparisons between landform positions within a site were made using a one-way ANOVA and a multiple comparison test. . . .

Source: N. Slobodian, K. Van Rees, and D. Pennock. (2002). Cultivation-induced effects on belowground biomass and organic carbon. *Soil Science Society of America Journal, 66*(3), p. 926.

- -

All age follow-up tests were significant.

Source: C. W. Luchies, J. Schiffman, L. G. Richards, and M. R. Thompson. (2002). Effects of age, step direction, and reaction condition on the ability to step quickly. *The Journals of Gerontology, 57A*(4), p. M247.

- -

A posteriori multiple comparisons among sites were made [following a] significant one-way ANOVA.

Source: C. W. Luchies, J. Schiffman, L. G. Richards, and M. R. Thompson. (2001). Stable carbon, nitrogen, and sulfur isotope ratios in riparian food webs on rivers receiving sewage and pulp-mill effluents. *Canadian Journal of Zoology, 79*(1), p. 7.

EXCERPT 12.5 • *The Omnibus F-Test*

The three groups of patients categorized by lifetime diagnosis (anorexia, bulimia, or bulimia-anorexia) showed few differences, and the differences that did emerge were predictable in light of prior research. The only omnibus F test that was significant was for obsessive-compulsive personality disorder ($F = 5.8$, $df = 2, 94$, $p = 0.004$).

Source: D. Westen and J. Harnden-Fischer. (2001). Personality profiles in eating disorders: Rethinking the distinction between axis I and axis II. *American Journal of Psychiatry, 158*(4), pp. 552–553.

In Excerpts 12.6 and 12.7, we see cases in which reference was made to the use of pairwise and nonpairwise (complex) comparisons. Of these two types of comparisons, the pairwise kind is used widely by applied researchers whereas the nonpairwise is used only rarely.

EXCERPTS 12.6–12.7 • *Pairwise and Complex Comparisons*

The three groups were compared using a one-way ANOVA followed by pairwise follow-up comparisons to evaluate differences among the means of the total MSQ.

Source: D. Stein, R. Pat-Horenczyk, S. Blank, and Y. Dagan. (2002). Sleep disturbances in adolescents with symptoms of attention-deficit/hyperactivity disorder. *Journal of Learning Disabilities, 35*(3), p. 271.

(MO + MC)/2 − (CO + IC)/2: This complex contrast compared the two intervention groups who received instruction in morphemic analysis clues (MO, MC) to those who did not receive morphemic analysis instruction (CO, IC).

Source: J. F. Baumann, E. C. Edwards, G. Font, and C. A. Tereshinski. (2002). Teaching morphemic and contextual analysis to fifth-grade students. *Reading Research Quarterly, 37*(2), pp. 161–162.

Test Procedures Frequently Used in Post Hoc Analyses

A wide array of statistical procedures is employed by applied researchers in their post hoc investigations. The five most frequently used test procedures were developed by Fisher, Duncan, Newman and Keuls, Tukey, and Scheffé. The tests developed by these statisticians carry the names of their inventors—and in some cases the test's label also contains a three-letter abbreviation or a three-word phrase. Thus you will see these five test procedures referred to by the labels **Fisher's LSD, Duncan's multiple range test, Newman-Keuls, Tukey's HSD,** and **Scheffé.** In Excerpts 12.8 through 12.12, we see examples where these post hoc procedures were utilized by applied researchers.

Various test procedures have been developed because researchers differ in the degree of control they want to have over Type I errors when more than one comparison is made. For example, if all possible pairwise comparisons are made among four group means, a total of six tests must be conducted in the post hoc investigation. If each of these six tests were to be conducted at any particular alpha level, the chance of at least one Type I error being made somewhere in the set of tests would

EXCERPTS 12.8–12.12 • *Test Procedures Frequently Used in Post Hoc Investigations*

The means of each treatment group were subjected to a one-way ANOVA ($P \leq 0.05$) and compared using Fisher's least significant difference procedure.

Source: M. J. Rowling, M. H. McMullen, and K. L. Schalinske. (2002). Vitamin A and its deritvatives induce hepatic glycine N-methyltransferase and hypomethylation of DNA in rats. *Journal of Nutrition, 132*(3), p. 367.

- -

Duncan post hoc tests were done to determine specific differences between personality disorder groups and the major depressive disorder group.

Source: A. E. Skodol, J. G. Gunderson, T. H. McGlashon, and I. R. Dyck. (2002). Functional impairment in patients with schizotypal, borderline, avoidant, or obsessive-compulsive personality disorder. *American Journal of Psychiatry, 159*(2), p. 277.

- -

The statistical significance between groups was determined by one-way analysis of variance followed by inspection of all differences between pairs of means by Newman-Keuls' test.

Source: M. E. D'Alessandro, Y. B. Lombardo, and A. Chicco. (2002). Effect of dietary fish oil on insulin sensitivity and metabolic fate of glucose in the skeletal muscle of normal rats. *Annals of Nutrition & Metabolism, 46*(3/4), p. 116.

- -

For each measure, post hoc multiple comparisons were conducted using the Tukey method to identify significant differences among specific institutional types.

Source: M. W. Peterson and M. K. Einarson. (2001). What are colleges doing about student assessment? Does it make a difference? *Journal of Higher Education, 72*(6), p. 639.

- -

Individual comparisons were performed by the Scheffé test.

Source: J. J. Diez. (2002). Hypothyroidism in patients older than 55 years: An analysis of the etiology and assessment of the effectiveness of therapy. *The Journals of Gerontology, 57A*(5), p. M317.

be greater than the nominal alpha level employed. (This situation is highly analogous to the problem discussed in earlier chapters where a separate test is used to see if two comparison groups are significantly different on each of multiple dependent variables.)

Instead of dealing with the problem of an inflated Type I error risk by adjusting the level of significance (as is done when the Bonferroni technique is applied), the Fisher, Duncan, Newman-Keuls, Tukey, and Scheffé procedures make an adjustment in the size of the critical value used to determine whether an observed difference between two means is significant. To compensate for the fact that more than one comparison is made, larger critical values are used. However, the degree to which the critical value is adjusted upward varies according to which test procedure is used.

When the critical value is increased only slightly (as compared with what would have been the critical value in the situation of a two-group study), the test procedure is considered to be **liberal.** On the other hand, when the critical value is increased greatly, the test procedure is referred to as being **conservative.** Liberal procedures provide less control over Type I errors, but this disadvantage is offset by increased power (i.e., more control over Type II errors). Conservative procedures do just the opposite; they provide greater control over Type I error risk but do so at the expense of lower power (i.e., higher risk of Type II errors). In terms of relative positioning along a liberal-conservative continuum, the five procedures I have been discussing would be arranged as follows:

Liberal   Fisher's LSD
  ↑   Duncan's Multiple Range Test
  ↓   Newman-Keuls
                 Tukey
Conservative   Scheffé

A sixth test procedure exists that is often used in a post hoc investigation, but it is different from the Fisher, Duncan, Newman-Keuls, Tukey, and Scheffé procedures. Referred to as the **Dunnett test,** this sixth way of comparing groups allows for only a certain kind of contrast to be made. To be more specific, the Dunnett test compares the mean of a particular group in the study against each of the remaining group means. Typically, the Dunnett test is used when a researcher cares only about how each of several versions of an experimental treatment affect the dependent variable, in terms of means, as compared against a control (or placebo) group. Dunnett's test involves pairwise comparisons (C versus E_1, C versus E_2, etc.) but not all possible pairwise comparisons since contrasts are not made among the experimental groups.

Excerpt 12.13 illustrates the use of Dunnett's test in a study involving four experimental groups and one control group. If each of the five groups had been compared, in a pairwise fashion, with each of the other groups, a total of 10 comparisons would have been examined. With Dunnett's procedure, only a small subset of these comparisons (each of the E-versus-C variety) was actually set up and tested.

Before turning our attention to the way researchers report the results of their post hoc analyses, a special comment needs to be made regarding the Scheffé test.

EXCERPT 12.13 • *Dunnett's Test*

Comparisons of the control group with each of the four experimental conditions on recall were conducted using Dunnett's *t*-ratio for control group comparisons.

Source: P. L. Witt and L. R. Wheeless. (2001). An experimental study of teachers' verbal and nonverbal immediacy and students' affective and cognitive learning. *Communication Education, 50*(4), p. 334–335.

This test procedure is the only one of those we have mentioned that can be used to make both pairwise and nonpairwise comparisons. Despite this extra versatility of the Scheffé procedure, it is used almost exclusively in studies characterized solely by pairwise comparisons.

The Null Hypotheses of a Post Hoc Investigation

In the next section, we will look at the different ways researchers present the results of their post hoc analyses. In those presentations, you will rarely see reference made, through symbols or words, to the null hypotheses that are associated with the test results. Consequently, you need to remember that all of the post hoc procedures are inferential in nature and are concerned with null hypotheses.

In any post hoc analysis, at least two contrasts will be investigated, each involving a null hypothesis. For example, in a study involving three groups (A, B, and C) and pairwise comparisons used to probe a significant result from a one-way ANOVA, three null hypotheses would be tested: $H_0: \mu_A = \mu_B$, $H_0: \mu_A = \mu_C$ and $H_0: \mu_B = \mu_C$.[1] With a similar analysis involving four groups, there will be six null hypotheses. With Dunnett's test, there will be one fewer null hypothesis than there are comparison groups.

The purpose of a post hoc analysis is to evaluate the null hypothesis associated with each contrast that is investigated. As I have pointed out several times, many applied researchers seem to forget this exceedingly important point. They often talk about their findings with reference only to their sample means, and they discuss their results in such a way as to suggest that they have proven something in a definitive manner. When they do so, they are forgetting that their "discoveries" are nothing more than inferences regarding unseen population means, with every inference potentially being nothing more than a Type I or Type II error.

---

[1]Although the null hypotheses of a post hoc investigation theoretically can be set up with something other than zero as H_0's pinpoint number, you are unlikely to ever see a researcher test anything except no-difference null hypotheses in a post hoc analysis.

Presentation of Results

Researchers sometimes summarize the results of their post hoc investigations through the text of the technical report. Usually it is not difficult to understand what the researcher has concluded when the results are presented in this fashion. Consider, for example, Excerpt 12.14. Can you tell how many comparison groups were involved in the study? How many pairwise comparisons were made? How many null hypotheses were rejected?[2]

EXCERPT 12.14 • *Results of a Post Hoc Investigation*

Specifically, Tukey post hoc tests ($p < 0.01$ or better for all significant contrasts) for pairwise comparisons between ethnic/racial groups (means provided in parentheses) indicated that South Asian students ($M = 6.04$ years) immigrated at an older age than those from all other racial/ethnic groups. In addition, Black ($M = 4.63$ years) and Asian ($M = 4.75$ years) students immigrated at a significantly older age than those from "other" racial/ethnic backgrounds ($M = 2.59$) and White students ($M = 0.58$ years). Finally, students from "other" racial/ethnic backgrounds immigrated at an older age than White students.

Source: M. D. Ruck and S. Wortley. (2002). Racial and ethnic minority high school students' perceptions of school disciplinary practices: A look at some Canadian findings. *Journal of Youth and Adolescence, 31*(3), p. 188.

If you take another look at Excerpt 12.14, you'll note that Tukey's procedure was referred to there as "Tukey post hoc tests." John Tukey developed several different tests for making pairwise comparisons among means, and researchers will often specify which particular Tukey test they used. Excerpts 12.15, 12.16, and 12.17 show reference to Tukey's HSD, Tukey's a, and Tukey's B. For all practical purposes, you can consider these different versions of Tukey's test to be nearly equivalent.

When the results of a post hoc analysis are presented graphically, one of three formats is typically used. These formats involve (1) a table of means with attached letters, (2) a table of means with one or more notes using group labels and less than or greater than symbols, and (3) a figure containing lines drawn above vertical bars. Although different formats are employed for displaying the results, these three

---

[2]In Excerpt 12.14, there are five comparison groups, 10 pairwise comparisons, and 9 rejected null hypotheses.

EXCERPTS 12.15–12.17 • *Different Versions of Tukey's Test Procedure*

Further, results of Tukey's HSD analysis indicated that members of in-group LMXs perceived significantly higher levels of personal feedback and supervisory communication satisfaction than their middle-group counterparts who, in turn, reported significantly greater amounts of satisfaction than their out-group peers.

Source: B. H. Mueller and J. Lee. (2002). Leader-member exchange and organizational communication satisfaction in multiple contexts. *Journal of Business Communication, 39*(2), p. 232.

- -

Post-hoc tests of differences between means found that they were not significantly different at placement and interview, but that depression was higher at follow-up than either interview, Tukey a (2, 156) = 2.42, $p < .01$, or placement, Tukey a (2, 156) = 2.16, $p < .01$.

Source: L. M. Glidden. (2000). Adopting children with developmental disabilities: A long-term perspective. *Family Relations, 49*(4), p. 401.

- -

Subjects were divided into tertiles according to their insulin sensitivity, and one-way analysis of variance (ANOVA) followed by Tukey's B post hoc test were used to test differences between groups.

Source: E. Rask, T. Olsson, S. Soderberg, and O. Johnson. (2001). Impaired incretin response after a mixed meal is associated with insulin resistance in nondiabetic men. *Diabetes Care, 24*(9), pp. 1641–1642.

formats are identical in that they reveal where significant differences were found among the comparison groups.

The first format for presenting post hoc results is a table in which **letters are attached to group means.** Such a table appears in Excerpt 12.18.

The table shown in Excerpt 12.18 contains, on the right side of the first row of numbers, the results of the one-way ANOVA the researchers used to compare the four sample means. The results of the post hoc investigation, using Scheffé's test procedure, are shown via letters next to the means. Using the note beneath the table as a guide, we can tell that five of the six pairwise comparisons turned out to be statistically significant. The mean of the low anxiety group was found to be statistically significant from the other three means (the means of the moderately low, the moderately high, and the high anxiety group), and the mean of the high anxiety group also was found to be statistically significant from the means of the other three

EXCERPT 12.18 • *Results of a Post Hoc Investigation Presented in a Table with Letters Attached to Group Means*

TABLE 1 *Exploration of the Quadradic Relationship N = 164*

Anxiety Group	n	Mean	SD	F	p	ω^2
Low	40	10.50a	2.65	5.08	.0022	.08
Mod. Low	42	11.62b	2.92			
Mod. High	42	11.23b	2.44			
High	40	9.55c	2.28			

Note: Anxiety groups were split based on quartile scores which were 5.35 (25%), 6.62 (50%), and 7.88 (75%). Means with different subscripts were different at the $p < .05$ level using a Scheffé correction.

Source: H. Weger and L. E. Polcar. (2002). Attachment style and person-centered comforting. *Western Journal of Communication, 66*(1), p. 94.

anxiety groups. In the only other comparison (moderately low versus moderately high), the means were too close together to cast doubt on the null hypothesis being tested.

When looking at a table in which the results of a post hoc investigation are shown via letters attached to the means, you need to read the note that explains what the letters mean. It's important to do this because all authors do not set up their tables in the same way. In some tables, the same letter attached to any two means indicates that the tested null hypothesis was *not* rejected; in other tables, common letters indicate that the tested null hypothesis *was* rejected. Excerpt 12.18 provides an example of the first (and more typical) situations. The second (less typical) situation can be illustrated best by these words that I recently saw in a note positioned beneath a table: "means sharing the same subscript were all significant at $p < .05$."

The second method for summarizing the results of a post hoc investigation also involves a table of group means, as did the first method. Instead of attaching letters to those means, however, the second method involves (1) an ordering of abbreviations or numbers that represent the group means and (2) the use of the symbols >, <, and = (positioned within those group abbreviations or numbers) to indicate the findings of the pairwise comparisons. Excerpt 12.19 illustrates this method.

In Excerpt 12.19, there are three comparison groups: 41 physically abused children, 38 neglected children, and 35 nonabused/nonneglected children. Three one-way ANOVAs were used to compare these groups, one ANOVA being used

EXCERPT 12.19 • *Another Table Showing the Results of a Post Hoc Investigation*

TABLE 1   *Means and Standard Deviations of Attachment Factors*

	Secure		Avoidant		Anxious/ Ambivalent	
Group	*M*	*SD*	*M*	*SD*	*M*	*SD*
(1) Physically abused (*n* = 41)	2.74	0.55	3.89	0.66	2.74	0.72
(2) Neglected (*n* = 38)	3.45	0.45	2.41	0.56	3.94	0.51
(3) Nonabused/ nonneglected (*n* = 35)	3.76	0.54	2.58	0.55	2.78	0.83
$F(2, 111)$	38.60**		71.98**		35.69**	
Scheffé	3 > 2 > 1*		1 > 2 = 3*		2 > 1 = 3*	

*$p \leq 0.05$; **$p \leq 0.001$

Source: R. Finzi, A. Ram, D. Har-Even, D. Shnit, and A. Weizman. (2001). Attachment styles and aggression in physically abused and neglected children. *Journal of Youth and Adolescence,* *30*(6), p. 776.

---

with each of the study's three dependent variables (secure, avoidant, and anxious/ ambivalent) that represented three different kinds of child–parent interactions. In Excerpt 12.19, each *F* value indicates the results of the ANOVA comparison of means located above the *F*. Beneath each *F* is the summary of the post hoc comparisons of that *F*'s means. This summary for the first dependent variable (3 > 2 > 1) tells us that the null hypothesis was rejected for each of the three pairwise comparisons. The results for the second dependent variable (3 > 2 = 1) were different. Here, a statistically significant difference was found between the mean of the physically abused children and each of the other two group means; however, the null hypothesis for the comparison of the neglected and nonabused/nonneglected groups was not rejected.

The third method for summarizing the results of a post hoc investigation involves a figure containing vertical bars, each of which corresponds to a different comparison group. In such a figure, the height of each bar corresponds to the mean score earned by the group represented by that bar. To show how the post hoc investigation turned out, the researcher will either (1) position letters above (or inside) the bars and explain, in a note, how to make sense out of those letters, or (2) position horizontal lines of differing lengths above the bars, with a note provided to clarify how to interpret the horizontal lines.

In Excerpt 12.20, we see an example of this third method being used. Notice that the researchers tell us that "bars labeled with different lowercase letters indicate significant difference (Tukey's HSD: $P < 0.05$)."

EXCERPT 12.20 • *Results of a Post Hoc Investigation Shown via Bars*

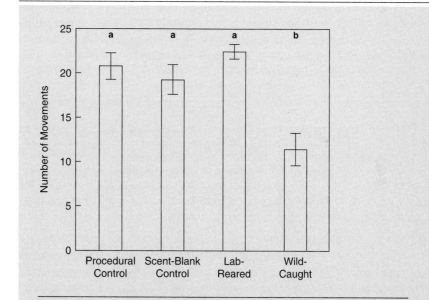

FIG. 1. *The mean ($\pm$ 1 SE) aggregate number of movements made by groups of three* **Etheostoma nigrum** *in three replicate trials following exposure to one of four treatments: (1) no solution (procedural control), (2) a solvent blank of tap water (scent-blank control), (3) skin extract solution from lab-reared conspecifics, (4) skin extract solution from wild-caught conspecifics. Bars labeled with different lowercase letters indicate significant differences (Tukey's HSD: $P < 0.05$)*

Source: J. C. Vokoun and D. B. Noltie. (2002). Evidence for the inheritance of alarm substance recognition in johnny darter (Etheostoma nigrum). *American Midland Naturalist, 147*(2), p. 402.

The Bonferroni Procedure as a Post Hoc Technique

Earlier in this chapter, we indicated that the Fisher, Duncan, Newman-Keuls, Tukey, and Scheffé tests have been designed to hold down the chances of a Type I error when comparisons are made among a set of group means. We also indicated that these test procedures are analogous in purpose to the Bonferroni technique's effort to deal with the "inflated Type I error risk problem" when comparisons are made between two groups on each of several dependent variables. The analogy is a strong one. In fact, many researchers use the Bonferroni technique in situations where others utilize the test procedures mentioned at the outset of this paragraph.

In Excerpts 12.21 and 12.22, we see two cases where the Bonferroni procedure was used in a post hoc investigation. In each case, the pairwise comparisons were made by means of regular independent sample t-tests. However, the level of significance used in these t-tests was made more demanding. In Excerpt 12.21, three post hoc pairwise comparisons were made among the comparison groups; therefore, alpha was changed from .05 to .017 for each post hoc test. In Excerpt 12.22, there were four student groups and six pairwise comparisons in the post hoc investigation; here, the adjusted alpha was set equal to .008.

EXCERPTS 12.21–12.22 • *Bonferroni Used as a Post Hoc Procedure*

Measures of strength were analyzed using a one-way analysis of variance (ANOVA), with frailty group (i.e., not frail, mildly frail, and moderately frail) as the independent factor. If group differences existed ($p < .05$), Bonferroni post hoc testing was done to identify the groups that were different.

Source: M. Brown, D. R. Sinacore, E. F. Binder, and W. M. Kohrt. (2000). Physical and performance measures for the identification of mild to moderate frailty. *The Journals of Gerontology, 55A*(6), p. M352.

- -

We ran a one-way analysis of variance (ANOVA) with the student groups [and] we performed a Bonferroni post hoc test to determine which specific groups differed.

Source: J. M. Olivero and R. Murataya. (2001). Homophobia and university law enforcement students. *Journal of Criminal Justice Education, 12*(2), p. 275.

Planned Comparisons

So far we have considered the comparison of group means using a two-step strategy that involves conducting a one-way ANOVA followed by a post hoc investigation. Researchers can, if they wish, bypass the ANOVA F-test and move directly to one or more specific comparisons of particular interest. Such comparisons among means (without reliance on a green light from a significant omnibus F-test) are called **planned comparisons**.[3] Although planned comparisons are used less frequently than post hoc comparisons, they show up in the research literature often enough to make it important for you to recognize and understand this kind of statistical test on means.

Excerpts 12.23, 12.24, and 12.25 illustrate the use of planned comparisons and are worth considering for two reasons. First, Excerpt 12.23 illustrates the point that planned comparisons are not logically tied to the omnibus F-test of the one-way ANOVA. Researchers can investigate planned comparisons directly without first conducting a one-way ANOVA, or they can make planned comparisons in conjunction with a one-way ANOVA even if the null hypothesis associated with the ANOVA F-test is not rejected.

Now consider Excerpts 12.24 and 12.25. As you can see, the planned comparisons in these studies were made via Duncan's test and Scheffé's test. Earlier in this chapter, you saw examples of the Duncan and Scheffé tests (as well as the test

EXCERPTS 12.23–12.25 • *Planned Comparisons*

The final memory test recall data were analyzed using two planned comparisons as opposed to an omnibus ANOVA.

Source: C. C. Williams and R. T. Zacks. (2001). Is retrieval-induced forgetting an inhibitory process? *American Journal of Psychology, 114*(3), p. 337.

- -

Planned comparisons were made by using Duncan's multiple range test.

Source: W. Byne, M. S. Buchsbaum, L. A. Mattiace, and E. A. Hazlett. (2002). Postmortem assessment of thalamic nuclear volumes in subjects with schizophrenia. *American Journal of Psychiatry, 159*(1), p. 62.

- -

We used a Scheffé test to examine planned comparisons between the four treatment conditions.

Source: K. D. Elsbach and G. Elofson. (2000). How the packaging of decision explanations affects perceptions of trustworthiness. *Academy of Management Journal, 43*(1), p. 85.

---

[3]The term *a priori comparison* means the same thing as *planned comparison*.

procedures developed Fisher, Newman-Keuls, and Tukey) being used in post hoc investigations. Here, we see the Duncan and Scheffé tests used to make planned comparisons. Therefore, it should be clear that you cannot look simply at the name of a test to decide whether it was used in a planned or post hoc manner; instead, you must consider whether it was applied in an effort to explain why an omnibus F turned out to be significant. Stated differently, Tukey, Newman-Keuls, and the other test procedures considered in our discussion of post hoc comparisons should not be thought of as being post hoc tests. They can be used within post hoc investigations *or* they can be used to make planned comparisons.

As is the case with most post hoc investigations, the contrasts set up in planned comparisons usually are pairwise in nature. (This was the case when the Duncan test was used in Excerpt 12.24 and when the Scheffé test was used in Excerpt 12.25.) Researchers can, however, set up one or more of their planned comparisons in a nonpairwise fashion.

Excerpt 12.26 illustrates the use of planned nonpairwise comparisons. In this large-scale longitudinal study, 666 youths were put into six subgroups based on their mothers' welfare and work patterns during the first five years of their children's lives. These six groups were called (1) working cyclers, (2) nonworking cyclers, (3) cycle to marriage, (4) short-term, (5) short-term work exit, and (6) long-term. The study's dependent variables were related to the children's cognitive and mental development.

Of the four contrasts articulated in Excerpt 12.26, the first two were nonpairwise contrasts in nature. The null hypothesis associated with the first nonpairwise contrast could be expressed in one of two ways, as H_0: $\mu_{Cyclers} = \mu_{Noncyclers}$ or as H_0: $(\mu_1 + \mu_2 + \mu_3)/3 = (\mu_4 + \mu_5 + \mu_6)/3$, where the subscript numbers stand for the subgroups. The null hypothesis for the second contrast could be expressed as H_0: $\mu_3 = (\mu_1 + \mu_2)/2$. The third and fourth contrasts, of course, were pairwise.

EXCERPT 12.26 • *Planned Pairwise and Nonpairwise Comparisons*

Planned contrasts were carried out: (1) Cyclers (Working Cyclers, Nonworking Cyclers, and Cycle to Marriage groups) versus Noncyclers (Short-Term, Short-Term Work Exit, and Long-Term groups), (2) Cycle to Marriage versus the other cyclers (Working and Nonworking Cyclers), (3) Working Cyclers versus Nonworking Cyclers, and (4) Short-Term Work Exit versus Long-Term.

Source: H. Yoshikawa and E. Seidman. (2001). Multidimensional profiles of welfare and work dynamics: Development, validation, and associations with child cognitive and mental health outcomes. *American Journal of Community Psychology, 29*(6), p. 923.

Comments

As we come to the end of this chapter on planned and post hoc comparisons, there are a few final things to consider. If you take the time to consider these end-of-chapter issues, you will be better able to decipher and critique research reports. These issues are positioned here at the end of the chapter because each of them has relevance to both post hoc and planned comparisons.

Terminology

Earlier in this chapter, you encountered six technical terms: post hoc, planned, comparison, contrast, pairwise, and nonpairwise. (A seventh term, *a priori*, appeared in a footnote.) We now need to consider two additional terms: "1 *df* F-test" and "orthogonal." After you add these two terms to your working vocabulary, you'll be able to understand just about any research report wherein the researchers discuss their post hoc and planned comparisons.

In reading discussions of post hoc and planned comparisons, you are likely to come across the term **one-degree-of-freedom F-test.** This term pops up every so often when nonpairwise contrasts are conducted via *F*-tests, and it simply refers to the fact that the first of the two *df* values of such an *F*-test will always be 1 no matter how many groups are involved in the comparison being made. In Excerpts 12.27, we see an example of such an *F*-test.

EXCERPT 12.27 • *A One-Degree-of-Freedom F-Test*

An a priori contrast indicated the predicted pattern. Participants in the no-dependency condition rated the influence of their joint performance significantly lower ($M = 5.77$) than did participants in asymmetrical and symmetrical task-dependency conditions ($Ms = 8.42$ and 8.43, respectively), $F(1, 78) = 19.59$, $MSE = 6.41$, $p < .0001$.

Source: L. E. Stevens and S. T. Fiske. (2000). Motivated impressions of a powerholder: Accuracy under task dependency and misperception under evaluation dependency. *Personality and Social Psychology Bulletin, 26*(8), p. 913.

In Excerpt 12.27, three comparison groups were involved in the contrast that was made. Whereas you might expect the first of the two *df* values next to the *F* to be 2, note that this particular *df* is equal to 1. Having this *df* value be equal to 1 makes sense once you realize that there really were only two means being compared by the *F*-test, the mean of those participants in the no-dependency condition of the study, on the one hand, and the combined mean of the participants in the two task-dependency conditions, on the other. And when two groups are compared via an *F*-test, the first of the *F*'s two *df* values (for between groups) would, of course, be a 1.

The second new term for us to consider is **orthogonal.** As illustrated in Excerpt 12.28, researchers occasionally use the term *orthogonal* when discussing the contrasts that they tested.

EXCERPT 12.28 • *Orthogonal Comparisons*

Preplanned orthogonal comparisons were used to compare treatment means at each sampling site. The comparisons for the greenhouse experiment were (i) Matua prairiegrass and Gala grazing bromegrass vs. Pennlate orchardgrass, and (ii) Matua prairiegrass vs. Gala grazing bromegrass.

Source: M. A. Sanderson, R. H. Skinner, and G. F. Elwinger. (2002). Seedling development and field performance of prairiegrass, grazing bromegrass, and orchardgrass. *Crop Science, 42*(1), p. 225.

In a researcher's planned (or post hoc) investigation, two contrasts are said to be orthogonal to one another if the information yielded by one contrast is new and different (i.e., independent) from what is revealed by the other contrast. For example, with three groups in a study (A, B, and C), a contrast comparing group A against the average of groups B and C would be orthogonal to a contrast comparing group B against group C because knowing how the first contrast turned out would give you no clue as to how the second contrast will turn out.

Assumptions

The various planned and post hoc test procedures mentioned earlier in this chapter will function as they are supposed to function only if four underlying assumptions hold true for the populations and samples involved in the study. These assumptions are the same ones that underlie a one-way ANOVA *F*-test, and they are referred to by the terms *randomness, independence, normality,* and *homogeneity of variance.* I hope you remember the main points that I made in Chapter 11 about these assumptions.

Although the various test procedures covered so far in this chapter generally are robust to the normality assumption, the same point cannot be made regarding the equal variance assumption—especially in situations where the sample sizes are dissimilar. If researchers conduct planned comparisons, they ought to talk about the issue of assumptions. If the study's sample sizes vary, a test should be applied to assess the homogeneity of variance assumption. With a post hoc investigation, the assumptions should have been discussed in conjunction with the omnibus *F*-test; those assumptions do not have to be discussed or tested a second time when the researcher moves from the one-way ANOVA to the post hoc comparisons.

If the equal variance assumption is tested and shown to be untenable (in connection with planned comparisons or with the one-way ANOVA), the researcher will likely make some form of adjustment when *a priori* or post hoc contrasts are tested. This adjustment might take the form of a data transformation, a change in the level of significance employed, or a change in the test procedure used to compare means. If the latter approach is taken, you are likely to see the Welch test applied to the data (because the Welch model does not assume equal population variances).

Many of the test procedures for making planned or post hoc comparisons were developed for the situation where the various samples are the same size. When used in situations where samples vary in size, researchers may indicate that they used a variation of one of the main techniques. For example, Kramer's extension of Duncan's multiple range test simply involves a modification of the regular Duncan test procedure to make it usable in studies where the *ns* vary. Don't let such extensions or modifications cause you to shy away from deciphering research reports in the same way you would if the regular planned or post hoc test had been used.

The Researcher's Choice of Test Procedure

As I pointed out near the outset of this chapter, the various post hoc procedures differ in terms of how liberal or conservative they are. Ideally, a researcher ought to choose among these procedures after considering the way they differ in terms of power and control of Type I errors. Realistically, however, the decision to use a particular test procedure is probably influenced most by what computer programs are available for doing the data analysis or by what procedure was emphasized in a specific textbook or by a specific instructor.

In Excerpt 12.29, we see where a team of researchers did the right thing: they explained *why* they chose the test procedure they used to make multiple comparisons among means. What they are saying here is that they wanted to avoid making a Type I error. Because of this, they chose the Tukey test because it is more conservative than most of the alternative test procedures (e.g., Duncan or Newman-Keuls).

Regardless of the reasons why the researcher chooses to use a particular test procedure, you are in full control of how *you* interpret the results presented in the research report. If a researcher uses a test procedure that is too liberal or too conservative for *your* taste, remember that you have the undisputed right to accept only a portion of the researcher's full set of conclusions. Or, you may want to reject *everything* that is "discovered" in the research study because your position on the liberal/conservative continuum is quite different from that of the researcher who performed the data analysis.

EXCERPT 12.29 • *Explaining Why a Test Procedure Was Used*

For multiple comparisons of mean yields, the Tukey Studentized Range (HSD) Test was chosen over other methods because it is less likely to detect borderline significance between factors that may, in fact, not be significant.

Source: P. C. Hamner, B. H. Bond, and J. K. Wiedenbeck. (2002). The effects of lumber length on part yields in gang-rip-first rough mills. *Forest Products Journal, 52*(5), p. 74.

Statistical Significance versus Practical Significance

We have considered the distinction between statistical significance and practical significance in earlier chapters. My simple suggestion at this point is to keep this distinction in mind when you come into contact with the results of planned and post hoc comparisons.

In Excerpt 12.30, we see a case in which an effect size was used in an effort to further explore a statistically significant pairwise comparison. In this study, the Tukey HSD procedure was used to make six pairwise comparisons among the four means. Three of these comparisons yielded a statistically significant result, and the estimated effect size index d turned out equal to .87 (i.e., large) for the comparison of the largest and smallest means. (In case you are wondering, the other two estimated effect sizes, had they been reported, would have been equal to about .72.)

The researcher who conducted the study associated with Excerpt 12.30 deserves high praise for demonstrating an awareness that statistical significance does not necessarily signify practical significance. Unfortunately, most researchers conduct their post hoc and planned comparisons without performing a power analysis, without computing a strength-of-association index, and without converting the observed difference between group means into effect size measures. When you come across studies like that associated with Excerpt 12.30, upgrade your evaluation of the researchers' work.

EXCERPT 12.30 • *Concern for Practical Significance in a Post Hoc Investigation*

The Tukey HSD post hoc test showed that the mean score for this social coping strategy was significantly lower for 9th graders ($M = 5.18$) than for 10th graders ($M = 5.78$, $p < .05$), 11th graders ($M = 5.79$, $p < .05$), and 12th graders ($M = 5.91$, $p < .05$), although there were no significant differences among grades 10–12. The effect size (d) of the largest difference (i.e., between grade 9 and grade 12) was .87.

Source: M. A. Swiatek. (2001). Social coping among gifted high school students and its relationship to self-concept. *Journal of Youth and Adolescence, 30*(1), p. 32.

Other Test Procedures

In this chapter, we have considered several test procedures that researchers use when comparing means within planned and post hoc investigations. You have seen how Fisher's LSD, Duncan's multiple range test, the Newman-Keuls test, the Tukey test, Scheffé's test, and Dunnett's test are used to hold down the chances of a Type I error when two or more contrasts were evaluated. You also saw how this same objective is sometimes achieved by using the Bonferroni technique to adjust the level of significance used in planned or post hoc tests.

Although a variety of test procedures have received our attention in this chapter, there are additional test procedures that we have not discussed. The tests mentioned in the preceding paragraph are the ones I believe you will encounter most often when you read research reports. However, you may come across one or more techniques not discussed in this text. (Within the past week, for example, I came across a research report in which the authors said that the significant finding from their one-way ANOVA was probed by the Ryan-Einot-Gabriel-Welsch multiple range test.) If this happens, I hope you will not be thrown by the utilization of a specific test procedure different from those considered here. If you understand the general purpose served by the planned and post hoc tests we *have* considered, I think you will have little difficulty understanding the purpose and results of similar test procedures that we have *not* considered.

Review Terms

A posteriori test	Multiple comparison test
A priori	Newman-Keuls
Comparison	Nonpairwise (or complex) comparison
Complex comparison	Omnibus *F*-test
Conservative	One-degree-of-freedom *F*-test
Contrast	Orthogonal
Duncan's multiple range test	Pairwise comparison
Dunnett test	Planned comparisons
Fisher's LSD	Post hoc comparisons
Follow-up test	Scheffé
Liberal	Tukey's HSD

The Best Items in the Companion Website

1. An interactive online quiz (with immediate feedback provided) covering Chapter 12.
2. Eight misconceptions about the content of Chapter 12.
3. An email message sent from the author to his students entitled "Seemingly Illogical Results."
4. Two funny jokes about statisticians.
5. One of two best passages from Chapter 12: "Your Right to Be Liberal or Conservative."

Fun Exercises inside Research Navigator

1. What is the quality of life for those who are HIV-positive?

In an effort to validate the Italian version of an HIV quality-of-life questionnaire, a team of researchers divided a sample of HIV-positive individuals into three subgroups: "asymptomatic" (no evidence of a problem), "symptomatic" (evidence of minor problems), and "AIDS" (evidence of major problems). After the people in these three categories took the quality-of-life questionnaire, a one-way ANOVA was used to compare the three group means on each of the instrument's many scales. If the omnibus *F* turned out to be significant on any of the scales, pairwise comparisons were made within the context of a post hoc investigation. Your job is to think about this study and then make a guess as to which test procedure was used to make the pairwise comparisons. After formulating your guess, locate the PDF version of this article in the Nursing, Health, and Medicine database of ContentSelect, look at Table 5 (on page 412), and then read the "statistical analysis" section on page 407.

E. Starace, L. Cafaro, N. Abrescia, A. Chirianni, C. Izzo, P. Rucci, & G. deGirolamo. Quality of life assessment in HIV-positive persons: Application and validation of the WHOQOL-HIV, Italian Version. *AIDS Care.* Located in the NURSING, HEALTH, AND MEDICINE database of ContentSelect.

2. Can you catch mistakes in a published article?

The central purpose of this study was to compare four groups of elderly individuals—English-speaking Alzheimer's patients, English-speaking normal controls, Spanish-speaking Alzheimer's patients, and Spanish-speaking normal controls—in terms of their ability to perform two tasks often included in an intelligence test. Before the researchers discussed those results, however, they presented the findings of four one-way ANOVAs that compared the groups on two demographic variables and two screening variables. Because the omnibus *F*-test from each of these one-way ANOVAs turned out significant, a post hoc investigation was conducted so as to make all possible pairwise comparisons. To see if you have an "eagle-eye" for catching mistakes, first find this research report in the Nursing, Health, and Medicine database of ContentSelect. Next, take a look at Table 1 at the bottom of page 360. Finally, see if you can find something wrong with one of the table's numbers and one of the letters that are used as superscripts to convey the results of the post hoc tests.

T. Argüelles, D. Loewenstein, & S. Argüelles. The impact of the native language of Alzheimer's disease and normal elderly individuals on their ability to recall digits. *Aging & Mental Health.* Located in the NURSING, HEALTH, AND MEDICINE database of ContentSelect.

Review Questions and Answers begin on page 516.

13

Two-Way Analyses of Variance

In Chapters 10 and 11, we saw how one-way ANOVAs can be used to compare two or more sample means in studies involving a single independent variable. In this chapter, I want to extend our discussion of analysis of variance to consider how this extremely popular statistical tool is used in studies characterized by two independent variables. It should come as no surprise that the kind of ANOVA to be considered here is referred to as a two-way ANOVA. Since you may have come across the term *multivariate analysis of variance* or the abbreviation *MANOVA,* it is important to clarify that this chapter does not deal with multivariate analyses of variance. The first letter of the acronym *MANOVA* stands for the word *multivariate,* but the letter *M* indicates that multiple dependent variables are involved in the same unitary analysis. Within the confines of this chapter, we will look at ANOVAs that involve multiple independent variables but only one dependent variable. Accordingly, the topics in this chapter (along with those of earlier chapters) fall under the general heading **univariate analyses.**

Similarities between One-Way and Two-Way ANOVAs

Like any one-way ANOVA, a two-way ANOVA focuses on group means. (As you will soon see, a minimum of four $\overline{X}$s are involved in any two-way ANOVA.) Because it is an inferential technique, any two-way ANOVA is actually concerned with the set of μ values that correspond to the sample means that are computed from the study's data. The inference from the samples to the populations will be made through the six-, seven-, or nine-step version of hypothesis testing. Statistical assumptions may need to be tested, and the research questions will dictate whether planned and/or post hoc comparisons are used in conjunction with (or in lieu of) the two-way ANOVA. Despite these similarities between one-way and two-way ANOVAs, the kind of ANOVA to which we now turn is substantially different from the kind we examined in Chapter 11.

The Structure of a Two-Way ANOVA

Before we discuss what kinds of research questions can be answered by a two-way ANOVA, it is essential that you understand how a two-way ANOVA is structured. Therefore, I now will explain (1) how factors and levels come together to form cells, (2) how randomization is used to "fill" the ANOVA's cells with the people, animals, or things from whom data are eventually collected, and (3) why this chapter deals exclusively with two-way ANOVAs having "between-subjects" factors.

Factors, Levels, and Cells

A two-way ANOVA always involves two independent variables. Each independent variable, or **factor,** is made up of, or defined by, two or more elements called **levels.** When looked at simultaneously, the levels of the first factor and the levels of the second factor create the conditions of the study to be compared. Each of these conditions is referred to as a **cell.**

To help you see how factors, levels, and cells form the basic structure of any two-way ANOVA, let's consider a recent study that involved movie performers who were recognized at the Academy Awards. In this study, the researcher took a 25-year period and found out, for each year, the then-current ages of the men and women who won the awards for best actor, best actress, best supporting actor, and best supporting actress. With winners for 25 years in each of the four award categories, there were a total of 100 pieces of data—each an award winner's age—that went into the two-way ANOVA.

The table in Excerpt 13.1 provides a kind of picture of the study we are considering, and it permits us to see the factors, levels, and cells of this particular two-way ANOVA. In this excerpt's table, the term *role* labels the two rows, while the term *sex* labels the two main columns. These are the two independent variables, or factors, involved in this study. The specific rows and columns indicate the levels that went together to make up the two factors. Thus the factor of role was made up of two levels, leading and supporting, while the sex factor was made up of two levels, male and female. If you take either row of Table 1 and combine it with either of the columns, you end up with one of the four cells associated with this particular two-way ANOVA. Each of these cells represents the "home" of one of the subgroups of 25 award recipients.

Within each cell shown in Excerpt 13.1, you will see a mean and a standard deviation. These two numerical values constitute a summary of the scores on the dependent variable—age—collected from the 25 performers who were associated with each of the four award categories. These data, of course, were very important to the two-way ANOVA that was conducted in conjunction with this study. The factors, levels, and cells provided the structure for the two-way ANOVA; without data on the dependent variable, however, there would have been no way to probe any of the research questions of interest.

EXCERPT 13.1 • *Factors, Level, and Cells*

TABLE 1 *Ages of Male and Female Winners of Oscar Awards*

| | | \multicolumn{4}{c}{SEX} | | | |
| | | \multicolumn{2}{c}{Male} | \multicolumn{2}{c}{Female} |

		Male M	Male SD	Female M	Female SD
ROLE	Leading	45.6	11.2	40.3	14.0
	Supporting	51.9	16.9	41.8	14.3

Source: M. Gilberg and T. Hines. (2000). Male entertainment award winners are older than female winners. *Psychological Reports, 86,* p. 176. [Adapted slightly for presentation here.]

As indicated earlier, all two-way ANOVAs involve two factors. Researchers will tell you what factors were involved in their studies, but they are not consistent in their descriptions. Sometimes factors are called *independent variables,* sometimes they are called *main effects,* and sometimes they are not called anything. Such variations in the way researchers label the two factors of their two-way ANOVAs are illustrated in Excerpts 13.2 through 13.4.

EXCERPTS 13.2–13.4 • *The Factors of a Two-Way ANOVA*

A two-way analysis of variance with treatment and story as independent variables showed that. . . .

Source: D. N. E. Fournier and M. F. Graves. (2002). Scaffolding adolescents' comprehension of short stories. *Journal of Adolescent and Adult Literacy, 46*(1), p. 36.

- -

Data were analyzed using two-way ANOVA with sex and habitat as main effects.

Source: A. S. Smith and E. Nol. (2000). Winter foraging behavior and prey selection of the Semipalmated Plover in coastal Venezuela. *The Wilson Bulletin, 112*(4), p. 468.

- -

A two-way ANOVA test of topic and source effects on compliance scores shows. . . .

Source: K. Marton and L. F. Stephens. (2001). The *New York Times'* conformity to AAPOR standards of disclosure for the reporting of public opinion polls. *Journalism and Mass Communication Quarterly, 78*(3), p. 495.

When describing their two-way ANOVAs, most researchers indicate how many levels were in each factor. They do this by using terms such as 2 × 2 ANOVA, 2 × 4 ANOVA, 3 × 5 ANOVA, and 2 × 3 ANOVA. When such notation is used, the first of the two numbers that precede the acronym ANOVA specifies how many levels went together to make up the first factor, while the second number indicates how many levels composed the second factor. Excerpts 13.5 and 13.6 illustrate the use of this kind of notation.

EXCERPTS 13.5–13.6 • *Delineating a Two-Way ANOVA's Dimensions*

A 2 × 2 ANOVA was employed for testing the hypotheses.

Source: S. P. Jain and D. Maheswaran. (2000). Motivated reasoning: A depth-of-processing perspective. *Journal of Consumer Research, 26*(4), p. 363.

- -

Statistical comparisons of test scores were made, based upon a 2 × 3 Analysis of Variance.

Source: D. Tiene. (2000). Sensory mode and "information load": Examining the effects of timing on multisensory processing. *International Journal of Instructional Media, 27*(2), p. 183.

The researchers who are most helpful in describing their two-way ANOVAs are the ones who indicate not only the names of the factors and the number of levels in each factor but also the names of the levels. An example of this kind of description appears in Excerpt 13.7.

Based on the information contained in Excerpt 13.7, you can and should create a picture (either on paper or in your mind) like the one presented earlier in Excerpt 13.1. Here, however, the picture would have three rows, four columns, and 12 cells. Collectively, the three rows would be labeled cognitive style, with the specific rows being field-dependent, field-neutral, and field-independent. Collectively, the four columns would be labeled type of image, with realistic color, realistic highlight color, contrived highlight color, and black-and-white used to name the specific columns.[1]

---

[1]The picture of Excerpt 13.7 could be set up with rows corresponding to type of image and columns corresponding to cognitive style. If we set it up that way, there would be four rows and three columns. With two-way ANOVAs, it makes no difference whether a particular factor is used to define the picture's rows or its columns.

EXCERPT 13.7 • *Naming Factors and Levels*

Based on the type of image (realistic color, realistic highlight color, contrived highlight color, black-and-white) and student cognitive style (field-dependent, field-neutral, field-independent), a 3×4 factorial analysis of variance (ANOVA) was employed to interpret the data.

Source: G. M. Worley and D. M. Moore. (2001). The effects of highlight color on immediate recall on subjects of different cognitive styles. *International Journal of Instructional Media, 28*(2), p. 172.

Shortly, we will consider the null hypotheses that are typically tested when researchers use a two-way ANOVA, and we also will look at the different reporting schemes used by researchers to report the results of such tests. I cannot overemphasize how important it is to understand the concepts of factor, level, and cell before considering what a two-way ANOVA tries to accomplish. Stated differently, if you can't create a picture that shows the structure of a researcher's two-way ANOVA, there is no way you will be able to understand the results or evaluate whether the researchers' claimed discoveries are supported by the empirical data.

Active versus Assigned Factors and the Formation of Comparison Groups

All two-way ANOVAs are the same in that the levels of the two factors jointly define the cells. However, there are different ways to "fill" each cell with the things (people, animals, or objects) from which measurements will be taken. In any given study, one of three possible procedures for forming the comparison groups will be used depending on the nature of the two factors. Since any factor can be classified as being "assigned" or "active" in nature, a two-way ANOVA could be set up to involve two assigned factors, two active factors, or one factor of each type.

An **assigned factor** deals with a characteristic of the things being studied that they "bring with them" to the investigation. In situations where the study focuses on people, for example, such a factor might be gender, handedness, birth order, intellectual capability, color preference, GPA, or personality type. If the study focused on dogs, an assigned factor might be breed, size, or age. The defining element of an assigned factor is that a person's (or animal's) status of this kind of independent variable is determined by the nature of that person (or animal) on entry into the study.

The second kind of factor is called an **active factor.** Here, a participant's status on the factor is determined within the investigation. This is because active factors deal with conditions of the study that are under the control of the researcher.

Simply put, this means that the researcher can decide, for any participant, which level of the factor that participant will experience. Examples of active factors include type of diet, time allowed to practice a task, gender of the counselor to whom the participant is assigned, and kind of reward received following the occurrence of desirable behavior. The hallmark of these and all other active factors is the researcher's ability to decide which level of the factor any participant will experience during the investigation.

If a two-way ANOVA involves two assigned factors, the researcher simply will put the available participants into the various cells of the ANOVA design based on the characteristics of the participants. This situation is exemplified by Excerpt 13.1. In that study dealing with movie stars who won Oscar awards, the two factors were role and sex. Each of the 100 movie stars was put into one of the four cells entirely based on their sex and winning an award for being in a leading or supporting role.

If the factors of a two-way ANOVA are both active, the researcher will form the comparison groups by randomly assigning participants to the various cells of the design. This is what happened in the study that supplied Excerpt 13.6. In that investigation, 236 college students were first exposed to a description of a fictitious island and then they took a test covering the details of that description. One of the study's two active factors was sensory mode, and its two levels were auditory and visual. Some students were given a printed description of the island, whereas others heard the description read to them. The second active factor was called map presentation, and it had three levels: simultaneous, sequential, and none. Some students received a map of the island to look at while they read or heard the verbal description, others got a chance to look at the map after being exposed to the verbal description, and still others had no chance to look at the map. With two levels of sensory mode and three levels of map presentation, there were six cells in the study. Each student was randomly assigned to one of these conditions of the study. Thus, it was the researcher who decided which level of each factor would be given to any participant. In that sense, the researcher had control over each of the study's independent variables.

If a two-way ANOVA involves one active factor and one assigned factor, the researcher will form the comparison groups by taking the participants who share a particular level on the assigned factor and randomly assigning them to the various levels of the active factor. This procedure for forming comparison groups was used in the study from which Excerpt 13.7 was drawn. In that study, each of the 276 college students was first classified (based on paper-and-pencil test) into one of three categories: field-dependent, field-neutral, and field-independent. These were the levels of the assigned factor, cognitive style. Then, the students associated with each of these cognitive style categories were randomly assigned to receive one of four versions of an instructional booklet that contained text and images dealing with the anatomy of the human heart. These booklets were identical except for the images. In one version of the booklet, no images had color; each of the other three versions had realistic color, realistic highlight color, or contrived highlight color. Each of these booklets corresponded to a level of the study's second factor, type of image. The thing to notice about this study is that the college students were randomly assigned to the levels of the type of image factor from *within* their respective levels of the cognitive style factor.

Between-Subjects and Within-Subjects Factors

Research
Navigator.c⊛m
Between-subjects
factor
Within-subjects
factor

Each of the factors in a two-way ANOVA can be described as being either between subjects or within subjects in nature. The distinction between these two kinds of factors revolves around the simple question, "Are the study's participants measured under (i.e., have exposure to) just one level of the factor, or are they measured repeatedly across (and thus exposed to) all levels of the factor?" If the former situation exists, the factor is a between-subjects factor; otherwise, it is a within-subjects factor.

To help clarify the difference between these two kinds of factors, let's consider a simple (yet hypothetical) study. Imagine that a researcher wants to see if a golfer's ability to putt accurately is influenced by whether or not the flag is standing in the hole and whether the golf ball's color is white or orange. Further imagine that 20 golfers agree to participate in our study, that all putts are made on the same green from the same starting spot 25 feet from the hole, and that putting accuracy (our dependent variable) is measured by how many inches each putted ball ends up away from the hole.

In our putting investigation, we might design the study so both of our independent variables (flag status and ball color) are between-subjects factors. If we did that, we'd create four comparison groups (each with $n = 5$) and have the golfers in each group putt under just one of the conditions of our study (e.g., putting an orange ball toward a flagless hole). Or, we might want to have both factors be within-subjects in nature. If that were our choice, we would have all 20 golfers putt under all four conditions of the study. There's also a third possibility. We could have one between-subjects factor and one within-subjects factor. For example, we could have all golfers putt both white and orange balls, with half of the golfers putting toward the hole with the flag in and the other half putting toward the hole with the flag out.

In this chapter, we will consider two-way ANOVAs involving two between-subjects factors. If a researcher indicates that he/she used a two-way ANOVA (without any specification as to the type of factors involved), you should presume that it's the kind of two-way ANOVA being discussed in this chapter. You can feel relatively confident doing this because most researchers use the generic phrase "two-way ANOVA" when both factors are of the between-subjects variety.[2] Occasionally, as illustrated in Excerpt 13.8, you'll see a clear indication that two between-subjects factors were involved in the ANOVA being discussed.

---

[2]If one or both of the factors are of the within-subjects variety, researchers will normally draw this to your attention by labeling the factor(s) in that way or by saying that they used a repeated-measures ANOVA, a mixed ANOVA, or a split-plot ANOVA. We will consider such ANOVAs in Chapter 14.

EXCERPT 13.8 • *Between-Subjects Factors*

This study used a 2 × 3 between-subjects factorial design with motivation level (low vs. high) and type of sensory evaluation instructions (evaluative criteria in conjunction with a rating scheme provided during the trial experience, evaluative criteria in conjunction with a rating scheme provided immediately after the trial experience, and no evaluative criteria given) as the between-subjects factors.

Source: S. Shapiro and M. T. Spence. (2002). Factors affecting encoding, retrieval, and alignment of sensory attributes in a memory-based brand choice task. *International Journal of Consumer Research, 28*(4), pp. 611–612.

Samples and Populations

The samples associated with any two-way ANOVA are always easy to identify. There will be as many samples as there are cells, with the subjects who share a common cell creating each of the samples. Thus there will be four distinct samples in any 2 × 2 ANOVA, six distinct samples in any 2 × 3 ANOVA, twelve distinct samples in any 3 × 4 ANOVA, and so on.

As is always the case in inferential statistics, a distinct population is associated with each sample in the study. Hence, the number of cells designates not only the number of samples (i.e., comparison groups) in the study, but also the number of populations involved in the investigation. While it is easy to tell how many populations are involved in any two-way ANOVA, care must be exercised in thinking about the nature of these populations, especially when one or both factors are active.

Simply put, each population in a two-way ANOVA should be conceptualized as being made up of a large group of people, animals, objects, or ideas that are similar to those in the corresponding sample represented by one of the cells. Suppose, for example, that the dart-throwing ability of college students is measured via a two-way ANOVA in which the factors are sex (male and female) and handedness (right and left). One of the four populations in this study would be right-handed male college students. Each of the other three populations in this study would be defined in a similar fashion by the combination of one level from each factor. If the four samples in this study were extracted from a larger group of potential participants, then each population would be considered tangible in nature. If, on the other hand, all available dart-throwers were used, then the populations would be abstract in nature.[3]

---

[3]I discussed the difference between tangible and abstract populations in Chapter 5.

If a two-way ANOVA involves one or two active factors, the populations associated with the study will definitely be abstract in nature. To understand why this is true, consider once again the study from which Excerpt 13.6 was taken. As discussed earlier, that study involved college students who received a description of a fictitious island. The study's two factors were sensory mode and map presentation. (The description was presented either in writing or read aloud to the participants; one-third had a map to look at while they took in the description, one-third looked at the map later, and one-third never saw the map.) The dependent variable was knowledge about the island, as measured by a 15-item test.

In this study, the populations were abstract because they were characterized by college students like those who were in this study following application of the two active factors. There undoubtedly were (and are) lots of college students similar to the ones who served as participants in this investigation. However, there probably was (or is) no one outside the study who was taught about the fictitious island under any of the six conditions of this study. Even if the college students in this study had been drawn from a larger, tangible population of potential participants, the six groups of actual participants became fully unique once they experienced the conditions of this experimental investigation.

Three Research Questions

To gain an understanding of the three research questions that are focused on by a two-way ANOVA, consider once again the study discussed near the beginning of this chapter that focused on the ages of male and female movie stars who had won an Oscar in a leading or supporting role. As you will recall, the two factors in that study's two-way ANOVA were sex and role, with 25 movie stars in each of four cells. So as to facilitate our current discussion, I have reproduced here the original four cells means of Excerpt 13.1, plus I have added four additional numbers that we'll need to consider.

		Male	*Female*	
			Sex	
Role	*Leading*	45.6	40.3	*42.95*
	Supporting	51.9	41.8	*46.85*
		48.75	*41.05*	

When the researchers applied a two-way ANOVA to the data provided by the 100 movie stars, they obtained answers to three research questions. Although these three research questions were tied to the specific independent and dependent variables involved in this study, the nature of their questions was identical to the nature of the three research questions that are posed and answered in any two-way ANOVA. These three questions, in their generic form, can be stated as follows: (1) Is there a statistically significant main effect for the first factor? (2) Is there a statistically significant main effect for the second factor? (3) Is there a statistically significant interaction between the two factors?

The first research question in the study dealing with the ages of Oscar-winning movie stars asked whether there was a statistically significant main effect for role. To get a feel for what this first research question was asking, you must focus your attention on the main effect means for the role factor. These means, located on the right side of the box containing the four cells, turned out equal to 42.95 and 46.85. The first of these means is simply the overall mean for the 50 movie performers who won an award in a leading role. (Since there were 25 males and 25 females in the top two cells, it is equal to the arithmetic average of 45.6 and 40.3.) The second main effect mean for the role factor is the overall mean for the 50 performers who won an award in a supporting role. Those 50 performers are located, so to speak, within the two cells on the bottom row of the box.

In any two-way ANOVA, the first research question asks whether there is a statistically significant **main effect** for the factor that corresponds to the rows of the two-dimensional picture of the study. Stated differently, the first research question is asking whether the main effect means associated with the first factor are further apart from each other than would be expected by chance. There will be as many such means as there are levels of the first factor. In the study we are considering, there were two levels (leading and supporting) of the first factor (role), with the first research question asking whether the difference between 42.95 and 46.85 was larger than could be accounted for by chance. In other words, the first research question asked, "Is there a statistically significant difference between the mean age of the 50 movie stars who won an Oscar in a leading role and the mean age of the 50 winners who were in supporting roles?"

The second research question in any two-way ANOVA asks whether there is a significant main effect for the factor that corresponds to the columns of the two-dimensional picture of the study. The answer to this question will be yes if the main effect means for the second factor turn out to be further apart from each other than would be expected by chance. In the study we are considering there are two such main effect means, one for males and one for females. These means turned out equal to 48.75 and 41.05, respectively. Simply put, the second research question in this study asked, "Is there a statistically significant difference between the mean age of the 50 Oscar-winning male movie stars and the mean age of their female counterparts?"

The third research question in any two-way ANOVA asks whether there is a statistically significant **interaction** between the two factors involved in the study. As you will see, the interaction deals with cell means, not main effect means. Therefore, there will always be at least four means involved in the interaction of any 2×2 ANOVA, six means involved in any 2×3 ANOVA, and so on.

Research Navigator.com
Main effect

Research Navigator.com
Interaction

Interaction exists to the extent that the difference between the levels of the first factor changes when we move from level to level of the second factor. To illustrate, consider again the study dealing with the ages of Oscar-winning movie stars. The difference between the mean age of male and female performers who won an award in a leading role was 5.3, with the mean in the upper left-hand cell (for males) being larger than the mean in the upper right-hand cell (for females). If this difference of 5.3 were to show up again when we examine the bottom row of cell means (with the same ordering of those means in terms of their magnitude), there would be absolutely no interaction. If this difference is either smaller or larger than 5.3 (or if it is 5.3 with a reverse ordering of the means), then interaction is present in the data.

When we look at the bottom row of cell means, we can see that the difference between them does not mirror what we saw on the top row of cell means. The difference on the bottom row is 10.1, not 5.3. Hence, there is some interaction between the role and sex factors. But is the amount of interaction contained in the four cell means more than what one would expect by chance? If so, then it can be said that a statistically significant interaction exists between the study's two factors.

It should be noted that the interaction of a two-way ANOVA can be thought of as dealing with the difference between the levels of the row's factor as one moves from one level to another level of the column's factor, or it can be thought of as dealing with the difference between the levels of the column's factor as one moves from one level to another level of the row's factor. For example, in the study of movie stars, the difference between the cell means in the left-hand column is 6.3 (with the lower mean being larger) whereas the difference between the means in the right-hand column is 1.5 (again with the lower mean being larger). Although these two differences (6.3 and 1.5) are not the same as the differences discussed in the preceding paragraph (5.3 and 10.1), note that in both cases the difference between the differences is exactly the same: 4.8. My point here is simply that there is only one interaction in a two-way ANOVA; the order in which the factors are named (or used to compare cell means) makes no difference whatsoever.

The Three Null Hypotheses (and Three Alternative Hypotheses)

There are three null hypotheses examined within a two-way ANOVA. One of these null hypotheses is concerned with the main effect of the row's factor, the second is concerned with the main effect of the column's factor, and the third is concerned with the interaction between the two factors. Rarely are these null hypotheses referred to in a research report. In Excerpt 13.9, however, we see a case where the researcher enumerated the main effect and interaction null hypotheses associated with his two-way ANOVA.

To explain how each of these null hypotheses should be conceptualized, I want to reiterate that the group of participants that supplies data for any cell of the two-way ANOVA is only a sample. As was pointed out earlier in this chapter, a population

EXCERPT 13.9 • *The Three Null Hypotheses of a Standard Two-Way ANOVA*

All main and interaction effects were assessed. The null hypotheses for main effects were as follows: (a) there will be no difference in applicant reactions to advertisements varied according to instructional program content (academic transfer, career education, compensatory education); and (b) there will be no difference in applicant reactions to advertisements varied according to job attribute content (intrinsic, extrinsic, work context). The null hypothesis for interaction effects was as follows: There will be no influence on applicant reactions to advertisements associated with the joint effects of instructional programs and job attributes.

Source: P. A. Winter. (1996). The application of marketing theory to community college faculty recruitment: An empirical test. *Community College Review, 24*(3), p. 6.

is connected to each cell's sample. Sometimes each of these populations will be concrete in nature, with participants randomly selected from a finite pool of potential participants. In many studies, each population will be abstract in nature, with the nature of the population tailored to fit the nature of the group within each cell and the condition under which data are collected from the participants in that group.

In the 2×2 ANOVA that dealt with the ages of Oscar winning movie stars, four populations were involved. It is best, I think, to view each of these populations as being abstract (rather than tangible) in nature. These populations could be considered to include all movie actors and actresses. Or, maybe they should include just those performers who have been nominated for an Academy Award for a leading or supporting role. Or, perhaps the populations could be construed as containing past and future recipients of these prestigious movie awards. We have flexibility in how we might want to think of the populations; however, we *must* consider this study to have had populations connected to it, for inferential procedures were used to analyze the data. If the 100 performers who supplied the data had been the only ones the researchers cared about, a two-way ANOVA would *not* have been used to analyze the data.

There were four populations. One of them should be conceptualized as being made up of male performers who are similar to the ones in this study who won an Oscar for their role as a leading actor. A second population should be conceptualized as being made up of female performers who are similar to the ones in this study who won an Oscar for their role as a leading actress. The third and fourth populations are like the first two except they should be conceptualized as being made up of supporting actors and actresses like those used in this study.

The first null hypothesis in any two-way ANOVA deals with the main effect means associated with the rows' factor of the study. This null hypothesis asserts that the population counterparts of these sample-based main effect means are equal to each other. Stated in symbols for the general case, this null hypothesis is as follows: H_0: $\mu_{row1} = \mu_{row2} = \ldots = \mu_{bottom\ row}$. For the study dealing with movie stars, this null hypothesis took the form H_0: $\mu_{leading} = \mu_{supporting}$.

The second null hypothesis in any two-way ANOVA deals with the main effect means associated with the columns factor. This null hypothesis asserts that the population counterparts of these sample-based main effect means are equal to each other. For the general case, the null hypothesis says H_0: $\mu_{column1} = \mu_{column2} = \ldots = \mu_{last\ column}$. For the study dealing with Oscar winners, this null hypothesis took the form H_0: $\mu_{males} = \mu_{females}$.

Before we turn our attention to the third null hypothesis of a two-way ANOVA, I need to clarify the meaning of the μs that appear in the null hypothesis for the main effects. Each of these μs, like the data-based sample mean to which it is tied, actually represents the average of cell means. For example, $\mu_{row\ 1}$ is the average of the μs associated with the cells on row 1, while $\mu_{column\ 1}$ is the average of the μs associated with the cells in column 1. Each of the other main effect μs similarly represents the average of the μs associated with the cells that lie in a common row or in a common column. This point about the main effect μs is important to note because (1) populations are always tied conceptually to samples and (2) the samples in a two-way ANOVA are located *in* the cells. Unless you realize that the main effect μs are conceptually derived from averaging cell μs, you might find yourself being misled into thinking that the number of populations associated with any two-way ANOVA can be determined by adding the number of main effect means to the number of cells. Hopefully, my earlier and current comments will help you to see that a two-way ANOVA has only as many populations as there are cells.

The third null hypothesis in a two-way ANOVA specifies that there is no interaction between the two factors. This null hypothesis deals with the cell means, not the main effect means. This null hypothesis asserts that whatever differences exist among the population means associated with the cells in any given column of the two-way layout are equal to the differences among the population means associated with the cells in each of the other columns. Stated differently, this null hypothesis says that the relationship among the population means associated with the full set of cells is such that a single pattern of differences accurately describes what exists within any column.[4]

To express the interaction null hypothesis using symbols, we must first agree to let j and j' stand for any two different rows in the two-way layout, and to let k

---

[4]The interaction null hypothesis can be stated with references to parameter differences among the cell means within the various rows (rather than within the various columns). Thus the interaction null hypothesis asserts that whatever differences exist among the population means associated with the cells in any given row of the two-way layout are equal to the differences among the population means associated with the cells in each of the other rows.

and k' stand for any two different columns. Thus the intersection of row j and column k designates cell jk, with the population mean associated with this cell being referred to as μ_{jk}. The population mean associated with a different cell in the same column would be symbolized as $\mu_{j'k}$. The population means associated with two cells on these same rows, j and j', but in a different column, k', could be symbolized as $\mu_{jk'}$ and $\mu_{j'k'}$, respectively. Using this notational scheme, we can express the interaction null hypothesis of any two-way ANOVA as follows:

$$H_0: \mu_{jk} - \mu_{j'k} = \mu_{jk'} - \mu_{j'k'}, \text{ for all rows and columns}$$
(i.e., for all combinations of both j and j', k and k')

To help you understand the meaning of the interaction null hypothesis, I have constructed sets of hypothetical population means corresponding to a 2 × 2 ANOVA, a 2 × 3 ANOVA, and a 2 × 4 ANOVA. In each of the hypothetical ANOVAs, the interaction null hypothesis is completely true.

$\mu = 20$	$\mu = 40$
$\mu = 10$	$\mu = 30$

$\mu = 10$	$\mu = 30$	$\mu = 29$
$\mu = 5$	$\mu = 25$	$\mu = 24$

$\mu = 2$	$\mu = 12$	$\mu = 6$	$\mu = 24$
$\mu = 4$	$\mu = 14$	$\mu = 8$	$\mu = 26$

Before turning our attention to the alternative hypotheses associated with a two-way ANOVA, it is important to note that each H_0 we have considered is independent from the other two. In other words, any combination of the three null hypotheses can be true (or false). To illustrate, I have constructed three sets of hypothetical population means for a 2 × 2 layout. Moving from left to right, we see a case in which only the row means differ, a case in which only the interaction null hypothesis is false, and a case in which the null hypotheses for both the row's main effect and the interaction are false:

$\mu = 10$	$\mu = 10$
$\mu = 5$	$\mu = 5$

$\mu = 20$	$\mu = 10$
$\mu = 10$	$\mu = 20$

$\mu = 10$	$\mu = 30$
$\mu = 20$	$\mu = 0$

Because the three null hypotheses are independent of each other, a conclusion drawn (from sample data) concerning one of the null hypotheses is specific to that particular H_0. The same data set can be used to evaluate all three null statements, but the data must be looked at from different angles in order to address all three null hypotheses. This is accomplished by computing a separate F-test to see if each H_0 is likely to be false.

If the researcher who conducts the two-way ANOVA evaluates each H_0 by means of hypothesis testing there will usually be three alternative hypotheses. Each H_0 is set up in a nondirectional fashion, and they assert that:

1. The row μs are *not* all equal to each other;
2. The column μs are *not* all equal to each other;
3. The pattern of differences among the cell μs in the first column (or the first row) *fails* to describe accurately the pattern of differences among the cell μs in at least one other column (row).

Presentation of Results

The results of a two-way ANOVA can be communicated through a table or within the text of the research report. We begin our consideration of how researchers present the findings gleaned from their two-way ANOVAs by looking at the results of the study dealing with the ages of Oscar-winning movie stars. We then consider how the results of several other two-way ANOVAs were presented. Near the end of this section, we will look at the various ways researchers organize their findings when two or more two-way ANOVAs have been conducted within the same study.

Results of the Two-Way ANOVA Study on Movie Stars

In the research report of the study dealing with the ages of movie stars, the findings were not presented in a two-way ANOVA summary table. If such a table had been prepared, it probably would have looked like Table 13.1. Notice that this summary table is similar to the summary table for a one-way ANOVA in terms of (1) the number and names of columns included in the table, (2) each row's *MS* being computed by dividing the row's *df* into its *SS*, (3) the total *df* being equal to one less than the number of participants used in the investigation, and (4) calculated values being presented in the *F* column. Despite these similarities, one-way and two-way ANOVA summary tables differ in that the latter contains five rows (rather than three) and three *F*-ratios (rather than one). Note that in the two-way summary table, the *MS* for the next-to-bottom row (which is usually labeled *error* or *within groups*)

TABLE 13.1 *ANOVA Summary Table for Influence of Role and Sex on Age*

Source	df	SS	MS	F	P
Role	1	380.25	380.25	1.87	ns
Sex	1	1,482.25	1,482.25	7.31	.008
Interaction	1	144.00	144.00	.71	ns
Within Groups	96	19,476.96	202.89		
Total	99	21,483.46			

was used as the denominator in computing each of the three F-ratios: $380.25/202.89$ $= 1.87$, $1,482.25/202.89 = 7.31$, and $144/202.89 = .71$.

There are three values in the F column of a two-way ANOVA summary table because there are three null hypotheses associated with this kind of ANOVA. Each of the three Fs addresses a different null hypothesis. The first two Fs are concerned with the study's main effects; in other words, the first two Fs deal with the two sets of main effect means. The third F deals with the interaction between the two factors, with the focus of this F being on cell means.

In the ANOVA summary table, look at the results for the two main effects. The F for role was smaller than the F for sex (with the F for role being *ns* whereas the F for sex was $p = .008$). These dissimilar results came about because the two main effect means for role (42.95 and 46.85) were closer together than were the two main effect means for sex (41.05 and 48.75). There was a 3.9 difference between the first pair of means but a 7.7 difference between the second pair. Statistically speaking, the observed difference of 3.9 was not large enough to cast doubt on the role null hypothesis (H_0: $\mu_{leading} = \mu_{supporting}$) whereas the observed difference of 7.7 was so large that it was highly unlikely ($p = .008$) that the sample data came from populations in which the sex null hypothesis (H_0: $\mu_{males} = \mu_{females}$) was true.

In the ANOVA summary table, you can see that the interaction F turned out to be small and not significant. If you examine the cell means associated with the study we are considering, you will notice that there was some interaction in the sample data. The difference between the mean ages for the male and female leading performers ($45.6 - 40.3 = 5.3$) was not the same as the difference between the mean ages for the male and female supporting performers ($51.9 - 41.8 = 10.1$). However, the amount of this interaction was "within the limits of chance sampling," meaning that this degree of observed interaction in the sample data would not be unexpected if the four samples had come from populations in which there was no interaction. Accordingly, the interaction null hypothesis was not rejected, as indicated by the letters *ns* that appear next to the F of .71.

Results from Various Two-Way ANOVA Studies

In Excerpt 13.10, we see the summary table from a study in which a 2×2 ANOVA was used. It is worth the effort to compare this table to Table 13.1 so as to identify differences in how the same kind of information can be presented, even for cases that are identical in terms of the number of levels and cells involved.

First, notice that the summary table in Excerpt 13.10 does not contain a column for sum of squares or a row for total. You are not at a disadvantage by not having these parts of the table, for you could (if you so desired) compute all five missing SS values and the df for total. The df_{Total} is the most important of these items, for it allows you to determine how many individuals were involved in the study. (Don't make the mistake of adding 1 to 305 and thinking that data were collected from 306 people!) The second thing to notice is that two of the row names

EXCERPT 13.10 • *Two-Way ANOVA Summary Table*

To test the major hypothesis, that there is a significant interaction between years and gender, we conducted a 2 × 2 Independent Groups analysis of variance (ANOVA). As seen in Table 3, the predicted interaction was highly significant, $F(1, 305) = 18.55$, $p < .001$.

TABLE 3 *Gender × Year ANOVA on BAS Scores*

Source	df	MS	F	p
Gender	1	2,109.70	0.69	.406
Year	1	55,320.58	18.10	< .001
Gender × Year	1	56,706.38	18.55	< .001
Error	305	3,056.24		

Note. ANOVA = analysis of variance. BAS = Body Attitude Scale.

Source: E. L. Sondhaus, R. M. Kurtz, and M. J. Strube. (2002). Body attitude, gender, and self-concept: A 30-year perspective. *Journal of Psychology, 135*(4), p. 419.

differ across the two tables we are considering. (In Table 13.1, the third row was termed *interaction* whereas that same row in Excerpt 13.10 is labeled with the *name* of the interaction: gender × year. Also, the fourth row was called *within groups* in Table 13.1 but *error* in Excerpt 13.10.) Finally, note that a number for *p* is presented on the first row in Excerpt 13.10 whereas the notation *ns* was used in Table 13.1 to designate a nonsignificant result.

Despite the differences between Table 13.1 and Excerpt 13.10, these two ANOVA summary tables are similar in several respects. In each case, the title of the table reveals what the dependent variable was. In each case, the names of the first two rows reveal the names of the two factors. In each case, the *df* values for the main effect rows of the table allow us to know that there were two levels in each factor. In each case, the three *F*-values were computed by dividing the *MS* values on the first three rows by the *MS* value located on the fourth row (i.e., within groups or error). And in each case, three calculated *F*-values are presented, one of which addresses each of the three null hypotheses associated with the two-way ANOVA.

Not all two-way ANOVAs, of course, are of the 2 × 2 variety. In Excerpt 13.11, we see the summary table for a 2 × 4 ANOVA. Although there were two levels of the gender factor and four levels of the education factor, this two-way ANOVA still produced three *F*-values, one for each main effect and one for the interaction between the two factors. Note that the row for total was positioned as

EXCERPT 13.11 • *Summary Table for a 2 × 4 ANOVA*

TABLE 2   *Analysis of Variance for Physical Characteristcs*

Source	df	Sums of Square	Mean Square	F	Pr > F
Total	157	139.7907			
Gender	1	7.1453	7.1453	8.26	0.0046
Education	3	2.7646	0.9215	1.06	0.3659
Gender by Education	3	5.0229	1.6743	1.93	0.1264
Error	150	129.8003	0.8653		

Source: T. Parmer. (1998). Characteristics of preferred partners: variations between African American men and women. *Journal of College Student Development, 39*(5), p. 465.

the top row in this table, not the bottom row. This was done to show that a two-way ANOVA, on a conceptual level, starts with the total *df* and *SS* values and then partitions each of them into four components that correspond with the two main effects, the interaction, and the error.

In reporting the outcome of their two-way ANOVAs, researchers often talk about the results within the text of the research report without including a summary table. In Excerpt 13.12, we see a case in which three sentences were used to summarize and interpret the results of a 2 × 2 ANOVA. This ANOVA came from a study involving college students, all of whom had high levels of communication apprehension (CA). The study's two factors were treatment (exposure or nonexposure to systematic desensitization) and pretesting (taking or not taking a pretest). The data from a posttest measure of CA, given to the participants in all four groups, served as the dependent variable.

Based on the information in Excerpt 13.12, you should be able to figure out what the three null hypotheses were, what decision was reached regarding each H_0, and how many college students supplied the researcher with the posttest data analyzed by the two-way ANOVA.[5]

When there are two or more dependent variables in a study along with two independent variables, researchers often choose a strategy for data analysis that involves conducting a separate two-way ANOVA on the data from each dependent variable. Sometimes, separate summary tables like the ones you saw in Table 13.1 or Excerpts 13.10 or 13.11 will appear in the same table. When you come across

---

[5]If you end up thinking that 77 students were involved in this study, try again.

EXCERPT 13.12 • *Results of a Two-Way ANOVA Presented in the Text*

The ANOVA applied to the posttest data for state CA indicated that neither the main effect for pretesting or the interaction effect was significant [$F(1,76) = .89$, *ns*; $F(1,76) = .62$, *ns*]. However, the ANOVA applied to the state CA for the effect of treatment proved to be significant [$F(1,76) = 18.11$, $p < .001$, $\omega^2 = .24$.] An inspection of the means for those receiving treatment compared to those not receiving treatment ($M = 13.6$, $SD = 4.6$; and $M = 17.7$, $SD = 3.4$, respectively) indicates that those exposed to systematic desensitization reported lower state CA than those not exposed to systematic desensitization.

Source: J. Ayres, T. Hopf, and A. Will. (2000). Are reductions in CA an experimental artifact? A Solomon four-group answer. *Communication Quarterly, 48*(1), p. 23.

such a table, you will have no difficulty interpreting the results. Sometimes, however, the results of separate two-way ANOVAs are combined into a single table that does not look at all like the "standard" two-way ANOVA summary table. Consider, for example, Excerpt 13.13.

EXCERPT 13.13 • *Results of Five Two-Way ANOVAs in One Table*

TABLE 3   F-Statistics for Main Dependent Variables

Dependent Variable	Advertising Main Effect (df = 1,710)	Peer Main Effect (df = 3,710)	Advertising by Peer Interaction Effect (df = 3,710)
Stereotypic beliefs about smokers	3.77**	1.29	2.59*
Belief that smokers are rebellious	.25	.42	.70
Belief that smokers are contented	1.25	.02	.88
Intentions to smoke	.92	.28	3.43*
Valenced thoughts about peers	2.74*	25.02**	2.60*

*$p < .05$.

**$p < .01$.

Source: C. Pechmann and S. J. Knight. (2002). An experimental investigation of the joint effects of advertising and peers on adolescents' beliefs and intentions about cigarette consumption. *Journal of Consumer Research, 29*(1), p. 13.

Excerpt 13.13 contains the results of five separate two-way ANOVAs, each of which used data on a different dependent variable. On each row of the table, the researcher presents just the *F*-values for the two main effects and the interaction. In the headings for the columns containing these *F*-values, we see the names of the study's two factors as well as the degrees of freedom associated with the *F*-tests. We can use those *df* numbers to figure out that each row of information came from a 2 × 4 ANOVA and that this study's data were gathered from 718 individuals.

If multiple two-way ANOVAs are conducted, researchers often summarize the results within the text of their research reports without any tables. Excerpt 13.14 illustrates this popular reporting technique. Notice that the same two factors were involved in all 10 of the two-way ANOVAs discussed in Excerpt 13.14. The dependent variable, however, was different in each separate analysis.

Follow-Up Tests

If none of the two-way ANOVA *F*s turns out to be significant, no follow-up test will be conducted. On the other hand, if at least one of the main effects is found to be significant, or if the interaction null hypothesis is rejected, you may find that a follow-up investigation is undertaken in an effort to probe the data. We will consider first the follow-up tests used in conjunction with significant main effect *F*-ratios. Then, we will examine the post hoc strategy typically employed when the interaction *F* turns out to be significant.

EXCERPT 13.14 • *Results of 10 Two-Way ANOVA Summarized in the Text*

Two-way ANOVA results [on the nine FSS subscales and global FSS scores] indicated nonsignificant gender by sport interactions and nonsignificant main effects for the Flow State Scales of challenge-skill balance, clear goals, unambiguous feedback, paradox of control, loss of self-confidence, transformation of time, autotelic experience, and total FSS score. For action-awareness, the interaction was nonsignificant ($p = .71$) as was the main effect for gender ($p = .12$). However, there was a significant main effect for spot setting $F(1,38) = 9.62$, $p = .004$, indicating that team-sport athletes have a significantly higher level of action-awareness merging than individual sport athletes during flow. For the concentration subscale, there were trends toward significance on the interaction ($p = .051$), the gender main effect ($p = .054$) and the sport main effect ($p = .053$).

Source: W. D. Russell. (2001). An examination of flow state occurrence in college athletes. *Journal of Sport Behavior, 24*(1), p. 113.

Follow-Up Tests to Probe Significant Main Effects

If the *F*-test for one of the factors turns out to be significant and if there are only two levels associated with that factor, no post hoc test will be applied. In this situation, the outcome of the *F*-test indicates that a significant difference exists between that factor's two main effect means, and the only thing the researcher needs to do to determine where the significant difference lies is to look at the two row (or two column) means. Whichever of the two means is larger is significantly larger than the other mean. If you take another look at Excerpt 13.12, you will see an example where (1) one main effect (but not the interaction) of a 2 $\times$ 2 ANOVA turned out significant, and (2) the researcher interpreted these results directly without using any follow-up tests.

If the two-way ANOVA yields a significant *F* for one of the two factors, and if that factor involves three or more levels, the researcher is likely to conduct a **post hoc** investigation in order to compare the main effect means associated with the significant *F*. This is done for the same reasons that a post hoc investigation is typically conducted in conjunction with a one-way ANOVA that yields a significant result when three or more means are compared. In both cases, the omnibus *F* that turns out to be significant needs to be "probed" so as to allow the researcher (and others) to gain insight into the pattern of population means.

Excerpt 13.15 illustrates how a post hoc investigation can help to clarify the meaning of a significant main effect in a two-way ANOVA. Actually, two two-way ANOVAs are being summarized in this excerpt, each having a different dependent

EXCERPT 13.15 • *A Post Hoc Investigation Following a Significant Main Effect*

The association between mother's attachment style and reports of psychological distress was examined by a two-way analysis of variance (ANOVA). The factors were the self-classification of attachment style (secure, avoidant, and anxious-ambivalent) and study group (severe CHD, mild CHD, and control). . . . The ANOVAs performed on threat appraisal and perceived coping abilities only yielded a significant main effect for attachment style, $F(2,141) = 3.29, p < .05, F(2,141) = 9.53, p < .01$, respectively. Scheffé post hoc tests indicated that (a) anxious-ambivalent mothers appraised motherhood tasks in more threatening terms ($M = 2.77$) than secure ones ($M = 2.28$) and (b) secure mothers perceived having more abilities to cope with these tasks ($M = 4.44$) than avoidant ($M = 4.13$) and anxious-ambivalent ones ($M = 3.91$).

Source: E. Berant, M. Mikulincer, and V. Florian. (2001). The association of mothers' attachment style and their psychological reactions to the diagnosis of infant's congenital heart disease. *Journal of Social and Clinical Psychology, 20*(2), pp. 218–219.

variable. In one of these ANOVAs, threat appraisal was the dependent variable; in the other ANOVA, the data reflected perceived coping ability. Notice how the Scheffé post hoc procedure showed, for each dependent variable, where statistically significant pairwise differences exist among the three main effect means for the attachment style factor.

If each of the factors in a two-way ANOVA turns out significant and if each of those factors contains three or more levels, then it is likely that a separate post hoc investigation will be conducted on each set of main effect means. The purpose of the two post hoc investigations would be the same: to identify the main effect means associated with each factor that are far enough apart to suggest that the corresponding population means are dissimilar. When both sets of main effect means are probed by means of post hoc investigations, the same test procedure (e.g., Tukey's) will be used to make comparisons among each set of main effect means.

Follow-Up Tests to Probe a Significant Interaction

When confronted with a statistically significant interaction, researchers will typically do two things. First, they will *refrain* from interpreting the *F*-ratios associated with the two main effects. Second, post hoc tests will be conducted and/or a graph will be prepared to help explain the specific nature of the interaction within the context of the study that has been conducted. Before turning our attention to the most frequently used follow-up strategies employed by researchers after observing a statistically significant interaction, I want to say a word or two about what they *do not do*.

Once the results of the two-way ANOVA become available, researchers will usually first look to see what happened relative to the interaction *F*. If the interaction turns out to be nonsignificant, they will move their attention to the two main effect *F*s and will interpret them in accordance with the principles outlined in the previous section. If, however, the interaction turns out to be significant, little or no attention will be devoted to the main effect *F*-ratios. This is because conclusions based on main effects can be quite misleading in the presence of significant interactions.

To illustrate how the presence of interaction renders the interpretation of main effects problematic, consider the three hypothetical situations presented in Figure 13.1. The number within each cell of each diagram is meant to be a sample mean, the numbers to the right of and below each diagram are meant to be main effect means (assuming equal cell sizes), and the abbreviated summary table provides the results that would be obtained if the samples were large enough or if the within-cell variability were small enough.

In situation 1, both main effect *F*s turn out nonsignificant. These results, coupled with the fact that there is no variability within either set of main effect means, might well lead one to think that the two levels of factor A are equivalent and to think that the three levels of factor B are equivalent. An inspection of the cell means, however, shows that those conclusions based on main effect means would cause one

(1)

A \ B				
	10	15	20	15
	20	15	10	15
	15	15	15	

Source	F
A	ns
B	ns
A × B	*

(2)

A \ B				
	5	10	15	10
	25	20	15	20
	15	15	15	

Source	F
A	*
B	ns
A × B	*

(3)

A \ B				
	10	10	10	10
	10	10	40	20
	10	10	25	

Source	F
A	*
B	*
A × B	*

FIGURE 13.1 ***Hypothetical Results from Three Two-Way ANOVAs***

to overlook potentially important findings. The two levels of factor A produced different means at the first and third levels of factor B, and the three levels of factor B were dissimilar at each level of factor A.

To drive home this point about how main effect *F*s can be misleading when the interaction is significant, pretend that factor A is gender (males on the top row, females on the bottom row), that factor B is a type of headache medicine given to relieve pain (brands X, Y, and Z corresponding to the first, second, and third columns, respectively), with each participant asked to rate the effectiveness of his or her medication on a 0 to 40 scale (0 = no relief; 40 = total relief) 60 minutes after being given a single dose of one brand of medication. If one were to pay attention to the main effect *F*s, one might be tempted to conclude that men and women experienced equal relief and that the three brands of medication were equally effective. Such conclusions would be unfortunate because the cell means suggest strongly (1) that males and females differed, on the average, in their reactions to headache medications X and Z, and (2) that the three medications differed in the relief produced (with Brand X being superior for females, Brand Z being superior for males).

In the second of our hypothetical situations, notice again how the main effect *F*s are misleading because of the interaction. Now, the main effect of factor A is significant, and one might be tempted to look at the main effect means and draw the conclusion that males experienced less relief from their headache medicines than did females. However, inspection of the cell means clearly shows that no difference exists between males and females when given Brand Z. Again, the main effect *F* for factor B would be misleading for the same reason as it would in the first set of results.

In the final hypothetical situation, both main effect *F*s are significant. Inspection of the cell means reveals, however, that the levels of factor A do not differ at the first or at the second levels of factor B, and that the levels of factor B do not differ at the first level of factor A. Within the context of our hypothetical headache study, the main effect *F*s, if interpreted, would lead one to suspect that females experienced more relief than males and that the three medicines differed in their effectiveness. Such conclusions would be misleading, for males and females experienced differential relief only when given Brand Z, and the brands seem to be differentially effective only in the case of females.

When the interaction *F* turns out to be significant, the main effect *F*s must be interpreted with extreme caution—or not interpreted directly at all. This is why most researchers are encouraged to look at the interaction *F* first when trying to make sense out of the results provided by a two-way ANOVA. The interaction *F* serves as a guidepost that tells the researchers what to do next. If the interaction *F* turns out to be *non*significant, this means that they have a green light and may proceed to interpret the *F*-ratios associated with the two main effects. If, however, the interaction *F* *is* significant, this is tantamount to a red light that says "Don't pay attention to the main effect means but instead focus your attention on the cell means."

One of the strategies used to help gain insight into a statistically significant interaction is a **graph of the cell means.** In a moment, we will look at such a graph that was included in a recent research report. First, however, you need to become acquainted with the study.

In this study, the researchers collected data on the success of IEPs (i.e., individualized education programs) in reading when used with young school children with mild disabilities. The students in this study came from one of two kinds of special education programs (resource and inclusive), with these being the levels of the type of program factor. The other independent variable was recommended IEP intensity, with three levels (low, medium, and high) based on how many minutes of reading instruction were recommended in the students' IEPs. The cell means shown here were presented in the research report; they reveal the mean number of minutes of reading instruction actually provided to each of the six groups of students.

		Recommended IEP Intensity		
		Low	Medium	High
Type of Program	Resource	*M* = 52.5	*M* = 50.7	*M* = 47.9
	Inclusive	*M* = 50.6	*M* = 45.0	*M* = 64.4

In Excerpt 13.16, we see a graph of the cell means from the IEP/reading study. Most researchers set up their graphs like the one in Excerpt 13.16 in that (1) the ordinate represents the dependent variable, (2) the points on the abscissa represent the levels of one of the two independent variables, and (3) the lines in the graph represent the levels of the other independent variable. In setting up such a graph, either of the two independent variables can be used to label the abscissa. For example, if the type of program factor in Excerpt 13.16 had been put on the abscissa, there would have been two points on the baseline (one for inclusive and one for resource) with three lines in the graph (one for each of the levels of program intensity).

Notice how the graph in Excerpt 13.16 allows us to see whether or not an interaction exists. First recall that the absence of interaction means that the difference between the levels of one factor remains constant as we move from one level to another level of the other factor. Now look at Excerpt 13.16. In the graph, the height

EXCERPT 13.16 • *The Graph of a Significant Interaction*

Two-way ANOVA on actual time allocated for reading revealed a significant interaction between type of program and level of [recomended] service intensity, $F(2,96)$ = 4.148, p < .02 (see Figure 2).

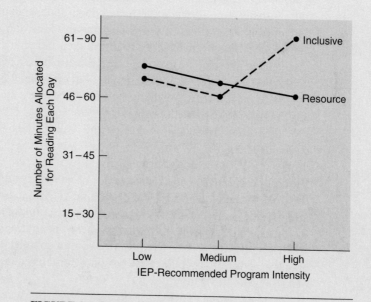

FIGURE 2 *Graph of interaction between IEP-recommended intensity and type of program.*

Source: C. A. Espin, S. L. Deno, and D. Albayrak-Kaymak. (1998). Individualized education programs education programs in resource and inclusive settings: How "individualized" are they? *Journal of Special Education, 32*(3), pp. 170, 172.

difference between (and the ordering of) the dashed and solid lines stays the same when you first consider the lines' left end points and then move your focus to the lines' mid points. So far, there is no interaction. However, things change when we consider the right end points of the two lines. Here, not only is there a much larger difference between the two lines, but the ordering of the two lines has also changed (for the dashed line is now higher than the solid line). Considered as a whole, this graph suggests that the differential amount of reading instruction actually provided to students from resource versus inclusive programs varies depending on IEP-recommended intensity.[6]

The graph of an interaction can be and often is set up such that vertical bars (rather than dots above the baseline) represent the cell means. I will illustrate this popular reporting technique with a graph taken from a recent study in which data were analyzed using a 2 × 2 ANOVA. This graph will make more sense if I first provide a brief overview of the investigation.

In the study associated with this two-way ANOVA, the same written information about the health risks of caffeine was given to sixty women, half of whom were coffee-drinkers. After reading health risk information, all 60 women filled out a questionnaire. This questionnaire was not connected to the study's dependent variable; instead, it represented the manipulated independent variable. For half of the coffee-drinkers and half of the non-coffee-drinkers, the form of the questionnaire they received had been designed to affirm their individual values. The other women received the alternate form of the questionnaire which did not provide this affirmation. After completing the questionnaire, all 60 women were asked to rate (on a 9-point scale) the extent to which they accepted the conclusions of the health-risk information they had been given.

The mean ratings provided by the four groups were as follows: affirmed coffee-drinkers = 7.23, affirmed non-coffee-drinkers = 5.81, non-affirmed coffee-drinkers = 4.15, and non-affirmed non-coffee-drinkers = 6.22. As you can see from Excerpt 13.17, each of the four samples of women is represented in the graph by a different bar, with the height the bars being determined by the sample means. This graph displays the statistically significant interaction found in the study, for the coffee-drinkers, on average, gave higher acceptance ratings than non-coffee-drinkers when both groups had received affirmation; in contrast, the coffee-drinkers, on average, gave lower acceptance ratings than non-coffee-drinkers when neither group had received affirmation.

Another strategy used by researchers to help understand the nature of a significant interaction is a statistical comparison of cell means. Such comparisons will normally be performed in one of two ways. Sometimes all of the cell means will be compared simultaneously in a pairwise fashion using one of the test procedures dis-

---

[6]Notice that the three lines in Excerpt 13.16 are not parallel. If the interaction F turns out to be significant, this will cause the lines in the graph to be nonparallel to a degree greater than what one expects by chance. For this reason, some authors define interaction as a departure from parallelism.

EXCERPT 13.17 • *Another Way to Graph an Interaction*

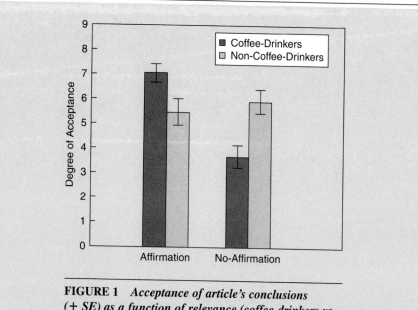

FIGURE 1 *Acceptance of article's conclusions (+ SE) as a function of relevance (coffee-drinkers vs. non-coffee-drinkers) and self-affirmation condition.*

Source: D. A. K. Sherman, L. D. Nelson, and C. M. Steele. (2000). Do messages about health risks threaten the self? Increasing the acceptance of threatening health messages via self-affirmation. *Personality and Social Psychology Bulletin, 26*(9), p. 1051.

cussed in Chapter 12. In other studies, cell means will be compared in a pairwise fashion one row and/or one column at a time using a post hoc strategy referred to as a simple main effects analysis. In the following five paragraphs, excerpts from actual studies are used to illustrate each of these post hoc strategies.

When a researcher probes a statistically significant interaction via **tests of simple main effects,** the various levels of one factor are compared in such a way that the other factor is "held constant." This is accomplished by comparing the cell means that reside in individual rows and/or in individual columns of the two-dimensional arrangement of cell means. This strategy of making tests of simple main effects is illustrated in Excerpt 13.18, which comes from the same study that gave us the graph of the interaction displayed in Excerpt 13.16.

In the first of the three sentences in Excerpt 13.18, the researchers report what happened when they compared the heights of the three points on the *solid line* in the graph. The cell means involved in this comparison—52.5, 50.7, and 47.9—were

Research
Navigator.com

Simple main
effects

EXCERPT 13.18 • *Tests of Simple Main Effects*

When this interaction was followed, it was seen that in resource programs, time allocated for reading did not change depending on IEP-recommended service intensity, $F(2,46) = 0.533$. By contrast, in inclusive programs, time allocated increased with IEP-recommended level of service intensity, $F(2,50) = 3.99$, $p < .03$. When differences among the three IEP service intensity groups in inclusive programs were further analyzed by Tukey's post hoc test, the only significant difference ($p < .05$) was between the high and medium IEP service intensity groups.

Source: C. A. Espin, S. L. Deno, and D. Albayrak-Kaymak. (1998). Individualized education programs in resource and inclusive settings: How "individualized" are they? *The Journal of Special Education, 32*(3), p. 170.

for the resource students whose IEP recommendations were classified as being low, medium, and high in intensity, respectively. An *F*-test was used to make this comparison, with this test being highly analogous to a one-way ANOVA comparison of three groups. As you can tell, the null hypothesis associated with this test was not rejected.

The second and third sentences in Excerpt 13.18 indicate what happened when the heights of the three points on the *dashed line* in the graph were compared. The cell means involved in this comparison—50.6, 45.0, and 64.4—were for the three groups of inclusive students. First, an omnibus *F*-test compared these three means; it was significant, thus suggesting that the three population means associated with these three samples were not all the same. This finding was then probed further via three pairwise comparisons using Tukey's test. Of the three Tukey comparisons that were made, only one revealed a statistically significant difference (the comparison of 64.4 and 45.0).

Sometimes two sets of tests of simple main effects are used to probe a statistically significant interaction. When this is done, one set of these post hoc tests compares cell means that lie in each row, and then a second set is used to compare the cell means that lie within each column. Excerpt 13.19 shows how tests of simple main effects can be applied in both directions to the cell means of a two-way ANOVA. As you will see, this excerpt comes from the same study that provided us with Excerpt 13.17.

A third strategy exists for statistically comparing cell means. Instead of comparing the means that reside within individual rows and/or columns of the two-dimensional layout of a two-way ANOVA, some researchers conduct **all possible pairwise comparisons among the cell means.** In Excerpt 13.20, we see an example where this approach was taken after the interaction null hypothesis was rejected.

With four cells means involved (because it was a 2 × 2 ANOVA), a total of six pairwise comparisons were made. Using the Newman-Keuls procedure to test each of the null hypotheses associated with these six comparisons, the researchers rejected one H_0 and failed to reject the other five.

EXCERPT 13.19 • *Tests of Simple Main Effects Applied in Both Directions*

As Figure 1 shows, within the no-affirmation condition, coffee-drinkers ($M = 4.15$) were less accepting of the conclusions than were non-coffee-drinkers ($M = 6.22$), $F(1, 28) = 10.77$, $p < .01$. However, in the affirmation condition, coffee-drinkers ($M = 7.23$) were more accepting of the article's conclusions than were non-coffee-drinkers ($M = 5.81$), $F(1, 30) = 5.85$, $p < .05$. Examining the results somewhat differently shows that the effects of the affirmation were most beneficial to the relevant participants. For the non-coffee-drinkers, there was no difference between the affirmation condition ($M = 5.81$) and the non-affirmation condition ($M = 6.22$), $F(1, 31) < 1.00$, *ns*. However, for the coffee drinkers, the affirmation had clear beneficial effects. Affirmed coffee-drinkers were much more accepting of the article's conclusions ($M = 7.23$) than were nonaffirmed coffee-drinkers ($M = 4.15$), $F(1, 27) = 33.26$, $p < .001$ (see Figure 1). Thus, for the coffee-drinking women, the self-affirmation reduced the defensive processing of the threatening message and persuaded them to accept that they should reduce their caffeine intake.

Source: D. A. K. Sherman, L. D. Nelson, and C. M. Steele. (2000). Do messages about health risks threaten the self? Increasing the acceptance of threatening health messages via self-affirmation. *Personality and Social Psychology Bulletin, 26*(9), p. 1050.

EXCERPT 13.20 • *Pairwise Comparison of All Cell Means*

A two-way analysis of variance for independent groups, with Face Presence and Pre-exposure as the independent variables, showed that there was a significant effect of Face Presence ($F(1,112) = 5.73$, $p < .05$), no significant effect of Pre-exposure ($F(1,112) = 0.64$) and a significant interaction between these two variables ($F(1,112) = 7.07$, $p < .01$). Face Presence reduced the number of correct identifications, but only when the face was not seen before speech began. A Newman-Keuls test demonstrated that the only groups to differ significantly were the two without pre-exposure, indicating that face presence was only effective when the face was not seen beforehand.

Source: S. Cook and J. Wilding. (2001). Earwitness testimony: Effects of exposure and attention on the Face Overshadowing Effect. *British Journal of Psychology, 92*(4), p. 626.

Planned Comparisons

In Chapter 12, we saw a case where planned comparisons were used in conjunction with a one-way ANOVA. It should come as no surprise that such comparisons can also be combined with the main and interaction *F*-tests of a two-way ANOVA. Not many researchers do this, but there are some who do. Consider, for example, Excerpt 13.21.

EXCERPT 13.21 • *Planned Comparisons in a Two-Way ANOVA*

Because our predicted effect occurs in only one of the four cells [of our] 2×2 ANOVA test, planned contrasts are the appropriate tests of our hypotheses. Planned contrasts supported hypothesis 1: those in the group/during-anticipation condition held significantly less favorable attitudes ($M = 1.05$, SD $= 1.30$, $n = 20$) than those in the group/before-anticipation and individual conditions ($M = 1.83$, SD $= 1.57$, $n = 63$; $F(1, 81) = 4.01$, $p < .05$). If, as expected, those in the group/before-anticipation condition formed an attitude prior to learning of the approaching discussion, then their attitudes should be relatively unaffected by the approaching discussion and therefore similar to the attitudes of those in the individual conditions. In support of this expectation, an omnibus test comparing the attitudes of those in the group/before-anticipation condition ($M = 1.85$, $SD = 1.48$, $n = 20$), individual/before-anticipation condition ($M = 2.18$, $SD = 1.47$, $n = 20$), and individual/during-anticipation condition ($M = 1.49$, $SD = 1.71$, $n = 23$) yielded no significant differences ($F(1, 60) = 2.08$, *NS*).

Source: A. E. Schlosser and S. Shavitt. (2002). Anticipating discussion about a product: Rehearsing what to say can affect your judgments. *Journal of Consumer Research, 29*(1), p. 105.

In the study from which Excerpt 13.21 was drawn, a 2×2 ANOVA was used. In this ANOVA, the levels of one factor were called *individual* and *group,* while the levels of the other factor were called *before* and *during.* Instead of focusing on the main and interaction effects, the researchers set up and tested two planned comparisons that addressed directly their two hypotheses. Both of these *a priori* tests were nonpairwise in nature. The first one compared one of the cell means against the combined mean of two other cell means. The second planned comparison involved was like a one-way ANOVA, for it was an omnibus comparison of three cell means.

The researchers associated with Excerpt 13.21 deserve credit for having specific plans in mind when they designed their study *and* when they analyzed their data. Their research questions guided their statistical analysis, and their analysis did not follow the conventional rules for making statistical comparisons in a two-way ANOVA. Far too many applied researchers erroneously think that (1) *F*-tests for main and interaction effects must be computed and (2) comparisons of cell means can be made only if the interaction is significant. This is unfortunate for several reasons, the main one being that planned comparisons of cell means can sometimes produce interesting findings that remain undetected by the standard *F*-tests of a two-way ANOVA.

Assumptions Associated with a Two-Way ANOVA

The assumptions associated with a two-way ANOVA are the same as those associated with a one-way ANOVA: randomness, independence, normality, and homogeneity of variance. As I hope you recall from the discussion of assumptions contained in Chapter 11, randomness and independence are methodological concerns; they are dealt with (or *should* be dealt with) when a study is set up, when data are collected, and when results are generalized beyond the participants and conditions of the researcher's investigation. Although the randomness and independence assumptions can ruin a study if they are violated, there is no way to use the study's sample data to test the validity of these prerequisite conditions.

The assumptions of normality and homogeneity of variance *can* be tested and in certain circumstances *should* be tested. The procedures used to conduct such tests are the same as those used by researchers to check on the normality and equal variance assumptions when conducting *t*-tests or one-way ANOVAs. Two-way ANOVAs are also similar to *t*-tests and one-way ANOVAs in that (1) violations of the normality assumption usually do not reduce the validity of the results, and (2) violations of the equal variance assumption are more problematic only when the sample sizes differ.

Since violations of the normality and equal variance are less disruptive to the *F*-tests of a two-way ANOVA when the *n*s are large and equal, many researchers will make an effort to set up the studies with equal cell sizes. Frequently, however, it is impossible to achieve this goal. On occasion, a researcher will start out with equal cell sizes but will end up with cell *n*s that vary because of equipment failure, subject dropout, or unusable answer sheets. On other occasions, the researcher will have varying sample sizes at the beginning of the study but will not want to discard any data so as to create equal *n*s because such a strategy would lead to a loss of statistical power. For either of these reasons, a researcher may end up with cell sizes that vary. In such situations, researchers will frequently concern themselves with the normality and homogeneity of variance assumptions.

In Excerpts 13.22 and 13.23, we see examples where the **normality assumption** and the **equal variance assumption** were tested. In these and other cases where assumptions are tested, researchers usually hope that the assumption's null hypothesis will not be rejected. When this is the case, they can proceed directly

EXCERPTS 13.22–13.23 • *Testing the Normality and Equal*
Variance Assumptions

Differences between hematological parameters and body mass were tested by two-way ANOVA using locality and season as factors. Because ratios such as the H:L index and percentages are often not normally distributed, we performed a Kolmogorov-Smirnov analysis to test for normality. Data of body mass and hematological parameters as well as H:L index in both urban and rural samples exhibited a normal distribution.

Source: G. Ruiz, M. Rosenmann, F. F. Novoa, and P. Sabat. (2002). Hematological parameters and stress index in Rufous-collared Sparrows dwelling in urban environments. *The Condor, 104*(1), p. 163.

[For the] 2 (treatment setting) $\times$ 2 (gender) ANOVA . . . , Levene's test for equality of variances indicated that homoscedasticity could be assumed.

Source: B. E. Bride. (2001). Single-gender treatment of substance abuse: Effect on treatment retention and completion. *Social Work Research, 25*(4), p. 227.

from these preliminary tests to their study's main tests. This is precisely what happened in Excerpts 13.22 and 13.23, for in each case the assumption being tested was not rejected but rather upheld by the sample data.

As indicated in Chapter 11, researchers have several options when it becomes apparent that their data sets are characterized by extreme nonnormality or heterogeneity of variance. One option is to apply a **data transformation** before testing any null hypotheses involving the main effect or cell means. In Excerpt 13.24, we see a case in which this was done. In other research reports, you are likely to see different kinds of data transformations used (e.g., the square root transformation and the arcsine transformation). Different kinds of transformations are available because nonnormality or heterogeneity of variance can exist in different forms. It is the researcher's job, of course, to choose an appropriate transformation that accomplishes the desired objective of bringing the data into greater agreement with the normality and equal variance assumptions.

Well-trained researchers will indicate that they were aware of the assumptions underlying the *F*-tests of a two-way ANOVA. On occasion, you will see researchers say that their tests are **robust,** meaning that the assumptions are of little concern because the statistical tests have been found to operate as designed even if the assumptions are violated. Sometimes, the assumptions will be tested and found to be tenable. Not infrequently, data transformations will be used to bring the sample data

EXCERPT 13.24 • *Using a Data Transformation*

> We used Cochran's test of homogeneity of variance. We found that the basic demographic data satisfied this criterion, hence we used no transformations. The hormone data for the [two-way] ANOVA did not meet this criterion, however, and we used the log (x + 1) transformation to make the variances homogeneous.
>
> *Source:* R. Boobstra, A. H. Hubbs, E. A. Lacey, and C. J. McColl. (2001). Seasonal changes in glucocorticoid and testosterone concentrations in free-living arctic ground squirrels from the boreal forest of the Yukon. *Canadian Journal of Zoology, 79*(1), p. 51.

into greater compatibility with assumptions. Finally, it is not uncommon to see a researcher assess the study's central null hypotheses with a test procedure that has less rigorous assumptions, either because the more rigorous assumptions associated with *F*-tests were tested and found to be untenable or because the researcher doesn't want to bother with test procedures that have lots of assumptions.

If a researcher conducts a two-way ANOVA but does not say anything at all about the normality and equal variance assumptions, then you have a right—even an obligation—to receive the researcher's end-of-study claims with a big grain of salt. You have a right to do this because *F*-tests can be biased if the assumptions are violated. That **bias** can be positive or negative in nature, thus causing the ANOVA's *F*-tests to turn out either too large or too small, respectively. If the former problem exists, the computed *p*-value associated with a calculated *F*-value will be too small, thereby exaggerating how much the sample data deviate from null expectations. In this situation, the nominal alpha level will understate the probability of a Type I error. If the bias is negative, the *p*-values associated with computed *F*-values will be too large. This may cause the researcher to not reject one or more null hypotheses that would have been rejected if evaluated with unbiased *p*s.

Effect Size Indices, Strength of Association Measures, and Power Analyses in Two-Way ANOVAs

As indicated in Chapter 8, various techniques have been developed to help researchers assess the extent to which their results are significant in a practical sense. It is worth repeating that such techniques serve a valuable role in quantitative studies wherein null hypotheses are tested, for it is possible for a result to end up being declared statistically significant even though it is totally unimportant from a practical standpoint. Earlier, we saw how these techniques have been used in conjunction with *t*-tests and one-way ANOVAs. We now will consider their relevance to two-way ANOVAs.

Research
Navigator.c⊛m

Effect size

In Excerpt 13.25, we see a case in which the researchers computed **effect size** indices for the main effect of age that turned out to be significant in two of the three 2 × 2 ANOVAs that were conducted, each one using data on a different dependent variable. The researchers tagged the two *d*s as being small because these effect size estimates were compared against the standards of .2, .5, and .8 (for small, medium, and large effects).

EXCERPT 13.25 • *Estimated Effect Size*

Age-related trends in the development of autonomy were examined by a 2 (Sex) × 2 (Age) analysis of variance (ANOVA) on attitudinal, emotional, and functional autonomy. . . . A significant main effect for age was found in attitudinal autonomy, $F(1, 400) = 3.75$, $p < 0.05$, and emotional autonomy, $F(1, 400) = 6.53$, $p < 0.01$. Cohen's *d* was computed to determine the effect size. For both dimensions small effects were found ($d = 0.19$ for attitudinal autonomy, $d = 0.29$ for emotional autonomy).

Source: M. J. Noom, M. Dekovic, and W. Meeus. (2001). Conceptual analysis and measurement of adolescent autonomy. *Journal of Youth and Adolescence, 30*(5), pp. 591–592.

Excerpt 13.26 illustrates an alternative method used by researchers to address the issue of practical significance versus statistical significance. Here, they used their data to compute an estimate of the **strength of association** for each *F*-test in their two-way ANOVA. As you can see, they used omega squared to do this. According to the standards for evaluating this kind of strength of association measure, both of the main effects would be said to have a very small impact on the dependent variable. How could this be the case if the main effect turned out to be statistically significant? Perhaps the samples sizes were quite large. (And perhaps you can check this out by examining the *df* numbers that accompany each of the *F*-values.)

Whereas the values of *d* in Excerpt 13.25 and the values of ω^2 in Excerpt 13.26 were computed in a post hoc manner, the power analysis in Excerpt 13.27 was conducted in the design phase of the investigation. Sometimes researchers do a **power analysis** after their data have been analyzed, and sometimes they do a power analysis before their data are gathered. In one situation, the purpose is to see if there *was* sufficient power to detect meaningful differences; in the other situation, the purpose is to design the study so that there *will be* sufficient power to detect meaningful differences. The researchers who conducted the study associated with Excerpt 13.27 deserved high praise for doing the better kind of power analysis.

Research
Navigator.c⊛m

Power analysis

EXCERPT 13.26 • *Estimated Strength of Association*

A 2 (Activity Status) $\times$ 4 (BMI Classification) ANOVA was performed [and] significant main effects for both activity status, $F(1, 519) = 6.48$, p $< .05$, $\omega^2 = .03$, and BMI classification, $F(3, 519) = 3.21$, p $< .05$, $\omega^2 = .02$, were found. The interaction between these two factors was not significant, $F(3, 519) = 0.20$, p $> .05$, $\omega^2 = .00$.

Source: B. J. Cardinal. (2001). Role modeling attitudes and physical activity and fitness promoting behaviors of HPERD professionals and preprofessionals. *Research Quarterly for Exercise and Sport, 72*(1), pp. 86–87.

EXCERPT 13.27 • *An A Priori Power Analysis*

The method used to establish the sample size for this investigation was a power analysis conducted according to procedures developed by Cohen (1988) for a factorial ANOVA design. The parameters for the power analysis were: (a) a planned alpha level ($\alpha = .05$), (b) a specified power level (b $= .80$), and (c) an estimated effect size ($\omega^2 = .06$). Cohen described the above effect size as "medium" in magnitude (1988, p. 397). The power analysis resulted in a cell size of 17 participants and a total sample size of 136 (8 cells $\times$ 17).

Source: P. A. Winter and C. L. Kjorlien. (2001). Business faculty recruitment: The effects of full-time versus part-time employment. *Community College Review, 29*(1), p. 23.

In your reading of the research literature, you are likely to encounter many studies in which a two-way ANOVA functions as the primary data analytic tool. Unfortunately, many of these researchers who use this tool formally address only the concept of statistical significance, with the notion of practical significance automatically (and incorrectly) superimposed on each and every result that turns out to be statistically significant. Consequently, you must remain vigilant for instances of this unjustified and dangerous misinterpretation of results.

The Inflated Type I Error Rate in Factorial ANOVAs

When data are subjected to a standard two-way ANOVA, three *F*-values are computed—one for each main effect and one for the interaction. If the same level of significance (e.g., .05) is used in assessing each F-value, you may have been thinking that the probability of a Type I error occurring somewhere among the three F-tests is greater than the alpha level used to evaluate each F-value. Accordingly, you may have been expecting me to point out how conscientious researchers make some form of adjustment to avoid having an inflated Type I error rate associated with their two-way ANOVAs.

Although it is clear that the computation of three F-values in a two-way ANOVA leads to a greater-than-alpha chance that one or more of the three null hypotheses will be incorrectly rejected, the vast majority of applied researchers do not adjust anything in an effort to deal with this "problem." This is because most applied researchers consider each F-test separately rather than look at the three F-tests collectively as a set. When the F-tests are viewed in that manner, the Type I error risk is *not* inflated, for the researcher's alpha level correctly specifies the probability that any given F-test will cause a true H_0 to be rejected.

When a given level of significance is used to evaluate each of the three F-values, it can be said that the **familywise error rate** is set equal to the alpha level. Each "family" is defined as the set of contrasts represented by an F-test and any post hoc tests that might be conducted if the F turns out to be statistically significant. The familywise error rate is equal to the common alpha level employed to evaluate all three F-tests because the chances of a Type I error, *within each family,* are equal to the alpha level.

If a researcher analyzes the data from two or more dependent variables with separate two-way ANOVAs, you may find that the Bonferroni procedure is used to adjust the alpha level. In Excerpt 13.28, we see a case in which this was done. In this study, there were two dependent variables: a multiple-choice verbal test (WORD) and a multiple-choice quantitative test (DS). The available group of participants was divided into two subgroups. One subgroup took the two tests in the normal fashion, recording on the answer sheets just their selected answers. Each individual in the other subgroup also answered the questions on each test, but in addition he or she was required to indicate, for each question, his or her confidence that the selected answer was correct. Altogether, four two-way ANOVAs were conducted (each having gender and BSRI grouping as its factors): the first subgroup's performance on the WORD test, that same group's performance on the DS test, the second subgroup's performance on the WORD test, and the second subgroup's performance on the DS test. In using the Bonferroni technique, the researchers divided their desired study-wide alpha level of .05 by 4, the number of two-way ANOVAs. They then used 0.0125 as the alpha criterion when evaluating the three F-tests from each analysis.

Researchers frequently conduct ANOVAs involving more than three factors. In such situations, the number of F-tests in the "standard" analysis increases dramatically as more and more factors are included. With three factors, for example, most researchers compute seven F-tests, whereas 16 F-tests are usually examined when there are four factors involved in the ANOVA. If a researcher uses one of these

EXCERPT 13.28 • *The Bonferroni Adjustment*

Also calculated was the percentage of "Extremely sure" self-assessments given by the participants, and four 2 (Gender: Men, Women) × 4 (BSRI: Gender-typed, Cross-gender-typed, Androgynous, Undifferentiated) ANOVAs were performed in order to detect possible effects of Gender and BSRI grouping on the percentage of "Extremely sure" answers (correct and incorrect answers on the WORD and DS subtests) given by the participants. The Bonferroni method of controlling the Type-I error rate was used to determine the significance level alpha ($\alpha/4 = 0.0125$).

Source: N. Koivula, P. Hassmen, and D. P. Hunt. (2001). Performance on the Swedish Scholastic Aptitude Test: Effects of self-assessment and gender. *Sex Roles, 44*(11/12), p. 638.

higher order factorial ANOVAs (with a single dependent variable), you are likely to see an alpha level of .05 used to evaluate each of the many F-tests computed. Thus the practice of using a familywise alpha (such as .05) is not restricted to two-way ANOVAs.

A Few Warnings Concerning Two-Way ANOVAs

Before concluding this chapter, I want to offer a few cautionary comments that I hope you will tuck away in your memory bank and then bring up to consciousness whenever you encounter a research report based on a two-way ANOVA. Although I have touched on some of these issues in previous chapters, your ability to decipher *and* critique research summaries may well improve if I deliberately reiterate a few of those earlier concerns.

Evaluate the Worth of the Hypotheses Being Tested

I cannot overemphasize how important it is to critically assess the worth of the hypotheses being tested within any study based on a two-way ANOVA. No matter how good the study may be from a statistical perspective and no matter how clear the research report is, the study cannot possibly make a contribution unless the questions being dealt with are interesting. In other words, the research questions that prompt the investigator to select the factors and levels of the two-way ANOVA must be worth answering and must have no clear answer before the study is conducted. If these things do not hold true, then the study has a fatal flaw in its foundation that cannot be overcome by large sample sizes, rigorous alpha levels, high reliability and validity estimates, impressive F-ratios that are statistically significant, elaborate post hoc analyses, tests of assumptions, and power analyses. The old saying that "you can't make a silk purse out of a sow's ear" is as relevant here as anywhere else.

Remember That Two-Way ANOVAs Focus on Means

As with most *t*-tests and all one-way ANOVAs, the focus of a two-way ANOVA is on means. The main effect means and the cell means serve as the focal points of the three research questions associated with any two-way ANOVA. When the main effect and interaction *F*-tests are discussed, it is essential for you to keep in mind that conclusions should be tied to means.

I recently read a study (utilizing a two-way ANOVA) that evaluated the impact of an outdoor rock-climbing program on at-risk adolescents. There were two main dependent variables: alienation and personal control. The researchers asserted, in the abstract of the research report, that "after experiencing the climbing program, the experimental group was less alienated than its control counterparts" and "demonstrated a stronger sense of personal control than did the control group." Many people reading those statements would think that *everyone* in the experimental group scored lower on alienation and higher on personal power than *anyone* in the control group. However, the group means and standard deviations included in the research report—on both measures (alienation and personal power)—make it absolutely clear that some of the members of the control group had better scores than did some of the members in the experimental group.

Many researchers fail to note that their statistically significant findings deal with means, and the literal interpretation of the researchers' words says that all of the folks in one group outperformed those in the comparison group(s). If the phrase *on average* or some similar wording does not appear in the research report, make certain that you insert it as you attempt to decipher and understand the statistical findings. If you don't, you will end up thinking that comparison groups were far more different from one another than was actually the case.

Remember the Possibility of Type I and Type II Errors

The third warning that I want to offer is not new. You have encountered it earlier in our consideration of *t*-tests and one-way ANOVAs. Simply stated, I want to encourage you to remember that regardless of how the results of a two-way ANOVA turn out, there is always the possibility of either a Type I or Type II error whenever a decision is made to reject or fail to reject a null hypothesis.

Based on the words used by many researchers in discussing their results, it seems to me that the notion of "statistical significance" is quite often amplified (incorrectly) into something on the order of a firm discovery—or even proof. Far too seldom do I see the word *inference* or the phrase *null hypothesis* in the technical write-ups of research investigations wherein the hypothesis testing procedure has been used. Although you do not have the ability to control what researchers say when they summarize their investigations, you most certainly *do* have the freedom to adjust the research summary to make it more accurate.

Sooner or later, you are bound to encounter a research report wherein a statement is made on the order of (1) "Treatment A works better than Treatment B" or (2) "Folks who possess characteristic X outperform those who possess characteristic Y." Such statements will come from researchers who temporarily forgot not only the difference between sample statistics and population parameters but also the ever-present possibility of an inferential error when a finding is declared either significant or nonsignificant. You can avoid making the mistake of accepting such statements as points of fact by remembering that no *F*-test *ever* proves anything.

Be Careful When Interpreting Nonsignificant F-tests

In Chapter 7, I pointed out that it is wrong to consider a null hypothesis to be true simply because the hypothesis testing procedure results in a fail-to-reject decision. Any of several factors (e.g., small sample sizes, unreliable measuring instruments, or too much within-group variability) can cause the result to be nonsignificant, even if the null hypothesis being tested is actually false. This is especially true when the null hypothesis is false by a small amount.

Almost all researchers who engage in hypothesis testing have been taught that it is improper to conclude that a null hypothesis is true simply because the hypothesis testing procedure leads to a fail-to-reject decision. Nevertheless, many of these same researchers use language in their research reports suggesting that they have completely forgotten that a fail-to-reject decision does not logically permit one to leave a study believing that the tested H_0 is true. In your review of studies that utilize two-way ANOVAs (or, for that matter, any procedure for testing null hypotheses), remain vigilant to erroneous statements as to what a nonsignificant finding means.

Review Terms

Active factor	Graph of an interaction
Assigned factor	Interaction
Biased *F*-test	Level
Cell	Main effect *F*
Data transformation	Main effect mean
Equal variance assumption	Omega squared
Estimated magnitude of effect	Post hoc tests
Eta squared	Power analysis
Factor	Simple main effect
Familywise error rate	Univariate analysis

The Best Items in the Companion Website

1. An interactive online quiz (with immediate feedback provided) covering Chapter 13.
2. Nine misconceptions about the content of Chapter 13.

3. An email message sent from the author to his students entitled "Can One Cell Create an Interaction?"
4. An interactive online resource entitled "Two-Way ANOVA (a)."
5. One of two best passages from Chapter 13: "You Can't Make a Silk Purse Out of a Sow's Ear."

Fun Exercises inside Research Navigator

1. **Who admits to cheating more: undergraduate males or females? Younger or older undergraduates?**

   As part of a study conducted in the UK, psychology students at four universities were administered a cheating questionnaire. In one analysis, the resulting data were subjected to a 2 (gender: male, female) × 2 (age: younger, older) ANOVA. The data that went into this two-way ANOVA were the scores on the cheating questionnaire. First, make a guess as to which of the ANOVA's three *F* tests turned out to be statistically significant. Then, locate the PDF version of the research report in the Education database of ContentSelect and read the first full paragraph on page 277 to find out what the two-way ANOVA actually revealed.

   L. S. Norton, A. J. Tilley, S. E. Newstead, & A. Franklyn-Stokes. The pressures of assessment in undergraduate courses and their effect on student behaviours. *Assessment and Evaluation in Higher Education.* Located in the EDUCATION database of ContentSelect.

2. **Do different groups/genders have different attitudes toward rape victims?**

   The *Attitudes toward Rape Victims Scale* (*ARVS*) was administered to three groups: upper-level undergraduates, Master's students in a counseling program, and professionals (who held a Master's or Doctoral degree) working as mental health practitioners. After subdividing each group on the basis of gender, the attitude scores were analyzed by a 2 × 3 ANOVA. Results showed that both main effects and the interaction were statistically significant. With high scores on the *AVRS* indicating more negative attitudes toward a rape victim, what do you think the tests of simple main effects revealed? (These tests were conducted "both directions," comparing the three groups for each gender and then comparing the two genders within each of the three groups.) After making a guess, refer to the PDF version of the research report in the Criminal Justice database of ContentSelect and check to see if you are correct by looking at the top paragraph on page of 922.

   B. H. White & S. E. R. Kurpius. Attitudes toward rape victims. *Journal of Interpersonal Violence.* Located in the CRIMINAL JUSTICE database of ContentSelect.

Review Questions and Answers begin on page 516.

14

Analyses of Variance with Repeated Measures

In this chapter, we consider three different ANOVAs that are characterized by repeated measures. In particular, the focus here is on one-way ANOVAs with repeated measures, two-way ANOVAs with repeated measures on both factors, and two-way ANOVAs with repeated measures on just one factor. Although there are other kinds of ANOVAs that involve repeated measures (e.g., a four-way ANOVA with repeated measures on all or some of the factors), the three types considered here are the ones you are most likely to encounter.

The one-way and two-way ANOVAs examined in this chapter are similar in many respects to the ANOVAs considered in Chapters 11 and 13. The primary difference between the ANOVAs of this chapter and those looked at in earlier chapters is that the ANOVAs to which we now turn our attention involve repeated measures on at least one factor. This means that the research participants will be measured once under each level (or combination of levels) of the factor(s) involved in the ANOVA.

Perhaps an example will help to distinguish between the ANOVAs considered in earlier chapters and their repeated measures counterparts examined in this chapter. If a researcher has a 2×3 design characterized by no repeated measures, each participant in the study can be thought of (1) as being located inside *one* of the six cells of the factorial design and (2) as contributing *one* score to the data set. In contrast, if a researcher has a 2×3 design characterized by repeated measures across both factors, each participant can be thought of (1) as being in *each of the six* cells and (2) as contributing *six* scores to the data set.

Before we turn our attention to the specific ANOVAs of this chapter, I'd like to make three introductory comments. First, each of the ANOVAs to be considered here will be univariate in nature. Even though participants are measured more than once with the same ANOVA, these statistical procedures are univariate in nature—not multivariate—because each participant provides only one score to the data set for each level or combination of levels of the factor(s) involved in the study. The ANOVAs of this chapter could be turned into multivariate ANOVAs if each participant were measured repeatedly within each cell of the design, with these within-cell repeated measurements corresponding to different dependent variables. Such multivariate repeated measures ANOVAs, however, are not considered in this chapter.

Second, it's important to understand the distinction between (1) two or more separate ANOVAs, each conducted on the data corresponding to a different dependent variable, with all data coming from the same participants, and (2) a single unified ANOVA in which there are repeated measures across levels of the factor(s) of the study. In Chapters 10, 11, and 13, you have seen many examples of multiple but separate ANOVAs being applied to different sets of data, each corresponding to a unique dependent variable. The ANOVAs to which we now turn our attention are different from those referred to in the preceding sentence in that the ones to be considered here always involve a single, consolidated analysis.

My final introductory point concerns different kinds of repeated measures factors. To be more specific, I want to distinguish between some of the different circumstances in a study that can create a **within-subjects factor.**[1] You will likely encounter three such circumstances as you read technical research reports.

One obvious way for a factor to involve repeated measures is for participants to be measured at different points in time. For example, a researcher might measure people before and after an intervention, with the factor being called *time* and its levels being called *pre* and *post.* Or, in a study focused on the acquisition of a new skill, the factor might be called *trials* (or *trial blocks*), with levels simply numbered 1, 2, 3, and so on. A second way for a factor to involve repeated measures is for participants to be measured once under each of two or more different treatment conditions. In such studies, the factor might well be called *treatments* or *conditions,* with the factor's levels labeled to correspond to the specific treatments involved in the study. A third kind of repeated measures factor shows up when the study's participants are asked to rate different things or are measured on different characteristics. Here, the factor and level names would be chosen to correspond to the different kinds of data gathered in the study.

In Excerpts 14.1 through 14.3, we see how different kinds of situations can lead to data being collected from each participant across levels of the repeated measures factor. Although the factors referred to in these excerpts are all within-subjects factors, they involve repeated measures for different reasons. In Excerpt 14.1, the data were collected at different *times;* in Excerpt 14.2, the data were collected under different *treatment conditions;* and in Excerpt 14.3, the data were collected on different *variables.*

---

[1]The terms *repeated-measures factor, within-subjects factor,* and *within-participants factor* are synonymous.

EXCERPTS 14.1–14.3 • *Different Kinds of Repeated Measures Factors*

In each ANOVA, the within-subjects factor was Time of Measurement (initial session vs. follow-up session).

Source: K. H. Breitenbecher and M. Scarce. (2001). An evaluation of the effectiveness of a sexual assault education program focusing on psychological barriers to resistance. *Journal of Interpersonal Violence, 16*(5), p. 398.

- -

The validity of the CSA accelerometer was assessed during light walking, brisk walking, and jogging around an outdoor 400-m track with a synthetic surface. The order of [3 exercise] tests was randomized. Instructions were given to "stroll," "walk briskly," and "Jog at a comfortable pace" for 5 min each. . . . One-way repeated measures analysis of variance (ANOVA) was used to examine the sensitivity of the CSA to changes in velocity.

Source: J. F. Nichols, C. G. Morgan, L. E. Chabot, J. F. Sallis, and K. J. Calfas. (2000). Assessment of physical activity with the Computer Science and Applications, Inc., accelerometer: Laboratory versus field validation. *Research Quarterly for Exercise and Sport, 71*(1), pp. 38–39.

- -

The AWPBI [Ability to Work with Problem Behaviors Inventory] provides a scale score for each of the three scales: (a) internalizing (18 items), (b) externalizing (12 items), and (c) thought disordered (8 items) . . . with behavior type being a within-subject factor.

Source: J. R. Nelson, A. Maculan, M. L. Roberts, and B. J. Ohlund. (2001). Sources of occupational stress for teachers of students with emotional and behavioral disorders. *Journal of Emotional and Behavioral Disorders, 9*(2), pp. 125, 127.

One-Way Repeated Measures ANOVAs

When researchers use a one-way repeated measures ANOVA, they usually will tip you off that their ANOVA is different from the kind we considered in Chapters 10 and 11 (where no repeated measures are involved). They do this by including the phrase "repeated measures" or "within-subjects" or "within-participants" as a descriptor of their ANOVA or of their ANOVA's single factor. Examples of this practice appear in Excerpts 14.4, 14.5, and 14.6.

Purpose

The purpose of a one-way repeated measures ANOVA is identical to the purpose of a one-way ANOVA not having repeated measures. In each case, the researcher is

EXCERPTS 14.4–14.6 • *Different Labels for a One-Way Repeated Measures ANOVA*

To assess the differences among DCN, CEV, and HEX, a 1-way within-subjects analysis of variance (ANOVA) was conducted.

Source: D. W. Chan. (2002). Perceptions of giftedness and self-concepts among junior secondary students in Hong Kong. *Journal of Youth and Adolescence, 31*(4), p. 246.

The effect of time was assessed [by a] one-factor repeated measures analysis of variance (ANOVA) (Weeks 2, 8, and 14).

Source: W. W. Campbell, T. A. Trappe, R. R. Wolfe, and W. J. Evans. (2001). The recommended dietary allowance for protein may not be adequate for older people to maintain skeletal muscle. *The Journals of Gerontology, 56A*(6), p. M375.

A one-way analysis of variance (ANOVA) was performed on the arcsine-transformed data for the young participants, with a within-subjects factor of trial ($k = 10$).

Source: M. P. Feeney and B. Hallowell. (2000). Practice and list effects on the synthetic sentence identification test in young and elderly listeners. *Journal of Speech, Language, and Hearing Research, 43*(5), p. 1163.

interested in seeing whether (or the degree to which) the sample data cast doubt on the null hypothesis of the ANOVA. That null hypothesis, for the within-subjects case as well as the between-subjects case, states that the μs associated with the different levels of the factor do not differ. Since the researcher who uses a one-way within-subjects ANOVA is probably interested in gaining an insight into how the μs differ, post hoc tests are normally used (as in a between-subjects ANOVA) if the overall null hypothesis is rejected and if three or more levels compose the ANOVA's factor.

To illustrate, suppose a researcher collects reaction-time data from six people on three occasions: immediately upon awakening in the morning, one hour after awakening, and two hours after awakening. Each of the six people would be measured three times, with a total of 18 pieces of data available for analysis. In subjecting the data to a one-way repeated measures ANOVA, the researcher would be asking whether the three sample means, each based on six scores collected at the same time during the day, are far enough apart to call into question the null hypothesis that says all three population means are equivalent. In other words, the purpose of the one-way repeated measures ANOVA in this study would be to see if the average reaction time of folks similar to the six people used in the study varies depending upon whether they are tested 0, 60, or 120 minutes after awakening.

It is usually helpful to think of any one-way repeated measures ANOVA in terms of a two-dimensional matrix. Within this matrix, each row corresponds to a different person and each column corresponds to a different level of the study's factor. A single score is entered into each cell of this matrix, with the scores on any row coming from the same person. Such a matrix, created for our hypothetical reaction-time study, is presented in Figure 14.1. Such illustrations normally do not appear in research reports. Therefore, you will need to create such a picture (in your mind or on a piece of scratch paper) when trying to decipher the results of a one-way repeated measures ANOVA. This will usually be easy to do because you will be given information as to the number of people involved in the study, the nature of the repeated measures factor, and the sample means that correspond to the levels of the repeated measures factor.

Presentation of Results

The results of a one-way repeated measures ANOVA may be presented in an ANOVA summary table. In Table 14.1, I have prepared such a table for our hypothetical study on reaction time. This summary table is similar in some ways to the one-way ANOVA summary tables contained in Chapter 11, yet it is similar, in other respects, to the two-way ANOVA summary tables included in Chapter 13. Table 14.1 is like a one-way ANOVA summary table in that a single F-ratio is contained

Hours Since Awakening

	Zero	One	Two
Person 1	1.7	1.1	1.7
Person 2	1.8	0.9	1.5
Person 3	1.6	1.2	1.4
Person 4	2.3	1.5	1.8
Person 5	2.0	1.5	1.3
Person 6	2.0	1.0	1.9
	$\bar{X} = 1.9$	$\bar{X} = 1.2$	$\bar{X} = 1.6$

FIGURE 14.1 *Illustration of the Data Setup for the One-Way Repeated Measures ANOVA in the Hypothetical Reaction-Time Study*

TABLE 14.1   *ANOVA Summary Table for the Reaction-Time Data Contained in Figure 14.1*

Source	df	SS	MS	F
Hours since awakening	2	1.48	.74	16.34*
People	5	.47	.09	
Residual	10	.45	.05	
Total	17	2.40		

*$p < .01$.

in the right-hand column of the table. (Note that this *F*-ratio is computed by dividing the *MS* for the study's factor by the *MS* for residual.) It is like a two-way ANOVA summary table in that (1) the row for people functions, in some respects, as a second factor of the study and (2) the numerical values on the row for residual are computed in the same way as if this were the interaction from a two-way ANOVA. (Note that the *df* for residual is computed by multiplying together the first two *df* values.) In fact, we could have used the term *hours × people* to label this row instead of the term *residual*.

Regardless of whether Table 14.1 resembles more closely the summary table for a one-way ANOVA or a two-way ANOVA, it contains useful information for anyone trying to understand the structure and the results of the investigation. First, the title of the table indicates what kind of data were collected. Second, we can tell from the Source column that the study's factor was Hours since awakening. Third, the top two numbers in the *df* column inform us that the study involved three levels (2 + 1 = 3) of the factor and six people (5 + 1 = 6). Fourth, the bottom number in the *df* column indicates that a total of 18 pieces of data were analyzed (17 + 1 = 18). Finally, the note beneath the table reveals that the study's null hypothesis was rejected, with .01 being one of three things: (1) the original level of significance used by the researcher, (2) the revised alpha level that resulted from a Bonferroni or pseudo-Bonferroni adjustment, or (3) the most rigorous of the standard alpha levels (i.e., .05, .01, .001) that could be beaten by the data.

In our hypothetical study on reaction time, Table 14.1 indicates that the null hypothesis of equal population means is not likely to be true. To gain an insight into the pattern of the population means, a post hoc investigation would probably be conducted. Most researchers would set up this follow-up investigation such that three pairwise contrasts are tested, each involving a different pair of means ($\overline{X}_0$ versus $\overline{X}_1$, $\overline{X}_0$ versus $\overline{X}_2$, and $\overline{X}_1$ versus $\overline{X}_2$).

In Excerpt 14.7, we see the results of a real study that used a one-way repeated-measures ANOVA. The data summarized by this table came from 57 individuals who independently rated photographs of 17 buildings in San Francisco. The

EXCERPT 14.7 • *Results of a One-Way Repeated Measures ANOVA Presented in a Summary Table*

TABLE 1   *Analysis of Variance*

Source	SS	df	MS	F	p
Respondents	1714	56	30.6		
Stimuli	449	16	28.1	14.3	<.001
Residual	1752	896	1.96		
Total	3915	968			

Source: A. E. Stumps. (2000). Evaluating architectural design review. *Perceptual and Motor Skills, 90,* p. 269.

F- and *p*-values on the second row of the table indicate that the average scores for the various scenes differed more than would be expected by chance. Note that only one *F*-ratio appears in the ANOVA summary table, for there is only one true factor in this study, stimuli (i.e., photographs).

Although it is helpful to be able to look at the ANOVA summary table, researchers often must delete such a table from their reports because of space considerations. In Excerpt 14.8, we see how the results of a one-way repeated measures ANOVA were presented wholly within the text of the report. Note how a post hoc test was used to compare the three group means because (1) the omnibus *F*-test yielded a statistically significant result and (2) more than two means were being compared.

EXCERPT 14.8 • *Results of a One-Way Repeated Measures ANOVA Presented without an ANOVA Summary Table*

A one-way repeated measures ANOVA revealed an effect of condition ($F(2, 34) = 18.4$, $p < .0001$). Tukey's HSD revealed that the Complete condition was not significantly different to the Organized condition ($p > .05$) but the Disorganized condition was significantly slower than both of these ($p < .05$).

Source: A. P. Banks and L. J. Millward. (2000). Running shared mental models as a distributed cognitive process. *British Journal of Psychology, 91*(4), p. 524.

Sometimes researchers will apply a one-way repeated measures ANOVA more than once within the same study. They do this for one of two reasons. On one hand, each participant in the study may have provided two or more pieces of data at each level of the repeated measures factor, with each of these scores corresponding to a different dependent variable. Given this situation, the researcher may utilize a separate one-way repeated measures ANOVA to analyze the data corresponding to each dependent variable. On the other hand, the researcher may have two or more groups of participants, with just one score collected from each of them at each level of the within-subjects factor. Here, the researcher may decide to subject the data provided by each group to a separate one-way repeated measures ANOVA. Excerpt 14.9 illustrates the first of these two situations.

EXCERPT 14.9 • *Two One-Way Repeated Measures ANOVAs Used with Different Dependent Variables*

Data were analyzed using one-way, repeated measures analysis of variance (ANOVA) and eta-squared effect size. Post-hoc comparisons were conducted as needed in the form of pair-wise contrasts between the baseline and each training period mean. . . . Vocal engagement increased significantly over time [$F(3, 17) = 4.51$, $p = .017$; $\eta^2 = .44$]. Post-hoc comparisons located differences between the baseline and all three training periods: for baseline and Training 1, results showed $F(1, 19) = 5.16$, $p = .035$; baseline and Training 2 yielded $F(1, 19) = 12.67$, $p = .002$; and for baseline and Training 3, $F(1, 19) = 9.55$, $p = .006$. Physical engagement increased over time, but not significantly [$F(3, 17) = 1.10$, $p = .377$; $\eta^2 = .16$].

Source: A. P. Banks and L. J. Millward. (2001). An in-service training program in music for child-care personnel working with infants and toddlers. *Journal of Research in Music Education, 49*(1), pp. 14–15.

The Presentation Order of Levels of the Within-Subjects Factor

The factor in a one-way repeated measures ANOVA can take one of three basic forms. In some studies, the within-subjects factor corresponds to time, with the levels of the factor indicating the different points in time at which data are collected. The second kind of within-subjects factor corresponds to different treatments or conditions given to or created for the participants, with a measurement taken on each person under each treatment or condition. The third kind of within-subjects factor is found in studies where each participant is asked to rate different things, take different tests, or in some other way provide scores on different dependent variables.

If the one-way repeated measures ANOVA involves data collected at different points in time, there is only one order in which the data can be collected. If, however, the within-subjects factor corresponds to treatment conditions or different dependent variables, then there are different ways in which the data can be collected. When an option exists regarding the order in which the levels of the factor are presented, the researcher's decision regarding this aspect of the study should be taken into consideration when *you* make a decision as to whether or not to accept the researcher's findings.

If the various treatment conditions, things to be rated, or tests to be taken are presented in the same order, then a systematic bias may creep into the study and function to make it extremely difficult—or impossible—to draw clear conclusions from the statistical results. The systematic bias might take the form of a **practice effect,** with participants performing better as they warm up or learn from what they have already done; a **fatigue effect,** with participants performing less well on subsequent tasks simply because they get bored or tired; or **confounding** with things that the participants do or learn outside the study's setting between the points at which the study's data are collected. Whatever its form, such bias can cause different treatment conditions (or the different versions of a measuring device) to look different when they are really alike or to look alike when they are really dissimilar.

To prevent the study from being wrecked by practice effects, fatigue effects, and confounding due to order effects, a researcher should alter the order in which the treatment conditions, tasks, questionnaires, rating forms, or whatever are presented to participants. This can be done in one of three ways. One design strategy is to randomize the order in which the levels of the within-subjects factor are presented. A second strategy is to utilize all possible presentation orders, with an equal proportion of the participants assigned randomly to each possible order. The third strategy involves counterbalancing the order in which the levels of the repeated measures factor are presented; here, the researchers make sure that each level of the factor appears equally often in any of the ordered positions.

In Excerpt 14.10, we see an example of how a pair of researchers randomized and **counterbalanced** the order in which the study's participants performed two tasks. (The two tasks were pitching horseshoes at a stake that was either tall or short.) The task order was counterbalanced because half of the participants performed the easy task prior to the hard task, while others performed the hard task before the easy task. The order was randomized because participants were randomly assigned to one or the other of the two task orders.

Carry-Over Effects

In studies where the repeated-measures factor is related to different kinds of treatments, the influence of one treatment might interfere with the assessment of how

Research
Navigator.c⊕m
Practice effect
Fatigue effect
Confounding

Research
Navigator.c⊕m
Counterbalanced

EXCERPT 14.10 • *Varying the Order in Which Tasks Are Presented*

Primary task performance during baseline performance trials was examined using a one-way repeated measures (RM) analysis of variance (ANOVA), with level of difficulty as the independent variable. . . . Participants either completed all trials of the difficult task before completing all trials of the easy task or vice-versa. This order was randomized and counterbalanced across the pool of participants.

Source: A. M. Prezuhy and J. L. Etnier. (2001). Attentional patterns of horseshoe pitchers at two levels of task difficulty. *Research Quarterly for Exercise and Sport, 72*(3), pp. 294, 296.

the next treatment works. If so, such a **carry-over effect** will interfere with the comparative evaluation of the various treatments. Even if the order of the treatments is varied, the disruptive influence of carry-over effects can make certain treatments appear to be more or less potent than they really are.

One way researchers can reduce or eliminate the problem of carry-over effects is to delay presenting the second treatment until after the first treatment has "run its course." In a recent study, Alzheimer patients took three different kinds of pills, with each kind of pill taken for four consecutive weeks. Between each set of four weeks, however, the patients took no pills whatsoever. These so-called "washout" weeks were built into the study to allow the effects of each of the drugs to wear off before the patient began taking the next drug.

The Sphericity Assumption

In order for a one-way repeated measures ANOVA to yield an *F*-test that is valid, an important assumption must hold true. This is called the **sphericity assumption,** and it should be considered by *every* researcher who uses this form of ANOVA. Even though the same amount of data will be collected for each level of the repeated measures factor, the *F*-test of a one-way repeated measures ANOVA is *not* robust to violations of the sphericity assumption. To be more specific, the *F*-value from this ANOVA will turn out to be too large to the extent that this assumption is violated.

The sphericity assumption says that the population variances associated with the levels of the repeated measures factor, in combination with the population correlations between pairs of levels, must represent one of a set of acceptable patterns. One of the acceptable patterns is for all the population variances to be identical and for all the bivariate correlations to be identical. There are, however, other patterns of variances and correlations that adhere to the requirements of sphericity.

The sample data collected in any one-factor repeated measures investigation can be used to test the sphericity assumption. This test was developed by J. W. Mauchly in 1940, and researchers now refer to it as the Mauchly sphericity test. If the application of **Mauchly's test** yields a statistically significant result (thus suggesting that the condition of sphericity does not exist), there are various things the researcher can do in an effort to help avoid making a Type I error when the one-way repeated measures ANOVA is used to test the null hypothesis of equal population means across the levels of the repeated measures factor. The two most popular strategies both involve using a smaller pair of *df* values to determine the critical *F*-value used to evaluate the calculated *F*-value. This adjustment results in a larger critical value and a greater likelihood that a fail-to-reject decision will be made when the null hypothesis of the one-way repeated measures ANOVA is evaluated.

One of the two ways to adjust the *df* values is to use a simple procedure developed by two statisticians, S. Geisser and S. W. Greenhouse. Their procedure involves basing the critical *F*-value on the *df* values that would have been appropriate if there had been just two levels of the repeated measures factor. This creates a drastic reduction in the critical value's *df*s, because it presumes that the sphericity assumption is violated to the maximum extent. Thus the **Geisser-Greenhouse** approach to dealing with significant departures from sphericity creates a **conservative *F*-test** (since the true Type I error rate will be smaller than that suggested by the level of significance).

The second procedure for adjusting the degrees of freedom involves first using the sample data to estimate how extensively the sphericity assumption is violated. This step leads to ε, a fraction that turns out to be smaller than 1.0 to the extent that the sample data suggest that the sphericity assumption is violated. Then, the "regular" *df* values associated with the *F*-test are multiplied by ε, thus producing adjusted *df* values and a critical value that are tailor-made for the study being conducted. When researchers use this second procedure, they often report that they have used the **Huynh-Feldt correction.**

In Excerpts 14.11 and 14.12, we see two cases in which the researchers took corrective action after the sphericity assumption was tested and found not to be tenable. In the first of these excerpts, the Geisser-Greenhouse procedure was used. In Excerpt 14.12, the sample data were first examined to see how extensively the assumption was likely to be violated, and then the Huynh-Feldt correction was applied. In both of these studies, the degrees of freedom associated with the critical value got smaller, thereby making the critical value larger. This change in the critical value eliminated the positive bias in the *F*-test that would have existed (due to a lack of sphericity) if the regular critical value had been used.

Regardless of which strategy is used to deal with the sphericity assumption, I want to reiterate my earlier statement that this is an important assumption for the ANOVAs being discussed in this chapter. If a researcher conducts a repeated measures ANOVA and does not say anything at all about the sphericity assumption, the conclusions drawn from that investigation probably ought to be considered with a *big* grain of salt. If the data analysis produces a statistically significant finding when no test of sphericity is conducted or no adjustment is made to the critical value's *df*, you have the full right to disregard the inferential claims made by the researcher.

EXCERPTS 14.11–14.12 • *The Sphericity Assumption*

Mauchly's test of sphericity was significant (Mauchly's $W = 0.643$, $df = 2$, $p < 0.01$) thus the more conservative Greenhouse-Geisser test was used for the analyses.

Source: R. J. R. Blair, E. Colledge, and D. G. V. Mitchell. (2001). Somatic markers and response reversal: Is there orbitofrontal cortex dysfunction in boys with psychopathic tendencies? *Journal of Abnormal Child Psychology, 29*(6), p. 505.

When tests of sphericity were violated, the Huynh-Feldt statistic was used.

Source: K. A. Phillips, R. S. Albertini, S. A. Rasmussen. (2002). A randomized placebo-controlled trial of fluoxetine in body dysmorphic disorder. *Archives of General Psychiatry, 59*(4), p. 383.

Two-Way Repeated Measures ANOVAs

We now turn our attention to ANOVAs that contain two repeated measures factors. As you will see, there are many similarities between this kind of ANOVA and the kind we examined in Chapter 13. However, there are important differences between two-way ANOVAs that do or don't involve repeated measures. For this reason, you need to be able to distinguish between these two kinds of analysis.

If researchers state that they have used a two-way ANOVA but say nothing about repeated measures, then you should presume that it is the kind of ANOVA we considered in Chapter 13. On the other hand, if researchers use the phrase "repeated measures," "within-subjects," or "within-participants" when describing each of their ANOVA's two factors, then you will need to remember the things you will learn in this section of the book. Excerpts 14.13 and 14.14 illustrate how researchers usually provide a tip-off that they used a two-way ANOVA with repeated measures.

Purpose

The purpose of a two-way repeated measures ANOVA is identical to the purpose of a two-way ANOVA not having repeated measures. In each case, the researcher uses inferential statistics to help assess three null hypotheses. The first of these null hypotheses deals with the main effect of one of the two factors. The second null hypothesis deals with the main effect of the second factor. The third null hypothesis deals with the interaction between the two factors.

Although two-way ANOVAs with and without repeated measures are identical in the number and nature of null hypotheses that are evaluated, they differ in two

EXCERPTS 14.13–14.14 • *Different Labels for a Two-Way Repeated Measures ANOVA*

Repeated measures analysis of variance (ANOVA) procedures were used to examine the effects of task (breathing vs. speaking) and condition (room air vs. tank air vs. CO_2) on each [dependent] variable.

Source: E. F. Bailey and J. D. Hoit. (2002). Speaking and breathing in high respiratory drive. *Journal of Speech, Language, and Hearing Research, 45*(1), p. 91.

- -

A 2×2 analysis of variance (ANOVA) was performed on the RT data, with Prime Type (morphemic vs. semantic) and Relatedness (related vs. unrelated) as within-subject factors.

Source: C. MacNevin and D. Besner. (2002). When are morphemic and semantic priming observed in visual word recognition? *Canadian Journal of Experimental Psychology, 56*(2), p. 115.

main respects. In terms of the way data are collected, the kind of two-way ANOVA considered in Chapter 13 requires that each participant be positioned in a single cell, with only one score per person going into the data analysis. In contrast, a two-way repeated measures ANOVA requires that each participant travel across all cells created by the two factors, with each person being measured once within *each* cell. (Such was the case in the study described in Excerpt 14.13. Each person in that investigation contributed six scores to the analysis (of each dependent variable), with each of those six scores being a measure of lung performance under one of the study's six conditions. Those six conditions were created by having the research participants either sit quietly or read some printed material while breathing room air, air from a tank with a normal level of CO_2, or air from a tank with a high level of CO_2.

The second main difference between two-way ANOVAs with and without repeated measures involves the ANOVA summary table. We will return to this second difference in the next section when we consider how researchers present the results of their two-way repeated measures ANOVAs. Right now, we need to concentrate on the three null hypotheses dealt with by this ANOVA and the way the necessary data must be collected.

To help you gain insight into the three null hypotheses of any two-way repeated measures ANOVA, let's consider an imaginary study. This study will involve the game "Simon," which is a battery-operated device with four colored buttons. After the player flips the start switch, a sequence of Simon's buttons lights up, with each light accompanied by a unique tone. The task of the person playing this game involves (1) watching and listening to what Simon does and then, after Simon stops, (2) pushing the same sequence of buttons that Simon just illuminated.

Suppose now that you are the player. If the red button on Simon lights up, you must press the red button. Then, if the red button lights up first followed by the green button, you must press these same two buttons in this same order to stay in the game. Every time you successfully mimic what Simon does, you'd receive a new string of lighted buttons that is like the previous one, and the new sequence would be one light longer. At first, it would be easy for you do duplicate Simon's varied but short sequences. But after the sequences lengthen, you would find it more and more difficult to mimic Simon.

For my study, imagine that I have each of six people play Simon. The dependent variable will be the length of the longest sequence that the player successfully duplicates. (For example, if the player works up to the point where he or she correctly mimics an eight-light sequence but fails on the ninth light, that person's score would be 8.) After three practice rounds, I would then ask each person to play Simon four times, each under a different condition defined by my study's two factors: tones and words. The two levels of the tones factor would be on and off, meaning that the Simon device would be set up either to provide the auditory cues or to be silent while the player played. The two levels of the word factor would be color names or people names. With color names, the player would be instructed to say out loud the color of the lights as Simon presents them in a sequence. (Those colors are red, blue, green, and yellow.) With people names, the player would be instructed to say out loud one of these names for each color: Ron for red, Barb for blue, Greg for green, and Yoko for yellow. Finally, imagine that I randomly arrange the order in which the four conditions of my study are ordered for each of the six Simon players.

Figure 14.2 contains the scores from my hypothetical study, with the order of each person's four scores arranged so as to fit accurately under the column headings. This figure also contains a 2 × 2 matrix of the four cell means, with the main effect means positioned on the right and bottom sides of the cell means.

As indicated earlier, there are three null hypotheses associated with any two-way repeated measures ANOVA. In our hypothetical study, the null hypothesis for the main effect of tones would state that there is no difference, in the populations associated with our samples, between the mean performance on the Simon game when players hear the tone cues as compared to when they don't hear the tone cues. In a similar fashion, the null hypothesis for the main effect of words would state that there is no difference, in the populations associated with our samples, between the mean performance on the Simon game when players say color words when trying to memorize each sequence as compared to when they say people's names. Finally, the interaction null hypotheses would state the positive (or negative) impact on players of having the tone cues is the same regardless of whether they are having to say color names or people names as Simon's buttons light up.

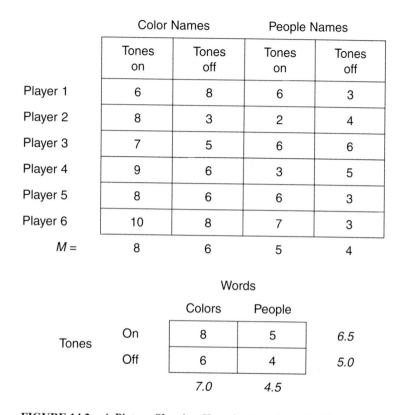

	Color Names		People Names	
	Tones on	Tones off	Tones on	Tones off
Player 1	6	8	6	3
Player 2	8	3	2	4
Player 3	7	5	6	6
Player 4	9	6	3	5
Player 5	8	6	6	3
Player 6	10	8	7	3
M =	8	6	5	4

Words

		Colors	People	
Tones	On	8	5	*6.5*
	Off	6	4	*5.0*
		7.0	*4.5*	

FIGURE 14.2 *A Picture Showing How the Data from the Simon Study Would Be Arranged*

The lower portion of Figure 14.2 shows the four cell means and the two main effect means for each of the two factors. The null hypothesis for tones would be rejected if the means of 6.5 and 5.0 are found to be further apart from each other than we would expect by chance. Likewise, the null hypothesis for words would be rejected if the means of 7.0 and 4.5 are found to be further apart from each other than would be expected by chance. The interaction null hypothesis would be rejected if the difference between the cell means on the top row (8 − 5 = 3) varies more from the difference between the cell means on the bottom row (6 − 4 = 2) than would be expected by chance.

Illustrations such as that presented in the upper portion of Figure 14.2 rarely appear in research reports. However, it is usually quite easy to construct pictures of cell means and main effect means. This picture-constructing task is easy because you almost always will be given information as to (1) the factors and levels involved in the study, (2) the nature of the dependent variable, and (3) the sample means. Having such a picture is highly important, for a study's results are inextricably tied to its table of cell and main effect means.

Presentation of Results

Occasionally, the results of a two-way repeated measures ANOVA will be presented using an ANOVA summary table. In Table 14.2, I have prepared such a table for the Simon study.

The summary table shown in Table 14.2 is similar, in some very important ways, to the two-way ANOVA summary tables contained in Chapter 13. Most importantly, it contains three calculated *F*-values, one for the main effect of words, one for the main effect of tones, and one for the words-by-tones interaction. These three *F*-values speak directly to the null hypotheses discussed in the previous section.

There are two main differences between the summary table shown in Table 14.2 and the summary tables we examined in Chapter 13. First, there are three error rows in Table 14.2, whereas there is just one such row in the summary table for a two-way ANOVA without repeated measures. If you will look closely at the workings inside Table 14.2, you will see that the *MS* for error 1 is used to obtain the calculated *F*-value for words, that the *MS* for error 2 is used to obtain the calculated *F*-value for tones, and that the *MS* for error 3 is used to obtain the calculated *F*-value for the interaction.[2]

The second difference between Table 14.2 and the ANOVA summary tables contained in Chapter 13 concerns the meaning of the *df* for total. As you can see,

TABLE 14.2   *ANOVA Summary Table of Performance Scores on Simon*

Source	*df*	*SS*	*MS*	*F*
Players	5	15.5	3.1	
Words	1	37.5	37.5	19.74*
Error 1	5	9.5	1.9	
Tones	1	13.5	13.5	12.27**
Error 2	5	5.5	1.1	
Words × tones	1	1.5	1.5	.29
Error 3	5	25.5	5.1	
Total	23	108.5		

*$p < .01$. **$p < .05$.

[2]The *df* numbers for these error rows are all equal to 5, but they were computed differently. Each was found by multiplying together the *df* for players and the *df* for the row immediately above the error being considered. For example, the *df* for error 2 was found by multiplying $df_{Players}$ by df_{Tones}.

this *df* number is equal to 23. If this were a regular two-way ANOVA, you could add 1 to df_{Total} in order to figure out how many people were in the study. You can't do that here, obviously, because there were only six people who functioned as players in our Simon study, yet df_{Total} is much larger than this. The problem gets solved completely when you realize that in all ANOVA summary tables, adding 1 to df_{Total} gives you the total number of pieces of data that were analyzed. That is true for ANOVAs with and without repeated measures. If there are no repeated measures, then the number of pieces of data will be the same as the number of people (for each person provides, in those cases, just one score). When there *are* repeated measures, however, you must remember that adding 1 to the *df* for the top row of the summary table (not the bottom row) will allow you to know how many people were involved.

If you ever encounter a summary table like that presented in Table 14.2, do not overlook the valuable information sitting in front of you. From such a table, you can determine how many people were involved in the study ($5 + 1 = 6$), what the dependent variable was (performance on the Simon game), what the two factors were (tones and words) and how many levels made up each factor ($1 + 1 = 2$ in each case), how many total pieces of data were involved in the analysis ($23 + 1 = 24$), and which null hypotheses were rejected.

In Excerpt 14.15, we see how a team of researchers summarized the results of their two-way repeated measures ANOVA in the text of their report. Note that this passage is extremely similar to the textual summary of a two-way ANOVA without repeated measures. There are two factors, three *F*-tests (two for main effects and one for the interaction), and a post hoc investigation applied to the main effect means of the three-level factor that turned out to be statistically significant.

EXCERPT 14.15 • *Results of a Two-Way Repeated Measures ANOVA Presented without an ANOVA Summary Table*

Mean azimuth errors were analyzed using a 2 (Hearing Aid) $\times$ 3 (Source Elevation) repeated-measures analysis of variance (ANOVA), employing the Huynh-Feldt correction to guard against violations of sphericity, which revealed significant main effects of Hearing Aid, $F(1, 5) = 16.13$, $p < .05$, and Source Elevation, $F(2, 10) = 33.78$, $p < .05$. The interaction was not significant ($p > .05$). A small increase in azimuth error from 17.8% unaided to 19.8% aided was observed and was responsible for the main effect of Hearing Aid. The main effect of source elevation was further investigated by means of post hoc pairwise Bonferroni-corrected t tests, indicating a difference in azimuth error between the peri-horizontal condition and both the upper- and lower-hemisphere conditions ($p < .05$).

Source: W. R. D'Angelo, R. S. Bolia, P. J. Mishler, and L. J. Morris. (2001). Effects of CIC hearing aids on auditory localization by listeners with normal hearing. *Journal of Speech, Language, and Hearing Research, 44*(6), p. 1212.

Although the ANOVA discussed in Excerpt 14.15 resembles, in many ways, the kind of two-way ANOVA considered in Chapter 13, there are two important differences. First, the researchers associated with Excerpt 14.15 demonstrated a concern for the sphericity assumption. (ANOVAs without repeated measures do not have this assumption.) Second, the *df* values for the three *F*-tests are not the same. The first of the two *df* numbers next to each *F*, of course, are not the same simply because there were two levels in one factor and three levels in the other factor. However, look at the second *df* next to each *F*. These *df*s vary because there were three different values for MS_{Error} involved in this analysis, each of which was used as the researchers (or a computer) calculated one of three *F*-ratios. Had this been a two-way ANOVA without repeated measures, just one MS_{Error} would have been used to get all three of the *F*s, thus causing each *F*'s second *df* to be equal to the same value.

Turning now to Excerpt 14.16, we see the summary of a 2 × 4 repeated measures ANOVA. This portion of the research report is important to read, for it shows another similarity between two-way ANOVAs with repeated measures and two-way ANOVAs without repeated measures. This similarity concerns what researchers typically do when the interaction turns out to be statistically significant. Note here that the significant interaction prompted the researchers to (1) refrain from interpreting the main effect *F*s and (2) conduct a post hoc investigation of the interaction. To probe the interaction, the researchers conducted tests of simple main effects, first comparing the four levels of Exposure at the first level of VF, and then

EXCERPT 14.16 • *Probing the Interaction of a Two-Way Repeated Measures ANOVA*

A two-way ANOVA was conducted on familiarity ratings with the repeated measures factors VF and Exposure. The main effect of VF was not significant ($F(1, 37) = 3.52$, $p < .07$). The main effect of Exposure was significant ($F(3, 111) = 9.89, p < .0001$) and was qualified by the VF × Exposure interaction ($F(3, 111) = 6.83, p < .0005$). For the LVF, familiarity ratings were highest for the faces presented the most frequently, as would be expected (effect of Exposure for LVF, $F(3, 111) = 10.71, p < .0001$; rating for eight exposures was greater than ratings for one and two exposures, Tukey's HSD, $ps < .01$; no significant difference between four and eight exposures). However, for the RVF, familiarity ratings were less systematic, with the highest familiarity ratings for faces presented four times (main effect of Exposure for RVF, $F(3, 111) = 5.99, p < .001$; rating for 4 exposures was greater than for one, two, and eight exposures, Tukey's HSD, $ps < .02$).

Source: R. J. Compton, S. Williamson, S. G. Murphy, and W. Heller. (2002). Hemispheric differences in affective response: Effects of mere exposure. *Social Cognition, 20*(1), pp. 7–8.

comparing those same four levels of Exposure at the second level of VF. Because these two tests yielded statistically significant *F*-ratios, the researchers used the Tukey HSD test to make pairwise comparisons among the four cell means involved in each test of simple main effects.

The Presentation Order of Different Tasks

Earlier in this chapter, we indicated how a repeated measures factor can take one of three basic forms: different points in time, different treatment conditions, or different dependent variables. With a two-way repeated measures ANOVA, any combination of these three kinds of factors is possible. The most popular combinations, however, involve either (1) two factors, each of which is defined by different versions (i.e., levels) of a treatment, or (2) one treatment factor and one factor that involves measurements taken at different points in time.

When the levels of one or both factors in a two-way repeated measures ANOVA correspond with different treatment conditions or different dependent variables, those levels should not be presented to the research participants in the same order. If they were, certain problems (such as a practice effect or a fatigue effect) might develop. And if that happened, the meaning of the *F*-tests involving the repeated measures factor(s) would be muddied.

As indicated earlier in this chapter, researchers ought to use different presentation orders for the levels of factors that involve different treatments, tasks, or tests. In Excerpt 14.17, we see a case that illustrates the technique of randomizing the orders in which treatment conditions occur. As you will see, this passage comes from that same research report from which Excerpt 14.15 was drawn.

EXCERPT 14.17 • *Different Presentation Orders in a Two-Way Repeated Measures ANOVA*

Two hearing-aid conditions (unoccluded, CIC hearing aid) were combined factorially with three source-elevation conditions (upper hemisphere, peri-horizontal region, lower hemisphere) for a total of six experimental conditions. A repeated measures design was employed so that each of the listeners participated in all six conditions. . . . The order in which the experimental sessions were conducted was randomized.

Source: W. R. D'Angelo, R. S. Bolia, P. J. Mishler, and L. J. Morris. (2001). Effects of CIC hearing aids on auditory localization by listeners with normal hearing. *Journal of Speech, Language, and Hearing Research, 44*(6), pp. 1211–1212.

The Sphericity Assumption

The calculated *F*-values that are computed in a two-way repeated measure ANOVA will turn out to be too large unless the population variances and correlations that correspond to the sample data conform to one or more acceptable patterns. This is the case even though the sample variances and correlations in a two-way repeated measures ANOVA are based upon sample sizes that are equal (a condition brought about by measuring the same subjects repeatedly). Therefore it is important that researchers, when using this kind of ANOVA, attend to the assumption concerning population variances and correlations. This assumption is popularly referred to as the sphericity assumption.

Any of three strategies can be used when dealing with sphericity assumption. As is the case with a one-way repeated measures ANOVA, the researcher can (1) subject the sample data to Mauchly's test for sphericity, (2) bypass Mauchly's test and instead use the Geisser-Greenhouse conservative *df*s for locating the critical value needed to evaluate the calculated *F*-values, or (3) utilize the sample data to compute ε (the index that estimates how badly the sphericity assumption is violated) and then reduce the critical value(s) *df*s to the extent indicated by the ε index.

If you take another look at Excerpt 14.15, you will see a case in which the third of these strategies was used in conjunction with a 2 × 3 repeated measures ANOVA. In that passage, the researchers indicate that they used the Huynh-Feldt correction to guard against violations of the sphericity assumption. The researchers who conducted that study, and others who use this or some other strategy to deal with this important assumption, deserve your respect for conducting their analysis with concern for sphericity. On the other hand, you should give demerits to those researchers who give no indication of knowing or caring about this important assumption.

Practical versus Statistical Significance

Throughout this book, I have tried to emphasize repeatedly the important point that statistical significance may or may not signify practical significance. Stated differently, a small *p* does not necessarily indicate that a research discovery is big and important. In this section, I'd like to show that well-trained researchers who use two-way repeated measures ANOVAs do *not* use the simple six-step version of hypothesis testing.

There are several options available to the researcher who is concerned about the meaningfulness of his or her findings. These options can be classified into two categories: *a priori* and post hoc. In the first category, one option involves conducting an *a priori* power analysis for the purpose of determining the proper sample size. A second option in that category involves checking to see if there is adequate power for a fixed sample size that already exists. In the post hoc category, the three options involve using the study's sample data to estimate effect sizes, strength of association indices, or the power of the completed analysis.

In Excerpt 14.18, we see a case in which a post hoc strategy was used to address the issue of practical significance. The specific technique used in this study was the computation of eta squared. According to the criteria established for interpreting values of η^2, the two main effects in this study each reflected a large deviation from the null hypothesis under investigation. (Those criteria, you may recall, are as follows: .01 = small, .06 = medium, and .15 = large.)

EXCERPT 14.18 • *Practical versus Statistical Significance*

The likelihood ratings for the alternative cause were analyzed using a 2 × 3 (Belief × ΔP) repeated measures ANOVA. This analysis revealed a significant main effect of belief, $F(1, 71) = 40.77$, $MSE = 1,056.67$, $\eta^2 = .37$, where causality judgments for the alternative cause were greater for the believable alternatives ($M = 60.2$) than for the unbelievable alternatives ($M = 40.2$). There was also a main effect of ΔP, $F(2, 142) = 50.0$, $MSE = 1,004.62$, $\eta^2 = .41$, where causality judgments for the alternative cause increased as a function of increases in ΔP ($Ms = 32.8$, 47.8, and 70.0). The Belief × ΔP interaction was not significant ($F < 1$).

Source: J. A. Fugelsang and V. A. Thompson. (2001). Belief-based and covariation-based cues affect causal discounting. *Canadian Journal of Experimental Psychology,* 55(1), p. 74.

Two-Way Mixed ANOVAs

Research
Navigator.c⊕m

Two-way mixed
ANOVA

We now turn our attention to the third and final kind of ANOVA to be considered in this chapter. It is called a **two-way mixed ANOVA.** The word *mixed* is included in its label because one of the two factors is between subjects in nature while the other factor is within subjects.

Labels for This Kind of ANOVA

Unfortunately, all researchers do not use the same label (that is, *two-way mixed ANOVA*) to describe the kind of ANOVA that has one between-subjects factor and one within-subjects factor. Therefore, the first thing you need to do relative to two-way mixed ANOVAs is familiarize yourself with the different ways researchers indicate that they have used this kind of ANOVA. If you don't do this, you might be looking at a study that involves a two-way mixed ANOVA and not even realize it!

When researchers use a two-way mixed ANOVA, some of them refer to it as a **two-way ANOVA with repeated measures on one factor.** Others call it an

ANOVA with one between-subjects factor and one within-subjects factor. Occasionally it is called a **split-plot ANOVA** or a **two-factor between-within ANOVA.** In Excerpts 14.19 through 14.22, we see four different ways researchers chose to describe the two factor mixed ANOVA that they used.

EXCERPTS 14.19–14.22 • *Different Labels for a Two-Way Mixed ANOVA*

The practice data were analyzed in a 2 (Groups) × 10 (Blocks) analysis of variance (ANOVA) with repeated measures on the last factor.

Source: G. Wulf, N. H. McNevin, T. Fuchs, F. Ritter, and T. Toole. (2000). Attentional focus in complex skill learning. *Research Quarterly for Exercise and Sport, 71*(3), p. 232.

- -

A 3 × 2 factorial design was used. Type of interpolated activity (same word stems, different word stems, or nonverbal control) was varied between subjects, and type of test (word stem completion or free recall) was a within-subject factor.

Source: S. Martens and G. Wolters. (2002). Interference in implicit memory caused by processing of interpolated material. *American Journal of Psychology, 115*(2), pp. 172–173.

- -

The data were submitted to a two-way ANOVA with Group (AD/HD vs. controls) as the between-participants factor and Trial Length (5, 10, 15 s) as the within-participants factor.

Source: E. J. S. Sonuga-Barke. (2002). Interval length and time-use by children with AD/HD: A comparison of four models. *Journal of Abnormal Child Psychology, 30*(3), p. 260.

- -

To test Hypothesis 2, we applied a between/within ANOVA, with condition (order of influence) as the between variable [and] agent/no-agent as the within variable.

Source: R. Schneider, M. Binder, and H. Walach. (2001). A two-person effort: On the role of the agent in EDA-DMILS experiments. *Journal of Parapsychology, 65*(3), p. 284.

Data Layout and Purpose

To understand the results of a two-way mixed ANOVA, you must be able to conceptualize the way the data were arranged prior to being analyzed. Whenever you deal with this kind of ANOVA, try to think of (or actually draw) a picture similar to the one displayed in Figure 14.3. This picture is set up for an extremely small-scale study, but it illustrates how each participant is measured repeatedly across levels of the within-subjects factor but not across levels of the between-subjects factor. In this picture, of course, the between-subjects factor is gender and the within-subjects factor is time of day. The scores are hypothetical, and they are meant to reflect the data that might be collected if we asked each of five males and five females to give us a self-rating of his or her typical energy level (on a 0–10 scale) at each of three points during the day: 8 A.M., 2 P.M., and 8 P.M.

Although a two-way mixed ANOVA always involves one between-subjects factor and one within-subjects factor, the number of levels in each factor will vary from study to study. In other words, the dimensions and labeling of Figure 14.3 only match our hypothetical two-way mixed ANOVA in which there is a two-level between-subjects factor, a three-level within-subjects factor, and five participants per group. Our picture can easily be adapted to fit *any* two-way mixed ANOVA because we can change the number of main rows and columns, the number of mini-rows (to indicate the number of participants involved), and the terms used to reflect the names of the factors and levels involved in the study.

The purpose of a two-way mixed ANOVA is identical to that of a completely between-subjects two-way ANOVA or of a completely within-subjects two-way ANOVA. In general, that purpose can be described as examining the sample means to see if they are further apart than would be expected by chance. Most researchers

Time of Day

Gender		8 A.M.	2 P.M.	8 P.M.
Male	Participant 1	6	3	8
	Participant 2	7	6	8
	Participant 3	4	2	10
	Participant 4	8	5	10
	Participant 5	5	4	9
Female	Participant 6	8	5	9
	Participant 7	6	6	7
	Participant 8	8	4	8
	Participant 9	7	4	9
	Participant 10	6	6	7

FIGURE 14.3   *Picture of the Data Layout for a 2 × 3 Mixed ANOVA*

take this general purpose and make it more specific by setting up and testing three null hypotheses. These null hypotheses, of course, focus on the populations relevant to the investigation, with the three null statements asserting that (1) the main effect means of the first factor are equal to one another, (2) the main effect means of the second factor are equal to one another, and (3) the two factors do not interact.

To help you understand these three null hypotheses, I have taken the data from Figure 14.3, computed main effect means and cell means, and positioned these means in the following picture:

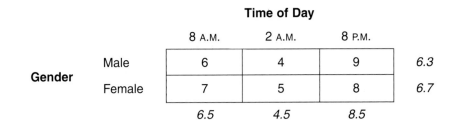

One of our three research questions concerns the main effect of gender. To answer this question, the mean of 6.3 (based on the 15 scores provided by the five males) will be compared against the mean of 6.7 (based on the 15 scores provided by the 5 females). The second research question, concerning the main effect of time of day, will be addressed through a statistical comparison of the column means of 6.5, 4.5, and 8.5 (each based on scores provided by all 10 participants). The third research question, dealing with the interaction between gender and time of day, will be dealt with by focusing on the six cell means (each based on five scores). This interaction question asks whether the change in the difference between the male and female means—which remains the same at 8 A.M. and 2 P.M. but then reverses itself at 8 P.M.—is greater than would be expected by chance sampling.

Presentation of Results

If the results of a two-way mixed ANOVA are presented in an ANOVA summary table, three *F*-values will be presented—two for the main effects and one for the interaction—just as is the case in the ANOVA summary tables for completely between-subjects and completely within-subjects ANOVAs. However, the summary table for mixed ANOVAs is set up differently from those associated with the ANOVAs considered earlier. To illustrate these differences, I have analyzed the energy level data originally shown in Figure 14.3. The results of this two-way mixed ANOVA are found in Table 14.3.

As Table 14.3 shows, the summary table for a mixed ANOVA has an upper section and a lower section. These two sections are often labeled **between subjects**

TABLE 14.3   *ANOVA Summary Table of the Energy Level Data Shown in Figure 14.3*

Source	df	SS	MS	F
Between Subjects	9			
Gender	1	0.83	0.83	0.50
Error (between)	8	13.34	1.67	
Within Subjects	20			
Time of day	2	80.00	40.00	28.17*
Gender × time of day	2	6.67	3.33	2.35
Error (within)	16	22.66	1.42	
Total	29	123.50		

*$p < .05$

and **within subjects,** respectively. In the upper section, there will be two rows of information, one concerning the main effect of the between-subjects factor and the other for the error that goes with the between-subjects main effect. In the lower section of the summary table, there will be three rows of information. The first of these rows is for the main effect of the within-subjects factor, the second is for the interaction between the two factors, and the third provides information for the within-subjects error term. As you can see from Table 14.3, the *MS* for the first error was used as a denominator in computing the *F*-value in the upper section of the summary table, while the *MS* for the second error was used as the denominator in computing the two *F*-values in the lower section.

Table 14.3 contains information that allows you to understand the structure of the study that provided the data for the two-way mixed ANOVA. To illustrate how you can extract this information from the table, pretend that you have not read anything about the study connected with Table 14.3. In other words, imagine that your first encounter with this study is this ANOVA summary table.

First of all, the *df* value for the between-subjects row of the table (9) allows you to know that data were gathered from 10 individuals. Second, the name of and the *df* value for the main effect in the upper portion of the table allow you to know that there were two groups in the study, with gender being the independent variable associated with this main effect. Third, the name of and *df* for the main effect in the lower portion of the table allow you to know that each of the 10 individuals was measured on three occasions, each being a particular time of the data. The table's title gives you a hint as to the kinds of scores used in this study, for you're told that this ANOVA was conducted on energy level data.

Table 14.3, of course, also contains the results of the ANOVA. To interpret these results, you now will need to look back and forth between the ANOVA summary table and the 2 × 3 table of cell and main effect means that we considered earlier. The first *F*-value (0.50) indicates that the two main effect means for males (6.3) and females (6.7) were not further apart from each other than we could expect by chance. Accordingly, the null hypothesis for gender was not rejected. The second *F*-value (28.17), on the other hand, shows that the null hypothesis for time of day was rejected. This finding came about because the main effect means of the within-subjects factor (6.5, 4.5, and 8.5) were further apart than could be expected by chance. The third *F*-value (2.35), for the interaction, was not statistically significant. Even though the differences between the male and female cell means were not constant across the data collection points during the day, the three male-female differences (-1.0, -1.0, and $+1.0$) did not vary enough to call into question the interaction null hypothesis.

Now let's consider Excerpt 14.23 which comes from a published study that used a 2×2 mixed ANOVA. There are two primary differences between the summary table shown in this excerpt and the one you saw earlier in Table 14.3. First, the upper and lower sections of the summary table in Excerpt 14.23 are not distinguished from each other by means of rows carrying the labels "between subjects" and "within subjects." (Nothing is really lost by not having those two rows, since

EXCERPT 14.23 • *Summary Table for Two-Way Mixed ANOVA*

TABLE 4 *Analysis of Variance for Postoperative Exercise Routine-Knowledge Test Knowledge Gain*

Source	Sum of Squares	df	Mean Square	F	p
Group (1, 2)	0.26	1	0.26	0.07	>.05
Error term	176.30	48	3.57		
Time (pre/post)	55.71	1	55.71	39.17	<.05
Group × time	1.95	1	1.95	1.37	>.05
Error term	68.29	48	1.42		

Source: A. Schrecengost. (2001). Do humorous preoperative teaching strategies work? *AORN Journal, 74*(5), p. 686.

[3]As illustrated in Table 14.3 and Excerpt 14.23, different terms are sometimes used to label the two rows that contain the *MS* values used as the denominators for the *F*s. You are likely to encounter ANOVA summary tables in which these two rows are labeled error 1 and error 2, error (a) and error (b), or error (b) and error (w). A few researchers label these error rows as "subjects within groups" and "_____ × subjects within groups," with the blank filled by the name of the within-subjects factor.

they do nothing more than *label* the two sections.) Second, each of the two error rows in Excerpt 14.23 is simply labeled "error term" whereas the terms *error between* and *error within* were used in Table 14.3. (Even though these two error rows in Excerpt 14.23 carry the same label, it is important to note that they are not interchangeable. The *MS* associated with the first of these errors was used as the denominator in computing the *F*-value that appears in the upper section of the table; in contrast, the *MS* associated with the second of these error rows was used as the denominator in computing each of the two *F*-values that appear in the lower section of the table.)[3]

Although it is helpful to be able to look at ANOVA summary tables when trying to decipher and critique research reports, such tables are usually not included in journal articles. Instead, the results are typically presented strictly within one or more paragraphs of textual material. To illustrate, consider Excerpt 14.24, wherein the results of a two-way mixed ANOVA are presented without a summary table.

Excerpt 14.24 is worth looking at closely for two reasons. First, it shows how *df* values can prove useful to you. Note that the first sentence says that a two-way ANOVA was used. It does not say "two-way *mixed* ANOVA" or "two-way ANOVA *with repeated measures on one factor*" or "two-way ANOVA *with one within-subjects factor.*" It just says "two-way ANOVA." The clear tip-off that a mixed ANOVA was used is that the second of the two *df* numbers next to the first *F* is 70 whereas the second of the two *df* numbers next to the other two *F*s is 210. If a regular two-way ANOVA had been used, each of the three *F*s would have had the same number as its second *df* number. The *df* numbers are also useful because they allow us to figure out, based on the first *F*'s pair of *df* numbers, that there were 75 children involved in this study.

EXCERPT 14.24 • *Results of a Two-way Mixed ANOVA Presented in the Text of the Research Report*

A two-way analysis of variance for age (3, 4, 5, 6, and 7 years) and quantity (zero, whole numbers, half, and quarter) showed main effects of age, $F(4, 70) = 22.65$, $p < .0001$, and quantity, $F(3, 210) = 93.33$, $p < .0001$. There was also an interaction between the factors, $F(12, 210) = 3.25$, $p < .0003$. Post-hoc Scheffé comparisons of the means ($p < .01$) showed that the age effect was different for each quantity. For whole numbers, zero, and half, the 4-, 5-, 6-, and 7-year-olds performed better than the 3-year-olds, but for quarter, only the 7-year-olds were more accurate than the other children.

Source: E. Bialystok and J. Codd. (2000). Representing quantity beyond whole numbers: Some, none, and part. *Canadian Journal of Experimental Psychology, 54*(2), p. 122.

The second reason for spending time with Excerpt 14.24 concerns the post hoc tests that were conducted. As with the other kinds of two-way ANOVAs that we considered earlier in this chapter and in Chapter 13, the statistically significant interaction in Excerpt 14.24 prompted the researchers to conduct a post hoc investigation. In doing this, sets of pairwise comparisons were made *within* each of the four levels of the quantity factor. In other words, these Scheffé contrasts compared the five age groups against each other, two at a time.

Related Issues

Earlier in this chapter, I indicated how the levels of within-subjects factors sometimes can and should be presented to subjects in varying orders. That discussion applies to mixed ANOVAs as well as to fully repeated measures ANOVAs. Excerpt 14.25 comes from a study where the three levels of the conditions factor were different kinds of auditory stimuli presented to people as they watched a movie. The study's dependent variable was brain-wave activity. As indicated in Excerpt 14.25, the order in which the three kinds of auditory stimuli were presented was counterbalanced. If three conditions had been presented in the same sequence to each of the study's participants, any effect of condition would have been confounded with order of presentation. Such confounding would have made it impossible to disentangle the effects of order and condition. By counterbalancing the presentation order of the conditions, the researchers eliminated such confounding from their study.

A second issue that you should keep in mind when examining the results of two-way mixed ANOVAs is the important assumption of **sphericity.** I discussed this assumption earlier when we considered fully repeated measures ANOVAs. It is relevant to mixed ANOVAs as well—but only the F-tests located in the within-subjects portion of the ANOVA summary are based upon the sphericity assumption. Thus the F-value for the main effect of the between-subjects factor is unaffected by a lack

Research
Navigator.c✿m

Sphericity

EXCERPT 14.25 • *Altering the Order in Which Levels of the Within-Subjects Factor Are Presented*

In addition, a repeated measures ANOVA of the peak latency of mismatch negativity was performed with group as the between-subject factor and condition as the within-subject factor. . . . The order of the three conditions was counterbalanced across the subjects.

Source: K. Kasai, K. Nakagome, K. Itoh, and I. Koshida. (2002). Impaired cortical network for preattentive detection of change in speech sounds in schizophrenia: A high-resolution event-related potential study. *American Journal of Psychiatry, 159*(4), pp. 547–548.

of sphericity in the populations connected to the study. In contrast, the *F*-values for the main effect of the within-subjects factor and for the interaction will be positively biased (i.e., turn out larger than they ought to) to the extent that the sphericity assumption is violated.

Well-trained researchers do not neglect the sphericity assumption when they use two-way mixed ANOVAs. Instead, they will do one of two things. One option is to adjust the degrees of freedom associated with the critical values (using the Geisser-Greenhouse or the Huynh-Feldt procedures), thereby compensating for possible or observed violation of the sphericity assumption. The other option is to apply Mauchly's test to the sample data to see if the assumption appears to be violated. In Excerpts 14.26 and 14.27, we see examples where researchers used these two options. Both sets of researchers deserve high marks for demonstrating a concern for the sphericity assumption.

A third issue to keep in mind when you encounter the results of two-way mixed ANOVAs concerns the distinction between statistical significance and practical significance. I first talked about this distinction in Chapter 7, and I have tried to bring up this issue as often as possible since then. I have done this because far too many researchers conduct studies that yield one or more findings that have very little practical significance even though a very low probability level is associated with the calculated value produced by their statistical test(s).

EXCERPTS 14.26–14.27 • *Option for Dealing with the Sphericity Assumption*

To address potential violations of the sphericity assumption in the ANOVAs, Greenhouse-Geisser-corrected degrees of freedom were employed in all *F*-tests involving main effects and interactions of repeated measures.

Source: T. P. Beauchaine, Z. Strassberg, M. R. Kees, and D. A. G. Drabick. (2002). Cognitive response repertoires to child noncompliance by mothers of aggressive boys. *Journal of Abnormal Child Psychology, 30*(1), p. 95.

- -

The data were initially examined using both Mauchly's Test of Sphericity and Levene's Test of Equality of Error Variances and the data satisfied the assumptions underlying a two factor ANOVA with repeated measures on one factor.

Source: M. V. Jones, R. D. Mace, S. R. Bray, A. W. MacRae, and C. Stockbridge. (2002). The impact of motivational imagery on the emotional state and self-efficacy levels of novice climbers. *Journal of Sport Behavior, 25*(1), p. 66.

Most researchers who conduct two-way mixed ANOVAs fail to address the question of practical significance. However, some researchers do this—and they deserve credit for performing a more complete analysis of the study's data than is usually the case. In Excerpt 14.28, we see an illustration of this good practice. In this study, the researchers computed a post hoc effect size. Though not labeled as such, the effect size mentioned in this excerpt is the same as the *d* index that researchers use when comparing two means. Using the standard criteria for interpreting *d* (where .20, .50, and .80 are considered to be small, medium, and large effects, respectively), the researchers associated with Excerpt 14.28 were justified in arguing (elsewhere in their article) that a *meaningful* difference existed between the means of the two groups of teachers. By computing *d,* these researchers helped the recipients of their research report see that the main effect of condition in their two-way mixed ANOVA was not just significant in a statistical sense, it was also significant in a practical sense.

EXCERPT 14.28 • *Concern for Practical Significance*

For the kindergarten data, a 2×2 (Experimental vs. Control by Fall vs. Spring) repeated-measures ANOVA of time spent on explicit phonological activities yielded a statistically significant condition effect, $F(1, 19) = 6.98$, $MSE = 30.72$, $p < .05$; a nonsignificant condition by time interaction, $F(1, 19) < 1$, $MSE = 21.96$; and a nonsignificant time effect, $F(1, 19) < 1$, $MSE = 21.96$. Across the year, experimental group kindergarten teachers spent significantly more time on activities directed toward phonological awareness ($M = 7.8$ minutes) than control group teachers ($M = 3.3$ minutes). The effect size (calculated as the difference between group means divided by the square root of the mean square error for condition) was .82.

Source: D. McCutchen, R. D. Abbott, L. B. Green, and S. N. Beretvas. (2002). Beginning literacy: Links among teacher knowledge, teacher practice, and student learning. *Journal of Learning Disabilities, 35*(1), p. 676.

Three Final Comments

As we near the end of this chapter, I would like to close by making three final comments. In each case, I will argue that you need to be alert as you read or listen to formal summaries of research studies. This is necessary so you can (1) know for sure what kind of analysis the researcher *really* used, and (2) filter out unjustified claims from those that warrant your close attention. If you do not put yourself in a position to do these two things, you are likely to be misled by what is contained in the research reports that come your way.

What Kind of ANOVA Was It?

In this chapter, we have considered three different kinds of ANOVAs: a one-way ANOVA with repeated measures, a two-way ANOVA with repeated measures on both factors, and a two-way ANOVA having repeated measures on just one factor. These three ANOVAs are different from each other, and they are also different from the one-way and two-way ANOVAs focused on in Chapters 11 and 13. Thus, for you to understand the structure and results of any one-way or two-way ANOVA, you need to know whether it did or did not involve repeated measures and, in the case of a two-way ANOVA having repeated measures, you need to know whether one or both of the factors involved repeated measures.

As indicated earlier, most researchers will clarify what kind of one-way or two-way ANOVA they have used. For example, if repeated measures are involved, they typically will use special terms—such as within-subjects or repeated measures—to describe the factor(s) in the ANOVA, or you may see the term *mixed* used to describe the kind of ANOVA considered near the end of this chapter. If no such term is used, this usually means that no repeated measures were involved.

Unfortunately, not all descriptions of one-way or two-way ANOVAs are clear as to the nature of its factor(s). At times, you'll be told that a one-way ANOVA was used when in reality it was a one-way ANOVA with repeated measures. Occasionally, this same thing will happen with two two-way ANOVAs. Or, you may be told that a two-way repeated measures ANOVA was used, thus causing you to think that there were two within-subjects factors, which will be wrong, because only one of the factors actually had repeated measures. To see an example of where the description of an ANOVA might mislead recipients of the research report, take another look at the first sentence in Excerpt 14.24.

Because the presence or absence of repeated measures does not affect the null hypothesis of a one-way ANOVA or the three null hypotheses of a two-way ANOVA, someone might want to argue that it really doesn't matter whether you can tell for sure if the factor(s) of the ANOVA had repeated measures. To that person I would ask just one simple question: "Do you know about the sphericity assumption and under what circumstances this assumption comes into play?"

Practical versus Statistical Significance

At various points in this chapter, I have tried to help you understand that statistical significance does not always signify practical significance. I've tried to accomplish that objective by means of the words I have written and the excerpts I have chosen to include. Before you leave this chapter, you should take another look at three particular passages from published studies that we looked at during our consideration of ANOVAs having repeated measures. These are Excerpt 14.9, Excerpt 14.18, and Excerpt 14.28.

There is a growing trend for researchers to do something in their studies, either as they chose their sample sizes or as they go about interpreting their results, so they and the recipients of their research reports do not make the mistake of thinking that statistical significance means big and important. However, you are bound to come across research claims that are based on the joint use of (1) one or more of the ANOVAs considered in this chapter and (2) the six-step version of hypothesis testing. When that happens, I hope you will remember two things. First, a very small p may indicate that nothing big was discovered, only that a big sample can make molehills look like mountains, and, conversely, a large p may indicate that something big was left undetected because the sample size was too small. The second thing to remember is that studies can be planned, using the nine-step version of hypothesis testing, such that neither of those two possible problems is likely to occur.

The Possibility of Inferential Error

Many researchers discuss the results of their studies in such a way that it appears that they have discovered ultimate truth. Stated differently, the language used in many research reports suggests strongly that sample statistics and the results of inferential tests are being reified into population parameters and indisputable claims. At times, such claims are based on the kinds of ANOVA considered in this chapter.

You need to remember that the result of any F-test might be a Type I error (if the null hypothesis is rejected) or a Type II error (if the null hypothesis is retained). This is true even if the nine-step version of hypothesis testing is used, and even if attention is paid to all relevant underlying assumptions, and even if the data are collected in an unbiased fashion with valid and reliable measuring instruments from probability samples characterized by zero attrition, and even if all other good things are done so the study is sound. Simply stated, inferential error is *always* possible whenever a null hypothesis is tested.

Review Terms

Between subjects
Bonferroni technique
Counterbalancing
Mixed ANOVA
Omega squared
One between, one within ANOVA
One between, two within ANOVA

Sphericity
Split-plot ANOVA
Three-way mixed ANOVA
Two between, one within ANOVA
Two-way mixed ANOVA
Within subjects

The Best Items in the Companion Website

1. An interactive online quiz (with immediate feedback provided) covering Chapter 14.
2. Ten misconceptions about the content of Chapter 14.
3. One of the best passages from Chapter 14: "Practical versus Statistical Significance in Mixed ANOVAs."

4. An online resource entitled "Within-Subjects ANOVA."
5. Two jokes about statistics.

Fun Exercises inside Research Navigator

1. **Do different conjunctions (*and* versus *or* versus *either/or*) in written material create different cognitive demands on college students?**

   In this experiment, college students read several short vignettes, each of which was followed by a sentence containing the word *and*, *or*, or *either/or*. Their task was to quickly determine whether or not each follow-up question was a legitimate "match" to the vignette to which it was paired. A separate 3 (conjunction: and, or, either/or) x 2 (match: yes, no) ANOVA with repeated measures on both factors was applied to the data for each of the two dependent variables: reaction time and accuracy. The results of these analyses suggested that one of the conjunctions was harder to deal with than the other two. Which one do you think it was? (Are you sure?) To find out if your guess is correct, refer to the PDF version of the research report in the Psychology database of ContentSelect and take a look at the first two paragraphs of the results along with Figures 1a and 1b.

   M. E. Pratarelli & A. Lawson. Conjunctive forms and conditional inference in questions and statements. *North American Journal of Psychology.* Located in the PSYCHOLOGY database of ContentSelect.

2. **Does the presence of a dog reduce stress for kids at the dentist's office?**

   To see if children's stress at the dental office could be reduced, the researchers of this study randomly assigned 40 children aged 7 to 11 to an experimental group (*n* = 20) and a control group (*n* = 20). Those in the experimental group were given a gentle and child-friendly Golden Retriever to be with them while they were in the dentist's office; those in the control group had no dog. Measures of stress were taken on two dependent variables at five points in time, with each set of data analyzed by means of a 2 (group) × 5 (time) mixed ANOVA. Data for one of the stress-related dependent variables came from ratings of a videotape of the child while he or she was in the dentist's office. Try to guess what the second dependent variable was. To find out if your guess is correct (and to see the results of this cute study), refer to the PDF version of the research report in the Nursing, Health, and Medicine database of ContentSelect. You'll find the second dependent variable described on page 143 and the main results for it presented on pages 145–147.

   L. Gentes, B. Thaler, M. E. Megel, M. M. Baun, F. A. Driscoll, S. Beiraghi, & S. Agrawl. The effect of a companion animal on distress in children undergoing dental procedures. *Issues in Comprehensive Pediatric Nursing.* Located in the NURSING, HEALTH, AND MEDICINE database of ContentSelect.

Review Questions and Answers begin on page 516.

15

The Analysis of Covariance

In the previous five chapters, we looked at several different kinds of analysis of variance. We focused our attention on one-way and two-way ANOVAs, with consideration given to the situations where (1) each factor is between subjects in nature, (2) each factor is within subjects in nature, and (3) both between-subjects and within-subjects factors are combined in the same study. We closely examined five different kinds of ANOVAs that are distinguished from one another by the number and nature of the factors. In this book, these five ANOVAs have been referred to as a one-way ANOVA, a two-way ANOVA, a one-way repeated measures ANOVA, a two-way repeated measures ANOVA, and a two-way mixed ANOVA.

Research
Navigator.c⊕m

Analysis of
covariance

We now turn our attention to an ANOVA-like inferential strategy that can be used instead of any of the ANOVAs examined or referred to in earlier chapters. This statistical technique, called the **analysis of covariance** and abbreviated by the six letters **ANCOVA,** can be used in any study regardless of the number of factors involved or the between-versus-within nature of the factor(s). Accordingly, the analysis of covariance is best thought of as an option to the analysis of variance. For example, if a researcher's study involves one between-subjects factor, data can be collected and analyzed using a one-way ANOVA *or* a one-way ANCOVA. The same option exists for any of the other four situations examined in earlier chapters. Simply stated, there is an ANCOVA counterpart to any ANOVA.

In Excerpts 15.1 through 15.3, we see how researchers typically indicate that their data were subjected to an analysis of covariance. Note how these excerpts illustrate the way ANCOVA can be used as an option to ANOVA regardless of the number of factors involved in the study or the between-versus-within nature of any factor.

The Three Different Variables Involved in Any ANCOVA Study

In any of the ANOVAs considered in earlier chapters, there are just two kinds of variables: independent variables and dependent variables. The data analyzed in

EXCERPTS 15.1–15.3 • *The Versatility of the Analysis of Covariance*

A one-way ANCOVA was used to explore the prediction that the difference in re-sponding was specifically related to the inability of children with psychopathic ten-dencies to shift away from the bad packs.

Source: R. J. R. Blair, E. Colledge, and D. G. V. Mitchell. (2001). Somatic markers and re-sponse reversal: Is there orbitofrontal cortex dysfunction in boys with psychopathic tenden-cies? *Journal of Abnormal Child Psychology, 29*(6), p. 505.

Data were subjected to a 2 (humor vs. relaxation) × 2 (instructional set type: ex-pectation of increase vs. decrease in discomfort threshold) analysis of covariance (ANCOVA).

Source: D. L. Mahony, W. J. Burroughs, and A. C. Hieatt. (2001). The effects of laughter on discomfort thresholds: Does expectation become reality? *Journal of General Psychology, 128*(2), p. 222.

The data were submitted to a two-way ANCOVA with Group (AD/HD vs. controls) as the between-participants factor and Trial Length (5, 10, 15 s) as the within-participants factor.

Source: E. J. S. Sonuga-Barke. (2002). Interval length and time-use by children with AD/HD: A comparison of four models. *Journal of Abnormal Child Psychology, 30*(3), p. 262.

---

those ANOVAs, of course, represent the dependent variable; the factors correspond with the study's independent variables. We've seen how ANOVAs can involve more than one factor, factors made up of different numbers of levels, and different kinds of factors (i.e., between-subjects versus within-subjects factors); nevertheless, each and every factor in the ANOVAs considered in this book represents an independent variable. Thus such ANOVAs could be said to contain two structural ingredients: one or more independent variables and data on one dependent variable.

In any analysis of covariance, three rather than two kinds of variables are involved. Like the ANOVAs we have considered, there will be scores that corre-spond with the dependent variable and one or more factors that coincide with the study's independent variable(s). In addition, there will be a variable that is called the covariate.[1] Since the **covariate** is a variable on which the study's participants

Research
Navigator.c⊛m
Covariate

---

[1]The term *concomitant variable* is synonymous with the term *covariate variable*.

are measured, it is more similar to the study's dependent variable than to the independent variable(s). The covariate and dependent variables have entirely different functions in any ANCOVA study, as the next section will make clear. Before discussing the covariate's function, however, let's consider a few real studies for the purpose of verifying that ANCOVA studies always have *three* structural ingredients.

Consider Excerpts 15.4 and 15.5, which come from studies involving one-way and two-way ANOVAs, respectively. In the study from which Excerpt 15.4 was drawn, two groups of undergraduate college students were compared: males and females. Thus, the independent variable was gender. The dependent variable was shame, measured by having the college students provide self-ratings of how much shame they would feel if they had been the person in a variety of written vignettes who did something embarrassing. The covariate variable was guilt, again a self-rating that was provided after each college student read the vignettes. In Excerpt 15.5, there were two independent variables, gender and coital status of each adolescent; the dependent variable was the adolescent's self-esteem; and the covariate variable was the age at which he or she began puberty.

EXCERPTS 15.4–15.5 • *The Three Kinds of Variables in Any ANCOVA Study*

A one-way ANCOVA, treating gender as the between-subjects factor, shame ratings as the dependent measure, and guilt ratings as the covariate, was conducted.

Source: T. J. Ferguson, H. L. Eyre, and M. Ashbaker. (2000). Unwanted identities: A key variable in shame-anger links and gender differences in shame. *Sex Roles, 41*(3/4), pp. 142–143.

- -

Therefore, a 2 × 2 analysis of covariance was conducted for gender (male, female) and coital status (virgin, nonvirgin) on self-esteem, with pubertal timing as the covariate.

Source: J. M. Spencer, G. D. Zimet, M. C. Aalsma, and D. P. Orr. (2002). Self-esteem as a predictor of initiation of coitus in early adolescents. *Pediatrics, 109*(4), p. 582.

The Covariate's Role

Like the analysis of variance, the analysis of covariance allows researchers to make inferential statements about main and interaction effects. In that sense, these two statistical procedures have the same objective. However, an ANCOVA will be superior to its ANOVA counterpart in two distinct respects, so long as a good covariate is used.[2] To understand what is going on in an analysis of covariance, you need to understand this dual role of the covariate.

One role of the covariate is to reduce the probability of a Type II error when tests are made of main or interaction effects, or when comparisons are made within planned or post hoc investigations. As pointed out on repeated occasions in earlier chapters, this kind of inferential error is committed whenever a false null hypothesis is not rejected. Since the probability of a Type II error is inversely related to statistical power, I will restate this first role of the covariate by saying that an ANCOVA will be more powerful than its ANOVA counterpart, presuming that other things are held constant and that a good covariate has been used within the ANCOVA.

As you have seen, the *F*-tests associated with a standard ANOVA are computed by dividing the *MS* for error into the *MS*s for main and interaction effects. If MS_{error} can somehow be made smaller, then the calculated *F*s are larger, *p*s are smaller, and there's a better chance that null hypotheses will be rejected. When a good covariate is used within a covariance analysis, this is exactly what happens. Data on the covariate function to explain away a portion of within-group variability, thus resulting in a smaller value for MS_{error}. This mean square is often referred to as "error variance."

In Excerpt 15.6, we see a case where a pair of researchers explain that they collected data on a covariate variable for the express purpose of reducing error variance. By doing this, they were increasing the power of group comparisons that focused on the study's dependent variable. Accordingly, Excerpt 15.6 exemplifies the first role of the covariate: increased statistical power brought about by a reduction in the error variance.

EXCERPT 15.6 • *The First Role of the Covariate: Increased Statistical Power*

An ANCOVA approach was chosen primarily to maximize power to detect systematic treatment effects. In randomized experiments, covariates in ANCOVA are included to reduce error (within-cell) variance, thereby increasing the power of statistical tests of treatments.

Source: G. B. Armstrong and L. Chung. (2000). Background television and reading memory in context: Assessing TV interference and facilitative context effects on encoding versus retrieval processes. *Communication Research, 27*(3), p. 340.

---

[2]The qualities of a "good" covariate will be described shortly.

In addition to its power function, the covariate in an analysis of covariance has another function. This second function can be summed up by the word *control*. In fact, some researchers will refer to the covariate of their ANCOVA studies as the *control variable*. Excerpt 15.7 illustrates nicely the fact that a covariate is sometimes used because of its control (or corrective) capability. It is worth noting, in this excerpt, that the covariate was used (to control for pretreatment group differences) even though the 95 participants were randomly assigned to the study's six treatment conditions. It should be noted that the researchers pointed out, in the full research report from which this excerpt was taken, that there was no attrition from any of the six groups.

EXCERPT 15.7 • *The Second Role of the Covariate: Control*

The research design is a 2 × 3 (expectancy × treatment) factorial design with a randomized assignment protocol in which hospital staff were blinded to the experimental manipulations.... Participants were randomly assigned to 1 of the 6 treatment conditions.... Analysis of covariance was used to control for pretreatment differences between groups.

Source: W. J. Matthews, J. M. Conti, and S. G. Sireci. (2001). The effects of intercessory prayer, positive visualization, and expectancy on the well-being of kidney dialysis patients. *Alternative Therapies in Health and Medicine, 7*(5), pp. 42–43.

The logic behind the control feature of ANCOVA is simple. The comparison groups involved in a study are likely to differ from one another with respect to one or more variables that the researcher may wish to hold constant. In an attempt to accomplish this objective, the researcher could use participants who have identical scores on the variable(s) where control is desired. That effort, however, would normally bring forth two undesirable outcomes. For one thing, only a portion of the available participants would actually be used, thus *reducing* the statistical power of inferential tests. Furthermore, the generalizability of the findings would be greatly restricted as compared with the situation where the analysis is based on a more heterogeneous group of people.

To bring about the desired control, ANCOVA adjusts each group mean on the dependent variable. Although the precise formulas used to make these adjustments are somewhat complicated, the rationale behind the adjustment process is easy to understand. If one of the comparison groups has an *above-average* mean on the *control variable* (as compared with the other comparison groups in the study), then that group's mean score on the *dependent variable* will be *lowered*. In contrast, any group that has a *below-average* mean on the *covariate* will have its mean score on the *dependent* variable *raised*. The degree to which any group's mean score on the dependent variable is adjusted depends on how far above or below average that group stands on the control variable. By adjusting the mean scores on the dependent variable in this fashion, ANCOVA provides the best estimates of how the comparison groups would have performed if they had all possessed identical means on the control variable(s).

To illustrate the way ANCOVA adjusts group means on the dependent variable, let's consider a recent study that was undertaken to see if a new interactive computer program would benefit incoming college freshmen. The content of the 14-week program used in this investigation focused on study skills, obtaining financial aid information, locating campus resources, etc. Two small groups were compared, both of which received the normal face-to-face assistance from the college administrators and faculty members. The treatment and control groups differed, however, in that the former used the computer program whereas the latter did not.

The primary data examined by the researcher in this study came from a personality instrument that was administered to the members of both groups at the beginning and at the end of the fall semester. This instrument measured the students' perceived locus of control, that is, the beliefs they had as to how extensively they themselves (rather than outside forces or luck) determined whether good or bad things happened to them. The second set of scores (i.e., from the posttest) represented the dependent variable, whereas the first set of scores (from the pretest) served as the control, or covariate, variable. In Excerpt 15.8, we see how the two groups performed on the "Luck" subscale of the locus-of-control instrument.

As you can see, the two groups began the study with different mean scores on the luck factor. With the mean pretest score for all 35 students being 3.542, it is clear that the 18 students in the treatment group started out, on the average, thinking that luck was less involved in their life events than were the 17 students in the control group.

If the obtained posttest means for the two groups had been directly compared (say, with an independent-samples *t*-test or *F*-test), a statistically significant result would be hard to interpret. That's because part or all of the posttest difference between the two groups might simply be a reflection of their different starting points.

To acknowledge the existence of the difference between the two groups on the covariate, ANCOVA adjusted the posttest means. If you examine the three sets of means in Excerpt 15.8, you'll easily see the basic logic of this adjustment procedure. The treatment group had an advantage at the outset, for its pretest mean (2.944) was lower than the grand average of both groups combined (3.542). Therefore that group's posttest mean was adjusted upward (from 2.833 to 3.04). The control group, in contrast, started out with a disadvantage, for its pretest mean (4.176) was higher than the grand average of all pretest scores. Consequently, the control group's posttest mean was adjusted downward (from 4.0 to 3.79). In *any* study, this

EXCERPT 15.8 • *The "Control" Function of ANCOVA*

A one-way (treatment versus control) analysis of covariance was used to test for differences between groups, with posttest scores as the dependent variable and the pretest scores as the covariate (see Table).

TABLE 1   *Mean Pretest and Mean and Adjusted Mean Posttest Scores for the Luck Factor*

				Posttest		
		Pretest		Obtained		Adjusted
Group	n	$\overline{X}$	SD	$\overline{X}$	SD	$\overline{X}$
Treatment	18	2.944	1.259	2.833	.858	3.04
Control	17	4.176	1.190	4.0	1.000	3.79

Source: E. Santa-Rita. (1997). The effect of computer-assisted student development programs on entering freshmen locus-of-control orientation. *College Student Journal, 31,* p. 83

is exactly how the control feature of ANCOVA works. Any group with an above-average mean on the covariate has its mean on the dependent variable adjusted downward, while any group with a below-average mean on the covariate has its mean on the dependent variable adjusted upward. These adjusted means constitute the best estimates of how the two groups would have performed, on the dependent variable, if they had possessed identical means on the control (i.e., covariate) variable(s) used in the study.

Although the logic behind ANCOVA's adjustment of group means on the dependent variable is easy to follow, the statistical procedures used to make the adjustment are quite complicated. The formulas used to accomplish this goal will not be presented here, because you do not need to understand the intricacies of the adjustment formula in order to decipher and critique ANCOVA results. All you need to know is that the adjustment process involves far more than simply (1) determining how far each group's covariate mean lies above or below the grand covariate mean and (2) adding or subtracting that difference to that group's mean on the dependent variable. As proof of this, take another look at Excerpt 15.8. Each group's pretest mean in that study was about six-tenths of a point away from the grand pretest mean. However, the covariance adjustment caused only .21 to be added to or subtracted from the posttest means.

Note that the two purposes of ANCOVA—increased power, on the one hand, and control of extraneous variables, on the other hand—occur simultaneously. If a researcher decides to use this statistical procedure solely to gain the increased power that ANCOVA affords, the means on the dependent variable will automatically be adjusted to reflect differences among the group means on the covariate variable. If, on the other hand, the researcher applies ANCOVA solely because of a desire to exert statistical control on a covariate variable, there will be, automatically, an increase in the statistical power of the inferential tests. In other words, ANCOVA accomplishes two objectives even though the researcher may have selected it with only one objective in mind.

At the beginning of this section, I stated that ANCOVA allows the researcher to make inferential statements about main and interaction effects in the populations of interest. Since you now know how data on the covariate variable(s) make it possible for the researcher to control one or more extraneous variables, I can now point out that ANCOVA's inferential statements are based on the adjusted means. The data on the covariate and the dependent variable are used to compute the adjusted means on the dependent variable, with ANCOVA's focus resting on these adjusted means whenever a null hypothesis is tested.

Null Hypotheses

As typically used, ANCOVA will involve the same number of null hypotheses as would be the case in a comparable ANOVA. Hence, you will usually find that there will be one and three null hypotheses associated with ANCOVAs that have one and two factors, respectively. The nature of these ANCOVA null hypotheses is the same as the null hypotheses I talked about in earlier chapters when we considered various forms of ANOVA, except that the μs in any covariance H_0 must be considered to be adjusted means.[3]

Although null hypotheses rarely appear in research reports that contain AN-COVA results, sometimes researchers refer to them. Two examples to illustrate this are contained in Excerpts 15.9 and 15.10. Had the null hypotheses in these two studies been written out symbolically, the first one would have taken the form H_0: $\mu'_{Placebo} = \mu'_{Orlistat}$, and the second one would have stated H_0: $\mu'_{Green} = \mu'_{Blue} = \mu'_{Red} = \mu'_{White}$, where the symbol μ' stands for an adjusted population mean. Of course, the meaning of μ' would not be the same in these two null hypotheses, for the dependent variables in the two studies were quite different.

---

[3] In a completely randomized ANCOVA where each factor is active in nature, the adjusted population means on the dependent variable are logically and mathematically equal to the unadjusted population means.

EXCERPTS 15.9–15.10 • *The Null Hypothesis in ANCOVA*

The null hypothesis—that the expected mean weight loss and change from baseline in HbA_{1c} at the end of 1 year of double-blind treatment did not differ significantly between the placebo and orlistat treatments—was tested using ANCOVA.

Source: D. E. Kelley, G. A. Bray, F. X. Pi-Sunyer, and S. Klein. (2002). Clinical efficacy of orlistat therapy in overweight and obese patients with insulin-treated type 2 diabetes: A 1-year randomized controlled trial. *Diabetes Care, 25*(6), p. 1035.

- -

The present study was designed to examine the effect of color on the performance of a target accuracy task (dart throwing). . . . A univariate ANCOVA indicated no significant differences ($p > .05$) between the performance means in the green, blue, red, and white conditions. . . . Based on the results of the present investigation, the null hypothesis that color would not produce significant performance differences on a dart throwing task could not be rejected.

Source: K. Araki and S. Huddleston. (2002). The effect of color on a target accuracy task. *International Sports Journal, 6*(2), pp. 86, 90.

The Focus, Number, and Quality of the Covariate Variable(s)

Suppose two different researchers each conduct a study in which they use the analysis of covariance to analyze their data. Further suppose that these two studies are conducted at the same point in time, in the same kind of setting, with the same independent variable(s) [as defined by the factor(s) and levels], and with the same measuring instrument used to collect data on the dependent variable from the same number and type of research participants. Despite all these similarities, these two ANCOVA studies might yield entirely different results because of differences in the focus, number, and quality of the covariate variable(s) used in the two investigations.

Regarding its focus, the covariate in many studies is set up to be simply an indication of each participant's status on the dependent variable at the beginning of the investigation. When this is done, the participant's scores on the covariate will be referred to as their pretest or baseline measures. Examples of this kind of covariate can be seen in Excerpts 15.7, 15.8, and 15.9. In one sense, this kind of ANCOVA study is simpler (but not necessarily of lower quality) because a single measuring instrument is used to collect data on both the covariate and the dependent variables.

There is no rule, however, that forces researchers to use pretest-type data to represent the covariate variable. In many studies, the covariate variable is entirely different from the dependent variable. For example, consider Excerpt 15.5. In that study, the dependent variable was self-esteem while the covariate variable "pubital timing."

Regardless of whether the covariate and dependent variables are the same or different, the adjustment process of ANCOVA is basically the same. First, the mean covariate score of all subjects in all comparison groups is computed. Next, each comparison group's covariate mean is compared against the grand covariate mean to see (1) if the former is above or below the latter, and (2) how much of a difference there is between these two means. Finally, each group's mean on the dependent variable is adjusted up or down (depending on whether the group was below or above average on the covariate), with larger adjustments made when a group's covariate mean is found to deviate further from the grand covariate mean.

The second way in which two ANCOVA studies might differ—even though they are identical in terms of independent and dependent variables, setting, and participants—concerns the number of covariate variables involved in the study. Simply stated, there can be one, two, or more covariate variables included in any ANCOVA study. Most often, only one covariate variable is incorporated into the researcher's study. Of the excerpts we have considered thus far, most came from studies wherein there was a single covariate variable. In Excerpt 15.11, we see a case in which two covariates were used. In this study, five separate ANCOVAs were conducted, each using a different measure of memory performance as the dependent variable. Each analysis involved two covariates, age and nonverbal intelligence.

Although it might seem as if ANCOVA would work better when lots of covariate variables are involved, the researcher has to pay a price for each such variable. We will consider this point later in the chapter. For now, all I want you to know is that most ANCOVAs are conducted with only one or two covariate variables.

The third way two seemingly similar studies might differ concerns the quality of the covariate variable. Earlier, we considered the two roles of the covariate: power and control. Covariate data will not help in either regard if (1) an irrelevant covariate variable is used or (2) the covariate variable is relevant conceptually but measured in such a way that the resulting data are invalid or unreliable.

EXCERPT 15.11 • *ANCOVA with Multiple Covariates*

One-way analyses of covariance (ANCOVAs) were computed to examine the effect of group on memory performance, with age and nonverbal intelligence being treated as covariates. . . . The comparisons of the memory scores were adjusted to take into account the differences in age and IQ between groups.

Source: P. W. Dawson, P. A. Busby, C. M. McKay, and G. M. Clark. (2002). Short-term auditory memory in children using Cochlear implants and its relevance to receptive language. *Journal of Speech, Language, and Hearing Research, 45*(4), p. 795.

In order for a covariate variable to be conceptually relevant within a given study, it must be related to the study's dependent variable. In studies where measurements on the covariate variable are gathered via a pretest and then posttest scores (using the same measuring instrument) are used to represent the dependent variable, the conceptual relevance of the covariate is clear. When the covariate and dependent variables are different, it may or may not be the case that the covariate is worthy of being included in the ANCOVA. Later in this chapter, we will return to this issue of relevant covariate variables.

Even if the covariate *variable* selected by the researcher is sensible, the *measurement* of the variable must be sound. In other words, the data collected on the covariate variable need to be both reliable and valid. Earlier in this book, we considered different strategies available for estimating reliability and validity. Competent researchers use these techniques to assess the quality of their covariate data; moreover, they present evidence of such "data checks" within their research reports.

Presentation of Results

Most researchers present the results of their ANCOVAs within the text of their research reports. Accordingly, we will now look at several passages that have been taken from recently published articles.

In Excerpt 15.12, we see the results of a one-way analysis of covariance. This passage is very similar to what you might see when a researcher uses a one-way ANOVA to compare the means of two groups. We're given information as to the independent and dependent variables, the calculated *F*-value, the sample means that were compared, and the decision about the null hypothesis ($p < .05$). Moreover, just like a one-way ANOVA, no follow-up test was needed because just two means were compared.

EXCERPT 15.12 • *Results of a One-Way ANCOVA*

A one-way, between-gender analysis of covariance on the total self-estimated score with total measured trait EI as the covariate indicated that males' self-estimates of EI (adjusted mean = 1659.3) were significantly higher ($F_{(1,257)} = 4.94$, $p < .05$) than those of females (adjusted mean = 1624.4).

Source: K. V. Petrides and A. Furnham. (2000). Gender differences in measured and self-estimated trait emotional intelligence. *Sex Roles, 42*(5/6), p. 455.

There is one thing about this passage that *is* different from textual presentations of results following a one-way ANOVA. Note the *df* numbers next to the *F*-value. If this were a one-way ANOVA, you'd add those numbers together and then add 1 in order to figure out how many people were involved in the study. Because these results come from an ANCOVA, you must add 2 to the sum of df_{Between} and df_{Within}, not 1. (This is because 1 degree of freedom is used up from the within-groups *df* because a covariate variable was involved in the study.) Knowing this, you can determine that there were 260 people in this study.

Now let's look at Excerpt 15.13. In this excerpt, we are given the results of two separate two-way ANCOVAs. Each analysis involved the same two factors (gender and country) and the same covariate variables, but they differed in terms of the dependent variable. In one analysis, the dependent variable was called *inattention symptoms;* in the other it was called *hyperactivity-impulsivity symptoms.*

EXCERPT 15.13 • *Results of Two Two-Way ANCOVAs*

Univariate 2×3 analyses of covariance were conducted for each of the dependent measures. A significant main effect for country was found for inattention symptoms, $F(2, 1,115) = 9.70, p < .001, \eta^2 = .02$, and for hyperactivity-impulsivity symptoms, $F(2, 1,115) = 4.14, p < .05, \eta^2 = .007$. Scheffe post hoc comparison tests using adjusted means indicated that Italian students reported significantly more inattention and hyperactivity-impulsivity symptoms than students from the United States (all *ps* < .05). Furthermore, students from New Zealand reported more inattention symptoms than did students from the United States ($p < .05$). There were no significant differences on either of the scores between students from Italy and New Zealand. Also, none of the univariate analyses revealed a significant main effect for gender or a Gender × Country interaction.

Source: G. J. DuPaul, E. A. Schaughency, L. L. Weyandt, and G. Tripp. (2001). Self-report of ADHD symptoms in university students: Cross-gender and cross-national prevalence. *Journal of Learning Disabilities, 34*(4), pp. 374–375.

Excerpt 15.13 deserves your close attention. I say that because it demonstrates that ANOVAs and ANCOVAs are highly similar in terms of the goals of any post hoc investigation of main effect means (and the techniques used within such an investigation). Moreover, this excerpt illustrates how competent researchers will concern themselves, when conducting an analysis of covariance, with practical significance as well as statistical significance.

Turning now to Excerpt 15.14, we see the results of a two-way mixed AN-COVA. This set of results is worth examining for two reasons. As you will see, tests of simple main effects were conducted in order to probe the interaction. Second, the levels of the within-subjects factor correspond with different dependent variables (verbal IQ and performance IQ). This kind of within-subjects factor was mentioned near the beginning of Chapter 14, but none of the excerpts in that chapter served to illustrate this kind of repeated measures factor. Now we see it in Excerpt 15.14. In a sense, this kind of factor is paradoxical, for its level creates one of the study's independent variables while, at the same time, each of those levels corresponds to one of the study's dependent variables!

EXCERPT 15.14 • *Results of a Mixed ANCOVA*

A two-way mixed ANCOVA, with cluster serving as the between-group factor, IQ Type (VIQ vs. PIQ) serving as the within-group variable, and FSIQ as the covariate, generated a significant Cluster $\times$ IQ Type interaction, $F(3, 49) = 9.31$, $p < .001$. This interaction was due to the fact that there was not a significant difference between VIQ and PIQ in the average group, $t(20) = 1.45$, $p = .163$. However, the PIQ was significantly higher than the VIQ in both the RD, $t(10) = 3.43$, $p = .006$, and the low RD, $t(12) = 2.27$, $p < .05$, group. In contrast, the VIQ was significantly higher than the PIQ in the high-average group, $t(8) = 2.34$, $p < .05$.

Source: M. A. Bonafina, J. H. Newcorn, K. E. McKay, V. H. Koda, and J. M. Halperin. (2000). ADHD and reading disabilities: A cluster analytic approach for distinguishing subgroups. *Journal of Learning Disabilities, 33*(3), pp. 300–301.

The Statistical Basis for ANCOVA's Power Advantage and Adjustment Feature

In an earlier section of this chapter, you learned that a good covariate variable is both conceptually related to the dependent variable and measured in such a way as to provide reliable and valid data. But how can researchers determine whether existing data (or new data that could be freshly gathered) meet this double criterion? Every researcher who uses ANCOVA ought to be able to answer this question whenever one or more covariate variables are incorporated into a study. With bad covariate variables, nothing of value comes in return for what is given up!

In order for ANCOVA to provide increased power (over a comparable ANOVA) and to adjust the group means, the covariate variable(s) must be correlated with the dependent variable. Although the correlation(s) can be either positive or negative in nature, ANCOVA will not achieve its power and adjustment objectives unless at least a moderate relationship exists between each covariate variable and the dependent variable. Stated differently, nuisance variability within the dependent variable scores can be accounted for to the extent that a strong relationship exists between the covariate(s) and the dependent variable.[4]

There are many ways to consider the correlation in ANCOVA, even when data have been collected on just one covariate variable. Two ways of doing this involve (1) looking at the correlation between the covariate and dependent variables for all participants from all comparison groups thrown into one large group, or (2) looking at the correlation between the covariate and dependent variables separately within each comparison group. The second of these two ways of considering the correlation is appropriate because ANCOVA makes its adjustments (of individual scores and of group means) on the basis of the pooled within-groups correlation coefficient.

One final point is worth making about the correlation between the covariate and dependent variables. Regarding the question of how large the pooled within-groups r needs to be before the covariate can make a difference in terms of increasing power, statistical theory responds by saying that the absolute value of this r should be at least .20. When r is at least this large, the reduction in the error SS compensates for df that are lost from the error row of the ANCOVA summary table. If r is between -2.0 and $+.20$, however, the effect of having a smaller number of error df without a proportionate decrease in the error SS is to make the error MS larger, not smaller. That situation would bring about a reduction in power.[5]

Assumptions

The statistical assumptions of ANCOVA include all the assumptions that are associated with ANOVA, plus three that are unique to the situation where data on a covariate variable are used in an effort to make adjustments and increase power. All three of these unique-to-ANCOVA assumptions must be met if the analysis is to function in its intended manner, and the researcher (and you) should consider these assumptions whenever ANCOVA is used—even in situations where the comparison

---

[4]When two or more covariate variables are used within the same study, ANCOVA works best when the covariates are *unrelated* to each other. When the correlations among the covariate variables are low, each such variable has a chance to account for a different portion of the nuisance variability in the dependent variable.

[5]Although we have used r in this paragraph, it is actually the population parameter ρ that needs to exceed $\pm.20$ in order for ANCOVA to have a power advantage.

groups are equally large. In other words, equal *n*s do *not* cause ANCOVA to be robust to any of the assumptions we now wish to consider.

The Independent Variable Should Not Affect the Covariate Variable

The first of these three new assumptions stipulates that the study's independent variable should not affect the covariate variable. In an experiment (where the independent variable is an active factor), this assumption clearly will be met if the data on the covariate variable are collected before the treatments are applied. If the covariate data are collected after the treatments have been applied, the situation is far murkier—and the researcher should provide a logical argument on behalf of the implicit claim that treatments do not affect the covariate. In nonexperimental (i.e., descriptive) studies, the situation is even murkier since the independent variable very likely may have influenced each subject's status on the covariate variable prior to the study. We will return to this issue—of covariance being used in nonrandomized studies—in the next major section.

To see an example of how the covariate can be affected by the independent variable in a randomized experiment, consider Excerpt 15.15. In this study, the data on the covariate variable (change scores over the 12-week duration of the study) were collected *after* the independent variable had been applied. Not only was there

---

EXCERPT 15.15 • *The Assumption That the Independent Variable Does Not Influence the Covariate Variable*

Subjects were randomly assigned to receive either 3g/day of E-EPA supplement in encapsulated form (three 500-mg capsules twice daily) or placebo (3g/day of medicinal liquid paraffin BP) in addition to the medication that they had been receiving. . . . The primary outcome measure was the percentage change in Positive and Negative Syndrome Scale total scores between baseline and 12 weeks. . . . An analysis of covariance using change in Positive and Negative Syndrome Scale total score as the dependent variable and change in dyskinesia score as a covariate was performed. . . . This study shows a significant advantage for E-EPA over placebo in the primary outcome measure [and] the results of the analysis of covariance suggest that reduction in Positive and Negative Syndrome Scale scores may at least in part be related to reduction in dyskinesia scores.

Source: R. Emsley, C. Myburgh, P. Oosthuizen, and S. J. van Rensburg. (2002). Randomized, placebo-controlled study of ethyl-eicosapentaenoic acid as supplemental treatment in schizophrenia. *American Journal of Psychiatry, 159*(9), pp. 1596–1597.

a possibility, therefore, that the independent variable affected covariate scores, the researchers seem to argue that this is exactly what happened!

Homogeneity of Within-Group Correlations (or Regression Slopes)

The second unique assumption associated with ANCOVA stipulates that the correlation between the covariate and dependent variables is the same within each of the populations involved in the study. This assumption usually is talked about in terms of regression slopes rather than correlations, and hence you are likely to come across ANCOVA research reports that contain references to the **assumption of equal regression slopes** or to the **homogeneity of regression slope assumption.** The data of a study can be employed to test this assumption—and it should *always* be tested when ANCOVA is used. As is the case when testing other assumptions, the researcher will be happy when the statistical test of the equal slopes assumption leads to a fail-to-reject decision. That outcome is interpreted as a signal that it is permissible to analyze the study's data using ANCOVA procedures.

Consider Excerpt 15.16. Notice that the researchers used the hypothesis testing procedure to check out the equal regression slope assumption. (The null hypothesis of this test said that the relationship between GPA, the covariate, and the unnamed dependent variable was the same, in the study's populations, for each of the classroom format groups.) The F-test used to do this did *not* lead to a rejection of the assumption's H_0 (as indicated by the notation "$p < 0.47$"). With this result in hand, the researchers went ahead and conducted an analysis of covariance to compare their groups' adjusted means.

If the equal-slopes H_0 is rejected, there are several options open to the researcher. In that situation, the data can be transformed and then the assumption can be tested again using the transformed data. Or, the researcher can turn to one of

EXCERPT 15.16 • *The Assumption of Equal Regression Slopes*

To determine if the slope homogeneity assumption was tenable, we performed an F-test on the interaction between GPA and classroom format. We failed to reject the null hypothesis ($F = 0.80, p < 0.47$). It is therefore concluded that the covariates relate similarly to the dependent measure for each group and that ANCOVA is a tenable approach.

Source: K. A. S. Lancaster and C. A. Strand. (2001). Using the team-learning model in a managerial accounting class: An experiment in cooperative learning. *Issues in Accounting Education, 16*(4), p. 562.

several more complicated analyses (e.g., the Johnson-Neyman technique) developed specifically for the situation where heterogeneous regressions exist. Or, the researcher can decide to pay no attention to the covariate data and simply use an ANOVA to compare groups on the dependent variable. These various options come into play only rarely, either because the equal-slopes assumption is not rejected when it is tested or because the researcher wrongfully bypasses testing the assumption.

Linearity

The third assumption connected to ANCOVA (but not ANOVA) stipulates that the within-group relationship between the covariate and dependent variables should be linear.[6] A statistical test exists that makes it possible to check out this **linearity** assumption, but not many applied researchers who use ANCOVA discuss the application of this test. In Excerpt 15.17, we see one of the rare instances in which the linearity assumption *was* tested. When no evidence is presented to show that the test on linearity was conducted, you have no option but to conclude that no attention was devoted to the linearity assumption. Since the impact of nonlinearity is to lower the statistical power of tests on the adjusted means, you have a right to be suspicious of any claims based on *nonsignificant* ANCOVA *F*-tests when nothing is said about linearity. On the other hand, when you come across an ANCOVA study in which the linearity assumption *was* tested (as in Excerpt 15.17), give the researcher some extra credit for not rushing into the ANCOVA analysis until after the data were examined to see if this rather delicate statistical procedure could be used.

EXCERPT 15.17 • *The Linearity Assumption*

ANCOVA procedures were used to analyze potential differences across groups for each of three post-intervention dependent variables: attitude, knowledge, and self-reported behavior. The independent variable was one of two alcohol education programs or the control group. The covariate for each measurement was the baseline survey of the corresponding dependent variable. The data were assessed for linearity of the covariate, equality of slopes, and independence of the covariate to satisfy assumptions for ANCOVA. No violations were identified.

Source: L. Sharmer. (2001). Evaluation of alcohol education programs on attitude, knowledge, and self-reported behavior of college students. *Evaluation and the Health Professions, 24*(3), p. 349.

---

[6]I first discussed the notion of linearity in Chapter 3; you may want to review that earlier discussion if you have forgotten what it means to say that two variables have a linear relationship.

Other Standard Assumptions

As indicated earlier, the "standard" assumptions of ANOVA (e.g., normality, homogeneity of variance, sphericity) underlie ANCOVA as well. You should upgrade or downgrade your evaluation of a study depending upon the attention given to these assumptions in the situations where F-tests are biased when assumptions are violated. Unfortunately, you are likely to come across *many* ANCOVA studies in which there is absolutely no discussion of linearity, equal regression slopes, normality, or homogeneity of variance.

ANCOVA Used with Intact Groups

In a randomized experiment, the various population means on the covariate variable can be considered identical. This is the case because of the random assignment of research participants to the comparison groups of the investigation. Granted, the sample means for the comparison groups on the covariate variable will probably vary, but the corresponding population means are identical.

When ANCOVA is used to compare **intact groups** (i.e., groups that are formed in a nonrandomized fashion), the population means on the covariate variable cannot be assumed to be equal. For example, if a study is set up to compare sixth-grade boys with sixth-grade girls on their ability to solve word problems in mathematics, a researcher might choose to make the comparison using ANCOVA, with reading ability used as the covariate variable. In such a study, the population means on reading ability might well differ between the two gender groups.

Although my concern over the equality or inequality of the covariate population means may initially seem silly (because of the adjustment feature of ANCOVA), this issue is far more important than it might at first appear. I say this because studies in theoretical statistics have shown that the ANCOVA's adjusted means turn out to be biased in the situation where the comparison groups differ with respect to population means on the covariate variable. In other words, the sample-based adjusted means on the dependent variable do not turn out to be accurate estimates of the corresponding adjusted means in the population when the population means on the covariate variable are dissimilar.

Because ANCOVA produces adjusted means, many applied researchers evidently think that this statistical procedure was designed so as to permit intact groups to be compared. Over the years, I have repeatedly come across research reports in which the researchers talk as if ANCOVA has the magical power to equate intact groups and thereby allow valid inferences to be drawn from comparisons of adjusted means. Excerpts 15.18 and 15.19 illustrate this view held by many applied researchers that ANCOVA works well with intact groups.

Besides ANCOVA's statistical inability to generate unbiased adjusted means when intact groups are compared, there is a second, logical reason why you should

EXCERPTS 15.18–15.19 • *The Use of ANCOVA with Intact Groups*

We used analysis of covariance to compare the AVR and its components (summary measures of retinal arteriolar and venular diameters) between persons who did and did not develop diabetes.

Source: T. Y. Wong, R. Klein, A. R. Sharrett, and M. I. Schmidt. (2002). Retinal arteriolar narrowing and risk of diabetes mellitus in middle-aged persons. *Journal of the American Medical Association, 287*(19), pp. 2529–2530.

- -

One-way analysis of covariance (ANCOVA) was conducted to see if there was a significant difference between deaf males and females on the metacognitive test.

Source: Y. Al-Hilawani. (2001). Examining metacognition in hearing and deaf/hard of hearing students: A comparative study. *American Annals of the Deaf, 146*(1), p. 48.

be on guard whenever you come across a research report in which ANCOVA was used in an effort to equate intact groups. Simply stated, the covariate variable(s) used by the researcher may not address one or more important differences between the intact groups. Here, the problem is that a given covariate variable (or set of covariate variables) is limited in scope. Simply stated, the covariate variable(s) used by the researcher might not address one or more important differences between the intact groups.

Consider, for example, the many studies conducted in schools or colleges where one intact group of students receives one form of instruction while a different intact group receives an alternative form of instruction. In such studies, it is common practice to compare the two groups' posttest means via an analysis of covariance, with the covariate being IQ, GPA, or score on a pretest. In the summaries of these studies, the researchers will say that they used ANCOVA "to control for initial differences between the groups." However, it is debatable whether academic ability is reflected in any of the three covariates mentioned (or even in all three used jointly). In this and many other studies, people's motivation plays no small part in how well they perform!

In summary, be extremely cautious when confronted with research claims based upon the use of ANCOVA with intact groups. If an important covariate variable was overlooked by those who conducted the study, pay no attention whatsoever to the conclusions based upon the data analysis. Even in the case where data on all important covariate variables were collected and used, you *still* should be tentative in your inclination to buy into the claims made by the researchers.

Before you finish this section concerning ANCOVA and intact groups, take time to read Excerpts 15.20 and 15.21. They represent exceptions to the rule, for

EXCERPTS 15.20–15.21 • *Why ANCOVA with Intact Groups Is Problematic*

CEKS pretest scores were submitted to a one-way analysis of variance (ANOVA) to determine pretest differences among the groups. The highly significant result, $F(2, 673) = 12.21, p = .001$, substantiated that initial group differences were present. This initial difference invalidates the use of an analysis of covariance because the covariate (pretest score) was not statistically independent of the treatment (group membership).

Source: H. E. Baker. (2002). Reducing adolescent career indecision: The ASVAB Career Exploration Program. *Career Development Quarterly, 50*(4), p. 366.

Lack of random assignment to groups also limits the interpretation of the results. Successive cohorts admitted to the SUPPP go through an identically rigorous admission process and have many similar characteristics, as the exploration of several background characteristics revealed. However, there are undoubtedly other background characteristics not examined here that may have introduced selection bias not accounted for in the analysis. Though one can make the case that the use of the ANCOVA is more precise than a statistical procedure that ignores differences in background measures altogether, it is still likely to be biased. The sameness of the cohorts cannot be unequivocally determined on the basis of the selected background measures alone.

Source: M. A. Copland. (2000). Problem-based learning and prospective principals' problem-framing ability. *Educational Administration Quarterly, 36*(4), p. 602.

the good thoughts expressed in these passages are seen quite rarely in research summaries. These researchers deserve high praise for understanding and pointing out that ANCOVA is *incapable* of equating intact groups.

Related Issues

Near the beginning of this chapter, I asserted that any ANCOVA is, in several respects, like its ANOVA counterpart. We have already considered many of the ways in which ANOVA and ANCOVA are similar, such as the way post hoc tests are typically used to probe significant main effects and interactions. At this point, we ought to consider three additional ways in which ANCOVA is akin to ANOVA.

As with ANOVA, the Type I error rate will be inflated if separate ANCOVAs are used to analyze the data corresponding to two or more dependent variables. To deal with this problem, the conscientious researcher will implement one of several available strategies. The most frequently used strategy for keeping the operational Type I error rate in line with the stated alpha level is the **Bonferroni adjustment technique,** and it can be used with ANCOVA as easily as it can with ANOVA.

In Excerpt 15.22, we see a case where the Bonferroni adjustment technique was used in conjunction with a two-way mixed ANCOVA that was used multiple times, each with data from a different dependent variable. Although this passage makes it seem that there were five dependent variables, there were eight. That is why the final sentence indicates that the adjusted alpha level was set equal to .006.

EXCERPT 15.22 • *Use of the Bonferroni Adjustment Technique*

Repeated measures analysis of covariance (with mood as a covariate) was used to evaluate longitudinal changes in participants' self-care attitudes and the intervention effect on morale, caregiver appraisal, and life situation. . . . Due to the number of variables analyzed, a more stringent significance level ($p = .006$) was required to report significance in the ANCOVA results.

Source: M. C. Clark and J. Lester. (2000). The effect of video-based interventions on self-care. *Western Journal of Nursing Research, 22*(8), p. 903.

The second issue that has a common connection to both ANOVA and AN-COVA is the important distinction between **statistical significance** and **practical significance.** Since it is possible, in either kind of analysis, for the data to produce a finding that is significant in a statistical sense but not in a practical sense, you should upgrade your evaluation of any ANCOVA study wherein the researcher conducts a power analysis, estimates the magnitude of observed effects, or computes a strength-of-association index. Because so many people mistakenly equate statistical significance and practical significance, let's take the time to consider three studies in which the researchers wisely tried to distinguish between these different concepts.

Earlier (in Excerpt 15.13), we saw an example in which eta squared was used to assess the practical significance of ANCOVA results. Now, in Excerpt 15.23, we see a case in which the issue of practical significance is addressed by means of post hoc estimates of effect size. In this passage, the researchers summarize the four one-way ANCOVAs that they conducted, each on a different dependent variable. As you can see and as the researchers admit, the effect size indices are not very impressive (when compared against the standard of .20 for a small effect), even in the presence of statistical significance as shown by the ANCOVA *F.*

In Excerpts 15.24 and 15.25, we see cases in which power analyses were conducted in conjunction with analyses of covariance. In the first of these excerpts, the power analysis was performed in the design phase of the study, before any data were

EXCERPT 15.23 • *ANCOVA and Effect Size Computations*

Initial examination of the mean scores for the four executive function domains revealed average scores for the good writer group and average scores for the poor writer group for three of the four domains. Controlling for reading decoding skills, analysis of covariance (ANCOVA) procedures yielded statistically significant group differences in the initiation domain, $F(1, 53) = 4.81$, $p < .01$, and in the set shifting domain, $F(1, 53) = 3.93$, $p < .03$. Effect sizes were .16 and .13, respectively, and generally fell within the small range. Group comparisons on the sustaining domain approached statistical significance, $F(1, 53) = 2.46$, $p < .09$, and the effect size was small at .09. The inhibition/stopping domain was not significantly different between groups, $F(1, 53) = 1.19$, $p < .31$.

Source: S. R. Hooper, C. W. Swartz, M. B. Wakely, R. E. L. de Kruif, and J. W. Montgomery. (2002). Executive functions in elementary school children with and without problems in written expression. *Journal of Learning Disabilities, 35*(1), p. 64.

EXCERPTS 15.24–15.25 • *ANCOVA and Power Analyses*

Treatment effect at 3 months was estimated using analysis of covariance. The measurement obtained at 3 months was the outcome variable, treatment assignment was the main effect, and baseline measurement of the variable was used as a covariate. An estimated sample size of 30 was determined to be necessary to detect a 30% reduction in insulin concentration with 80% power and a 2-tailed α level of .05.

Source: C. Hadigan, C. Corcoran, N. Basgoz, and B. Davis. (2000). Metformin in the treatment of HIV lipodystrophy syndrome: A randomized controlled trial. *Journal of the American Medical Association, 284*(4), p. 473.

- -

Because the correlation coefficient between science scores (covariate) and posttest scores was significantly high ($r = .54$, $p = .001$), one-way ANCOVA was conducted on achievement scores. The results showed a significant difference for the treatments, $F(2, 56) = 5.28$, $MSE = 29.58$, $p < .01$. Approximately 16% of the difference in achievement was explained by the treatments. Observed power was .82.

Source: S. H. Song and J. M. Keller. (2001). Effectiveness of motivationally adaptive computer-assisted instruction on the dynamic aspects of motivation. *Educational Technology, Research and Development, 49*(2), p. 18.

collected. In fact, the purpose of this power analysis was to determine how much sample data should be gathered. In Excerpt 15.25, the power analysis was done after the fact. Of these two kinds of power analyses, the first kind ought to impress you more and cause you to respect more fully the results of the investigation.

The third point I want to make in this section is simple: **Planned comparisons** can be used in ANCOVA studies just as easily as they can be used in ANOVA studies. Excerpt 15.26 is a case in point. Within the researchers' five-group study, they investigated some of their questions by means of a 2×3 ANCOVA, and they dealt with their remaining questions by means of a set of orthogonal contrasts. In a very real sense, the tests conducted within *both* parts of this comprehensive analysis were planned comparisons.

EXCERPT 15.26 • *ANCOVA and Planned Comparisons*

Participants were randomly assigned to a no-TV control group or to one of four treatment conditions. . . . Hypotheses were tested using separate ANCOVAs for the two dependent measures. . . . The first set of analyses tested main effects and their interaction, on recall and recognition test scores. A second set of analyses included all five original conditions, using orthogonal planned contrasts to test individual hypotheses.

Source: G. B. Armstrong and L. Chung. (2000). Background television and reading memory in context: Assessing TV interference and facilitative context effects on encoding versus retrieval processes. *Communication Research, 27*(3), pp. 337, 341.

A Few Warnings

Before concluding our discussion of ANCOVA, I want to offer a few warnings about deciphering research reports that present results from this form of statistical analysis. As you consider these comments, however, do not forget that ANCOVA legitimately can be thought of as a set of statistical procedures made possible by adding covariate data to an ANOVA-type situation. Because of this fact, all the tips and warnings offered at the conclusions of Chapters 10 through 14 should be kept in mind when you consider the results from a study that used ANCOVA. In addition to being aware of the concerns focused upon in those earlier chapters, you should also remain sensitive to the following three unique-to-ANCOVA cautions when considering research claims based on covariance analyses.

The Statistical Focus: Adjusted Means

In a covariance analysis, all *F*-tests (other than those concerned with underlying assumptions) deal with adjusted means on the dependent variable, not the unadjusted means. This holds true for the *F*-tests contained in the ANCOVA summary table, the *F*-tests involved in any planned comparisons, and the *F*-tests involved in any post hoc investigation. For this reason, adjusted means should be presented—either in a table or within the textual discussion—whenever the researcher attempts to explain the meaning of any *F*-test result. It is helpful, as we have seen, to have access to the means on the covariate variable and the unadjusted means on the dependent variable. However, it is the adjusted means on the dependent variable that constitute the central statistical focus of any ANCOVA.

Unfortunately, many researchers fail to present the adjusted means in their research reports. When this happens, you are boxed into a corner where you cannot easily decide for yourself whether a statistically significant finding ought to be considered significant in a practical sense. Since making this kind of decision is one of the things consumers of the research literature ought to do on a regular basis, I must encourage you to downgrade your evaluation of any ANCOVA-based study that fails to contain the adjusted means that go with the *F*-test(s) focused on by the researcher.

The Importance of Underlying Assumptions

ANCOVA's *F*-tests that compare adjusted means function as they are supposed to function only if various underlying assumptions are valid. Moreover, the condition of equal sample sizes does not bring about a situation where the assumptions are rendered unimportant. In other words, equal *n*s do not cause ANCOVA to become robust to its underlying assumptions.

Whenever you consider research claims based upon ANCOVA, check to see whether the researcher says anything about the statistical assumptions upon which the analysis was based. Upgrade your evaluation of the research report when there is expressed concern over the assumption of equal regression slopes, the assumption of a linear relationship between the covariate and dependent variables, and the assumption that scores on the covariate variable are not influenced by the independent variable. If these assumptions are not discussed, you should downgrade your evaluation of the study.

If an assumption is tested, give the researchers some bonus credit if they use a lenient rather than rigorous alpha level in assessing the assumption's H_0. I say this because researchers deserve credit if they perform statistical tests in such a way that the "deck is stacked against them" in terms of what they would like to show. Since the typical researcher who uses ANCOVA wants the linearity and equal-slopes assumptions to be met, a lenient level of significance (such as .10, .15, .20, or even .25) gives the data more of a chance to reveal an improper situation than would be the case if alpha is set equal to .05, .01, or .001. When testing assumptions, Type II errors are generally considered to be more serious than errors of the first kind, and the level of significance should be set accordingly.

ANCOVA versus ANOVA

My final warning has to do with your general opinion of ANCOVA-based studies as compared with ANOVA-based studies. Because ANCOVA is more complex (due to the involvement of a larger number of variables and assumptions), many consumers of the research literature hold the opinion that data-based claims are more trustworthy when they are based on ANCOVA rather than ANOVA. I strongly encourage you to *refrain* from adopting this unjustified point of view.

Although ANCOVA (as compared with ANOVA) does, in fact, involve more complexities in terms of what is involved both on and beneath the surface, it is an extremely delicate instrument. To provide meaningful results, ANCOVA must be used very carefully—with attention paid to important assumptions, with focus directed at the appropriate set of sample means, and with concern over the correct way to draw inferences from ANCOVA's F-tests. Because of its complexity, ANCOVA affords its users more opportunities to make mistakes than does ANOVA.

If used skillfully, ANCOVA can be of great assistance to applied researchers. If not used skillfully, however, ANCOVA can be dangerous. Unfortunately, many people think of complexity as being an inherent virtue. In statistics, that is often *not* the case. As pointed out earlier in the chapter, the interpretation of ANCOVA F-tests is problematic whenever the groups being compared have been formed in a nonrandom fashion—and this statement holds true even if (1) multiple covariate variables are involved, and (2) full attention is directed to all underlying assumptions. In contrast, it would be much easier to interpret the results generated by the application of ANOVA to the data provided by participants who have been randomly assigned to comparison groups. Care is required, of course, whenever you attempt to interpret the outcome of *any* inferential test. My point is simply that ANCOVA, because of its complexity as compared to ANOVA, demands a higher—not lower—level of care on your part when you encounter its results.

Review Terms

Adjusted means	Homogeneity of regression slopes
Analysis of covariance	Intact groups
ANCOVA	Linearity
Assumption of equal regression slopes	Planned comparison
Bonferroni adjustment technique	Post hoc investigation
Concomitant variable	Practical significance
Covariate variable	Statistical significance

The Best Items in the Companion Website

1. An interactive online quiz (with immediate feedback provided) covering Chapter 15.
2. Nine misconceptions about the content of Chapter 15.
3. One of the best passages from Chapter 15: "Are ANCOVA Studies Better Than ANOVA Studies?"
4. The first two e-articles.
5. The first of the two jokes, for it deals with the analysis of covariance.

Fun Exercises inside Research Navigator

1. Do reminders of death have a differential impact on college men versus college women?

In a three-stage experiment, 101 male and female college students first completed a questionnaire concerning their sensation-seeking behavior. Then they were randomly assigned to one of two groups. Those in one group were asked what they thought about their impended death; those in the other group were asked about watching TV. Finally, members of both groups completed a questionnaire dealing with the appeal of risk-taking behaviors (such as bungee jumping and hang gliding). Scores on sensation-seeking served as the covariate in a 2 (death/TV) × 2 (gender) ANCOVA. Results indicated that being reminded of death had an impact on one of the gender groups but not the other. Which group do you think was affected, and do you think the death reminder increased or decreased the appeal of risk-taking behaviors? To find out, locate the PDF version of the research report in the Helping Professions database of ContentSelect, read the three full paragraphs on page 126, and look at Table 1.

G. Hirschberger, V. Florian, M. Mikulincer, J. L. Goldenberg, & T. Pyszczynski. Gender differences in the willingness to engage in risky behavior. *Issues in Comprehensive Journal of Psychology.* Located in the HELPING PROFESSIONS database of ContentSelect.

2. In a study on college students' opinions about prayer and counselors, why wasn't the covariate used?

In this study, 67 college students were randomly assigned to two groups, both of which read a two-page vignette describing a counseling session. The vignettes were identical except for one sentence located near the end of the second page. In one vignette (given to one of the groups), the counselee mentioned prayer prior to the counselor disclosing the use of prayer. In the other vignette (given to the other group), the counselee never said anything about prayer and yet the counselor still disclosed the use of prayer. Evaluations of each vignette's counselor by the research participants served as the study's dependent variable. Religiosity scores, gathered from the vignette readers, were supposed to be used as the covariate within an ANCOVA comparison of the two groups. However, those religiosity scores were not used and the ANCOVA was not conducted. Why do you think the researchers made this decision? To find out, locate the PDF version of the research report in the Psychology database of ContentSelect and read (on page 273) the first two sentences of the second paragraph of the "Results."

S. J. Nyman & T. K. Daugherty. Congruence of counselor self-disclosure and perceived effectiveness. *Journal of Psychology.* Located in the PSYCHOLOGY database of ContentSelect.

Review Questions and Answers begin on page 516.

16

Bivariate, Multiple, and Logistic Regression

In Chapter 3, we considered how bivariate correlation can be used to describe the relationship between two variables. Then, in Chapter 9, we looked at how bivariate correlations are dealt with in an inferential manner. In this chapter, our focus is on a topic closely related to correlation. This topic is called **regression.**

As you will see, three different kinds of regression will be considered here: **bivariate regression, multiple regression,** and **logistic regression.** Bivariate regression is similar to bivariate correlation, for both are designed for situations in which there are just two variables. Multiple and logistic regression, on the other hand, were created for cases where there are three or more variables. Although many other kinds of regression procedures have been developed, the three considered here are by far the ones used most frequently by applied researchers.

The three regression procedures considered in this chapter are like correlation in that they are concerned with relationships among variables. Because of this, you may be tempted to think that regression is simply another way of talking about, or measuring, correlation. Resist that temptation! That's because these two statistical procedures differ in three important respects: their purpose, the way variables are labeled, and the kinds of inferential tests applied to the data.

The first difference between correlation and regression concerns the purpose of each technique. As indicated in Chapter 3, bivariate correlation is designed to illuminate the relationship, or connection, between two variables. The computed correlation coefficient may suggest that the relationship being focused on is direct and strong, or indirect and moderate, or so weak that it would be unfair to think of the relationship as being either direct or indirect. Regardless of how things turn out, each of the two variables is equally responsible for the nature and strength of the link between the two variables.

Whereas correlation concentrates on the relationship that exists *between* variables, regression focuses on the variable(s) that exist on one or the other *ends* of the link. Depending on which end is focused on, regression will be trying to accomplish one or the other of two goals. These two goals involve prediction on the one hand and explanation on the other.

In some studies, regression is utilized to **predict** scores on one variable based upon information regarding the other variable(s). For example, a college might use regression in an effort to predict how well applicants will handle its academic curriculum. Each applicant's college GPA would be the main focus of the regression, with predictions made on the basis of available data on other variables (e.g., an entrance exam, the applicant's essay, and recommendations written by high school teachers). If used in this manner, regression's focus would be on the one variable toward which predictions are made: college GPA.

In other investigations, regression is used in an effort to **explain** why the study's people, animals, or things score differently on a particular variable of interest. For example, a researcher might be interested in why people differ in the degree to which they seem satisfied with life. If such a study were to be conducted, a questionnaire might be administered to a large group of individuals for the purpose of measuring life satisfaction. Those same individuals would also be measured on several other variables that might explain why some people are quite content with what life has thrown at them while others seem to grumble incessantly because they think life has been cruel and unfair to them. Such variables might include health status, relationships with others, and job enjoyment. If used in this manner, regression's focus would be on the variables that potentially explain why people differ in their levels of life satisfaction.

Excerpts 16.1 and 16.2 illustrate the two different purposes of regression. In the first of these excerpts, the clear objective was to see if ECGs could predict a very important later outcome (survival or mortality). If shown to have prognostic capabilities, the ECGs could then bring forth intervention for those individuals predicted to have a subsequent and fatal heart attack. In Excerpt 16.2, the goal was not prediction but rather explanation. In this study, the researchers wanted to gain insight into the reasons why a gender gap exists between the salaries paid to men and women.

The second difference between regression and correlation concerns the labels attached to the variables. This difference can be seen most easily in the case where data on just two variables have been collected. Let's call these variables A and B. In a correlation analysis, variables A and B have no special names; they are simply the study's two variables. With no distinction made between them, their location in verbal descriptions or in pictorial representations can be switched without changing what's being focused on. For example, once r becomes available, it can be described as the correlation between A and B *or* it can be referred to as the correlation between B and A. Likewise, if a scatter diagram is used to show the relationship between the two variables, it doesn't matter which variable is positioned on the abscissa.

In a regression analysis involving A and B, an important distinction between the two variables must be made. In regression, one of the two variables needs to be identified as the **dependent variable** and the other variable must be seen as the

EXCERPTS 16.1–16.2 • *The Two Purposes of Regression: Prediction and Explanation*

The main objective of this study was to determine the predictive value of the initial ECG [electrocardiogram] for in-hospital mortality. . . . The c statistic was calculated to determine the ability of the model to discriminate between patients with and without diagnostic ECGs. Relevant variables were then used to construct a series of forward logistic regression models with inhospital mortality as the dependent variable.

Source: R. D. Welch, R. J. Zalenski, P. D. Frederick, and J. A. Malmgren. (2001). Prognostic value of a normal or nonspecific initial electrocardiogram in acute myocardial infarction. *Journal of the American Medical Association, 286*(16), p. 1976.

- -

Multiple regression analysis was used to test Hypothesis 3 and ascertain if career determinants could explain the gender differences in career progression. . . . The income gaps between men and women were explained by gender differences in career determinants, such as work hours, career interruptions, and having a nonemployed spouse.

Source: C. Kirchmeyer. (2002). Gender differences in managerial careers: Yesterday, today, and tomorrow. *Journal of Business Ethics, 37*(1), pp. 5, 16.

independent variable.[1] This distinction is important because (1) the scatter diagram in bivariate regression always is set up such that the vertical axis corresponds with the dependent variable while the horizontal axis represents the independent variable and (2) the names of the two variables cannot be interchanged in verbal descriptions of the regression. For example, the regression of A on B is not the same as the regression of B on A.[2]

Excerpts 16.3 and 16.4 come from two studies that were quite different. In the first study, only two variables were involved in the single regression that was conducted. In the second study, seven variables were involved in each of four separate regressions. Despite these differences, notice how the researchers associated with each excerpt clearly designate the status of each variable as being a dependent variable or an independent variable.

---

[1]The terms *criterion variable, outcome variable,* and *response variable* are synonymous with the term *dependent variable,* while the terms *predictor variable* or *explanatory variable* mean the same thing as *independent variable.*

[2]When the phrase "regression of ___ on ___" is used, the variable appearing in the first blank will be the dependent variable whereas the variable(s) appearing in the second blank will be the independent variable(s).

EXCERPTS 16.3–16.4 • *Dependent and Independent Variables*

To assess the relationship between intake of antioxidants from food and cognitive function at baseline, we performed linear regression analysis with antioxidant intake as the dependent variable and baseline MMSE score as independent variable.

Source: M. J. Engelhart, M. I. Geerlings, A. Ruitenberg, and J. C. van Swieten. (2002). Dietary intake of antioxidants and risk of Alzheimer disease. *Journal of the American Medical Association, 287*(24), p. 3225.

- -

The four metaphor category variables—*roles, scope, membership, and objectives*—served as dependent variables in four separate regression equations. The independent variables for these models were power distance, individualism, performance emphasis, reward emphasis, tight control, and employee orientation.

Source: C. B. Gibson and M. E. Zellmer-Bruhn. (2001). Metaphors and meaning: An intercultural analysis of the concept of teamwork. *Administrative Science Quarterly, 46*(2), p. 293.

The third difference between correlation and regression concerns the focus of inferential tests and confidence intervals. With correlation, there is just one thing that can be focused upon: the sample correlation coefficient. With regression, however, you will see that inferences focus on the correlation coefficient, the regression coefficient(s), the intercept, the change in the regression coefficient, and something called the odds ratio. We will consider these different inferential procedures as we look at bivariate regression, multiple regression, and logistic regression.

Although correlation and regression are not the same, correlational concepts serve as some (but not all) of regression's building blocks. With that being the case, you may wonder why this chapter is positioned here rather than immediately after Chapter 9. If this question has popped into your head, there is a simple answer. This chapter is located here because certain concepts from the analysis of variance and the analysis of covariance also serve as building blocks in some regression analyses. For example, researchers sometimes base their regression predictions (or explanations) on the interactions between independent variables. Also, regressions are sometimes conducted with one or more covariate variables controlled or held constant. Without knowing about interactions and covariates, you would be unable to understand these particular components of regression analyses.

We now turn our attention to the simplest kind of regression used by applied researchers. Take good mental notes as you study this material, for the concepts you will now encounter provide a foundation for the other two kinds of regression to be considered later in the chapter.

Bivariate Regression

The simplest kind of regression analysis is called **bivariate regression.** First, we need to clarify the purpose of and the data needed for this kind of regression. Then, we will consider scatter diagrams, lines of best fit, and prediction equations. Finally, we will discuss inferential procedures associated with bivariate regression.

Purpose and Data

As you would suspect based on its name, bivariate regression involves just two variables. One of the variables will serve as the dependent variable while the other functions as the independent variable. The purpose of this kind of regression can be either prediction or explanation; however, bivariate regression is used most frequently to see how well scores on the dependent variable can be predicted from data on the independent variable.

To illustrate how bivariate regression can be used in a predictive manner, imagine that Sam, a 30-year-old weight lifter, has been plagued by a shoulder injury that for months has failed to respond to nonsurgical treatment. Consequently, arthroscopic surgery is scheduled to repair Sam's bad shoulder. Even though he knows that arthroscopic procedures usually permit a rapid return to normal activity, he would like to know how long he'll be out of commission following surgery. His presurgery question to the doctor is short and sweet: "When will I be able to lift again?" Clearly, Sam wants his doctor to make a prediction.

Although Sam's doctor might be inclined to answer this question concerning down time by telling Sam about the *average* length of convalescence for weight lifters following arthroscopic shoulder surgery, that's really not what Sam wants to know. Obviously, some people bounce back from surgery more quickly than do others. Therefore Sam wants the doctor to consider his (i.e., Sam's) individual case and make a prediction about how long he'll have to interrupt his training. If Sam's doctor has seen the results of a recent study dealing with weight lifters who had arthroscopic shoulder surgery, and if the doctor has a computer program that can perform a bivariate regression, he could provide Sam with a better-than-average answer to the question about postsurgical down time.

In the actual study conducted with people like Sam, there were 10 weight lifters who had shoulder injuries. Although data on several variables were collected in this real investigation, let's consider the data on just two: age and number of postsurgical days of down time. Excerpt 16.5 presents the data on these two variables.

Scatter Diagrams, Regression Lines, and Regression Equations

The component parts and functioning of regression can best be understood by examining a scatter diagram. In Figure 16.1, such a picture has been generated using

EXCERPT 16.5 • *Data on Two Variables*

TABLE 1 *Age and Postsurgical Time Away from Sport for 10 Weight Lifters*

Patient	Age	Return to sport (days)
1	33	6
2	31	4
3	32	4
4	28	1
5	33	3
6	26	3
7	34	4
8	32	2
9	28	3
10	27	2

Source: W. K. Auge and R. A. Fischer. (1998). Arthroscopic distal clavicle resection for isolated atraumatic osteolysis in weight lifters. *American Journal of Sports Medicine, 26*(2), p. 191. (Note: Table 1 was modified slightly for presentation here.)

the data from Excerpt 16.5. There are 10 dots in this "picture," each positioned so as to reveal the age and postsurgical convalescent time for one of the weight lifters.

The scatter diagram in Figure 16.1 was set up with days of convalescence on the ordinate and age on the abscissa. These two axes of the scatter diagram were labeled like this because it makes sense to treat convalescence as the dependent variable. It is the variable toward which predictions will eventually be made for Sam and other weight lifters who are similar to those who supplied the data we are currently considering. Age, on the other hand, is positioned on the abscissa because it is the independent variable. It is the variable that "supplies" data used to make the predictions.[3]

As you can see, a slanted line passes through the data points of the scatter diagram. This line is called the **regression line** or the **line of best fit,** and it will function as the tool our hypothetical doctor will use in order to predict how long Sam will have to refrain from lifting. As should be apparent, the regression line is positioned so as to be as close as possible to all of the dots. A special formula determines

[3]Since we are dealing with regression (and not correlation), it would be improper to switch the two variables in the scatter diagram. The dependent variable always goes on the ordinate; the independent variable always goes on the abscissa.

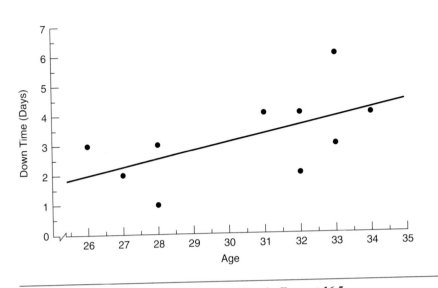

FIGURE 16.1   *Regression Analysis Using Data in Excerpt 16.5*

the precise location of this line; however, you do not need to know anything about that formula except that it is based on a statistical concept called *least squares.*[4]

Let's make a prediction for Sam, pretending now that we are his doctor. All we need to do is turn to the scatter diagram and take a little trip with our index finger or our eyes. Our trip begins on the abscissa at a point equal to Sam's age. (Remember, Sam is 30 years old.) We move vertically from that point up into the scatter diagram until we reach the regression line. Finally, we travel horizontally (to the left) from that point on the regression line until reaching the ordinate. Wherever this little trip causes us to end up on the ordinate becomes our prediction for Sam's down time. According to our information, our prediction is that Sam will be out of commission for approximately three days.

Notice that our prediction of Sam's down time would have been shorter if he had been younger and longer if he had been older. For example, we would have predicted about two days if he had been 26 years old, or four days if he had been 34. These alternative predictions for a younger or older Sam are brought about by the tilt of the regression line. Because there is a positive correlation between the independent and dependent variables, the regression line tilts from lower left to upper right.

Although it is instructive to see how predictions are made by means of a regression line that passes through the data points of a scatter diagram, the exact same

[4]The *least squares principle* simply means that when the squared distances of the data points from the regression line are added together, they yield a smaller sum than would be the case for any other straight line that could be drawn through the scatter diagram's data points.

objective can be achieved more quickly and more scientifically by means of something called the **regression equation.** In bivariate, linear regression, this equation always has the following form:

$$Y' = a + b \cdot X,$$

where Y' stands for the predicted score on the dependent variable, a is a constant, b is the **regression coefficient,** and X is the known score on the independent variable. This equation is simply the technical way of describing the regression line. For the data shown in Excerpt 16.5 (and Figure 16.1), the regression equation turns out like this:

$$Y' = -5.05 + (.27)X.$$

To make a prediction for Sam by using the regression equation, we simply substitute Sam's age for X and then work out the simple math. When we do this, we find that $Y' = 3.05$. This is the predicted down time (in days) for Sam. The fact that this value is very similar to what we predicted earlier (when we took a trip through the scatter diagram) should not be at all surprising. That's because the regression equation is nothing more than a precise mechanism for telling us where we'll end up if, in a scatter diagram, we first move vertically from some point on the abscissa up to the regression line and then move horizontally from the regression line to the ordinate.

Whereas scatter diagrams and regression lines appear only rarely in research reports, regression equations show up quite frequently. In Excerpt 16.6, we see a case in point. As you can see from this passage, the regression equation was built so as to predict height from arm span. In this study, each person's height and arm

EXCERPT 16.6 • *The Regression Equation in Bivariate Regression*

The purpose of this study is to determine the accuracy of arm span as a measure of height in young and middle-age adults. . . . A convenience sample of 83 subjects was studied. Subjects were between the ages of 20 and 61 years, with a mean age of 41.63 years ($SD = 11.10$). Fifty-seven (69%) were women, and 26 (31%) were men. . . . The first analysis was a simple regression of height on arm span to determine how well arm span, alone, predicted height. The prediction equation is as follows: Height = 0.87 (arm span) + 20.54.

Source: J. K. Brown, K. T. Whittemore, and T. R. Knapp. (2000). Is arm span an accurate measure of height in young and middle-age adults? *Clinical Nursing Research, 9*(1), pp. 90–91.

span was measured in centimeters. Thus, the two numbers in the regression formula (0.87 and 20.54) must be interpreted as being in the scale of centimeters, not inches.

Let's use the regression equation presented in Excerpt 16.6 to make some height predictions. When I measure my own arm span, I find that it is equal to 175.1 cm. Using the regression equation, I find that my predicted height is equal to 20.54 + 0.87(175.1) = 172.88 cm. This predicted value turns out to be extremely close to my actual height of 172.70 cm. Now it's your turn. Get a metric measuring device, measure your arm span, and then use the regression formula in Excerpt 16.6 to calculate your predicted height. After doing this, check to see how closely your predicted height matches your actual height. You may be surprised (as I was) at how closely arm span predicts height!

It should be noted that there are two kinds of regression equations that can be created in any bivariate regression analysis. One of these is called an **unstandardized regression equation.** This is the kind we have considered thus far, and it has the form $Y' = a + b \cdot X$. The other kind of regression equation (that can be generated using the same data) is called a **standardized regression formula.** A standardized regression equation has the form $z'_y = \beta \cdot z_x$. These two kinds of regression equations differ in three respects. First, a standardized regression equation involves z-scores on both the independent and dependent variables, not raw scores. Second, the standardized regression equation does not have a constant (i.e., a term for a). Finally, the symbol β is used in place of b (and is called a **beta weight** rather than a regression coefficient).

Interpreting a, b, r, and r^2 in Bivariate Regression

When used for predictive purposes, the regression equation has the form $Y' = a + bX$. Now that you understand how this equation works, let's take a closer look at its two main ingredients, a and b. In addition, let's now pin down the regression meaning of r and r^2.

Earlier, I referred to a as the "constant." Alternatively, this component of the regression equation is called the **intercept.** Simply stated, a indicates where the regression line in the scatter diagram would, if extended to the left, intersect the ordinate. It indicates, therefore, the value of Y' for the case where $X = 0$. In many studies, it may be quite unrealistic (or downright impossible) for there to be a case where $X = 0$; nonetheless, $Y' = a$ when $b = 0$.

In Excerpt 16.6, the constant in the regression equation for the 83 people was equal to 20.54. That is not a very realistic number, for it indicates the predicted height for a person with zero arm span. Likewise, the value of a for the regression line in Figure 16.1 is equal to -5.05. This number is nonsensical, of course, for it indicates the predicted down time following surgery for a weight lifter whose age is 0! Clearly, a may be totally devoid of meaning within the context of a study's independent and dependent variables. Nevertheless, it has an unambiguous and not-so-nonsensical meaning within a scatter diagram, for *a* indicates the point where the regression line intercepts the ordinate.

The other main component of the regression is *b,* the regression coefficient. When the regression line has been positioned within the data points of a scatter diagram, *b* simply indicates the **slope** of that line. As you probably recall from your high school math courses, slope means "rise over run." In other words, the value of *b* signifies how many predicted units change (either up or down) in the dependent variable there are for any one unit increase in the independent variable. In Figure 16.1, the regression equation has a slope equal to .27. This means that the predicted down time for our hypothetical patient Sam would be about one-fourth of a day longer if the surgery is put off a year.

When researchers use bivariate regression, they occasionally will focus on either *b* or *β* more than anything else. Consider, for example, Excerpt 16.7. Here, the researcher presents the beta weight (rather than the regression coefficient), and as you can see, it turned out to be negative. This means that the slope of the regression line was negative, tilting from upper left to lower right. This negative tilt came about because of the inverse relationship between worry and sleep time. (As this example illustrates, the sign of *β* or *b* indicates the kind of relationship that exists between the two variables.)

When summarizing the results of a regression analysis, researchers will normally indicate the value of *r* (the correlation between the independent and dependent variables) or r^2. You already know, of course, that such values for *r* and r^2 measure the strength of the relationship between the independent and dependent variables. However, each has a special meaning, within the regression context, that is worth learning.

As you might expect, the value of *r* will be high to the extent that the scatter diagram's data points are located close to the regression line. Though that is undeniably true, there is a more precise way to conceptualize the regression meaning of

EXCERPT 16.7 • *Focusing on the Regression Coefficient*

I calculated a simple regression using sleep length as the criterion and WDQ scores as the predictor variable to test the relationship between worry and habitual sleep length. [This analysis] indicated a negative relationship between worry and sleep length ($\beta = -.24$). . . . The results of the present study indicate that worry is negatively related to habitual sleep length. In other words, individuals who sleep less tend to worry more often.

Source: W. E. Kelly. (2002). Worry and sleep length revisited: Worry, sleep length, and sleep disturbance ascribed to worry. *Journal of Genetic Psychology, 163*(3), p. 301.

r. Once the regression equation has been generated, that equation could be used to predict Y′ for each person who provided the scores used to develop the equation. In one sense, that would be a very silly thing to do, for predicted scores are unnecessary in light of the fact that *actual* scores on the dependent variable are available for these people. However, by comparing the predicted scores for these people against their actual scores (both on the dependent variable), we would be able to see how well the regression equation works. The value of *r* does exactly this. It quantifies the degree to which the predicted scores match up with the actual scores.

Just as *r* has an interpretation in regression that focuses on the dependent variable, so it is with r^2. Simply stated, the coefficient of determination indicates the proportion of variability in the dependent variable that is "explained" by the independent variable. As illustrated in Excerpt 16.8, r^2 is usually turned into a percent when it is reported in research reports.

EXCERPT 16.8 • *Percent of Variability in the Dependent Variable That Is Explained by the Independent Variable*

The current research, therefore, has two purposes. First, we investigated the effectiveness of CBM math concept tasks in predicting success on statewide math achievement tests. Second, we compared the predictive power of these tasks for students with and without learning disabilities. . . . A Pearson product-moment correlation revealed a strong relationship between the 11-item CBM and the CAT ($r = .83$). Correlations for general education students ($r = .80$; $n = 90$) and students with learning disabilities ($r = .61$; $n = 81$) were high. . . . To determine how much of the variance in the CAT could be explained by CBM, regression analyses were used. Results of simple regression using total CBM scores (0–11) show that the CBM accounted for approximately two thirds of the variance in the CAT for the entire study population. This figure was only slightly lower (.63) for the general education group. Thirty-eight percent of the variance was explained in the group in special education.

Source: R. Helwig, L. Anderson, and G. Tindal. (2002). Using a concept-grounded, curriculum-based measure in mathematics to predict statewide test scores for middle school students with LD. *Journal of Special Education, 36*(2), pp. 105, 107–108.

Inferential Tests in Bivariate Regression

The data used to generate the regression line or the regression equation are typically considered to have come from a sample, not a population. Thus the component parts of a regression analysis—*a*, *b*, and *r*—are typically considered to be sample statistics, not population parameters. Accordingly, it should not come as a surprise that researchers conduct one or more inferential tests whenever they perform a regression analysis.

The most frequently conducted test focuses on r. The null hypothesis in such a test will probably be set up to say that the correlation in the population is equal to 0 (i.e., H_0: $\rho = 0$). This kind of test was discussed in Chapter 9, and the considerations raised there apply equally to tests of r within the context of bivariate regression. In Excerpt 16.9, we see a case in which such a test was performed. Near the end of this excerpt, the researchers present the value of r^2 rather than r. If they had wanted to, they could have reported $r = .20$ in the place where they reported $r^2 = .04$. It doesn't matter, for a test on r is mathematically equivalent to a test on r^2.

EXCERPT 16.9 • *Testing r (or r²) for Significance in Bivariate Regression*

It was hypothesized that physical self-efficacy would be a significant predictor of adherence. To test whether this was the case, a simple regression analysis was run using the physical self-efficacy pretest as the predictor variable and adherence as the criterion variable. Analysis revealed that physical self-efficacy did not significantly predict total adherence, $r^2 = .04$, $F(1, 60) = 2.6$, $p > .05$.

Source: N. M. Glaros and C. M. Janelle. (2001). Varying the mode of cardiovascular exercise to increase adherence. *Journal of Sport Behavior, 24*(1), p. 53.

In bivariate regression, a test on r is mathematically equivalent to a test on b. Therefore, you will never see a case where both r and b are tested, because these two tests would be fully redundant with each other. However, researchers have the freedom to have their test focus on either r or b. In Excerpt 16.10, we see a case where a team of researchers chose to test b. The null hypothesis in this kind of test says that the population value of the regression coefficient is 0. Stated differently, the null hypothesis in such tests is that the regression line has no tilt, thus meaning

EXCERPT 16.10 • *Testing b in Bivariate Regression*

Moreover, the regression of IQ on year of testing ($b = .05$) was not significant ($p \geq .7$).

Source: S. J. Wadsworth, R. K. Olson, B. F. Pennington, and J. C. DeFries. (2000). Differential genetic etiology of reading disability as a function of IQ. *Journal of Learning Disabilities, 33*(2), p. 194.

that the independent variable provides no assistance in predicting scores on the dependent variable.

In some studies, an inferential test will be conducted to compare two or more regression lines. In Excerpt 16.11, we see a situation in which three regression lines were compared. Each of the regression lines was individually tested to see if its slope was significantly different from zero. Then, the researchers statistically compared the slope of the regression line based on data from the psychotic individuals with the slopes of the other two regression lines.

EXCERPT 16.11 • *Statistically Comparing Regression Lines*

To describe the linear changes in cortisol levels across the seven time points in the afternoon cortisol test, regression lines were computed for each of the three groups. . . . [The] slope of the linear regression line was virtually flat for the psychotic major depression subjects ($b = -0.14, p = 0.71$), indicating a relatively constant cortisol level throughout the afternoon. In contrast, the nonpsychotic major depression subjects ($b = -0.90, p < 0.01$) and the healthy volunteers ($b = -0.96, p < 0.01$) showed the expected pattern of decreasing cortisol levels over time. Statistical comparisons of change in cortisol levels over time [showed that] the pattern of relatively constant cortisol levels observed for the subjects with psychotic major depression was statistically different from the reduction observed for both the normal comparison subjects ($z = 2.78, p < 0.01$) and the nonpsychotic major depression subjects ($z = 3.20, p < 0.01$).

Source: J. K. Belanoff, M. Kalehzan, B. Sund, S. K. F. Ficek, and A. F. Schatzberg. (2001). Cortisol activity and cognitive changes in psychotic major depression. *American Journal of Psychiatry, 158*(10), p. 1614.

Multiple Regression

Research
Navigator.c⊛m

Multiple
regression

We now turn our attention to the most popular regression procedure of all, **multiple regression.** This form of regression involves, like bivariate regression, a single dependent variable. In multiple regression, however, there are two or more independent variables. Stated differently, multiple regression involves just one Y variable but two, three, or more X variables.[5]

In three important respects, multiple regression is identical to bivariate regression. First, a researcher's reason for using multiple regression is the same as the

---

[5]Recall that the dependent variable (Y) is sometimes referred to as the criterion, outcome, or response variable while the independent variable (X) is sometimes referred to as the predictor or explanatory variable.

reason for using bivariate regression, either prediction (with a focus on the dependent variable) or explanation (with a focus on the independent variables). Second, a regression equation is involved in both of these regression procedures. Third, both bivariate and multiple regression almost always involve inferential tests and a measure of the extent to which variability among the scores on the dependent variable has been explained or accounted for.

Though multiple regression and bivariate regression are identical in some respects, they also differ in three extremely important ways. As you will see, multiple regression can be done in *different ways* that lead to different results, it can be set up to accommodate *covariates* that the researcher wishes to control, and it can involve (as predictor variables) one or more *interactions* between independent variables. Bivariate regression has none of these characteristics.

In upcoming sections, these three unique features of multiple regression will be discussed. We begin, however, with a consideration of the regression equation that comes from the analysis of data on one dependent variable and multiple independent variables. This equation functions as the most important stepping stone between the raw scores collected in a study and the findings extracted from the investigation.

The Regression Equation

When a regression analysis involves one dependent variable and two independent variables, the regression equation takes the form

$$Y' = a + b_1 \cdot X_1 + b_2 \cdot X_2$$

where Y' stands for the predicted score on the dependent variable, a stands for the constant, b_1 and b_2 are regression coefficients, and X_1 and X_2 represent the two independent variables. In Excerpt 16.12, we see a regression equation that has this exact form.

EXCERPT 16.12 • *A Regression Equation for the Case of Two Independent Variables*

The regression formula predicting overweight reduction was:

$$Y = 6.34 + 7.06X_1 + 4.17X_2$$

where X_1 is the change in eating between meals and X_2 is the change in eating while doing another activity.

Source: M. Golan, M. Fainaru, and A. Weizman. (1998). Role of behaviour modification in the treatment of childhood obesity with the parents as the exclusive agents of change. *International Journal of Obesity, 22*, p. 1221.

As indicated previously, multiple regression can accommodate more than two independent variables. In such cases, the regression equation will simply be extended to the right, with an extra term (made up of a new *b* multiplied by the new *X*) added for each additional independent variable. The presence of these extra terms, of course, does not alter the fact that the regression equation contains only one *Y'* term (located on the left side of the equation) and only one *a* term (located on the right side of the equation).

Excerpt 16.13 illustrates what a regression equation looks like when more than two independent variables are involved in the analysis. In the study associated with this excerpt, the researchers wanted to see if students' performance on a critical thinking task could successfully predict their GPAs. To assess critical thinking skills, college students were given a paper-and-pencil test called the WGCTA. Based on each student's responses, five subscale scores were computed. In the prediction equation shown in Excerpt 16.13, the dependent variable (GPA) is represented as *Y.* Each of the WGCTA subscales appears in parentheses on the right side of the equation.

EXCERPT 16.13 • *Regression Equation with Multiple Independent Variables*

The regression equation, computed using all of the WGCTA subscales, was $Y = 2.3 + .03$ (Inference) $+ .003$ (Recognition of Assumptions) $+ .03$ (Deduction) $+ .06$ (Interpretation) $- .03$ (Evaluation of Arguments).

Source: B. M. Gadzella, M. Baloglu, and R. Stephens. (2002). Prediction of GPA with educational psychology grades and critical thinking scores. *Education, 122*(3), p. 621.

Whereas the regression coefficients—that is, the *b*s—in Excerpt 16.12 were both positive (as indicated by the two + signs on the right side of the equation), a negative regression coefficient appears in Excerpt 16.13. A negative *b* simply implies an inverse relationship between the independent variable associated with that regression coefficient and the study's dependent variable. Surprisingly, in the sample of students used in the study that provided Excerpt 16.13, there was an indirect relationship between the students' GPAs and their ability to evaluate arguments.

Regardless of whether the multiple regression is being conducted for predictive or explanatory purposes, the researcher is usually interested in comparing the independent variables to see the extent to which each one helps the regression analysis achieve its objective. In other words, there is usually interest in finding out the degree to which each independent variable contributes to successful predictions or valid explanations. Although you (as well as a fair number of researchers) may be tempted to look at the bs in order to find out how well each independent variable works, this should not be done because each regression coefficient is presented in the units of measurement used to measure its corresponding X. Thus if one of the independent variables in a multiple regression is height, its b will differ in size depending on whether height measurements are made in centimeters, inches, feet, or miles.

To determine the relative importance of the different independent variables, the researcher needs to look at something other than an **unstandardized regression equation** like those we have seen thus far. Instead, a **standardized regression equation** can be examined. This kind of regression equation, for the case of three independent variables, would take the form

$$z_y' = \beta_1 \cdot z_{x1} + \beta_2 \cdot z_{x2} + \beta_3 \cdot z_{x3}.$$

As you will note, this equation presents the dependent and independent variables in terms of z, it has no constant term, and it uses the symbol β instead of b. These βs are like standardized regression coefficients, and they are called **beta weights.**

Although standardized regression equations are rarely included in research reports, researchers often extract the beta weights from such equations and present the numerical values of these βs. In Excerpts 16.14 and 16.15, we see two instances

EXCERPTS 16.14–16.15 • *Beta Weights*

The regression analysis shows that the owner's managerial skills is the first explanatory variable for sales volume (beta = .32). The second explanatory variable is previous experience in the industry, the third strategic planning (beta = .24 and .23, respectively), and the fourth is the venture's organizational resources (beta = .13).

Source: M. Lerner and T. Almor. (2002). Relationships among strategic capabilities and the performance of women-owned small ventures. *Journal of Small Business Management,* 40(20), p. 121.

- -

Acculturative stress, self esteem, social support, influence of religion, perception of religiosity, contribution, agreement, and education were entered together as predictors in a multiple regression analysis of overall anxiety. Significant independent predictors were acculturative stress ($\beta = .52$), contribution ($\beta = -.25$), and education ($\beta = .14$).

Source: Joseph D. Hovey and Cristina G. Magana. (2002). Cognitive, affective, and physiological expressions of anxiety symptomatology among Mexican migrant farmworkers: Predictors and generational differences. *Community Mental Health Journal,* 38(3), p. 232.

where this was done. Notice that the beta weights are referred to as "beta" in the first of these excerpts, while the symbol β is used in the second excerpt.

Before concluding our discussion of regression equations, two important points need to be made. First, you may come across the term **dummy variable** in reference to one or more of the independent variables used with a multiple regression analysis. This term refers to a dichotomous variable that is coded, for each measured person, as either a 1 or a 0. As you see the technique of multiple regression used in different studies, you are likely to see a wide variety of dummy variables: gender (male, female), race (black, white), residence (urban, rural), marital status (married, unmarried), and so on. Second, be aware of the fact that the beta weights associated with the independent variables can change dramatically if the analysis is repeated with one of the independent variables discarded or another independent variable added. Thus beta weights do not provide a pure and absolute assessment of any independent variable's worth.

Three Kinds of Multiple Regression

Different kinds of multiple regression exist because there are different orders in which data on the independent variables can be entered into the analysis. In this section, we will consider the three most popular versions of multiple regression. These are called simultaneous multiple regression, stepwise multiple regression, and hierarchical multiple regression.

In **simultaneous multiple regression,** the data associated with all independent variables are considered at the same time. This kind of multiple regression is analogous to the process used in preparing vegetable soup where all ingredients are thrown into the pot at the same time, stirred, and then cooked together. In Excerpt 16.16, we see an example of simultaneous multiple regression.

Research
Navigator.com

Simultaneous
multiple
regression

EXCERPT 16.16 • *Simultaneous Multiple Regression*

A simultaneous multiple regression analysis was conducted using age, race, SES, intelligence, metamemory, and presence or absence of instructions to predict the percentage of correct responses to nonmisleading questions. . . . A [second] simultaneous multiple regression analysis was conducted using age, race, SES, intelligence, metamemory, and presence or absence of instructions to predict the percentage of correct responses to misleading questions.

Source: L. F. Geddie, J. Beer, S. Bartosik, and K. L. Wuensch. (2001). The relationship between interview characteristics and accuracy of recall in young children: Do individual differences matter? *Child Maltreatment, 6*(1), p. 65.

The second kind of multiple regression analysis is analogous to the process of preparing a soup in which the ingredients are tossed into the pot based on the amount of each ingredient. Here the stock goes in first (because there's more of that than anything else), followed by the vegetables, the meat, and finally the seasoning. Each of these different ingredients is meant to represent an independent variable, with "amount of ingredient" equated to the size of the bivariate correlation between a given independent variable and the dependent variable. Here, in **stepwise multiple regression,** the computer determines the order in which the independent variables become a part of the regression equation. In Excerpt 16.17, we see an example of this kind of multiple regression.

Research
Navigator.c⊛m
Stepwise multiple
regression

EXCERPT 16.17 • *Stepwise Multiple Regression*

A stepwise multiple regression analysis was used to examine the relationship between mean wordlikeness scores, collapsed across participants, and the frequency of the medial CC sequence. Mean wordlikeness scores, averaged over the three nonwords containing the same CC sequence, served as the dependent variable. The independent variables were the three measures of pattern frequency: Celex frequency, HML frequency, and Moe et al. (1982) frequency. Each was entered into the regression equation in a stepwise fashion if it accounted for a significant proportion of variance in the dependent variable at the $\alpha < .05$ significance level.

Source: B. Munson. (2001). Phonological pattern frequency and speech production in adults and children. *Journal of Speech, Language, and Hearing Research, 44*(4), p. 782.

Research
Navigator.c⊛m
Hierarchical
multiple
regression

Instead of preparing our vegetable soup by simply tossing everything into the pot at once or by letting the amount of an ingredient dictate its order of entry, we could put things into the pot on the basis of concerns regarding flavor and tenderness. If we wanted garlic to flavor everything else, we'd put it in first even though there's only a small amount of it required by the recipe. Similarly, we would hold back some of the vegetables (and not put them in with the others) if they are tender to begin with and we want to avoid overcooking them. **Hierarchical multiple regression** is like cooking the soup in this manner, for in this form of regression the independent variables are entered into the analysis in stages. Often, as illustrated in Excerpt 16.18, the independent variables that are entered first correspond with things the researcher wishes to control. After they are allowed to explain as much variability in the dependent variable as they can, then the other variables are entered to see if they can contribute above and beyond the independent variables that went in first.

EXCERPT 16.18 • *Hierarchical Multiple Regression*

To examine the unique contribution of secure attachment and prosocial orientation to the prediction of proactive and reactive aggression, we performed two hierarchical multiple regression analyses. For both analyses we used the following entry format: the control variables of child age and gender, parent education and marital status, and household income (Step 1); secure attachment (Step 2); and prosocial orientation (Step 3).

Source: R. F. Marcus and C. Kramer. (2001). Reactive and proactive aggression: Attachment and social competence predictors. *Journal of Genetic Psychology, 162*(3), p. 268.

R, R^2, ΔR^2, and Adjusted R^2 in Multiple Regression

In multiple regression studies, the extent to which the regression analysis achieves its objective is usually quantified by means of R, R^2, or adjusted R^2. Sometimes two of these will be presented, and occasionally you will see all three reported for the same regression analysis. These elements of a multiple regression analysis are not superficial and optional add-ons; instead, they are as central to a regression analysis as the regression equation itself.

In bivariate regression, r provides an indication of how well the regression equation works. It does that by quantifying the degree to which the predicted scores match up with the actual scores (on the dependent variable) for the group of individuals used to develop the regression equation. The R of multiple regression can be interpreted in precisely the same way. **Multiple R** is what we would get if we computed Pearson's r between Y and Y' scores for the individuals who provided scores on the independent and dependent variables.

Although the value of R sometimes appears when the results of a multiple regression are reported, researchers are far more likely to report the value of R^2 or to report the percentage equivalent of R^2. By so doing, the success of the regression analysis is quantified by reporting the proportion or percentage of the variability in the dependent variable that has been accounted for or explained by the study's independent variables. Excerpt 16.19 illustrates the way researchers use R^2 in an explained variance manner.

When a multiple regression analysis is conducted with the data from all independent variables considered simultaneously, only one R^2 can be computed. In stepwise and hierarchical regression, however, several R^2 values can be computed, one for each stage of the analysis wherein individual independent variables or sets of independent variables are added. These R^2 values will get larger at each stage, and the *increase* from stage to stage is referred to as **R^2 change.** Another label for the increment in R^2 that's observed as more and more independent variables are

EXCERPT 16.19 • R^2 as an Index of Explained Variance

A multiple regression analysis was used to determine the predictive ability of health perceptions, knowledge, gender, exercise, personal characteristics, and self-esteem on health behaviors. . . . Coefficient of determination (R^2) was 0.248, indicating that these variables explained 25.0 percent of the variance in the total nutrition score.

Source: R. Misra and S. Aguillon. (2001). Predictors of health behaviors in rural adolescents. *Health Education, 101*(1), p. 26.

used as predictors is ΔR^2, where the symbol Δ stands for the two-word phrase "change in."

Excerpt 16.20 illustrates the concept of R^2 *change*. The first predictor variable, when used alone in step 1 of the analysis, produced an R^2 value of .126. When the second predictor variable was added, in step 2, the R^2 value rose to .217. Rounded off to two decimal places, these coefficients of determination were .13 and .22, respectively. The increase from .13 to .22, referred to by the researchers as "R^2 change," was .09.

Either in place of or in addition to R^2, something called **adjusted R^2** is often reported in conjunction with a multiple regression analysis. If reported, adjusted R^2 will take the form of a proportion or a percentage. It is interpreted just like R^2, for it indicates the degree to which variability in the dependent variable is explained by the set of independent variables included in the analysis. The conceptual difference between R^2 and adjusted R^2 is related to the fact that the former, being based on

Research
Navigator.c⊕m

Adjusted R^2

EXCERPT 16.20 • R^2 Change in Stepwise or Hierarchical Multiple Regression

Multiple regression analyses were conducted with SIRI-P as the dependent variable and predictor variables INT [intentionality] and KSS [knowledge] entered in that order. [In step 1], intentionality accounted for 12.6% of the variance when entered alone into the equation. When knowledge was entered as the second step, the model accounted for 21.7% of the variance in SIRI-P (R^2 change = .09). It appears that knowledge accounts for a further 9% of the variance.

Source: S. Maine, R. Shute, and G. Martin. (2001). Educating parents about youth suicide: Knowledge, response to suicidal statements, attitudes, and intention to help. *Suicide and Life-Threatening Behavior, 31*(3), p. 328.

sample data, always yields an overestimate of the corresponding population value of R^2.

Adjusted R^2 removes the bias associated with R^2 by reducing its value. Thus this adjustment anticipates the amount of so-called **shrinkage** that would be observed if the study were to be replicated with a much larger sample. As you would expect, the size of this adjustment is inversely related to study's sample size.[6]

When reporting the results of their multiple regression analyses, some researchers (who probably do not realize that R^2 provides an exaggerated index of predictive success) report just R^2. Of those who are aware of the positive bias associated with R^2, some will include only adjusted R^2 in their reports while others will include both R^2 and adjusted R^2. In Excerpt 16.21, we see an example of the latter situation.

EXCERPT 16.21 • *Adjusted R^2*

The final regression equation [predicting] overall sleep quality included variable sleep length, noise disturbance, going to bed thirsty, and worrying about the ability to fall asleep at bedtime as significant sleep quality predictors, $R^2 = .24$, adjusted $R^2 = .22$. . . .

Source: F. C. Brown, W. Buboltz, and B. Soper. (2002). Relationship of sleep hygiene awareness, sleep hygiene practices, and sleep quality in university students. *Behavioral Medicine,* 28(1), p. 36.

Inferential Tests in Multiple Regression

Researchers can apply several different kinds of inferential tests when they perform a multiple regression. The three most frequently seen tests focus on β, R^2, and ΔR^2. Let's consider what each of these tests does and then we will look at an excerpt in which all three of these tests were used.

When the beta weight for a particular independent variable is tested, the null hypothesis says that the parameter value is equal to 0. If this were true, that particular independent variable would be contributing nothing to the predictive or explanatory objective of the multiple regression. Because of this, researchers frequently will test each of the betas in an effort to decide (1) which independent

---

[6]The size of the adjustment is also influenced by the number of independent variables. With more independent variables, the adjustment is larger.

variables should be included in the regression equation that is in the process of being built or (2) which independent variables included in an already-developed regression equation turned out to be helpful. Beta weights are normally tested with two-tailed *t*-tests.[7]

When R^2 is tested, the null hypothesis says that none of the variance in the dependent variable is explained by the collection of independent variables. (This H_0, of course, has reference to the study's population, not its sample.) This null hypothesis normally is evaluated via an *F*-test. In most studies, the researcher will be hoping that this H_0 will be rejected.[8]

When ΔR^2 is tested, the null hypothesis says that the new independent variable(s) added to the regression equation is totally worthless in helping to explain variability in the dependent variable. As with the null hypotheses associated with tests on beta weights and R^2, this particular H_0 has reference to the study's population, not its sample. A special *F*-test is used to evaluate this null hypothesis. This kind of test, of course, logically fits into the procedures of stepwise and hierarchical multiple regression; it would never be used within the context of a simultaneous multiple regression.[9]

Consider now Excerpt 16.22. In the study associated with this excerpt, the researchers conducted a hierarchical multiple regression on data collected from a large group of adolescents from Quebec, Canada. The dependent variable in this study was psychological depression, with this construct measured with a French version of the Beck Depression Inventory (BDI). This excerpt is worth examining closely because it contains tests of the beta weights, a test of R^2 (in step 1), and a test of R^2 change (in steps 2 and 3).

Two additional features of Excerpt 16.22 are noteworthy. First, the size of the beta weight associated with pubertal status changed as the analysis moved from step 1 to step 2. In fact, this independent variable changed from being statistically significance in step 1 to being nonsignificant in step 2. Such a change in the assessed value of an independent variable is not uncommon in stepwise and multiple regression. Hence, the predictive value of any given independent variable is not absolute; rather, its usefulness depends upon the context (i.e., whether other independent variables are also involved in the multiple regression and, if there are other predictor variables, what kinds of relationships exist among the independent and dependent variables).

---

[7]The *df* for this kind of *t*-test is equal to the sample size minus one more than the number of independent variables.

[8]The first *df* for this kind of *F*-test is equal to the number of independent variables; the second *df* value is equal to the sample size minus one more than the number of independent variables.

[9]The *df* for this kind of *F*-test is equal to (a) the number of new independent variables and (b) the sample size minus one more than the total number of old and new independent variables.

EXCERPT 16.22 • *Inferential Tests in Multiple Regression*

A hierarchical analysis was performed in which BDI scores served as the dependent variable. In the first step, pubertal status was found to account for a small but significant percentage of variance of the BDI scores, $F(1, 488) = 4.23$; $R^2 = .01$, $p < .05$. Gender was entered in the second step of this analysis and accounted for an additional small percentage of variance, R^2 change $= .01$, $F(2, 487) = 5.64$, $p < .01$. The unique contribution of gender was found to be significant ($\beta = .11$, $p < .05$), but the contribution of pubertal status was not ($\beta = .05$, $p = ns.$) In the third step of this analysis, scores on instrumentality, expressivity, body image, self-esteem, and negative stressful life events were entered in the equation. These variables accounted for a significant percentage of the variance in BDI scores, R^2 change $= .51$, $F(7, 482) = 105.21$, $p < .001$. Overall, among these variables, the unique contributions of body image ($\beta = -.23$, $p < .001$); self esteem ($\beta = -.50$, $p < .001$); and negative life events ($\beta = .20$, $p < .001$) were significant.

Source: D. Marcotte, L. Fortin, P. Potvin, and M. Papillon. (2002). Gender differences in depressive symptoms during adolescence: Role of gender-typed characteristics, self-esteem, body image, stressful life events, and pubertal status. *Journal of Emotional and Behavioral Disorders, 10*(1), p. 33.

The second thing to notice about Excerpt 16.22 is the fact that the size of R^2 (in step 1) and the size of the first of the two R^2 change values (in Step 2) are both exceedingly small. Yet both turned out to be statistically significant. This happened because the sample size was quite large. (You can figure out the value of *n* by applying the information contained in footnotes 8 and 9.)

Logistic Regression

Research Navigator.c⊕m

Logistic regression

The final kind of regression considered in this chapter is called logistic regression. Originally, only researchers from medical disciplines (especially epidemiology) used this form of regression. More recently, however, logistic regression has been discovered by those who conduct empirical investigations in other disciplines. Its popularity continues to grow at such a rate that it may soon overtake multiple regression and become the most frequently used regression tool of all!

Before considering how logistic regression differs from the forms of regression already considered, let's look at their similarities. First, logistic regression deals with relationships among variables (not mean differences), with one variable being the dependent (i.e., outcome or response) variable while the other(s) is/are the independent (predictor or explanatory) variable(s). Second, the independent variables can be continuous or categorical in nature. Third, the purpose of logistic regression can be either prediction or explanation. Fourth, tests of significance can be and usually are conducted, with these tests targeted either at each individual independent variable or at the combined effectiveness of the independent variables. Finally, logistic regression can be conducted in a simultaneous, stepwise, or hierarchical manner dependent on the timing of and reasons for independent variables entering the equation.

There are, of course, important differences between logistic regression, on the one hand, and either bivariate or multiple regression, on the other hand. These differences will be made clear in the next three sections. As you will see, logistic regression revolves around a core concept called the **odds ratio** that was not considered earlier in the chapter because it is not a feature of either bivariate or multiple regression. Before looking at this new concept, we need to focus our attention on the kind of data that go into a logistic regression and also the general reasons for using this kind of statistical tool.

Variables

As does any bivariate or multiple regression, logistic regression always involves two main kinds of variables. These are the study's *dependent* and *independent* variables. In the typical logistic regression (as in some applications of multiple regression), a subset of the independent variables is included for control purposes, with the label *control* (or *covariate*) designating any such variable. Data on these three variables constitute the only ingredients that go into the normal logistic regression, and the results of such analyses are inextricably tied, on a conceptual level, to these three kinds of variables. For these reasons, it is important for us to begin with a careful consideration of the logistic regression's constituent parts.

In any logistic regression, as in any bivariate or multiple regression, there is one and only one dependent variable. Here, however, the dependent variable is dichotomous (i.e., binary) in nature. Examples of such variables used in recent studies include whether or not a person survives open heart surgery, whether or not an elderly and ill married person considers his/her spouse to be the primary caregiver, whether or not a young child chronically suffers from nightly episodes of coughing, and whether or not an adolescent drinks at least eight ounces of milk a day. As illustrated by these examples, the dependent variable in a logistic regression can represent either a true dichotomy or an artificial dichotomy.

In addition to the dependent variable, at least one independent variable is involved in any logistic regression. Almost always, two or more such variables will be involved. As in multiple regression, these variables can be either quantitative or qualitative in nature. If of the former variety, scores in the independent variable are construed to represent points along a numerical continuum. With qualitative independent variables, however, scores carry no numerical meaning and only serve the purpose of indicating group membership.[10] In any given logistic regression, the independent variables can be all quantitative, all qualitative, or a some of each. Moreover, independent variables can be used individually and/or jointly as an interaction.

When using logistic regression, applied researchers normally collect data on several independent variables, not just one. In the study alluded to earlier in which the dependent variable dealt with nighttime coughing among preschool children, the independent variables dealt with the child's sex and birth weight, the possible presence of pets and dampness problems in the home, whether or not the parents smoked or had asthma, and whether or not the child attended a day care center. It is not unusual to see this many independent variables utilized within logistic regression studies.

As indicated earlier, a subset of the independent variables in a typical logistic regression are control variables. Such variables are included in a logistic regression so the researcher can assess the "pure" relationship between the remaining independent variable(s) and the dependent variable. In a very real sense, control variables are included because of suspected confounding that would muddy the water if the connection between the independent and dependent variables were examined directly.

In any given logistic regression wherein control is being exercised by means of the inclusion of covariate variables, it may be that only one such variable is involved, or that two or three are used, or that all but one of the independent variables are covariates. It all depends, of course, on the study's purpose and the researcher's ability to identify and measure potentially confounding variables. In the study concerned with preschoolers and chronic coughing at night, all but one of the independent variables were included for control purposes; by so doing, the researchers considered themselves better able to examine the direct influence of day care versus home care on respiratory symptoms.

In Excerpt 16.23, we see a case in which the three kinds of variables of a typical logistic regression are clearly identified. It is worth the time to read this excerpt closely with an eye toward noting the nature and number of these three kinds of variables.

As in all such logistic regressions, the study associated with Excerpt 16.23 had one dependent variable that was dichotomous in nature. In addition, this particular study involved a single independent variable along with several control variables. Many logistic regression studies have this kind of combination of variables. In some logistic regression studies, there will be multiple independent variables and a single control variable. In others, there will be multiple independent variables as well as multiple control variables. It all depends on the goals of the investigation and the researcher's ability to collect data on independent and control variables that are logically related to the dependent variable.

---

[10]Such variables, you will recall, are called *dummy variables.*

EXCERPT 16.23 • *Dependent, Independent, and Control Variables*

Logistic regression was used to understand whether youths with SED [serious emotional disturbance] designations were more likely to be incarcerated for violent offenses. . . . The study sample included youths incarcerated in the California Youth Authority (CYA) facilities. . . . *Dependent Variable:* "Primary commitment offense" was divided into two categories: (1) nonperson crimes (for example, possession or sale of drugs and property and drug-related nonviolent crimes like burglary or auto theft) and (2) violent crimes (for example, assault, rape, robbery, and murder). *Independent Variable:* Serious emotional disturbance is defined by the presence or absence of a record of receipt of special education services for serious emotional disturbance as defined by the California Department of Education. *Control Variables:* "Child demographics" included ethnicity, gender, and date of birth. "Family demographics" included parental marital status (never married or other) at time of incarceration and number of siblings.

Source: M. Jonson-Reid, J. H. Williams, and D. Webster. (2001). Severe emotional disturbance and violent offending among incarcerated adolescents. *Social Work Research, 25*(4), p. 215.

Objectives of a Logistic Regression

Earlier in this chapter, we pointed out that researchers use bivariate and multiple regression in order to achieve one of two main objectives: explanation or prediction. So it is with logistic regression. In many studies, the focus is on the noncontrol independent variables, with the goal being to identify the extent to which each one plays a role in explaining why people have the status they do on the dichotomous dependent variable. In other studies, the focus is primarily on the dependent variable and how to predict whether or not people will end up in one or the other of the two categories of that outcome variable.

Excerpt 16.24 illustrates the kind of logistic regression in which explanation is the goal. In this interesting study, loggers in the state of Pennsylvania were classified into two groups based on how they would deal with a plot of forested land. The focus in this study was on the independent variables, for the researchers' stated goal was to gain an understanding of factors that explain why certain loggers would use an "improvement thinning" approach to the land in question, while others would use a "diameter-limit" approach.

In Excerpt 16.25, we see a case in which logistic regression was used for predictive purposes. In the article associated with this excerpt, the researchers first presented evidence regarding the problems created when the head administrator of a nursing home resigns to take a job elsewhere. The researchers then described their effort to identify characteristics of job applicants that could be used to predict whether

EXCERPT 16.24 • *Logistic Regression and Explanation*

We undertook a statewide study of Pennsylvania loggers to see what factors, such as demographics, attitudes, and training, might influence loggers' forest management decisions. . . . To do this we included in the survey a timber harvest scenario. A black-and-white photograph was included as a full-page insert, with a paragraph describing the conditions of the stand and a table listing the species, diameter, and overall quality of 10 numbered trees. The survey asked which trees they would cut, and why. . . . Respondents in the Diameter-Limit group tended to remove the larger-diameter, higher-quality trees; those in the Improvement Thinning group removed trees of all diameters, focusing on inferior timber species and poor quality trees. . . . We titled the dependent variable for this analysis "Harvest Proposal" (coded 0 = Improvement Thinning, 1 = Diameter-Limit). Thus, in an exploratory approach, we used logistic regression analysis to test whether loggers' forest management decisions were related to demographics, attitudes, or logging-related characteristics.

Source: M. J. Keefer, J. C. Finley, A. E. Luloff, and M. E. McDill. (2002). Characterizing loggers' forest management decisions. *Journal of Forestry, 100*(6), pp. 9, 10, 11.

EXCERPT 16.25 • *Logistic Regression and Prediction*

This study has two main objectives: First, to determine which factors, attitudes, and personal characteristics of NHAs [nursing home administrators] are associated with tenure in the administrator position, and second, to construct a predictive model that can help decision makers avoid hiring administrators who are likely to leave their positions prematurely. . . . The binary dependent variable used in the logistic regression model was whether the NHA stayed in his/her previous position for less than 3 years or at least 3 years. . . . After controlling for voluntary and involuntary separations, logistic regression results show that NHAs who have evidenced a pattern of short tenures and frequent job changes in the past are also likely to be potential leavers in future positions. Hence, instability appears to be an administrative trait that can be easily assessed by reviewing the tenure history on a prospective administrator's resume and verifying this information through reference checks. Interestingly, this "tendency to turnover" as a personality characteristic has been observed in other studies (Casio, 1992; Kettliz, Zbib, & Motwani, 1998; Mowday & Lee, 1987), but the strength of this variable in our logistic regression model was quite surprising. It was clearly the most significant independent variable predicting tenure.

Source: D. A. Singh and R. C. Schwab. (2000). Predicting turnover and retention in nursing home administrators: Management and policy implications. *The Gerontologist, 40*(3), pp. 310, 312, 316.

they would stay or leave, within a three-year period, if hired. Logistic regression was used to accomplish this objective. You probably will not be surprised at what the researchers discovered was the most valuable (i.e., predictive) independent variable.

Odds, Odds Ratios, and Adjusted Odds Ratios

Because the concept of **odds** is so important to logistic regression, let's consider a simple example that illustrates what this word does (and doesn't) mean. Suppose you have a pair of dice that are known to be fair and not loaded. If you were to roll these two little cubes and then look to see if you rolled a pair (two of the same number), the answer would be yes or no. Altogether, there are 36 combinations of how the dice might end up, with six of these being pairs. On any roll, therefore, the probability of getting a pair is 6/36, or .167. (Naturally, the probability of not getting a pair would be .833.) Clearly, it's more likely that you'll fail than succeed in your effort to roll a pair. But we can be even more precise than that. We could say that the odds are 5-to-1 against you, meaning that you are five times more likely to roll a nonpair than a pair.

Most researchers utilize logistic regression so they can discuss the explanatory or predictive power of each independent variable using the concept of odds. They want to be able to say, for example, that people are twice as likely to end up one way on the dependent variable if they have a particular standing on the independent variable being considered. For example, in one recent study on the impact of child maltreatment on later delinquency, the researchers summarized their finding by saying that "youth maltreated during adolescence are about five times as likely to be arrested as are those never maltreated." In another study, the researchers found that "Snowboarders who wore protective wrist guards were half as likely to sustain wrist injuries as those who did not wear guards."

After performing a logistic regression, researchers will often cite the **odds ratio** for each independent variable, or at least for the independent variable(s) not being used for control purposes. The odds ratio is sometimes reported as **OR,** and it is analogous to r^2 in that it measures the strength of association between the independent variable and the study's dependent variable. However, the odds ratio is considered by many people to be a more user-friendly concept than the coefficient of determination. Because the odds ratio is so central to logistic regression, let's pause for a moment to consider what this index means.

Imagine that two very popular TV programs end up going head-to-head against each other in the same time slot on a particular evening. For the sake of our discussion, let's call these programs A and B. Also imagine that we conduct a survey of folks in the middle of this time slot in which we ask each person two questions: (1) What TV show are you now watching? and (2) Are you a male or a female? After eliminating people who either were not watching TV or were watching something other than program A or B, let's suppose we end up with data like that shown in Figure 16.2.

Research Navigator.com

Odds ratio

TV Program Being Watched

		Program A	Program B
Gender	Male	200	100
	Female	50	150

FIGURE 16.2 *Hypothetical Data Showing Gender Preferences for Two TV Programs*

As you can see, both TV programs were equally popular among the 500 people involved in our study. Each was being watched by 250 of the folks we called. Let's now look at how each gender group spread itself out between the two programs. To do this, we'll arbitrarily select Program A and then calculate, first for males and then for females, the odds of watching Program A. For males, the odds of watching Program A are $200 \div 100$ (or 2 to 1); for females, the odds of watching this same program are $50 \div 150$ (or 1 to 3). If we now take these odds and divide the one for males by the one for females, we obtain the ratio of the odds for gender relative to Program A. This OR would be equal to $(2 \div 1) \div (1 \div 3)$, or 6. This result tells us that among our sampled individuals, males are six times more likely to be watching Program A than women. Stated differently, gender (our independent variable) appears to be highly related to which program is watched (our dependent variable).

In our example involving gender and the two TV programs, the odds ratio was easy to compute because there were only two variables involved. As we have seen, however, logistic regression is typically used in situations where there are more than two independent variables. When multiple independent variables are involved, the procedures for computing the odds ratio become quite complex; however, the basic idea of the odds ratio stays the same.

Consider Excerpts 16.26 and 16.27. Notice that the phrase "were half as likely" appears in the first of these excerpts, whereas the phrase "were at nearly 3 times the risk" appears in the second of these excerpts. Most people can understand conclusions such as these even though they are unfamiliar with the statistical formulas needed to generate an odds ratio type of conclusion. In addition, I suspect you can see, without difficulty, that whether an odds ratio ends up being greater than 1 or less than 1 is quite arbitrary. It all depends on the way the sentence is structured. For example, the researchers who gave us Excerpt 16.26 would have presented an OR of 2.0 (and they would have said "were twice as likely") if the position of the words "Caucasian women" and "African Americans" had been reversed.

When the odds ratio is computed for a variable *without* considering the other independent variables involved in the study, it can be conceptualized as having

EXCERPTS 16.26–16.27 • *The Odds Ratio and Adjusted Odds Ratio*

In terms of race, African-Americans (OR = 0.50) were half as likely to be using estrogen for prevention of osteoporosis when compared with Caucasian women.

Source: M. M. Amonkar and R. Mody. (2002). Developing profiles of postmenopausal women being prescribed estrogen therapy to prevent osteoporosis. *Journal of Community Health*, 27(5), pp. 344–345.

- -

Children in compact extended-cab pickup trucks were at nearly 3 times the risk of injury (OR, 2.96) compared with children in other vehicles after adjusting for age, restraint use, point of impact, vehicle weight, and crash severity.

Source: F. K. Winston, M. J. Kallen, M. R. Elliott, R. A. Menon, and D. R. Durbin. (2002). Risk of injury to child passengers in compact extended-cab pickup trucks. *Journal of the American Medical Association, 287*(9), p. 1150.

Research
Navigator.c⊕m

Adjusted odds
ratio

come from a bivariate analysis. Such an OR is said to be a crude or unadjusted odds ratio. If, as is usually the case, the OR for a particular variable is computed in such a way that it takes into consideration the other independent variable(s), then it is referred to as an **adjusted odds ratio.** By considering all independent variables jointly so as to assess their connections to the dependent variable, researchers often say that they are performing a multivariate analysis.

To see an example of an adjusted odds ratio, consider once again Excerpt 16.27. Notice that this excerpt contains the words "after adjusting for age, restraint use, point of impact, vehicle weight, and crash severity." Because these variables (such as child's age) were taken into account, the number 2.96 in the excerpt is really an adjusted odds ratio. Although it was referred to as being an OR, it really should have been called an **AOR** (the standard abbreviation for an adjusted odds ratio). Surprisingly, the researchers used the phrase "adjusted OR" seven times when presenting their results. Perhaps they thought we would know that 2.96 was an AOR because they indicated clearly that it had been adjusted for five different variables (each of which was included in the study simply for control purposes).

Tests of Significance

When using logistic regression, researchers usually conduct tests of significance. As in multiple regression, such tests can be focused on the odds ratios (which are like regression coefficients) associated with individual independent variables or on the full regression equation. Whereas tests on the full regression equation typically represent the most important test in multiple regression, tests on the odds ratios in logistic regression are considered to be the most critical tests the researcher can perform.

When the odds ratio or adjusted odds ratio associated with an independent variable is tested, the null hypothesis says that the population counterpart to the sample-based OR is equal to 1. If the null hypotheses were true (with OR = 1), it would mean that membership in the two different categories of the dependent variable is unrelated to the independent variable under consideration. For this null hypothesis to be rejected, the sample value of OR must deviate from 1 further than would be expected by chance.

Researchers typically use one of two approaches when they want to test an odds ratio or an adjusted odds ratio. One approach involves setting up a null hypothesis, selecting a level of significance, and then evaluating the H_0 either by comparing a test statistic against a critical value or by comparing the data-based p against α. In Excerpts 16.28 and 16.29, we see two examples in which this first approach was used.

EXCERPTS 16.28–16.29 • *Testing an OR or an AOR for Significance*

The odds of having made a suicide attempt was significantly higher for subjects with bipolar disorder than for subjects with recurrent unipolar depression (odds ratio = 6.2, Wald χ^2 = 15.7, df = 1, p = 0.0001).

Source: J. B. Potash, H. S. Kane, Y. Chiu, and S. G. Simpson. (2000). Attempted suicide and alcoholism in bipolar disorder: Clinical and familial relationships. *American Journal of Psychiatry, 157*(12), pp. 2048–2049.

- -

African Americans were more likely than non-Hispanic whites to sleep prone (AOR = 1.45; P < .001). African American infants were more likely to live in large families, which is also a risk factor for prone sleep. Hispanic/Latino infants were less likely than non-Hispanic whites to sleep prone (AOR 0.81; P < .01).

Source: H. A. Pollack and J. G. Frohna. (2002). Infant sleep placement after the back to sleep campaign. *Pediatrics, 109*(4), p. 610.

Notice in Excerpt 16.28 that the researchers used the **Wald test** to see if the odds ratio was statistically significant. This test is analogous to the *t*-test in multiple regression that is used to see if a beta weight is statistically significant. These two tests are only analogous, however, for they differ not only in terms of the null hypothesis but also in the kind of calculated and critical values used to test the H_0. As illustrated in Excerpt 16.28, the Wald test is tied to a theoretical distribution symbolized by χ^2 rather than t. (This is the chi-square distribution.) In Excerpt 16.29, the test used to test the adjusted odds ratios is not specified. The researchers probably used the Wald test, but they may have used an alternative test procedure.

The second way a researcher can test an odds ratio is through the use of a confidence interval. The CI rule of thumb for deciding whether to reject or retain the null hypothesis is the same as when CIs are used to test means, rs, the difference between means, or anything else. If the confidence interval overlaps the pinpoint number in the null hypothesis, the null hypothesis will be retained; otherwise, H_0 is rejected. Excerpt 16.30 illustrates the use of CIs to test three adjusted ORs. Take the time to look closely at each CI, note its ends, and then consider the p-value associated with the CI. By so doing, you ought to get a good feel for the way in which CIs can be used to test null hypotheses in a logistic regression.

EXCERPT 16.30 • *Testing Adjusted ORs for Signficance via Confidence Intervals*

Minority children aged at least 12 months were significantly more likely to have a skeletal survey performed than were white children in the same age group (adjusted OR, 8.75; 95% CI, 3.48–22.03; $P < .001$). Racial differences in ordering of skeletal surveys for children younger than 12 months had only borderline significance (adjusted OR, 2.01; 95% CI, 1.00–4.04; $P = .05$). There was no difference in ordering of skeletal surveys by insurance status (adjusted OR, 0.93; 95% CI, 0.51–1.69; $P = .81$).

Source: W. G. Lane, D. M. Rubin, R. Monteith, and C. W. Christian. (2002). Racial differences in the evaluation of pediatric fractures for physical abuse. *Journal of the American Medical Association, 288*(13), p. 1606.

As indicated previously, it is possible in logistic regression to test whether the collection of independent and control variables do a greater-than-chance job of accounting for the status of people on the dependent variable. This test is typically made with a special form of the chi-square test. This test has the same symbol (χ^2) as the test used to evaluate individual ORs or AORs; with this version, however, researchers usually talk about it in terms of it being a test of the "model." In Excerpt 16.31, we see an example of this kind of test.

EXCERPT 16.31 • *Testing the Full Logistic Regression Model*

In the hierarchical multiple logistic regression analysis, only adolescents' reported frequency of discussing with their mothers how to prevent AIDS retained significance (adjusted odds ratio [AOR] = 2.62, 95% CI = 1.35–5.13, p = .005). Although adolescents' perceived level of family support was not associated with their STD history, a trend (i.e., p = .10) was noted. Among the demographic covariates entered in block one, adolescents' age retained significance in the model (AOR = 1.33, 95% CI = 1.08–1.63, p = .005); however, enrollment in school did not retain significance. The overall model was significant (χ^2 with 2 df = 16.7, p < .0002).

Source: R. A. Crosby, G. M. Wingood, R. J. DiClemente, and E. S. Rose. (2002). Family-related correlates of sexually transmitted disease and barriers to care: A pilot study of pregnant African American adolescents. *Family and Community Health, 25*(2), pp. 21–22.

Final Comments

Research Navigator.com

Multicollinearity

As we conclude this chapter, we should consider four additional regression-related issues. These concerns deal with multicollinearity, control, practical significance, and cause. If you will keep these issues in mind as you encounter research reports based on bivariate, multiple, and logistic regression, you will be in a far better position to both decipher and critique such reports.

In multiple and logistic regression, the independent and control variables should not be highly correlated with one another. If they are, a condition called **multicollinearity** is said to exist. Excerpts 16.32 and 16.33 illustrate the way dedicated researchers will demonstrate that they know about this potential problem and examine their data to see whether their regressions would be "messed up" by an undesirable network of intercorrelations among their independent variables. These excerpts also show that multicollinearity is an issue not just for multiple regressions but also for logistic regression.

In the discussions of both hierarchical multiple regression and logistic regression, we saw that researchers often incorporate control or covariate variables into their analyses. Try to remember that such **control** is very likely to be less than optimal. This is the case for three reasons. First, one or more important confounding variables might be overlooked. Second, potential confounding variables that *are* measured are likely to be measured with instruments possessing less than perfect reliability. Finally, recall that the analysis of covariance undercorrects when used with intact groups that come from populations that differ on the covariate variable(s). Regression suffers from this same undesirable characteristic.

My next concern relates to **the distinction between statistical significance and practical significance.** We have considered this issue in connection with tests

EXCERPTS 16.32–16.33 • *Multicollinearity*

Before a multiple regression analysis for IPG use was performed, the possibility of multicollinearity was checked. The highest intercorrelation among the independent variables was −.421 between "perceived IPG utility" and "perceived IPG complexity," which was not strong enough to cause multicollinearity problems in the multiple regression.

Source: M. Kang. (2002). Interactivity in television: Use and impact of an interactive program guide. *Journal of Broadcasting and Electronic Media, 46*(3), pp. 338–339.

- -

To determine whether or not this multicollinearity is a concern, we dropped the "truth" exposure variable from the logistic regression models and examined whether the odds ratios were influenced. Results showed that all of the odds ratios remained stable.

Source: M. Farrelly, C. G. Healton, K. C. Davis, and P. Messeri. (2002). Getting to the truth: Evaluating national tobacco countermarketing campaigns. *American Journal of Public Health, 92*(6), p. 906.

focused on means and *r*s, and it is just as relevant to the various inferential tests used by researchers within regression analyses. In Excerpt 16.34, we see a case in which a team of researchers attended to the important distinction between useful and trivial findings. These researchers deserve high praise for realizing (and warning their readers) that inferential tests can yield results that are statistically significant without being important in a practical manner.

EXCERPT 16.34 • *Practical versus Statistical Significance*

There appears to be no meaningful relationship between the portfolio of IS applications and the organizational operating characteristics we studied. Although the regression is significant ($F = 2.01$, $p = 0.01$), the adjusted R^2 is only 4.2 percent. With 393 observations, we were able to detect only a weak link between operational characteristics and the benefits from the overall IS portfolio.

Source: A. Ragowsky, M. Stern, and D. A. Adams. (2000). Relating benefits from using IS to an organization's operating characteristics: Interpreting results from two countries. *Journal of Management Information Systems, 16*(4), pp. 191–192.

In many research reports, researchers make a big deal about a finding that seems small and of little importance. Perhaps such researchers are unaware of the important distinction between practical and statistical significance, or it may be that they know about this distinction but prefer not to mention it due to a realization that their statistically significant results do not matter very much. Either way, it is important that *you* keep this distinction in mind whenever you are on the receiving end of a research report.

Recently, I came across an article (in a technical research journal) concerning youth and adolescents, their use of sunscreen and tanning beds, and their rate of sunburns. It turned out that there was a statistically significant connection between age (one of the predictor variables) and sunburning (one of the outcome variables.) This finding was based on an adjusted odds ratio produced by a logistic regression. How large do you think this AOR was? Tucked away in one of the article's tables, I found it. The table contained this information: "adjusted OR = 1.09 (1.01–1.18)." In my opinion, this finding has questionable worth because the number 1.09 is so close to the null hypothesis value of 1.00. You have the right to make similar kinds of judgments when you read or listen to research reports.

As we turn to my last concern, recall the important point made in Chapter 3 that a bivariate correlation—even if found to be statistically significant with a large r^2 value—should not be automatically interpreted to mean that a **causal link** exists between the two variables on which data have been collected. The same point holds for bivariate, multiple, and logistic regression. Even when the results suggest strongly that the regression has achieved its predictive or explanatory objective, the analysis is correlational in nature. Even when multiple control variables are included in the model, a regression analysis is simply correlational in nature.

In Excerpt 16.35, we see a case in which a team of researchers provides their readers with a clear warning about cause-and-effect. In essence, that warning says

EXCERPT 16.35 • *Regression and Cause-and-Effect*

The goal of the current study was to compare the relationship between mental health problems and health status in a large sample of low-income children with and without serious emotional disorders (SED). . . . SED status contributed significantly to predictions of all three health-status indicators. . . . Neither this study [using hierarchical multiple regression] nor the research reviewed for it provides an explanation of the relationship between physical and mental health problems, of course; one might cause the other, or a third variable may influence both types of health problems.

Source: T. Combs-Orme, C. A. Helfinger, and C. G. Simpkins. (2002). Comorbidity of mental health problems and chronic health conditions in children. *Journal of Emotional and Behavioral Disorders, 10*(2), pp. 117, 121.

not to think that the study's primary independent variable (mental health) had a causal influence on the study's dependent variable (physical health). I salute these researchers for providing this warning and for explaining, in the excerpt's final sentence, why it would be wrong to impute cause-and-effect into the study's findings.

Review Terms

Adjusted R^2
Adjusted odds ratio
Beta weight
Bivariate regression
Criterion variable
Dummy variable
Dependent variable
Explanation
Explanatory variable
Goodness-of-fit test
Hierarchical regression
Independent variable
Intercept
Line of best fit
Logistic regression
Model
Multicollinearity
Multiple regression

Odds ratio
Outcome variable
Prediction
Predictor variable
Regression coefficient
Regression equation
Regression line
Response variable
Shrinkage
Simultaneous regression
Slope
Standardized regression coefficient
Stepwise regression
Unstandardized regression equation
Wald test
R
R^2
ΔR^2

The Best Items in the Companion Website

1. An interactive online quiz (with immediate feedback provided) covering Chapter 16.
2. Ten misconceptions about the content of Chapter 16.
3. An interactive online resource entitled "Bivariate Regression."
4. An email message sent by the author to his students entitled "Logistic Regression."
5. Several e-articles illustrating the use of bivariate regression, multiple regression, and logistic regression.

Fun Exercises inside Research Navigator

1. Do the same variables predict suicidal thoughts in college men and women?

In this study, 139 undergraduate females and 75 undergraduate males completed two personality inventories: the *Suicide Probability Scale* (which measures level of suicidal thinking) and the *MMPI-2* (which measures several kinds of psychopathology). Separately for the females and the males, the researchers performed a hierarchical multiple regression, using scores from the *SDS* as the dependent variable and scores from the various *MMPI-2* scales as the independent variables. In which group, males or females, do you think the *MMPI-2* scores better predicted suicidal thinking? Do you think the best predictors for males were also the best predictors for females? After you make your guess, refer to the PDF version of the research report in the Psychology database of ContentSelect and consult pages 600–604 (and Tables 5 and 6) to see if *your* predictions were correct!

B. A. Kopper, A. Osman, & F. X. Barrios. Assessment of suicidal ideation in young men and women: The incremental validity of the *MMPI-2* content scales. *Death Studies.* Located in the PSYCHOLOGY database of ContentSelect.

2. Are the predictors of adolescent violence different for boys versus girls?

In this study of adolescent violence, data on 2,643 high school seniors were analyzed by means of two logistic regressions, one for boys and one for girls. In each regression, the dependent variable was whether or not the adolescent had engaged in violent behavior during the previous 12-month period. In addition, the two regressions had the same independent variables (alcohol use, drug use, religious beliefs, grades, etc.) and the same demographic control variables (race and location of residence). Do you think these two logistic regressions produced the same results? In particular, do you think the independent variables of alcohol use, drug use, and grades showed up as predicting violent behavior for both gender groups? To see if your hunches are correct, refer to the PDF version of the research report in the Helping Professions database of ContentSelect and read (on page 14) the final two paragraphs of the "Results" section.

R. Bachman & R. Peralta. The relationship between drinking and violence in an adolescent population: Does gender matter? *Deviant Behavior.* Located in the HELPING PROFESSIONS database of ContentSelect.

Review Questions and Answers begin on page 516.

17

Inferences on Percentages, Proportions, and Frequencies

In your journey through the previous eight chapters, you have examined a variety of inferential techniques that are used when at least one of the researcher's variables is quantitative in nature. The bulk of Chapter 9, for example, dealt with inferences concerning Pearson's *r*, a bivariate measure of association designed for use with two quantitative variables. Beginning in Chapter 10, you saw how inferential techniques can be used to investigate one or more groups in terms of means (and variances), with the dependent variable in such situations obviously being quantitative in nature. In Chapter 16, we considered how inferential procedures can be with regression techniques involving at least one quantitative variable.

In the present chapter, your journey takes a slight turn, for you will now look at an array of inferential techniques designed for the situation where *none* of the researcher's variables is quantitative. In other words, the statistical techniques discussed in this chapter are used when all of a researcher's variables involve questions concerning membership in categories. For example, a researcher might wish to use sample data to help gain insights as to the prevalence of AIDS in the general population. Or, a pollster might be interested in using sample data to predict how each of three political candidates competing for the same office would fare "if the election were to be held today." In these two illustrations as well as in countless real studies, the study's data do not reflect *the extent* to which each subject possesses some characteristic of interest but instead reveal how each subject has been classified into one of the categories established by the researcher.

When a study's data speak to the issue of group membership, the researcher's statistical focus will be on frequencies, on percentages, or on proportions. For example, the hypothetical pollster referred to in the previous paragraph might summarize the study's data by reporting, "Of the 1,000 voters who were sampled, 428 stated that they would vote for candidate A, 381 stated that they would vote for candidate B, and 191 reported that they would vote for candidate C." Instead of providing us with **frequencies** (i.e., the number of people in each response category), the same data could be summarized through **percentages.** With this approach, the researcher would report that "candidates A, B, and C received 42.8 percent, 38.1 percent, and 19.1 percent of the votes, respectively." Or, the data could be converted into **proportions,** with the researcher asserting that "the proportionate popularity of candidates A, B, and C turned out to be .428, .381, and .191, respectively." The same information, of course, is communicated through each of these three ways of summarizing the data.

Regardless of whether the data concerning group membership are summarized through frequencies, percentages, or proportions, it can be said that the level of measurement used within this kind of study is nominal (rather than ordinal, interval, or ratio). As I pointed out in Chapter 3, a researcher's data *can* be nominal in nature. In focusing on inferential techniques appropriate for means, r, R, and R^2, we spent the last several chapters dealing with procedures that are useful when the researcher's data are interval or ratio in nature. In the present chapter, however, we restrict our consideration to statistical inferences appropriate for nominal data.

Although a multitude of inferential procedures have been developed for use with nominal-level data, we will consider here only six of these procedures that permit researchers to evaluate null hypotheses. These procedures are the sign test, the binomial test, Fisher's Exact Test, the chi-square test, McNemar's test, and Cochran's test. These are the most frequently used of the test procedures designed for nominal-level data, and a knowledge of these procedures will put you in a fairly good position to understand researchers' results when their data take the form of frequencies, percentages, or proportions.

I will also illustrate how z-tests can be used, in certain situations, to answer the same kinds of research questions as those posed by the six basic test procedures considered in this chapter. Moreover, I will show how the Bonferroni technique can be used with any of these test procedures to control against an inflated Type I error rate. The distinction between statistical significance and practical significance will also be considered. Finally, we will examine a few cases in which confidence intervals have been built around sample percentages or proportions.

The Sign Test

Research
Navigator.c⊕m

Sign test

Of all inferential tests, the **sign test** is perhaps the simplest and easiest to understand. It requires that the researcher do nothing more than classify each participant of the study into one of two categories. Each of the participants put into one of these categories receives a plus sign (i.e., a $+$); in contrast, a minus sign (i.e., a $-$) is given to each participant who falls into the other category. The hypothesis testing procedure is then used to evaluate the null hypothesis that says the full sample of participants comes from a population in which there are as many pluses as minuses. If the sample is quite lopsided with far more pluses than minuses (or far more minuses than pluses), the sign test's H_0 will be rejected. On the other hand, if the frequencies of pluses and minuses in the sample are equal or nearly equal, the null hypothesis of the sign test will be retained.

The sign test can be used in any of three situations. In one situation, there is a single group of people, with each person in the group evaluated as to some characteristic (e.g., handedness) and then given a + or a − depending on his or her status on that characteristic. In the second situation, there are two matched groups; here, the two members of each pair are compared, with a + given to one member of each dyad (and a − given to his or her mate) depending on which one has more of the characteristic being considered. In the third situation, a single group is measured twice, with a + or a − given to each person depending on whether his or her second score is larger or smaller than his or her first score.

In Excerpt 17.1, we see a case in which the sign test was used with paired samples. This excerpt comes from a morbid study in which the researchers asked, Is the killer older or younger than the victim when one of two siblings kills the other sibling? The sample data in Excerpt 17.1 come from three counties in which one or both of the siblings was a juvenile. In applying each sign test, the researchers focused on each pair of siblings and assigned a + and a − to indicate the older and younger siblings, respectively. As you can see, the lopsided nature of the sample data caused the sign test's null hypothesis to be rejected for both the Canadian and Chicago groups. (The Britain sample was too small for the sign test to be applied.)

As illustrated by Excerpt 17.2, the sign test can be used just as easily when a single group is measured on two occasions. In the study associated with this excerpt, a single group of patients received a medical intervention. At the time of the

EXCERPTS 17.1–17.2 • *The Sign Test*

In these cases [where at least one of the two siblings was a juvenile], unlike those in which both parties were adults, the great majority of killers were indeed older than their victims: 21 of 25 in Canada ($p < .001$ by sign test), 3 of 3 in Britain, and 9 of 10 ($p = .01$) in Chicago.

Source: M. Daly, M. Wilson, C. A. Salmon, M. Hiraiwa-Hasegawa, and T. Hasegawa. (2001). Siblicide and seniority. *Homicide Studies*, 5(1), p. 37.

Using a simple sign test and a 1-sided alternative hypothesis against the null hypothesis (i.e., that the procedures were equally likely to help the subjects or not help them), the P value associated with 12 of 17 improvements was .015, a statistically significant result.

Source: J. S. Edman, W. H. Williams, and R. C. Atkins. (2000). Nutritional therapies for ulcerative colitis: Literature review, chart review study, and future research. *Alternative Therapies in Health and Medicine*, 6(1), p. 58.

posttest evaluation, each person's status was noted as improved (+) or not improved (−). Under the null hypothesis, we would expect, out of 17 signs, somewhat of an even split of + and − signs to show up. Allowing for sampling error, we might expect anywhere between 7 and 10 plus signs. However, the sample yielded 12 pluses, a result that caused the null hypothesis to be rejected.

The Binomial Test

The **binomial test** is similar to the sign test in that (1) the data are nominal in nature, (2) only two response categories are set up by the researcher, and (3) the response categories must be mutually exclusive. The binomial test is also like the sign test in that it can be used with a single group of people who are measured just once, with a single group of people who are measured twice (e.g., preintervention and postintervention), or with two groups of people who are matched or are related in some logical fashion (e.g., husbands and wives). The binomial and sign tests are even further alike in that both procedures lead to a data-based *p*-level that comes from tentatively considering the null hypothesis to be true.

The only difference between the sign test and the binomial test concerns the flexibility of the null hypothesis. With the sign test, there is no flexibility. This is because the sign test's H_0 always says that the objects in the population are divided evenly into the two response categories. With the binomial test, on the other hand, researchers have the flexibility to set up H_0 with any proportionate split they wish to test.

In Excerpt 17.3, we see a case that shows the versatility of the binomial test. In the study associated with this excerpt, the researchers wanted to see if there were seasonal variations in the number of cases of cryptosporidiosis. They first determined the total number of cases that showed up during the entire year and the number of cases that showed up during a particular five-month period. Next, they

EXCERPT 17.3 • *The Binomial Test*

Differences between observed and expected proportions were tested using the binomial test with exact *p*-values. . . . Overall, the number of cases occurring between July and November inclusive (63%) was significantly higher than expected (42%) assuming no seasonal variation ($p < 0.01$).

Source: S. E. Majowicz, P. Michel, J. J. Aramini, S. A. McEwen, and J. B. Wilson. (2001). Descriptive analysis of endemic cryptosporidiosis cases reported in Ontario, 1996–1997. *Canadian Journal of Public Health, 92*(1), pp. 62–63.

figured out the percentage of cases associated with the July through November period. Finally, they used the binomial test to compare their observed percentage for this period, 63 percent, against the null value of 42 percent. The 21 percent difference between these two values was larger than would be expected by chance, so the null hypothesis of no seasonal variation was rejected.

In the study associated with Excerpt 17.3, the null number of 42 percent came about because the researchers split the year into two uneven parts, a five-month part (July through November) and a seven-month part (December though June). If they had divided the year into two six-month periods, the null number would have been 50 percent. In that hypothetical situation or in any real situations where the null hypothesis is set up in an even fashion (with H_0 specifying a 50-50 split in the population), the binomial test and the sign test are mathematically identical.

Fisher's Exact Test

Research Navigator.c⊕m

Fisher's Exact Test

The sign test and the binomial tests, as we have seen, can be used when the researcher has dichotomous data from either a single sample or from two related samples. However, researchers often conduct studies for the purpose of comparing two independent samples with respect to a dichotomous dependent variable. In such situations, **Fishers' Exact Test** often serves as the researcher's inferential tool.[1]

The null hypothesis of Fisher's Exact Test is highly analogous to the typical null hypothesis of an independent-samples *t*-test. With that kind of *t*-test, most researchers evaluate a null hypothesis that says H_0: $\mu_1 = \mu_2$ (or alternatively as H_0: $\mu_1 - \mu_2 = 0$). Using the symbols P_1 and P_2 to stand for the proportion of cases (in the first and second populations, respectively) that fall into one of the two dichotomous categories of the dependent variable, the null hypothesis of Fisher's Exact Test can be expressed H_0: $P_1 = P_2$ (or alternatively as H_0: $P_1 - P_2 = 0$).

In Excerpt 17.4, we see an example of Fisher's Exact Test. As this excerpt makes clear, the raw data of Fisher's Exact Test are *n*s (i.e., frequencies) of the two groups. To get a feel for what was happening statistically, think in terms of percentages. Among the males referred to in this excerpt, 50 percent (9 out of 18) had committed a violent crime. Among the females, only 10 percent (1 out of 10) had. Fisher's Exact Test compared these two percentages and found them to differ more than could be expected by chance. Hence, the null hypothesis was rejected.

It should be noted that the null hypothesis of Fisher's Exact Test does *not* say that each of the study's two populations will be divided evenly into the two dichotomous categories. Rather, it simply says that the split in one population is the

---

[1]The word *exact* in the title of this test gives the impression that the Fisher test is superior to other test procedures. This is unfortunate, since many other tests (e.g., the sign test and the binomial test) possess just as much "exactness" as does Fisher's test.

EXCERPT 17.4 • *Fisher's Exact Test*

Considering both index and original crimes, there was a statistically significant association between male gender and violent crimes. Nine of 18 male subjects committed a violent crime, compared with one of the 10 females (Fisher's Exact Test, $p < .05$).

Source: M. R. Munetz, T. P. Grande, and M. R. Chambers. (2001). The incarceration of individuals with severe mental disorders. *Community Mental Health Journal, 37*(4), p. 367.

same as the split in the other population. Thus, if 6 of the 18 males had committed a violent crime compared with 3 of the 10 females, the two sample percentages would be 33 and 30, respectively. These two values, being quite similar, would not lead to a rejection of H_0.

If you will look again at Excerpt 17.4, you will see that the researchers summarized their findings by saying that there was a significant *association* between gender and violent crime. It is not unusual to see this term (or the term *relationship*) used to describe the goal or the results of a Fisher's Exact Test. This way of talking about Fisher's Exact Test is legitimate and should not throw you when you encounter it. If the two sample proportions turn out to be significantly different, then there is a nonzero relationship (in the sample data) between the dichotomous variable that "creates" the two comparison groups and the dichotomous dependent variable. Hence, the use of Fisher's Exact Test accomplishes the same basic goal as does a test of significance applied to a phi or tetrachoric correlation coefficient.[2]

Chi-Square Tests: An Introduction

Research
Navigator.c✦m

Chi square

Although inferential tests of frequencies, percentages, or proportions are sometimes made using the sign test, the binomial test, or Fisher's Exact Test, the most frequently used statistical tool for making such tests is called **chi square.** As you will see, the chi-square procedure can be used, in certain circumstances, instead of the sign, binomial, or Fisher tests. In addition, the chi-square procedure can be used to answer research questions that cannot be answered by any of the inferential tech-

[2]Again we have a parallel between Fisher's Exact Test and the independent-samples *t*-test, since the *t*-test's comparison of the two sample means is mathematically equivalent to a test applied to the point-biserial correlation coefficient that assesses the relationship between the dichotomous grouping variable and the dependent variable.

niques covered thus far in this chapter. Because the chi-square test is so versatile and popular, it is important for any reader of the research literature to become thoroughly familiar with this inferential technique. For this reason, I feel obliged to consider the chi-square technique in a careful and unhurried fashion.

Different Chi-Square Tests

The term *chi-square test* technically describes any inferential test that involves a critical value being pulled from and/or a data-based *p*-value being tied to one of the many chi-square distributions. Each such distribution is like the normal and *t* distributions in that it (1) has one mode, (2) is asymptotic to the baseline, (3) comes from a mathematical formula, and (4) helps applied researchers decide whether to reject or fail to reject null hypotheses. Unlike the normal and *t* distributions (but like any *F* distribution), each chi-square distribution is positively skewed. There are many chi-square distributions simply because the degree of skewness tapers off as the number of degrees of freedom increases. In fact, the various chi-square distributions are distinguished from one another solely by the concept of degrees of freedom.

Certain of the inferential tests that are called chi square (because they utilize a chi-square distribution) have nothing to do with frequencies, proportions, or percentages. For example, a comparison of a single sample's variance against a hypothesized null value is conducted by means of a chi-square test. However, these kinds of chi-square tests are clearly in the minority. Without a doubt, most chi-square tests *do* involve the types of data being focused on throughout this chapter. In other words, it is a relatively safe bet that any chi-square test that you encounter will be dealing with nominal data.

Even when we restrict our consideration of chi square to those cases that involve nominal data, there still are different types of chi-square tests. One type is called a one-sample chi-square test (or a chi-square goodness-of-fit test), a second type is called an independent-samples chi-square test (or a chi-square test of homogeneity of proportions), and the third type is called a chi-square test of independence. We will consider each of these chi-square tests shortly, and then later in the chapter we will see how a chi-square test can also be used with related samples. Before we look at any of these chi-square tests, however, it is appropriate first to consider how to tell that a researcher is presenting results of a chi-square test.

Chi-Square Notation and Language

Excerpts 17.5 through 17.8 illustrate the variation in how applied researchers refer to the chi-square tests used in their studies. Although the studies from which these excerpts were taken differ in the number of samples being compared and the number of nominal categories in the data, it should be noted that each of these studies had the same statistical focus as all of the other tests considered in this chapter: frequencies, proportions, or percentages.

EXCERPTS 17.5–17.8 • *Different Ways of Referring to Chi Square*

A chi-square statistic (with alpha set at .05 with 2 degrees of freedom) was used to compare the percentages of each group that fell within, above, and below the critical range.

Source: N. E. Nereo, B. A. Farber, and V. J. Hinton. (2002). Willingness to self-disclose among late adolescent female survivors of childhood sexual abuse. *Journal of Youth and Adolescence, 31*(4), p. 307.

Generally, immigrants in the present sample were less educated than nonimmigrants ($\chi^2[5, N = 95] = 29.34, p < .0001$).

Source: J. D. Hovey and C. G. Magana. (2002). Cognitive, affective, and physiological expressions of anxiety symptomatology among Mexican migrant farmworkers: Predictors and generational differences. *Community Mental Health Journal, 38*(7), p. 234.

The statistical significance of observed differences in categorical outcome variables was determined using chi-squared analysis.

Source: S. M. Sookram, S. Barker, K. D. Kelly, and W. Patton. (2002). Can body temperature be maintained during aeromedical transport? *Journal of the Canadian Association of Emergency Physicians, 4*(3), p. 174.

Pearson's chi square statistics were used to investigate the relationship between the dependent variables.

Source: M. L. Boninger, J. D. Towers, R. A. Cooper, B. E. Dicianno, and M. C. Munin. (2001). Shoulder imaging abnormalities in individuals with paraplegia. *Journal of Rehabilitation Research and Development, 38*(4), p. 403.

Excerpt 17.5 is clear-cut since the authors used the phrase "chi-square statistic." In Excerpt 17.6, we see the Greek symbol for chi square, χ^2. Excerpt 17.7 contains a very slight variation of this test's name: *chi squared*.[3] Finally, in Excerpt 17.8, the phrase "Pearson's chi square" is used.

The adjective *Pearson* is the technically correct way to indicate that the chi-square test has been applied to frequencies (rather than, for example, to variances).

[3]From a technical standpoint, the term *chi squared* is more accurate than *chi square*. However, most applied researchers use the latter label when referring to this inferential test.

However, very few applied researchers use this adjective (or the more formal label, *Pearson's approximation to chi square*). Accordingly, it's fairly safe to presume that any chi-square test you encounter is like those considered in this chapter, even though the word *Pearson* does not appear in the test's label. (Of course, this would not be a safe bet if the term *chi-square test* is used within a context where it is clear that the test's statistical focus deals with something other than frequencies, proportions, or percentages.)

Three Main Types of Chi-Square Tests

We now turn our attention to the three main types of chi-square tests used by applied researchers—the one-sample chi-square test, the independent-samples chi-square test, and the chi-square test of independence. Although applied researchers typically refer to all three using the same label (*chi-square test*), the null hypotheses of these tests differ. Accordingly, you need to know which kind of chi-square test has been used in order to understand what is meant by a statistically significant (or nonsignificant) finding.

The One-Sample Chi-Square Test

With this kind of chi-square test, the various categories of the nominal variable of interest are first set up and considered. Second, a null hypothesis is formulated. The H_0 for the **one-sample chi-square test** is simply a specification of what percentage of the population being considered falls into each category. Next, the researchers determine what percentage of their sample falls into each of the established categories. Finally, the hypothesis testing procedure is used to determine whether the discrepancy between the set of sample percentages and those specified in H_0 is large enough to permit H_0 to be rejected.

Excerpt 17.9 provides us with an example of a one-sample chi-square test. The single sample was made up of 255 people who responded to five different website advertisements. Each of the five ads represented one of the response categories. In essence, the null hypothesis in this study said that the five ads have equal "drawing power," and this H_0 would have been retained if the number of hits had been similar across the five ads. However, the chi-square test showed that there was more variability among the frequencies than would be expected by chance. Hence, the null hypothesis was rejected.

If you look again at Excerpt 17.9, you will see that the χ^2's *df* is not equal to one less than the number of people in the sample. Instead, it is equal to one less than the number of categories. This is the way the *df* for all one-sample chi-square tests are computed. That's because the sample percentages, across the various categories, must add up to 100. Because of this fact, you could figure out the final category's percentage once you have been given the percentages for all other categories. The

EXCERPT 17.9 • *One-Sample Chi-Square Test*

Several approaches were developed to discover which test advertisements obtained more consumer response. The first analysis involved an examination of website "hits." When viewing the frequencies of the number of "hits" the website received, the WEB MENTION and TECHADVANCE advertisements received the most "hits" (76 and 55, respectively). Fewer "hits" were recorded for the WEB LOOK ALIKE advertisement (48), the STANDARD advertisement (42), and the COMPETITIVE advertisement (34). A one-sample chi-square test produced a significant finding ($\chi^2 = 20.0$, $df = 4$, $p < .001$).

Source: J. A. Bellizzi. (2000). Drawing prospects to e-commerce Websites. *Journal of Advertising Research, 40(1/2)*, p. 45.

final category's percentage, therefore, is not free to vary but rather has a value that's known as soon as the percentages for the other categories are recorded.

There's one additional thing you should know about the one-sample chi-square test. The null hypothesis is often set up in a "no difference" fashion. This kind of H_0 states that the population percentages are equal across the various categories. However, the null hypothesis can be set up such that these percentages are dissimilar. For example, in comparing the handedness of a group of college students, we might set up the H_0 with the right- and left-handed percentages equal to 90 and 10, respectively. These numbers come from census figures, and our little study would be asking the simple question, "Do the census figures seem to hold true for the population of college students associated with the sample used in our study?"

Because the one-sample chi-square test compares the set of observed sample percentages with the corresponding set of population percentages specified in H_0, this kind of chi-square analysis is often referred to as a **goodness-of-fit test.** If these two sets of percentages differ by an amount that can be attributable to sampling error, then there is said to be a good fit between the observed data and what would be expected if H_0 were true. In this situation, H_0 is retained. On the other hand, if sampling error cannot adequately explain the discrepancies between the observed and null percentages, then a bad fit is said to exist and H_0 is rejected. The researcher's level of significance, in conjunction with the data-based *p*-value, makes it easy to determine what action should be taken whenever this chi-square goodness-of-fit test is applied.

On occasion, researchers will use the chi-square goodness-of-fit test to see if it is reasonable to presume that the sample data have come from a normally distributed population. Of course, for researchers to have this concern, their response variable must be quantitative, not qualitative. If researchers have data that are interval or ratio in nature and if they want to apply this kind of a test of normality, the baseline beneath the theoretical normal distribution can be subdivided into segments, with each segment assigned a percentage to reflect the percentage of cases in a true normal distribution that would lie within that segment. These percentages are then put into H_0. Then, the sample is examined to determine what percentage of the observed cases fall within each of the predetermined segments, or categories. Finally, the chi-square goodness-of-fit test compares the observed and null percentages across the various categories to see whether sampling error can account for any discrepancies.[4]

The Independent-Samples Chi-Square Test

Researchers frequently wish to compare two or more samples on a response variable that is categorical in nature. Since the response variable can be made up of two or more categories, we can set up four different kinds of situations to which the **independent-samples chi-square test** can be applied: (1) two samples compared on a dichotomous response variable, (2) more than two samples compared on a dichotomous response variable, (3) two samples compared on a response variable that has three or more categories, and (4) more than two samples compared on a response variable that has three or more categories. As you will see, considering these four situations one by one will allow you to generate some valuable insights about chi square and its relationship with other inferential tests we have covered.

When two independent samples are compared with respect to a dichotomous dependent variable, the chi-square test can be thought of as analogous to an independent-samples t-test. With the t-test, the null hypothesis usually tested is H_0: $\mu_1 = \mu_2$. With the chi-square test, the null hypothesis is H_0: $P_1 = P_2$, where the notation P_1 and P_2 stand for the percentage of cases (in the first and second populations) that fall into one of the two response categories. Thus the null hypothesis for this form of the chi-square test simply says that the two populations are identical in the percentage split between the two categories of the response variable.

In Excerpt 17.10, we see an example of this first kind of independent-samples chi-square test. The two groups were child care providers who either had or had not participated in a training session. The two categories of the response variable were set up to correspond with yes and no answers to the question, "Are you interested in serving children with disabilities?"

To help you understand the chi-square test that was applied to the data of Excerpt 17.10, I have constructed a **contingency table.** In such a table, the data of a

Research
Navigator.c⊛m
Contingency table

---

[4]The Kolmogorov-Smirnoff one-sample test is another goodness-of-fit procedure that can be used as a check on normality. It has several properties that make it superior to chi square in situations where concern rests with the distributional shape of a continuous variable.

EXCERPT 17.10 • *Two-Group Independent-Samples Chi-Square Test with a Dichotomous Response Variable*

A random survey of 41 child care providers was done. Of the 41 surveyed, 18 had participated in the training and 23 had not. Respondents were asked whether they were interested in serving children with disabilities. Among the providers who had participated in the training, 17 of 18 reported that they were interested with one responding that it was not. Among the providers who had not received the training, 12 reported that they were interested and 11 reported that they were not. Chi-square analysis of this distribution indicated a significant difference ($\chi^2[df = 1] = 8.21$, $p < .01$). The providers who had received the training were significantly more likely to report being interested in serving children with disabilities.

Source: S. Osborne, C. Garland, and N. Fisher. (2002). Caregiver training: Changing minds, opening doors to inclusion. *Infants and Young Children, 14*(3), p. 50.

study are arranged in a 2×2 matrix for the purpose of showing how each group split itself up on the dichotomous response variable. Contingency tables are worth looking at (if they are provided in research reports) or creating (if they're not provided), for they make it easier to understand the chi-square null hypothesis and why the data led to the rejection or retention of H_0.

		Would Serve Children with Disabilities	
		Yes	No
Received Training	Yes	17	1
	No	12	11

The null hypothesis associated with Excerpt 17.10 did *not* specify that each of the two populations—providers who went through training and those who didn't—had a 50-50 split between the two categories of the response variable (with half of each population saying "yes" in response to the question about serving disabled children). Instead, H_0 said that the two populations were identical to each other in the percentage (or proportion) of providers falling into each of the response categories. Thus, the null hypothesis of the study would not have been rejected if about the same percentage of the trained providers and untrained providers had said "yes," regardless of whether that percentage was close to 80, 33, 67, or any other value.

Since the null hypothesis deals with percentages (or proportions), it is often helpful to convert each of the cell frequencies of a contingency table into a percentage (or proportion). I have created such a table for Excerpt 17.10. As before, the rows and columns correspond to the groups and the response categories, respectively. Now, however, the cells on either row indicate the percentage split of that row's child care providers across the yes and no responses to the question. This contingency table shows why the chi-square null hypothesis was rejected, for the two samples clearly differed in their willingness to serve disabled children.

		Would Serve Children with Disabilities	
		Yes	*No*
Received Training	*Yes*	94.4%	5.6%
	No	52.2%	47.8%

Earlier, I stated that a chi-square test that compares two groups on a dichotomous response variable is analogous to an independent *t*-test. This kind of chi square is even more similar to Fisher's Exact Test, since these two tests have the same null hypothesis and also utilize the same kind of data. Because of these similarities, you may have been wondering why some researchers choose to use a Fisher's Exact Test while others subject their data to an independent-samples chi-square test. Although I will address this question more fully later in the chapter, suffice it to say that Fisher's test works better when the researcher has a small number of subjects.

The second kind of independent-samples chi-square test to consider involves a comparison of three or more samples with respect to a dichotomous response variable. Excerpt 17.11 illustrates this second kind of chi-square test. In the study associated with this excerpt, there were three comparison groups, referred to by the labels CFS, ME, and FN. If we were to create a contingency table to help us understand this chi-square test, our table would have three rows (one for each of the three groups) and two columns (one for each of the two response categories). Each of the six cells would then be filled with a percentage. Those percentages would be 54 and 46 for the CFS group, 28 and 72 for the ME group, and 19 and 81 for the FN group.

In Excerpt 17.11, notice that a 2 appears immediately to the right of the symbol for chi square, inside the parentheses. This number was the chi square's *df*. In this or any other contingency table, the *df* for χ^2 is determined by multiplying 1 less than the number of rows times 1 less than the number of columns. In this case, *df* = (3 − 1)(2 − 1) = 2.

EXCERPT 17.11 • *Three-Group Independent-Samples Chi-Square Test with a Dichotomous Response Variable*

First, Likert-type items were analyzed using chi-square tests. For the question, "What is the likelihood that the person is correctly diagnosed," there was a significant difference between the three groups, $\chi^2(2, N = 105) = 10.48$, $p < .01$. Fifty-four percent of individuals in the CFS condition indicated that the person was likely or very likely to have been correctly diagnosed, as compared with 28 and 19% from the ME and FN conditions, respectively.

Source: L. A. Jason, R. R. Taylor, S. Plioplys, Z. Stepanek, and J. Shlaes. (2002). Evaluating attributions for an illness based upon the name: Chronic fatigue syndrome, myalgic encephalopathy and Florence Nightingale disease. *American Journal of Community Psychology, 30*(1), p. 140.

With three or more groups being compared, this second version of the independent-samples chi-square test is analogous to a one-way analysis of variance. Whereas a one-way ANOVA focuses on means, this kind of chi-square test focuses on proportions. Thus whereas the null hypothesis in a three-group one-way ANOVA would state H_0: $\mu_1 = \mu_2 = \mu_3$, the null hypothesis in a three-group chi-square of the kind being considered would state H_0: $P_1 = P_2 = P_3$, where P stands for the percentage of cases in the population that fall into the first of the two available response categories (and where each subscript number designates a different population). The numerical value of the common P in the chi-square null hypothesis is not specified by the researcher but instead is determined by the data and can be any value between 0 and 100. Thus, the null hypothesis in Excerpt 17.11 would have been retained if the same percentage of individuals in each group had said "very likely" or "likely" in response to the question that was asked, regardless of whether that common percentage was 10, 16, 22, or any other value.[5]

The third kind of independent-samples chi-square test we need to consider involves two comparison groups and a response variable that has three or more categories. Excerpt 17.12 contains an example of this kind of chi-square test. Here, the two groups were made up of males and females. The four categories of the response variable were created to indicate whether these research participants were able to correctly identify the voices of a male voice and a female voice that they had heard

---

[5]The null hypothesis would also be retained if these sample percentages were all just slightly different, with *slightly* defined as "within the expected limits of sampling error, presuming that H_0 is true."

EXCERPT 17.12 • *Two-Group Independent-Samples Chi-Square Test with a Four-Category Response Variable*

In order to check for sex differences in these data, a count was made of the number of male and female listeners identifying neither voice correctly, male voice only, female voice only, or both voices. These frequencies were compared with chance expectation, and were found not to differ significantly from chance ($\chi^2 = 2.04(3), p > .05$).

Source: S. Wilding and J. Wilding. (2001). Earwitness testimony: Effects of exposure and attention on the Face Overshadowing Effect. *British Journal of Psychology, 92*(4), p. 621.

a week earlier. As you can see, the results of the chi-square test indicated that no statistically significant difference existed in the ability of the male and female participants to successfully perform the voice-recognition task.

Although no frequencies or percentages appear in Excerpt 17.12, you still should be able to imagine or sketch out the contingency table for this particular chi-square test. Such a table would have two rows (for the two groups) and four columns (to indicate how each person did when trying to identify the voices). The *df* for this table would be equal to $(2 - 1)(4 - 1)$, and the resulting *df* appears immediately to the right of the chi-square calculated value.

Whenever a chi-square test compares two groups on a response variable that has two or more categories, the null hypothesis states simply that the two populations are distributed in the same fashion across the various response categories. Thus the H_0 for the chi-square test in Excerpt 17.12 specified that the male participants and the female participants performed equally well on the voice-recognition task. As with the other kinds of independent-samples chi-square tests being considered, the null percentages for the various categories of the response variable do not have to be specified by the researcher at the outset of the hypothesis testing procedure because H_0 simply says that "whatever is the case in the first population is also the case in the second population." This means, of course, that H_0 can be true even though the percentages vary in size across the response categories; however, the way they vary must be the same in each population if H_0 is true.

The fourth kind of independent-samples chi-square test involves three or more comparison groups and a response variable made up of three or more categories. An example of this kind of chi-square test appears in Excerpt 17.13.

The null hypothesis in this fourth kind of independent-samples test is very much like the H_0 for a one-way ANOVA except that the one-way ANOVA focuses on means whereas the chi-square test focuses on proportions (or percentages). With the chi-square test, the null hypothesis simply says that the various populations are

EXCERPT 17.13 • *An Independent-Samples Chi-Square Involving Three Groups and a Four-Category Response Variable*

Table 2 presents the between-group differences in severity of sleep disturbances according to the different MSQ categories. Differences in these frequencies for the 12 cells (4 sleep problems by 3 participant groups) were significant, $\chi^2 = 14.06, p < .05$.

TABLE 2 *Severity of Sleep Disturbances by Group*

| | Sleep Disturbance | | | | | | | |
| | None | | Mild | | Moderate | | Severe | |
Group	n	%	n	%	n	%	n	%
ADHD Medicated	17	49	2	6	5	14	11	31
ADHD Nonmedicated	18	56	8	25	0	0	6	19
Control	46	60	13	17	6	8	12	15

Source: D. Stein, R. Pat-Horenczyk, S. Blank, and Y. Dagan. (2002). Sleep disturbances in adolescents with symptoms of attention-deficit/hyperactivity disorder. *Journal of Learning Disabilities, 35*(3), pp. 271–272.

identical to one another in the way subjects are distributed across the various categories of the response variable. Hence, if the percentages within the second and third rows of the table in Excerpt 17.13 had been identical to or only slightly different from the percentages in the first row, the chi-square calculated value would have been small, the data-based *p*-value would have been large, and the null hypothesis would have been retained. Such was not the case, however, because each row of percentages is quite dissimilar from the other two.

Chi Square as a Correlational Probe

In many studies, a researcher is interested in whether a nonchance relationship exists between two nominal variables. In such studies, a single sample of subjects is measured, with each subject classified into one of the available categories of the first variable and then classified once more into one of the categories of the second variable. After the data are arranged into a contingency table, a chi-square test can be used to determine whether a statistically significant relationship exists between the two variables.

In Excerpts 17.14 through 17.16, we see three terms used in conjunction with chi-square tests that let you know that the researchers were using chi square in a correlational manner. The first two of these terms—*association* and *relationship*—are not new, for we saw them used in Chapter 3 while considering bivariate correlation. The third term, however, is new. A chi-square **test of independence** is simply a test to see whether a relationship (or association) exists between the study's two variables.

When a chi-square test is used as a correlational probe, it does not produce an index that estimates the strength of the relationship between the two variables that label the contingency table's rows and columns. Instead, the chi-square test simply addresses the question, "In the population of interest, are the two variables related?" Focusing on the sample data, this question takes the form, "In the contingency table, is there a nonchance relationship between the two variables?"

To illustrate what I mean by "nonchance relationship," imagine that we go out and ask each of 100 college students to name a relative. (If anyone responds with a

EXCERPTS 17.14–17.16 • *Terms Used When Chi Square Is Used as a Correlational Probe*

Chi-square tests revealed no association between the method of recruitment with gender, education level, marital status and occupational status.

Source: L. E. Waters and K. A. Moore. (2002). Reducing latent deprivation during unemployment: The role of meaningful leisure activity. *Journal of Occupational and Organizational Psychology, 75*(1), p. 19.

- -

This finding indicates a statistically significant relationship between location and use of tobacco ($\chi^2 = 42.59$; $p = .000$).

Source: S. Atav and G. A. Spencer. (2002). Health risk behaviors among adolescents attending rural, suburban, and urban schools: A comparative study. *Family and Community Health, 25*(2), p. 58.

- -

A chi square test of independence was used to determine if a relationship exists between receipt of material about ADHD and use of positive teaching strategies.

Source: C. S. Glass. (2001). Factors influencing teaching strategies used with children who display attention deficit hyperactivity disorder characteristics, *Education, 122*(1), p. 74.

gender-free name like Pat, we would ask the respondent to indicate whether the relative is a male or a female.) We would also keep track of each respondent's gender. After collecting these two pieces of information from our 100th student, we might end up with sample data that look like this:

**Gender of
the Relative**

		Male	Female
**Gender of
the Student**	Male	30	20
	Female	23	27

In the 2 × 2 contingency table for our hypothetical study, there is a relationship between the two variables—student's gender and relative's gender. More of the male students responded with the name of a male relative while more of the female students thought of a female relative. (Or, we could say that there was a tendency for male relatives to be thought of by male students while female relatives were thought of by female students.) But is this relationship something other than what would be expected by chance?

If there were *no* relationship in the population between the two variables in our gender study, the population frequencies in all four cells of the contingency table would be identical. But a sample extracted from that population would not likely mirror the population perfectly. Instead, sampling error would likely be in the sample data, thus causing the observed contingency table to have dissimilar cell frequencies. In other words, we would expect a relationship to pop up in the sample data even if there were no relationship in the population. Such a relationship, in the sample data, would be due entirely to chance. Although we should expect a "null population" (i.e., one in which there is no relationship between the two variables) to yield sample data in which a relationship *does* exist between the two variables, such a relationship ought to be small, or weak. It *is* possible for a null population to yield sample data suggesting a strong relationship between the two variables, but this is *not* very likely to happen. Stated differently, if researchers end up with a contingency table in which there is a meager relationship, they have only weak evidence for arguing that the two variables of interest are related in the population. If, in contrast, a pronounced relationship shows up in the contingency table built with the sample data, the researchers possess strong evidence for suggesting that a relationship does, in fact, exist in the population.

Returning to our little gender study, the chi-square test can be used to label the relationship that shows up in the sample data as being either meager or pronounced. Using the hypothesis testing procedure in which the level of significance is set equal to .05, the null hypothesis of no relationship in the population cannot be rejected. This means that the observed relationship in the contingency table could easily have come from a sample pulled from a population characterized by H_0. This means that the observed relationship is not of the nonchance variety.

In addition to using a chi-square test to see if a nonchance relationship exists in the sample data, researchers can convert their chi-square calculated value into an index that estimates the strength of the relationship that exists in the population. By making this conversion, the researcher obtains a numerical value that is analogous to the correlation coefficient generated by Pearson's or Spearman's technique. Several different conversion procedures have been developed.

The phi coefficient can be used to measure the strength of association in 2 × 2 contingency tables. I discussed this correlational procedure in Chapters 3 and 9 and pointed out in those discussions how phi is appropriate for the case of two dichotomous variables. Now, I can extend this discussion of phi by pointing out its connection to chi square. If a chi-square test has been applied to a 2 × 2 contingency table, the phi index of association can be obtained directly by putting the chi-square calculated value into this simple formula:

$$\text{phi} = \sqrt{\frac{\chi^2}{N}}$$

where N stands for the total sample size. Researchers, of course, are the ones who use this formula in order to convert their chi-square calculated values into phi coefficients. As illustrated by Excerpt 17.17, you will not have to do this!

For contingency tables that have more than two rows or columns, researchers can convert their chi-square calculated value into a measure of association called the

---

EXCERPT 17.17 • *Chi Square and Phi*

What we want to know is whether the sixteenth-century norms prohibiting core-disgusting actions are more likely to be part of contemporary manners than the sixteenth-century norms prohibiting actions unlikely to elicit core disgust. Prohibitions against core-disgusting actions were indeed more likely to survive than prohibitions against actions that aren't core-disgusting: $\chi^2(1, N = 57) = 17.411, p < .0001$ (two-tailed), $\Phi^2 = .305$.

Source: S. Nichols. (2002). On the genealogy of norms: A case for the role of emotion in cultural evolution. *Philosophy of Science*, 69(2), pp. 249–250.

contingency coefficient. This index of relationship is symbolized by *C*, and the connection between *C* and chi square is made evident by the following formula for *C*:

$$C = \sqrt{\frac{\chi^2}{N + \chi^2}}$$

In Excerpt 17.18, we see an illustration of how the contingency coefficient can be computed following a chi-square test of independence.[6]

EXCERPT 17.18 • *Chi Square and the Contingency Coefficient*

To test for familiarity with facilities, a 3 (location of game: home, away, neutral) $\times$ 3 (outcome: win, lose, draw) chi-square test was performed. The association between the two variables was significant [$\chi^2(4, n = 3914) = 206.90, p < .001, C = .23$].

Source: T. D. Brown, J. L. Van Raalte, B. W. Brewer, and C. R. Winter. (2002). World Cup soccer home advantage. *Journal of Sport Behavior,* 25(2), p. 137.

The formula for *C* shows that this index of association will turn out equal to zero when there is no relationship in the contingency table (since in that case, the calculated value of χ^2 will itself turn out equal to zero) and that it will assume larger values for larger values of χ^2. What this formula does not show is that this index usually cannot achieve a maximum value of 1.00 (as is the case with Pearson's *r*, Spearman's rho, and other correlation coefficients). This problem can be circumvented easily if the researcher computes **Cramer's measure of association** because Cramer's index is simply equal to the computed index of relationship divided by the maximum value that the index could assume, given the contingency table's dimensions and marginal totals.

In Excerpt 17.19, we see a case in which Cramer's measure of association, symbolized as *V*, was computed in conjunction with a 4 $\times$ 2 contingency table. The researcher called her table of percentages a **crosstabulation;** this is simply another label for a contingency table. In the final sentence of this excerpt, notice that the researcher first presents the results of the chi-square analysis (which suggested the

---

[6]A variation of *C* is called the *mean square contingency coefficient.* This index of relationship uses the same formula as that presented for phi.

EXCERPT 17.19 • *Chi Square and Cramer's V*

To answer the question posed by previous researchers of whether race or ethnicity was associated with being portrayed as a "bad guy" or a "good guy," a crosstabulation with chi square and Cramer's V was used. Caucasian characters were nearly equally split between "bad guys" (54.5%) and "good guys" (45.5%), appearing slightly more often in the "bad guy" category than in the "good." The vast majority, 78.1%, of Black and African American characters appeared as "good guys," with 21.9% as "bad guys." Hispanic and Latino characters appeared slightly more often as "bad guys" (52.9%) than "good guys" (47.1%). Finally, in this sample, Asians and Asian Americans never appeared as "good guys," while four characters in all appeared as "bad guys." The differences among the cells were statistically significant ($\chi^2 = 15.98$, $p < .001$, Cramer's $V = .22$).

Source: E. Scharrer. (2001). Tough guys: The portrayal of hypermasculinity and aggression in televised police dramas. *Journal of Broadcasting and Electronic Media, 45*(4), p. 627.

presence of a relationship), and then she presents the value for Cramer's *V* (indicating the estimated *strength* of that relationship).

Issues Related to Chi-Square Tests

Before we conclude our discussion of chi-square tests, a few related issues need to be addressed. Unless you are aware of the connection between these issues and the various chi-square tests we have covered, you will be unable to fully understand and critique research reports that contain the results of chi-square tests. Accordingly, it is important for you to be sensitive to the following issues.

Post Hoc Tests

If an independent-samples chi-square test is used to compare two groups, interpretation of the results is straightforward regardless of what decision is made regarding the null hypothesis. If there are three or more comparison groups involved in the study, the results can be interpreted without difficulty so long as H_0 is not rejected. If, however, the independent-samples chi-square test leads to a rejection of H_0 when three or more groups are contrasted, the situation remains unclear.

When three or more samples are compared, a statistically significant outcome simply indicates that it is unlikely that all corresponding populations are distributed in the same way across the categories of the response variable. In other words, a rejection of H_0 suggests that at least two of the populations differ, but this outcome by itself does not provide any insight as to which specific populations differ from one another. To gain such insights, the researcher must conduct a post hoc investigation.

In Excerpt 17.20, we see a case where a post hoc investigation after an "omnibus" chi-square test yielded a statistically significant result. In the study associated with this excerpt, there were four groups of psychiatric patients, with each person classified as having or not having a panic attack after breathing air containing an abnormal amount of CO_2. Hence, the original chi-square test was conducted on a 4×2 (group by response) contingency table. In the post hoc investigation, all possible pairwise comparisons were made among the four groups, each conducted with a 2×2 (group by response) chi-square test.

EXCERPT 17.20 • *Post Hoc Investigation Following a Significant Chi Square*

Fifty panic disorder subjects, 21 depressed subjects, 10 subjects with premenstrual dysphoric disorder, and 34 normal comparison subjects underwent the 5% CO_2 inhalation procedure. Chi square analysis revealed a significant difference in panic rates [52%, 24%, 30%, and 9%, respectively] across groups ($\chi^2 = 22.04$, $df = 3$, $p < 0.001$). Follow-up 2×2 comparisons revealed significant differences in panic rates in response between panic disorder subjects and both depressed and normal comparison subjects but not subjects with premenstrual dysphoric disorder. Panic rates for the depressed subjects did not differ from those for the subjects with premenstrual dysphoric disorder or for the normal comparison subjects.

Source: J. M. Kent, L. A. Papp, J. M. Martinez, and S. T. Browne. (2001). Specificity of panic response to CO_2 inhalation in panic disorder: A comparison with major depression and premenstrual dysphoric disorder. *American Journal of Psychiatry, 158*(1), pp. 61–62.

Whenever two or more separate chi-square tests are performed within a post hoc investigation, with each incorporating the same level of significance as that used in the initial (omnibus) chi-square test, the chances of a Type I error being made somewhere in the post hoc analysis will exceed the nominal level of significance. This is not a problem in those situations where the researcher judges Type II errors to be more costly than Type I errors. Be that as it may, the scientific community seems to encourage researchers to guard against Type I errors.

In Excerpt 17.20, you saw a case in which a post hoc investigation involved six pairwise comparisons (each performed as a 2×2 chi-square) among the four groups. If each of these post hoc chi-square tests had been conducted at a .05 level of significance, the study would have suffered from an inflated Type I error rate. However, the researchers were aware of this potential problem. In their research report, the researchers stated that their post hoc chi-square tests involved "values corrected for multiple comparisons (Bonferroni correction)." This use of the Bonferroni test is identical in purpose to what we saw in Chapter 12 where the focus was on group means. There, we saw a case where pairwise comparisons were made via regular *t*-tests accompanied by a Bonferroni adjustment. Here, Bonferroni was employed for precisely the same reason.

Small Amounts of Sample Data

To work properly, the chi-square tests discussed in this chapter necessitate sample sizes that are not too small. Actually, it is the **expected frequencies** that must be sufficiently large for the chi-square test to function as intended. An expected frequency exists for each category into which sample objects are classified, and each one is nothing more than the proportion of the sample data you would expect in the category if H_0 were true and if there were absolutely no sampling error. For example, if we were to perform a taste test in which each of 20 individuals is asked to sip four different beverages and then indicate which one is the best, the expected frequency for each of the four options would be equal to 5 (presuming that H_0 specifies equality among the four beverages). If this same study were to be conducted with 40 participants, each of the four expected values would be equal to 10.

If researchers have a small amount of sample data, the expected values associated with their chi-square test will also be small. If the expected values are too small, the chi-square test should not be used. Various rules of thumb have been offered over the years to help applied researchers know when they should refrain from using the chi-square test because of small expected values. The most conservative of these rules says that none of the expected frequencies should be smaller than 5; the most liberal rule stipulates that chi square can be used so long as the average expected frequency is at least 2.

In Excerpt 17.21 we see a case where the researchers' decision to use chi square or Fisher's Exact Test was tied to the size of the expected values. Using the data presented in this excerpt, it is possible to determine the expected value associated with each of the three analyses. For the first analysis, all four expected values turned out to be larger than 22. Accordingly, the data corresponding to "living with a nonrelative friend or family" were analyzed via chi square. With each of the other two sets of data ("had residential placements" or "lived with a boyfriend or girlfriend with children"), two of the four cells had expected values smaller than 5. For this reason, the researchers used Fisher's Exact Test rather than chi square when analyzing these sets of data.

The option of turning to Fisher's Exact Test when the expected frequencies are too small is available in those situations where the sample data create a 2×2 contingency table. This option does not exist, however, if their researcher is using (1) a one-sample chi-square test with three or more categories or (2) chi square with

EXCERPT 17.21 • *Use of Fisher's Exact Test Rather Than Chi Square Because of Small Expected Frequencies*

For variables showing low expected cell frequencies, we used Fisher's Exact test to judge significance levels in place of chi squares. . . . Of 15 different living situations, 3 showed significant differences between participants classified as deviant versus nondeviant. As shown in Table 2 [not shown here], significantly more deviant than nondeviant participants lived with a nonrelative friend or family [30/62 vs. 33/111], $\chi^2(1) = 5.98$, $p = .014$; had residential placements [9/62 vs. 3/111], Fisher's Exact test, $p = .009$; and lived with a boyfriend or girlfriend with children [8/62 vs. 3/111], Fisher's Exact test, $p = .018$.

Source: S. H. McConaughy and M. E. Wadsworth. (2000). Life history reports of young adults previously referred for mental health services. *Journal of Emotional and Behavioral Disorders, 8*(4), p. 207.

a contingency table that has more than two rows and/or more than two columns. In these situations, the problem of small expected frequencies will be solved by the researcher's redefining of the response categories such that two or more of the original categories can be collapsed together. For example, if men and women are being compared regarding their responses to a five-option Likert-type question, the researcher might convert the five original categories into three new categories by (1) merging together the "strongly agree" and "agree" categories into a new single category called "favorable response," (2) leaving the "undecided" category unchanged, and (3) merging together the "disagree" and "strongly disagree" categories into a new single category called "unfavorable response." By so doing, the revised contingency table might not have any expected frequencies that are too small.

Yates' Correction for Continuity

When applying a chi-square test to situations where $df = 1$, some researchers use a special formula that yields a slightly smaller calculated value than would be the case if the regular formula were employed. When this is done, it can be said that the data are being analyzed using a chi-square test that has been **corrected for discontinuity.** This special formula was developed by a famous statistician named **Yates,** and occasionally the chi-square test has Yates' name attached to it when the special formula is used. Excerpt 17.22 shows that Yates' correction is used in conjunction with chi-square analyses. It is not used with any of the other statistical procedures considered in this book.

EXCERPT 17.22 • *Yates' Correction for Discontinuity*

I tested the effect of human scent on seed removal by comparing removal rates and the total amount of removal between seeds that had been handled with bare hands (hereafter scented seeds) and seeds that had not been handled directly (hereafter no-scent seeds). . . . Overall, 88% of scent seeds were removed compared with 55% of no-scent seeds. The total number of seeds removed was significantly greater for scented than for no-scent seeds (Yates-corrected $\chi^2 = 25.13$, $df = 1$, $P < 0.001$).

Source: Daniel G. Wenny. (2002). Effects of human handling of seeds on seed removal by rodents. *American Midland Naturalist, 147*(2), pp. 404–405.

Statistical authorities are not in agreement as to the need for using Yates' special formula. Some argue that it should *always* be used in situations where $df = 1$ because the regular formula leads to calculated values that are too large (and thus to an inflated probability of a Type I error). Other authorities take the position that the Yates adjustment causes the pendulum to swing too far in the opposite direction because Yates' correction makes the chi-square test overly conservative (thus increasing the chances of a Type II error). Ideally, researchers should clarify why the Yates formula either was or wasn't used on the basis of a judicious consideration of the different risks associated with a Type I or a Type II error. Realistically, however, you are most likely to see the Yates formula used only occasionally and, in those cases, used without any explanation as to why it was employed.

McNemar's Chi-Square

Earlier in this chapter, we saw how a chi-square test can be used to compare two independent samples with respect to a dichotomous dependent variable. If the two samples involved in such a comparison are related rather than independent, chi square can still be used to test the **homogeneity of proportions** null hypothesis. However, both the formula used by the researchers to analyze their data and the label attached to the test procedure are slightly different in this situation where two related samples are compared. Although there is no reason to concern ourselves here with the unique formula used when correlated data have been collected, it *is* important that you become familiar with the way researchers refer to this kind of test.

A chi-square analysis of related samples is usually referred to simply as **McNemar's test.** Sometimes, however, it is called McNemar's change test, McNemar's chi-square test, McNemar's test of correlated proportions, or McNemar's test

EXCERPTS 17.23–17.24 • *McNemar's Chi-Square Test*

To determine whether a change had occurred in the self-reported presence of physical discomfort before and after the assessment, McNemar's test was used. . . . The percent reporting discomfort decreased from 65 percent to 15 percent following the assessment ($p = 0.001$).

Source: L. A. Tiraboschi, J. E. Weiss, and M. B. Blayney. (2002). Evaluating the effectiveness of an office ergonomics program. *Professional Safety, 47*(1), pp. 41–42.

Eligible patients from the restorative and usual care offices were identified concurrently. The pool of potential usual care patients was sufficiently large to permit the use of a computerized algorithm designed to match patients according to age (within 5 years), sex, race, self-care, or basic activities of daily living (ADLs) function at admission to home care, and baseline cognitive status. . . . Differences in patient characteristics between the restorative and usual care groups at start of care were assessed using the McNemar test for binary variables.

Source: M. E. Tinetti, D. Baker, W. T. Gallo, and A. Nanda. (2002). Evaluation of restorative care vs usual care for older adults receiving an acute episode of home care. *Journal of the American Medical Association, 287*(16), pp. 2099, 2101.

for paired data. Occasionally, it is referred to symbolically as $Mc\chi^2$. Excerpts 17.23 and 17.24 illustrate the use of McNemar's test.

McNemar's chi-square test is very much like a correlated-samples *t*-test in that two sets of data being compared can come either from a single group that is measured twice (e.g., in a pre/post sense) or from matched samples that are measured just once. Excerpt 17.23 obviously falls into the first of these categories because data from a single group are compared at two points in time, before and after an intervention. (This intervention involved ergonomic assessments and individualized training to the office and administrative workers who served as research participants.) In Excerpt 17.24, we see a case where two comparison groups were first matched and then compared on several dichotomous variables. Because these groups were matched, neither chi-square nor Fisher's Exact Test could be used. Instead, McNemar's test was employed to make the desired comparisons.

Although the McNemar chi square is similar to a correlated *t*-test with respect to the kind of sample(s) involved in the comparison, the two tests differ dramatically in terms of the null hypothesis. With the *t*-test, the null hypothesis involves population means; in contrast, the null hypothesis of McNemar's chi-square test is concerned with population percentages. In other words, the null hypothesis of Mc-Nemar's test always takes the form H_0: $P_1 = P_2$ while the *t*-test's null hypothesis always involves the symbol μ (and it usually is set up to say H_0: $\mu_1 = \mu_2$).

The Cochran Q Test

A test developed by Cochran is appropriate for the situation where the researcher wishes to compare three or more related samples with respect to a dichotomous dependent variable. This test is called the **Cochran Q test,** with the letter Q simply being the arbitrary symbol used by Cochran to label the calculated value produced by putting the sample data into Cochran's formula. This test just as easily could have been called Cochran's chi-square test inasmuch as the calculated value is compared against a chi-square critical value to determine whether the null hypothesis should be rejected.

The Cochran Q test can be thought of as an "extension" of McNemar's chi-square test, since McNemar's test is restricted to the situation where just two correlated samples of data are compared while Cochran's test can be used when there are any number of such samples. Or, the Cochran Q test can be likened to the one-factor repeated-measures analysis of variance covered in Chapter 14; in each case, multiple related samples of data are compared. (That ANOVA is quite different from the Cochran test, however, because the null hypothesis in the former focuses on μs whereas Cochran's H_0 involves Ps.)

In Excerpt 17.25, we see a case where Cochran's Q test was used. In this study, 326 adolescents were asked to respond yes or no as to whether they felt they had control over three kinds of stressors. The data were cast into a 3×2 contingency table, with each row corresponding to one of the three stressors, and the two columns corresponding to the response categories (yes or no) indicating whether or not the adolescent believed he or she had control over the stressor. A regular chi-square test could not be used because the data on each row of this contingency table came from the same group.

In the study associated with Excerpt 17.25, the null hypothesis for Cochran's Q test could be stated as H_0: $P_{\text{Family}} = P_{\text{School}} = P_{\text{Peer}}$, where each P stands for the population percentage of adolescents who believe a given stressor is controllable. As you can see, the Cochran Q test led to a rejection of this null hypothesis. (In this excerpt, there are two numbers inside a set of parentheses next to the letter Q. The first of these numbers is the *df* associated with the Cochran test; the second number is the sample size.)

When Cochran's test leads to a rejection of the omnibus null hypothesis, the researcher will probably conduct a post hoc investigation. Within this follow-up investigation, the researcher most likely will set up and test pairwise comparisons. Such post hoc tests can be made via McNemar's test, as illustrated in Excerpt

17.25. (The researchers used the word "adjustment" when presenting the results of their three McNemar tests—only two of which yielded a statistically significant result—because they adjusted the level of significance by means of the Bonferroni technique.)

EXCERPT 17.25 • *Cochran's Q Test*

Using Cochran's Q nonparametric statistic, we also examined whether the adolescents perceived differences in controllability across the three stressors. This test assesses whether matched sets of frequencies differ significantly among themselves. Perceived controllability ratings for the three stressors were considered to be "matched" groups because the same adolescent rated all three stressors on perceived controllability. Of the 326 students who provided controllability ratings for each stressor, 53% rated the family stressor as controllable, 64% rated the school stressor as controllable, and 53% rated the peer stressor as controllable, yielding a significant overall Cochran's $Q(2, 326) = 10.46, p < .01$. Follow-up tests indicated that students found school stressors to be more controllable than both family and peer stressors (McNemar's adjusted $\chi^2 = 8.47, p < .01$, and $\chi^2 = 8.89, p < .01$, respectively).

Source: M. A. Griffith, E. F. Dubow, and M. F. Ippolito. (2000). Developmental and cross-situational differences in adolescents' coping strategies. *Journal of Youth and Adolescence, 29*(2), p. 194.

The Use of z-Tests When Dealing with Proportions

As you may recall from Chapter 10, researchers will sometimes use a *z*-test (rather than a *t*-test) when their studies are focused on either the mean of one group or the means of two comparison groups. It may come as a surprise that researchers will sometimes apply a *z*-test when dealing with dependent variables that are qualitative rather than quantitative in nature. Be that as it may, you are likely to come across cases where a *z*-test has been used by researchers when their data take the form of proportions, percentages, or frequencies.

If a researcher has a single group that is measured on a dichotomous dependent variable, the data can be analyzed by a one-sample chi-square test *or* by a *z*-test. The choice here is immaterial, since these two tests are mathematically equivalent and will always lead to the same data-based *p*-value. The same thing holds true for the case where a comparison is made between two unrelated samples.

Such a comparison can be made with an independent-samples chi-square test or a z-test, for the *p*-value of both tests will be the same.

Whereas the z-tests we have just discussed and the chi-square tests covered earlier (for the cases of a dichotomous dependent variable used with a single sample or two independent samples) are mathematically equivalent, there is another z-test that represents a **large sample approximation** to some of the tests examined in earlier sections of this chapter. To be more specific, researchers will sometimes use a z-test, if they have large samples, in places where you might expect them to use a sign test, a binomial test, or a McNemar test. In Excerpts 17.26 and 17.27, we see two examples of a z-test being used in connection with test procedures considered in this chapter. In the first of these excerpts, a large-sample approximation to the sign test was used. In Excerpt 17.27, a large-sample approximation to the binomial test was used.

EXCERPTS 17.26–17.27 • *Use of z-Tests with Percentages (and Large Samples)*

Only seven participants (7 percent) moved their preferences on the response scale in the nonpredicted direction. This difference between predicted and nonpredicted changes was statistically significant by sign test ($z = 3.08$, $p < 0.001$).

Source: J. H. Hibbard, P. Slovic, E. Peters, and M. L. Finucane. (2002). Strategies for reporting health plan performance information to consumers: Evidence from controlled studies. *Health Services Research, 37*(2), p. 306.

- -

However, a majority of respondents (63%; 43 out of 68) chose the grocery credit over the massage or facial (using the normal approximation of the binomial distribution; $z = 2.2$; $p < .05$).

Source: R. Kivetz and I. Simonson. (2002). Self-control for the righteous: Toward a theory of precommitment to indulgence. *Journal of Consumer Research, 29*(2), pp. 2099, 2101.

A Few Final Thoughts

As you have seen, a wide variety of test procedures have been designed for situations where the researcher's data take the form of frequencies, percentages, or proportions. Despite the differences among these tests (in terms of their names, the number of groups involved, and whether repeated measures are involved), there are many commonalities that cut across the tests we have considered. These commonalities exist because each of these tests involves the computation of a data-based p-value that is then used to evaluate a null hypothesis.

In using the procedures considered in this chapter within an applied research study, a researcher will follow the various steps of hypothesis testing. Accordingly, many of the "side issues" dealt with in Chapters 7 and 8 are relevant to the proper use of any and all of the tests we have just discussed. In an effort to help you keep these important concerns in the forefront of your consciousness as you read and evaluate research reports, I feel obliged to conclude this chapter by considering a few of these more generic concerns.

My first point is simply a reiteration that the data-based p-value is always computed on the basis of a tentative belief that the null hypothesis is true. Accordingly, the statistical results of a study are always tied to the null hypothesis. If the researcher's null hypothesis is silly or articulates something that no one would defend or expect to be true, then the rejection of H_0, regardless of how "impressive" the p-value, does not signify an important finding.

If you think that this first point is simply a "straw man" that has no connection to the real world of actual research, consider this *real* study that was conducted not too long ago. In this investigation, chi square compared three groups of teachers in terms of the types of instructional units they used. Two kinds of data were collected from the teachers: (1) their theoretical orientation regarding optimal teaching-learning practices and (2) what they actually did when teaching. The results indicated that skill-based instructional units tended to be used more by teachers who had a skill-based theoretical orientation, that rule-based instructional units were used more so by teachers who had a rule-based theoretical orientation, and that function-based instructional units were utilized to a greater extent by teachers who possessed a function-based theoretical orientation. Are you surprised that this study's data brought forth a rejection of the chi-square null hypothesis of no relationship between teachers' theoretical orientation and type of instructional unit used? Was a study needed to reach this finding?

The second point I wish to reiterate is that the chances of a Type I error increase above the researcher's nominal level of significance in the situation where multiple null hypotheses are evaluated. Although there are alternative ways of dealing with this potential problem, you are likely to see the Bonferroni technique employed most often to keep control over Type I errors. Excerpt 17.28 illustrates the use of this technique in conjunction with the chi-square test. The researchers who conducted the study associated with this excerpt deserve high praise for using the Bonferroni technique even though it forced them to retain the null hypothesis. It is worth noting that the data-based p-level in this study was quite small (.003), yet this did not beat the Bonferroni-corrected alpha level of .002.

EXCERPT 17.28 • *The Bonferroni Technique Used With Chi Square*

All two-by-two chi-square analyses were two-sided and Yates corrected. . . . To control for multiple comparisons, we applied a Bonferroni correction (0.05/22, setting the significance level at 0.002). . . . [Results for marital status] did not reveal a significant group difference ($\chi^2 = 9.0$, $df = 1$, $p = 0.003$) after Bonferroni correction.

Source: A. Feinstein, J. Owen, and N. Blair. (2002). A hazardous profession: War, journalists, and psychopathology. *American Journal of Psychiatry, 159*(9), pp. 1571–1572.

My third point concerns the distinction between statistical significance and practical significance. As I hope you recall from our earlier discussions, it is possible for H_0 to be rejected, with an "impressive" data-based p-value (e.g., $p < .0001$), even though the computed sample statistic does not appear to be very dissimilar from the value of the parameter expressed in H_0. I also hope you remember my earlier contention that conscientious researchers will either design their studies and/or conduct a more complete analysis of their data with an eye toward avoiding the potential error of figuratively making a mountain out of a molehill.

There are several ways researchers can demonstrate sensitivity to the distinction between practical significance and statistical significance. In our examination of t-tests, F-tests, and tests on correlation coefficients, we have seen that these options include (1) computing, in the design phase of the investigation, the proper sample size; (2) calculating, after the data have been collected, the magnitude of the discrepancy between the estimated and null values of the population parameter; and (3) computing, once again after the data have been gathered, a strength-of-association index. These three options are as readily available to researchers who use the various test procedures covered in this chapter as they are to those who conduct t-tests, F-tests, or tests involving one or more correlation coefficients.

In Excerpts 17.29 and 17.30, we see two cases in which researchers showed that they were aware of this important distinction between practical significance and statistical significance. In the first of these excerpts, the researchers conducted an *a priori* power analysis for the purpose of determining how large their sample needed to be. In Excerpt 17.30, estimated effect size indices were computed after a chi-square test had revealed a statistically significant difference between the two comparison groups. The researchers associated with both of these studies deserve credit for being concerned with the *meaningfulness* of their findings.

EXCERPTS 17.29–17.30 • *Practical versus Statistical Significance*

Associations between categoric variables were analyzed using the Fisher exact test or the χ^2 test. . . . To detect a difference of 5%, with 95% confidence interval (CI) and a power of 80%, a sample size of 90 patients or more was needed.

Source: F. J. Garcia and A. L. Nager. (2002). Jaundice as an early diagnostic sign of urinary tract infection in infancy. *Pediatrics, 109*(5), p. 847.

The free response data demonstrated that Control Intervention-Media Images participants were more likely to make Negative-Self statements (proportion = .28) than participants in the Control Intervention-Car Images condition (proportion = 0), $\chi^2(1, N = 50) = 8.14, p = .004$. We calculated the effect size of the difference between two proportions (ES_p) according to the arcsine transformation procedure described by Cohen (1977) and Lipsey (1990). ES_p is interpreted in the same way as Cohen's *d*. This analysis revealed that the effect size of this difference was large ($\mathrm{ES}_p = 1.12$).

Source: H. D. Posavac, S. D. Posavac, and R. G. Weigel. (2001). Reducing the impact of media images on women at risk for body image disturbance: Three targeted interventions. *Journal of Social and Clinical Psychology, 20*(3), pp. 333–334.

Review Terms

Binomial test
Chi square
Cochran Q test
Contingency coefficient
Contingency table
Cramer's measure of association
Expected frequency
Fisher's Exact Test
Frequencies
Goodness-of-fit test
Homogeneity of proportions
Independent samples

Large-sample approximation
McNemar's chi-square test
Observed frequency
One-sample chi-square test
Pearson chi square
Percentages
Proportions
Sign test
Test of independence
Test of normality
Yates' correction for continuity

The Best Items in the Companion Website

1. An interactive online quiz (with immediate feedback provided) covering Chapter 17.
2. Ten misconceptions about the content of Chapter 17.
3. One of the best passages from Chapter 17: "Consider the Null Hypothesis before Looking at the *p*-Level."

4. Four interactive online resources.
5. The first of the two jokes, for it deals with one of the statistical tests covered in Chapter 17.

Fun Exercises inside Research Navigator

1. If women could choose their first child's sex, would mothers want girls?

In this study, 230 college men and 239 college women were asked, among other things, (1) whether they wanted their future first-born child to be a boy or a girl, and (2) whether they would determine (i.e., actively choose) that child's sex, if such were an option. Several chi-square tests were conducted in this study. One compared the stated preferences of the full groups of men and women, while another compared the stated preferences of just those individuals who said that they would determine their first-born's sex. What do you think these chi-square tests revealed? And do you think either group of women stated a preference for a girl? To find out what this study revealed, refer to the PDF version of the research report in the Psychology database of ContentSelect, look at Tables 1 and 2, and read the results on page 233.

D. Swetkis, F. D. Gilroy, & R. Steinbacher. Firstborn preference and attitudes toward using sex selection technology. *Journal of Genetic Psychology*. Located in the PSYCHOLOGY database of ContentSelect.

2. Does psychotherapy help people get off antidepressant drugs?

This study focused on individuals who had been on antidepressant drugs. One group was made up of 30 individuals who had been receiving psychotherapy for one year; the other group, matched to the first group (on the basis of age and sex), had not been in therapy. For the dependent variable, each person in each group was classified as either taking or not taking antidepressant drugs. The percentage still taking antidepressants was 47% (14 out of 30) in one group and 97% (29 out of 30) in the other group. A comparison of these two percentages, using McNemar's test for paired data, indicated a statistically significant difference (with $p < 0.001$). Which of the two groups—those in therapy or those not in therapy—do you think had all but one of its members still using antidepressant drugs at the point data were collected? Are you sure of your guess? To find out if you are right, refer to the PDF version of the research report in the Nursing, Health, and Medicine database of ContentSelect, go to page 630, and read the first two paragraphs in the section entitled "Antidepressant prescribing and patients in comparison group 1."

M. Ashworth, J. Wastie, F. Reid, & S. Clement. The effects of psychotherapeutic interventions upon psychotropic prescribing and consultation rates in one general practice. *Journal of Mental Health*. Located in the NURSING, HEALTH, AND MEDICINE database of ContentSelect.

Review Questions and Answers begin on page 516.

18

Statistical Tests on Ranks (Nonparametric Tests)

In the previous chapter, we examined a variety of test procedures designed for data that are qualitative, or nominal, in nature. Whether dealing with frequencies, percentages, or proportions, those tests involved response categories devoid of any quantitative meaning. For example, when a Fisher's Exact Test was used in Excerpt 17.4 to compare males and females regarding the violent or nonviolent nature of the crime they had committed, neither the grouping variable (gender) nor the response variable (type of crime) involved categories that had any numerical meaning.

We now turn our attention to a group of test procedures that utilize the simplest kind of quantitative data: ranks. In a sense, we are returning to this topic (rather than starting from scratch), since in Chapter 9, I pointed out how researchers can set up and evaluate null hypotheses concerning Spearman's rho and Kendall's tau. As I hope you recall, each of these correlational procedures involves an analysis of ranked data.

Within the context of this chapter, we consider five of the many test procedures that have been developed for use with ordinal data. These **nonparametric** procedures are the median test, the Mann-Whitney *U* test, the Kruskal-Wallis one-way analysis of variance of ranks, the Wilcoxon matched-pairs signed-ranks test, and the Friedman two-way analysis of variance of ranks. Excerpts 18.1 through 18.5 show how researchers typically refer to these nonparametic test procedures.[1]

The five test procedures considered in this chapter are not the only ones that involve ranked data, but they are the ones used most frequently by applied researchers. Because these five tests are used so often, we will examine each one sep-

---

[1]The term *nonparametric* is simply a label for various test procedures that involve ranked data. In contrast, the term *parametric* is used to denote those tests (e.g., *t* and *F*) that are built on a different statistical view of the data—and usually a more stringent set of assumptions regarding the population(s) associated with the study's sample(s).

EXCERPTS 18.1–18.5 • *Five Test Procedures That Involve Ranked Data*

We tested for the difference in the distributions of percent change using the median test, which is a nonparametric test.

Source: S. L. McFall, A. M. Yerkes, and L. D. Cowan. (2000). Outcomes of a small group educational intervention for urinary incontinence: Episodes of incontinence and other urinary symptoms. *Journal of Aging and Health, 12*(2), p. 258.

- -

The Mann-Whitney *U* test was used to examine differences in rates of health care contact among the groups.

Source: J. B. Luoma, C. E. Martin, and J. L. Pearson. (2002). Contact with mental health and primary care providers before suicide: A review of the evidence. *American Journal of Psychiatry, 159*(6), p. 912.

- -

We also examined the effect of loss of a particular leg (1, 2, 3, 4) on foraging ability with a Kruskal-Wallis ANOVA.

Source: C. C. Amaya, P. D. Klawinski, and D. R. Formanowicz. (2001). The effects of leg autonomy on running speed and foraging ability in two species of wolf spider (Lycosidae). *American Midland Naturalist, 145*(1), p. 202.

- -

Pretest and posttest mean scores were compared using the Wilcoxon matched-pairs signed ranks test.

Source: P. Agron, E. Takada, and A. Purcell. (2002). California Project LEAN's food on the run program: An evaluation of a high school-based student advocacy nutrition and physical activity program. *Journal of the American Dietetic Association* (Supplement: Adolescent nutrition: A springboard for health), p. S104.

- -

To examine differences by domain in the relative frequency of hoped-for and feared selves, as well as differences in priority ratings, the Friedman two-way analysis of variance by ranks test was used.

Source: C. M. Yowell. (2000). Possible selves and future orientation: Exploring hopes and fears of Latino boys and girls. *Journal of Early Adolescence, 20*(3), p. 257.

arately in an effort to clarify the research "setting" for which each test is appropriate, the typical format used to report the test's results, and the proper meaning of a rejected null hypothesis. First, however, we need to consider the three ways in which a researcher can obtain the ranked data needed for any of the five tests.

Obtaining Ranked Data

One obvious way for a researcher to obtain ranked data is to ask each research participant to rank a set of objects, statements, ideas, or other things. When this is done, numbers get attached to the things by the persons doing the ranking, with the numbers being 1, 2, 3, and so on used to indicate an ordering from best to worst, most important to least important, strongest to weakest, and the like. The resulting numbers are **ranks.**[2]

In Excerpt 18.6, we see a case where ranks were used in a research study. In the study associated with this excerpt, the research participants (shoppers at a farmer's market) provided these data by ranking the items in two lists provided by the researchers.

EXCERPT 18.6 • *Obtaining Ordinal Data by Having People Rank a Set of Things*

In separate questions consumers were asked why they come to the PTFM. In the first question, consumers were shown a list and asked to rank four possible reasons for coming to the farmers market: to buy local food, to buy fresh food, to buy inexpensive food, and to meet a farmer. . . . In a related question consumers were asked to rank some advantages of coming to the PTFM from a list (quality, freshness, support local economy, variety, or other).

Source: S. Andreatta and W. Wickliffe. (2002). Managing farmer and consumer expectations: A study of a North Carolina farmers market. *Human Organization, 61*(2), p. 171.

A second way for a researcher to obtain ranks is to observe or arrange the study's participants such that each one has an ordered position within the group. For example, we could go to the Boston Marathon, stand near the finish line and hold a list of all contestants' names, then record each person's standing (first, second,

---

[2]Ranks are often confused with ratings. Ranks indicate an ordering of things, with each number generated by having a research participant make a *relative* comparison of the things being ranked. **Ratings,** on the other hand, indicate amount, and they are generated by having a research participant make an *independent* evaluation of each thing being rated (perhaps on a 0-to-100 scale).

third, or whatever) as he or she completes the race. Or, we might go into a class-room, ask the students to line up by height, and then request that the students count off beginning at the tall end of the line.[3]

The third way for a researcher to obtain ranks involves a two-step process. First, each participant is independently measured on some variable of interest with a measuring instrument that yields a score indicative of that person's absolute stand-ing with respect to the numerical continuum associated with the variable. Then, the scores from the group of participants are compared and converted into ranks to in-dicate each person's relative standing within the group.

In Excerpt 18.7, we see a case in which this two-step process was used. The data originally collected by the researchers came from measuring the force exerted by each of several infants. These measurements took the form of kilograms. Each infant was measured in such a way that his or her score reflected the notion of "amount of force" for that particular infant, *without* any consideration of the other infants. In step 2, the infants were compared (in terms of their scores from step 1) and ordered from high to low. As the researchers point out, "ratio scale data . . . were transformed into ranks."

EXCERPT 18.7 • *Converting Ratio-Level Data into Ranks*

The infant scale researchers used contained a digital display system. The scale dis-played cricoid force in kilograms, with a displayed resolution of 0.005 kg. The scale's specifications included an accuracy of 0.1% one digit of reading for any weight more than 0.002 kg. The scale was calibrated by the manufacturer and oper-ated according to the manufacturer's instructions. . . . Statistical analysis was used to determine if there was a significant difference between the cricoid force applied and the amount of recommended force. Ratio scale data obtained regarding applied cricoid force [were] transformed into ranks, and nonparametric statistical analysis was performed using the Wilcoxon Signed-Rank test.

Source: C. A. Koziol, J. D. Cuddeford, and D. D. Moos. (2000). Assessing the force generated with application of cricoid pressure. *AORN Journal, 72*(6), pp. 1023–1024.

---

[3]Although none of the tests discussed in this chapter could be applied to just the ranks obtained in our running or line-up-by-height examples, two of the tests could be used if we simply classified each sub-ject into one of two or more subgroups (e.g., gender) in addition to noting his or her order on the run-ning speed or height variable.

Reasons for Converting Scores on a Continuous Variable into Ranks

It may seem odd that researchers sometimes engage in the two-step, data-conversion process whereby scores on a variable of interest are converted into ranks. Since the original scores typically are interval or ratio in nature, whereas the ranks are ordinal, such a conversion might appear to be ill-advised in that it brings about a "loss of information." There are, however, three reasons why researchers might consider the benefits associated with the scores-to-ranks conversion to outweigh the loss-of-information liability.

One reason why researchers often change raw scores into ranks is that the test procedures developed for use with ranks involve fewer assumptions than do the test procedures developed for use with interval- or ratio-level data. For example, the assumptions of normality and homogeneity of variance that underlie t- and F-tests do not serve as the basis for some of the tests considered in this chapter. As Excerpts 18.8 and 18.9 make clear, researchers sometimes convert their raw scores into ranks because the original data involved nonnormality and/or heterogeneity of variance.

A second reason why researchers convert raw scores to ranks is related to the issue of sample size. As you will recall, t- and F-tests tend to be robust to violations of underlying assumptions when the samples being compared are the same size and large. When the ns differ or are small, however, nonnormality and/or heterogeneity of variance in the population(s) can cause the t- or F-test to function differently than

EXCERPTS 18.8–18.9 • *Nonnormality and Heterogeneous Variances as Reasons for Converting Scores to Ranks*

A nonparametric statistic (Kruskal-Wallis) was used to examine group differences because the homogeneity of variance assumption was not met (i.e., Levene test of homogeneity of variance was found to be significant).

Source: J. Kistner, M. Balthazor, S. Risi, and C. David. (2001). Adolescents' perceptions of peer acceptance: Is dysphoria associated with greater realism? *Journal of Social and Clinical Psychology, 20*(1), p. 73.

- -

Because the data were not normally distributed, statistical comparisons between groups were performed using the nonparametric Mann-Whitney U test.

Source: B. Negrini, K. J. Kelleher, and E. R. Wald. (2000). Cerebrospinal fluid findings in aseptic versus bacterial meningitis. *Pediatrics, 105*(2), p. 317.

intended. For this reason, some researchers will turn to one of the five test procedures discussed in this chapter if their *n*s differ. In Excerpt 18.10, we see a case where concerns about sample size prompted the researchers to use nonparametric tests.

EXCERPT 18.10 • *Sample Size as a Reason for Converting Scores to Ranks*

Because of the small size of the study groups, the significance of differences between groups was assessed with the Mann-Whitney *U* test, and the significance of change within groups was assessed with the Wilcoxon matched-pairs signed ranks test.

Source: B. S. Gershuny, L. Baer, M. A. Jenike, W. E. Minichiello, and S. Wilhelm. (2002). Comorbid posttraumatic stress disorder: Impact on treatment outcome for obsessive-compulsive disorder. *American Journal of Psychiatry, 159*(5), p. 852.

Regarding sample size, it is legitimate to ask the simple question, "When are samples so small that parametric tests should be avoided even if the *n* are equal?" Unfortunately, there is no clear-cut answer to this question because different mathematical statisticians have responded to this query with conflicting responses. According to one statistician, researchers should use nonparametric tests if their sample size is 6 or less, even if all samples are the same size. According to a different statistician, parametric tests can be used with very small samples as long as the *n*s don't differ. I mention this controversy simply to alert you to the fact that some researchers use nonparametric tests because they have small sample sizes, even though the *n*s are equal.[4]

The third reason for converting raw scores to ranks is related to the fact that raw scores sometimes appear to be more precise than they really are. In other words, a study's raw scores may provide only ordinal information about the study's subjects even though the scores are connected to a theoretical numerical continuum associated with the dependent variable. In such a case, it would be improper to

[4]The two statisticians referred to in this paragraph are Sidney Siegel and John Gaito.

treat the raw scores as if they indicate the absolute distance that separates any two participants that have different scores when in fact the raw scores only indicate, in a relative sense, which person has more of the measured characteristic than the other.

Consider, for example, the popular technique of having participants respond to a **Likert-type attitude inventory.** With this kind of measuring device, the respondent indicates a level of agreement or disagreement with each of several statements by selecting one of four or five options that typically include "strongly agree" and "strongly disagree" on the ends. In scoring a respondent's answer sheet, consecutive integers are typically assigned to the response options (e.g., 1, 2, 3, 4, 5) and then the respondent's total score is obtained by adding together the individual scores earned on each of the inventory's statements. In this fashion, two people in a study might end up with total scores of 32 and 29.

With Likert-type attitude inventories, the total scores derived from the participant responses are probably only ordinal in nature. For one thing, the arbitrary assignment of consecutive integers to the response options does not likely correspond to any participant's view of how the response options relate to another. Moreover, it is probably the case that certain of the inventory's statements are more highly connected than others to one's reason for holding a positive or negative attitude toward the topic being focused on—yet all statements are equal in their impact on a respondent's total score. For these reasons, it is not very plausible to presume that the resulting total scores possess the characteristic of equal intervals that is embodied in interval (and ratio) levels of measurement.

Excerpts 18.11 and 18.12 illustrate how a concern for level of measurement will sometimes prompt researchers to use nonparametric tests. When, in the first of these excerpts, the researcher states that the data were not "metric," he was pointing out that the study's numbers did not possess the quality of equal intervals. (Rulers and thermometers yield numbers that possess this characteristic, for an interval of 2 means the same thing anywhere along the scale; in contrast, the numbers associated with most psychological inventories are not characterized by equal intervals.) In Excerpt 18.12, the researchers point out that each participant's measured "degree of stress" produced data that positioned people into categories that were related to one another only in terms of less than or greater than notions.

Now that we have considered how and why a researcher might end up with ranked data, let us take a look at each of the five test procedures that deserve the label "popular nonparametric test." As noted earlier, these test procedures are the median test, the Mann-Whitney *U* test, the Kruskal-Wallis one-way ANOVA, the Wilcoxon matched-pairs signed-ranks test, and the Friedman two-way ANOVA. In looking at each of these test procedures, I want to focus our attention on the nature of the research setting for which the test is appropriate, the way in which the ranked data are used, the typical format for reporting results, and the meaning of a rejected null hypothesis.

EXCERPTS 18.11–18.12 • *Measurement Scale Concerns as the Reason for Using Nonparametric Tests*

Because the data is not definitely metric, the MannWhitney test for ordinal data was used.

Source: A. Hetsroni. (2000). The relationship between values and appeals in Israeli advertising: A smallest space analysis. *Journal of Advertising, 29*(3), p. 63.

Degrees of psychosocial stressors on DSM-III-R axis IV were regarded as ordinal categorical data, and Wilcoxon's rank sum test was used to make comparisons between the two groups.

Source: M. Nakao, G. Yamanaka, and T. Kuboki. (2002). Suicidal ideation and somatic symptoms of patients with mind/body distress in a Japanese psychosomatic clinic. *Suicide and Life-Threatening Behavior, 32*(1), p. 83.

The Median Test

The **median test** is designed for use when a researcher wishes to compare two or more independent samples. If two such groups are compared, the median test is a nonparametric analog to the independent-samples *t*-test. With three or more groups, it is the nonparametric analog to a one-way ANOVA.

A researcher might select the median test in order to contrast two groups defined by a dichotomous characteristic (e.g., male versus female, or experimental versus control) on a dependent variable of interest (e.g., throwing ability, level of conformity, or anything else the researcher wishes to measure). Or, the median test might be selected if the researcher wishes to compare three or more groups (that differ in some qualitative fashion) on a measured dependent variable. An example of this latter situation might involve comparing football players, basketball players, and baseball players in terms of their endurance while riding a stationary bicycle.

The null hypothesis of the two-group version of the median test can be stated as $H_0: M_1 = M_2$, where the letter M stands for the median in the population and the numerical subscripts serve to identify the first and second populations. If three or more groups are compared using the median test, the null hypothesis takes the same form except that there would be additional Ms involved in H_0. The alternative hypothesis says that the two Ms differ (if just two groups are being compared) or that at least two of the Ms differ (in the situation where three or more groups are being contrasted).

To conduct a median test, the researcher follows a simple three-step procedure. First, the comparison groups are temporarily combined and a single median is determined for the entire set of scores. (This step necessitates that ranks be assigned either to all participants or at least to those who are positioned near the middle of the pack.) In the second step, the comparison groups are reconstituted so that a contingency table can be set up to indicate how many people in each comparison group lie above and below the "grand median" identified in the first step. This contingency table will have as many columns as there are comparison groups, but it will always have two rows (one labeled "above the median," the other labeled "below the median"). Finally, an independent-samples chi-square test is applied to the data in the contingency table to see if the samples differ (in the proportion of cases falling above the combined median) by more than what would be expected by chance alone, presuming that H_0 is true.

In Excerpt 18.13, we see a case where a median test was used in a study designed to assess a bladder-control intervention with individuals who were prone to having accidents. In this study, there were two groups, one that received the intervention and one that didn't. Each individual was measured on three occasions, with the median test referred to in Excerpt 18.13 used to compare the two groups in terms of "difference" scores calculated as the decrease (or increase) in episodes between time 1 and time 3. It was these difference scores that were used in the three-step procedure described in the preceding paragraph.

Although there is no indication in Excerpt 18.13 as to how the data were analyzed, the median test involved a chi-square test applied to the data of a 2×2 contingency table. I like to think of this contingency table as being set up so that the columns correspond with the groups (treatment and control) and the rows correspond to being above or below the grand median. Each person in the study was positioned in one of the four cells of this contingency table. If the two frequencies in each column had been about the same, there would not have been evidence to support the intervention's effectiveness. However, the actual frequencies in the contingency table produced a statistically significance value for chi square, with a

EXCERPT 18.13 • *The Median Test Used to Compare Two Groups*

In this analysis, difference scores were computed for each subject (i.e., number of frequency and/or leakage episodes at Time 1 minus number of episodes at Time 3). Then, these differences were compared between the groups using the median test. Hypothesis 2 was supported, because there was a greater median reduction in number of episodes from Time 1 to Time 3 in the treatment group than in the control group ($P = 0.05$, one-tailed).

Source: T. Dowd, K. Kolcaba, and R. Steiner. (2000). Using cognitive strategies to enhance bladder control and comfort. *Holistic Nursing Practice, 14*(2), p. 98.

greater-than-chance number of people from the treatment group (control group) positioned above (below) the grand median.

In Excerpt 18.13, the second sentence makes it seem as if the main thing going on in a median test is a statistical comparison of two sample medians to see if they are far enough apart from each other to permit a rejection of H_0. Many people have this misconception about the median test. There is only one median involved in a median test (the grand median based on the data from all groups), and the question being asked is whether the comparison groups differ significantly in terms of the percentage of each group that lie above this single median. Given any set of scores, it would be possible to change a few scores and thereby change the group medians (making them closer together or further apart) *without* changing the median test's calculated value or *p*. To me, this constitutes proof that the median test is *not* focusing on the individual medians of the comparison groups!

In trying to interpret the results of the median test, one should recognize that the grand median computed from the sample data is unlikely to match the common median found in H_0. Because of this, the actual null hypothesis being tested is not that the populations being compared have the same median but rather that the various populations have the same proportion of scores above the value of the median of the combined *samples*. With larger samples, of course, there is likely to be a smaller discrepancy between the median value used to set up the contingency table and the common value of *M* hypothesized to exist in the populations. With small samples, however, it turns out that the median test (despite its name) is not really a test of equal population medians.

As mentioned earlier, the median test can compare two groups or more than two groups. In Excerpt 18.14, we see a case where the median test was used to compare three groups. These three groups were schizophrenic patients with delusions

EXCERPT 18.14 • *The Median Test Used to Compare Three Groups*

Schizophrenic patients with delusions of influence gave globally more "yes" responses than noninfluenced schizophrenic patients and comparison subjects in both the trials with angular biases (median = 56.5 for influenced patients; median = 39.0 for noninfluenced patients; median = 33.0 for comparison subjects) and temporal biases (median = 53.5 for influenced patients; median = 49.5 for noninfluenced patients; median = 29.0 for comparison subjects). The median test for "yes" responses revealed that the differences between groups were significant both for the 84 trials with angular biases ($\chi^2 = 7.67$, *df* = 2, *p* < 0.03) and the 84 trials with temporal biases ($\chi^2 = 20.49$, *df* = 2, *p* < 0.001).

Source: N. Franck, C. Farrer, N. Georgieff, and M. Marie-Cardine. (2001). Defective recognition of one's own actions in patients with schizophrenia. *American Journal of Psychiatry, 158*(3), p. 456.

of influence, schizophrenic patients who did not have this kind of delusion, and "normal" controls. As you will see, the median test was used twice in this study, once on data dealing with angular biases and then a second time on data dealing with temporal biases. Within each of these two sets of data, the score for each individual was equal to the summed performance across 48 trials.

The Mann-Whitney U Test[5]

Research
Navigator.c⊛m

Mann-Whitney
U test

The **Mann-Whitney *U* test** is like the two-sample version of the median test in that both tests allow a researcher to compare two independent samples. While these two procedures are similar in that they are both considered to be nonparametric tests, the Mann-Whitney *U* test is the more powerful of the two. In other words, if the two comparison groups truly do differ from each other, the Mann-Whitney *U* test (as compared to the median test) is less likely to produce a Type II error. This superiority of the Mann-Whitney test comes about because it utilizes more information from the subjects than does the median test.

When using the Mann-Whitney *U* test, the researcher examines the scores made available by measuring the research participants on the variable of interest. Initially, the two comparison groups are lumped together. This is done so that each person can be ranked to reflect his or her standing within the combined group. After the ranks have been assigned, the researcher reconstitutes the two comparison groups. The previously assigned ranks are then examined to see if the two groups are significantly different.

If the two samples being compared came from identical populations, then the **sum of ranks** in one group ought to be approximately equal to the sum of ranks in the other group. For example, if there were four people in each sample and if H_0 were true, we would not be surprised if the ranks in one group were 2, 4, 5, and 8 while the ranks in the other group were 1, 3, 6, and 7. Here, the sum of the ranks are 19 and 17, respectively. It *would* be surprising, however, to find (again assuming that H_0 is true) that the sum of the ranks are 10 and 26. Such an extreme outcome would occur if the ranks of 1, 2, 3, and 4 were located in one of the samples while the ranks of 5, 6, 7, and 8 were located in the other sample.

To perform a Mann-Whitney *U* test, the researcher computes a sum-of-ranks value for each sample and then inserts these two numerical values into a formula. It is not important for you to know what that formula looks like, but it *is* essential that you understand the simple logic of what is going on. The formula used to analyze the data will produce a calculated value called *U*. Based on the value of *U*,

[5]This test is also referred to as the Wilcoxon test, as the Wilcoxon rank-sum test, and as the Wilcoxon-Mann-Whitney test.

the researcher (or a computer) can then derive a *p*-value that indicates how likely it is, under H_0, to have two samples that differ as much or more than do the ones actually used in the study. Small values of *p*, of course, are interpreted to mean that H_0 is unlikely to be true.

In Excerpt 18.15, we see a case where the Mann-Whitney *U* test was used within a study that involved 10 fifth-grade children. Three of these children successfully demonstrated a skill they had been taught whereas the other seven did not acquire the skill. The Mann-Whitney *U* test compared the ages of these two groups of children, yielding a statistically significant finding.[6]

EXCERPT 18.15 • *The Mann-Whitney U Test*

The procedures for training the prerequisite performances and testing transfer that had been successfully used with older participants . . . clearly proved inadequate for our 5-year-old preschoolers. Excluding Child 6, who left the program prematurely, only 3 of the 10 children (30%) in Experiments 1 and 3 learned the AB-X relations with the procedures that had been used successfully with 6-year first-grade (and older) students. Although this age difference may not seem significant, present findings suggest that it was. Even among our 5-year-olds, age appeared to be relevant. The 3 children who completed the original AB-X training successfully were older (*M* = 5.6 yr, Range: 5.3–5.7) than the 7 children who failed this training (*M* = 5.2 yr, Range: 4.9–5.5) (Mann-Whitney *U* = 2, *p* = 0.03).

Source: F. Carpentier, P. M. Smeets, and D. Barnes-Holmes. (2002). Establishing transfer of compound control in children: A stimulus control analysis. *Psychological Record, 52*(2), p. 154.

Although it is quite easy for a researcher to obtain a calculated value for *U* from the sample data and to compare that data-based number against a tabled critical value, the task of interpreting a statistically significant result is a bit more difficult, for two reasons. First, the null hypothesis being tested deals not with the ranks used to compute the calculated value but rather with the continuous variable that lies behind or beneath the ranks. For example, if we used a Mann-Whitney *U*

---

[6]Knowing the formula for *U* and seeing that the calculated value turned out equal to 2 in Excerpt 18.15, I was able to determine that the three children who acquired the skill in this study must have been the oldest, second-oldest, and fifth-oldest among the 10 children, or perhaps the oldest one, the third-oldest, and fourth-oldest. No other combinations could have produced the study's results.

test to compare a sample of men against a sample of women with respect to their order of finish after running a 10-kilometer race, the data collected might very well simply be ranks, with each person's rank indicating his or her place (among all contestants) upon crossing the finish line. The null hypothesis, however, would deal with the continuous variable that lies beneath the ranks, which in our hypothetical study is running speed.

The second reason why statistically significant results from Mann-Whitney U tests are difficult to interpret is related to the fact that the rejected null hypothesis says that the two populations have identical distributions. Consequently, rejection of H_0 could come about because the populations differ in terms of their central tendencies, their variabilities, and/or their distributional shapes. In practice, however, the Mann-Whitney test is far more sensitive to differences in central tendency, so a statistically significant result is almost certain to mean that the populations have different average scores. But even here, an element of ambiguity remains because the Mann-Whitney U test could cause H_0 to be rejected because the two populations differ in terms of their means, or in terms of their medians, or in terms of their modes.

In the situation where the two populations have identical shapes and variances, the Mann-Whitney U test focuses on means, and thus H_0: $\mu_1 = \mu_2$. However, applied researchers rarely know anything about the populations involved in their studies. Therefore, most researchers who find that their Mann-Whitney U test yields a statistically significant result legitimately can conclude only that the two populations probably differ with respect to their averages. Another way of drawing a proper conclusion from a Mann-Whitney U test that causes H_0 to be rejected is to say that the scores in one of the populations tend to be larger than scores in the other population. This statement could only be made in a tentative fashion, however, since the statistically significant finding might well represent nothing more than a Type I error.

If you return to Excerpt 18.15 and try to interpret the results, you will find this to be more difficult than you would probably like. There is a temptation to think that the Mann-Whitney U test turned out as it did because of the reported difference between the two sample means. However, such thinking is not proper. If U turns out to be small and significant, we are not able to say that the two populations probably differ with respect to *any* specific measure of central tendency. All we can justifiably say is that age seems to make a difference in situations characterized by the tasks, trainers, tests, and children like those involved in this particular study.

One other feature of the Mann-Whitney U test is worth mentioning. By contrast with most statistical tests (e.g., t, F, and χ^2), the null hypothesis associated with the Mann-Whitney U test is rejected when the researcher's data-based calculated value turns out to be equal to or *smaller than* the tabled critical value. Thus, if the U in Excerpt 18.15 had turned out equal to 1, p would have been smaller than .03. If U had been equal to 0, p would have been even smaller.

The Kruskal-Wallis H Test

Research Navigator.c⊛m
Kruskal-Wallis

In those situations where a researcher wishes to use a nonparametric statistical test to compare two independent samples, the Mann-Whitney U test is typically used to analyze the data. When researchers wish to compare three or more such groups, they more often than not utilize the **Kruskal-Wallis H test.** Hence, the Kruskal-Wallis procedure can be thought of as an "extension" of the Mann-Whitney procedure in the same way that a one-way ANOVA is typically considered to be an extension of an independent-samples t-test.[7]

The fact that the Kruskal-Wallis test is like a one-way ANOVA shows through when one considers the mathematical derivation of the formula for computing the test's calculated value. On a far simpler level, the similarity between these two test procedures shows through when we consider their names. The parametric test we considered in Chapter 11 is called a one-way ANOVA whereas the nonparametric analog to which we now turn our attention is called the Kruskal-Wallis one-way ANOVA of ranks. Excerpts 18.16 and 18.17 show how the notion of an analysis of variance pops up in the way researchers describe the Kruskal-Wallis test.

EXCERPTS 18.16–18.17 • *The Kruskal-Wallis Test Referred to as an Analysis of Variance*

The Kruskal-Wallis one way analysis of variance was used to compare the differences between the [three treatment] groups in the amounts of blood products used and in the secondary outcomes.

Source: N. McGill, D. O'Shaughnessy, R. Pickering, and M. Herbertson. (2002). Mechanical methods of reducing blood transfusion in cardiac surgery: Randomised controlled trial/Commentary. *British Medical Journal, 324*(7349), p. 1300.

- -

In an effort to determine if living arrangements interfered with grandparents' activities, we conducted the Kruskal-Wallis one-way ANOVA.

Source: S. A. Spence, S. R. Black, J. P. Adams, and M. R. Crowther. (2001). Grandparents and grandparenting in a rural southern state. *Journal of Family Issues, 22*(4), p. 529.

[7]When just two groups are compared, the ANOVA F-test and the independent-samples t-test yield identical results. In a similar fashion, the Kruskal-Wallis and Mann-Whitney tests are mathematically equivalent when used to compare two groups.

The Kruskal-Wallis test works very much as the Mann-Whitney test does. First, the researcher temporarily combines the comparison groups into a single group. Next, the people in this one group are ranked on the basis of their performance on the dependent variable. Then, the single group is subdivided so as to reestablish the original comparison groups. Finally, each group's sum of ranks is entered into a formula that yields the calculated value. This calculated value, in the Kruskal-Wallis test, is labeled *H*. When the data-based *H* beats the critical value or when the *p*-value associated with *H* turns out to be smaller than the level of significance, the null hypothesis is rejected.

In Excerpt 18.18, we see a case in which the Kruskal-Wallis test was used to compare three groups, two of which included people with Tourette's syndrome. As you can see, when these three groups were compared, the Kruskal-Wallis test produced a calculated value (*H*) equal to 0.95, an accompanying *p* of 0.62, and a decision not to reject the null hypothesis.

EXCERPT 18.18 • *Use of the Kruskal-Wallis Test*

The study subjects included 12 Tourette's syndrome patients with high autoantibody levels (seven male subjects and five female subjects, age range = 10–19 years, mean = 14.4) and 12 Tourette's syndrome patients with low autoantibody levels (nine male subjects and three female subjects, age range = 14–40 years, mean = 21.5). Twelve comparison subjects with sera with staining intensities below the 75th percentile for both antineural and antinuclear autoantibodies were also selected (six male subjects and six female subjects, age range = 11–35 years, mean = 18.2). . . . The effect of medication on stereotypies was assessed, and no differences between groups were found (Kruskal-Wallis $H = 0.95$, $df = 2$, $p = 0.62$).

Source: J. R. Taylor, S. A. Morshed, S. Parveen, and M. T. Mercadante. (2002). An animal model of Tourette's syndrome. *American Journal of Psychiatry, 159*(4), p. 659.

The Kruskal-Wallis *H* test and the Mann-Whitney *U* test are similar not only in how the subjects are ranked and in how the groups' sum-of-ranks values are used to obtain the test's calculated value but also in the null hypothesis being tested and what it means when H_0 is rejected. Technically speaking, the null hypothesis of the Kruskal-Wallis *H* test is that the populations associated with the study's comparison groups are identical with respect to the distributions on the continuous variable that lies beneath the ranks used within the data analysis. Accordingly, a rejection of the H_0 could come about because the population distributions are not the same in central tendency, in variability, and/or in shape. In practice, however, the Kruskal-

Wallis test focuses primarily on central tendency. In fact, two well-known statisticians—Leonard Marascuilo and Maryellen McSweeney—recently asserted that "the Kruskal-Wallis test is not too sensitive to differences in spread or form" and that "rejection of H_0 via the H statistic is almost certain to be equivalent to differences in mean, median, center, or some other measure of shift."[8]

While the Mann-Whitney and Kruskal-Wallis tests are similar in many respects, they differ in the nature of the decision rule used to decide whether H_0 should be rejected. With the Mann-Whitney test, H_0 is rejected if the data-based U turns out to be smaller than the critical value. In contrast, the Kruskal-Wallis H_0 is rejected when the researcher's calculated H is *larger* than the critical value.[9] In Excerpt 18.18, therefore, it was the small value of H, 0.95, that prompted the researchers to say that "The effect of medication on stereotypies was assessed, and no differences between groups were found."

Whenever the Kruskal-Wallis H test leads to a rejection of H_0, there remains uncertainty as to which specific populations are likely to differ from one another. In other words, the Kruskal-Wallis procedure functions very much as an "omnibus" test. Consequently, when such a test leads to a rejection of H_0, the researcher will normally turn to a post hoc analysis so as to derive more specific conclusions from the data. Within such post hoc investigations, comparison groups are typically compared in a pairwise fashion.

The post hoc procedure used most frequently following a statistically significant H test is the Mann-Whitney U test. Excerpts 18.19 and 18.20 illustrate the use of the Mann-Whitney U test in post hoc investigation following rejection of the Kruskal-Wallis null hypothesis. When used in this capacity, most researchers use the Bonferroni procedure for adjusting the level of significance of each post hoc comparison. For example, in the study associated with Excerpt 18.20, there were three pairwise comparisons, each evaluated with alpha set equal to .017.

The Wilcoxon Matched-Pairs Signed-Ranks Test

Researchers frequently wish to compare two related samples of data generated by measuring the same people twice (e.g., in a pre/post sense) or by measuring two groups of matched individuals just once. If the data are interval or ratio in nature and if the relevant underlying assumptions are met, the researcher will probably utilize a correlated t-test to compare the two samples. On occasion, however, that kind of parametric test cannot be used because the data are ordinal or because the t-test

---

[8]L. A. Marascuilo and M. McSweeney. (1977). *Nonparametric and distribution-free methods for the social sciences.* Monterey, Calif.: Brooks/Cole, p. 305.

[9]If U or H turns out equal to the critical value, H_0 is rejected. Such an outcome, however, is quite unlikely.

EXCERPTS 18.19–18.20 • *Use of the Mann-Whitney U Test within a Post Hoc Investigation*

Results for the bactericidal study were coded and analyzed using the Kruskal-Wallis test. Post hoc testing was done using the Mann-Whitney *U* test.

Source: V. S. Rabenberg, C. D. Ingersoll, M. A. Sandrey, and M. T. Johnson. (2002). The bacterial and cytotoxic effects of antimicrobial wound cleansers. *Journal of Athletic Training, 37*(1), p. 52.

Differences in the rate of pCO_2 increase between susceptible individuals, nonsusceptible individuals, and controls were tested for by the Kruskal-Wallis test and post hoc by the Mann-Whitney U test.

Source: M. Anetseder, M. Hager, C. Muller, and N. Roewer. (2002). Diagnosis of susceptibility to malignant hyperthermia by use of a metabolic test. *The Lancet, 359*(9317), p. 1580.

Research
Navigator.c⊕m

Wilcoxon
matched-pairs
signed-ranks test

assumptions are untenable (or considered by the researcher to be a nuisance). In such situations, the two related samples are likely to be compared using the **Wilcoxon matched-pairs signed-ranks test.**

In conducting the Wilcoxon test, the researcher (or a computer) must do five things. First, each pair of scores is examined so as to obtain a *change* score (for the case where a single group of people has been measured twice) or a *difference* score (for the case where the members of two matched samples have been measured just once). These scores are then ranked, either from high to low or from low to high. The third step involves attaching a + or a − sign to each rank. (In the one-group-measured-twice situation, these signs will indicate whether a person's second score turned out to be higher or lower than the first score. In the two-samples-measured-once situation, these signs will indicate whether the people in one group earned higher or lower scores than their counterparts in the other group.) In the fourth step, the researcher simply looks to see which sign appears less frequently and then adds up the ranks that have that sign. Finally, the researcher labels the sum of the ranks that have the least frequent sign as *T,* considers *T* to be the calculated value, and compares *T* against a tabled critical value.

In Excerpt 18.21, we see a case where the Wilcoxon matched-pairs signed-ranks test was used in a study dealing with the caregivers of Alzheimer's patients. As you will see, the Wilcoxon test was used twice in this study, once for each of the two dependent variables (stress and coping ability). In each case, the Wilcoxon test yielded a statistically significant result.

EXCERPT 18.21 • *Wilcoxon's Matched-Pairs Signed-Ranks Test*

The Wilcoxon Signed Rank test for ordinal data was used in statistical analysis of the data to compare the level of stress and coping ability prior to the therapist's visit, with the level of stress and coping ability after the caregiver implemented the recommendations. With an alpha level of .05, stress $P = .015$ and coping $P = .028$. Thus both self-reported stress level and coping ability demonstrated a significant change following the home visit by the occupational therapist.

Source: M. M. Sheldon and M. H. Teaford. (2002). Caregivers of people with Alzheimer's dementia: An analysis of their compliance with recommended home modifications. *Alzheimer's Care Quarterly, 3*(1), p. 80.

In using the Wilcoxon test, the researcher's conclusion either to reject or to retain H_0 is based on a decision rule like that used within the Mann-Whitney U test. Simply stated, that decision rule gives the researcher permission to reject H_0 when the data-based value of T is equal to or smaller than the tabled critical value. This is because a direct relationship exists between T and p.

Although it is easy to conduct a Wilcoxon test, the task of interpreting the final result is more challenging. The null hypothesis says that the populations associated with the two sets of sample data are each symmetrical around the same common point. This translates into a statement that the population of change (or difference) scores is symmetrical around a median value of zero. Interpreting the outcome of a Wilcoxon matched-pairs signed-ranks test is problematic because the null hypothesis could be false because the population of change/difference scores is not symmetric, because the population median is not equal to zero, or because the population is not symmetrical around a median other than zero. Accordingly, if the Wilcoxon test leads to a statistically significant finding, neither you nor the researcher will know the precise reason why H_0 has been rejected.

There are two different ways to clarify the situation when one wants to interpret a significant finding from the Wilcoxon test. First, such a test can be interpreted to mean that the two populations, each associated with one of the samples of data used to compute the difference/change scores, are probably not identical to each other. That kind of interpretation is not too satisfying, since the two populations could differ in any number of ways. The second interpretation one can draw if the Wilcoxon test produces a small p-value is that the two populations probably have different medians. (This is synonymous to saying that the population of difference/change scores is probably not equal to zero.) This interpretation is legitimate, however, only in the situation where it is plausible to assume that both populations have the same shape.

Friedman's Two-Way Analysis of Variance of Ranks

The **Friedman test** is like the Wilcoxon test in that both procedures were developed for use with related samples. The primary difference between the Wilcoxon and Friedman tests is that the former test can accommodate just two related samples whereas the Friedman test can be used with two or more such samples. Because of this, the Friedman test can be thought of as the nonparametric equivalent of the one-factor repeated-measures ANOVA that we considered in Chapter 14.[10]

To illustrate the kind of situation to which the Friedman test could be applied, suppose you and several other individuals are asked to independently evaluate the quality of the five movies nominated for this year's Best Picture award from the Academy of Motion Pictures. I might ask you and the other people in this study to rank the five movies on the basis of whatever criteria you typically use when evaluating movie quality. Or, I might ask you to rate each of the movies (possibly on a 0-to-100 scale), thus providing me with data that I could convert into ranks. One way or the other, I could end up with a set of five ranks from each person indicating his or her opinion of the five movies.

If the five movies being evaluated are equally good, we would expect the movies to be about the same in terms of the sum of the ranks assigned to them. In other words, movie A ought to receive some high ranks, some medium ranks, and some low ranks if it is truly no better or worse than the other movies up for the big award. That would also be the case for each of the other four movies. The Friedman test treats the data in just this manner, because the main ingredient is the sum of ranks assigned to each movie.

Once the sum of ranks are computed for the various things being compared, they are inserted into a formula that yields the test's calculated value. I will not discuss here the details of that formula, or even present it. Instead, I want to focus on three aspects of what pops out of that formula. First, the calculated value is typically symbolized as χ_r^2 (or sometimes simply as χ^2). Second, large values of χ_r^2 suggest that H_0 is not true. Third, the value of χ_r^2 is referred to a null distribution of such values so as to determine the data-based *p*-value and/or to decide whether or not the null hypothesis should be rejected.

In Excerpt 18.22, we see a case where the Friedman test was used to compare college students' attitudes toward three different forms of communication: written, oral, and email. Each of the students who participated in this study was asked to rate (on a 10-point scale in which high scores indicated more positive attitudes) each form of communication. Thus the data collected in this real study were very

---

[10]Although the Friedman and Wilcoxon tests are similar in that they both were designed for use with correlated samples of data, the Friedman test actually is an extension of the sign test.

EXCERPT 18.22 • *Friedman's Two-Way Analysis of Variance of Ranks*

Part 3 [of the survey given to business communication students at two comprehensive, Midwestern universities] used an anchored 10-point Likert scale to determine students' attitudes toward written, oral, and e-mail communication. . . .

The students surveyed for this research generally have a positive attitude toward written, oral, and e-mail communication; all means exceed 5 on the 10-point scale. E-mail communication earned the highest mean (7.42), followed closely by written communication (7.41); the oral communication mean (5.47) was nearly two points lower.

The calculated means indicate that students view oral communication less favorably than they do either written or e-mail communication. Results from a Friedman two-way ANOVA procedure showed that differences among the means are statistically significant ($\chi^2 = 71.2118, p < .001$).

Source: P. A. Merrier and R. Dirks. (1997). Student attitudes toward written, oral, and e-mail communication. *Business Communication Quarterly, 60*(2), p. 89.

similar to the data involved in our hypothetical movie study; the only key differences concern the number of things being compared (three forms of communication versus five movies) and the score range of the rating scale (0–10 versus 0–100).

If the Friedman test leads to a rejection of the null hypothesis when three or more things (such as movies in our hypothetical example or forms of communication in Excerpt 18.22) are compared, you are likely to see a post hoc follow-up test utilized to compare the things that have been ranked. Although many test procedures can be used within such a post hoc investigation, you will likely see the Wilcoxon matched-pairs signed-ranks test employed to make all possible pairwise comparisons. In using the Wilcoxon test in this fashion, the researcher should use the Bonferroni adjustment procedure to protect against an inflated Type I error rate.

Large-Sample Versions of the Tests on Ranks

Near the end of Chapter 17, I pointed out how researchers will sometimes conduct a *z*-test when dealing with frequencies, percentages, or proportions. Whenever this occurs, researchers put their data into a special formula that yields a calculated value called *z*, and then the data-based *p*-value is determined by referring the calculated value to the normal distribution. Any *z*-test, therefore, can be conceptualized as a "normal curve test."

In certain situations, the *z*-test represents nothing more than an option available to the researcher, with the other option(s) being mathematically equivalent to the *z*-test. In other situations, however, the *z*-test represents a **large-sample approximation** to some other test. In Chapter 17, I pointed out how the sign, binomial, and McNemar procedures can be performed using a *z*-test if the sample sizes are large enough. The formula used to produce the *z* calculated value in these large-sample approximations varies across these test procedures, but that issue is of little concern to consumers of the research literature.

Inasmuch as tests on nominal data can be conducted using *z*-tests when the sample(s) are large, it should not be surprising that large-sample approximations exist for several of the test procedures considered in the present chapter. To be more specific, you are likely to encounter studies in which the calculated value produced by the Mann-Whitney *U* test is not *U*, studies in which the calculated value produced by the Kruskal-Wallis one-way analysis of variance of ranks is not *H*, and studies in which the calculated value produced by the Wilcoxon matched-pairs signed-ranks test is not *T*. Excerpts 18.23 through 18.25 illustrate such cases.

EXCERPTS 18.23–18.25 • *Large-Sample Versions of the Mann-Whitney, Kruskal-Wallis, and Wilcoxon Tests*

The Mann-Whitney *U* test revealed that the difference in mean CMAPSCR was statistically significant: $U = 6.5$, $Z = -2.477$, $p = .013$.

Source: J. A. Rye and P. A. Rubba. (2002). Scoring concept maps: An expert map-based scheme weighted for relationships. *School Science and Mathematics, 102*(1), p. 41.

- -

The median ages of the patients in the diagnostic groups were 26 years for those with schizophrenia, 27 for those with psychotic bipolar disorder, and 31 for those with psychotic depression ($\chi^2 = 5.9$, $df = 2$, $p = 0.05$, Kruskal-Wallis test).

Source: T. J. Craig, E. J. Bromet, S. Fennig, and M. Tanenberg-Karant. (2000). Is there an association between duration of untreated psychosis and 24-month clinical outcome in a first-admission series? *American Journal of Psychiatry, 157* (1), p. 62.

- -

Wilcoxon matched-pairs signed-rank tests revealed that significantly more women received treatment during the first year of the study than in the second year ($z = -4.02$, $df = 242$, $p < 0.001$). . . .

Source: P. K. Keel, D. J. Dorer, K. T. Eddy, and S. S. Delinsky. (2002). Predictors of treatment utilization among women with anorexia and bulimia nervosa. *American Journal of Psychiatry, 159* (1), p. 141.

In Excerpts 18.23 and 18.25, we see that the calculated value in the large-sample versions of the Mann-Whitney and Wilcoxon tests is a *z*-value. In contrast, the calculated value for the large-sample version of the Kruskal-Wallis test is a chi-square value. These excerpts thus illustrate nicely the fact that many of the so-called large-sample versions of nonparametric tests yield a *p*-value that is based on the normal distribution. Certain of these tests, however, are connected to the chi-square distribution.

The Friedman test procedure—like the Mann-Whitney, Kruskal-Wallis, and Wilcoxon procedures—can be conducted using a large sample approximation. Most researchers do this by comparing their calculated value for χ_r^2 against a chi-square distribution in order to obtain a *p*-value. If you look again at Excerpt 18.22, you will see a case in which the Friedman test was conducted in this fashion.

It should be noted that the median test is inherently a large-sample test to begin with. That is the case because this test requires that the data be cast into a 2 $\times$ 2 contingency table from which a chi-square calculated value is then derived. Because this chi-square test requires sufficiently large expected cell frequencies, the only option to the regular, "large-sample" median test is Fisher's Exact Test. Fisher's test, used within this context, could be construed as the "small-sample" version of the median test.

Before concluding this discussion of the large-sample versions of the tests considered in this chapter, it seems appropriate to ask the simple question, "How large must the sample(s) be in order for these tests to function as well as their more exact, small-sample counterparts?" The answer to this question varies depending on the test being considered. The Mann-Whitney *z*-test, for example, works well if both *n*s are larger than 10 (or if one of the *n*s is larger than 20) while the Wilcoxon *z*-test performs adequately when its *n* is greater than 25. The Kruskal-Wallis chi-square test works well when there are more than three comparison groups or when the *n*s are greater than 5. The Friedman chi-square test functions nicely when there are more than four things being ranked or more than 10 subjects doing the ranking.

Although not used very often, other large-sample procedures have been devised for use with the Mann-Whitney, Kruskal-Wallis, Wilcoxon, and Friedman tests. Some involve using the ranked data within complex formulas. Others involve using the ranked data within *t*- or *F*-tests. Still others involve the analysis of the study's data through two different formulas, the computation of an average calculated value, and then reference to a specially formed critical value. Although not now widely used, some of these alternative procedures may gain popularity among applied researchers in the coming years.

Ties

Whenever researchers rank a set of scores, they may encounter the case of **tied observations.** For example, there are two sets of ties in this hypothetical set of 10 scores: 8, 0, 4, 3, 5, 4, 7, 1, 4, 5. Or, ties can occur when the original data take the form of ranks. Examples here would include the tenth and eleventh runners in a race crossing the finish line simultaneously, or a judge in a taste test indicating that two of several wines equally deserve the blue ribbon.

With the median test, tied scores do not create a problem. If the tied observations occur within the top half or the bottom half of the pooled group of scores, the ties can be disregarded since all of the scores are easily classified as being above or below the grand median. If the scores in the middle of the pooled data set are tied, the "above" and "below" categories can be defined by a numerical value that lies adjacent to the tied scores. For example, if the 10 scores in the preceding paragraph had come from two groups being compared using a median test, high scores could be defined as anything above 4 while low scores could be defined as less than or equal to 4. (Another way of handling ties at the grand median is simply to drop those scores from the analysis.)

If tied observations occur when the Mann-Whitney, Kruskal-Wallis, Wilcoxon, or Friedman tests are being used, researchers will typically do one of three things. First, they can apply average ranks to the tied scores. (The procedure for computing average ranks was described in Chapter 3 in the section dealing with Kendall's Tau.) Second, they can drop the tied observations from the data set and subject the remaining, untied scores to the statistical test. Third, they can use a special version of the test procedure developed so as to handle tied observations.

In Excerpts 18.26 and 18.27, we see two cases in which the third of these three options was selected. In both of these cases, the phrase *corrected for ties* is an un-

EXCERPTS 18.26–18.27 • *Using Special Formulas to Accommodate Tied Observations in the Data*

Women appointed in Decades 1 and 2 published no *JRME* articles before their terms began, but women in Decade 3 published more than twice as many articles prior to appointment than did their male counterparts, a statistically significant rank-order difference for Decade 3 (Mann-Whitney U, corrected for ties, $Z = -1.96, p < .05$).

Source: J. T. Humphreys and S. L. Stauffer. (2000). An analysis of the editorial committee of the Journal of Research in Music Education, 1953–1992. *Journal of Research in Music Education, 48*(1), pp. 72–73.

- -

. . . the overall trend in the proportion of squirrels becoming vigilant did not differ significantly among treatments (Friedman's test, $df = 2$, χ_r^2 (corrected for ties) = 3.82, $p = 0.15$).

Source: K. J. Warkentin, A. T. H. Keeley, and J. F. Hare. (2001). Repetitive calls of juvenile Richardson's ground squirrels (Spermophilus richardsonii) communicate response urgency. *Canadian Journal of Zoology, 79*(1), pp. 571–572.

ambiguous signal that the tied scores were left in the data set and that a special formula was used to compute the calculated value.

Ties can also occur within the Friedman test. This could happen, for example, if a judge were to report that two of the things being judged were equally good. Such tied observations are not discarded from the data set, since that would necessitate tossing out all the data provided by that particular judge. Instead, the technique of assigning average ranks would be used, with the regular formula then employed to obtain the calculated value for the Friedman test.

The Relative Power of Nonparametric Tests

It is widely believed that nonparametric procedures are inferior to parametric techniques because the former supposedly have lower power than the latter. This concern about power is appropriate, since any test having low power is likely to lead to a Type II error when H_0 is false. It is unfortunate, however, that nonparametric tests have come to be thought of as being less able to detect true differences between populations. I say this because nonparametric tests, in certain situations, are *more* powerful than their parametric counterparts.

If researchers have collected interval- or ratio-level data from two independent samples, they could compare the two groups by means of a parametric test (say an independent-samples *t*-test) or by means of a nonparametric test (say the Mann-Whitney *U* test). Similar statements could be made for the cases where data have been collected from three or more independent samples, from two correlated samples, or from a single sample that is measured in a repeated-measures sense. For these situations where data can be analyzed either with a parametric test or with a nonparametric test, it is possible to compare the power of one test procedure versus the power of a different test procedure. Such comparisons allow us to talk about a test's **relative power.**

If the assumptions of normality and homogeneity of variance are valid, then *t*- and *F*-tests will be more powerful than their nonparametric counterparts. On the other hand, if these assumptions are violated, nonparametric tests can, in certain circumstances, provide researchers with greater protection against Type II errors. As illustrated earlier in Excerpts 18.8 and 18.9, researchers often explain that they utilized a nonparametric test because their data sets were skewed and/or had nonequivalent variances. By deciding to use nonparametric procedures, these researchers may have increased the sensitivity of their tests over what would have been the case if they had used *t*- or *F*-tests.

The relative power of any nonparametric test as compared with its parametric counterpart varies depending on the distributional shape in the population(s) associated with the study. Because of this, I believe that applied researchers should explain why they decided to use whatever techniques they employed. The issue of relative power ought to be included in such explanations. Unfortunately, the typical applied research investigation suffers from inadequate power, and consequently it behooves the researcher to utilize the most powerful analytical technique available.

A Few Final Comments

As we approach the end of this chapter, five final points need to be made. These points constitute my typical end-of-chapter warnings to those who come into contact with technical research reports. By remaining sensitive to these cautions, you will be more judicious in your review of research conclusions that are based on nonparametric statistical tests.

My first warning concerns the quality of the research question(s) associated with the study you find yourself examining. If the study focuses on a trivial topic, no statistical procedure has the ability to "turn a sow's ear into a silk purse." This is as true of nonparametric procedures as it is of the parametric techniques discussed earlier in the book. Accordingly, I once again urge you to refrain from using data-based *p*-levels as the criterion for assessing the worth of empirical investigations.

My second warning concerns the important assumptions of random samples and independence of observations. Each of the nonparametric tests considered in this chapter involves a null hypothesis concerned with one or more populations. The null hypothesis is evaluated with data that come from one or more samples that are assumed to be representative of the population(s). Thus the notion of randomness is just as essential to any nonparametric test as it is to any parametric procedure. Moreover, nonparametric tests, like their parametric counterparts, are based on an assumption of **independence.** Independence simply means that the data provided by any individual are not influenced by what happens to any other person in the study.[11]

My third warning concerns the term **distribution-free,** a label that is sometimes used instead of the term *nonparametric.* As a consequence of these terms being used as if they were synonyms, many applied researchers are under the impression that nonparametric tests work equally well no matter what the shape of the population distribution(s). This is not true for the two reasons discussed earlier. On the one hand, the power of each and every nonparametric test varies depending on the shape of the population distribution(s). On the other hand, the proper meaning of a rejected null hypothesis is frequently influenced by what is known about the distributional shape of the populations.

My next-to-last warning is really a reiteration of an important point made earlier in this book regarding overlapping distributions. If two groups of scores are

---

[11]With the median, Mann-Whitney, and Kruskal-Wallis tests, independence is assumed to exist both within and between the comparison groups. With the Wilcoxon and Friedman tests, the correlated nature of the data causes the independence assumption to apply only in a between-subjects sense.

compared and found to differ significantly from each other (even at impressive *p*-levels), it is exceedingly likely that the highest scores in the low group are higher than the lowest scores in the high group. When this is the case, as it almost always is, a researcher should not claim—or even suggest—that the individuals in the high group outperformed the individuals in the other group. What can be said is that people in the one group, on the average, did better. Those three little words *on the average* are essential to keep in mind when reading research reports.

To see clearly what I mean about "overlapping distributions," consider Excerpt 18.28. If the sentence in this excerpt seems familiar, that's because I have taken the last sentence out of Excerpt 18.15 and put it here so you can examine it closely.

EXCERPT 18.28 • *Overlapping Distributions*

The 3 children who completed the original AB-X training successfully were older ($M = 5.6$ yr, Range: 5.3–5.7) than the 7 children who failed this training ($M = 5.2$ yr, Range: 4.9–5.5) (Mann-Whitney $U = 2$, $p = 0.03$).

Source: F. Carpentier, P. M. Smeets, and D. Barnes-Holmes. (2002). Establishing transfer of compound control in children: A stimulus control analysis. *Psychological Record, 52*(2), p. 154.

In this excerpt, the researchers report that they found a statistically significant difference (using the Mann-Whitney U test) between the ages of the two groups of fifth graders. Because of this, they assert that the 3 children in the "success" group *were older* than the 7 children in the "failure" group. But is this really true? In other words, were all three of the "success" children older than all seven of the "failure" children?

By looking at the ranges provided in Excerpt 18.28, you can see the presence of overlapping distributions. The age range for the "success" group extends from 5.7 down to 5.3, while the age range for the "failure" group extends from 5.5 down to 4.9. As these ranges make clear, at least one of the seven children in the "failure" group was older than at least one of the three children in the "success" group. (If you review footnote 6, you will find some verification for this claim of overlapping distributions.)

I think Excerpt 18.28 provides a powerful example of why you need to be vigilant when reading or listening to research reports. Researchers frequently say that the members of one group outperformed the members of one or more comparison groups. When the researchers fail to include the three important words *on the average* when making such statements, you should mentally insert this phrase into the statement that summarizes the study's results. You can feel safe doing this, for nonoverlapping distributions are very, very rare.

My final warning concerns the fact that many nonparametric procedures have been developed besides the five focused on within the context of this chapter. Such tests fall into one of two categories. Some are simply alternatives to the ones I have discussed, and they utilize the same kind of data to assess the same null hypothesis. For example, the Quade test can be used instead of the Friedman test. The other kind of nonparametric test not considered here has a different purpose. The Jonckheere-Terpstra test, for instance, allows a researcher to evaluate a null hypothesis that says a set of populations is ordered in a particular way in terms of their average scores. I have not discussed such tests simply because they are used infrequently by applied researchers.

Review Terms

Distribution-free	Parametric test
Friedman two-way analysis of variance	Ranks
	Ratings
Independence	Relative power
Kruskal-Wallis one-way analysis of variance by ranks	Sum of ranks
	Tied observations
Large-sample approximation	Wilcoxon-Mann-Whitney test
Likert-type attitude inventories	Wilcoxon matched-pairs signed-ranks test
Mann-Whitney *U* test	
Median split	Wilcoxon-Pratt test
Median test	Wilcoxon rank-sum test
Nonparametric test	Wilcoxon test

The Best Items in the Companion Website

1. An interactive online quiz (with immediate feedback provided) covering Chapter 18.
2. Ten misconceptions about the content of Chapter 18.
3. One of the best passages from Chapter 18: "The Importance of the Research Question(s)."
4. The interactive online resource entitled "Wilcoxon's Matched-Pairs Signed-Ranks Test."
5. The website's final joke: "The Top 10 Reasons Why Statisticians Are Misunderstood."

Fun Exercises inside Research Navigator

1. **Do people with multiple sclerosis (MS) have high-level language problems?**

   The data of this study came from three groups of elderly individuals who were given a newly developed test battery designed to assess high-level language skills. The test's tasks included (among other things) repeating long sentences, resolving ambiguities, making inferences, and understanding metaphors. The three comparison groups were (1) four MS individuals with self-reported language problems, (2) five MS individuals who said that they did not have language problems, and (3) nine individuals without MS who were matched with the MS participants in terms of age, gender, and educational level. The total scores earned on the test battery were first analyzed by a Kruskall-Wallis one-way ANOVA. Because that analysis yielded a significant *H*, the researchers then used the Mann-Whitney *U* test to make all possible pairwise comparisons within a post hoc investigation. What do you think the three Mann-Whitney tests revealed? To find out, first locate the PDF version of the research report in the Communication Sciences and Disorders database of ContentSelect and then read (on pages 339–340) the third paragraph of the study's "Results."

   K. Laakso, K. Brunnegård, L. Hartelius, & E. Ahlsén. Assessing high-level language in individuals with multiple sclerosis: A pilot study. *Clinical Linguistics and Phonetics.* Located in the COMMUNICATION SCIENCES AND DISORDERS database of ContentSelect.

2. **Acupuncture, massage, or both: which therapy best helps HIV patients?**

   In this study, three therapies for dealing with HIV-infected patients were compared: acupuncture, massage, and acupuncture plus massage. There were six groups of patients; three were "treatment" groups that received the different therapies, and each of those groups had its own set of "matched controls." Using data on blood cell counts as the dependent variable, the researchers evaluated each therapy group in two ways: (1) by comparing its blood counts pre-therapy versus post-therapy and (2) by comparing its post-therapy, level against that of its control group. Wilcoxon's matched pairs signed-ranks test was used for each intragroup (i.e., pre-post) comparison. For the intergroup comparisons, the researchers used a nonparametric test that seems inappropriate based on the study's design. What test do you think they *should* have used? After coming up with an answer to that question, go to the PDF version of the research report in the Nursing, Health, and Medicine database of ContentSelect and read (on pages 745–746) the "Results" section of the research report.

   M. Henrickson. Clinical outcomes and patient perceptions of acupuncture and/or massage therapies in HIV-infected individuals. *AIDS Care.* Located in the NURSING, HEALTH, AND MEDICINE database of ContentSelect.

Review Questions and Answers begin on page 516.

Epilogue

The warnings sprinkled throughout this book were offered with two distinct groups of people in mind. The principal reason for raising these concerns is to help those who are on the *receiving* end of research claims. However, these same warnings should be considered by those who are *doing* research. If both parties are more careful in how they interact with research studies, fewer invalid claims will be made, encountered, and believed.

There are two final warnings. The first has to do with the frequently heard statement that begins with these three words, "Research indicates that. . . ." The second is concerned with the power of replication. All consumers of research, as well as all researchers, should firmly resolve to heed the important messages contained in this book's final two admonitions.

First, you must protect yourself against those who use research to intimidate others in discussions (and in arguments) over what is the best idea, the best practice, the best solution to a problem, or the best anything. Because most people (1) are unaware of the slew of problems that can cause an empirical investigation to yield untenable conclusions and (2) make the mistake of thinking that statistical analysis creates a direct pipeline to truth, they are easily bowled over when someone else claims to have research evidence on his or her side. Don't let this happen to you! When you encounter people who promote their points of view by alluding to research ("Well, research has shown that. . . ."), ask them politely to tell you more about the research project(s) to which they refer. Ask them if they have seen the actual research reports(s). Then pose a few exceedingly legitimate questions.

If the research data were collected via mailed questionnaires, what was the response rate? No matter how the data were collected, did the researchers present evidence as to the reliability and validity of the data they analyzed? Did they attend to the important assumptions associated with the statistical techniques they used? If they tested null hypotheses, did they acknowledge the possibility of inferential error when they rejected or failed to reject any given H_0? If their data analysis produced one or more results that were significant, did they distinguish between statistical and practical significance? If you ask questions such as these, you may find that the person who first made reference to what research has to say may well become a bit more modest when arguing his or her point of view. And never, ever forget that you not only have a *right* to ask these kinds of questions, you have an *obligation* to do so (presuming that you want to be a discerning recipient of the information that comes your way).

Second, be impressed with researchers who replicate their own investigations—and even more impressed when they encourage others to execute such replications. The logic behind this admonition is simple and shines through if we consider this little question: Who are you more willing to believe, someone who demonstrates something once or someone who demonstrates something twice? (Recall that a correlation matrix containing all bivariate rs among seven or more variables is more likely than not to be accompanied by the notation "$p < .05$" *even if all null hypotheses are true,* unless the level of significance is adjusted to compensate for the multiple tests being conducted. Similarly, the odds are greater than 50-50 that a five-way ANOVA or ANCOVA will produce a statistically significant result *simply by chance,* presuming that each F's p is evaluated against an alpha criterion of .05.)

It is sad but true that most researchers do not take the time to replicate their findings before they race off to publish their results. It would be nice if there were a law stipulating that every researcher had to replicate his or her study before figuratively standing up on a soapbox and arguing passionately that something important has been discovered. No such law is likely to appear on the books in the near future. Hence, *you* must protect yourself from overzealous researchers who regard publication as more important than replication. Fortunately, there *are* more than a few researchers who delay making any claims until they have first checked to see if their findings are reproducible. Such researchers deserve your utmost respect. If their findings emanate from well designed studies that deal with important questions, their discoveries may bring forth improvements in your life and the lives of others.

Review Questions

CHAPTER 1

1. Where is the abstract usually found in a journal article? What type of information is normally contained in the abstract?
2. What information usually follows the review of literature?
3. If an author does a good job of writing the method section of the research report, what should a reader be able to do?
4. The author of this chapter's model article used the term *participants* to label the people from whom data were collected (see Excerpt 1.5). What is another word that authors sometimes use to label the data suppliers?
5. If a researcher compares the IQ scores of 100 boys with the IQ scores of 100 girls, what would this researcher's dependent variable be?
6. What are three ways authors present the results of their statistical analyses?
7. Will a nontechnical interpretation of the results usually be located in a research report's results section or in its discussion section?
8. What is the technical name for the bibliography that appears at the end of a research report?
9. If a research report is published, should you assume that it is free of mistakes?
10. Look again at these four parts of the model article: the next-to-last sentence of the abstract (see Excerpt 1.1), the researcher's hypothesis (see Excerpt 1.4), the first sentence of the results section (see Excerpt 1.8), and the first sentence of the discussion section (see Excerpt 1.9). With respect to this study's purpose and findings, how many of these four sentences are consistent with one another?

CHAPTER 2

1. What does each of the following symbols or abbreviations stand for: N, M, s, Mdn., Q_3, SD, R, σ, Q_2, s^2, Q_1, σ^2, μ?
2. If a cumulative frequency distribution had been used to summarize the male data in Excerpt 2.1, what would the cumulative frequency be for age 15?
3. Each of several people from your home town is asked to indicate his or her favorite radio station, and the data are summarized using a picture containing

vertical columns to indicate how many people vote for each radio station. What is the name for this kind of picture technique for summarizing data?

4. True or False: In any set of data, the median is equal to the score value that lies halfway between the high and low scores.

5. Which two of the following four terms fit the 2,371 scores summarized in Excerpt 2.4?
   a. positively skewed
   b. negatively skewed
   c. skewed left
   d. skewed right

6. If the variance of a set of scores is equal to 9, how large is the standard deviation for those scores?

7. If the standard deviation for a set of 30 scores is equal to 5, how large do you think the range is?

8. What measure of variability is equal to the numerical distance between the 25th and 75th percentile points?

9. Which of the following three descriptive techniques would let you see each and every score in the researcher's data set?
   a. grouped frequency distribution
   b. stem-and-leaf display
   c. box-and-whisker

10. True or False: The distance between the high and low scores in a data set can be determined by doubling the value of the interquartile range.

CHAPTER 3

1. Following are the quiz scores for five students in English (E) and History (H).

   Sam: E = 18, H = 4
   Sue: E = 16, H = 3
   Joy: E = 15, H = 3
   John: E = 13, H = 1
   Chris: E = 12, H = 0

   Within this same group of quiz-takers, what is the nature of the relationship between demonstrated knowledge of English and history?
   a. *high-high, low-low*
   b. *high-low, low-high*
   c. little systematic tendency one way or the other

2. If 20 individuals are measured in terms of two variables, how many dots will there be if a scatter diagram is built to show the relationship between the two variables?

3. Which of the following five correlation coefficients indicates the weakest relationship?
   a. $r = +.72$
   b. $r = +.41$
   c. $r = +.13$
   d. $r = -.33$
   e. $r = -.84$

4. If Excerpt 3.7 had been set up like Excerpt 3.8, how many rows, columns, and correlation coefficients would there be inside the correlation matrix?

5. What is the name of the correlational procedure used when interest lies in the relationship between two variables measured in such a way as to produce each of the following?
   a. two sets of raw scores
   b. two sets of ranks (with ties)
   c. two sets of truly dichotomous scores
   d. one set of raw scores and one set of truly dichotomous scores

6. What does the letter s stand for in the notation r_s?

7. If a researcher wanted to see if there is a relationship between people's favorite color (e.g., blue, red, yellow, orange) and their favorite TV network, what correlational procedure would you expect to see used?

8. True or False: If a bivariate correlation coefficient turns out to be closer to 1.00 than to 0.00, you should presume that a causal relationship exists between the two variables.

9. Based on the information shown in Excerpt 3.9, what is the coefficient of determination between knowledge and fatalism among parents?

10. True or False: If a researcher has data on two variables, there will be a high correlation if the two means are close together (or a low correlation if the two means are far apart).

CHAPTER 4

1. The basic idea of reliability is captured nicely by what word?

2. What is the name of the reliability procedure that leads to a coefficient of stability? To a coefficient of equivalence?

3. Regardless of which method is used to assess reliability, the reliability coefficient cannot be higher than ____ or lower than ____.

4. Why is the Cronbach alpha approach to assessing internal consistency more versatile than the Kuder-Richardson 20 approach?

5. Look at Excerpt 4.7. If internal consistency had been assessed by the split-half technique (rather than Kuder-Richardson 20), would the reliability coefficient have turned out equal to .83?

6. True or False: As reliability increases, so does the standard error of measurement.

7. What might cause the correlation coefficient used to assess concurrent or predictive validity to turn out *low* even though scores on the new test are *high* in accuracy?

8. Persuasive evidence for discriminant validity is provided by correlation coefficients that turn out close to
   a. +1.00
   b. 0.00
   c. −1.00

9. Should reliability and validity coefficients be interpreted as revealing something about the measuring instrument, or should such coefficients be interpreted as revealing something about the scores produced by using the measuring instrument?

10. True or False: If a researcher presents impressive evidence regarding the reliability of his or her data, it is safe to assume that the data are valid too.

CHAPTER 5

1. In which direction does statistical inference move: from the population to the sample or from the sample to the population?

2. What symbols are used to denote the sample mean, the sample variance, and the sample value of Pearson's correlation? What symbols are used to denote these statistical concepts in the population?

3. True or False: If the population is abstract (rather than tangible), it's impossible for there to be a sampling frame.

4. In order for a sample to be a probability sample, what must you or someone else be able to do?

5. Which of the following eight kinds of samples are considered to be probability samples?

   cluster samples   simple random samples
   convenience samples   snowball samples
   purposive samples   stratified random samples
   quota samples   systematic samples

6. If you want to determine whether a researcher's sample is a random sample, which of these two questions should you ask?
   a. Precisely how well do the characteristics of the sample mirror the characteristics of the population?
   b. Precisely how was the sample selected from the population?

7. True or False: Studies having a response rate lower than 30 percent are not allowed to be published.

8. The best procedure for checking on a possible nonresponse bias involves doing what?
   a. Comparing demographic data of respondents and nonrespondents.
   b. Comparing survey responses of respondents and a sample of nonrespondents.
   c. Comparing survey responses of early versus late respondents.
9. If randomly selected individuals from a population are contacted and asked to participate in a study, and if those who respond negatively are replaced by randomly selected individuals who agree to participate, should the final sample be considered a random subset of the original population?
10. Put the words *tangible* and *abstract* into their appropriate places within this sentence: If a researcher's population is _____, the researcher ought to provide a detailed description of the sample, but if the researcher's population is _____, it is the population that ought to be described with as much detail as possible.

CHAPTER 6

1. True or False: Sampling errors can be eliminated by selecting samples randomly from their appropriate populations.
2. If many, many samples of size *n* are drawn randomly from an infinitely big population, and if the data from each sample are summarized so as to produce the same statistic (e.g., *r*), what would the resulting set of sample statistics be called?
3. The standard deviation of a sampling distribution is called the _____.
4. True or False: You can have more faith in a researcher's sample data if the standard error is large (rather than small).
5. The two most popular levels of confidence associated with confidence intervals are ____ and ____.
6. If the first confidence interval reported in Excerpt 6.6 had been a 99 percent CI, the lower end of the CI would have been:
   a. lower than 0.70
   b. higher than 0.70
   c. equal to 0.70
7. One type of estimation is called interval estimation; the other type is called _____ estimation.
8. True or False: When a researcher includes a reliability or validity coefficient in the research report, such a coefficient should be thought of as a point estimate.
9. Which type of interval is superior to the other, a confidence interval or a standard error interval?

10. In Excerpts 6.14 and 6.15, there are three confidence intervals built around reliability coefficients. In how many of these cases does the reliability coefficient lie exactly midway between the CI's ends?

CHAPTER 7

1. How could the null hypothesis in Excerpt 7.2 be rewritten so as to make explicit a pinpoint numerical value?
2. Suppose a researcher takes a sample from a population, collects data, and then computes the correlation between scores on two variables. If the researcher wants to test whether the population correlation is different from 0, which of the following would represent the null hypothesis?
   a. $H_0: r = 0.00$
   b. $H_0: r \neq 0.00$
   c. $H_0: \rho = 0.00$
   d. $H_0: \rho \neq 0.00$
3. True or False: If the alternative hypothesis is set up in a nondirectional fashion, this decision will make the statistical test one-tailed (not two-tailed) in nature.
4. The null hypothesis is rejected if the sample data turn out to be _____ (consistent/inconsistent) with what one would expect if H_0 were true.
5. Which level of significance offers greater protection against Type I errors, .05 or .01?
6. Does the critical value typically appear in the research report?
7. If a researcher sets $\alpha = .05$ and then finds out (after analyzing the sample data) that $p = .03$, will the null hypothesis be rejected or not rejected?
8. If a researcher's data turn out such that H_0 cannot be rejected, is it appropriate for the researcher to conclude that H_0 most likely is true?
9. If a null hypothesis is rejected because the data are extremely improbable when compared against H_0 (with $p < .00000001$), for what reason might you legitimately dismiss the research study as being totally unimportant?
10. True or False: Even if the results of a study turn out to be statistically significant, it is possible that those results are fully insignificant in any practical sense.

CHAPTER 8

1. Is it possible for a researcher to conduct a study wherein the result *is* significant in a statistical sense but *is not* significant in a practical sense?
2. What are the two popular strength-of-association indices that are similar to r^2?

3. Statistical power equals the probability of not making what kind of error?
   a. Type I
   b. Type II

4. What kind of relationship exists between statistical power and sample size?
   a. direct
   b. indirect
   c. power and sample size are unrelated

5. The statistical power of a study must lie somewhere between ___ and ___.

6. What are the numerical values for small, medium, and large effect sizes (as suggested by Cohen) when comparing two sample means?

7. If a study is conducted to test H_0: $\mu = 30$ and if the results yield a confidence interval around the sample mean that extends from 26.44 to 29.82, will H_0 be rejected?

8. When the Bonferroni adjustment procedure is used, what gets adjusted?
   a. H_0
   b. H_a
   c. α
   d. p

9. If a researcher wants to use the nine-step version of hypothesis testing instead of the six-step version, what three additional things must he or she do?

10. If the researcher's sample size is too _____, the results can yield statistical significance even in the absence of any practical significance. On the other hand, if the sample size is too _____, the results can yield a nonsignificant result even though the null hypothesis is incorrect by a large margin.
    a. small; large
    b. large; small

CHAPTER 9

1. If a researcher reports that a sample correlation coefficient turned out to be statistically significant, which of the following most likely represents the researcher's unstated null hypothesis?
   a. H_0: $\rho = -1.00$
   b. H_0: $\rho = 0.00$
   c. H_0: $\rho = +1.00$

2. If a researcher reports that "$r(58) = -.61, p < .05$," how many pairs of scores were involved in the correlation?

3. When a researcher checks to see if a sample correlation coefficient is or isn't significant, the inferential test most likely will be conducted in a _____ (one-tailed/two-tailed) fashion.

4. Suppose a researcher has data on 5 variables, computes Pearson's r between every pair of variables, and then displays the rs in a correlation matrix. Also suppose that an asterisk appears next to three of these rs, with a note beneath

the table explaining that the asterisk means $p < .05$. Altogether, how many correlational null hypotheses were set up and tested on the basis of the sample data?

5. In the situation described in Question 4, how many of the *r*s would have turned out to be statistically significant if the Bonferroni technique had been applied?

6. Is it possible for a researcher to have a test-retest reliability coefficient of .25 that turns out to be statistically significant at $p < .001$?

7. A confidence interval built around a sample correlation coefficient will lead to a rejection of the typical correlational null hypothesis if the CI overlaps which of the following numbers?
   a. -1.0
   b. $-.50$
   c. 0.00
   d. $+.50$
   e. $+1.00$

8. Is it possible for r^2 to be low (i.e., close to zero) and yet have $p < .01$?

9. True or False: To the extent that the *p*-value associated with r is small (e.g., $p < .01, p < .001$, or $p < .001$), the researcher more confidently can argue that a cause-and-effect relationship exists between the two variables that were correlated.

10. Attenuation makes it _____ (more/less) likely that a true relationship will reveal itself through the sample data by means of a statistically significant correlation coefficient?

CHAPTER 10

1. If 20 eighth-grade boys are compared against 25 eighth-grade girls, should these two comparison groups be thought of as correlated samples or as independent samples?

2. In the null hypothesis of an independent-samples *t*-test comparison of two group means, what kind of means are referred to?
   a. sample means
   b. population means

3. If the *df* associated with a correlated-samples *t*-test is equal to 18, how many pairs of scores were involved in the analysis?

4. Based on the information contained in the following ANOVA summary table, the researcher's calculated value would be equal to what number?

Source	df	SS	MS	F
Between groups	1	12		
Within groups	18	54		

5. If a researcher uses an independent-samples *t*-test to compare a sample of men with a sample of women on each of 5 dependent variables, and if the researcher uses the Bonferroni adjustment technique to protect against Type I errors, what will he/she adjust?
   a. each group's sample size
   b. each *t*-test's calculated value
   c. the degrees of freedom
   d. the level of significance

6. True or False: Whereas strength-of-association indices *can* be computed in studies concerned with the mean of a single sample, they *cannot* be computed in studies concerned with the means of two samples.

7. Suppose a researcher compares two groups and finds that $M_1 = 60$, $SD_1 = 10$, $M_2 = 55$, and $SD_2 = 10$. Based on this information, how large would the estimated effect size be? According to Cohen's criteria, would this effect size be considered small, medium, or large?

8. If a researcher uses sample data to test the homogeneity of variance assumption in a study involving two independent samples, what will the null hypothesis be? Will the researcher hope to reject or fail to reject this null hypothesis?

9. If the measuring instrument used to collect data has less than perfect reliability, the confidence interval built around a single sample mean or around the difference between two sample means will be _____ (wider/narrower) than would have been the case if the data had been perfectly reliable.

10. Suppose a one-way analysis of variance is used to compare the means of two samples. Also suppose that the results indicate that $SS_{Total} = 44$, $MS_{Error} = 4$, and $F = 3$. With these results, how large was the sample size, assuming both groups had the same *n*?

CHAPTER 11

1. If a researcher uses a one-way ANOVA to compare four samples, and the statistical focus is on _____ (means/variances), there will be _____ (how many) inferences, and the inference(s) will point toward the _____ (samples/populations).

2. In a one-way ANOVA involving five comparison groups, how many independent variables are there? How many factors?

3. If a one-way ANOVA is used to compare the heights of three groups of first-grade children (those with brown hair, those with black hair, and those with blond hair), what is the independent variable? What is the dependent variable?

4. For the situation described in Question 3, what would the null hypothesis look like?

5. Based on the information contained in the ANOVA summary table presented below, what is the numerical value for SS_{Total}?

Source	df	SS	MS	F
Between groups	4			3
Within groups			2	
Total	49			

6. Which of these two researchers would end up with a statistically significant finding after they each perform a one-way ANOVA?
   a. The *F*-value in Bob's ANOVA summary table is larger than the appropriate critical *F*-value.
   b. The *p*-value associated with Jane's calculated *F*-value is larger than the level of significance.

7. Suppose a one-way ANOVA comparing three sample means (8.0, 11.0, and 19.0) yields a calculated *F*-value of 3.71. If everything about this study remained the same except that the largest mean changed from 19.0 to 17.0, the calculated value would get _____ (smaller/larger).

8. Suppose a researcher wants to conduct 10 one-way ANOVAs, each on a separate dependent variable. Also suppose that the researcher wants to conduct these ANOVAs such that the probability of making at least one Type I error is equal to .05. To accomplish this objective, what alpha level should the researcher use in evaluating each of the *F*-tests?

9. A one-way ANOVA is *not* robust to the equal variance assumption if the comparison groups are dissimilar in what way?

10. Is it possible for a one-way ANOVA to yield a statistically significant but meaningless result?

CHAPTER 12

1. Which term more accurately describes Tukey's test: planned or post hoc?
2. What are the differences among these three terms: post hoc comparison, follow-up comparison, *a posteriori* comparison?
3. If a one-way ANOVA involves five groups, how many pairwise comparisons will there be if the statistically significant omnibus *F* is probed by a post hoc investigation that compares every mean with every other mean?
4. Will a conservative test procedure or a liberal test procedure more likely yield statistically significant results?
5. True or False: If three sample means are $M_1 = 60$, $M_2 = 55$, and $M_3 = 50$, it is impossible for the post hoc investigation to say $M_1 > M_2 < M_3$.
6. Which kind of comparison is used more by applied researchers, pairwise comparisons or nonpairwise comparisons?

7. True or False: When conducting post hoc investigations, some researchers use the Bonferroni technique in conjunction with *t*-tests as a way of dealing with the inflated Type I error problem.

8. True or False: Whereas regular *t*-tests and the one-way ANOVA's omnibus *F*-test have no built-in control that addresses the difference between statistical significance and practical significance, planned and post hoc tests have been designed so that only meaningful differences can end up as statistically significant.

9. If a researcher has more than two comparison groups in his or her study, it _____ (would/would not) be possible for him/her to perform a one-degree-of-freedom *F* test.

10. True or False: In a study comparing four groups (A, B, C, and D), a comparison of A versus B is orthogonal to a comparison of C versus D.

CHAPTER 13

1. If a researcher performs a univariate 3×3 ANOVA, how many independent variables are there? How many dependent variables?

2. How many cells are there in a 2×4 ANOVA? In a 3×5 ANOVA?

3. Suppose the factors of a 2×2 ANOVA are referred to as Factor A and Factor B. How will the research participants be put into the cells of this study if Factor A is assigned while Factor B is active?

4. How many research questions dealt with by a two-way ANOVA are concerned with main effects? How many are concerned with interactions?

5. Suppose a 2 (gender) $\times$ 3 (handedness) ANOVA is conducted, with the dependent variable being the number of nuts that can be attached to bolts within a 60-second time limit. Suppose that the mean scores for the six groups, each containing 10 participants, turn out as follows: right-handed males = 10.2, right-handed females = 8.8; left-handed males = 7.8, left-handed females = 9.8; ambidextrous males = 9.0, ambidextrous females = 8.4. Given these results, what are the main effect means for handedness equal to? How many scores is each of these means based on?

6. True or False: There is absolutely no interaction associated with the sample data presented in Question 5.

7. How many different mean squares serve as the denominator when the *F*-ratios are computed for the two main effects and the interaction?

8. True or False: You should not expect to see a post hoc test used to compare the main effect means of a 2×2 ANOVA, even if the *F*-ratios for both main effects turn out to be statistically significant.

9. How many simple main effects are there for Factor A in a 2×3 (A $\times$ B) ANOVA?

10. True or False: Whenever a two-way ANOVA is used, there is a built-in control mechanism that prevents results from being statistically significant unless they are also significant in a practical sense.

CHAPTER 14

1. If you see the following factors referred to with these names, which one(s) should you guess probably involve repeated measures?
   a. treatment groups
   b. trial blocks
   c. time period
   d. response variables

2. How does the null hypothesis of a between-subjects one-way ANOVA differ from the null hypothesis of a within-subjects one-way ANOVA?

3. If a 2 × 2 ANOVA is conducted on the data supplied by 16 research participants, how many individual scores would be involved in the analysis if both factors are between subjects in nature? What if both factors are within subjects in nature?

4. If the two treatments of a one-way repeated measures ANOVA are presented to 20 research participants in a counterbalanced order, how many different presentation orders will there be?

5. True or False: Since the sample means of a two-way repeated measures ANOVA are each based on the same number of scores, this kind of ANOVA is robust to the sphericity assumption.

6. If eight research participants are each measured across three levels of factor A and four levels of factor B, how many rows (including total) will there be in the ANOVA summary table? How many *df* will there be for the total row?

7. How many null hypotheses are typically associated with a two-way mixed ANOVA? How many of them deal with main effects?

8. If each of 10 males and 10 females is measured on three occasions with the resulting data analyzed by a two-way mixed ANOVA, how many main effect means will there be for gender and how many scores will each of these sample means be based on?

9. Suppose the pretest, posttest, and follow-up scores from four small groups (with $n = 3$ in each case) are analyzed by means of a mixed ANOVA. How large would the interaction F be if it turned out that $SS_{Groups} = 12$, $SS_{Total} = 104$, $MS_{Error(w)} = 2$, $F_{Groups} = 2$, and $F_{Time} = 5$?

10. True or False: One of the nice features of any repeated measures ANOVA is the fact that any statistically significant result is guaranteed to be significant in a practical sense as well.

CHAPTER 15

1. ANCOVA was developed to help researchers decrease the probability that they will make a Type _____ (I/II) error when they test hypotheses.
2. What are the three kinds of variables involved in any ANCOVA study?
3. In ANCOVA studies, is it possible for something other than a pretest (or baseline measure) to serve as the covariate?
4. Suppose the pretest and posttest means for a study's experimental (E) and control (C) groups are as follows: $M_{E(pre)} = 20$, $M_{E(post)} = 50$, $M_{C(pre)} = 10$, $M_{C(post)} = 40$. If this study's data were to be analyzed by an analysis of covariance, the control group's adjusted posttest mean might turn out equal to which one of these possible values?
   a. 5
   b. 15
   c. 25
   d. 35
   e. 45
5. For ANCOVA to achieve its objectives, there should be a _____ (strong/weak) correlation between each covariate variable and the dependent variable.
6. True or False: Like the analysis of variance, the analysis of covariance is robust to violations of its underlying assumptions so long as the sample sizes are equal.
7. One of ANCOVA's assumptions states that the _____ variable should not affect the _____ variable.
8. ANCOVA works best when the comparison groups _____ (are/are not) formed by random assignment.
9. In testing the assumption of equal regression slopes, does the typical researcher hope the assumption's null hypothesis will be rejected?
10. True or False: Because ANCOVA uses data on at least one covariate variable, results cannot turn out to be statistically significant without also being significant in a practical sense.

CHAPTER 16

1. In a scatter diagram constructed in conjunction with a bivariate regression analysis, which of the two axes will be set up to coincide with the dependent variable?
2. In the equation $Y' = 2 + 4(X)$, what is the numerical value of the constant and what is the numerical value of the regression coefficient?
3. In bivariate regression, can the slope end up being negative? What about the Y-intercept? What about r^2?

4. True or False: In bivariate regression, a test of H_0: $\rho = 0$ is equivalent to a test that the Y-intercept is equal to 0.

5. In multiple regression, how many X variables are there? How many Y variables?

6. True or False: You will never see an adjusted R^2 reported among the results of a simultaneous multiple regression.

7. In stepwise and hierarchical multiple regression, do the beta weights for those independent variables entered during the first stage remain fixed as additional independent variables are allowed to enter the regression equation at a later stage?

8. In logistic regression, the dependent variable is _____ (dichotomous/continuous) in nature.

9. An odds ratio of what size would indicate that a particular independent variable has no explanatory value?

10. In logistic regression, does the Wald test focus on individual ORs or does it focus on the full regression equation?

CHAPTER 17

1. True or False: When the sign test is used, the null hypothesis says that the sample data will contain an equal number of observations in each of the two response categories, thus yielding as many pluses as minuses.

2. Which test is more flexible, the sign test or the binomial test?

3. What symbol stands for chi square?

4. Suppose a researcher uses a 2×2 chi square to see if males differ from females with regard to whether or not they received a speeding ticket during the past year. Of the 60 males in the study, 40 had received a ticket. The sample data would be in full agreement with the chi-square null hypothesis if ____ of the 90 females received a ticket.

5. How many degrees of freedom would there be for a chi-square comparison of freshmen, sophomores, juniors, and seniors regarding their answers to the question: "How would you describe the level of allegiance to your school?" (The response options are low, moderate, and high.)

6. Whose name is often associated with the special chi-square formula that carries the label "correction for continuity"?

7. McNemar's chi-square test is appropriate for _____ (two/more than two) groups of data, where the samples are _____ (independent/correlated), and where the response variable contains _____ (two/more than two) categories.

8. If a pair of researchers got ready to use a one-factor repeated measures ANOVA but then stopped after realizing that their data were dichotomous, what statistical test could they turn to in order to complete the data analysis?

9. True or False: Techniques for applying the concept of *statistical power* to tests dealing with frequencies, percentages, and proportions have not yet been developed.
10. Can confidence intervals be placed around sample percentages?

CHAPTER 18

1. Why do researchers sometimes use nonparametric tests with data that are interval or ratio?
2. The median test is used with _____ (independent/correlated) samples.
3. If the median test is used to compare two samples, how many medians will the researcher need to compute based on the sample data?
4. A Mann-Whitney U test is designed for situations where there are ___ (how many) samples that _____ (do/don't) involve repeated measures.
5. Which of the test procedures discussed in this chapter is analogous to the correlated-samples *t*-test considered earlier in Chapter 10? Which one is analogous to the one-way ANOVA considered in Chapter 11?
6. Which of the nonparametric tests involves a calculated value that is sometimes symbolized as χ^2?
7. True or False: The large-sample versions of the Mann-Whitney, Kruskal-Wallis, and Wilcoxon tests all involve a calculated value that is labeled z.
8. Are random samples important to nonparametric tests?
9. True or False: Because they deal with ranks, the tests considered in this chapter have lower power than their parametric counterparts.
10. The term *distribution free* ___ (should/should not) be used to describe the various nonparametric tests discussed in this chapter.

Answers to Review Questions

CHAPTER 1

1. The abstract is usually found near the beginning of the article. It normally contains a condensed statement of the study's objective(s), participants, method, and results.
2. Statement of purpose
3. Replicate the investigation
4. Subjects
5. IQ (i.e., intelligence)
6. In paragraphs of text, in tables, and in figures
7. In the discussion section
8. References
9. No
10. All four

CHAPTER 2

1. Size of the data set, mean, standard deviation, median, upper quartile point, standard deviation, range, standard deviation, middle quartile point (or median), variance, lower quartile point, variance, mean
2. 45
3. Bar graph
4. False
5. a
6. Three
7. 20
8. Interquartile range
9. b
10. False

CHAPTER 3

1. a
2. 20
3. c
4. 4 rows, 4 columns, 10 correlation coefficients

5. **a.** Pearson's r
   b. Kendall's Tau
   c. phi
   d. point biserial
6. Spearman
7. Cramer's V
8. False
9. .09
10. False (Correlation says *nothing* about the two means!)

CHAPTER 4

1. Consistency
2. Test-retest reliability; parallel-forms reliability (or alternate-forms reliability or equivalent-forms reliability)
3. 1.0; 0.0
4. Cronbach's alpha is not restricted to situations where the data are dichotomous
5. Probably not
6. False
7. Poor measurement of the criterion variable
8. b
9. The score obtained by using the measuring instrument
10. False

CHAPTER 5

1. From the sample to the population
2. M, s^2, r, μ, σ^2, ρ
3. True
4. Assign a unique ID number to each member of the population
5. Cluster samples, simple random samples, stratified random samples, and systematic samples
6. b
7. False
8. b
9. No
10. Abstract; tangible

CHAPTER 6

1. False
2. A sampling distribution
3. Standard error
4. False
5. 95 percent; 99 percent
6. a
7. Point
8. True
9. A confidence interval
10. None of them

CHAPTER 7

1. H_0: $\mu_{users} - \mu_{nonusers} = 0$ (or $\sigma_\mu^2 = 0$)
2. c
3. False
4. Inconsistent
5. .01
6. No
7. Rejected
8. No
9. A silly null hypothesis
10. True

CHAPTER 8

1. Yes
2. Eta squared and omega squared
3. b
4. a
5. 0, 1.0
6. Small = .20, medium = .50, large = .80
7. H_0 would be rejected
8. c
9. Specify the effect size, specify the desired power, and determine (via formula, chart, or computer) the proper sample size.
10. b

CHAPTER 9

1. b
2. 60
3. Two-tailed
4. 10

5. Most likely none of them
6. Yes
7. c
8. Yes, if the sample size is large enough
9. False
10. Less likely

CHAPTER 10

1. Independent samples (because two groups with different ns cannot be correlated)
2. b
3. 19
4. Four
5. d
6. False
7. .50; medium
8. H_0: $\sigma_1^2 = \sigma_2^2$; not rejected
9. Wider
10. Five

CHAPTER 11

1. Means; one; populations
2. One of each
3. hair color; height
4. H_0: $\mu_1 = \mu_2 = \mu_3$
5. 114
6. Bob
7. Smaller
8. .005
9. Group size
10. Yes

CHAPTER 12

1. Neither. It depends on whether the researcher who uses the Tukey test first examines the ANOVA F to see if it is okay to compare means using the Tukey test.
2. Nothing. They are synonyms.
3. 10
4. A liberal test procedure
5. True
6. Pairwise
7. True
8. False
9. Would
10. True

CHAPTER 13

1. Two; 1
2. 8; 15
3. Participants will be randomly assigned to levels of Factor B from within each level of Factor A.
4. Two; 1
5. The main effect means would be equal to 9.5, 8.8, and 8.7 (for right-handed, left-handed, and ambidextrous individuals, respectively). Each would be based on 20 scores.
6. False
7. One
8. True
9. Three
10. False

CHAPTER 14

1. b, c, d
2. They do not differ in any way.
3. 16; 64
4. Two
5. False
6. 8; 95
7. Three; two
8. 2; 30
9. Two
10. False

CHAPTER 15

1. Type II error
2. Independent, dependent, and covariate (concomitant) variables
3. Yes
4. e
5. Strong
6. False
7. Independent; covariate
8. Are
9. No
10. False

CHAPTER 16

1. The vertical axis (i.e., the ordinate)
2. The constant is 2; the regression coefficient is 4.
3. Yes; yes; no
4. False
5. At least two; just one
6. True
7. No
8. Dichotomous
9. 1.0
10. Individual ORs

CHAPTER 17

1. False. (The null hypothesis is a statement about population parameters, not sample statistics.)
2. The binomial test
3. χ^2
4. 60
5. Six
6. Yates
7. Two; correlated; two
8. Cochran's Q test
9. False
10. Yes

CHAPTER 18

1. Because researchers know or suspect that the normality and/or equal variance assumptions are untenable, especially in situations where the sample sizes are dissimilar.
2. Independent
3. One
4. Two; don't
5. The Wilcoxon matched-pairs signed-ranks test; the Kruskal-Wallis one-way ANOVA of ranks
6. Friedman's two-way analysis of variance of ranks
7. False (The Kruskal-Wallis test, when conducted with large samples, yields a calculated value symbolized as χ^2.)
8. Yes
9. False
10. Should not

Credits

Excerpts 1.1–1.10   Reprinted with permission of author and publisher from Wininger, S. R. The anxiolytic effect of aqua aerobics in elderly women. *Perceptual and Motor Skills,* 2002, 94, 338–340. © Perceptual and Motor Skills 2002.

Excerpt 2.1   R. A. Ellis, M. O'Hara, and K. M. Sowers. (2000). Profile-based intervention: Developing gender-sensitive treatment for adolescent substance abusers. *Research on Social Work Practice, 10*(3), p. 332. © 2000 by Sage Publications. Reprinted by Permission of Sage Publications.

Excerpt 2.2   B. D. Cejda, C. B. McKenney, and H. Burley. (2001). The career lines of chief academic officers in public community colleges. *Community College Review, 28*(4), p. 39.

Excerpt 2.3   M. S. Ferrara, M. McCrea, C. L. Peterson, and K. M. Guskiewicz. (2001). A survey of practice patterns in concussion assessment and management. *Journal of Athletic Training, 36*(2), p. 146.

Excerpt 2.4   M. Sabrin. (2002). A ranking of the most productive business ethics scholars: A five-year study. *Journal of Business Ethics, 36*, p. 364. With kind permission of Kluwer Academic Publishers.

Excerpt 2.5   Reproduced with permission of authors and publisher from Glencross, M. J., and Cherian, V. I. Attitudes toward applied statistics of postgraduate education students in Transkei. *Psychological Reports,* 1992, 70, 67–75. © Psychological Reports 1992.

Excerpt 2.6   From "Differential Genetic Etiology of Reading Disability as a Function of IQ" by S. J. Wadsworth, R. K Olson, B. F. Pennington, and J. C. DeFries, 2000, *Journal of Learning Disabilities, 33*, 192–199. Copyright 2000 by PRO-ED, Inc. Reprinted with permission.

Excerpt 2.7   G. Gunter-Hunt, J. E. Mahoney, and C. E. Sieger. (2002). A comparison of state advance directive documents. *Gerontologist, 42*(1), p. 53. Copyright © The Gerontological Society of America. Reproduced by permission of the publisher.

Excerpt 2.8   T. M. Smith. (2002). An analysis of northern hardwood lumber buyers' use of electronic commerce. *Forest Products Journal, 52*(2), p. 64.

Excerpt 2.21   Republished with permission of the American Society for Engineering Management, from E. M. Van Aken, R. L. Groesbeck, and G. D. Coleman. (2001). Integrated organizational assessment process and tools: Application in an engineer-to-order company. *Engineering Management Journal, 13*(4), p. 24; permission conveyed through Copyright Clearance Center, Inc.

Excerpt 2.26   C. C. Persad, N. Abeles, R. T. Zacks, and N. L. Denburg. (2002). Inhibitory changes after age 60 and their relationship to measures of attention and memory. *The Journals of Gerontology, 57B*(3), p. P226. Copyright © The Gerontological Society of America. Reproduced by permission of the publisher.

Excerpt 3.1   D. M. Clayton and A. M. Stallings. (2000). Black women in Congress: Striking the balance. *Journal of Black Studies, 30*(4), pp. 593–594. © 2000 by Sage Publications. Reprinted by Permission of Sage Publications.

Excerpt 3.7   D. L. Alden, A. Mukherjee, and W. D. Hoyer. (2000). The effects of incongruity, surprise and positive moderators on perceived humor in television advertising. *Journal of Advertising, 29*(2), p. 8.

Excerpt 3.8   S. L. McFall, A. M. Yerkes, and L. D. Cowan. (2000). Outcomes of a small group educational intervention for urinary incontinence: Health-related quality of life. *Journal of Aging and Health, 12*(3), p. 311. © 2000 by Sage Publications. Reprinted by Permission of Sage Publications.

Excerpt 3.9   J. R. Ramirez, W. D. Crano, R. Quist, and M. Burgoon. (2002). Effects of fatalism and family communication on HIV/AIDS awareness variations in Native American and Anglo parents and children. *AIDS Education and Prevention, 14*(1), p. 36. Reprinted by permission of Guilford Press.

Excerpt 3.10   From "Discourse Complexity of College Writers With and Without Disabilities: A Multi-dimensional Analysis" by N. Gregg, C. Coleman, R. B. Stennett, and M. Davis, 2002, *Journal of Learning Disabilities, 35*, 23–38. Copyright 2000 by PRO-ED, Inc. Reprinted with permission.

Excerpt 3.21   M. Sabrin. (2002). A ranking of the most productive business ethics scholars: A five-year study. *Journal of Business Ethics, 36*, p. 373. With kind permission of Kluwer Academic Publishers.

Excerpt 6.2   J. L. Moul. (1998). Differences in selected predictors of anterior cruciate ligament tears between male and female NCAA Division I collegiate basketball players. *Journal of Athletic Training, 33*(2), p. 119.

Excerpt 6.3   L. Gary, L. W. Miller, B. L. Philipp, and E. M. Blass. (2002). Breastfeeding is analgesic in healthy newborns. Reproduced with permission from *Pediatrics*, Vol. 109, Page 592, Figure 1, Copyright 2002.

Excerpt 6.4   Gerone, L. J. & McKeever, W. F. Failure to support the right-shift theory's hypothesis of a "heterozygote advantage" for cognitive abilities, *British Journal of Psychology,* Vol. 90, Part 1 (February 1999), pp. 109–123. Reproduced with permission from the *British Journal of Psychology,* © The British Psychological Society.

Excerpt 6.8   C. S. Avvampato. (2001). Effect of one leg crossed over the other at the knee on blood pressure in hypertensive patients. *Nephrology Nursing Journal, 28*(3), p. 326.

Excerpt 6.9   E. A. Gilpin, A. J. Farkas, S. L. Emery, C. F. Ake, and J. P. Pierce. (2002). Clean indoor air: Advances in California, 1990–1999. *American Journal of Public Health, 92*(5), p. 787.

Excerpt 9.14   M. E. Kenny, L. A. Gallagher, R. Alvarez-Salvat, and J. Silsby. (2002). Sources of support and psychological distress among academically successful inner-city youth. *Adolescence, 37*(145), p. 167.

Excerpt 9.15   M. D. Calero; M. L. Arnedo; E. Navarro; M. Ruiz-Pedrosa; C. Carnero. (2002). Usefulness of a 15-item version of the Boston Naming Test in neuropsychological assessment of low-educational elders with dementia. *The Journals of Gerontology, 57B*(2), p. P190. Copyright © The Gerontological Society of America. Reproduced by permission of the publisher.

Excerpt 9.26   M. J. Monteith, C. I. Voils, and L. Ashburn-Nardo. (2001). Taking a look underground: Detecting, interpreting, and reacting to implicit racial biases. *Social Cognition, 19*(4), p. 409. Reprinted by permission of Guilford Press.

Excerpt 10.2   P. Szatmari, S.E. Bryson, D. L. Streiner, and F. Wilson. (2000). Two-year outcome of preschool children with autism or Asperger's Syndrome. *American Journal of Psychiatry, 157*(12), p. 1984. Copyright 2000, the American Psychiatric Association; http://AJP.psychiatryonline.org. Reprinted by permission.

Excerpt 10.5   From "Lexical Access in College Students With Learning Disabilities: An Electrophysiological and Performance-Based Investigation" by S. S. Rubin and C. M. Johnson, 2002, *Journal of Learning Disabilities, 35*, 257–267. Copyright 2002 by PRO-ED, Inc. Reprinted with permission.

Excerpt 10.11   D. A. Latif. (2000). Ethical cognition and selection-socialization in retail pharmacy. *Journal of Business Ethics, 25*(4), p. 352. With kind permission of Kluwer Academic Publishers.

Excerpt 10.15   S. Carney-Crompton and J. Tan. (2002). Support systems, psychological functioning, and academic performance of nontraditional female students. *Adult Education Quarterly, 52*(2), p. 145. © 2002 by Sage Publications. Reprinted by Permission of Sage Publications.

Excerpt 10.29   F. T. Delbeke, P. Van Eenoo, and P. DeBacker. (1998). Detection of human chorionic gonadotrophin misuse in sports. *International Journal of Sports Medicine, 19,* p. 288.

Excerpt 11.1   B. Kracher, A. Chatterjee, and A. R. Lundquist. (2002). Factors related to the cognitive moral development of business students and business professionals in India and the United States: Nationality, education, sex and gender. *Journal of Business Ethics, 35*(42), p. 262. With kind permission of Kluwer Academic Publishers.

Index

Note: All numbers appearing in Roman type refer to pages; all numbers appearing in bold italics refer to Excerpts.